RIVERSIDE COMMUNITY COLLEGE
1916

EDUCATION AND SCHOOLING I[...]

LA209.2 .G87 1992

P9-AFZ-618

DATE DUE

OC 28 '94	JE 1 0 '00		
AP 21 '95	DE 2 0 '00		
JE 1 '95	MY 2 1 '01		
AG 3 '95	AU 6 '01		
OC 27 '95	AP 21 '03		
MR 2 9 96	AP 21 '05		
MY 17 '92			
FE 25 '97			
MY 29 '97			
NO 24 '97			
DE 17 97			
MY 30 98			
AP 20 99			
NO 2 '0			

DEMCO 38-296

Education
and Schooling
in America

Education and Schooling in America

Third Edition

GERALD L. GUTEK
Loyola University Chicago

ALLYN AND BACON
Boston London Toronto Sydney Tokyo Singapore

Riverside Community College
Riverside Community College
Library
AUG '94   4800 Magnolia Avenue
Riverside, California 92506

LA209.2 .G87 1992
Gutek, Gerald Lee.
Education and schooling in
America

e Joseph
reese
dy Lyle Rymer
hran
ckinson
1

Copyright © 1992, 1988, 1983 by Allyn and Bacon
A Divison of Simon & Schuster, Inc.
160 Gould Street
Needham Heights, Massachusetts 02194

All rights reserved. No part of the material protected by this copyright
notice may be reproduced or utilized in any form or by any means,
electronic or mechanical, including photocopying, recording, or by any
information storage and retrieval system, without the written permission
of the copyright owner.

Library of Congress Cataloging-in-Publication Data

Gutek, Gerald Lee.
   Education and schooling in America/Gerald L. Gutek. — 3rd ed.
      p.   cm.
   Includes bibliographical references and index.
   ISBN 0-205-13203-0
   1. Education — United States — History.   I. Title.
   LA209.2.G87   1992
   370'.973 — dc20   91-28442
                                                            CIP

Printed in the United States of America
10 9 8 7 6 5 4 3 2   96 95 94 93

The author wishes to thank the copyright owners for permission to reprint the following photographs in the text:
Pages 18, 119, 257, 262, 270, 277, 286, 392, 404, 420, 428 © Frank Siteman 1990; pages 65, 73, 80, 82, 103, 113
(sculpture by Epstein), 133, 193, 238, 243, 265, 304, 317, 332 from the Picture Collection, The Branch Libraries,
the New York Public Library; page 66, *The New England Primer Improved* (Pittsburgh: United Presbyterian
Board of Publication, n.d.); page 67, Charles C. Coffin, *Building the Nation* (New York: Harper & Brothers,
1882, p. 25); pages 71, 75, 100, 131, 133, 150, 321, Library of Congress; page 78, *Sander's Pictorial Primer*
(Chicago: S.C. Griggs & Co., 1886, p. 20); pages 79, 148, 366 from the collection of the National Archives; page
146 courtesy of the Fort Laramie Historical Association and the National Park Service, U.S. Department of the
Interior; page 163 reprinted with permission of the Japanese Information Service, Consulate General of Japan,
Chicago.

Riverside Community College
Riverside Community College
4800 Magnolia Avenue
Riverside, California 92506

*To my wife, Patricia
and to my daughters,
Laura and Jennifer*

___ BRIEF CONTENTS ___

CONTENTS

__ PREFACE

Education and Schooling in America developed from my teaching of American Education at Loyola University Chicago. American Education, a preservice undergraduate course designed to introduce prospective teachers to schooling in American society, is similar to the courses titled Introduction to Education, Introduction to the Foundations of Education, or Introduction to Educational Policy Studies that are offered in colleges and universities throughout the country. Over the course of 20 years of teaching this course, I experimented with various approaches to organizing it. For some years, the course was presented as an historical overview. In other years, it was divided into separate sections, with some units being historical and other units contemporary. At still other times, it consisted of reading and discussing a number of short paperbacks that dealt with positions on educational issues. While each of these approaches had its strengths, all presented weaknesses.

During the course of my career as a professor of foundations of education, I also served on the local school board in my community. I served as dean of Loyola University's School of Education from 1979 to 1985 and worked with my colleagues in the school to sustain program approval by the Illinois Teacher Certification Board and the National Council for the Accreditation of Teacher Education. From these experiences, I developed a perspective or orientation that I incorporated into the first edition of *Education and Schooling in America,* in 1983; into the second edition, in 1988; and now into this, the third edition.

First, I believe that it is important to provide prospective teachers with a sense of continuity that integrates the educational past with the present. Too often, teacher education, in its enthusiasm for change, yields too quickly to an overeager presentism. Books that exhibit this tendency tend to confuse novelty with significance. Prospective teachers who are prepared for the profession in a strictly presentist manner tend to lack needed depth in the development of their field. Although as an historian of education I thoroughly enjoy working with the past, I came to realize that historical treatments, especially in preservice teacher education programs, need to be connected with the present and its problems. *Education and Schooling in America* therefore uses a pattern of organization that presents an overview of the history of each topic treated, bringing the subject up to the most recent developments.

Second, I believe that teachers need to make connections between what they do in the classroom and what is going on in the out-of-school society and in other classrooms. Teachers also need to make connections with how grade levels and educational institutions relate to each other. Making these connections helps teachers to avoid the sense of isolation and limitations that may develop from the day-to-day immersion of teaching in a particular classroom setting. The recognition that one is involved in a process that has cumulative effects on a student's life and learning grows out of making these connections between grade levels and schools.

I would like to thank the following individuals, who reviewed this book for Allyn and Bacon: June Almes, Lock Haven University; Arthur W. Anderson, Florida Atlantic University; Steve Kokovich, Muskingum College; Ernest E. Lohman, Keene State College; and Carmine C. Sippo, Wagner College. Their suggestions, as well as those of students and teachers who have used the text, have been incorporated into this third edition.

The chapters "Teacher Preparation, Demand, Supply, and Salaries" and "Teaching as a Profession," which were placed near the end of the second edition, now appear much earlier in the book. The new placement of these chapters is in response to comments that prospective teachers want to examine these "immediate" concerns before probing more theoretical areas. In the second edition, I introduced a new chapter titled "International Education." Since we live in a world of greater interdependency between nations and peoples, I believe that teachers need an international perspective that broadens their outlook from the domestic to the world scene. In this edition, the chapter on international education appears immediately after the one on multicultural education so that instructors can build relationships between the two.

Finally, I have resisted the temptation to try to include everything. To do so in an introductory book tends to confuse the important with the temporary and to make the treatment current but superficial. What appears in this edition is my attempt to create a knowledge base, a stable core, that introduces prospective teachers to education and schooling in the United States.

I hope that the third edition of *Education and Schooling in America* will be useful to our nation's future teachers.

G. L. G.

1

Education and Schooling in American Society

Chapter 1 is designed to provide a perspective on the book and its contents. The title, *Education and Schooling in America*, reflects the book's focus; it suggests that education and schooling are distinct with distinguishing meanings and purposes. However, in American life and society, as in other societies, education and schooling exist in relationship and ideally are mutually supportive of each other. The book takes the position that, whereas teachers are engaged primarily in schooling, it is necessary and useful for them to relate schooling to education. Because Americans have often regarded education and schooling as synonymous, this chapter examines their relationships and differences. Among the general focusing questions that will be answered as you read this chapter are:

1. What distinctions and relationships exist between education and schooling?
2. What is the process of enculturation?
3. Who are the major informal educators?
4. What are the cultural role and the social functions of the school?

Education

Because the concept of education is broader in scope and more comprehensive than schooling, education is discussed first. Education is a total lifelong process that begins with one's birth and ends only with one's death. Before entering a school, children know many things, have a stock of experiences and ideas, and have a generalized system of values and ethics. They know and use language and can communicate with others. Children are already social beings who relate to and interact with their peers. All these important human developments took place as the child interacted with his or her environment, parents, family members, and playmates. The kind of learning that takes place in early childhood is generalized; it is not structured deliberately or organized. Educators often refer to this generalized kind of learning as informal education, enculturation, or socialization.

Enculturation

Although informal education has various names, the term *enculturation* is useful in describing the process. It means literally that at only the moment of our birth are we "culture-free" and immediately thereafter are enveloped by the culture into which we are born in much the same way that an infant is wrapped in a blanket. Our learning of the culture, its requirements, knowledge, values, behaviors, and expectations begins immediately and is ongoing. We acquire our culture by living and participating in it. We have no choice about the matter. We simply are born into a culture. However, a culture is a heritage and a way of life that is complex. While our entry into the culture may be simple, our living and learning or our taking on of the culture is complex.

Informal Education

Although enculturation is more or less automatic, much of it is done deliberately by a large number of informal educational agents. These persons or agencies are not trained teachers or schools, but they have a large and pervasive educational impact. Informal educators include the following:

1. *Parents or guardians* with whom children have their initial contact and with whom they live during their formative years are primary or direct educators who impart language, knowledge, and values to their children. The values that parents convey to children are important to later school and life success. If parental values are supportive of schooling, the teacher can build on these predispositions. If parental attitudes are negative to schooling, then children's attitudes are also likely to be negative.

2. *Brothers, sisters, playmates, and the peer group* also exert important influences on child development. The child's patterns of socialization such as assertiveness, competitiveness, and cooperativeness are generally based on peer group experience. The peer group grows in significance as the person passes from childhood to adolescence and to early adulthood. In the United States, in particular, the adolescent subculture is of special importance. With its own styles of speech, music, dress, and behavior, the adolescent subculture is an important force in a person's total education. Many persons have reflected on the joys, challenges, and traumas of their adolescence. Teachers recognize the importance of the peer group as a formative educational force.

3. *The neighborhood,* the child's immediate residential area, is an early and crucial agent in enculturation. It is from the neighborhood that the child learns the styles of behavior that are accepted or rejected when a person leaves the home. Neighborhoods have their own speech styles, communication patterns, and socialization networks. They also have informal criteria that govern a person's acceptance into the neighborhood community.

Many American educators, such as John Dewey and William H. Kilpatrick, portrayed American society as a community of neighborhoods in which a social consensus arose that united and integrated American life, institutions, and values. Throughout the modern era, but especially in the twentieth century, a great transformation took place as the United States changed from a small-town rural society into an urban, industrial, technological society. While the modernization process has brought us many innovations and inventions that have improved our lives in a material sense, it also has generated rapid change, mobility, and social dislocation that has eroded the feeling of community and neighborliness. Teachers need to recognize that social change has also altered American family and community life.

The neighborhood's, or the community's, attitude to schooling is an important factor in the school's success. If the community regards the school and teacher as aliens, then the school tends to be isolated from the community and draws little financial or moral support from it. On the other hand, when the school is viewed as a vital institution, it enjoys community support, protection, and affection.

4. *The church* is also an important educational force for many Americans and their children. Religious outlooks on the meaning and purpose of life and on human values are powerful determinants affecting a person's informal education or enculturation. The religious practices in the home and family and the instruction given to children by the various denominations help to form a person's world view. In the United States, separation of church and state also has meant the separation of the church and the public school. Nevertheless, teachers need to recognize the powerful role of religious institutions in shaping attitudes and values.

5. *Radio, television, movies, the popular press, or mass media* are pervasive educational forces in modern society. Combining entertainment with information delivery, the media have shaped American attitudes and values. Teachers need to listen to the radio programs and view the television programs that their students are listening to or watching to identify some of the factors that are shaping students' attitudes and values.

Through the medium of television, students are aware of events taking place in space, internationally, and in their own nation. Television also presents images conveying life-style and values. As a transmitter of public affairs information, the television commentator acts as an informal teacher. Consider the impact of such events on the education of children and youth: the tragic explosion of the space craft *Challenger* with the death of its crew, including Christa McAuliffe, a social studies teacher; the nuclear explosion at Chernobyl in the Soviet Union; the war in the Persian Gulf. These events, amply covered by television, represent only a few of the momentous occasions that have shaped our perceptions.

Even though television represents a dramatic and moving information explosion, it is also confusing. Despite the sophistication of the modern television portrayal of events, the structure and explanations of these events are often unclear. Their very immediacy and drama lack perspective. These events occur quickly, their suddenness is direct, but their impact in the totality of learning is unclear. While their drama is usually greater than that of the classroom, their structure and perspective are often undeveloped.

In *Crisis in the Classroom*, Charles Silberman examined the role of the media in transmitting information. While the media may be competent in reporting the immediate and urgent issues of the day, Silberman contends that it might miss or fail to recognize truly important problems. The dramatic event may be captured vividly by the television camera, but its meaning may be lost in the confusion of immediate reaction. The transmission of knowledge in schools, on the other hand, is seasoned by time and has a distance from the event or situation that is helpful in creating a sense of perspective. However, classroom instruction pales before the quickness of the rapid-fire televised portrayal of an event.

Silberman finds the basic weakness of television to be that of reinforcing the status quo in a world where people need to understand and know how to deal with change. Media persons, Silberman argues, rarely view themselves as educators. They rarely ask the educational questions that they should. For example, what really constitutes significant information? How does the television portrayal of a situation shape public conceptions of events? What values or lessons are conveyed in the televised commentary?[1]

In this chapter, we can identify only a few of the many informal educators. There are many more, however, such as libraries, social organizations, ethnic groups, museums, art galleries, parks, recreation centers, athletic teams, and so on. These informal agencies of education enculturate us and shape our outlook and values. What we have learned outside either advances or retards what takes place inside the school.

Schooling

Education is the process that brings children into their culture. Education takes place inside the schools and outside them. Although many agencies, such as the home, church, community, and media, are informal educators, advanced cultures use schooling as the process designed specifically to facilitate cultural transmission and enculturation. As a special learning environment, staffed by specialists in education, the school is designed to educate by providing the young with a structured and organized access to the culture's tools, skills, knowledge, and values.

As a specialized cultural agency, the school cannot be isolated from the culture it serves. It must be related intimately to that particular society and cultural heritage. American education draws its content and values from its heritage and society.[2]

In addition to conserving and transmitting the cultural heritage, the school is an agency of social renewal and change. The heritage that the school transmits is vast and complex. To the school falls the immense problem of selecting some parts of the heritage for transmission and rejecting others. As a selective agency, the school serves moral purposes. Educators charged with introducing the young to participation in their culture must make their selection according to a criteria acceptable to the society. American educators have generally followed a democratic social philosophy.

American teachers have the twofold responsibility of introducing each generation to its heritage and of providing the knowledge and skills needed to continue to reformulate the democratic ethic in the face of contemporary challenges.

As part of its task, the school tries to identify cultural elements most likely to produce integrated individuals within an integrated society. An integrated society is not a monolith characterized by common conformity, but a harmonious blend of divergent elements in a unified social fabric. For example, the United States is a nation of immigrants of various ethnic, racial, and religious persuasions. Although commonly committed to the democratic process, Americans enjoy a wide range of political, social, and religious beliefs. A democratic society may encourage many forms of cultural pluralism and adhere simultaneously to underlying ethical, social,

1. Charles E. Silberman, *Crisis in the Classroom: The Remaking of American Education* (New York: Random House, 1970), pp. 30–41.
2. George S. Counts, *Education and American Civilization.* (New York: Teachers College Press, Columbia University, 1952), p. 34.

and political precepts that unite it. The school communicates these values in a graduated environment by selecting cultural elements, skills, and knowledge according to the maturity level of the learner.

Schooling does not occur in social isolation. As a dynamic and ongoing experience rooted in the past, it also actively affects the present situation and influences the future as each new generation is educated. Because our schools have a history, prospective teachers need to understand their origins or roots as educators. The past can be used to interpret the present and to help shape the future. Because schooling deals with current problems, prospective teachers need to examine educational philosophies, theories, methods, curricula, organization, psychology, and administration that are the working tools of the professional educator. For an overview of the structure of schools in the United States, see Figure 1-1. Prospective teachers also need to think in terms of the future to prepare students to live in the twenty-first century.

American Perceptions of Schooling

Americans have often equated education with the school as an institution and with schooling as a process of instruction and value formation. These identifications have contributed to the creation of one of the world's most complex and comprehensive educational systems. Although the public schools' performance is periodically criticized, indicators point to the continued growth and development of public schooling in the United States. By 1995, an enrollment of more than 44 million students is predicted in public elementary and secondary schools. It is further anticipated that these students will be taught by almost 2.6 million teachers.

Undergirding the growth of American public education has been a commitment to the school as a powerful agency of promoting the general social, political, and economic welfare of the nation and its citizens. More than sixty years ago, in 1930, the distinguished educator George S. Counts, commenting on the popular faith of Americans in their schools, wrote:

> *Confront practically any group of citizens with a difficult problem in the sphere of human relations and they will suggest education as the solution. . . . Perhaps the most striking aspect of this phenomenon, however, lies in the fact that education is identified with the work of the school. As a consequence the faith in education becomes a faith in the school, and the school is looked upon as a worker of miracles. In fact, the school is the American road to culture.*[3]

Despite periodic waves of criticism, the American faith in the school has persisted. Whenever a major problem confronts the American people, programs are added to the curriculum to address it. When many young men were physically unfit for service in the armed forces in World War I, physical education requirements were increased. To reduce accidents on the highways, driver education was introduced in the high schools. During the 1980s, substance abuse prevention education

---

3. George S. Counts, *The American Road to Culture: A Social Interpretation of Education in the United States* (New York: John Day, 1930), pp. 16–17.

FIGURE 1–1 The Structure of Education in the United States.

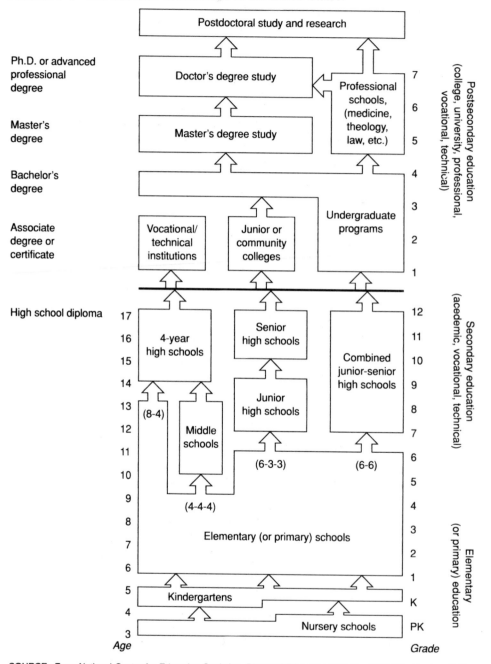

SOURCE: From National Center for Education Statistics, *Digest of Education Statistics 1989* (Washington, D.C.: U.S. Government Printing Office, 1989), p. 5.

NOTE: Adult education programs, while not separately delineated above, may provide instruction at the elementary, secondary, or higher education level. Chart reflects typical patterns of progression rather than all possible variations.

was added to the curriculum as a response to the widespread national epidemic of drug and substance abuse. AIDS education is still another response to a serious national and world health problem.

However, while education in the formal sense of schooling can be a potent instrument for dealing with the nation's problems, the school is only one of several educational agencies. Schools can help, but they alone cannot be expected to solve major problems like drug abuse and environmental pollution. The degree to which the schools' programs are related to and integrated with the society's total response and commitment determines, in large part, the degree to which these problems will be solved. Schools alone cannot solve society's problems.

In addition to the historic American faith in the school that Counts wrote about, more recent indicators of how Americans perceive schooling are useful in assessing the relationships between education and schooling. Some idea of how Americans perceive their schools is provided by *The Gallup/Phi Delta Kappa Polls of Attitudes Toward the Public Schools*, which has been published since 1969. Despite the importance attached to public schooling, only 18 percent of the respondents to the poll in 1969 claimed that they knew "quite a lot" about their local public schools, while 42 percent admitted to knowing "very little" about them. In 1987, eighteen years later, the response was virtually unchanged. This finding strongly suggests that to make informed decisions about public schooling, the public needs to be much better educated about the organization, structure, curricula, and financing of the public schools.[4]

Responding to the question "How important are schools to one's future success?" 76 percent of the respondents in 1973 and 80 percent in 1982 found them to be "extremely important." Attesting to the consistency of the American belief in the school's potential as a socioeconomic force, 84 percent of the respondents in 1982 and 88 percent in 1988 found it "very important" that "America's strength in the future depends on developing the best education system in the world."[5]

Education, Schooling, and Social Change

Throughout this book, you will find historical sections that explain the context of the subject under discussion. This mode of presentation assumes that the changes that are taking place and will take place in the future are part of a continuum of educational events. The present condition of schooling in the United States developed from our educational history. The future of the public schools will be shaped by the way in which existing conditions are developed in the light of new situations, issues, and problems. The educational policy of the future will then become part of the continuum of education and schooling.

In the 1980s, the pattern of declining enrollments that had impacted schools in the 1970s ended. The demand for additional teachers increased, and shortages of

4. Stanley Elam, ed., *The Gallup/Phi Delta Kappa Polls of Attitudes Toward the Public Schools, 1969–88: A 20-Year Compilation and Educational History* (Bloomington, Ind.: Phi Delta Educational Foundation, 1989), p. 5.

5. Ibid., p. 9.

teachers appeared in some areas. In addition, the accelerating inflation and rising expenditures of the 1970s were checked. The 1980s also witnessed a revival of the public's interest in education, spurred by *A Nation at Risk* and other national reports on the condition of education in the United States. For many Americans, the 1980s was a decade of economic prosperity and social stability. Not all, however, shared this sense of economic and social well-being. During the decade, a number of serious economic trends developed that have important implications for education and schools. In the 1990s, the United States and its citizens face a number of serious problems. School administrators and teachers will need to be aware of these issues and contribute to their solution.

During the 1980s, many American families faced increasing economic pressures that are continuing in the 1990s. Since 1973, the growth in real family income, or purchasing power, has slowed and a growing disparity among income levels in the United States has developed. Between 1979 and 1986, the median adjusted income for the bottom two-fifths of American families decreased by 2 percent, while there was a 10 percent increase for the upper two-fifths. Between 1980 and 1986, families with children made no gains in real income despite a 16 percent increase in the number of working mothers. As of 1987, the wealthiest 40 percent of American families were receiving 67.8 percent of the national family income, while the poorest 40 percent were receiving 15.4 percent.[6] This trend has placed many families with children in situations of economic risk.

Some observers of the American economic and social scene have pointed out that an economically disadvantaged "underclass" has developed in the United States. The condition of poverty is especially oppressive for the nation's children. In 1987, one-fifth of American children were estimated to be living in poverty, an increase of 24 percent over 1979. While poverty impacts children throughout the population, it falls most heavily on children of minority groups. One out of every six white children, one in every three Hispanic children, and one in every two African-American children lives in conditions of poverty. Poverty impacts not only children in the inner cities, but those in rural areas as well. Since 1978, rural poverty rates have grown at twice the rate of those in urban areas. It is estimated that one in every four rural children lives in conditions of poverty.[7]

A new phenomenon on the American socioeconomic scene in the 1980s was the rise of the homeless population. Estimates of homeless persons in the United States range from 500,000 to 2.2 million. Homelessness has had its impact on families with children, who are estimated to comprise one-third of the homeless in the United States.[8]

The old stereotype nurtured by reading series like *Dick and Jane* and the television programs of the 1950s was of a two-parent family in which the father was the sole wage earner and the mother stayed at home to rear children and run the household. By the 1990s, economic reality had shattered this stereotypic image of the American family. Since 1975, the number of working mothers has increased by

6. Staff Report of the Select Committee on Children, Youth, and Families, *Children and Families: Key Trends of the 1980s* (Washington, D.C.: U.S. Government Printing Office, 1989), pp. 3, 12.
7. Ibid., p. 11.
8. Ibid., p. 13.

nearly 50 percent. In 1988, 65 percent of mothers with children under eighteen were employed outside of the home. These working mothers contributed 41.3 percent to the total family earnings of married couple families with children.[9]

Because of the increase in single parent families and the increase in the number of working mothers, the demand for and the expense of child care has increased dramatically. Families were spending $11.5 billion on child care each year, an average of $3,000 per each child in full-time care. In 1987, for example, child care cost 10 percent of available family income. For the low-income family, the cost of child care was 26 percent.[10]

The growing economic problems faced by a large number of American families and their children have serious implications for schooling. Inherited perceptions of family life that many teachers hold need to be reconstructed in the light of new social and economic conditions. In particular, the role that the family has played as an informal educational force is undergoing serious changes.

Conclusion

The total process of education in the United States involves the interplay of schools, as formal educational agencies, with informal educational agencies, such as the family, the peer group, the media, churches, libraries, and museums. The roles of these agencies are subject to alteration due to the impact of social and educational change. In their history, Americans have relied on the school as a powerful force of education, and they continue to do so. Our intent in this book is to introduce prospective teachers to schooling, bearing in mind that schooling is related to and an important part of the large cultural process of education.

DISCUSSION QUESTIONS

1. Distinguish between education and schooling.
2. Write a short biographical sketch in which you identify the agents of enculturation that have shaped your attitudes and values.
3. Discuss the influence of your current peer group on your education.
4. How did your neighborhood community influence your educational decisions?
5. Examine the educational role of radio, television, and motion pictures.
6. List the informal educators who have an impact on schooling, in order of priority.
7. Discuss the ways Americans perceive the school's role.
8. Identify current social and economic trends and assess their impact on schooling.

FIELD EXERCISES

1. Visit a museum or art gallery and identify the ways in which that agency acts as an informal educator.

9. Ibid., p. 4.
10. Ibid., p. 5.

2. Watch the television programs that children or adolescents are likely to view. Identify the life-styles and values conveyed in these programs.

3. Read a newspaper and identify the ways in which it acts as an educational agency.

4. Interview members of your family and try to ascertain their views on education and schooling.

5. Interview a school principal and try to determine his or her perceptions of the public's attitudes and support of public schooling.

6. Interview several classroom teachers and try to determine the relationships they see between the home and the school.

SUGGESTED READINGS

BASTIAN, ANN, FRUCHTER, NORM, GITTELL, MARILYN, GREER, COLIN, AND HASKINS, KENNETH. *Choosing Equality: the Case for Democratic Schooling*. Philadelphia: Temple University Press, 1986.

BAYDO, GERALD R., ed. *The Evolution of Mass Culture in America—1877 to the Present*. Arlington Heights, Ill.: The Forum Press, 1982.

BURGESS, ROBERT G. *Sociology, Education and Schools: An Introduction to the Sociology of Education*. New York: Nichols, 1986.

COUNTS, GEORGE S. *Education and American Civilization*. New York: Teachers College Press, Columbia University, 1952.

CREMIN, LAWRENCE A. *Public Education*. New York: Basic Books, 1976.

ELAM, STANLEY, ed. *The Gallup/Phi Delta Kappa Polls of Attitudes Toward the Public Schools, 1969–88: A 20-Year Compilation and Educational History*. Bloomington, Ind.: Phi Delta Kappa Educational Foundation, 1989.

GIROUX, HENRY A., AND SIMON, ROGER I. *Popular Culture, Schooling, and Everyday Life*. Granby, Mass.: Bergin and Garvey, 1989.

STAFF REPORT OF THE SELECT COMMITTEE ON CHILDREN, YOUTH, AND FAMILIES. *Children and Families: Key Trends in the 1980s*. Washington, D.C.: U.S. Government Printing Office, 1989.

SILBERMAN, CHARLES E. *Crisis in the Classroom: The Remaking of American Education*. New York: Random House, 1970.

TAYLOR, ELLA. *Prime-Time Families: Television Culture in Postwar America*. Berkeley: University of California Press, 1989.

U.S. DEPARTMENT OF HEALTH AND HUMAN SERVICES. *Single Parent Families*. Washington, D.C.: U.S. Government Printing Office, 1981.

WILLIAM T. GRANT FOUNDATION COMMISSION ON WORK, FAMILY, AND CITIZENSHIP. *The Forgotten Half: Pathways to Success for America's Youth and Young Families*. Washington, D.C.: William T. Grant Foundation Commission on Work, Family, and Citizenship, 1989.

2

Teacher Preparation, Demand, Supply, and Salaries

Today, the preparation of teachers for the public and private schools of the United States is a large and complex undertaking. It involves the cooperative efforts of teacher educators in colleges and universities, of officials in state departments of education, of experienced teachers and administrators, and of the public. Since many readers of this book are preparing for careers as professional educators, this chapter provides statistical information on current trends that concern prospective teachers. Chapter 3, "Teaching as a Profession," provides an introduction to the issues related to being prepared as a teacher and entering the teaching profession. Chapters 2 and 3 examine the immediate context of teaching, and are followed by sections that explore the foundations, governance, and institutionalization of education.

Specifically, Chapter 2 provides a perspective on the historical development of the teaching profession, examines programs designed to prepare teachers, and describes the teacher certification process. Among the general focusing questions that will be answered as you read this chapter are the following:

1. What has been the historical condition of American teacher education?
2. How are resourceful teachers prepared?
3. What is the process of teacher certification?
4. What is the current condition of teacher supply and demand?
5. What are the trends in teachers' salaries?

Historical Evolution of American Teacher Education

During the colonial era of the seventeenth and eighteenth centuries, the preparation and status of teachers varied, depending upon the school in which they taught. Latin Grammar teachers and college professors enjoyed greater social status than elementary school teachers. Usually lacking a college degree, elementary school teachers were expected to conform to the dominant local religious tenets; maintain discipline; and teach reading, writing, arithmetic, and catechism.

Teacher hiring practices varied from colony to colony. In New England, school committees hired teachers with approval by the town minister. In the Middle Atlantic colonies, the society or the church operating the school appointed the teacher. In the South, wealthy plantation owners hired tutors to educate their children.

The Common School and Teacher Education

During the nineteenth century, the common-school movement focused attention on teaching and teacher preparation. Proponents of the public school, such as Horace Mann and Henry Barnard, realized that the success of common schools required well-prepared teachers. An early contributor to teacher education was Samuel Hall, a Congregational minister who headed the Normal Department of Phillips Andover Academy. Hall argued that teachers should be prepared in the science of teaching, in the principles of school management, and in the methods of teaching spelling, reading, arithmetic, geography, grammar, writing, composition, history, and other common school subjects.[1] Good teachers, Hall wrote, should have such personal qualifications as common sense, an ability to understand human behavior, affection for children, decisiveness, and ethical standards.

James G. Carter, a colleague of Horace Mann in the Massachusetts legislature, was convinced that common-school education could be improved only by competent teachers who had been prepared in normal schools designed for teacher education. Carter recommended that normal schools also contain a "model," or demonstration, school in which prospective teachers would do practice teaching under the supervision of skilled and experienced educators.[2]

Horace Mann deliberately supported the normal school as a necessary element in the success of the common school. To improve teaching in the common schools, he organized teacher institutes, established normal schools, and worked to increase teachers' salaries. Teachers' institutes were periodic in-service meetings in which teachers gathered to share mutual problems and to hear educational lectures. The normal schools were teacher training institutions that prepared prospective teachers specifically in common-school subjects, pedagogy, and instructional methodology.

Convinced by Carter and Mann, Governor Edward Everett signed the law establishing normal schools in Massachusetts. These early normal schools taught the content and method of teaching reading, writing, grammar, arithmetic, geography, spelling, composition, vocal music, drawing, physiology, algebra, philosophy, methodology, and Scripture. Other states followed the Massachusetts' example of establishing normal schools to prepare common-school teachers.

By the 1870s, normal schools had been established throughout the country and were regarded as the standard institution for preparing elementary school teachers.

1. Samuel Hall, *Lectures to School-Masters on Teaching* (Boston: Carter, Hendee, 1833), pp. 20–21.
2. James G. Carter, "Outline of an Institution for the Education of Teachers," 1825, in Henry Barnard, *Normal Schools and Other Institutions, Agencies, and Means Designed for the Professional Education of Teachers* (Hartford, Conn.: Case, Tiffany, 1851), pp. 78–81.

Although often criticized for a lack of academic rigor, normal schools advanced professional teacher preparation in the United States. Their very existence disputed the common notion that anyone could teach, regardless of preparation. They also were transitional institutions that later developed into teachers' colleges. The normal-school professors produced a professional literature on educational history, philosophy, curriculum, and methods of instruction. The concept of the model school led to the practice that prospective teachers should have a supervised clinical experience that included practice teaching.

Transition to Teachers College

By the late nineteenth century, colleges and universities assumed a role in teacher education. Their involvement was stimulated by growing high school enrollments and a need to prepare larger numbers of qualified secondary school teachers. Because high school teachers were expected to have college degrees, many normal schools became four-year degree-granting colleges, and many existing colleges and universities established departments of pedagogy to prepare teachers as well. For example, the University of Iowa established the first permanent chair of pedagogy in 1873. Iowa's example was followed by the University of Wisconsin in 1879 and by Indiana and Cornell universities in 1886. In 1892, Teachers College, a leading teacher education institution, became a part of Columbia University. By 1900, colleges and universities had become involved in teacher education.

As existing colleges and universities developed teacher education programs, the normal schools became teachers' colleges. By the 1940s, most of the normal schools had been transformed into teachers' colleges. The transition from normal schools to teachers' colleges involved the following stages: requiring high school graduation as an admission requirement, adding a liberal arts and science component to the teacher preparation program, lengthening the curriculum from two to four years, securing authority to grant degrees from the state legislature, and improving quality of instruction. During the 1950s, many teachers' colleges were reorganized into comprehensive state universities that granted degrees in other fields besides professional education.[3]

Emergence of Professional Study

In the early twentieth century, pedagogy had become a recognized field of research and teaching in most universities. In the 1880s and 1890s, the ideas of American educators were shaped by pedagogical insights of the German philosopher Johann Herbart, who sought to organize instructional concepts on psychological principles. In 1892, American Herbartians, such as Frank and Charles McMurry, Charles De Garmo, C. C. Van Liew, and Elmer Brown, organized the National Herbartian Society to advance systematic inquiry into education as a discipline. The American

---

3. Paul Woodring, "A Century of Teacher Education," in William Brickman and Stanley Lehrer, eds., *Century of Higher Education* (New York: Society for the Advancement of Education, 1962), p. 158.

Herbartians enriched the curriculum through their emphasis on culture, history, and literature. They also stressed systematic instruction based on the Herbartian methodological sequence of preparation, presentation, association, generalization, and application.[4]

Along with the Herbartian stress on systematic methodology, G. Stanley Hall's pioneering work in educational psychology provided teachers with new insights into childhood and adolescence. The scientific movement in education, with its research into measurement, evaluation, and testing, was advanced by Edward L. Thorndike.

As school systems expanded and urban school districts grew larger, professional educators became involved in complex administrative and organizational issues. Professional educational programs were expanded to include supervision, administration, curriculum, public relations, financing, and school law. In addition to the curricular, scientific, and administrative aspects of education, educational history, philosophy, and psychology remained an important foundational base in teacher education. Courses in educational foundations or policies examined the aims and purposes of education, the organization of the curriculum, the function of the school, and the relationship of the school to society. Contemporary programs of teacher education are based on this history of teacher education. The next section examines the preparation of teachers for modern American society.

Preparing Resourceful Teachers

The contemporary teacher fulfills many roles in today's society.[5] The most obvious but often most difficult role is that of educating children and youth. To fulfill their primary educational role, teachers need to command a wide repertoire of personal and educational resources. Teachers should be

1. Educated persons who have command of and can use effectively the fundamental skills of thinking and communicating. They should possess an understanding of human beings and society based on a knowledge of the culture in which they live.
2. Resourceful educators who know thoroughly the skills and subjects that they are teaching. They should know and be able to do what they expect others to do. In addition to knowing their subjects, the resourceful educator should know how to teach them by planning and organizing instruction according to the readiness and needs of learners.

---

4. Johann Herbart, *Outlines of Educational Doctrine* (New York: Macmillan, 1901).
5. Many articles and books have been written on teaching and the teacher's role. Varying perspectives are provided by the following. Bel Kaufman's *Up the Down Staircase* (Englewood Cliffs, N.J.: Prentice-Hall, 1964) is a novel, based on experience, that describes the frustrations but also rewards of teaching in a large inner-city urban school. Larry Cuban's *How Teachers Taught: Constancy and Change in American Classrooms 1890–1980* (New York: Longman, 1984) presents a perspective on teaching at key historical periods. *American Teachers: Histories of a Profession at Work*, edited by Donald Warren (New York: Macmillan, 1989), contains essays by leading authorities in teacher education. Tracy Kidder's *Among Schoolchildren* (Boston: Houghton Mifflin, 1989) is an engaging account of a teacher's day-to-day interactions with children.

3. Motivated and interested in teaching as their primary career. Teaching is not a part-time commitment. It should be a career commitment that one genuinely wants to make one's own.
4. Committed to using their own general knowledge, professional expertise, and force of personality to help learners to know, to think, and to grow as responsible persons and citizens.

While a teaching career is demanding of a person's energy and time, it also brings challenges that provide the means for personal growth, realization, and integration. The resourceful teacher needs to be a continuing researcher and an active agent who makes learning happen. Teaching requires a quiet time to research, prepare, and plan for learning. It also requires an active—doing—and interactive time in which the teacher stimulates and brings about learning.

In addition to the primary role of educator, teachers have been assigned many subsidiary roles by contemporary society. Some of these subsidiary functions have been assumed by teachers; others have been thrust on them because of socio-economic change. For example, the teacher is expected to be:

1. A counselor, model, and guide to students in many areas that go beyond teaching a particular skill and subject.
2. The school's representative to parents and other community members.
3. An educator who is active in professional organizations and in the ongoing development of the teaching profession.

Teacher Education Programs

Today's teacher education programs are the product of the early efforts of normal schools, the experimentation of educational researchers, accumulated experience in teaching children in the schools, state certification requirements, the guidelines of accreditation bodies, and the forces of public opinion. As the products of evolutionary forces, teacher education programs are under continuous review, reexamination, and redesign. The major objective of teacher education programs is to prepare resourceful teachers who can use their knowledge, talents, and expertise to educate children and youth effectively.

Although many variations exist, teacher education programs generally consist of five major components: (1) general education, (2) specialized education, (3) professional education, (4) pre–student teaching clinical and field experiences, and (5) supervised clinical experiences. The following sections examine these components.

General Education The *general education* component is designed to prepare teachers who are educated persons by providing academic work in the liberal arts and sciences. The general education component involves the study of language and literature, history and social sciences, humanities and fine arts, mathematics, and natural and physical sciences. In addition, some programs require foreign language study. Moreover, there may be specific institutional requirements; for example, denominational colleges and universities may require courses in theology. The student's choice of elective subjects completes the program.

Depending upon the particular program, courses in the general education component generally occupy between a third and a half of the four-year bachelor's degree program.

The general education component is usually based on (1) courses in the liberal arts and sciences that the particular college or university requires of all students in degree programs and (2) courses of a broad and general nature identified as providing the intellectual background needed by educated individuals. The general education component is designed to provide teachers with the intellectual resources needed to (1) understand knowledge and culture so that the teaching specialty is related to a broader world view and (2) communicate effectively in writing and in speech.

Specialized Education   The *specialized education* component, sometimes called the *depth*, or *major area, of study*, concentrates on the subjects, fields, or levels that the student is preparing to teach. In the specialized education component, elementary teacher preparation generally differs from that of secondary school teachers. Prospective elementary teachers enroll in courses that prepare them to teach the skills and subjects of the elementary curriculum, such as language arts, mathematics, social studies, sciences, music, art, and physical education. These courses are typically organized as methods and materials in the teaching of reading, the teaching of art, the teaching of language arts, children's literature, and others directly related to elementary education.

Prospective secondary teachers are prepared to teach the specialized subjects in the high school curriculum—English, foreign languages, mathematics, history, chemistry, and other academic subjects. In addition, they enroll in professional education courses related to teaching the subject at the secondary level.

The specialized education component is designed to ensure that teachers are specialists as well as generalists. It seeks to provide them with the in-depth knowledge needed in their particular teaching specialty.

Professional Education   Teacher education programs contain a *professional education* component that consists of the humanistic and behavioral foundations of education. This component involves study in the history, philosophy, sociology, and psychology of education, the exceptional child, human growth and development, and often tests and measurements. In addition to the foundational courses, work is required in educational methodology and audiovisual media. The humanistic and behavioral foundations are intended to provide a theoretical base for practice. History of education traces the evolution of educational institutions and processes. Sociology of education examines the relationship of schooling to society. Philosophy of education examines the broad aims and purposes of education. Educational psychology analyzes the learning process, the motivation of students, and the evaluation of their progress. In methodological courses, prospective teachers learn to plan and organize instructional units.

Pre-Student Teaching Clinical and Field Experiences Contemporary teacher education programs include *pre-student teaching clinical and field experiences* designed to provide a direct familiarization with educational settings and situations. In fact, this component of the teacher education program is considered so important that many states require students in teacher education programs to acquire a specific number of hours in such direct contacts with schools prior to student teaching. While the terms *clinical experiences* and *field experiences* are similar and often used interchangeably, there are some subtle distinctions between them. A clinical experience takes place in a facility used in a professional educational program, usually but not always a school, and is supervised by a professional educator. A field experience occurs in a school or school-like setting outside the college or university at which the teacher education program is located and may or may not be directly supervised by college or school personnel. The types of clinical or field experience vary with the particular teacher education program and its location. Generally, the clinical or field experience seeks to

1. Place the teacher education student in a classroom situation in a school.
2. Provide exposure to a variety of school situations such as inner city, suburban, and rural, if possible.
3. Provide opportunities for observing and perhaps participating in educational activities in a multicultural setting.
4. Provide opportunities for working with teachers and students.
5. Provide opportunities for some exposure to educational activities in nonschool settings, such as youth groups, zoos, and museums.

For students in teacher education programs, clinical and field experiences have the benefit of

1. Confirming the decision to be a teacher.
2. Confirming that the person has decided to teach at the appropriate grade level and in the right subject matter area.
3. Providing exposure to teaching and schools before immersion in student teaching.
4. Providing direct experience with how schools and other educational agencies work.

Typically, the clinical or field experience places the teacher education student in a school classroom to observe actual teaching situations and perhaps assist the classroom teacher in instructional activities. As part of the clinical or field experience, the student is generally expected to maintain a journal that records particular experiences or to prepare a paper that analyzes the experience and to attend a seminar where experiences are shared with colleagues. A typical entry in a pre-student teaching journal may include the following:

1. An identification of the school setting, its location, grade level, the instructional activity, and the time and date that it occurred.
2. A description of the instructional episode or event that is being observed. Questions to be answered include: What are the teacher's objectives and goals? How does this particular episode relate to those that precede and follow it? What is the learners' readiness for the particular unit or lesson of instruction?

3. An analysis of the learning situation, unit, lesson, or event that includes a commentary on the teacher's and students' behavior. What sequence of events occurred? How was the achievement of the skill or subject matter measured and verified?

4. A conclusion that generates questions and issues to be discussed in the pre–student teacher seminar. What occurred that may be used or not used in the coming student teaching experience?

Supervised Clinical Experience   The *supervised clinical experience*, often called "student or practice teaching," places prospective teachers in classroom situations in which they are responsible for planning, organizing, and providing instruction to students.[6] Preliminary to the supervised clinical experience, the student teacher is assigned to a school and is placed under the supervision of an experienced classroom teacher. This assignment is arranged by the college or university's director or coordinator of clinical experiences and the appropriately responsible school administrator, often the building principal.

Before beginning the actual clinical experience, the student teacher should visit the school and its community to develop a perspective into the characteristics of the community in which the school is located. Reading the local newspaper may provide insights into social, political, and other community events. A visit to the school enables the student teacher to meet the building principal, department chairpersons,

A student teacher conducts a lesson under the supervision of a cooperating teacher.

6. Adam Drayer, *Problems in Middle and High School Training: A Handbook for Student Teachers and Beginning Teachers* (Boston: Allyn & Bacon, 1979).

and the cooperating teacher. Such preliminary visits should be discussed and planned in cooperation with the college or university director of clinical experiences and should follow the policies of the school in which the student teacher will be a guest.

Although the supervised clinical experience involves several persons indirectly, such as the building principal and department chairperson, the primary involvement is that of

1. *The student teacher*, who is expected to demonstrate subject matter knowledge, skills in instructional methods, and a professional attitude in teaching children or youth in a classroom setting.
2. *The cooperating teacher*, who is regularly assigned to provide instruction to the students. For a successful experience, it is imperative that both cooperating teacher and student teacher work together. The cooperating teacher should discuss the overall instructional plan with the student teacher and clearly state his or her expectations. In turn, the student teacher should be prepared to respond to and implement the cooperating teacher's suggestions.
3. *The college or university supervisor*, who, as an expert in instruction, serves as a facilitator, constructive critic, and counselor for the student teacher.

Many teacher education programs also include a seminar in which student teachers meet periodically to share their experiences, to discuss problems, and to arrive at generalizations based on their teaching experiences. Seminars may also involve resource persons from the education faculty who provide assistance from their fields of expertise to aid the student teachers.

Teacher Certification

Historical Patterns

The certification of teachers is a form of licensure that is administered by the states.[7] Each state, through its teachers' certification board or other state agency, grants a license to teach to individuals who meet its specified requirements for teaching. As with teacher preparation programs, certification, too, has been shaped by historical forces.

In the seventeenth- and eighteenth-century colonial period, religious doctrinal conformity rather than educational competency determined the criteria for hiring teachers. In the early nineteenth century, a confusing array of local government units, such as districts, townships, and counties, licensed teachers. Often, each unit administered its own examination and issued it own certificate. The confusing array of local teacher certification patterns created problems; for example, (1) there was a lack of uniformity of the professional standards for entry into teaching, and (2) while licensed in one locality, teachers often found that their certificates were unacceptable elsewhere.

7. John Tryneski, ed., *Requirements for Certification of Teachers, Counselors, Librarians, Administrators for Elementary and Secondary Schools* (Chicago: University of Chicago Press, 1990).

As a result of the nineteenth-century common-school movement, there was a corresponding attempt to establish minimal standards for entry into teaching on a statewide basis. State superintendents of education or state departments of education assumed control of teacher certification. Gradually, each state, often through its teacher certification board, developed its own licensing requirements as a means to govern entry into teaching. The states' intention was to make certain that only adequately prepared persons were teaching in their public schools. To ensure minimal quality standards, state funds were provided only to school districts employing teachers with certification.

Although differences in certification requirements exist from state to state, most states require possession of a bachelor's degree and evidence of completion of specified courses in professional education. Several states also require a fifth year of preparation for the granting of a teaching credential. In addition to specifying degree and professional education requirements, state certification laws generally prescribe a minimum age requirement for entry into teaching and require evidence of citizenship, good physical health, and good moral character. Some local boards of education, particularly those in large urban districts, may require additional requirements or examinations for employment in their school systems.

Contemporary Patterns

Because teacher certification is a state prerogative, each state has its own requirements. Certification is generally administered by the state teacher certification board, which

1. Grants approved program status to colleges or universities engaged in teacher preparation.
2. Determines that applicants for certification meet the specified legal and professional requirements.
3. Issues the appropriate certificates.

Historically, there have been two patterns by which individuals have been granted a certificate by the state certification board: on an individual basis or as a graduate of an approved program. Certification on an individual basis means that the applicant for a certificate provides the state board with evidence that the necessary requirements have been fulfilled—perhaps by earning a degree and completing required professional education courses. Many state boards are moving from the cumbersome individual basis to the more generally recognized approved program basis of certification.

Teacher Competency Testing   During the 1980s, especially as part of the reform movement generated by *A Nation at Risk*, criticism was directed to the general academic and instructional competency of teachers. In particular, critics contended that declining Scholastic Aptitude Test scores and other indicators of academic achievement demonstrated that the academic competency of teachers needed to be

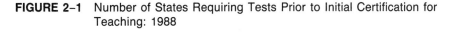

FIGURE 2–1   Number of States Requiring Tests Prior to Initial Certification for Teaching: 1988

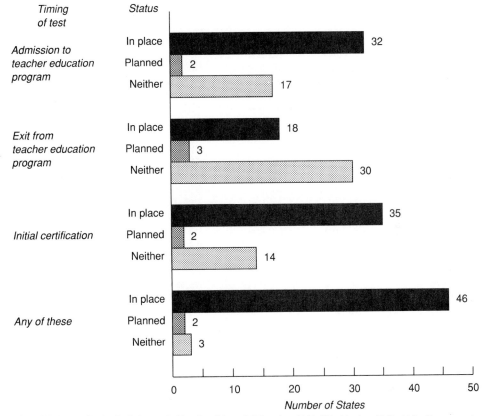

SOURCE: From Curtis O. Baker, ed. *The Condition of Education 1989* (Washington, D.C.: U.S. Government Printing Office, 1989), p. 71.

improved. As a result of this criticism, many states in the late 1980s adopted mandatory teacher competency testing as one possible means of raising the academic performance of American elementary and secondary students. Although it is highly controversial, teacher competency testing is designed to measure specific abilities and skills needed for educating students effectively, increase teachers' accountability for students' academic achievement, and upgrade the quality of the teaching force.

As shown in Figure 2–1 and Table 2–1, as of 1988, 46 states required some form of competency testing as part of teacher certification. By using these tests, the states that require them hope to screen out candidates who are deficient in basic skills and knowledge related to teaching. The specific time for administering competency teacher examinations varies from state to state. Thirty-two states require a test prior to admission to a teacher education program. The other states that require teacher

TABLE 2-1 Teacher Preparation Assessment Requirements, by State; 1988

State	Admission to Teacher Education	Exit from Teacher Education	Initial or Provisional Certification	Regular or Permanent Certification	Recertification or Maintenance of Certification
Alabama	BS	(1)	No test	CK	No test
Alaska[2]	No test	No test	No test	No test	No test
Arizona	BS, PS	No test	BS, PS	No test	No test
Arkansas	BS	IO	PS, CK	PS, CK	No test
California	BS	No test	[3]BS, CK	[3]BS, CK	No test
Colorado	BS	No test	[4]BS	No test	No test
Connecticut	BS	No test	BS, CK	BS, CK, IO	No test
Delaware	No test	No test	BS	BS	No test
District of Columbia	(2)	(2)	BS, CK	BS, CK	No test
Florida	[5]No test	BS, PS, IO	BS, PS	BS, PS, CK, IO	[6]CK
Georgia	No test	No test	CK	CK, IO	CK
Hawaii	BS	IO	BS, PS, CK, IO	IO	IO
Idaho	No test	No test	[7]BS, PS, CS	No test	No test
Illinois	[8]No test	No test	BS, CK	BS, CK	No test
Indiana	No test	No test	BS, PS, CK	No test	No test
Iowa	No test	No test	No test	No test	IO
Kansas	BS	No test	No test	BS, PS, IO	No test
Kentucky	BS	PS, CK, IO	PS, CK, IO	PS, CK, IO	No test
Louisiana	CK	IO	No test	BS, PS, CK	No test
Maine	No test	No test	BS, PS, IO	No test	No test
Maryland	No test	No test	BS, PS, CK	No test	No test
Massachusetts	No test	IO	No test	IO	No test
Michigan	[9]BS	[9]CK	[9]CK	No test	No test
Minnesota	BS	IO	No test	No test	No test
Mississippi	BS	IO	BS, PS, CK	IO	No test
Missouri	BS	[10]PS, CK, IO	IO	IO	IO
Montana	No test	No test	BS, PS	BS, PS	No test
Nebraska	BS	No test	No test	BS	No test
Nevada	BS	PS, CK	PS, CK	PS, CK	CK
New Hampshire	BS	No test	No test	No test	IO
New Jersey	BS, IO	IO	CK, IO	CK	No test
New Mexico	BS	IO	BS, PS, CK	BS, PS, CK, IO	IO
New York	No test	No test	BS, PS	BS, PS	BS, PS
North Carolina	BS	PS, CK	PS, CK, IO	IO	IO
North Dakota	BS	PS, CK	No test	No test	No test
Ohio[11]	BS, IO	BS, PS, CK, IO	BS, PS, CK	No test	No test
Oklahoma	BS, PS	No test	CK	CK	No test
Oregon	BS, CK	No test	BS	IO	No test
Pennsylvania[11]	No test	No test	BS, PS, CK	No test	No test
Rhode Island	No test	IO	BS, PS, IO	No test	No test
South Carolina	BS	PS, CK, IO	PS, CK	PS, CK	No test
South Dakota	BS	No test	No test	No test	No test
Tennessee	PS	No test	PS, CK	No test	No test
Texas	BS	IO	PS, CK	IO	IO
Utah	No test	No test	IO	IO	No test
Vermont	No test	No test	No test	No test	No test
Virginia	BS, PS, CK, IO	No test	BS, PS, CK	IO	No test
Washington	BS	[12]No test	[12]No test	No test	No test

State	Admission to Teacher Education	Exit from Teacher Education	Initial or Provisional Certification	Regular or Permanent Certification	Recertification or Maintenance of Certification
West Virginia	BS	CK, IO	CK, IO	No test	No test
Wisconsin	[13]BS	[14]CK	[14]BS, CK	[14]BS, CK	No test
Wyoming	BS	No test	No test	No test	No test

SOURCE: From Curtis O. Baker, ed., *The Condition of Education 1989* (Washington, D.C.: U.S. Government Printing Office, 1989), p. 127.

Key to types of tests required:
    BS = Basic skills;
    PS = Professional skills;
    CK = Content knowledge;
    IO = In-class observation.

[1]Requirements or tests are under development.
[2]No State policy, some tests administered by universities.
[3]May be waived by the State.
[4]Basic skills test required for persons holding out-of-State certificates.
[5]Provided student's score is in the 40th or higher percentile on the ACT.
[6]Optional in lieu of other requirements.
[7]Also required for reinstatement of expired license.
[8]Institutions must test for reading, language arts, and mathemtatics; no specific test is required.
[9]Required in 1990.
[10]Required beginning in 1992.
[11]Tests for admission to and exit from teacher education programs are established by the college or university.
[12]Professional skills test planned.
[13]Required fall of 1989.
[14]Required spring of 1991.

competency testing position a test either prior to the completion of the teacher education program or prior to initial certification.[8]

Approved Program Certification

In matters relating to teacher certification, it should be noted that the teacher education program of the college or university is closely related to state certification requirements. While the college or university grants the degree to the prospective teacher, it is the state teacher certification board that grants the certificate. The process by which colleges or universities receive approved program recognition from the state certification board involves several carefully defined steps:

1. The state certification board develops standards that colleges or universities must meet in their teacher education programs. Such standards typically include library resources, field work, student teaching, professional courses, and other items related to teacher preparation.
2. The college or university seeking approved program status prepares an institutional self-study that documents how the institution meets the required standards.

8. National Center for Education Statistics, *The Condition of Education 1989*, I (Elementary and Secondary Education) (Washington, D.C.: U.S. Government Printing Office, 1989), p. 70.

3. The college or university is visited by a team appointed by the state board with the approval of the institution that ascertains if the institution is actually complying with the prescribed standards. This team prepares a report that leads eventually to the granting or the denial of approved program status by the state certification board to the college or university.

Reciprocity and NCATE

Prospective teachers also encounter the problem of reciprocity of certification between states. A teaching certificate is issued by a state certification board and is valid in the state of issuance. In our mobile society, however, teachers often are employed in states other than the one that granted initial certification. For many years, the complex and varying state teacher certification patterns made reciprocity difficult.

To reduce the complexities of teacher certification, the American Association of Colleges for Teacher Education (AACTE), a national organization of institutions involved in teacher preparation, has contributed to the advancement of uniform standards. Through the efforts of professional education organizations, the National Council for Accreditation of Teacher Education (NCATE) was established to accredit teacher education programs in colleges and universities.[9] Upon invitation, NCATE evaluates each institution according to the following criteria:

1. It must already be accredited by the proper regional accrediting agency and be recognized by the appropriate state department of education.
2. It must be a nonprofit institution of higher learning offering not less than four years of college work leading to the bachelor's degree.
3. It must offer a four-year curriculum to prepare either elementary or secondary teachers, or both, or offer graduate programs in education.

Proponents of NCATE see it as a national organization for the evaluation and accreditation of qualified teacher education programs. According to the concept of reciprocity, the states would automatically license graduates of NCATE accredited programs. By 1977, 31 states had accepted NCATE accreditation for teacher certification. This has contributed significantly to uniformity in teacher certification. NCATE detractors allege that it has inflexibly overemphasized requirements not justified by research.

Teacher Supply and Demand

The question of teacher supply and demand directly concerns prospective teachers. In gross terms, teacher supply and demand is based on two major factors: (1) the number of students to be educated and (2) the number of teachers available to

---

9. Patricia Sinclair, ed., *National Professional Accrediting Agencies: How They Function* (Washington, D.C.: National Education Association, 1973); *Standards for the Accreditation of Teacher Education* (Washington, D.C.: National Council for Accreditation of Teacher Education, 1982).

educate them. If the student population increases at a faster rate than the number of available teachers, teacher shortage results. If more teachers are available than are needed to educate students, a teacher surplus results. Calculating and predicting teacher supply and demand is not simple, however, as many complex variables come into play.

Demographic factors influence teacher supply and demand in that the number of children enrolled in the schools determines to a large extent the number of teachers employed to educate them. Average daily attendance as shown in Table 2–2 is an important means of estimating the number of teachers needed in a particular state. Social, political, and economic factors also influence teacher supply and demand. What priority does the nation, the state, the local community, and the individual give to education? If they give education a high priority, taxpayers will be willing to provide the teachers needed to educate children. If they give it a low priority, then the educational service provided to children is likely to be reduced. Inevitably, social and political priorities for education must be translated into economics and finance. Local school districts must have both the resources and the willingness to pay teachers. Here, the issue of wealthy versus poor school districts and the degree to which the federal and state governments support education is relevant.

Demographic Factors

From the end of World War II until 1970, there was an increase in school-aged population and a general teacher shortage. The demands placed on local school districts were particularly intense in the suburban areas that developed around the large cities. The suburbs adjacent to New York, Philadelphia, Boston, Chicago, St. Louis, Dallas, Los Angeles, and other large cities grew as more affluent Americans were attracted to the life-style that suburbia promised. Families with school-aged children moved in droves to the existing suburbs and caused development of new suburbs. The suburban school districts with their expanding school system were a ready market for teachers. By the 1950s, the situation had stabilized as colleges and universities prepared large numbers of teachers and many school districts built new physical facilities for the growing school-aged population.

Throughout the 1960s, there was a teacher shortage. By the end of that decade, however, the shortage became a surplus as the decreasing American birthrate resulted in declining enrollments in the elementary and secondary schools.

The 20-year period from 1970 to 1990 was marked by two contrasting school enrollment trends: declining enrollments from 1971 through 1984 and increasing enrollments since 1985 (see Table 2–3). From 1971 until 1984, overall public and private elementary and secondary school enrollments declined because of a decreasing school-aged population. For example, total enrollments declined from 46,318,000 in 1980 to 44,625,000 in 1984. The school year of 1985 marked a turning point in enrollments; they began to climb upward for the first time since 1971. In 1990, enrollments had reached 46,112,000. Between 1989 and 1995, overall elementary and secondary school enrollments are expected to increase by 8 percent,

TABLE 2-2 Average Daily Attendance in Public Elementary and Secondary Schools, by State: 1969–70 to 1987–88

State	1969-70	1975-76	1979-80	1980-81	1983-84	1984-85	1985-86	1986-87	1987-88
1	2	3	4	5	6	7	8	9	10
United States	**41,934,376**	**41,269,720**	**38,288,911**	**37,703,744**	**36,362,978**	**36,404,261**	**36,523,103**	**136,863,867**	**37,050,707**
Alabama	777,123	716,371	711,432	701,925	679,742	684,211	686,716	690,256	689,340
Alaska	72,489	81,564	79,945	83,745	80,264	96,257	98,535	96,004	94,917
Arizona	391,526	455,692	481,905	476,149	482,185	477,520	494,504	518,277	534,812
Arkansas	414,158	428,720	423,610	417,080	404,282	405,077	408,601	409,388	405,196
California[2]	4,418,423	4,366,617	4,044,736	4,014,917	4,098,300	4,139,461	4,245,090	4,429,792	4,531,459
Colorado	500,388	527,434	513,475	508,750	503,162	505,321	507,876	513,587	514,838
Connecticut	618,881	596,175	507,362	501,085	452,061	446,981	452,058	444,285	441,150
Delaware	120,819	116,553	94,058	89,609	84,118	84,407	84,936	86,655	87,821
District of Columbia	138,600	119,255	91,576	85,773	77,859	76,023	76,241	76,822	79,801
Florida	1,312,693	1,435,570	1,464,461	1,389,487	1,388,717	1,416,104	1,442,921	1,489,146	1,536,866
Georgia	1,019,427	998,898	989,433	988,612	978,530	989,713	1,004,799	1,023,127	1,033,459
Hawaii	168,140	162,903	151,563	151,713	150,137	150,572	151,174	152,287	155,220
Idaho	170,920	182,215	189,199	190,144	194,533	197,902	198,141	198,449	199,563
Illinois	2,084,844	1,990,158	1,770,435	1,765,357	1,616,711	1,600,380	1,604,265	1,574,128	1,584,745
Indiana	1,111,043	1,049,889	983,444	944,424	893,464	883,592	870,463	873,733	877,942
Iowa	624,403	574,773	510,081	501,403	467,965	461,392	454,341	453,150	450,858
Kansas	470,296	419,022	382,019	374,451	368,354	369,524	371,655	378,073	384,660
Kentucky	647,970	622,484	619,868	614,676	585,861	579,441	577,190	579,226	578,550
Louisiana	776,555	768,097	727,601	715,844	724,153	732,864	732,230	736,474	729,492
Maine	225,146	227,841	211,400	207,554	200,159	198,125	198,358	197,539	197,225
Maryland	785,989	793,848	686,336	664,866	602,077	596,478	592,383	595,618	601,415
Massachusetts	1,056,207	1,070,996	935,960	950,675	806,193	779,869	745,991	727,680	749,030
Michigan	1,991,235	1,971,774	1,758,427	1,711,139	1,514,671	1,490,452	1,481,068	1,476,471	1,473,542
Minnesota	864,595	827,239	748,606	710,836	663,780	669,930	669,385	674,245	679,729
Mississippi	524,623	479,076	454,401	446,515	437,790	435,587	448,117	473,424	479,402
Missouri	906,132	864,958	777,269	756,536	715,182	712,197	714,230	724,710	725,661
Montana	162,664	156,473	144,608	141,641	139,387	139,905	138,829	139,199	139,018
Nebraska	314,516	296,915	270,524	263,797	252,484	250,647	250,975	252,457	252,399

26

Nevada	113,421	128,106	134,995	138,481	139,115	140,402	143,941	149,136	153,252
New Hampshire	140,203	159,836	154,187	150,316	144,733	144,655	147,561	149,963	152,000
New Jersey	1,322,124	1,310,042	1,140,111	1,121,272	1,037,865	1,043,047	1,029,797	1,024,611	1,008,749
New Mexico	259,997	256,764	253,453	240,496	246,451	248,758	252,892	243,340	248,231
New York	3,099,192	3,012,893	2,530,289	2,475,055	2,321,800	2,309,169	2,276,842	2,266,283	2,247,588
North Carolina	1,104,295	1,120,207	1,072,150	1,055,651	1,022,138	1,018,795	1,014,795	1,020,702	1,016,742
North Dakota	141,961	126,277	118,986	111,759	111,630	109,427	108,947	109,074	109,512
Ohio	2,246,282	2,103,243	1,849,283	1,801,914	1,693,851	1,675,530	1,660,718	1,664,709	1,612,592
Oklahoma	560,993	558,528	548,065	542,800	553,236	552,835	553,370	550,949	547,149
Oregon	436,736	425,126	418,593	417,009	401,398	401,154	401,476	402,855	406,054
Pennsylvania	2,169,225	2,064,312	1,808,630	1,754,782	1,601,944	1,571,831	1,560,746	1,554,642	1,539,310
Rhode Island	163,205	158,752	139,195	135,096	123,501	122,653	122,109	122,024	124,559
South Carolina	660,292	591,900	569,612	580,132	602,183	559,340	558,716	564,508	567,091
South Dakota	158,543	141,120	124,934	121,663	117,192	117,137	118,269	118,902	119,868
Tennessee	836,010	826,335	806,696	797,237	774,346	769,862	762,225	766,521	766,651
Texas	2,432,420	2,549,517	2,608,817	2,647,288	2,745,339	2,879,823	2,923,741	2,977,783	2,991,242
Utah	287,405	289,171	312,813	323,048	356,072	366,574	379,249	386,306	397,214
Vermont	97,772	98,015	95,045	90,884	86,404	85,734	85,875	85,985	87,760
Virginia	995,580	1,018,034	955,105	938,794	900,378	901,994	904,347	911,261	914,354
Washington	764,735	723,083	710,929	704,655	685,068	688,759	696,372	708,584	721,952
West Virginia	372,278	366,395	353,264	351,823	343,320	336,196	330,145	324,791	319,330
Wisconsin	880,609	858,407	770,554	743,505	699,089	696,071	694,351	682,560	698,963
Wyoming	81,293	82,147	89,471	91,381	93,804	94,583	95,547	94,176	92,434
Outlying areas									
American Samoa	—	7,461	—	—	—	10,580	10,816	10,559	10,579
Guam	20,315	26,318	—	22,343	—	23,632	23,220	23,409	23,172
Northern Marianas	—	—	—	—	—	5,548	4,921	5,071	5,851
Puerto Rico	—	669,400	656,709	671,661	—	649,651	636,268	629,922	621,731
Virgin Islands	—	21,793	—	23,312	—	—	23,811	22,814	22,103

SOURCE: From National Center for Education Statistics, *Digest of Education Statistics 1990* (Washington, D.C. U.S. Government Printing Office, 1991), p. 59.

[1]Revised from previously published data.

[2]Data for California are not strictly comparable with those for other States because California's attendance figures include excused absences.

—Data not available.

TABLE 2-3 Public and Private School Enrollment, Kindergarten Through Grade 12, Fall 1970-86

Fall of Year	Public School			Private School			Private School Enrollment as a Percentage of Total Enrollment		
	Total K-12	K-8	9-12	Total K-12	K-8	9-12	Total K-12	K-8	9-12
	Enrollment (in thousands)						Percent		
1970	46,193	32,648	13,545	5,655	4,485	1,170	10.9	12.1	8.0
1971	46,575	32,518	14,057	5,378	4.252	1,126	10.4	11.6	7.4
1972	45,344	31,329	14,015	5,203	4,048	1,155	10.3	11.4	7.6
1973	44,945	30,783	14,162	4,945	3,761	1,184	9.9	10.9	7.7
1974	44,957	30,682	14,275	4,867	3,695	1,172	9.8	10.7	7.6
1975	44,520	30,017	14,503	5,001	3,821	1,180	10.1	11.3	7.5
1976	44,201	29,660	14,541	4,804	3,603	1,201	9.8	10.8	7.6
1977	43.153	28,648	14,505	5,025	3,777	1,248	10.4	11.6	7.9
1978	41,976	27,745	14,231	4,978	3,734	1,244	10.6	11.9	8.0
1979	41,343	27,349	13,994	4,663	3,541	1,122	10.1	11.5	7.4
1980	—	27,088	—	—	3,537	—	—	11.5	—
1981	40,897	27,374	13,523	4,701	3,582	1,119	10.3	11.6	7.6
1982	40,131	27,127	13,004	4,702	3,584	1,118	10.5	11.7	7.9
1983	39,701	26,909	12,792	4,868	3,650	1,218	10.9	11.9	8.7
1984*	39,794	27,073	12,721	4,306	3,249	1,057	9.8	10.7	7.7
1985	39,788	27,024	12,764	4,872	3,657	1,215	10.9	11.9	8.7
1986	40,237	27,491	12,746	4,757	3,591	1,166	10.6	11.6	8.4

SOURCE: From Curtis O. Baker, ed., *The Condition of Education 1989* (Washington, D.C.: U.S. Government Printing Office, 1989), p. 109.

NOTE: Detail may not add to total due to rounding.

—Not available.

*An unexplained drop occurred in the number and proportion of private school students in 1984, according to the Bureau of the Census. However, the 1984 data appear to be an anomaly since the 1985 and 1986 figures for private school students are very similar to those for 1983 and are consistent with the level from 1979 through 1983.

or 3.1 million students. Enrollment projections for 1995 estimate an elementary and secondary school population of 49,112,000.[10] The current and projected increase in student enrollments provide clear evidence that the employment prospects for teachers will be favorable throughout the first half of the 1990s.

Although overall enrollments increased from 1980 to 1990 and are projected to increase through 1995, the growth rates differ for elementary (kindergarten through eighth grade) and secondary schools (grades 9 through 12) (see Figure 2-2). Elementary enrollments, which were 31,666,000 in 1980, reached 33,540,000 in 1990. They are projected at 35,123,000 for 1995. Secondary schools, however, are currently experiencing declining enrollments as the smaller age-group cohort reaches high school age. Secondary school enrollments dropped from 14,652,000 in 1980 to 13,822,000 in 1985, and in 1990 they reached their low point at 12,563,000. In the

10. National Center for Education Statistics, *Digest of Education Statistics 1989*, pp. 3, 9.

FIGURE 2–2 Trends in Public School Enrollment,
Fall 1972–1997

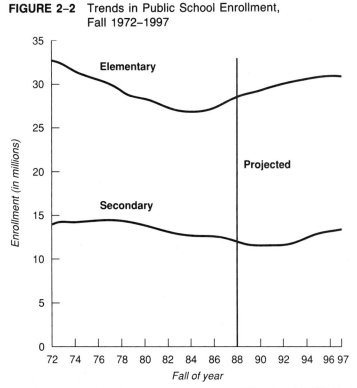

SOURCE: From Curtis O. Baker, ed. *The Condition of Education 1989* (Washington,
D.C.: U.S. Government Printing Office, 1989), p. 53.

first half of the 1990s, secondary enrollments will begin an upward trend and are
projected to reach 13,999,000 in 1995.[11]

In response to the teacher surplus and resultant poorer employment prospects
of the late 1970s and early 1980s, the number of individuals entering and completing
teacher education programs decreased. As enrollments increased, the supply of
teachers did not keep up with the demand. The enrollment patterns and projections
for the 1990s, viewed nationally, indicate favorable employment prospects for most
teachers; generally we find a trend toward increasing demand. In the following
sections we will describe the different prospects in various regions.

Population Shifts

Historically, Americans have been very mobile. Due to this mobility, centers of
population have shifted periodically. Several important shifts of population have

11. Ibid., p. 9.

affected school enrollments. At the end of the nineteenth century, there was a major movement of population from the rural to the urban areas of the country. After World War II, there was a massive influx of people to the suburbs that ring the nation's large cities. Seen regionally, for most of the first two-thirds of the twentieth century, the industrial states of the Northeast and Middle West were the major centers of population; however, during the 1970s, substantial increases occurred in the population of the Sunbelt states of the South and West, with a corresponding decline in several northern and northeastern states, especially in the large cities.

Projections for the early 1990s find the greatest enrollment growth in public elementary and secondary schools for the western states, where a 12 percent increase is expected by 1993. The greatest increase is expected in California, with an enrollment increase of 650,000 by 1993. Substantial increases are also projected in Arizona, Nevada, and New Mexico. Stable enrollment patterns with smaller increases are projected for Idaho, Montana, Oregon, and Wyoming. To meet the needs of the larger school population, an 8 percent increase in the number of teachers is expected by 1993; substantial increases are projected for Arizona and Nevada.

Enrollments in the southern states are expected to increase by 806,000, which follows the anticipated national average growth rate of 6 percent. This overall projected increase continues the growth of the 1980s. However, the pattern of growth is expected to vary considerably from state to state. For example, Florida's enrollments are projected to increase by 13 percent, while West Virginia's are expected to decrease by 10 percent. Enrollment increases are projected for Delaware, Florida, Georgia, Maryland, Texas, and Virginia; decreases are predicted for Arkansas, Kentucky, and West Virginia. Therefore, although the general increase in enrollments in the southern states is projected to create a 6 percent increase overall in the demand for teachers, the actual demand will vary from state to state. The demand is expected to be greatest in Maryland, while Mississippi is likely to have a significant decline.

Enrollment increases of 3 percent are projected for the northeastern states. This projected increase signals a slight upward growth pattern that reverses the 4 percent decline of the 1980s. By 1993, the northeastern region is expected to have a total of 7.4 million students, a 3 percent increase over 1988. Based on these projections, the number of teachers in the Northeast is expected to increase by 12 percent by 1993, an increase of 57,000. The states likely to have the largest increases in the teaching force are Connecticut, New Jersey, and New York.

Enrollment increases of 2 percent, the smallest among the nation's regions, are projected for the midwestern states. The largest increase is expected in Minnesota, where it is estimated to be 6 percent by 1993. The most significant decrease, 4 percent, is expected in Iowa. The number of new teachers needed in the midwestern states is generally anticipated to remain stable.[12]

---

12. *State Projections to 1993 for Public Elementary and Secondary Enrollments, Graduates, and Teachers* (Washington, D.C.: National Center for Education Statistics, 1988), pp. 5, 27.

Early Childhood Education

A combination of social, economic, and educational trends has produced an increased demand for early childhood educators. In the 1970s, the sharpest growth in the labor force occurred in the category of women who were the mothers of children under six years of age. Although the number of children in the age level from three to five declined from 1966, the increase in the number of working mothers produced a greater demand for preprimary education. Along with these socioeconomic factors, there is also a greater sensitivity to the educational needs and potentialities of preprimary-aged children.

In 1987, 5,931,000 children, ages three through five, were enrolled in preprimary programs. By 1993, preprimary enrollments are expected to reach 7.2 million. Equally impressive has been the dramatic increase in the percentages of children enrolled in preprimary programs. In 1965, 27.1 percent of children, ages three to five,

FIGURE 2-3 Projected Annual Demand for New Hiring of
Teachers, by Level, 1989–1997

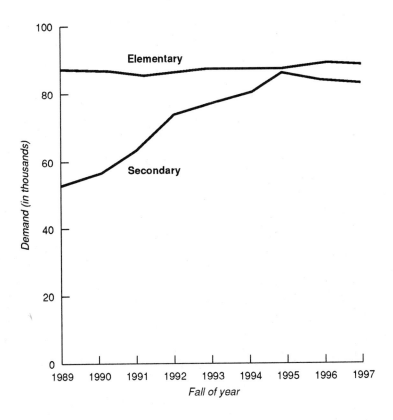

SOURCE: From Curtis O. Baker, ed. *The Condition of Education 1989* (Washington, D.C.: U.S. Government Printing Office, 1989), p. 47.

were enrolled. By 1975, 48.7 percent were enrolled, and by 1985, the figure had reached 54.6 percent.[13] Since then, the percentage of children enrolled has been relatively stable at slightly more than 54 percent. The popularity of preprimary programs suggests encouraging prospects for those seeking to be early childhood educators.

Trends in Teacher Demand and Supply

The indications for the employment of teachers, including those entering the profession for the first time, are generally favorable. Factors that impact hiring new teachers, such as student enrollment, pupil–teacher ratios, the number of individuals who retire or leave teaching, demographic movement and relocation of the school-age population, and the funding of education, are favorable to increases in the number of teachers. These factors vary from state to state and from local district to local district; however, the annual projection for new public school teachers is expected to range from 161,000 in 1992 to 174,000 in 1996 (Figure 2–3 and Table 2–4).[14]

By 1995, the total demand for new public school elementary and secondary teachers is expected to reach 24 percent. Until 1997, the demand for elementary teachers is likely to be greater than that for secondary teachers. However, the need for secondary teachers is meanwhile expected to increase by 57 percent.[15] As shown in Table 2-4 and Figure 2-4, the projected annual demand for new public school

TABLE 2–4   Projected Annual Demand for New Hiring of Classroom Teachers in Public Elementary and Secondary Schools, Fall 1989–97

	Projected Demand for New Hiring of Teachers		
Fall of Year	Total	Elementary	Secondary
1989	140,000	87,000	53,000
1990	143,000	87,000	57,000
1991	149,000	85,000	64,000
1992	161,000	87,000	74,000
1993	166,000	88,000	78,000
1994	169,000	88,000	81,000
1995	174,000	88,000	86,000
1996	174,000	89,000	84,000
1997	171,000	89,000	83,000

SOURCE: From Curtis O. Baker, ed., *The Condition of Education 1989* (Washington, D.C.: U.S. Government Printing Office, 1989), p. 108.

13. National Center for Education Statistics, *Digest of Education Statistics 1989*, p. 57.
14. Ibid.
15. Curtis O. Baker, *The Condition of Education 1989* (Washington, D.C.: U.S. Government Printing Office, 1989), p. 46.

FIGURE 2–4   Percent Change in Number of Classroom Teachers in Public Schools, by State, Fall 1988 to Fall 1993

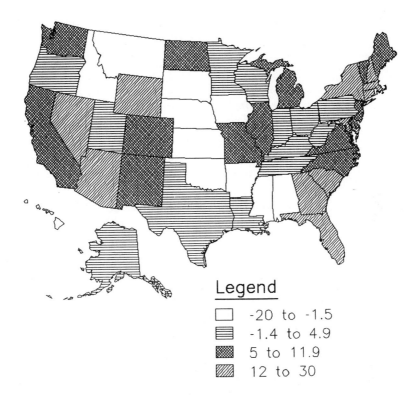

SOURCE: From National Center for Education Statistics, *State Projections to 1993 For Public Elementary and Secondary Enrollment, Graduates, and Teachers* (Washington, D.C.: U.S. Government Printing Office, 1987), p. 29.

teachers in 1992 is estimated at 161,000, with 87,000 being elementary and 74,000 secondary teachers. In 1994, projected new hirings of public school teachers will increase to 169,000, 88,000 at the elementary and 81,000 at the secondary level. For 1996, a further increase is projected, with new hires of teachers estimated at 174,000 – 89,000 elementary and 84,000 secondary.[16]

Subject and Specialty Needs

A shortage of teachers is expected in mathematics, industrial arts, chemistry, physics, vocational agriculture, special education, and bilingual education. If fund-

16. Ibid., p. 108.

ing improves, it is likely that there will be a growing demand for teachers of the gifted. A teacher surplus will probably also continue in home economics, health education, the social sciences, and art. (See Figure 2–5.)

According to teacher placement officials, teacher surplus and shortages will exist in the following areas:

Considerable teacher shortage in mathematics, industrial arts, physics, learning disabilities, vocational agriculture, chemistry, general science, speech correction, and bilingual education.

Slight teacher shortage in special education areas such as reading, mental retardation, multiple handicapped, gifted, earth science, biology, school psychology, and business.

Balanced supply and demand in English, instrumental music, library science, elementary and secondary school counseling, vocal music, Spanish, driver's training, journalism, and speech.

FIGURE 2–5   Fields with Largest Proportional Teacher Shortages in Public Elementary/Secondary Schools

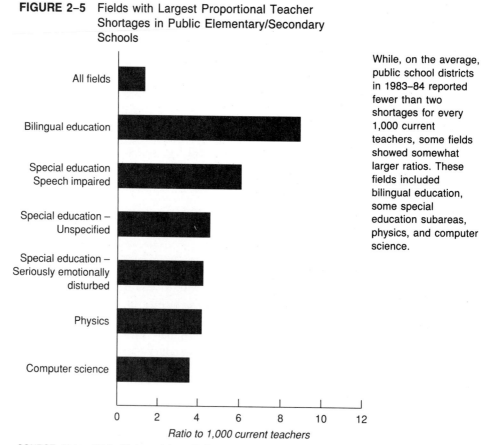

While, on the average, public school districts in 1983–84 reported fewer than two shortages for every 1,000 current teachers, some fields showed somewhat larger ratios. These fields included bilingual education, some special education subareas, physics, and computer science.

Ratio to 1,000 current teachers

SOURCE: Valena White Plisko and Joyce D. Stern, eds., *The Condition of Education: 1985 Edition* (Washington, D.C.: U.S. Government Printing Office, 1985), p. 147.

Slight surplus in French, German, elementary education, home economics, health education, social science, and art.
Considerable surplus in physical education.

Pupil–Teacher Ratios

A crucial factor that relates to the employment demand for teachers is that of pupil–teacher ratios. Pupil–teacher ratios are determined by the number of students enrolled and the number of full-time teachers available to provide instruction. The employment of teachers corresponds closely to the number of pupils assigned to a particular classroom teacher. Considerable variation in pupil–teacher ratios exists from school district to school district. The lower the number of pupils to teachers,

TABLE 2–5   Pupil–Teacher Ratios in Public Elementary and Secondary Schools; School Years 1959–60 through 1987–88

School year	K–12	Elementary	Secondary
1959–60	26.0	28.7	21.5
1969–61	25.8	28.4	21.7
1961–62	25.6	28.3	21.7
1962–63	25.7	28.5	21.7
1963–64	25.5	28.4	21.5
1964–65	25.1	27.9	21.5
1965–66	24.7	27.6	20.8
1966–67	24.1	26.9	20.3
1967–68	23.7	26.3	20.3
1968–69	23.2	25.4	20.4
1969–70	22.7	24.8	20.0
1970–71	22.3	24.4	19.9
1971–72	22.3	24.9	19.3
1972–73	21.8	24.0	19.1
1973–74	21.3	23.0	19.3
1974–75	20.8	22.6	18.7
1975–76	20.4	21.7	18.8
1976–77	20.3	21.8	18.5
1977–78	19.7	21.1	18.2
1978–79	19.3	21.0	17.3
1979–80	19.1	20.6	17.2
1980–81	18.8	20.3	16.9
1981–82	18.9	20.5	16.9
1982–83	18.7	20.4	16.6
1983–84	18.5	20.4	16.2
1984–85	18.1	20.0	15.7
1985–86	17.9	19.6	15.7
1986–87	17.7	19.1	16.0
1987–88˙	17.6	19.5	15.3

SOURCE: From Curtis O. Baker, ed., *The Condition of Education 1989* (Washington, D.C.: U.S. Government Printing Office, 1989), p. 107.
˙Preliminary.

FIGURE 2–6   Pupil/Teacher Ratios in Public Elementary
and Secondary Schools

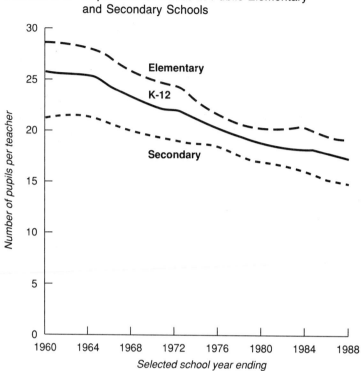

SOURCE: From Curtis O. Baker, ed., *The Condition of Education 1989* (Washington, D.C.: U.S. Government Printing Office, 1989), p. 45.

the larger the number of teachers needed. It has been generally assumed that a lower pupil–teacher ratio will result in higher student academic achievement. However, this assumption has been controversial, and research results are inconclusive.

While student enrollments in public schools decreased in the late 1970s and early 1980s, the number of teachers increased. This factor caused a sharp decline in the pupil–teacher ratios in the public schools. As shown in Table 2–5 and Figure 2–6, between 1959 and 1988, the pupil–teacher ratio in public elementary schools declined from 28.7:1 to 19.5:1, a decrease of 32 percent. During the same period, the pupil–teacher ratio in public secondary schools declined from 21.5:1 to 15.3:1, a decrease of 29 percent.[17]

Teacher Salaries and Benefits

In many societies, the esteem that a profession enjoys is measured by the economic rewards it receives. Historically, teachers have not been compensated adequately for their contributions to the education of children and youth. In the past, particularly in the colonial and early national periods, many teachers were poorly prepared.

17. Baker, *The Condition of Education 1989*, p. 44.

Today, however, teachers are prepared in carefully designed programs. Because of sustained effort, American teachers' salaries have risen slowly over time.

Although local and state variations must be considered, the following generalizations apply to teachers' salaries:

1. The average salary paid to secondary teachers is often higher than that paid to elementary school teachers.
2. Teachers holding master's degrees receive higher average salaries than do those with bachelor's degrees.
3. The average teachers' salaries in large- and medium-sized school systems are higher than those in smaller districts.
4. The salaries paid to beginning teachers with a bachelor's degree are generally lower than are those paid to individuals entering other fields with a bachelor's degree.

The recent history of teachers' compensation shows an impressive increase in teachers' salaries. In 1968, public school teachers received an average annual salary of $7,423, with elementary teachers receiving $7,208 and secondary teachers receiving $7,692. Ten years later, in 1978, the average annual salary had risen to $14,198, with elementary teachers receiving $13,845 and secondary teachers receiving $14,602.[18] In 1988, the national average public school teachers' salary had risen to $30,788, with elementary teachers receiving $30,106 and secondary teachers receiving $31,722.[19] To put it another way, teachers' salaries, which had lost purchasing power due to the high inflation rates of the 1970s, rose faster than the lower inflation rates of the 1980s. Between 1980 and 1988, the value of teachers' salaries, after being adjusted for inflation, rose by 19 percent.[20]

Salary Schedules

The individual teacher's salary is determined in most school districts by location on a salary schedule. A number of states have determined the minimum salaries to be paid to teachers in the state. Such state minimum salary levels are actually lower than the salaries paid to most teachers, but they provide a starting point for the salary schedules that local school districts establish. Teacher salary schedules are established as a result of negotiation between the local school board and the local teachers' organization or bargaining unit. After both parties agree, the salary schedule for teachers in the district is established. Items included in the typical teachers' salary schedule are:

1. The initial, starting, base salary for teachers with a bachelor's degree, a master's degree, and a master's degree with additional earned credit hours. In ascending order, the salaries are generally higher depending on the advanced degrees earned by the teacher.
2. The maximum salary that a teacher can reach at the different degree levels.
3. A series of steps—based on experience in the district and/or merit—that determines the annual salary increment to be paid each year in addition to the base salary.

18. Ibid., p. 106.
19. Laurence T. Ogle, ed. *The Condition of Education 1990*, I (Washington, D.C.: U.S. Government Printing Office, 1990), p. 90.
20. National Center for Education Statistics, *Digest of Education Statistics 1989*, p. 1.

The salary schedule also may specify the extra pay or stipend that teachers receive for supervisory or extracurricular activities outside of classroom instruction.

Teachers may earn extra income from the school district for performing certain added duties, such as coaching athletic teams, acting as moderators or advisors for clubs and student organizations, advising and assisting in the production of plays, school newspapers, and yearbooks, and serving as chaperons for special events.

The typical salary schedule is designed to encourage teachers to improve their professional competency by enrolling in graduate courses or advanced degree programs. Service to the school district is rewarded by increments based on years of experience. Salary schedules are usually renegotiated periodically by school boards and teacher associations or unions at times specified in their professional agreements or in contracts.

Agreement on a salary schedule is often preceded by negotiations between the local school board and the teachers' organization. A number of issues can lead to possible conflict in the negotiation process. Teachers' organizations generally have argued that salary schedules should be based on the level of academic preparation, earned degrees, and years of teaching experience. In light of recent inflationary trends in the economy, teachers' organizations have sought to tie increments to cost-of-living increases, based on the consumer price index. School boards tend to resist cost-of-living increases because their revenues, based on the local property tax and state aid formulas, are relatively fixed and do not increase with inflation. There has also been a tendency for school boards to base increments on merit as determined by performance evaluations. Teachers' organizations that oppose merit increments argue that most instruments for rating teachers are ambiguous or unscientific and generate distrust between the supervisory staff and teachers.

Career Ladders

Growing out of recent educational reforms has been the tendency to establish *career ladders* for teachers. As with merit pay, career ladders are designed to recognize and reward teachers for excellence in teaching.[21] Based upon performance evaluations, career ladders involve differentiated award levels and roles. Originally, the career ladder was intended as a more flexible alternative to the often rigid salary schedule. However, career ladders have become additions to the salary schedule rather than a substitution for it.

Although career ladders vary, they generally have the following goals:

1. Improving the quality of instruction by rewarding outstanding teacher performance
2. Establishing a performance-based system of teacher rewards

21. For these recent developments in teacher compensation and career advancement, see H. C. Johnson, Jr., ed., *Merit Money and Teachers' Careers* (Lanham, Md.: University Press of America, 1985), and Harry Hatry and John Griener, *Issues and Case Studies in Teacher Incentive Plans* (Washington, D.C.: Urban Institute, 1985).

3. Increasing the earning power of teachers by providing incentives that will attract and retain highly competent persons in the profession.

Career ladders may be used to identify, recognize, and reward demonstrated competency in teaching. In some cases, they also may be used to assign added responsibilities to teachers who have demonstrated their teaching ability. Such added duties might be providing supervision or monitoring new teachers.

Fringe Benefits

Individuals entering professions and occupations are attracted to fringe benefits, as well as to the annual salary or wage. Somewhat difficult to define, *fringe benefits* refers to added benefits, inducements, and rewards enjoyed by people working in a field. The most obvious fringe benefit is a financial reward; however, a broader concept of fringe benefits includes the opportunities for personal satisfaction and social significance provided by a given profession or occupation.

Despite its challenges and day-to-day frustrations, teaching is a socially significant activity that provides many opportunities for personal integration and satisfaction. The teacher's preservice and in-service education is related so directly to career activities that it is a means of continual professional renewal and meaning. The school year of nine to ten months allows time for personal growth and continuing education.

Teachers traditionally have used summer months for advanced professional education or for travel that enriches their teaching careers. Teaching also provides opportunities to work with colleagues who face similar problems and experience similar rewards.

In negotiations with boards of education, teachers' organizations and unions have sought to achieve tangible fringe benefits for their members. Among benefits enjoyed by many teachers are the following:

> *Leaves of absence*, with pay or partial pay, are designed to encourage teachers to engage in advanced professional study, to travel, to participate in educational exchange programs at home or abroad, and to write and develop teaching materials and strategies.
> *Sick leaves* are generally provided by the statutory provisions of many of the states and in the policies of school districts. Generally, the amount of sick leave that can be accumulated is based on the length of service to the district. Most districts also provide sick days with pay for illness or death of a member of the immediate family.
> *Insurance benefits*, such as group life, hospitalization, medical-surgical, major medical, dental, liability, disability, and other forms, may be provided by larger school districts. Often, a school district and its employees each contribute to various insurance plans.

Some school districts also provide cost-of-living increases based on increases in the consumer price index. Fringe benefits are negotiated between the school board and representatives of the teachers' association and are specified in their agreement or contract.

Teacher Retirement

All states have established retirement systems for teachers. Teachers and the employing school districts usually contribute to the retirement fund. Retirement benefits are based on the average annual salary and the number of years employed in teaching.

Conclusion

Teacher education and certification in the United States is a product of historical forces and contemporary trends. Present-day teacher education programs have been designed to prepare resourceful teachers who are liberally educated and professionally prepared. Today's teacher preparation programs combine theory and practice, with a greater focus on clinical experience in the classroom. Teacher education programs are generally approved by the various states; many are also accredited by NCATE.

Teacher supply and demand is changeable and is based on a number of demographic and economic factors. Within the United States, the movement of population to and away from particular states influences teacher demand in those states. In addition, the financial ability of school districts to staff classrooms and the establishing of pupil–teacher ratios also determines the number of teachers who will be employed in the particular school district. Although they have increased in recent years, teacher salaries vary considerably from state to state and from district to district within a particular state.

DISCUSSION QUESTIONS

1. Trace the historical evolution of teacher preparation and certification.
2. Examine the author's conception of a resourceful teacher. Do you agree or disagree?
3. Describe the origins and current process of teacher certification.
4. Describe "approved program" status.
5. Analyze the process of accreditation by NCATE.
6. Identify the variables that affect teacher supply and demand.
7. Examine current population trends in relationship to teacher supply and demand.
8. Identify the states that are likely to experience increased teacher demand.
9. Identify the teaching areas and subject matter areas that are likely to experience teacher shortage or surplus.
10. How do teacher–pupil ratios determine teacher demand?
11. Explain and discuss the purpose of a teacher salary schedule.

FIELD EXERCISES

1. Identify the major components of a teacher preparation program and then relate these components to the teacher preparation program at your college or university.

2. Invite the director or coordinator of clinical experiences at your college or university to your class to describe clinical experiences and student or practice teaching.

3. Invite the teacher certification officer of your college or university to visit your class to describe the certification process.

4. Invite several students who have completed practice teaching to visit your class and to share their experience with you.

5. Invite a cooperating teacher to visit your class to discuss his or her work with student teachers.

6. Record teacher supply and demand in a given state for the past ten years. Predict anticipated teacher supply and demand in that state for the next two years.

7. Invite a representative of your college or university teacher placement department to visit your class to discuss teacher supply and demand.

8. Invite a professor of economics to visit your class to discuss the general economic factors that are likely to have an impact on schools and teachers.

9. Invite an educational administrator for a local school district to visit your class to discuss the establishing and functioning of the salary schedule in his or her district.

SUGGESTED READINGS

ANDERSON, LORIN W. *The Effective Teacher: Study Guide and Readings.* New York: Random House, 1989.

BURDEN, PAUL R., ed. *Establishing Career Ladders in Teaching: A Guide for Policy Makers.* Springfield, Ill.: C. W. Thomas, 1989.

CUBAN, LARRY. *How Teachers Taught: Constancy and Change in American Classrooms 1890–1980.* New York: Longman, 1984.

FEISTRITZER, C. EMILY, ed. *The American Teacher.* Washington, D.C.: Feistritzer, 1983.

———. *The Condition of Teaching: A State by State Analysis.* Princeton, N.J.: The Carnegie Foundation for the Advancement of Teaching, 1983.

———. *The Making of a Teacher: A Report on Teacher Education and Certification.* Washington, D.C.: National Center for Educational Information, 1984.

GINSBURG, MARK B. *Contradictions in Teacher Education and Society: A Critical Analysis.* New York: Falmer Press, 1988.

GRIFFIN, GARY A., AND EDWARDS, S., eds. *Student Teaching: Problems and Promising Practices.* Austin: University of Texas at Austin, 1982.

HABERMAN, MARTIN, AND STINNETT, T. M. *Teacher Education and the New Profession of Teaching.* Berkeley, Calif.: McCutchan, 1973.

HATRY, HARRY, AND GRIENER, JOHN. *Issues and Case Studies in Teacher Incentive Plans.* Washington, D.C.: Urban Institute, 1985.

JOHNSON, H. C. *Merit Money and Teachers' Careers.* Lanham, Md.: University Press of America, 1985.

KAUFMAN, BEL. *Up the Down Staircase.* Englewood Cliffs, N.J.: Prentice-Hall, 1964.

KIDDER, TRACY. *Among Schoolchildren.* Boston: Houghton Mifflin, 1989.

ROTH, ROBERT A., AND MASTAIN, RICHARD. *Manual on Certification and Preparation of Educational Personnel in the United States.* Sacramento, Calif.: National Association of State Directors of Teacher Education and Certification, 1984.

SMITH, DAVID D., ed. *Essential Knowledge for Beginning Educators.* Washington, D.C.: American Association of Colleges for Teacher Education, 1983.

SMYTH, JOHN AND GITLIN, ANDREW. *Beyond Teacher Evaluation: Critical Educative and Transformative Alternatives.* New York: Falmer Press, 1988.

Standards for the Accreditation of Teacher Education. Washington, D.C.: National Council for Accreditation of Teacher Education, 1982.

TRYNESKI, JOHN, ed. *Requirements for Certifica-*

tion of Teachers, Counselors, Librarians, Administrators for Elementary and Secondary Schools. Chicago: University of Chicago Press, 1990.

WARREN, DONALD, ed. *American Teachers: His-tories of a Profession at Work*. New York: Macmillan, 1989.

WOOLFOLK, ANITA E. *Research Perspectives on the Graduate Preparation of Teachers*. Englewood Cliffs, N.J.: Prentice-Hall, 1989.

3

Teaching
as a Profession

Chapter 3 examines teaching as a profession and the issues that affect teachers as professional educators. It also deals with several matters that affect prospective teachers, such as preparing credentials, locating a teaching position, and the issuance of a teaching contract. The ethical and legal relationships of tenure and academic freedom are examined. There is also a brief discussion of teachers' organizations and the issue of collective bargaining. The chapter is designed to familiarize prospective teachers with the major issues that they face as professional educators.

The general focusing questions that will be answered as you read this chapter include the following:

1. Does teaching meet the criteria of other professions?
2. What are the phases of teacher appointment?
3. How do teachers attain tenure?
4. What is the relationship between teacher organization and collective bargaining?
5. How do judicial decisions affect teaching?

Is Teaching a Profession?

The question "Is teaching a profession?" has stimulated prolonged and often heated debate. Sociologists and educational theorists have examined the question as an academic matter. For teachers, however, the question is a "bread and butter" issue that affects their social status, income, and civil and academic freedom. There is no easy answer to the question, for the criteria of what constitutes a profession are not universally accepted. In the medieval period, the three recognized professions were law, medicine, and theology. In modern times, however, the claimants to the title of *professional* have multiplied.

In contemporary America, the term *professional* has been used imprecisely to cover a wide range of occupations. For example, it is used to identify "professional" actors, dancers, photographers, barbers, truck drivers, pilots, and many other occupational categories, as well as the older recognized professions of law, medicine, and theology and the more recently recognized professions of architecture and

43

engineering. Although there is a professional literature and ethics associated with teaching, there are also critics who dispute that teachers have a unique professional culture. These critics contend either that teachers are born and not prepared or that anyone can teach who has knowledge of that which he or she purports to teach. In other words, they deny that teachers possess a professional culture. To deal with the question of teaching as a profession, we will examine a number of generally accepted criteria:[1]

1. *A profession involves intellectual activities and commands a body of specialized knowledge.* Teaching involves intellectual activities designed to transmit the cultural heritage and its knowledge, skills, and values to the young. Teachers are prepared in the liberal arts and sciences, as well as in the knowledge and methods of teaching. The body of knowledge pertains to human learning and develops increasingly effective methods of instruction.

2. *A profession performs specific functions that provide essential personal and social services.* For example, the legal profession has the specific function of preserving rights and adjudicating disputes among members of society; the medical profession functions to maintain the health of persons in society. In a similar fashion, teaching functions to educate the members of a society in an organized and systematic fashion, especially the children, who are being introduced to their society's knowledge, skills, and values.

3. *Unlike a craft, a profession rests on theory drawn from basic foundational disciplines that can be applied to practice.* A craft, such as baking, rests on the ability to make good breads, pies, and cakes. Although bakers must know how to follow a recipe and to mix ingredients in their proper proportion, it is not necessary for them to understand the chemistry involved in the leavening of bread. In contrast, medical practice rests on scientific disciplines—anatomy, biology, physiology, and chemistry. Teaching, too, rests on foundational disciplines, such as philosophy, history, sociology, psychology, and economics. These foundations of education, an important part of teachers' preparation, are the base for practice.

4. *Entry into a profession requires an extended period of preparation, usually in a professional school of a college or university.* What constitutes a proper and appropriate professional preparation remains a debatable issue among members of professions and the public. Even in the long-standing professions of law and medicine, there were once two approaches for professional entry: by way of university education or by way of apprenticeship with a practicing physician or lawyer. Today, the medical profession has combined these two approaches by requiring (a) possession of a bachelor's degree, usually in the arts and sciences, (b) completion of a three- to four-year course of study in a medical school, and (c) an extensive internship in a hospital under the supervision of skilled physicians.

Entry into teaching falls short of the extended period of preparation required for physicians and lawyers. Historically, many elementary school teachers took teaching positions only after two years of preparation. Even today, most states require only the bachelor's degree for entry into teaching. Several states now require that the teacher take a fifth year of study after entry into the field. It is common for many teachers to continue their professional preparation by earning master's and doctoral degrees. However, the important point is that individuals may begin their careers as teachers with only the four years of preparation required for the bachelor's degree.

1. The criteria stated are the author's own compilation based on Robert Howsam et al., *Educating a Profession* (Washington, D.C.: American Association of Colleges for Teacher Education, 1976); E. H. Schein, *Professional Education* (New York: McGraw-Hill, 1972); James M. Hughes and Frederick M. Schultz, *Education in America* (New York: Harper & Row, 1976), pp. 73–101; and other sources.

5. *A profession establishes its own standards for admission into the profession and determines the ethical codes that govern its members.* Although there are state requirements and examinations for licensure in professions such as law, medicine, and architecture, the members of these professions must be judged to be in good standing by their professional peers. In the case of teachers, however, the admission standards are not established by teachers' organizations but rather by the state. Teachers have little or no power to admit a candidate to their profession, because certification is done by the state and hiring is done by administrators.

6. *Members of a profession enjoy a broad range of autonomy and freedom in making professional judgments and decisions.* The teacher's decision is often questioned, however, especially in grading or evaluating pupils. Teachers may find their decisions challenged by their students, parents, and administrators. It is often assumed by those who challenge teachers' judgments that decision making in education is subjective.

Historically, teachers have been subject to community pressures and controls that circumscribe their personal as well as their professional lives. In part, these community infractions on teachers' personal lives stemmed from the low social and economic status associated with teaching. Another factor in these controls is that parents and other community members often see teachers as models for imitation by the young. As a result, they often expect teachers to follow higher standards of behavior than they themselves follow.

Teachers do enjoy protection of their professional autonomy by virtue of tenure laws, however. After a minimal probational period, teachers are granted tenure by employing school districts and can be dismissed only for serious cause or because of the need to reduce the teaching force. Tenure protects the autonomy and academic freedom of teachers.

7. *The members of the profession are united in a highly organized professional organization with clearly defined ethics and standards.* The issue of the appropriate form of professional organization has provoked ongoing dispute among teachers. Rather than uniting them, the competition among rival teachers' organizations, such as the National Education Association (NEA) and the American Federation of Teachers (AFT), has divided them. While the NEA takes the stance that teachers are served best by a large, umbrellalike professional organization, the AFT argues that teachers will gain improved salaries, working conditions, and status by following the trade union model.

These seven criteria, though not exhaustive, illustrate the essential characteristics of a profession. They also show that, while teaching shares much with other professions, areas exist in which teachers need to work for more professionalization:

1. Many teachers who see themselves as classroom practitioners need to overcome their distrust of theory and analysis of educational issues and problems. They must be willing to move from a craft mentality to a professional outlook grounded on the theoretical principles that relate to (a) purpose and organization of education and schools, (b) nature of the learning process and human growth and development, and (c) ethical rights and responsibilities of teachers and students.

2. Because the period of professional preparation is shorter than in other professions and the standards of initial entry are not as demanding, teachers should work to improve the standards of admission to teaching and continue to advance their own knowledge by in-service preparation. Although this means that more extensive preparation will be costly initially in terms of time and money, the long-range professional benefits will outweigh these costs.

A recent proposal for extending and restructuring teacher preparation, which aims to enhance professionalization, has been made by the Holmes Group Consortium. The Holmes Group has recommended that undergraduate programs in education be discontinued. Prospective teachers would complete undergraduate programs in the liberal arts and sciences and then enter rigorous master's degree programs in education. The graduate program would include a one-year supervised teaching internship.[2]

3. Because teachers are not united in a single professional organization, they need to examine and resolve the obstacles that impede unification. They need to overcome their differences on the style of organization appropriate to represent them. They also need to overcome their segmentation and isolation as elementary, secondary, and college teachers and unite in a general professional organization.

4. As is true for all professionals, teachers need to resist attempts to circumscribe their academic freedom and professional autonomy. Freedom carries with it responsibility. The prudent exercise of freedom means that teachers must know and protect the areas in which they are competent, but they must also know where their competence ends. It also means that teachers need to be willing to protect the freedom of their colleagues to teach and of their students to learn.

Teacher Appointment

The first section of this chapter examined the nature of a profession. While that discussion was theoretical, its contents are significant to the career on which you are embarking as a teacher. In this section, we turn to the more practical matter of teacher appointment, or actual entry into teaching.

The process of teacher appointment begins long before the person is hired for a teaching position and involves several steps or stages:

1. The individual decides to be a teacher and applies for admission to a state-recognized education program in an accredited college or university.
2. The admissions committee of the college or university accepts or rejects the applicant.
3. If accepted, the student is guided through the courses and sequences of the teacher preparation program by an advisor; the teacher preparation program leads to admission, at a later stage, to practice teaching, a supervised clinical experience.
4. The individual receives a bachelor's degree and a state teaching certificate.
5. The individual is employed as a teacher by a school district for a probationary period.
6. After a specified number of years of successful performance as a probationary teacher, the teacher is recommended for and granted tenure by the school board upon the recommendation of the superintendent of the district.

Each of these six stages is crucial in the professional career of teachers.

Teacher Placement

Once a person has completed the teacher preparation program, been granted the bachelor's degree, and received the appropriate state certification, then comes the very important process of finding the initial teaching position. Locating the most suitable teaching position is a two-way process: (1) The prospective teacher needs to identify a position that will permit maximum challenges and opportunities for professional growth, development, and reward, and (2) the employing school dis-

2. "Holmes Group Recommends Major Changes in Teacher Training," *Phi Delta Kappan*, 67, No. 10 (June 1986), pp. 766–767.

trict needs to identify a professionally prepared person who will become a valuable member of the district's professional staff as a skilled and resourceful teacher.

In a school district, the superintendent or his or her delegated representative (an assistant superintendent for personnel or building principal, depending upon the size of the district and its employment practices) conducts the recruitment process. Once a vacancy occurs, or a new position is authorized by the school board, the school administrator announces and advertises the position and begins a search to fill it. The administrator may use several sources to identify possible candidates for the position, such as (1) the college or university teacher placement division, (2) commercial teacher placement agencies, (3) recommendations that come from an informal network of school administrators with which the hiring administrator may be familiar, and (4) unsolicited letters, inquiries, and applications from teachers seeking employment.

For the beginning teacher seeking the initial appointment, the college or university placement office is generally the most satisfactory way of finding an entry-level position. It is best to begin working with the college or university teacher placement office during your senior year and to prepare a credential that is on file in the placement office and available to prospective employing school districts. Usually the college or university placement service is available to the institution's students and alumni for a minimal fee. It is important that the credentials in the placement office be prepared with care. The credential file is a collection of documents that provides prospective employers with specific information about an individual teaching candidate. The usual credentials file contains a résumé, a statement of the candidate's academic preparation, courses, degrees, and types of certification and letters of recommendation.

In the credential file and in the employment process, the candidate's résumé is of particular importance. It should convey clearly and directly to the potential employer not only the candidate's professional preparation and interests but also the person's ability to organize, prepare, and present information accurately and clearly. Poorly prepared résumés discourage prospective employers from interviewing potential candidates for positions.

Candidate's Résumé

Before you prepare your résumé, or vita, for the credential file, it is good practice to consult with the advisors at the placement department on the proper format. Your academic advisor or the director of teacher education can also offer valuable suggestions. The following items are intended to suggest categories that are appropriate for inclusion on your résumé:

> *Personal Information*: Name, address, telephone number, date of birth, and military service. If your school address is temporary, you should include your permanent residence.
> *Educational Background*: Names and years of elementary, high school, and college attendance; degree or degrees earned; major and minor subjects; other educational experiences relevant to teaching.

Teaching Certificates: Types of teaching certificates held and subject or grade-level specialization; when issued or about to be issued; when due to expire.

Employment Experience: A listing of places of employment and employers or supervisors.

References: Individuals that the prospective employer can contact to obtain additional information. The individuals whom you list as references should be appropriate and know you and your aptitude for teaching. Obviously, they should be people with whom you have had successful, rather than unsatisfactory, relationships.

Honors: Scholarships, awards, prizes, and various kinds of recognition received by the candidate.

Professional Memberships: Memberships in professional educational organizations, associations, or related service activities, such as Future Teachers of America, Student Education Association, and speech and drama club.

Interests or Hobbies: A statement of interests or hobbies relevant to teaching, such as debate, photography, or travel.

Academic or Professional Preparation Statement

The teacher placement office that you use to establish and file your credentials is likely to have a prepared form on which to detail your academic and professional preparation. As is true of your résumé, the academic statement should be prepared accurately and carefully. This statement indicates your professional preparation to prospective employing school districts. It conveys to them information about the areas and subjects that you have been prepared to teach. It may also suggest to the administrator conducting the search additional teaching combinations.

The academic statement that appears in the credentials is based on the candidate's degree program and the courses that appear on the academic transcript. It should indicate the degree earned and the date the degree is expected or was awarded; it should also provide specific details about the teaching major or area of educational specialization. The academic statement conveys to a prospective employer the candidate's academic preparation and competence to teach a particular area or subject.

Letters of Recommendation

As indicated, the letters of recommendation in the candidate's credential file are very important. They inform the prospective employer of the evaluation and impressions that appropriate people have made of your potential as a teacher. When you prepare your credential file, it is important that you ask appropriate individuals to write letters of reference. Among appropriate references are college or university professors who have been involved in your academic preparation, particularly your program advisor and professors associated with your major subject or educational specialization; your cooperating teacher or college or university supervisor during student teacher or clinical experience, because this will convey to the hiring administrator your competence in the classroom; and carefully selected previous employers who can write about your work record, punctuality, attendance, and other job-related matters.

The Interview Process

The interview process is important for both the candidate being interviewed and for the prospective employer. The smoothest interviews occur when both parties have prepared themselves on the specific requirements of the position to be filled; the most difficult and awkward situations occur when the parties to the interview are poorly prepared. It is incumbent on the interviewer to make the person being interviewed comfortable so that the job requirements can be dealt with as objectively as possible. The candidate should also review the requirements of the position and his or her background for it prior to the interview.

Interviews take place after the prospective employer has reviewed and screened the credentials of applicants and has narrowed the search to those most likely to suit the requirements for the position. Depending upon the size of the school district which has the position available, the interview can occur in several settings. Very large school districts, particularly large urban ones, may send an administrative team to college or university campuses to conduct the interviewing process. When this occurs, the college or university placement office may arrange the interviewing schedule. In the case of smaller school districts, the candidates are likely to be invited to visit and be interviewed in the district. In either case, the candidate should take the time to do some preliminary research on the school district, its population, its socioeconomic and ethnic characteristics, and its particular educational needs and problems. Common courtesy dictates that both interviewers and candidates be punctual and follow the schedule arranged for the interviews.

The interview is a "two-way street" in that the candidate explores the possibilities of teaching in the school district to determine if it is the kind of district in which he or she wishes to begin a career, and administrators conducting the interview seek to determine if the candidate is suited to the educational requirements of the position and the character of the district. Although the interview is important, it should not be used as the sole determinant in answering these questions.

The topics that will be raised in the interview vary, but usually include the following:

1. The candidate's philosophy of education
2. The attitude of classroom discipline and management
3. Specifics about the content and methods of the candidate's area of specialization in relationship to the requirements of the position
4. The candidate's familiarity with methods of instruction and materials that are used in the areas of specialization
5. The candidate's interest in extracurricular activities, curriculum development, and other matters related indirectly to the teaching assignment.

In addition to the questions that the interviewer raises, the candidate should have questions concerning the position. It is generally advisable to ask these questions when the interviewer invites them. Often, the interviewer may answer these questions during the course of the interview in a more or less informal way. For example:

1. The extent to which the community is involved and supportive of the school system
2. The general expectations that the community and the school district has of its teachers

3. The school district's educational philosophy and mode of curricular organization
4. Innovations that are being conducted in the district
5. The process of curriculum revision, textbook selection, and determination of teacher planning for instruction
6. Salary and other fringe benefits

After the interview, there is a waiting period while the district administrators complete the interviewing process and determine who will be invited to accept a contract. The salary and increments are generally fixed in the district's salary schedule, so little negotiation takes place between the prospective teacher as an individual and the school district as the employer. Once the interviewing administrator has offered the position to the successful candidate and he or she has accepted it, the district superintendent recommends that the board of education issue a contract to the new teacher. It should be noted that it is only the board of education that can authorize the employment of a teacher and issue the contract.

Teacher Employment Contracts

The statutory authority to employ teachers, specified in school codes, is vested in boards of education. This authority includes the power to enter into a contract and fix the terms of a teacher's employment and compensation. The issuing of an employment contract to a teacher represents an important commitment for both the individual teacher and the employing district. For the candidate for a teaching position, the issuing of an employment contract represents the end of searching for a position and sustaining interviews. For the district, it also represents the conclusion of a search to find a teacher who is expected to educate the children of the district according to its educational philosophy and curriculum. The issuing of a contract is related to the district's hiring process. In most districts, the superintendent or an administrator appointed by him or her announces and advertises the position, reviews applicant's credentials, identifies and interviews candidates who appear to be qualified for the position, and recommends employment of the candidate to the board of education. The board of education, meeting as a board, acts at an official session to enter into a contractual agreement with the teacher.

An employment contract generally contains the following basic provisions:

1. Identification of the signatories of the contract (that is, the teacher and the board of education)
2. A statement of the legal capacity of each party to enter the contract
3. A definition of the specific assignment
4. A statement of the salary and how it is to be paid
5. Signatures of the teacher and the board's authorized agent

Some states require the use of prescribed contract forms; in other states, the school district designs its own contract format.

A contract is legally binding on both parties—the teacher and the officials of the school district. A school board that breaks a contract is required to pay damages to the teacher to compensate for loss of salary; in some situations, a teacher may be entitled to reinstatement. A teacher who breaks a contract may be liable for the school district's expenses in finding a suitable replacement and for any additional salary costs that the district might incur.

The Matter of Tenure

Teacher Evaluation

Once employed in the initial teaching position, the teacher enters the period probationary to granting tenure. Administrators must be certain that the teachers whom they recommend for tenure are competent educators. Because the issuing of tenure is a long-term commitment for it, the employing board of education, too, must be certain that the teachers to whom it grants tenure have been excellent in performing their teaching tasks. To recommend teachers for tenure, superintendents or administrators entrusted with maintaining the quality of instruction need to supervise carefully and judiciously the members of the professional staff. Supervision, however, is difficult and often controversial, for the criteria for judging teacher performance are subject to debate.

In an era of accountability, the evaluation of teachers, as well as of other school administrators and personnel, is of critical importance. Evaluation can be defined as the gathering of the data and its analysis to ascertain the quality of instructional or educational practices in terms of objectives, criteria, and standards determined by the school board and generally regarded as appropriate for professional educators. With the assistance of the professional administrators and staff, the school board — the employing body — of a particular school district establishes objectives relating to the education of children attending district schools.

In addition to the specific objectives appropriate to a particular school district, there are also the generally recognized criteria that differentiate good teaching from inadequate performance. Teachers should expect to be evaluated in terms of specific and stated criteria. Evaluation should not be designed as a coercive measure, but rather as an instrument to identify strengths and weaknesses and to assist in staff development. In the school districts using merit increments, it is necessary to use criteria to identify teachers deserving increases. It is also necessary in determining promotion from probationary to tenure status. In other words, a close relationship exists between evaluation and factors like salary increments and differentiation, promotion, tenure, and dismissal.

Unfortunately, controversy abounds regarding accurate instruments of evaluating teacher performance. A number of rating scales provide bases for evaluation, however. In recent years, there has been a distinction between *formative* and *summative* evaluation. Formative evaluation is continuous, diagnostic, remedial, and individualized and is designed toward the continuous improvement of instruction. Summative, based on the word *summary*, tends to be terminal and uniform. Summative evaluation often relates to the administrative decisions of tenure, dismissal, and promotion. In many school districts, teacher evaluation has been transformed into the broader concept of performance evaluation involving both teachers and administrators in setting instructional objectives and establishing standards for evaluating teacher performance and student achievement.

Tenure and Academic Freedom

While teaching involves many duties and responsibilities, it invariably means that teachers are free to communicate, share, and discuss ideas with students. As the Athenians discovered in the days of Socrates, working with ideas can pose a risk to established traditions and institutions. Effective teaching carries with it the possibility of change. People who fear change may also fear teaching, which may be a catalyst for change.

Academic freedom refers to the right of teachers to teach within the area of their competence. For example, teachers of history or biology have the right and indeed the obligation to teach the concepts, information, and methods related to their field of educational competence. Although academic freedom has often been controversial, in the proper exercise of academic freedom the teacher is teaching what is within his or her area of expertise. This freedom does not extend to areas in which the teacher lacks competence.

In addition to academic freedom, teachers should enjoy the civil rights available to other citizens. No restrictions should be placed on the teacher's freedom as a citizen. For example, teachers have the same right of political expression and action as other citizens of the United States.

Cases involving academic freedom often relate to the teaching of controversial issues or the use of controversial books or other instructional materials. When such cases reach the courts, they generally have been decided on specific circumstances. The specific questions considered include the following:

1. What is the educational relevance of the controversial issue or material?
2. What is the teacher's objective in examining the issue or using the material?
3. What is the age and maturity of the students involved in the particular learning situation?

Although the courts have generally protected the teacher's right to investigate controversial issues or to use controversial materials, academic freedom does not protect teaching that is incompetent or irrelevant or is clearly being used for religious or political indoctrination in the public schools.[3]

Tenure laws were enacted to protect the academic freedom of teachers. By implication, they also protect the right of learners to learn. Prior to the enactment of tenure laws, teachers were sometimes summarily dismissed for their political, religious, and economic beliefs rather than for their educational incompetence. When used according to their original intent, tenure laws protect teachers from (1) special-interest groups who seek to remove teachers whose views may differ from theirs and (2) arbitrary action by school boards or administrators.

3. Louis Fischer, David Schimmel, and Cynthia Kelly, *Teachers and the Law* (New York: Longman, 1981), p. 139.

In using tenure provisions properly, it is necessary that administrators carefully consider the teaching competence of individuals whom they are recommending for tenure and that boards of education grant tenure to teachers who have demonstrated professional competency. Quickly made and ill-considered tenure decisions frequently defeat the purposes for which tenure was created. Tenure laws should be used to safeguard good teaching and not misused to protect incompetent individuals.

Teacher employment and dismissal are subject to teacher tenure or dismissal laws. These laws establish due-process provisions that govern teacher dismissal. In most states, tenure laws have a statewide applicability that is mandatory on all school districts in the state.

Permanent tenure laws specify that teachers, after demonstrating a prescribed period of satisfactory probationary service, cannot be dismissed except for specific reasons, such as incompetence, neglect of duty, insubordination, or declining enrollment. In a few states, tenure laws may not have statewide applicability. New York, for example, excludes rural school districts. The California law is optional for districts with enrollments under 250 pupils. In Texas, permissive tenure laws permit local districts to follow statewide provisions if they so wish.

Today, tenure laws are extremely controversial as declining enrollments and financial retrenchment have caused some school districts to reduce the size of their teaching force. Tenure laws were enacted originally to prevent the removal of teachers for reasons other than incompetence; however, some critics contend that the broad interpretation and rigidity in enforcing tenure laws have made the removal of incompetent teachers time consuming and extremely difficult. They also charge that tenure laws work to prevent entry of new teachers into the profession and create a static educational situation. Defenders of tenure laws claim that they protect teachers from capricious administrative action or from politically motivated dismissals.

Although varying from state to state, tenure laws generally include detailed and very specific prescriptions detailing the process by which teachers attain tenure, the procedures required for the granting of tenure, and the procedures for dismissing teachers who have been granted tenure in a school district.

Attaining Tenure

When employed and issued an initial contract by the employing school district, the individual begins the probationary period. During the probationary period, the teacher's contract with the school district is for a definite and specified period of time, usually the school year, and is subject to renewal on a regular, usually annual, basis. The length of time for the probationary period varies from state to state. The process of being granted tenure also depends upon the given state. In some states, tenure is awarded automatically after satisfactory completion of the probationary period; in other states, the local school board, upon the recommendation of the superintendent, takes official action to grant tenure to the teachers who have completed the probationary period.

Dismissal of Tenured Teachers

The grounds and procedures for dismissing tenured teachers are specified in the tenure statutes of the various states. Among the grounds for dismissal of tenured teachers are incompetency, insubordination, and immorality. Depending upon the nature of the specific charge, tenure regulations may indicate a required period of remediation, provisions for filing charges, and the process for conducting hearings and appeals.

In dismissing teachers, boards of education are to follow due-process procedures:

1. Issuing a timely and adequate notice specifying the reasons for the proposed termination
2. Providing an opportunity to the teacher facing termination for self-defense and the cross-examination of witnesses
3. Conducting a public hearing, with the publication of adequate notice

Teacher Organizations

Educators, like other professionals, have organized to promote and protect their interests. Although both the NEA and the AFT represent the interests of teachers, they are often rivals. They differ in style, organization, and strategy.

The origins of the NEA, the older of the two national teachers' organizations, go back to 1857, when a small group of educators met in Philadelphia to establish the National Teachers Association. In 1870, the National Teachers Association was reorganized as the National Education Association, with the broad aims of advancing the interests of teachers and promoting public education in the United States.

Today, the NEA, the largest educational organization in the world, is a confederation of affiliated state and local educational associations that includes departments, commissions, divisions, and committees relating to nearly every teaching subject and interest. It is an inclusive organization that embraces teachers and administrators at all levels of institutional organization.

The NEA is governed by a representative assembly composed of delegates appointed by local and state associations. As the legislative unit of the association, the assembly establishes its broad governing policies. The NEA board of directors, consisting of one representative from each state, implements the legislation passed by the representative assembly. In addition, other specialized organizations are affiliated with the NEA, such as the American Association of Elementary-Kindergarten Educators, the American Association of Industrial Arts, the American Association of School Administrators, the American Association of School Librarians, the Association of Teacher Education, the Music Educators National Conference, the National Science Teachers Association, and other educational associations.

As a large confederation of educational associations, the NEA performs a wide range of services for its members. It publishes professional journals and books; it conducts research; it defends teachers from violation of their academic freedom and tenure; it encourages a favorable public opinion of education; it promotes legislation favorable to teachers; and it seeks to improve teacher welfare provisions.

The AFT, organized in 1916, is affiliated with the American Federation of Labor–Congress of Industrial Organization (AFL–CIO).[4] Whereas the NEA claims to be a broad professional organization, the AFT has specifically limited its membership to classroom teachers and has identified with organized labor. To achieve its goals, the AFT also has used the organizational strategy of the labor movement, including the strike, when necessary.

The organization of the AFT consists of state federations that are formed from the local unions within the state. Membership in the AFT entitles the member to affiliation with the AFL–CIO, subscription to *American Teacher* magazine, and the services of the national office. The governing body of the AFT is its annual convention; its administrative body consists of the president and a number of vice-presidents who are elected for two-year terms. In addition to the general improvement of education, the AFT has the following objectives: (1) to gain recognition of the right of teachers to organize, negotiate, and bargain collectively, (2) to seek improved teachers' salaries, and (3) to secure better health and retirement benefits for teachers.

Since the late 1950s, rivalry has developed between the NEA and the AFT. In asserting that educators can accomplish their objectives best through their own professional organization, NEA leaders claim that professional strength resides in the broad range of affiliations encompassed in their organization. In contrast, the AFT believes that affiliation with organized labor strengthens the bargaining position of teachers. The AFT leadership asserts that it is effective for teachers to use collective bargaining techniques developed by organized labor. According to the AFT, labor affiliation brings its membership the support of the national AFL–CIO and provides union teachers with the support of local trade and labor councils.

Both the NEA and AFT are active in recruiting teachers and organizing local units. Both organizations have turned to collective-bargaining techniques and to the strike as a last resort. The NEA has approximately 1.5 million members, the AFT, 500,000. The trend of the future is likely to be the further organization of teachers into local units of either the NEA or the AFT. Although there has been some tentative discussion of a merger of the two national organizations, this seems unlikely at the present time. Nevertheless, it can be expected that teachers will be more forceful in presenting their demands to the school districts that employ them.

Collective Bargaining

In recent years, as teachers have organized into associations and unions, the issue of collective bargaining has been subject to great controversy. Historically, the individual teacher and the school board reached agreement on the conditions of employment and salaries. With the appearance of salary schedules and other benefits, teachers have enjoyed more power in improving working conditions, salaries, and other benefits by negotiating with school boards as a unified group. As unionization

---

4. The definitive history of the AFT is William E. Eaton's *The American Federation of Teachers, 1916–1961* (Carbondale: Southern Illinois University Press, 1975).

has proceeded throughout much of the country, the teachers' union or association has often used professional negotiators to represent them. Today, the majority of American teachers are covered by collective-bargaining agreements.

Collective bargaining has been pursued actively by both the NEA and the AFT. These organizations have promoted collective-bargaining legislation in the various states. Although this legislation varies, it generally provides for

1. Recognition of teachers' rights to organize and bargain collectively.
2. Provisions for teachers in a given school district to determine the bargaining agent that will represent them.
3. A description of the scope and procedures in which negotiations are to occur between the teachers' agent and the school board.
4. A description of action to be taken should an impasse occur in the negotiations.

Today, many states have enacted legislation that permits teachers to select an organization, such as the NEA or AFT, to represent them as the bargaining agent in contract negotiations with employing school boards. Some states also have described procedures to be followed if negotiations reach a stalemate.

Since the 1960s, the number of teachers' strikes has increased dramatically. Such strikes occur when negotiations between a school board and a teachers' union or association reach an impasse. The teacher strike represents use of a weapon that has long been associated with trade and industrial unions. Those who advocate the strike as a last resort claim that it is the most potent weapon that teachers have to improve the conditions and benefits of their work. Opponents of teachers' strikes claim that such activities represent unprofessional behavior on the part of individuals who claim to be professional educators serving the public welfare.

Teachers and the Law

School or education law is a dynamic field that has experienced an explosion of litigation since the 1950s. The rights and responsibilities of school boards, administrators, teachers, students, and parents have been defined in a series of court cases during the past several decades. State and federal courts have ruled on issues that involve religious questions, special education, sex and racial discrimination, censorship, corporal punishment, academic freedom, teacher employment, and many other matters that have shaped U.S. education. This section examines selected legal developments that affect teachers directly.

Teachers, like all citizens, have the civil right of freedom of expression and the recourse to due process in the case of unjustified deprivation of this right. While the decisions of state and federal courts that deal with education generally have consequences for teachers, the cases described in this section relate directly to teachers and the law. Since the law relating to education, schooling, and teaching is extensive, representative recent cases have been selected to illustrate three categories: employment of teachers, freedom of expression, and students' rights in relation to schools and teachers.[5]

5. For an excellent treatment of how the law has shaped U.S. education, see David Tyack, Thomas James, and Aaron Benavot, *Law and the Shaping of Public Education, 1785–1954* (Madison: University of Wisconsin Press, 1987).

Employment of Teachers

The U.S. Supreme Court in *Mt. Healthy Board of Education* v. *Doyle* (1976) ruled that the First Amendment does not demand that a discharged employee be placed in "a better position as a result of the exercise of constitutionally protected activity than he would have occupied had he done nothing."[6] This decision permits an employer to evaluate an employee's performance and to reach a decision not to rehire based on that evaluation.

In *Ambach* v. *Norwick* (1979) the U.S. Supreme Court upheld a New York law that required United States' citizenship as a requirement for teaching in the state's public schools. In this case the Court ruled that barring aliens from permanent certification as public school teachers did not violate the equal protection clause of the Fourteenth Amendment.[7]

The U.S. Supreme Court in *Wygant* v. *Jackson Board of Education* (1986) ruled that white teachers could not be laid off from their jobs to preserve the jobs of minority groups' members.[8] While the Court ruled in this case that "societal discrimination" was an insufficient reason for racially discriminatory layoffs, they might be permissible if they were part of an employer's "narrowly tailored" remedy for past patterns of discrimination. The Court, in this decision, was extremely careful to distinguish between racially based layoffs and racially conscious hiring according to affirmative action policies.

Teacher's Freedom of Expression

In *Pickering* v. *Board of Education* (1968), the U.S. Supreme Court used the "balance of interest test" to uphold the claims of a teacher that his First and Fourteenth Amendment rights had been violated when he was dismissed for writing a letter that was published in a local newspaper, criticizing the school board and the district superintendent for their distribution of school funds. While the Court upheld the teacher's right in this case, it also established procedures regarding public employees', including public school teachers' right to freedom of expression in regard to their employing state agency. The Court held that a decision on the exercise of freedom of expression must consider employees' rights as well as their duties and responsibilities. The proper test, according to the Court, is whether the government's interest in limiting a public employee's "opportunities to contribute to public debate is . . . significantly greater than its interest in limiting a similar contribution by any member of the general public." According to the Court, there were six situations in which the state could conceivably limit a public employee's freedom of expression:

1. To maintain discipline and harmony among employees
2. To maintain confidentiality
3. When an employee's position provides access to factual information such that refutation of his or her statements might be difficult

---

6. *Mt. Healthy Board of Education* v. *Doyle* 429 U.S. 274 (1977).
7. *Ambach* v. *Norwick* 441 U.S. 68 (1979).
8. *Wygant* v. *Jackson Board of Education* 106 S. Ct. 842 (1986).

4. When an employee's statements impede the proper performance of work
5. When the statements made are so clearly without foundation that the employee's basic capacity to perform his or her occupational duties is questionable
6. When close personal loyalty and confidence are jeopardized.[9]

Although teachers have the right to academic freedom and to freedom of expression, they are also expected to follow the policies and the designated curriculum adopted by the employing board of education. In *Palmer* v. *Board of Education of the City of Chicago* (1980), a teacher refused to teach children to recite the pledge of allegiance to the flag and to commemorate patriotic observances designated by the Chicago Board of Education. While the Court recognized the teacher's right as an individual to freedom of belief, it affirmed that the Board of Education, as a state agency, had a compelling interest in the education of children for the benefit of society and had a legitimate right to enforce its policies.[10]

Student Rights, Schools, and Teachers

Tinker v. *Des Moines Independent Community School District* (1969) was one of the earliest U.S. Supreme Court decisions regarding students' First Amendment rights. This case occurred during the period of student protests against United States's involvement in the war in Vietnam. It involved three students who wore black armbands to classes as a symbol of their protest against the war. The Court ruled that the students were properly exercising their rights, despite the objections of the school district, in that no substantial interference with school procedures and routines could be attributed to their action.[11]

The U.S. Supreme Court, in *Goss* v. *Lopez* (1975), established minimal due process for suspending students for short periods of time that were not to exceed ten days. The Court ruled that a school was required only to give a student notice of charges; it was not required to afford the student the right to counsel or to call or cross-examine witnesses. The Court also ruled that suspensions for more than ten days might require more formal procedures.[12]

The courts have generally dismissed suits that charge educational malpractice by school boards and teachers in which claimants allege indirect injury of not achieving an adequate education. In *Peter W.* v. *San Francisco Unified School District*, a former student charged that, although he had graduated from high school, he had severely limited reading and writing skills. The California court ruled that there was no way to prove the school's negligence or malpractice because the achievement of literacy is influenced by a wide variety of factors that exist outside of the school and its formal instructional process.[13]

In *Bethel School District No. 403* v. *Fraser* (1986), the U.S. Supreme Court ruled that First Amendment rights to freedom of speech did not prevent school

9. *Pickering* v. *Board of Education* 391 U.S. 563 (1968).
10. *Palmer* v. *Board of Education of the City of Chicago*, 603 F 2d. 1271 (7th Cir. 1979), cert. denied 444 U.S. 1026, 100 S. Ct. 689 (1980).
11. *Tinker* v. *Des Moines School Independent Community School District* 393 U.S. 503 (1969).
12. *Goss* v. *Lopez* 419 U.S. 565 (1975).
13. *Peter W.* v. *San Francisco Unified School District* 60, Cal. App. 3d 814, 131 Cal. Rptr. 854 (1976).

officials from disciplining a student who used offensive and lewd language during a school assembly. According to the Court's decision, "[I]t is a highly appropriate function of public school education to prohibit the use of vulgar and offensive terms in public discourse."[14]

In *Hazelwood School District* v. *Kuhlmeier* (1988), the U.S. Supreme Court upheld the decision of a high school principal to prevent publication of an edition of a school newspaper that contained articles dealing with student pregnancy and the effects of divorce on young people. This decision, representing a more circum-scribed interpretation of the constitutional rights of students, placed greater reliance on school administrators to use "reasonableness" as their standard for reviewing student-generated publications.[15]

Although it has been possible in this chapter to describe only a few of the court decisions that affect teachers, prospective as well as experienced teachers should be aware of the role that the judicial system has in shaping educational practices.[16]

Conclusion

Chapter 3 has examined the nature of a profession and the degree to which teaching fits the criteria. It examined the theoretical, legal, and practical issues related to entry into teaching. Chapter 3 explored such practical matters as finding a teaching position, gaining tenure as a teacher, and joining the ranks of professional educators.

DISCUSSION QUESTIONS

1. In your opinion, does teaching meet the criteria of a profession?
2. Identify and discuss the characteristics of the well-qualified professional educator.
3. Examine the arguments for and against tenure.
4. Define *academic freedom*.
5. Compare and contrast the approaches to teacher education used by the NEA and AFT.
6. Discuss the appropriate format and contents of a prospective teacher's résumé.
7. Examine the rights and limitations on teachers' freedom of expression.

FIELD EXERCISES

1. Invite several teachers to your class to participate in a panel on "teaching as a career." Ask them to identify the characteristics of the professional educator and to comment on the challenges, problems, and satisfactions they have experienced.
2. Invite a representative of your college or university teacher placement office to visit your class to discuss the procedures for preparing a placement credential.

14. *Bethel School District No. 403* v. *Fraser* 474 U.S. 814, 1046 (1986).
15. *Hazelwood School District* v. *Kuhlmeier* 108 S.Ct. 562 (1988).
16. A useful summary of school-related law is Kern Alexander and M. David Alexander, *The Law of Schools, Students, and Teachers* (St. Paul, Minn.: West, 1984).

3. Invite a school administrator to visit your class to discuss the hiring interview.

4. Prepare a sample résumé.

5. Simulate the teacher hiring interview by having students play the roles of interviewer and interviewee.

6. Invite a professor of school law to your class to discuss "The Teacher and the Law."

SUGGESTED READINGS

ALEXANDER, KERN, AND DAVID, ALEXANDER M. *The Law of Schools, Students, and Teachers*. St. Paul, Minn.: West, 1984.

BURKE, PETER J., CHRISTENSEN, JUDITH C., AND FESSLER, RALPH. *Teacher Career Stages: Implications for Staff Development*. Bloomington, Ind.: Phi Delta Kappa Educational Foundations, 1984.

CHENG, CHARLES W. *Teacher Unions and the Power Structure*. Bloomington, Ind.: Phi Delta Kappa Educational Foundation, 1981.

CRESSWELL, ANTHONY M., AND MURPHY, MICHAEL J. *Teachers, Unions and Collective Bargaining*. Berkeley, Calif.: McCutchan, 1976.

EATON, WILLIAM E. *The American Federation of Teachers, 1916–1961*. Carbondale: Southern Illinois University Press, 1975.

FINKELSTEIN, BARBARA. *Governing the Young: Teacher Behaviour in Popular Primary Schools in the Nineteenth-Century United States*. New York: Falmer Press, 1988.

FISCHER, LOUIS, SCHIMMEL, DAVID, AND KELLY, CYNTHIA. *Teachers and the Law*. New York: Longman, 1981.

FLYGARE, THOMAS J. *Collective Bargaining in the Public Schools*. Bloomington, Ind.: Phi Delta Kappa Educational Foundation, 1977.

GLICKMAN, CARL. *Developmental Supervision: Alternative Practices for Helping Teachers Improve Instruction*. Alexandria, Va.: Association for Supervision and Career Development, 1981.

HOLLY, MARY LOUISE, AND McLOUGHLIN, CAVEN S. *Perspectives on Teacher Professional Development*. New York: Falmer Press, 1988.

KERCHNER, CHARLES T., AND MITCHEL, DOUGLAS. *The Changing Idea of a Teachers' Union*. New York: Falmer Press, 1988.

LIEBERMAN, ANN, ed. *Building a Professional Culture in Schools*. New York: Teachers College Press, 1988.

McNEIL, JOHN, AND WILES, JON. *The Essentials of Teaching: Decisions, Plans, Methods*. New York: Macmillan, 1990.

MONKS, ROBERT L., AND PROULX, ERNEST I. *Legal Basics for Teachers*. Bloomington, Ind.: Phi Delta Kappa Educational Foundation, 1986.

PARKAY, FORREST W., AND HARDCASTLE, BEVERLY. *Becoming a Teacher: Accepting the Challenge of a Profession*. Boston: Allyn & Bacon, 1989.

RAPHAEL, RAY. *The Teacher's Voice: A Sense of Who We Are*. Portsmouth, N.H.: Heinemann, 1985.

ROBINSON, VIRGINIA. *Making Do in the Classroom: A Report on the Misassignment of Teachers*. Washington, D.C.: Council for Basic Education, American Federation of Teachers, 1985.

WEIS, LOIS. *Crisis in Teaching: Perspectives on Current Reforms*. Albany: State University of New York Press, 1989.

4

The Historical Foundations of American Education

Chapter 4 provides an historical narrative of the significant events and movements that shaped the basic patterns of American education. It is designed to provide an overview that creates a perspective on later developments. The general focusing questions that will be answered as you read this chapter include the following:

1. What educational ideas and institutions were transported from Europe to North America?
2. What were the similarities and differences between educators in the New England, Middle Atlantic, and southern colonies?
3. How did Benjamin Franklin, Thomas Jefferson, and other theorists contribute to educational thought in the early years of the new nation?
4. How did the common school movement produce major social and educational change in the United States?
5. What have been the major trends in education in the twentieth century?

European Settlement

The early history of American education began as Europeans discovered and then settled in the New World. While the English, who established a chain of colonies along the Atlantic coast, had the greatest impact on American education, the French, Spanish, and Dutch also founded colonies and schools. The French established a far-flung but sparsely populated empire that reached from Canada down the Mississippi River Valley to Louisiana. French priests, in particular the Jesuits, journeyed with the explorers and fur traders to convert and educate the Indians in Christian ways. Jesuits and religious communities of nuns, such as the Ursulines, taught the children of the French settlers in such towns as Quebec and New Orleans. When French dreams of an American empire ended with the English victory in the French and Indian Wars in 1763, their educational efforts also waned.

The Spanish, both in the southwestern region and in California, established an empire known as New Spain. With the *conquistadores* also came priests, especially Franciscans, who worked to convert the Indians to Catholicism. The missions of the Franciscan friars usually included schools for the Indians to learn agricultural and vocational skills. The priests often had to protect the Indians living near their missions from the cruelty and exploitation of the conquerors. The Spanish influence had a long-lasting impact, especially in language.

The Dutch, too, sought to establish a North American empire, but it was short-lived, as they fell victim to British power. The Dutch colony of New Amsterdam became New York when it fell into British hands, but the remnants of the Dutch heritage survived in the Dutch Reformed Church and its schools. In addition to the Dutch, various communities of German Pietists, particularly Moravians, located in the North American colonies in the late seventeenth and eighteenth centuries. The Moravians worked to convert the Indians to their version of Christianity and translated the Bible and other religious books into the Indian languages. While these various groups contributed to the foundations of American education by transplanting European ideas into the New World setting, the English colonists had the most significant impact.

Education in the English Colonies

To a large extent, the English colonists in North America sought to relive their European educational experience in the New World. The schools and colleges that they founded expressed their commitment that they were in America to stay and that their religion, culture, and language would be transmitted to their children through organized education. The educational ideas that they brought with them as a common heritage were diversified by the varying conditions of the regions in which they settled. Puritan New England, the culturally pluralistic Middle Atlantic colonies, and the plantation-owning South shared a common heritage that was reshaped by the American environment. First, we examine the common educational heritage brought by the English to North America; then we examine its regional variations.

The English colonists shared what was essentially a similar educational heritage. Although of differing religious persuasions, they inherited from the Renaissance the belief that the well-educated person knew the classical languages of Latin and Greek. From the Reformation, they inherited a belief that schooling should be steeped in religious doctrine so that the young would be nurtured in their faith and be ready to defend it.

The colonists' conception of institutionalized education was decidedly centered on social class. The children of workers and peasants should have a minimum primary education, in vernacular schools, to learn reading, writing, arithmetic, and religion. While the lower-class children were to have only a few years of primary schooling, the male offspring of the middle and upper classes would attend the Latin Grammar school, a college preparatory institution, and then go on to college. Thus, the colonists believed in a two-track system of schools—one for the poor and another for the wealthy.

Then, as now, much of a person's education went on in informal situations such as the family, church, farm, and shop. Lawrence Cremin, in his definitive work on colonial education, holds that throughout the North American colonies the family was the basic social and economic agency.[1] In particular, the New England Puritans regarded the family as fundamental to a healthy religious and civil society.

The family household was the place of sustained religious, literary, and vocational instruction. Parents taught their children to read the Bible and other religious books. Children's chores introduced them to the world of work. Children were expected to embrace the cherished values of piety and respect for parents, elders, and civil and religious authorities.[2] The informal education of the family was the foundation upon which the formal education—the school—was built.

It was upon this common educational tradition that the English established their schools in America. Although they shared a common European intellectual tradition, the colonists of the New England, Middle Atlantic, and southern colonies had to adapt and reshape this heritage when faced with America's wilderness, to meet the unique needs of their region of settlement.

New England

The New England Puritans, who followed the theology of John Calvin, were intensely religious. Subscribing completely to Calvin's doctrine of predestination, they believed that only the righteous would be saved and that the unrighteous would be damned. The righteous Puritans, an elect set apart, were to be literate, hardworking, diligent, frugal, and law-abiding men, women, and children. The Puritan ethic stressed that schooling was to be a means of cultivating these values. Formal education, or schooling, reinforced by the informal educational agencies of home and church, was designed to bring up children properly in Calvinist doctrine and laws of the Commonwealth. The Puritans saw schooling as a means of preserving their religious, social, and political beliefs by transmitting them to their children.

While the concept of separation of church and state is an important principle in American education today, just the opposite was true in the colonial era. In Puritan New England, particularly in Massachusetts, church, state, and school were closely related. Schools were often governed by the same trustees who governed the church.

Puritan View of Childhood   Elsewhere in this book, particularly in Chapter 13, on early childhood education, you will encounter the ideas of such educators as Rousseau, Pestalozzi, Froebel, and Montessori, who emphasized the dignity and importance of childhood as a time of human growth and development. The New England Puritan would have rejected such theories as permissive poison that would

---

1. Lawrence A. Cremin, *American Education: The Colonial Experience, 1607–1783* (New York: Harper & Row, 1970), pp. 135–136.
2. Bernard Bailyn, *Education in the Forming of American Society* (New York: W. W. Norton, 1972), p. 16.

spoil the child by sparing the rod. For the Puritans, the infant was conceived in sin and born in corruption.[3] Savage and primitive creatures, children needed training, discipline, and indoctrination so that they could control their weak human natures. Not childish, the good child behaved like an adult. To break children's willful behavior, schoolmasters were to use corporal punishment when necessary. Puritan ministers, such as the famous clergyman Jonathan Edwards, admonished parents:

> *Let children obey their parents, and yield to their instructions, and submit to their orders, as they would inherit a blessing and not a curse. For we have reason to think, from many things in the word of God, that nothing had a greater tendency to bring a curse on persons in this world, and on all their temporal concerns, than undutiful, unsubmissive, disorderly behavior in children towards their parents.[4]*

Puritan Stress on Schooling   The Puritans stressed schooling as a means of establishing and maintaining a proper society peopled by righteous men and women. Literate people, they believed, would be good citizens, whereas ignorant people would soon corrupt society. As early as 1642, the Massachusetts General Court required parents and guardians to see that their children could read and understand religious principles and the civil laws. The Law of 1642 was one of the first educational ordinances in the New World. In 1647, the Massachusetts General Court enacted the Old Deluder Satan Law, requiring towns of 50 of more families to appoint a teacher of reading and writing. Towns of 100 or more families were to employ a Latin teacher as well, to prepare students for college entry. The Old Deluder Satan Law stated:

> *It being one Chiefe project of ye ould deluder, Satan, to keepe men from the knowledge of ye Scriptures, as in former times by keeping ym in an unknowne tongue, so in these lattr times by perswading from ye use of tongues, yt so at least ye true sence & meaning of ye originall might be clouded by false glosses of saint seeming deceivers, yt learning may not be buried in ye grave of our fathers in ye church and commonwealth, the Lord assisting our endeavors, –*
>
> *It is therefore ordred, yt evry towneship in this jurisdiction, aftr ye Lord hath increased ym number of 50 housholdrs, shall then forthwth appoint one within their towne to teach all such children as shall resort to him to write & reade, whose wages shall be paid eithr by ye parents or mastrs of such children, or by ye inhabitants in genrall, by way of supply, as ye major part of those yt ordr ye prudentials of ye towne shall appoint; provided, those yt send their children be not oppressed by paying much more yn they can have ym taught for in othr townes; & it is furthr ordered, yt where any towne shall increase to ye numbr of 100 families or housholdrs, they shall set up a grammar schoole, ye mr thereof being able to instruct youth so farr as they shall be fited for ye university, provided, yt if any towne neglect ye performance hereof above one yeare, yt every such towne shall pay 5 £ to ye next schoole till they shall performe this order.[5]*

3. Stanford Fleming, *Children and Puritanism: The Place of Children in the Life and Thought of the New England Churches, 1620–1847* (New Haven, Conn.: Yale University Press, 1933).
4. H. Norman Gardiner, ed., *Selected Sermons of Jonathan Edwards* (New York: Macmillan, 1904), p. 148.
5. Nathaniel Shurtleff, ed., *Records of the Governor and Company of the Massachusetts Bay in New England* (Boston: n.p., 1853), II, p. 203.

These early Massachusetts laws of 1642 and 1647 were significant in American educational history in that they (1) illustrated the concern of civil government over schooling, (2) established a tone or atmosphere that gave civil authorities some control of schools, and (3) pointed to taxation for school support. The enactment of these laws demonstrated Puritan stress on schooling.

Schooling in New England   The New England town schools, such as those required by the Massachusetts laws of 1642 and 1647, were vernacular schools that offered the basic curriculum of reading, writing, arithmetic, and religion. Reading, the primary subject, was taught according to the ABC method, in which children learned the letters of the alphabet, then syllables and words, and finally sentences. The first reader was a Hornbook, a single sheet of parchment covered by a transparent material, that contained the alphabet, vowels, and syllables, the doctrine of the Trinity, and the Lord's Prayer. The *New England Primer*, a widely used colonial schoolbook, which first appeared in 1690, was called New England's Little Bible. The *Primer* contained 24 rhymes, one for each letter of the alphabet, illustrated by a woodcut drawing. The first rhyme, "In Adam's Fall, We Sinned All," was evidence of the close relationship between reading and religion that was so dear to the Puritans. The *New England Primer* also contained vowels, syllables, "An Alphabet of Lessons for Youth," "The Dutiful Child's Promises," the Lord's Prayer, the

The Hornbook, an instructional material used in colonial schooling, was printed on parchment, and included the alphabet, vowels, and Lord's Prayer.

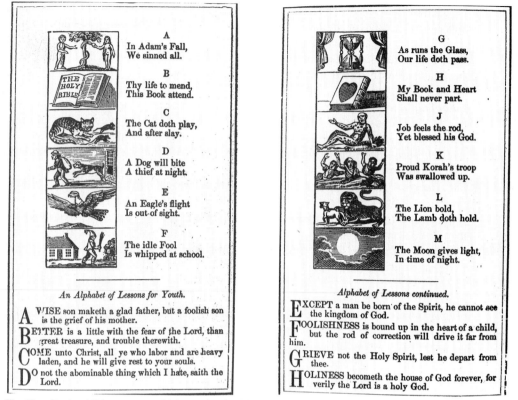

The New England Primer was a widely used colonial textbook.

Apostle's Creed, the Ten Commandments, "The Duty of Children Towards Their Parents," "Names and Order of the Books of the Old and New Testaments," and an abbreviated version of the Westminster Catechism.[6]

The preparation of teachers in the New England town schools varied considerably. Teaching might be a temporary situation as one prepared for a higher-status career as a minister or lawyer. Teachers were occasionally indentured servants who were "paying off" their passage to the New World.

The town school was typically a one-room building that enrolled children—both boys and girls—of various ages. The typical method was the recitation, in which children individually repeated before the teacher lessons they had memorized earlier. The catechetical method, in which children repeated memorized responses to questions, was popular. As indicated earlier, a failure to produce the required response or a breach of discipline was often dealt with harshly by the teacher. With the exception of the women who taught in Dame Schools, the colonial teachers were men. The educational preparation and social status of the town schoolteacher was generally less than that of the Latin Grammar schoolmaster.

6. Paul Leicester Ford, ed., *The New England Primer* (New York: Dodd, Mead, 1899).

A New England school board examines students.

Schooling in the Southern Colonies

The southern colonies of Maryland, Virginia, Georgia, and the Carolinas had a different social, economic, religious, and educational situation than New England.

Because the subtropical climate favored crops such as tobacco, rice, sugar, indigo, and cotton, the chief unit of agriculture was the plantation, supported by a work force of black slaves. The plantation economy and society produced rigid class distinctions among both whites and blacks. The owners of large plantations associated with each other but not with the small farmers, known as "poor whites" who had been pushed to the infertile scrub lands of the "back country." The black slaves were organized in a hierarchical fashion according to their job assignment on the plantation.

The plantation owners, as a class, considered themselves descendants of the Cavaliers, the English aristocrats who had supported the Stuart kings against Cromwell's "Roundheads." According to the "Cavalier myth," these displaced aristocrats immigrated to the American South, where they reestablished the old aristocratic way of life in the plantation society. Historically, the "Cavalier myth" is more legend than fact.

Social class distinctions and the often long distances between plantations retarded the development of a formal school system in the southern colonies. Although schools existed in the Tidewater cities, the plantation owners often employed tutors who lived with the family and taught their children. Frequently, the sons of leading families were sent to England for their preparation and higher education.

For the poor whites, education was largely informal. The boys learned to hunt, fish, and farm from their fathers; girls learned to sew, weave, and cook from their mothers. Formal schooling in the backwoods areas was minimal. Occasionally, the Anglican Missionary Society, the Society for the Propagation of the Gospel in Foreign Parts, conducted a few schools. Benevolent plantation owners sometimes would build a school on a piece of land that had been worn out by successive plantings of tobacco. In many respects, however, the prevalent attitude was that parents were responsible for educating their children. The poor white population included many illiterates due to the limited number of schools available, a condition that inhibited progress in the South in later years.

The black slaves, who worked on the plantations, had been uprooted from their societies in Africa. Seized by slave traders or sold into slavery, they were torn away from their families and tribal societies. When they arrived in the southern colonies, they were trained to perform specific functions of the plantation economy. Some slaves were trained to be field workers, others tended livestock, and others were trained as blacksmiths, wheelwrights, and mill hands. At the top of the slave society were the household servants, such as butlers, maids, valets, and coachmen. On most plantations, the slaves were not taught to read or write. In fact, the formal education of slaves was forbidden in most of the South. There were exceptions, however, as some masters taught slaves, particularly household servants, to read. Some slaves also taught themselves to read. Fearful of slave insurrections, the majority of southern plantation owners made no attempt to provide formal education to their slaves.

Although much of the education in the South was informal, there were some instances of formal education. Virginia and North Carolina made the apprenticeship of orphans and pauper children compulsory. When so apprenticed, orphans were indentured to masters of specific trades to learn a particular skill. The master was also required to provide instruction in reading and writing.

More formal education in the South was also provided by various private denominational schools, supported by private endowments or gifts. But this kind of schooling was sporadic and lacked the support given by the New England Puritans.

Schooling in the Middle Atlantic Colonies

Because of their location between New England and the southern colonies, New York, New Jersey, Pennsylvania, and Delaware were called the Middle Atlantic colonies. These colonies were ethnically, linguistically, and religiously diverse. Unlike Puritan New England, which was religiously homogeneous, the middle colonies were settled by Dutch Calvinists, Anglicans, Lutherans, Quakers, Presbyterians, Roman Catholics, and Jews. The presence of English, Dutch, Swedes, French, Danes, Jews, Irish, Scottish, and Germans resulted in cultural and language pluralisms. Whereas the New England colonists shared common religious and cultural traditions, such was not the case in the Middle Atlantic colonies. Different ethnic, language, and religious groups sought to preserve their unique heritage by establishing their own parochial schools. If the precedents for the American public school system were established in New England, the roots of the private and parochial schools were planted in the middle colonies.

Representative examples of schooling in the Middle Atlantic colonies are provided by New York and Pennsylvania.

Until 1664, New Amsterdam, later New York, was a Dutch colony. The most powerful religious denomination there was the Dutch Reformed Church, a Calvinistic church that believed in an educated ministry and laity. While the Dutch West India Company financed schools, the Reformed Church controlled and maintained vernacular reading and writing schools. After the English occupation, these Dutch schools continued as the Dutch community sought to preserve its cultural identity as a minority group in the English colony. The English established several charity schools, supported by the Church of England, which provided instruction in reading, writing, arithmetic, catechism, and religion. Because New York was a commercial colony, a number of informal commercial training situations developed in which young people learned various skills, such as navigation, surveying, printing, and accounting. These "training situations" occurred in apprenticeship arrangements or in private venture schools, operated by teachers for a profit. The "private venture schools" were an educational response to the demand for practical skills and knowledge.

Schooling in Pennsylvania was similar to that in New York. The Quakers, who originally settled in William Penn's colony, had fairly liberal ideas about education. Quaker elementary schools stressed religion, reading, writing, and arithmetic. The Quakers rejected corporal punishment as inhuman and were attentive to children's individual needs. In addition to the Quaker schools, parochial schools were established by German Pietists to transmit the Germanic culture and language. As in New York, private venture schools prepared individuals for certain commercial trades.

Education in the Early National Period

After the 13 colonies had won their political independence from Great Britain, they had to learn to become Americans rather than transplanted English subjects. In the early national period from 1776 to the 1830s, a cultural transformation took place in which educational ideas and institutions were repatterned to fit the needs of the United States. Major trends of the early national period that influenced education included the following:

1. Education became a state rather than a federal responsibility.
2. Concepts of civic or citizenship education emerged that eclipsed religious domination of education theory.
3. American cultural nationalism became a significant theme in American educational thought.
4. Experimentation occurred with various philanthropic approaches to schooling.

Education Becomes a State Prerogative

Under the Articles of Confederation, Congress enacted the Northwest Ordinance of 1785, which divided the territory into townships of six square miles each, which were further subdivided into 36 sections. The income from the sixteenth section was reserved to support schools. Two years later, the Ordinance of 1787 encouraged education as "necessary to good government and the happiness of mankind." Although the Ordinances of 1785 and 1787 predated the federal Constitution, they anticipated a federal concern for education that would grow in the late nineteenth and twentieth centuries. These ordinances also showed that the federal government was prepared to use land—a readily available asset in the new republic—to support education.

The U.S. Constitution, ratified in 1788, did not mention education. Under the "reserved powers clause" of the Tenth Amendment, ratified in 1791, educational prerogatives remained with the individual states of the Union. Following the New England tradition, many states delegated substantial educational responsibility to local school districts. Although education remained a state function, local school districts and boards were delegated an important role in matters of educational support and control.

Planning for Civic Education

After the American Revolution ended the colonial period, the citizens of the Republic became conscious of their new cultural and political identities. Various leaders of the new nation, such as Benjamin Franklin, Thomas Jefferson, Benjamin Rush, and Noah Webster, sought to devise new educational strategies and institutions to educate Americans in the processes of republicanism. These leaders wanted to replace Old World values and commitments with new loyalties. For them, organized education was a potent instrument to foster Americanism in the nation's citizens and children. The proponents of a new philosophy of civic education stressed the concepts of republicanism, science, and nationalism as key elements in American education.[7] These concepts were to have an impact on the common school movement of the mid-nineteenth century.

Republicanism, based on the political theory of John Locke, asserted that government arises from the consent of the governed. When a government violates the inalienable rights of "life, liberty, or property," its citizens have a right to replace it with a new government. Unlike a monarchy, with power vested in a king, authority in a republic arises with the citizens—those who constitute the government. Education for republican citizenship was designed to cultivate the skills, knowledge, and attitudes needed for a democratic government and society.

The concept of "nationalism" stressed a sense of American identity and a common commitment and loyalty to the United States as an independent and sovereign nation. The concept of a "science" was based on the Enlightenment belief that individuals could discover the laws of the universe. Calling for experimentation, a scientific attitude claimed that old commitments had to be re-examined and changed if need be for progress. For the theorists of the early national period, a

---

7. Allen O. Hansen, *Liberalism and American Education in the Eighteenth Century* (New York: Macmillan, 1926).

philosophy of education suited for the republic would prepare patriotic Americans who would be eager to experiment and create a scientific and progressive society.[8]

Benjamin Franklin and an English Language Academy

Benjamin Franklin (1706–1790), an early advocate for American independence, was esteemed as the young Republic's elder statesman. Although his own formal schooling was minimal, Franklin was recognized as a scientist and philosopher in both Europe and America. A prominent Philadelphian, he helped to found the American Philosophical Society. The admonitions of *Poor Richard's Almanack* were read by Americans who eagerly accepted his emphasis on the values of frugality, diligence, thrift, hard work, and inventiveness. Franklin's philosophy exalted the common sense of the self-made and largely self-educated person.

Franklin, a practical man, distrusted the classical emphasis that dominated education. An advocate of utilitarian and scientific education, he proposed the establishment of an English grammar school in Philadelphia in 1749.[9] Franklin's

Benjamin Franklin (1706–1790) was a statesman, philosopher, and educational theorist.

8. Frederick Rudolph, *Essays on Education in the Early Republic* (Cambridge, Mass.: Harvard University Press, 1965).
9. Edmond Wright, *Franklin of Philadelphia* (Cambridge, Mass.: Harvard University Press, 1989).

proposal is significant in that it (1) presented an alternative to the Latin Grammar school and (2) anticipated the academy and high school. In contrast to the classical language curriculum of the Latin Grammar school, Franklin's plan incorporated humanistic and utilitarian studies.

Grammar, composition, rhetoric, and public speaking were a part of English language studies; instruction was to be in English, the language of commerce and politics, rather than in Latin. Vocational training included carpentry, shipbuilding, engraving, printing, painting, cabinetmaking, carving, and gardening.

Mathematics, including arithmetic, geometry, astronomy, and accounting, was to be an applied subject. History was to provide students with a sense of time and with biographical models that illustrated the lives of famous historical persons. Greek, Roman, English, and colonial history were offered.

Although English was the language of instruction, students could study a second language related to their vocational needs. Prospective clergy would study Latin and Greek; physicians would study Latin, Greek, and French; and merchants would study French, German, and Spanish. Other subjects in the curriculum were science, agriculture, technology, physical education, and character education.

Franklin's proposed school was a significant innovation because it introduced many practical skills into the formal school that had been ignored or left to private venture teachers. With prophetic insight into America's future, Franklin gave special attention to science, invention, and technology.

Franklin's proposed academy was established in Philadelphia, located in the same building as the Latin Grammar school. However, there was a profound difference between the two institutions. Franklin's school's enriched curriculum, responsive to the needs of the rising commercial class, was an improvement over the narrowly prescribed Latin Grammar curriculum.

Thomas Jefferson and State-Supported Schooling

Thomas Jefferson (1743–1826), son of a wealthy and socially prominent plantation owner, was born in Virginia. He attended the local vernacular and Latin Grammar schools and later graduated from William and Mary College. Because of his study of politics, philosophy, architecture, and science, Jefferson was elected to the American Academy of Arts and Sciences and served as president of the American Philosophical Society from 1797 to 1815.[10] As a leading statesman during the formative republican period, Jefferson held the positions of member of the Virginia legislature, delegate to the Continental Congress, governor of Virginia, minister to France, secretary of state, vice-president, and president.

Jefferson stated that his epitaph should refer to only three of his accomplishments: writing the Declaration of Independence, writing the Virginia Bill of Rights, and founding the University of Virginia. As the author of the Declaration of

---

10. Noble E. Cunningham, Jr., *In Pursuit of Reason: The Life of Thomas Jefferson* (Baton Rouge: Louisiana State University Press, 1987).

Thomas Jefferson (1743–1826) was the third president of the United States and the founder of the University of Virginia.

Independence, Jefferson stated his political belief that every person was endowed with inalienable rights of "life, liberty, and pursuit of happiness."[11]

In 1779, Jefferson introduced his "Bill for the More General Diffusion of Knowledge" into the Virginia legislature. Jefferson's proposal was based on the following beliefs: (1) Schools in the new Republic had the political function of educating a literate citizenry, (2) the state was responsible for providing schools, (3) state schools should be secular rather than religious, and (4) schools should also exercise the selective function of identifying intellectually able persons.[12]

In Jefferson's plan, Virginia's counties were subdivided into wards, each of which had an elementary school to provide instruction in reading, writing, arithmetic, and history. All white children in Virginia were to attend ward schools for three years of publicly supported elementary education. After completing three years of elementary school, parents could continue to enroll their children by paying tuition. Although minimal by today's standards, Jefferson's proposal for a state commitment to support education was significant for its time.

11. Roy J. Honeywell, *The Educational Work of Thomas Jefferson* (Cambridge, Mass.: Harvard University Press, 1931).
12. Jefferson's educational ideas are analyzed in Gordon C. Lee, "Learning and Liberty: The Jeffersonian Tradition in Education," in *Crusade Against Ignorance: Thomas Jefferson on Education* (New York: Teachers College Press, Columbia University, 1962).

The second stage of Jefferson's plan called for establishing 20 grammar (secondary) schools in Virginia. It was at this stage that the selective function became operative. Jefferson believed that state schools should identify the most academically able persons and prepare them for positions of civic leadership. To this end, the most able student who was unable to pay tuition would be given a scholarship.

These scholarship students were to continue in the grammar school for two or three years, where they would study Latin, Greek, English, geography, and higher mathematics. The most promising student from among this group would then receive an additional six years of education, and the rest of the class unable to pay tuition would be dismissed. The highest-ranking 20 students, selected annually, were to complete grammar school. At the end of this period, 10 would become elementary teachers in the ward schools, and the remaining 10 would go on to higher studies at the College of William and Mary.

Although not enacted, Jefferson's bill is noteworthy for the perspective that it provides on education in a republican society. To encourage citizenship education among the general population, he wanted every white child to have at least three years of publicly supported schooling. At the same time, he wanted secondary and higher schools to identify and prepare a selected number of academically promising students for leadership positions.

Noah Webster

Noah Webster (1758–1843) is often called the Schoolmaster of the Republic because of his influence on the development of language and language teaching in the United States.[13] A cultural nationalist, Webster believed that although the United States had won its political independence from England, it had yet to secure sovereignty over its language. A unique American language, Webster believed, was the means by which Americans would achieve their cultural identity and unity. To create a distinctive American language, Webster wrote *The American Spelling Book* and his definitive *American Dictionary*.

When the Constitution became the law of the land in 1789, Webster argued that the United States needed its own system of "language as well as government." The language of Great Britain, he claimed, "should no longer be our standard; for the taste of her writers is already completed, and her language on the decline."[14] Arguing that a sense of national identity could be conveyed through a distinctive national language and literature, Webster wanted to reshape the English language used in the United States into a uniquely American language. A distinctively American language would (1) eliminate the residues of European usage, (2) create a uniform American speech free of local usage, and (3) promote conscious American cultural nationalism and pride.

---

13. Harry R. Warfel, *Noah Webster: Schoolmaster to America* (New York: Octagon, 1936); Ervin C. Shoemaker, *Noah Webster, Pioneer of Learning* (New York: Columbia University Press, 1936); Richard M. Rollins, *The Long Journey of Noah Webster* (Philadelphia: University of Pennsylvania Press, 1980).
14. Noah Webster, *Dissertations on the English Language* (Boston: Isaiah Thomas, 1789), p. 20.

Noah Webster (1758–1843), author of the *American Dictionary* and the *American Spelling Book,* was called "the schoolmaster of the Republic."

Webster believed that a unique American language should be transmitted deliberately and systematically in the nation's schools. As they learned the American language, children also would learn to think and act as Americans. Because the values in these American schools would be shaped by the students' reading, Webster devoted himself to writing spelling and reading books. The first part of his *Grammatical Institute of the English Language*, published in 1783, was later printed as *The American Spelling Book*, which was popular throughout the United States in the early nineteenth century. It has been estimated that 15 million copies had been sold by 1837. Webster's great work, *The American Dictionary*, was completed in 1825, after 25 years of painstaking research.[15]

The educational plans of Franklin, Jefferson, and Webster demonstrated that these early leaders of the Republic were searching for an educational system for the new nation. They especially wanted to create an education that would foster effective citizenship.

Social and Educational Change in Nineteenth-Century America

The foundations of the American public school system were established during the social transformation of the nineteenth century. The common, or public, school

15. Henry Steele Commager, ed., *Noah Webster's American Spelling Book* (New York: Teachers College Press, Columbia University, 1962).

system was developed and implemented in the years before the Civil War in the northern states. After the war ended, it was extended to the South. The second half of the nineteenth century saw the rise of the American public high school. Land grant colleges and universities were funded by the Morrill Act of 1862. These educational changes need to be considered in the context of important socio-economic and political changes that transformed the United States from a rural-agricultural society into an industrial and urban nation. Throughout much of the nineteenth century, the United States was a developing nation. By the beginning of the twentieth century, it was a leading world power.

When it began in New England, the common school movement was one of many reforms, such as the abolition of black slavery, women's rights, temperance, and penal reform. The Abolitionist movement marked the beginning of the end of slavery; the common school movement marked the beginning of the American public school system. Before the common school won the commitment of large numbers of people, some states experimented with various nonpublic philanthropic alternatives.

Philanthropic Education

During the phenomenal industrial and urban growth of the early nineteenth century, some business and political leaders recognized that a mass education system was needed to train immigrant and working-class children. Large cities, such as New York and Philadelphia, inaugurated voluntary or philanthropic schools, usually Lancasterian, as an educational response. Often, wealthy benefactors funded these schools.

Support of voluntary and philanthropic schools rested on the premise that education was a private rather than a state function. Philanthropists who supported voluntary schools wanted to provide minimal, basic literacy and character training to children from the lower social and economic classes.

In contrast to those who used education for social control, others wanted popular education to stimulate social change. For example, many workers' associations wanted schools to provide knowledge to working classes. Eventually, working-class leaders hoped to gain political power by educational rather than by revolutionary means.

William Maclure (1763–1840), a scientist, geologist, and philanthropist, argued, in *Opinions on Various Subjects*, that industrial schools should be established for the working classes.[16] In such schools, working-class children would learn to recognize the real political and economic interests of their class. Maclure, who anticipated vocational education, designed a curriculum that stressed basic science and its agricultural and industrial application. He also introduced the Pestalozzian method of education (see Chapter 13) to the United States. Maclure believed in using education for social change rather than for social control.

The Sunday school was a philanthropic endeavor that reflected the impact of the industrial revolution on working-class families. In both England and the United

---

16. William Maclure, *Opinions on Various Subjects, I* (New Harmony, Ind.: School Press, 1821), pp. 65–70.

States, children toiled as cheap laborers in the factories and mines. Because they worked a six-day week, Sunday was the only day available for school. Sunday school instruction was limited to the basics of reading, writing, religion, and character formation. With the inauguration of the common school, the Sunday school declined as an agency of basic education. Today, it is used exclusively for religious education.

The infant school was another response to early industrialization. Because women worked in factories, the infant school was a place where children could stay while their mothers were absent. The infant school concept, a prototype of the modern day-care center, was developed by Robert Owen (1771–1858), a British industrialist and communitarian socialist, at New Lanark in Scotland.[17] Basically, the infant school was a nursery school where young children, ranging from ages two to six years, received moral, physical, and intellectual training.

The monitorial school was one of the most popular alternatives to common schools. Monitorial education was devised by Joseph Lancaster (1778–1838), who claimed that it was possible to educate large numbers of children effectively, efficiently, and cheaply.[18] According to Lancasterian monitorial education, a master teacher was to train advanced students to teach basic skills to beginning students. Because students did most of the teaching, costs were low. To accommodate large enrollments, Lancaster developed large factorylike schools. Using a semimilitary system, lessons were reduced to small elements, and each instructional phase was assigned to a particular monitor. Children of relatively similar ability were grouped together so that instruction could proceed uniformly. Each phase of instruction had its appropriate lesson plan. Instruction in writing and arithmetic was also arranged into groups based on ability levels. To keep costs down, inexpensive materials were used. Large wall charts were used instead of books to teach reading. Students traced letters with their fingers on sand tables instead of using pen, ink, and paper.

The Lancasterian monitorial system was confined to basic skill learning. After enjoying popularity in the early nineteenth century, the monitorial method was discarded and replaced by common public schools.

The Common School

The common school movement of the nineteenth century was one of the major events in American cultural, social, and educational history. Although defined in various ways, common schools were publicly supported and controlled institutions that offered a curriculum of reading, writing, arithmetic, penmanship, grammar, history, geography, and health. They also instilled the values of punctuality, hard work, and industry. The common school grew out of New England's tradition of local control. As the frontier moved westward, common schools were built in the new towns and settlements. Common schools were also used to assimilate, or Americanize, the children of immigrants.

17. Harold Silver, *Robert Owen on Education* (Cambridge: Cambridge University Press, 1969), pp. 109–110.
18. Carl F. Kaestle, *Joseph Lancaster and the Monitorial School Movement* (New York: Teacher's College Press, Columbia University, 1973), pp. 176–180.

An important argument for common schooling came from political and educational reformers such as James Carter, Horace Mann, and Thaddeus Stevens, who were concerned with the extension of civic education. Democratic processes and procedures required literate voters who were capable of electing public officials. American nationalism was also a motive behind the common school movement. Common schools could encourage shared values and loyalties and cultivate a sense of Americanness among people of ethically, racially, and linguistically diverse backgrounds. In addition, the middle classes wanted a more utilitarian education that would prepare skilled workers.

In 1827 Massachusetts instituted the support of common schools via compulsory taxation. Other states in New England and in the Midwest followed Massachusetts. The movement to publicly supported education took a slower course in the Middle Atlantic states, where Lancasterianism held on. Public schools did not develop in the South until the post–Civil War Reconstruction era.

While the common school movement varied from state to state, some general observations can be made. First, the state enacted legislation that permitted the voters of a given district to tax themselves to support common schools. This permissive legislation recognized school districts as units with administrative and taxing powers. Second, the state encouraged districts to organize by providing funds from the general school fund to those districts that had voted to support public

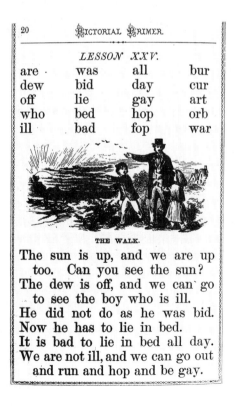

Lesson XXV, "The Walk," from Charles W. Sander's, *Sander's Pictorial Primer*. This lesson is from a representative nineteenth-century reader.

A child laborer employed in a mill; the success of compulsory education required restrictions on child labor.

schools. Third, the state required the formation of school districts and the levying of local taxes to provide elementary education for the children resident in the district.

Henry Barnard: A Common School Leader   Henry Barnard (1811–1900), a leader in the common school movement, was secretary of the Connecticut Board of Education from 1838 to 1842. He also served as state commissioner of the public schools in Rhode Island, 1845–1849, chancellor of the University of Wisconsin, 1858–1860, and U.S. commissioner of education, 1867–1870. Barnard was recognized, along with Horace Mann, as one of the founders of the common school. As a journalist, he popularized public education through the *Connecticut Common School Journal* and the *American Journal of Education*. He introduced teachers to the ideas of European education reformers like Pestalozzi, Froebel, and Herbart.[19]

Barnard traveled throughout Connecticut and reported on the condition of public schools to the members of the state board. While he believed that common schooling should establish a solid foundation in basic skills, he also wanted teachers to emphasize civic values, the principles of health and diet, and the methods of

19. Merle Curti, *The Social Ideas of American Educators* (New York: Littlefield, Adams, 1959), pp. 139–168.

Henry Barnard (1811–1900) was a common-school leader and U.S. commissioner of education.

accurate observation and clear reflection. Barnard's *First Annual Report*, in 1838, advised Connecticut teachers on subjects ranging from writing to religion.[20] Reading, writing, and arithmetic, the primary branches of learning, he wrote, were the foundations of later education and of work. The most important subject was the English language, which included spelling, reading, speaking, grammar, and composition. Practical arithmetic should also be stressed.

Barnard also urged more adequate teacher education, the establishment of normal schools, and increased financial compensation for teachers.

The Country School

Although the urban public school found in larger cities like Boston, New York, and Philadelphia represented one version of the common school, the one-room rural or country school of the nineteenth century came to typify common schooling for many Americans, especially in the midwestern and western states and territories. According to historian Wayne Fuller, these one-room, ungraded schools were the farmers' "solution to the problem of educating their scattered, isolated children . . . and the foundation of that cherished American institution, the neighborhood school."[21]

The rural schools were organized and governed by elected boards. The board's responsibilities included determining the location of the school, building and main-

20. John S. Brubacher, *Henry Barnard on Education* (New York: McGraw-Hill, 1931).
21. Wayne E. Fuller, *The Old Country School: The Story of Rural Education in the Middle West* (Chicago: University of Chicago Press, 1982), p. 43.

taining the school, hiring the teacher, and levying taxes to support the district's educational effort. In many instances, the board, acting as its own certification agency, conducted an examination to determine if the applicants for the teaching position were qualified. The board members divided the administrative duties of operating the school. The president of the board was responsible for conducting the meetings, the secretary for maintaining the records, and the treasurer for collecting the revenues and paying the teacher's salary and the other expenses. The board also supervised its single staff member, the teacher.

Architecturally, the country school was a simple white or red wooden frame building in which the school-aged children of the district were educated in one room. At the front of the room was located the teacher's large wooden desk and chair. The pupils sat at desks arranged in rows facing the teacher, with two children usually seated at each large desk. The school was heated by a large cast-iron wood-burning stove, the fuel provided by the children's parents. Behind the teacher was located a large blackboard. On the walls hung portraits of George Washington and Abraham Lincoln and perhaps a large map of the United States.

Although males continued to teach in the country schools, many women had entered the teaching ranks by mid-nineteenth century. Some of the teachers had completed the two-year normal school; others had no formal preparation for teaching beyond their own common school education. The standard curriculum was reading, writing, arithmetic, spelling, and perhaps history, geography, and public speaking or elocution. The standard method used was the recitation, in which each student would stand before the teacher and recite the lesson that had been assigned and memorized as homework. While some teachers might group students, the usual approach was to hear each student's individual recitation.

By the end of the nineteenth century, the one-room rural school was under attack by a growing body of professional educators, namely, professors of school administration in the newly organized departments of education. The professional educators claimed that the ungraded country school was inefficient and offered a much too limited curriculum to the students. They further argued that direct supervision of the rural school by the board of education placed instruction under the control of amateurs rather than professional educators. School administrators argued that the many rural school districts should be consolidated into larger districts where buildings could be larger and the curriculum more varied. Those who preferred the more centralized model of common schooling looked to the larger cities, such as St. Louis, where William T. Harris was developing the science of educational administration.

William Torrey Harris: Public School Consolidator After the Civil War, a great transformation occurred in American life as industrialism created an increasingly urban and technological society. The rapid growth of big cities and the massive influx of central and eastern European immigrants required educational leaders capable of administering efficiently the growing urban school systems. William Torrey Harris (1835–1909) was such an administrator of a large urban public school system. As the major statesman of American education after the Civil War era, Harris sought to consolidate the work of the earlier common school

William T. Harris (1835–1909) was a leader in school administration, St. Louis superintendent of schools, and U.S. commissioner of education.

leaders and to relate American public education to the needs of an industrial society.[22]

From 1868 until 1880, Harris was superintendent of schools in St. Louis, a growing commercial and industrial city. An interesting national crossroads, its location between North and South gave St. Louis a population harboring both southern and northern sentiments. Racially and ethnically diverse, it had a large black community as well as a large immigrant population, especially German Americans. In this urban diversity, Harris established the basic administrative and organizational patterns for schools in an industrial society. As he dealt with the quantitative problems of organizing, classifying, and structuring a modern school system, Harris earned a reputation as being an efficient, effective, but conservative administrator.

Harris believed that a society had reached a high level of civilization when its social institutions, such as the family, state, church, and school, were well developed. To promote civilized life, the school was to emphasize the values of self-discipline, civic commitment, obedience to law and order, and respect for private property in the young. Harris saw the school's role to be that of efficiently transmitting the cultural heritage to the young through a curriculum that was a graded, structured, and cumulative sequence of studies.

In the United States, schools were to prepare individuals for life in a technological society of growing complexity and specialization. By stressing work, diligence, punctuality, and perseverance, schools prepared people to contribute to an emergent technological society. Under Harris's command, the schools were to prepare a trained labor force and managerial class for the nation's new industrial economy.

22. Selwyn K. Troen, *The Public and the Schools: Shaping the St. Louis System, 1838–1920* (Columbia: University of Missouri Press, 1975), pp. 1–4.

Believing strongly in the importance of early childhood education, Harris established the first successful public school kindergarten in St. Louis in 1873. After the kindergarten, children would then be prepared for the elementary school curriculum of mathematics, geography, literature and art, history, and grammar. When the elementary curriculum was completed, secondary students would then study classics, mathematics, and language.

As an administrator, Harris believed that efficient teachers were needed to transmit the curricular subjects effectively. He urged teachers to emphasize silence, industriousness, regularity, and discipline in their classrooms and to impress upon students the need of incorporating these values into their daily lives.[23] Harris's style of school management and classroom discipline rewarded children who conformed to adult standards and existing social values.

Harris and other urban school superintendents of the late nineteenth century faced the problems of overcrowded classrooms, poorly prepared teachers, and wide divergence in students' backgrounds. Harris's superintendency in St. Louis was marked by careful planning, the ordering of educational priorities, and efficient administrative procedures. His attention to planned administration led him to classify and group students meticulously. He developed the graded school where the work of each year was organized into a specific grade. To make compulsory attendance effective, school administrators had to compile and maintain statistics and attendance reports. Further, the school administrator was concerned with noninstructional matters such as the school's physical facilities, lighting, heating, architecture, and ventilation.

Although Harris wanted schools to preserve existing social institutions and values rather than to change them, he also was prepared to deal with social issues. Believing that public schools should assimilate immigrants into American society, he also believed that Americanization should be gradual, evolutionary, and non-coerced. To this end, he encouraged bilingual and bicultural education for St. Louis's large German community that was designed to bring German-speaking children into the larger English-speaking American society.

Because of his work in St. Louis, Harris gained a national reputation and was recognized as the elder statesman of American education. As the U.S. commissioner of education from 1889 to 1906, he became the authority on American public education. He was a member of the most important educational associations and commissions and was particularly influential in the National Education Association.

The establishment of common schools was an important stage in the development of the American public school system, as the various state legislatures enacted laws to tax for public support. Educational leaders such as Mann, Barnard, and Harris developed the pioneering models of effective school administration in the United States. With common schools as its basic foundation, it was possible to extend public education through the secondary level and to create a complete system of public supported and controlled educational institutions.

---

23. William T. Harris, *Compulsory Education in Relation to Crime and Social Morals* (Washington, D.C.: printed privately, 1885), pp. 4–9.

The High School

While the common school created the base for public education in the United States, it was the public high school that linked public elementary schools with state colleges and universities. In the early nineteenth century, the colonial Latin Grammar school declined and was replaced by the academy, a secondary school serving the educational needs of the middle-class youth by offering a wide range of curricula and subjects for both college preparatory and terminal students. Generally private institutions, a few academies were semipublic and received some funds from cities or states. Characterized by loosely organized instructional programs, educational quality varied considerably from academy to academy, with variations in the competency of instructors and aptitude of the students.[24]

After the 1870s, the academies declined and were replaced by the public high school. However, a small number of private academies continued to educate a small percentage of the secondary school–aged population.

The high school became the major institution of American secondary education in the second half of the nineteenth century. In the 1870s, a series of court cases such as Michigan's *Kalamazoo* case in 1874 ruled that school districts could establish and support public high schools with tax funds. By the years 1889–1890, the 2,526 public high schools in the United States were enrolling 202,063 students, in comparison with the 1,632 private academies that enrolled 94,391 students.[25]

The rise of the high school can be explained by the impact of convergent socioeconomic forces. The United States experienced a great transformation from an agricultural and rural to an industrial and urban society. By 1930, more than 25 percent of the U.S. population was located in seven great urban areas of New York, Chicago, Philadelphia, Boston, Detroit, Los Angeles, and Cleveland. Urbanization stimulated a growing need for specialization of occupations, professions, and careers.

The high school represented an institutional response to the educational needs of modern society. It educated the growing number of students who were continuing their formal education beyond the eight years of elementary schooling. It served terminal students who were completing their formal schooling in the high school and continued to provide college preparatory schooling for those who would enter institutions of higher education.

As a school for adolescents of varying social, economic, racial, religious, and ethnic backgrounds, the comprehensive high school was a new kind of secondary institution. In contrast to European secondary schools, which separated the academic from terminal students, the American high school was a comprehensive institution that sought social integration in an environment of curricular differentiation.

When the high school became the dominant institution of American secondary education, it became possible for a student to attend a sequence of publicly sup-

24. Theodore R. Sizer, *The Age of Academies* (New York: Teachers College Press, Columbia University, 1964).
25. Edward Krug, *The Shaping of the American High School, 1880–1920* (New York: Harper & Row, 1964).

ported and controlled institutions, beginning with the kindergarten, extending to the elementary school and through high school, and reaching the college and university. The high school linked elementary and higher educational institutions and completed the American educational ladder.

Twentieth-Century Trends in Education

After the consolidation of public education in the early twentieth century, the public schools tended to become formalized and routine. The Progressive Movement was an effort to reform and liberalize not only education but also politics and society. John Dewey (1859–1952) exercised a great influence on twentieth-century American education. His *How We Think* (1910) stressed problem solving as a method of science and education. *Individualism Old and New* (1929) examined social change in relation to American civilization. *Democracy and Education* (1916) remains his classic statement of educational philosophy.

Dewey's Laboratory School

Dewey's work at the Laboratory School of the University of Chicago, which he directed from 1896 to 1904, operationalized his Experimentalist philosophy of education. Dewey's books, *The School and Society* (1898) and *The Child and the Curriculum* (1902) describe his work at the Laboratory School. By solving personal, social, and intellectual problems, children exercised their intelligence and used the knowledge and science accumulated by the human race. Dewey detailed three levels of learning activity used at the Laboratory School: (1) Children exercised their senses and developed physical coordination, (2) children used materials and tools present in the environment, and (3) children used their intelligence to discover, examine, and use ideas.[26]

After Dewey concluded his work at the Chicago Laboratory School, he returned to writing in formal philosophy and the philosophy of education at Columbia University. Dewey's educational philosophy exerted a profound influence on the "new education" of the twentieth century.

Progressivism in Education

The origins of Progressive Education began with the Naturalistic educators of the late eighteenth and nineteenth centuries. Rousseau, Pestalozzi, and Froebel developed educational theories that challenged traditional practices. The eighteenth-century Enlightenment and nineteenth-century social reform produced the notion of "progress" by which people could shape their environment by using reason and science.

In the United States, the early twentieth century was the era of the Progressive Movement in politics. Robert LaFollette, Theodore Roosevelt, and Woodrow

---

26. Arthur G. Wirth, *John Dewey as Educator: His Design and Work in Education, 1894–1904* (New York: John Wiley, 1966), pp. 96–99; Herbert M. Kliebard, *The Struggle for the American Curriculum 1893–1958* (Boston: Routledge & Kegan Paul, 1986), pp. 59–88.

Wilson campaigned against graft, corruption, and monopoly. LaFollette's Wisconsin Idea encouraged a working relationship between education and political reform. The social work of Jane Addams, the journalism of Lincoln Steffens, and the legal opinions of Oliver W. Holmes, Jr., expressed progressivism in society, literature, and law. Progressivism in education and politics challenged traditionalism and sought to reform society.[27]

An interesting synthesis of the theories and practices of progressivism and social efficiency took place in Gary, Indiana, a new city designed in 1906 near the massive U.S. Steel mills. In the twentieth century's early decades, Gary was a genuine multicultural city whose population included immigrants from southern and eastern Europe and African-Americans from the South who came to work in the steel mills. The design of a new city called for the design of a new school system to serve the educational needs of the growing population. Gary's superintendent of schools, William A. Wirt (1874–1938), decided to use John Dewey's Experimentalist philosophy to create schools that would serve the social and education needs of the entire community, adults as well as children. He designed an extended curriculum that included mechanical drawing, architecture, drafting, typing, commercial arithmetic, and bookkeeping, as well as the traditional academic subjects.[28] These vocational and technical courses were offered to students enrolled in the public schools and to adults in evening and Saturday programs. In addition, the schools' gymnasiums and auditoriums were also available for use by community organizations.

Along with his progressive desire that schools should be community centers, Wirt was determined to implement cost saving in Gary's schools. Like many early twentieth-century educational administrators, he was influenced by the social and economic efficiency movement. Wirt developed the "work-study-play system," in which students were organized into platoons designed to ensure full utilization of the buildings throughout the school day. While some students were engaged in physical education or assembly programs, others used the academic classrooms and the vocational education shops.

Progressive educators believed that schooling could exercise a reforming influence. However, schools first had to be reformed. A number of educators formed the Progressive Education Association in 1919 under the leadership of Stanwood Cobb.[29]

In the 1920s, Progressive Education was characterized by efforts to liberate the child's creative impulses as educators such as Marietta Johnson and Caroline Pratt devised instructional methods to release the child's creativity. Johnson, as director of the School of Organic Education at Fairhope in Alabama, stressed the child's interests and needs and emphasized music, singing, dancing, stories, and creative artwork to awaken the child's creativity. Caroline Pratt, founder of the Greenwich

---

27. Lawrence A. Cremin, *The Transformation of the School* (New York: Knopf, 1962).
28. Ronald D. Cohen, *Children of the Mill: Schooling and Society in Gary, Indiana, 1906–1960* (Bloomington: Indiana University Press, 1990), p. 12.
29. Patricia Albjerg Graham, *Progressive Education: From Arcady to Academe, A History of the Progressive Education Association, 1919–1955* (New York: Teachers College Press, Columbia University, 1967).

Village Play School, developed the principle that children would learn the truths of the universe through their play activities.

While the more child-centered educators neglected social issues, other progressive educators worked for social reform. Several of this socially oriented wing of Progressive Education were members of Columbia University's Teachers College faculty in the late 1920s and during the 1930s. Teachers College professors such as Harold Rugg, William H. Kilpatrick, and George S. Counts are of major significance in the history of Progressive Education. Rugg sought to integrate both creativity and social reform into his theory of education. Kilpatrick worked to provide progressivism with a coherent methodology of instruction. Counts popularized the view that schools should be agencies of active social reform.

Critics of Progressivism

Progressive Education had a number of critics, such as the Essentialist educators William Chandler Bagley and Isaac Kandel, who argued that the purpose of education was to cultivate intellectual skills and knowledge. The Essentialists believed that schools should train children systematically in the basic subjects of reading, writing, arithmetic, history, English, and foreign languages. They believed that schools should stress hard work and discipline and should transmit the cultural heritage rather than seek to inaugurate social, economic, or political change.

In the post-Sputnik era of the 1950s, Arthur Bestor, in *Educational Wastelands* and *The Restoration of Learning*, attacked the "educationist establishment" and urged a return to basic education grounded on intellectual disciplines. Max Rafferty, in his *Suffer, Little Children*, charged that progressive reformers had weakened educational standards.

Racial Integration and School Desegregation

In *Brown* v. *Board of Education of Topeka*, in 1954, the U.S. Supreme Court ruled that racial segregation in public schools was unconstitutional. The *Brown* case marked the beginning of a concerted movement for civil rights and racial integration. In September 1957, Congress passed a civil rights act that established a commission to investigate charges of the denial of voting rights and equal protection of the laws due to color, race, religion, or national origin. In 1960, the passage of another civil rights act empowered federal courts to appoint referees to examine state voting qualifications that denied the right to vote because of race or color. The Civil Rights Act of 1964, the most far-reaching law of its kind, protected voting rights and guaranteed civil rights in employment and education. It guaranteed equal access to public accommodations and strengthened the machinery for preventing employment discrimination. In education, the act empowered the federal government to file school desegregation suits and to withhold federal funds from districts that practiced discrimination in federal programs. The Civil Rights Act of 1968 protected the civil rights of workers and provided severe penalties for interfering with the rights of those attending school or working.

Along with the civil rights acts, several Supreme Court decisions advanced racial integration in the schools, such as *Griffin* v. *School Board of Prince Edward County*, in 1964.[30] In Prince Edward County in Virginia, the board of supervisors had refused to levy taxes for the 1959–1960 school year, with the result that the public schools were closed. A private association, the Prince Edward School Foundation, formed to operate private schools for white children, drew its major financial support from state and county tuition grants. The Supreme Court ruled that the closing of the Prince Edward County public schools had denied African-American students the equal protection of the laws guaranteed by the Fourteenth Amendment since the county supervisors' action had forced children to attend racially segregated schools that received county and state support.

In 1969, the Supreme Court, in *Alexander* v. *Holmes County Board of Education*, discarded the "all deliberate speed" criterion for school desegregation when it reversed lower court decisions that granted an extension of time to some Mississippi school districts for desegregation.[31] The Court ruled that every school district in the land was to terminate dual school systems "at once" and operate only unitary schools.

In 1971, in *Swann* v. *Charlotte-Mecklenburg Board of Education*, the Supreme Court ruled that busing was an acceptable means of achieving school desegregation.[32] It also stated that future school construction must not be used to perpetuate or reestablish segregated schools. Following the *Swann* decision, district courts began attacking de facto segregation in northern and western urban areas such as San Francisco, Philadelphia, Pittsburgh, Detroit, Los Angeles, Denver, and Boston. The first phase of the legal thrust against racial inequality was directed against de jure segregation in the South. The second phase of the movement toward racial equality was the attack launched against de facto segregation in the large northern cities.

Recent Trends

During the 1970s, public schools experienced a "time of troubles" caused by declining pupil enrollments, rising expenditures, and static revenues. From 1971 to 1984, elementary and secondary school enrollments decreased steadily, reflecting the national decline in the school-aged population. Since many state funding formulas are based on the number of students in attendance, the decline in the school population brought with it a decline in revenues. This decline in revenues occurred at a time when many local school districts rejected increasing the local property tax to raise needed funds for schools. Although revenues were either decreasing or remaining static in many school districts, the nation's school systems experienced rising costs for teachers' and administrators' salaries, fuel, and maintenance because of the high rate of inflation of the 1970s.

During the 1980s, the demographic and economic situation improved for American elementary and secondary schools. Since 1985, enrollments are again

30. *Griffin* v. *School Board of Prince Edward County*, 377 U.S. 218 (1964).
31. *Alexander* v. *Holmes County Board of Education*, 396 U.S. 19 (1969).
32. *Swann* v. *Charlotte-Mecklenburg Board of Education*, 402 U.S. 554 (1971).

increasing. For example, enrollments in kindergarten through eighth grade increased from 27 million in 1985 to 28.4 million in 1988.[33] Increasing enrollments brought added funds to schools in states where funding was based on average daily student attendance. In addition, the economy was stabilized in the 1980s as the inflationary cycle ended. Projections, however, for the 1990s indicate some economic uncertainty with the possibility of inflation again occurring.

The 1980s witnessed a concerted focusing of attention by political leaders, the media, and the public on the condition of education in the United States. In 1983, *A Nation at Risk: The Imperative for Educational Reform* was issued by the National Commission on Excellence in Education.[34] The commission decried the poor performance of American students in mathematics and science, the increase in functional illiteracy, and declining American economic productivity. Reminiscent of the Sputnik era of the late 1950s, the national mood was for the urgent reform of American public education. Reform initiatives, especially at the state level, increased the number of academic credits needed for high school graduation, increased the required courses in mathematics and science, developed student and teacher competency testing, and recommended merit pay and career ladders for teachers. The general thrust of the school reform climate of the 1980s is very likely to extend into the 1990s.

Conclusion

Chapter 4 has presented a general historical overview of major educational developments in the United States. More detailed and specific background will be presented in relation to the topics treated in subsequent chapters. From the era of the common school movement to the present, the general trend in American education has been to shape conditions that increased the educational opportunities of larger numbers of persons. This trend to provide greater educational opportunities was marked particularly by the emergence of the tax-supported public elementary and secondary school.

DISCUSSION QUESTIONS

1. Trace the major institutional developments in colonial education.
2. Examine the Puritan impact on schooling.
3. Examine the concept of civic education as exemplified in the theories of education of the early national era.
4. Define the common school and trace the common school movement.
5. Examine the impact of William T. Harris on educational administration in an urban era.
6. Examine the major trends in twentieth-century education.

33. National Center for Education Statistics, *Digest of Education Statistics 1989* (Washington, D.C.: U.S. Government Printing Office, 1989), p. 1.
34. National Commission on Excellence in Education, *A Nation at Risk: The Imperative for Educational Reform* (Washington, D.C.: U.S. Department of Education, 1983.)

7. Examine the impact of the country school in shaping the American historical view of public schooling.

8. How did the Gary Plan of William Wirt embody progressive educational ideology?

FIELD EXERCISES

1. Write a short biographical sketch of your own education.

2. Interview several experienced teachers and ask them to identify the major changes that have occurred in the public schools.

3. Set up a roundtable discussion in which members of the class act out the roles of Franklin, Jefferson, Rush, and Webster and carry on a dialogue on educational theory.

4. Invite an historian of education to visit your class to present his or her interpretation of American educational history.

5. Examine several textbooks from different periods of history.

6. Visit a local library or your college library and identify the primary sources that could be used in writing a history of a local elementary or secondary school.

7. Using oral history, interview several senior citizens for their recollections of their elementary or secondary schooling.

SUGGESTED READINGS

BAILYN, BERNARD. *Education in the Forming of American Society: Needs and Opportunities for Study*. New York: W. W. Norton, 1972.

BLINDERMAN, ABRAHAM. *Three Early Champions of Education: Benjamin Franklin, Benjamin Rush, and Noah Webster*. Bloomington, Ind.: Phi Delta Kappa Educational Foundation, 1976.

BROWN, RICHARD D. *Knowledge Is Power: The Diffusion of Information in Early America, 1700–1865*. New York: Oxford University Press, 1989.

COHEN, RONALD D. *Children of the Mill: Schooling and Society in Gary, Indiana, 1906–1960*. Bloomington: Indiana University Press, 1990.

COOPER, ARNOLD. *Between Struggle and Hope: Four Black Educators in the South, 1894–1915*. Ames: Iowa State University Press, 1989.

CREMIN, LAWRENCE A. *American Education: The Colonial Experience, 1607–1783*. New York: Harper & Row, 1970.

———. *American Education: The National Experience 1783–1876*. New York: Harper & Row, 1980.

———. *American Education: The Metropolitan Experience, 1876–1980*. New York: Harper & Row, 1988.

CUBAN, LARRY. *How Teachers Taught: Constancy and Change in American Classrooms, 1890–1980*. New York: Longman, 1984.

FULLER, WAYNE, E. *The Old Country School: The Story of Rural Education in the Middle West*. Chicago: University of Chicago Press, 1982.

GULLIFORD, ANDREW. *America's Country Schools*. Washington, D.C.: Preservation Press, 1984.

GUTEK, GERALD L. *Education in the United States: An Historical Perspective*. Englewood Cliffs, N.J.: Prentice-Hall, 1986.

———. *Cultural Foundations of Education: A Biographical Introduction*. New York: Macmillan, 1991.

HESLEP, ROBERT D. *Thomas Jefferson and Education*. New York: Random House, 1969.

LAGEMANN, ELLEN CONDLIFFE. *A Generation of Women: Education in the Lives of Progressive Reformers*. Cambridge, Mass.: Harvard University Press, 1979.

RAVITCH, DIANE. *The Troubled Crusade: American Education, 1945–1980.* New York: Basic Books, 1983.

SPRING, JOEL. *The American School, 1642–1990: Varieties of Historical Interpretation of the Foundations and Development of American Education.* New York: Longman, 1990.

STABLER, ERNEST. *Founders: Innovators in Education, 1830–1980.* Edmonton: University of Alberta Press, 1986.

TYACK, DAVID, AND HANSOT, ELISABETH. *Managers of Virtue: Public School Leadership in America, 1820–1980.* New York: Basic Books, 1982.

WAGONER, JENNINGS L., JR. *Thomas Jefferson and the Education of a New Nation.* Bloomington, Ind.: Phi Delta Kappa Educational Foundation, 1976.

WARREN, DONALD, ed. *American Teachers: Histories of a Profession at Work.* New York: Macmillan, 1989.

_5_

Philosophy
and Education

Chapter 5 explores the relationships between philosophy and education. To aid in analyzing this chapter, you might focus your attention on the following questions:

1. Why should teachers be aware of issues in philosophy of education?
2. What are the major divisions in philosophy, and how do they relate to educational issues and problems?
3. What are the major educational philosophies?
4. What general guidelines to educational policy can be derived from the various systematic philosophies of education?
5. How can prospective teachers formulate their own educational philosophies?

Education and Philosophy

Philosophy of education is one of the most important subjects that prospective teachers study. At times, teachers become immersed so immediately in the urgent tasks of teaching that they do not consciously examine the philosophical consequences of their activities. Preparing lessons and attendance reports, leading field trips, or participating in parent conferences are only a few of the many immediate activities that occupy a teacher's day. However, when teachers look beyond the daily demands on their time, they often find themselves reflecting on the general and long-term issues of significance for themselves, their students, and the society in which they live.

Perhaps the most direct but also the most significant question that arises upon reflection is, What difference does it make? Another way of stating this question is to ask, What is true? What is good? What is beautiful? What does it mean to lead a life that is true, good, and beautiful? Certainly, a genuine education should focus on these questions.

Philosophy as Speculation

Since the earliest recorded history, individuals have speculated about the nature of reality and of the meaning of life itself. In doing so, these persons have dealt with one of the most basic but also most pervasive concerns of human existence. The history of philosophy records the efforts of Plato, Aristotle, Plotinus, Zeno, Epicurus, Augustine, Aquinas, Locke, Rousseau, Kant, Hegel, Marx, Bertrand Russell, William James, John Dewey, and others to answer these basic questions.[1] These philosophers and many others have speculated about the nature of reality. When they recounted or recorded their speculations, they attempted to describe the nature of reality. Based upon their insights into reality, philosophers also have sought to prescribe values and ideals.

If you reflect on education—either as enculturation in the informal sense or as formal schooling—it becomes clear that the educative process involves both descriptive and prescriptive components. Much of what goes on in school involves descriptions that identify and explain certain features of reality. The kindergarten child who has brought a favorite toy to school for "show and tell" is describing an aspect of his or her reality to the other children. The books that students read and discuss in history, chemistry, and other subjects account for or describe specific dimensions of reality. The statement "John Kennedy was elected president of the United States in 1960" describes an historical event. The statement "The chemical formula for water is H_2O" describes a different sort of reality.

While schooling is descriptive, much of it is also *prescriptive* in that it seeks to inculcate desired or approved ethical and aesthetic behavioral standards. Whenever our language is conveyed with the words *ought* or *should* or *ought not* or *should not*, we are prescribing behavior. When we say, "You should wash your hands before eating," "You should not cheat on examinations," "You should be a good citizen," or "You should not litter parks and playgrounds," we are prescribing or recommending behavior.

The descriptive and the prescriptive phases of education are ultimately philosophical. While the descriptive phase seeks to describe reality, the prescriptive seeks to guide behavior by recommending some actions over other actions.

Relationships of Philosophy and Education

As is true for other bodies of knowledge, philosophy is subdivided into areas of specialization. In this section, we define and describe metaphysics, epistemology, axiology, and logic and relate them to education.[2]

Metaphysics

Metaphysics, the most abstract and speculative subdivision of philosophy, seeks to answer questions about the nature of ultimate reality. What is it about life and the universe that is really real? The branch of metaphysics that examines the nature of reality is known as *ontology*, and that which seeks to explain the origin and structure of the universe is known as *cosmology*.

1. For biographical commentaries on leading thinkers on education, see Gerald L. Gutek, *Cultural Foundations of Education: A Biographical Introduction* (New York: Macmillan, 1991).
2. Gerald L. Gutek, *Philosophical and Ideological Perspectives on Education* (Englewood Cliffs, N.J.: Prentice Hall, 1988), pp. 1–12.

Based upon their speculations about the nature of reality, philosophers have constructed metaphysical descriptions about the nature of the universe and the life and place of human beings in that universe. In the most general sense, much of the school's curriculum also describes various aspects of reality. For example, history and the social sciences describe social life on this planet. The natural and physical sciences are descriptive of the structures, patterns, and relationships of physical and natural phenomena. Each area of knowledge or science describes in a detailed way one phase of reality. Metaphysics, in contrast, seeks to describe all of reality in general rather than in specific terms.

The curriculum is comprised, in part, of knowledge derived from the various social, natural, and physical sciences. Regardless of the particular pattern of curricular organization, the total curriculum provides the learner with a sense of reality. It represents a particular society's conception of reality. Although educators may not carry their curricular conceptions to the most general level of discussion, metaphysical concerns are always present — either consciously or unconsciously — in the curriculum. As students learn what "was" or "is," they gain a world view.

Epistemology

While metaphysics examines reality, *epistemology* probes questions such as "What is knowledge?" and "How do we know?" Metaphysics is concerned with the content of our knowledge; epistemology deals with the process of knowing. In terms of education, epistemology relates closely to how we think, know, and learn. The use of various instructional methods, such as the lecture, the experiment, and the project, rests on the assumption that there is an effective and efficient method of teaching and learning. The various philosophies of education examined in this chapter argue that a particular epistemological strategy is to be preferred over other strategies. To develop this theme further, we look at several of these strategies.

One of the oldest and most widely accepted theories of knowing is that of *revelation*, which means that God has revealed Himself or has disclosed truth to certain specially inspired men and women. God has given a message to these persons, who have recorded it in a sacred or holy book or document. For the Christian and the Jew, the sacred book is the Bible; for the Muslim, the Koran; and for the Hindu, the Bhagavad-Gita. A basic requirement in revelation is that the knowledge seeker must believe on faith that the truths of the sacred book are divinely inspired. When this condition is met, the sacred book becomes the authoritative source for knowing. Educationally, students study the sacred book by reading and often memorizing its passages. Learned people, often priests, seek to explain and to apply the unchanging message to the present. Religious schools place great emphasis on studying and interpreting the sacred literature.

Another approach to truth is *rationalism*. The Western intellectual tradition, from the Greek classical period through the eighteenth-century Enlightenment to the present, has emphasized human reason as the most valid authority for recognizing and establishing knowledge. As an epistemological doctrine, rationalism asserts that reason is the source from which we derive universally valid judgments. The rationalist strategy of knowing propounds first principles as *a priori* statements that are universally true and then derives subsidiary principles from them. For example, if we accept as universally true the general statement that human beings are mortal, we can then reason that all men and women will die. Or if we accept as true that everyone is "endowed with inalienable rights of life, liberty, and property," it is possible to establish governmental systems to protect these rights. The rationalist tradition, which is pervasive in Western thought, has influenced our ideas of government, law, and society.

Empiricism, still another epistemological theory, stresses observation and experience. Empiricists hold that knowledge originates in sensory experience of the environment and that ideas are products of observed phenomena. Modern science is empirically based, and Pragmatist philosophers, such as John Dewey, have constructed a theory of knowledge based on the scientific method. Educational methods like the scientific, project, and activity methods assume that human experience is the best guide to truth. For Pragmatists, truth is neither eternal, as it is for those who hold to revelation, nor universal, as it is for Rationalists; rather, it is tentative and subject to further research and investigation.

Axiology

As philosophy is a quest for truth, so is it also a search for the good and the beautiful. This search for goodness and beauty leads both philosophers and educators in the axiological dimension of education. *Axiology*, the study of values, is subdivided into ethics, which examines morality and conduct, and aesthetics, which is concerned with beauty. In education, axiology leads to a consideration of many value-laden questions, such as:

> What is the good and beautiful life?
> What does it mean to be a good human being or a good citizen?
> What are appropriate standards of behavior?
> What is right and wrong?
> Are values permanent or changing?
> Are values universal or particular to a given time, place, and culture?
> What standards should a person use to judge a book, a musical composition, a play, or other works of art?
> Should schools reflect prevailing cultural values, or should they seek to change them?

All education and all forms of schooling are immersed in the value dimension of life. There is no education that is value-free. Either consciously or unconsciously, teachers are value agents. They, themselves, represents models of value; they either reinforce or challenge the values of students.

The school is an agency that is prescriptive as well as descriptive. It prescribes certain approved ways of behaving for students. Prescriptive language is conveyed by the words *should* or *shouldn't*, *ought* or *ought not*. In performing its prescriptive function, the school is a corrective agency. In a very obvious way, teachers correct spelling, addition, subtraction, and many other behaviors on the basis that they are either right or wrong. In a less obvious way, teachers also prescribe more complex and subtle forms of personal, social, political, aesthetic, and intellectual behavior.

In these more complex areas of life, the answers are not those of simple spelling or addition; often they are not clearly defined or commonly accepted. In a racially, ethnically, religiously, economically, and socially pluralistic society like the United States, competing and often conflicting standards of behavior make it difficult to arrive at a generally acceptable common core of values.

Logic

Logic, the study of correct reasoning, examines the rules of valid inference, which enables us to move correctly from one argument to another. As there is a logical way of thinking, there is also a logic that can be used to order instruction. Logical patterns are either *deductive* or *inductive*. Deduction, as a form of reasoning, moves from a known principle to an unknown, from the general to the specific, or from a premise to a logical conclusion. Deductive reasoning is particularly appropriate to a rationalist position. In contrast, induction is the process of developing generalized explanations, hypotheses, or laws from collections of facts. It is the kind of reasoning that moves from a particular instance to a general conclusion.

Philosophies of Education

Now that we have identified the subdivisions in philosophy, we can explore the major educational philosophies. In this chapter, we examine traditional philosophical positions—Idealism, Realism, Thomism, Perennialism, and Essentialism. In the following chapter, we examine the more recently developed philosophies of Experimentalism, Progressivism, Reconstructionism, Existentialism, and Philosophical Analysis. In our investigation of philosophies of education, we use a "systems approach" that looks at the particular philosophic position as a complete system of thought. That is, each philosophy presents a developed perspective on metaphysics, epistemology, axiology, and logic. From this perspective, implications can be drawn for educational areas such as the aims of education, the nature of the school, the organization of the curriculum, the appropriate methodology to be used in instruction, and the nature of the teaching–learning relationship.

Idealism, Realism, Thomism, and Experimentalism represent complete philosophical systems that can be applied to educational issues. Education is only one of many dimensions to which the philosophy applies. In the case of Perennialism, Essentialism, Progressivism, and Reconstructionism, these educational theories do not present fully developed metaphysical, epistemological, and axiological perspectives.

In this chapter, we begin with a discussion of a particular philosophical and theoretical position and then apply that position to specific educational issues. We examine each philosophical position and then state its meaning for education.

Idealism

Idealist metaphysics asserts that ultimate reality is spiritual or mental. The existence of matter and of the body depends upon the spiritual force that gives its energy and life. Reality can be understood to be ideas in relationship to each other. Although the Idealist metaphysical orientation is difficult to understand, it might be perceived as a relationship between the mind of God or the Absolute and the minds of humans.[3]

For Idealists, there is one source, a single point of origin, from which all reality flows. This supreme and all-encompassing source is given various names, but they all refer to the same World Mind or originator. For Jews and Christians, God is a spiritual and a personal Creator. For Hindus, Brahma is the all-encompassing World Being. While the religious conception of God may be compatible with Idealism, not all Idealists perceive of the World Mind in religious terms. Nor, for that matter, are all religious people Idealists.

The all-pervasive World Mind is also referred to as the Absolute, the Over Soul, and the Macrocosm. Whether defined in the theological sense or in a strictly philosophical sense, the World Mind is the source of all ideas and is the force that keeps these ideas in existence. Everything that exists, including human beings, originates as a concept or an idea in the World Mind, which is eternal, perfect, unchanging, and orderly. The ideas of the World Mind are in a perfect time and space relationship.

Human reality is also spiritual, mental, and intellectual. What is most real about a human being is his or her mind or intelligence. The human mind contains concepts or ideas, as does the World Mind. Whereas the ideas in the World Mind are complete, the ideas in the human mind are limited. What is important is that the reality in the World Mind and the human mind is of the same substance—ideas.

Idealist epistemology, or theory of knowledge, is closely related to the philosophy's metaphysical position. While the Mind of the Absolute, or God, or the World Mind is perfect, the human being's mind is imperfect and limited. Human beings are prisoners of their bodies. At birth, the human mind is encased in a body and is subject to the world of appearance, to hunger, cold, noise, to the senses and the appetites. The shock of birth itself pushes the ideas of the mind far back into the recesses of the unconscious. All that is to be known is latently present in the mind but it is repressed. The process of knowing, for Idealists, involves bringing these ideas forward into consciousness.

If knowing means bringing latent ideas to consciousness, then instruction, or teaching and learning, is designed to facilitate this process. The process of instruction can be illustrated by the Socratic dialogues, written by Plato.[4] In these dialogues, Socrates typically questions students about the meaning of life, truth, beauty, virtue, or courage. At first, the students reply by stating opinions that refer to particular instances of truth or beauty. However, Socrates's skillful and unrelenting questioning forces the students to recognize their ignorance and abandon their diverse and often erroneous opinions. Eventually, they are led by Socrates to conclude that particular instances of courage, beauty, or truth are based on a general and more abstract concept of these virtues.

3. Idealism as an educational philosophy is treated in J. Donald Butler, *Idealism in Education* (New York: Harper & Row, 1966).
4. For a discussion of the Socratic-Platonic method, see Jerome Eckstein, *The Platonic Method: An Interpretation of the Dramatic-Philosophical Aspects of the Meno* (New York: Greenwood, 1968).

The teacher who follows the Idealist strategy of instruction is, like Socrates, a midwife of ideas. The instructional task is twofold: First, the learner must realize that the senses can deceive and that opinions can be erroneous; then, once the learner is ready to abandon the world of appearances, he or she can turn within and find the truth that is present in the mind. Although the teacher can stimulate learning, only the learner can bring to consciousness and illuminate the ideas in the mind. Because learning is a recalling or remembering of ideas already present, the process is referred to as "re-cognition" or rethinking.

Since each particular idea leads back to one great idea that encompasses all existence, Idealists emphasize the interrelatedness of ideas. The metaphysics, epistemology, axiology, and logic of Idealism are all interrelated. This connectedness or interrelatedness can be illustrated by considering the relationship of the school to civilization. Idealists argue that the school, as an institution, is a civilizing agency. Its primary function is to civilize the young by imposing and transmitting the cultural heritage upon them.

Idealists regard civilization as the slow process of accumulating knowledge and of developing values over the centuries of human life on this planet. Each generation of human beings has inherited knowledge from its predecessors and has added to that cultural legacy. Each generation has likewise inherited and has further refined the values to be transmitted to the young.

Civilization, then, is the continually accumulating growth of knowledge and the advancement of morality to higher stages of development. In the continuing evolution of civilization, certain enduring trends have persisted into the present while others enjoyed but a fleeting existence. To preserve its intellectual and moral legacy, humankind has created social, religious, political, and educational institutions. Each of these institutions has a particular role to perform in protecting and preserving civilization. For example, the family is designed to rear children, the government to maintain law and order, the church to provide a comprehensive view of truth and morality in a religious context, and the school to transmit the intellectual, cultural, and moral heritage to the young so that they can share in and add to it.[5]

The Idealist's conception of the school as a civilizing institution can be seen by examining their views of curriculum and behavior. Seen as the repository of the cultural inheritance, the curriculum is a carefully organized, sequential, subject matter arrangement. Those subjects that contain the greatest intellectual and value possibilities are given priority over those that are more technical and vocational. In deciding what should be included and what should be excluded from the curriculum, Idealists have been guided by the wisdom of the past. Those books and works of art that are classics are given priority, for they embody a universal meaning that transcends the special interests of a particular generation. Children are prepared for the future by learning about the cultural accomplishments of the past.

In terms of subject matter, Idealists emphasize reading and writing as necessary tools in comprehending the cultural legacy. Arithmetic is a tool for sharpening

---

5. John Paul Strain, "Idealism: A Clarification of an Educational Philosophy," *Educational Theory*, 25 (Summer 1975), pp. 263–271.

reasoning. History and geography provide a perspective into temporal and spatial relationships. History also portrays the record of past accomplishments. The biographies of great men and women can be used as models for imitation by the young. Language and literature, both one's own vernacular and that of foreign origins as well, are useful in understanding and expressing the cultural inheritance. The preferred works of literature are selected carefully as both literary and moral exemplars that can be imitated by students. While science has a place in the Idealist curriculum, it should be treated conceptually and related deliberately to the humanistic dimension of education. For the Idealist, the subjects of the curriculum should be organized separately and carefully and presented through systematically written books that stand as compendiums of recorded knowledge.

In Idealism, the axiological or value dimension of education is closely related to the cognitive or knowledge domain. In fact, the books selected for instructional purposes should convey ethical and aesthetic as well as intellectual models. Certain values, such as discipline, order, and self-control, stand out as important for both life and school success.

For the Idealists, children possess immense spiritual and intellectual potential. It is the responsibility of the school and the teacher to help children realize their potential. The primary habit to be stressed is self-control. As they acquire self-control, they learn to use their minds to repress immediate impulses and instincts. By moving beyond immediate satisfaction and gratification, they learn to defer action and to place decision making in a temporal perspective. Through schooling, children are introduced to the routines and standards of civilization.

Idealists also assert that truly disciplined persons have a sense of order. In a child's education, discipline is a mutual responsibility of the home and the school. Together, parents and teachers are to cultivate habits of cleanliness, neatness, orderliness, punctuality, courtesy, obedience, and accuracy. The educated person, according to the Idealist value criterion, would (1) be polite and courteous in social behavior, (2) respect society's moral codes, and (3) realize that civilized progress requires discipline and perseverance.

In aesthetics, Idealists use models that portray the persistent ideals of civilization. They encourage students to know and to read the great literary classics, to attend and to reenact the great dramas, to view and to appreciate the great paintings, and to hear and to perform the great musical compositions. The crucial standard in measuring a classic is conveyed by the word *great*, which means that a given work of art or a book possesses qualities that enable it to endure and to appeal to people across the span of time.

Idealist teachers are to be models of knowledge and values that students can imitate. They should be able to integrate their lives harmoniously. As students imitate their teachers, they, too, are expected to develop a sense of order and perspective.

The Idealist conception of education and of schooling is conservative and traditional. It seeks to preserve the cultural heritage of the past by transmitting it to children, the immature members of society, so that they continue and extend human civilization into the future. A great priority is placed on studying and learning systematically organized bodies of knowledge and on cultivating socially acceptable standards of behavior.

The critics of Idealism contend that it is too abstract and vague to be of real use in schools. They argue that its objectives can be neither specified nor verified empirically. Many of its claims, while inspirational, cannot be used to guide practice. Further, the critics allege that Idealism is too oriented to the past and does not relate effectively to contemporary problems or to future directions in education.

Realism

As with Idealism, Realism is a traditional educational philosophy that is oriented to a subject matter curriculum and to teacher-centered instruction. The metaphysical and epistemological bases of Realism, however, are quite different from those of Idealism. Metaphysically, Realist philosophers assert that (1) an objective order of reality exists that is independent of human knowing or willing, (2) patterns and relationships exist between the objects found in reality, (3) human beings are capable of knowing about these objects and their relationships, and (4) human action and behavior are most intelligent when based on knowledge of the objective order of reality.[6]

Stated most directly, the Realist metaphysical position means that you and I certainly exist, and we live in a world of objects—other people, the planets, animals,

ΑΡΙΣΤΟΤΕΛΗΣ.

The ancient Greek philosopher, Aristotle, was the father of Realism.

---

6. An excellent statement of Realist philosophy is provided by John Wild, *Introduction to Realist Philosophy* (New York: Harper and Brothers, 1948), p. 6.

plants, trees, houses, schools, rocks, oceans, and so on. Everything that exists is related to other objects but is also independent of them. These objects possess two essential characteristics: matter and form. They are made of something; they are material. This matter has a structure that gives it a shape, form, or design.

Epistemologically, Realists assert that human beings can know the objects that they encounter. We can know about objects because we possess sensory powers — sight, hearing, touch, taste, feeling, and smelling — that enable us to acquire information — sensory data — about objects. This information is then conveyed to our minds, where we sort it out in a manner that is similar to the operation of a computer. Our mind determines what there is about an object that is always found in that class of objects (that is, essential to that object) or that is sometimes found in the object. We abstract "necessary," or essential, qualities of the object into a concept that signifies the general class or category of objects. For example, we see many kinds or types of dogs. There are large dogs, small dogs, pedigreeds, and mixed breeds. There are poodles, pomeranians, pekinese, and pugs. From this varied experience with different types of dogs, we can arrive at a general concept of "dog," that which is necessary for a particular object to be in one category and not in another. Our ability to conceptualize rests on our twofold and related powers of sensation and abstraction.

Realist metaphysics and epistemology have direct implications for the purposes of the school and for curriculum organization. As with Idealism, Realism asserts that each social institution has a primary or specialized function to perform. In a rationally organized society, each institution — such as the family, government, church, or school — performs its function and does not encroach on the domain of other institutions. The school's primary function, in Realist terms, is to educate students about the world, the reality in which they live. The school's task, then, is to transmit knowledge, or information, to students so that they can act rationally.

The Realist curricular pattern is a subject matter organization. If we return to the Realist conception of reality, we can see that objects are either like or unlike each other. The simple game of animal, vegetable, or mineral indicates how we classify objects according to similarities or differences. We can extend these three broad classifications to all the objects that we encounter and can derive more complicated and sophisticated kinds of classifications. For example, concepts that deal with the composition and properties of substances can be classified under the discipline, or subject matter, of chemistry. Concepts dealing with plants and their life, structure, and growth can be classified with botany. Concepts that relate to government, diplomacy, political organization, and management can be classified as political science. A visit to the card catalogue of a library illustrates the divisions of knowledge and the subdivisions that exist within these areas. Based on these divisions of knowledge, the curriculum at each level of schooling represents a more complex arrangement of these categories of knowledge or subjects.

Realist epistemology suggests how our concepts about reality should be organized, taught, and studied. Essentially, research is designed to tell us about the objects we encounter so that we can know, appreciate, and use them. In their research, scientists and scholars seek to know objects more precisely. The more accurate our knowledge of objects, the more accurately do our concepts conform to the object in reality. Scientists and scholars in the various disciplines, often university professors, publish their research in books and articles and disseminate their findings and interpretations in lectures. College students, including prospective elementary and secondary school students, attend courses taught by these scholars or read books and articles written by them. Knowledge acquired is then reorganized into the elementary and secondary school curriculum. Within the subjects of the curriculum, teachers organize instructional units and lessons that adapt the subject matter to the learners' readiness, ability, and needs.

The actual Realist curriculum resembles that of the Idealists in that it follows a subject matter mode of organization. The elementary school curriculum emphasizes reading, writing, arithmetic, and research as necessary skills and language arts, science, mathematics, history, and social science as significant content areas. The secondary school curriculum refines these subjects further into more complex and substantial bodies of knowledge, such as English and foreign languages, literature, natural and physical sciences, history, and social sciences. The college curriculum is still more refined, subdivided, and sophisticated.

Realist instructional methodology involves three necessary elements: (1) a teacher who possesses and knows how to teach some skill or knowledge, (2) the actual skill or body of knowledge, and (3) a student who lacks that skill or knowledge and who wants to learn it. This methodological strategy implies that a skill or body of knowledge must always be present in the teaching–learning relationship. In its absence, teaching degenerates into indoctrination or becomes an interpersonal relationship that lacks conscious instruction. Essentially, the teacher must know both the subject matter and how to teach it effectively.[7]

In terms of axiology, or ethical and aesthetic values, Realists tend to follow the ancient dictum of Aristotle, "Man is a rational being." This means that human beings have the power to think, to frame alternatives, and to choose from among them. It is this power of choice that liberates human beings and gives them the possibility of being free men and women. When we make our choices, we should be guided by knowledge rather than by our appetites, emotions, or unfounded opinions. As choice makers, our best guide is knowledge, such as that contained in the liberal arts and sciences. The word *liberal* here means that which liberates, or frees.

Thomism

As a philosophy, Thomism closely resembles Realism. Indeed, it is a form of religious or theistic Realism that is associated with Roman Catholic theology and education. Its name is derived from that of Thomas Aquinas (1225–1274), a Dominican expert on theology and philosophy who taught at the University of Paris in the thirteenth century. Aquinas effected a synthesis of Christian theology and Aristotelian philosophy.[8]

7. William O. Martin, *Realism in Education* (New York: Harper & Row, 1969), pp. 3–18.
8. John W. Donohue, *St. Thomas Aquinas and Education* (New York: Random House, 1968), pp. 23–57.

Thomism was a philosophy developed by Thomas Aquinas (1225–1274), a theologian at the medieval University of Paris.

Like Realists, Thomists assert the existence of an objective order of reality that we can come to know. For them, this reality has been created by God, a perfect spiritual being who is the cause and source of all existence. Human beings are endowed with a soul, a spirit that gives them the power of reason and free will. The soul is immortal and has the possibility of the direct vision of God after the death of the body.

Epistemologically, the Thomist, like other Realists, asserts that we come to know the physical world through a twofold process of sensation and abstraction. Our knowledge of reality moves to a greater completion by revelation of God's word in the Scriptures, traditions, and teaching authority of the Church. Thomists contend that there is no conflict between faith and reason or between theology and science. Faith and reason are held to be complementary to each other and contribute to a more complete knowledge of reality.

The axiology of Thomism incorporates the values of Christianity and of reason. Since God is a Universal Creator, truth, goodness, and beauty are also universal, eternal, and unchanging. Although the circumstances of modern life may change, the principles that should guide action are found in the truths of faith and reason.

The aims of education, the function of the school, the curriculum, and the teacher–learner relationship are best viewed in Thomism by examining human nature. Human beings have twofold but complementary aspects to their nature. We have, they assert, a spiritual soul and a physical body. It is the soul that relates us most closely to God and that gives us the power of intellect. The body, living at a given time and place, has physical, economic, social, and political needs. The basic aim of education is to help men and women to experience divine truth and love so that they will live the kind of earthly life that will lead them to eternal life. Subsidiary educational aims are directed to meeting economic, social, political, intellectual, and aesthetic needs. While the school provides for its students' physical, social, and religious development, its essential function is intellectual.

The Thomistic curriculum reflects the dualistic character of human nature in that certain subjects are religious, based on or derived from theology, and others are social, political, cultural, and economic. The elementary school curriculum would include reading and language arts, arithmetic, history and geography, and religion. The secondary curriculum would include theology and religious education, language and literature, art and music, physical and natural sciences, history and social sciences, and in some cases logic. The milieu of the school is also very important in the students' education in that it should provide opportunities for religious liturgies, ceremonies, and observances that reinforce and exemplify the formal curriculum. In higher education, the Thomists prefer a traditional liberal arts and science curriculum that is arranged hierarchically. Theology and philosophy are given priority in the curriculum and are regarded as the disciplines that integrate the total educational experience.

As is true of Idealism and Realism, the Thomist curriculum follows a subject matter arrangement. Thomists define a subject as *scientia*, a body of knowledge consisting of established principles and interpretations and conclusions based on these principles. The teacher is a mature person who possesses knowledge of these principles, their derivations, and applications and can transmit them to the student. The learner is regarded as possessing a capacity for actively acquiring and using these bodies of knowledge. Further, Thomists hold that teaching is highly integrative in that it incorporates both the contemplative and active modes of life. It is contemplative in that the teacher must be a researcher who quietly plans for instruction. Teaching, itself, is an activity by which the teacher motivates students and presents carefully organized bodies of knowledge to them.

The Second Vatican Council   Thomism as an educational philosophy continues to influence Catholic education; however, several developments of a theoretical nature have occurred in Catholic schools as a result of the Second Vatican Council that met from 1962 to 1965.[9] Two principal council themes were liturgical changes in which the vernacular language would be used rather than the traditional Latin and an emphasis on the world community that stressed ecumenism, social justice, and the common human welfare.

The liturgical changes of Vatican II did not alter essentials of Catholic worship but rather sought to engage the congregation in more active participation as a community of believers. For children, induction into religious ritual became more active and participatory than in the traditional Latin service.

For educational theory, Vatican II encouraged changes in attitude. In particular, it ended the "seige mentality" in which Catholic schools were seen as citadels preparing young defenders of the faith against theological adversaries. An educational consequence of the Second Vatican Council was an ecumenical opening to the world that, while retaining essential doctrines, encouraged Catholic teachers to develop an understanding of other religious cultures.

The values to be exemplified by Catholic school teachers were identified as faith qualities, Gospel values, and the Christian tradition. Such teachers were to share the "responsibility for establishing a community of faith within the context of the local Church and the universal Church." It was further recommended that Catholic school teachers "consciously and actively" integrate Christian faith with human experience.[10]

Perennialism

Perennialism is an educational theory that is derived from the general philosophical orientation provided by Realism and Thomism. The word *perennial* means that true educational principles are lasting, continuing, and recurring. Perennialist educators claim that truth, goodness, and beauty are eternal and unchanging. Although human beings have adapted themselves to varying geographical, historical, social, political, and economic circumstances, Perennialists claim that human nature has remained the same throughout the ages. The enduring quality and defining charac-

9. The impact of the Second Vatican Council on Catholic educational theory is examined in John W. Donohue, *Catholicism and Education* (New York: Harper & Row, 1973).
10. Russell M. Bleich et al., *The Pre-Service Formation of Teachers for Catholic Schools* (Washington, D.C.: National Catholic Educational Association, 1982), p. 5.

teristic of human beings have been their rationality and their quest for truth. Education is designed to prepare human beings to use their rationality and to seek, find, and use the truth.

One of America's leading Perennialist advocates was Robert Maynard Hutchins (1899–1977), who argued that the real purpose of education was to draw out the elements of our common human nature, which were the same in any time or place. He argued further that (1) education implies teaching, (2) teaching implies knowledge, (3) knowledge is truth, and (4) since the truth is everywhere the same, education should also be everywhere the same.[11] Hutchins advocated an intellectual education based upon the arts and sciences and the enduring classics of Western civilization.

The Paideia Proposal   There has been a resurgence of Perennialism with the launching of the Paideia proposal and program by Mortimer J. Adler (born 1902), a long-standing associate of Robert Hutchins. Based on a Greek word referring to the total upbringing of a child, the Paideia proposal calls for the same general education, based on the same objectives, and developing the same skills, for all students. Such common learning must be general or nonspecialized and liberal or nonvocational.[12]

The Paideia curriculum is organized into three modes of teaching and learning: (1) acquiring organized knowledge, (2) developing intellectual and learning skills, and (3) enlarging the understanding of ideas and values. The first curricular mode, knowledge acquisition, identifies the following subjects as the necessary fundamental elements of education: language, literature, and fine arts; mathematics and natural sciences; geography, history, and social studies.[13] Skill development, the second curricular mode, is designed to cultivate such basic language skills as reading, writing, speaking, and listening and such basic mathematical and scientific skills as observing, measuring, calculating, and estimating. The third curricular mode, enlarging one's understanding, relies on "maieutic" teaching, which uses the Socratic mode to bring forth ideas. It seeks to stimulate students' understanding, appreciation, and creativity by exposure to original books and works of art.[14]

Essentialism and Basic Education

With persistent regularity, various movements in American education have urged a return to the teaching of the essential or basic skills or subjects in the schools. Although there have been advocates of fundamental learning throughout the history of education, contemporary American education has witnessed four important movements: (1) the Essentialism of the 1930s, (2) the academic critics of the 1950s, (3) the "Back to Basics" of the 1970s, and (4) the neoconservatism of the 1980s.

---

11. Robert M. Hutchins, *The Higher Learning in America* (New Haven, Conn.: Yale University Press, 1936), pp. 65–68.
12. Mortimer J. Adler, *The Paideia Proposal: An Educational Manifesto* (New York: Macmillan, 1982), p. 18. See also, Mortimer J. Adler, *Paideia Problems and Possibilities: A Consideration of Questions Raised by the Paideia Proposal* (New York: Macmillan, 1983) and Mortimer J. Adler, *The Paideia Program: An Educational Syllabus* (New York: Macmillan, 1984).
13. Adler, *Paideia Proposal*, pp. 23–24.
14. Ibid., pp. 25–29.

Because these movements have many similar elements, we will treat them from the common theoretical perspective of Essentialism, or basic education, and will use the terms interchangeably.

In terms of philosophical orientation, Essentialism bears a strong resemblance to the traditional philosophies of Idealism, Realism, Thomism, and Perennialism. Essentialists argue that (1) schools should be academic rather than social agencies, (2) curricular organization should be based on carefully selected and well-defined skills and subjects, (3) the teacher should be an authority figure, and (4) learning should be teacher directed.

The term *Essentialist* was used to identify a group of educators who organized the Essentialist Committee for the Advancement of American Education in 1938. The leading spokesperson for the committee was William C. Bagley, who wrote the "Essentialist Platform."[15] The Essentialists developed both a critique and a program for American education. The Essentialist critique attacked tendencies in American education that were regarded as weakening the academic standards of the schools. Among the Essentialist criticisms were the following: (1) The standards of achievement of American students in fundamental skills and subjects were deficient in comparison to other countries, (2) increasing numbers of students in junior and senior high schools were functionally illiterate because of reading deficiencies, (3) many school systems had abandoned rigorous standards of scholastic achievement for promotion and merely passed students on schedule to higher grades, (4) progressive educators had weakened instruction by replacing exacting subjects with ill-defined projects and activities, and (5) an erroneous theory of child freedom had been used to eliminate discipline, order, and sequence from American schools.

To remedy the weaknesses that they perceived in American education, the Essentialists developed an educational theory that defined the role of the school, the nature of the curriculum, and the function of the teacher in terms of the learning of basic skills and subjects.

The school, according to the Essentialists, had the special function of transmitting the intellectual and social skills and knowledge that were a product of the long course of human civilization. This body of social and intellectual skills and knowledge constituted the "essentials" that were indispensable to the maintenance of a civilized society. Bagley's "Essentialist Platform" defined the essentials as (1) the basic civilized skills of reading, recording, computing, and measuring, (2) a perspective in time that acquainted the student with the past, (3) a widening of the space horizon through the study of geography, (4) health instruction and the inculcating of health practices, (5) the elements of natural science, (6) the fine arts, and (7) the industrial arts.[16]

In addition to a curriculum based on fundamental skills and subjects, the Essentialists argued that it was the responsibility of the teacher to organize and direct the school's instructional program. As a mature adult, the teacher was to guide, control, and direct the instruction of the immature. Instruction should be

---

15. William C. Bagley, "An Essentialist Platform for the Advancement of American Education," *Educational Administration and Supervision*, 24 (April 1938), pp. 241–256.
16. Ibid., pp. 251–254.

logical, structured, ordered, and sequential. Further, students should be impressed with the fact that learning required hard work and sustained effort.[17]

In the mid-1950s and early 1960s, a demand for more academic rigor in the schools occurred that was similar to the earlier Essentialist movement. Leading critics, such as Arthur Bestor, Max Rafferty, and Hyman Rickover, attacked declining academic standards, permissiveness, and "life adjustment" education and argued for a return to standards of academic excellence. In particular, Arthur Bestor, a professor of history and a founder of the Council for Basic Education, presented the arguments of the critics of the 1950s in his books *Educational Wastelands* and *The Restoration of Learning*. Bestor charged that (1) academic standards in American schools had deteriorated because of an anti-intellectual philosophy that had divorced education from the scientific and scholarly disciplines and (2) a narrowly educated coalition of professional educators and bureaucrats had gained control of the teaching profession by manipulating certification requirements.[18] Bestor asserted that the trend to anti-intellectualism could be reversed if the schools returned to an academic program based on the rigorous study of intellectual disciplines. For Bestor, it was imperative that the secondary school curriculum should stress the systematic study of the intellectual disciplines of English, foreign languages, history, mathematics, and science.

In the 1970s, the general Essentialist point of view was revitalized by the "Back to Basics" movement. Although this contemporary Essentialism exhibits a variety of rather diverse tendencies that range from patriotism to drill, its most articulate forum has been the Council for Basic Education. A. Graham Down has stated that the council perceives of basic education as more than the "three R's." It means that students "should receive competent instruction in all the fundamental disciplines, especially English, mathematics, history, geography, government, science, foreign languages, and the arts."[19] The 1980s saw the continuation of Essentialism in the decade's neoconservative reforms that stressed the "new basics" found in *A Nation at Risk*.

In summary, the Essentialist position is a subject matter, teacher-centered theory of education. It assigns to schools a strictly academic function that views instruction as essentially an art of transmitting literary and mathematical skills in the elementary school and subjects, based on learned disciplines, in the secondary school. It is generally cautious of educational innovations of a methodological nature, preferring to reply on a curricular emphasis.

Conclusion

In this chapter, we have examined the general relationships that exist between philosophy and education. In particular, we have identified the areas of philosophy—metaphysics, epistemology, axiology, and logic—and have indicated

17. William C. Bagley, "Just What Is the Crux of the Conflict Between the Progressives and the Essentialists?" *Educational Administration and Supervision*, 26 (1940), pp. 508–511.

18. Arthur E. Bestor, *Educational Wastelands* (Urbana: University of Illinois Press, 1953); *The Restoration of Learning* (New York: Knopf, 1955).

19. A. Graham Down, "Why Basic Education?" *The National Elementary Principal*, 57 (October 1977), pp. 28–32.

their implications for education. The traditional educational philosophies of Idealism, Realism, Thomism, Perennialism, and Essentialism were examined. In the next chapter, we describe and analyze recently developed philosophies: Experimentalism, Progressivism, Reconstructionism, Existentialism, and Philosophical Analysis. Areas of agreement among the traditional, pragmatic, and emerging philosophies are summarized in the listing that follows.

Philosophies of Education

Traditional Philosophies	*Areas of Agreement*
Idealism	Subject matter curriculum
Realism	Knowledge arranged in a hierarchy
Thomism	Authority of the teacher
Perennialism	The school as an intellectual agency
Essentialism	Content over method

Pragmatic Philosophies	
Experimentalism	Emphasis on change
Progressivism	An activity or problem-solving curriculum
Reconstructionism	Focus on learner-centered instruction
	Use of experience and scientific method
	Relative "truth" and value

Emerging Philosophies	
Existentialism	Distrust of philosophical systems and categories
Philosophical Analysis	

DISCUSSION QUESTIONS

1. Analyze a class in the course in which this textbook is being used. To what degree is the language used in this class descriptive or prescriptive?
2. In class discussion in this course, try to determine the students' metaphysical, epistemological, and axiological views.
3. Analyze a chapter in a textbook in professional education. Try to arrive at the author's underlying philosophy.
4. Read and review a book in the philosophy of education.
5. Compare and contrast the philosophies of education treated in this chapter.
6. What is the philosophical rationale for basic education?

FIELD EXERCISES

1. Visit a class in an elementary or secondary school. Observe the degree to which the language used in instruction in that class is descriptive or prescriptive.
2. Examine the curriculum guide that is being used in a particular school. Identify the general philosophical statements and try to determine how consistent the curriculum is with that statement.

3. Interview the instructor in this course and attempt to identify his or her philosophical assumptions.

4. Interview teachers at the kindergarten, primary, intermediate, and upper grade levels and try to identify their philosophical assumptions. Is there a relationship between their philosophy of education and the particular grade that they teach?

5. Interview an older friend, neighbor, or relative. Through questioning, attempt to identify his or her philosophy of education.

6. Compile newspaper and periodical clippings of articles on educational policies and issues. Analyze the articles in terms of their philosophical orientation.

SUGGESTED READINGS

ADLER, MORTIMER J. *The Paideia Proposal: An Educational Manifesto*. New York: Macmillan, 1982.

———. *Paideia Problems and Possibilities*. New York: Macmillan, 1983.

———. *The Paideia Program: An Educational Syllabus*. New York: Macmillan, 1984.

BESTOR, ARTHUR E. *Educational Wastelands*. Urbana: University of Illinois Press, 1953.

———. *The Restoration of Learning*. New York: Knopf, 1955.

BEYER, LANDON E. *Knowing and Acting: Inquiry, Ideology & Educational Studies*. New York: Falmer Press, 1988.

BLOOM, ALLAN. *The Closing of the American Mind*. New York: Simon and Schuster, 1987.

BUTLER, J. DONALD. *Idealism in Education*. New York: Harper & Row, 1966.

DONOHUE, JOHN W. *St. Thomas Aquinas and Education*. New York: Random House, 1968.

———. *Catholicism and Education*. New York: Harper & Row, 1973.

FITZGIBBONS, ROBERT E. *Making Educational Decisions: An Introduction to Philosophy of Education*. New York: Harcourt Brace Jovanovich, 1981.

GUTEK, GERALD L. *Philosophical and Ideological Perspectives on Education*. Englewood Cliffs, N.J.: Prentice Hall, 1988.

———. *Cultural Foundations of Education: A Biographical Introduction*. New York: Macmillan, 1991.

HUTCHINS, ROBERT M. *The Higher Learning in America*. New Haven, Conn: Yale University Press, 1936.

KNIGHT, GEORGE R. *Philosophy and Education: An Introduction in Christian Perspective*. Berrien Springs, Mich.: Andrews University Press, 1980.

———. *Issues and Alternatives in Educational Philosophy*. Berrien Springs, Mich.: Andrews University Press, 1982.

MARTIN, WILLIAM O. *Realism in Education*. New York: Harper & Row, 1969.

MORRIS, VAN CLEVE, AND PAI, YOUNG. *Philosophy and the School*. Boston: Houghton Mifflin, 1976.

POWER, EDWARD J. *Philosophy of Education: Studies in Philosophies, Schooling, and Educational Policies*. Englewood Cliffs, N.J.: Prentice-Hall, 1982.

RUSK, ROBERT R., AND SCOTLAND, JAMES. *Doctrines of the Great Educators*. New York: St. Martin's Press, 1979.

TROXELL, EUGENE A., AND SNYDER, WILLIAM S. *Making Sense of Things: An Invitation to Philosophy*. New York: St. Martin's Press, 1976.

WILD, JOHN. *Introduction to Realist Philosophy*. New York: Harper and Brothers, 1948.

6

Modern Educational Philosophies

Chapter 5 examined traditional philosophies of education: Idealism, Realism, Thomism, Perennialism, and Essentialism. In Chapter 6, more recently developed educational philosophies—Experimentalism, Progressivism, Reconstructionism, Existentialism, and Philosophical Analysis—are described and analyzed. The traditional philosophies have existed for centuries. For example, Idealism and Realism originated in ancient Greece; Thomism emerged in the medieval era. The philosophies treated in this chapter are developments of the late-nineteenth and twentieth centuries. The general focusing questions that will be answered as you read this chapter include the following:

1. What is the Experimentalist concept of human nature and education?
2. What is the Progressive orientation to social and educational reform?
3. How do Social Reconstructionists propose to solve the contemporary social crisis?
4. How is Existentialism a philosophical response to the impersonal trends of mass society?
5. How do Philosophical Analysts deal with the problem of meaning?

Experimentalism

The Experimentalist philosophy of education was developed by John Dewey (1859–1952), one of America's leading advocates of Pragmatism. To establish the context of Experimentalism, it is first necessary to describe Pragmatism.

The Pragmatic temperament is typically associated with the American predilection for the practical, for practice, for usefulness. In the American historical experience, the westward movement of the population into new frontiers required an elastic and flexible attitude that enabled the pioneers to adapt to different and initially inhospitable environments and to transform them into congenial and productive living places. The westward-moving frontier created a willingness to experiment. It fostered an attitude in which people were close to and interacted with their environment.

Near the end of the nineteenth century, several thinkers placed the pragmatic American orientation into a philosophical context. In addition to the American pragmatic temperament, the Darwinian scientific revolution had also stimulated the development of Pragmatism. Charles Darwin's theory of evolution postulated that living organisms had evolved over the centuries as a result of successful adaptation to their environments. Rather than being created in final and fixed form, the various species of living creatures survived because of their ability to adapt to changing circumstances. It was in this context of the American attitude to change and the Darwinian scientific revolution that Charles Sanders Peirce, a mathematician, William James, a psychologist, and John Dewey, a philosopher, each in his own way, contributed to what became Pragmatism. Essentially, the Pragmatist viewpoint emphasized that

1. Human beings are intelligent, flesh-and-blood organisms who live in, interact with, and are capable of transforming their environment in ways that enhance life.
2. The world in which we live is an open, ever-changing universe in which human beings create their own purposes.
3. The most intelligent human behavior uses the scientific method to solve problems.
4. To be valuable and valid, ideas must be tested in human experiences: Ideas must work and have consequences that can be measured by their impact on our lives.

John Dewey

While Peirce and James contributed to Pragmatism, John Dewey had the greatest impact on educational philosophy. Dewey, a native of Vermont, grew up in Burlington, a small New England city, where he experienced the democratic ethic and process.[1] After attending local elementary and high schools, Dewey went on to college and to the recently established Johns Hopkins University, a graduate-level institution that was at the forefront of scholarly research. At Johns Hopkins, Dewey specialized in philosophy. From 1894 to 1904, Dewey was a professor at the University of Chicago, where he founded the well-known Laboratory School, which enrolled children of elementary school age in an experimental educational setting. Many of Dewey's philosophical ideas either originated in or were tested at the Laboratory School.[2] This experimental and progressive school emphasized that learning is an active process in which children act on their ideas to solve problems. After leaving the University of Chicago, Dewey joined the philosophy department of Columbia University. He was a prolific author whose articles and books dominated American philosophy of education during the first half of the twentieth century. In particular, Dewey's *Democracy and Education* put forth his general

---

1. Gerald L. Gutek, *Cultural Foundations of Education: A Biographical Introduction* (New York: Macmillan, 1991), pp. 326–343.
2. For accounts of Dewey's University of Chicago Laboratory School, see Katherine C. Mayhew and Anna C. Edwards, *The Dewey School* (New York: Appleton-Century, 1936); see also, Arthur G. Wirth, *John Dewey as Educator: His Design for Work in Education, 1894–1904* (New York: John Wiley, 1966); Herbert M. Kliebard, *The Struggle for the American Curriculum, 1893–1958* (Boston: Routledge & Kegan Paul, 1986), pp. 59–88.

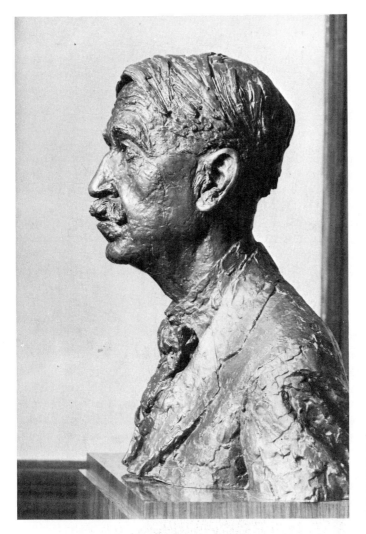

John Dewey (1859–1952) was one of America's leading philosophers. Dewey's Experimentalism had a great impact on educational theory and practice in the twentieth century.

stance on educational philosophy; his *Experience and Education* summed up his impressions of progressive education.[3]

Dewey's brand of Pragmatism is referred to as Experimentalism or as Instrumentalism. The following brief definitions of these terms illustrate his general philosophical orientation:

> *Experimentalism* is a philosophy that emphasizes that we learn by using the scientific method to solve our problems; life is like a laboratory in which we experiment to solve our problems.
>
> *Instrumentalism*, another name for Experimentalism, emphasizes that objects in the environment are instruments that become our tools to accomplish tasks and to solve

3. John Dewey, *Democracy and Education* (New York: Macmillan, 1906); John Dewey, *Experience and Education* (New York: Macmillan, 1938).

problems. More important, ideas are also instruments or tools that can be used to accomplish our purposes.

With this general orientation, we can examine the Experimentalist conception of metaphysics, epistemology, axiology, and logic—the basic subdivisions of philosophy.

Metaphysics

Unlike the traditional philosophies of Idealism, Realism, and Thomism, Experimentalism is not concerned with metaphysical issues. The traditional philosophies build their whole philosophical structure on a metaphysical base. For example, Idealism builds its structure on the Absolute Idea, and Realism builds its structure on the matter–form hypothesis. Experimentalists view such metaphysical bases as empirically nonverifiable; they cannot be tested in human experience. Rather than searching for metaphysical absolutes, Dewey identified the human being, or human organism, and the environment as the base of human experience. Human beings live within and interact with an environment. They can alter the environment but are also changed by that environment. In educational terms, the learner lives within an environment, often a school situation. That learning environment has problems within it that are occasions for learning to occur.

Epistemology

Experimentalists are heavily involved with epistemology, or the process of how we know and learn. In fact, Experimentalism is a process-oriented philosophy. Dewey and other Pragmatists assert that we know most accurately when we use the scientific method to solve our problems. In educational terms, learning is problem solving.

Dewey developed a five-step method of problem solving called the "Complete Act of Thought":

1. The person encounters a problem that is a condition or factor that is new and different from previous experience. This new situation means that the learner is involved in a *problematic situation*.
2. To begin to resolve the problematic situation, it is necessary to identify and define exactly what is causing the problem. In other words, the person needs to *define the problem*.
3. Once the problem has been defined, the person can investigate the various factors or characteristics of the situation. Such an investigation involves *reflecting on past experience* with similar situations, *doing research*, and *gathering information* that may be useful in solving the problem.
4. After the problem has been researched sufficiently, the person constructs some possible ways of solving the problem. These possible solutions, called *tentative hypotheses*, can be stated as "if-then" statements: If I choose to do such-and-such, then this is likely to happen.

5. The last step in problem solving is to choose the tentative hypothesis that is most likely to solve the problem and to test it by acting upon it. In Dewey's method of problem solving, it is necessary to act; merely conjecturing consequences is incomplete.

For Dewey and the Experimentalists, the "Complete Act of Thought," or problem solving according to the scientific method, is not only the way in which we think correctly but also the most effective method of teaching and learning. Problem solving can be used, for example, by primary-aged children who are experimenting with establishing a balanced aquarium or with gardening. It can be used by more advanced students to define and deal with a wide range of problems. Each time students solve a problem successfully, they add the solution to their repertoire of experience. Each problem-solving episode will lead to other problems and to an increase in the student's network of experience.

Axiology

Dewey placed great emphasis on publicly shared experience, which he saw as a foundation of a democratic society. In a democracy, the people share much: They hold commonly shared values and aspirations; they are free and indeed expected to participate in enjoying the benefits and solving the problems of their society. A democratic society, Dewey reasoned, is an open and experimental community.

Dewey and the Experimentalists stressed the educational possibilities of the human group. Children were to work together in defining and solving problems. Each participant contributed his or her unique skills and resources to solving the group's common problems. This mutual sharing was a socially enriching form of human experience.

Ethics and aesthetics in Experimentalism were arrived at socially, publicly, and experimentally. As society changed, ethical norms and aesthetic standards would also be subject to change. Unlike the more traditional philosophies, which based ethics and aesthetics on unchanging universals, Experimentalists claimed them to be variable with time and relative to culture.

Logic

For Experimentalists like Dewey, logic followed the inductive route of going from the particular instance or case to the general principle. Correct reasoning followed the scientific method. It was empirical and publicly verifiable.

School and Society

When he founded his Laboratory School in Chicago at the turn of the century, Dewey saw his new experimental school as a "miniature society" and an "embryonic community." Throughout his career, Dewey continued to stress the close and intimate relationship of the school to the society that it served. Unlike the strictly academic institution of the Idealists and Realists, Dewey's school was part of society and involved in its problems. Learning was not to be isolated within the four walls of the school; rather, schooling was part of the ongoing life of the society.

Progressivism

Progressive Education has had its zealous proponents and its vociferous detractors. Advocates of Basic Education trace many social ills and educational weaknesses to the influence of progressive educators. Progressives see themselves as agents of an education that liberates human beings. It is difficult to define or describe Progressive Education, for many different educators — often with conflicting viewpoints — gathered under the umbrellalike standard of Progressivism.[4] An historical perspective is useful in understanding Progressive Education.

Progressive Education in Historical Perspective: Antitraditionalism

The major outlooks of Progressive Education can be examined in two dimensions: (1) the long-standing attack on the traditionalism of formal schooling and (2) the Progressive Movement in American society, politics, and education. As these two dimensions of Progressivism are examined, it should be noted that Progressive Education is more a mood, a temperament, a posture, and an ideology than a fully developed philosophy.

Throughout history, the school has been a formal institution, governed by routine and regulation, in which learning is defined as the study and mastery of literary materials, especially books. In such a setting, teachers tend to lecture and students tend to recite prescribed lessons. Throughout history, there have been educators who sought to change schooling into an active rather than a passive center of learning.

Many of the individuals who have been identified as educational reformers such as Comenius, Rousseau, Pestalozzi, Froebel, Francis Parker, and John Dewey contributed to the ideas and practices associated with Progressive Education. Although they differed in particulars, these educational reformers generally asserted the following:

1. Children should be viewed as active rather than as passive agents in the learning process. Education should begin with the child's interests, needs, and problems rather than with a curriculum prescribed and organized by adults.
2. Learning is an active process in which learners investigate and explore their own environment, thoughts, and emotions.
3. Teachers should be flexible, facilitating learning by stimulating the interests of children, arranging the environment in ways that excite curiosity and interests.

4. The definitive history of progressivism in education is Lawrence A. Cremin's, *The Transformation of the School: Progressivism in American Education, 1876–1957* (New York: Knopf, 1961); the Progressive Education Association has been examined in Patricia A. Graham's *Progressive Education: From Arcady to Academe* (New York: Teachers College Press, Columbia University, 1967).

4. The school environment should be designed to encourage learning; it should be capable of flexible arrangements that can be varied to accommodate the different projects that arise in child and student life.

5. The atmosphere or milieu of the school and the personality of the teacher should be open and permissive. There should be no psychological or physical coercion or punishment.

Progressivism in American Life and Education

Progressive Education in the United States not only shared a broad antitraditionalist orientation but was also part of the Progressive Movement in American society, politics, and education. Historians have identified the period 1900–1920 as the "Progressive Era" in American history. In these two decades, leaders such as Theodore Roosevelt, Woodrow Wilson, and Robert LaFollette dominated American politics and inaugurated a series of regulatory reforms to control trusts and monopolies and to open political processes to more direct, popular participation. Social reformers such as Jane Addams worked in the settlement house movement to aid youths in the big cities and to assist in the assimilation of immigrants. Dewey, Addams, and others associated with Progressive Education saw it as an instrument of broad social reform.

In the years from the end of World War I to the beginning of the New Deal, 1919–1932, political Progressivism was eclipsed by a conservative reaction. However, Progressive Education flourished in the 1920s and 1930s, especially in private schools and many teacher education institutions. In the 1920s, Progressive Education lost many of its broad social and political reform impulses and concentrated on the liberation of the child through the liberalizing of the school.

Progressive Education Orientation

In 1919, educators of a Progressive orientation met in Washington, D.C., to organize the Progressive Education Association. The new organization enlisted various types of Progressive educators to its ranks, such as Deweyite Experimentalists and advocates of child freedom. Progressives who followed Dewey's pragmatic Experimentalist philosophy included professors of education like William H. Kilpatrick, Harold Rugg, George S. Counts, and John Childs, who were to make their own contributions to Progressive Education. Progressive educators often differed among themselves and lacked a unifying comprehensive educational philosophy. However, they agreed in their antagonism to the following traditional school practices:

1. The teacher who rules the classroom in an authoritarian manner
2. The exclusive reliance on textbooks and bookish methods of instruction
3. Passive learning that stressed the memorization of facts as its own end
4. The attempt to isolate schools from social change, conflicts, and issues
5. The use of psychological coercion and physical punishment as a means of maintaining order and discipline

Progressives not only opposed traditional practices but also developed their own educational principles. The principles adopted by the Progressive Education Association included the following:

1. Children should be free to develop naturally.
2. Interest, arising from direct experience, is the best stimulus for learning.
3. The teacher should be a researcher into educational processes and a guide to learning.
4. Close cooperation should exist between the school and home.
5. The progressive school should be a laboratory for educational reform and experimentation.[5]

Progressive educators devised alternative instructional models that stressed activities, field trips, problem solving, projects, and other nontraditional educational approaches. These alternatives centered on the child rather than on the subject matter; they emphasized activities rather than passive memorization and recitations; they encouraged cooperative and socially involved group learning rather than individualized lesson learning and personal competition among children. Progressives often viewed the use of democratic procedures in schools to be a prelude to community social reform. Progressives, who generally took a culturally relativistic approach to values, often challenged traditional customs and norms.

As was true of the Experimentalists, Progressives were generally not concerned with abstract philosophical speculation or metaphysics. Progressivism was an antitraditional educational theory rather than a systematic philosophy of education. In terms of epistemology, Progressives saw knowledge as tentative rather than absolute and unchanging. They preferred to concentrate on the process of learning rather than on the content of knowledge. Their axiological approach was equally tentative and relative. As with the Experimentalists, their tendency was to see values, ethics, and aesthetics in tentative and relativistic terms. By examining several of the major types of Progressive educators, it is possible to gain a better insight into the variety of educational positions that clustered together under the Progressive orientation.

Progressive educators of a Deweyite persuasion saw education as a process by which learners used the scientific method to solve problems. Frequently, the project method was used in progressive schools. This method was designed by William Heard Kilpatrick (1871–1965), a leader in Progressive Education and a professor at Columbia University's Teachers College.[6] Kilpatrick opposed traditional schooling as being authoritarian, too formal, abstract, and removed from the learner's interests. In contrast, Kilpatrick claimed that his project method motivated children to take the initiative for their education by encouraging them to plan, direct, and execute their own learning.[7] Students would work in groups on a variety of projects. Some students might design stage properties and costumes for the school play. Others might investigate local politics by studying city government and taking field trips to various municipal agencies. Students might also work on construction

---

5. Graham, *Progressive Education: From Arcady to Academe*, p. 51.
6. Samuel Tenenbaum, *William Heard Kilpatrick: Trail Blazer in Education* (New York: Harper and Brothers, 1951).
7. William H. Kilpatrick, *The Project Method* (New York: Teachers College Press, Columbia University, 1921).

Students working together on a geography project, a form of cooperative learning.

projects in which they designed and built school museums, gardens, and play areas. Kilpatrick believed that the project method encouraged scientific attitude, cooperative democratic behavior, and practical skills.

In addition to Experimentalists, another important group of Progressive educators were child-centered persons who wanted to liberate childhood from repressive child-rearing practices and authoritarian schooling. Convinced that learning should come directly from the children's interests and needs, Progressive champions of child freedom opposed having adults impose their objectives and values on children. Children should be free to learn according to their own impulses, needs, wants, and desires.

An early pioneer of child-centered Progressivism was Francis W. Parker (1837–1902). In his work at the Chicago Normal School, Parker distilled the educational concepts of Rousseau, Pestalozzi, and Froebel as a base for his own educational method, which encouraged children to learn directly from nature and the objects present in their environment. Through his talks and lectures to teachers, Parker was an early disciple of child freedom.[8]

Marietta Pierce Johnson (1864–1938), founder of the School of Organic Education at Fairhope, Alabama, was also a well-known advocate of child-centered Progressivism. Her theory of organic education sought to educate the whole child—

8. Francis Parker, *Talks on Pedagogics* (New York: John Day, 1937). For a biography of Parker, see Jack Campbell, *Colonel Francis W. Parker: The Children's Crusader* (New York: Teachers College Press, Columbia University, 1967).

mentally, emotionally, and physically, as well as cognitively. Seeking to prolong childhood as a time of crucial human growth and development, Johnson delayed introducing formal exercises in reading and writing until age 10. Organic education emphasized the development of creativity through field trips, handicrafts, and imaginative drama.[9] The concept of the "whole child" was emphasized by Progressive educators to bring about a broadened and enriched curriculum that included more than strictly academic subjects.

Child-centered Progressive educators like Johnson opposed imposing adult standards and requirements upon children. In particular, they were opposed to using the school as an agency for indoctrinating children. In the 1930s, child-centered Progressives split off from their Social Reconstructionist colleagues.

Found among child-centered Progressives were neo-Freudian educators, who were influenced by Sigmund Freud's psychoanalytical theory. Exalting the principle that children should have freedom of self-expression, they wanted to purge child rearing and educational practices of anything that repressed children's impulses. Neo-Freudian educators traced many emotional and psychological maladjustments to the repression of needs and drives in early childhood. They wanted teachers to undergo psychoanalysis so that they could be free to create nonrepressive classroom environments.

George Green, a leader in the application of psychoanalysis to schooling, found the classroom to be an emotionally charged environment for both children and teachers. He recommended that teachers use psychoanalytic methods to identify children's needs and to promote the cause of child freedom.[10]

In cultivating the "whole child" concept, some Progressive educators turned to art as both a way of learning and as a means of releasing children's creativity. Harold Rugg, Caroline Pratt, and other Progressives developed the concept of the artist-teacher, an educator whose teaching was a form of artistry. Caroline Pratt (1867–1954), who founded the Play School in New York's Greenwich Village, stressed creativity as the basis of learning. Emphasizing the creative use of direct experience, the children in Pratt's Play School took numerous field trips to parks, zoos, art galleries, fields, forests, and museums. When they returned to the Play School after their field trips, the children were encouraged to portray what they had seen and experienced. They were encouraged to act as artists and to use a variety of artistic media, such as clay, paints, paper, cardboard, and crayons to externalize their concepts. Progressives like Pratt viewed children as artists who had an intense desire to express reality as they had experienced it.

Social Reconstructionism

As indicated earlier in this chapter, the early stage of the Progressive Education movement closely related educational reform to social reform. By the 1920s, however, the social reform impulse in Progressive Education subsided and was eclipsed by the child-centered orientation. During the Great Depression of the 1930s, some

9. Marietta Johnson, *Thirty Years with an Idea* (University: University of Alabama Press, 1974).
10. George H. Green, *Psychoanalysis in the Classroom* (New York: Putnam, 1922).

Progressives, such as George S. Counts, believed that Progressive Education should seek to create a cooperative society in which wealth would be shared more equitably. Counts later broadened his call to all educators in his *Dare the School Build a New Social Order?*[11] Counts's challenge to the educational profession was the genesis of the Social Reconstructionist philosophy of education. Basically, Count's argument was the following:

1. Western civilization, including that in the United States, has experienced a great transformation from an agricultural and rural society into one that is industrial and technological.
2. Although material change has occurred, Western civilization's values have lagged behind the course of technological change.
3. Human beings are still following archaic individualistic and selfish patterns of behavior.
4. World War I and the Great Depression were symptoms of a lack of cooperative planning.
5. Education needs to reduce the cultural lag between humankind's material knowledge and values; it needs to prepare people to plan and to implement a design for a cooperative society.

Counts's call to "build a new social order" attracted adherents from the ranks of Progressive educators. Eventually, Social Reconstructionism developed into a distinctive educational ideology that contained both an analysis of society and a plan for social reform.

Social Reconstructionists argue that civilization is in a state of profound cultural crisis. If schools continue to mirror the social status quo, then, Reconstructionists claim, schooling will merely transmit societal ills and injustices. Schools will really be training children to play the roles required in an archaic and self-destructive society. Rather than relying on metaphysics as a theoretical rationale, Reconstructionist educators use the findings and methods of social sciences such as economics, anthropology, sociology, and psychology to provide the basis for their plans of social reform.

Social Reconstructionists want to use education as a means of designing policies that will bring about a new society. Such an education, they argue, cannot be neutral; it must be committed to bringing about deliberate social change. It must prepare future generations to be social engineers who can use science and technology to create a new and better world society.

According to Reconstructionists, educators, teachers, students, and schools should

1. Identify major social problems by critically examining the present condition of society.
2. Analyze social problems, issues, and controversies with the aim of resolving them in ways that enhance human growth and development.
3. Be committed to bringing about constructive social change and reform.
4. Cultivate a planning attitude among students that will be carried into adult citizenship activities.
5. Join in promoting definite programs of social, educational, political, and economic reform.

11. George S. Counts, *Dare the School Build a New Social Order?* (New York: John Day, 1932).

Social Reconstructionists believe that a new society can be created only as educators challenge obsolete conceptions of education and schooling and initiate carefully planned change that will lead to social reform. Because social sciences such as anthropology, economics, sociology, political science, and psychology are useful in providing the background and methods for planned social change, they should be emphasized in the curriculum. Education should awaken the students' consciousness about social problems by encouraging them to question the status quo and to examine controversial issues in religion, society, economics, politics, and education. By examining rather than ignoring controversial issues, the Reconstructionists believe, students will develop alternatives to the status quo.

The Reconstructionist teacher should encourage and respect divergent thinking by students. Divergent thinking should not be purely intellectual but should be used instrumentally to create alternative political, social, and economic institutions and processes.

Social Reconstructionists assert that a truly progressive education should create a world order in which people plan their own future. It should be future rather than past oriented. Reconstructionists contend that traditional schooling is based on the past to the neglect of the future. If people are to control their own destinies, it is important that schools include futuristic studies in the curriculum.

Reconstructionists insist that teachers lead students to examine critically their culture. They should identify major areas of controversy, conflict, and inconsistency and seek to resolve them.[12] For example, the curriculum should include units on such problems as overpopulation, environmental pollution, world poverty, violence, and war. Education should examine these world problems and seek to resolve them so that people can improve the quality of life on the planet.

The Reconstructionists believe that technology has created an interdependent world. Events in one region of the earth will have an impact in other regions. The new education must stress the reality of an interdependent and international world. Reconstructionists seek to internationalize the curriculum so that students learn that they are living in an interdependent world culture.

Existentialism

Existentialism is a recent development in both philosophy and educational philosophy. Although its roots can be traced back into the beginnings of Western thought, Existentialism gained its greatest popularity after World War II. Some commentators observed that Existentialism was a reaction to the attempt of totalitarian regimes to destroy personal choice and freedom. In a contemporary sense, Existentialism presents a philosophical alternative to the standardization and mass conformity of the modern technological society. As with other recent developments in philosophy, Existentialism does not easily fit the metaphysical, epistemological, axiological, and logical divisions of the more traditional philosophical systems. Indeed, Existentialism is antithetical to attempts at systematization.

12. Theodore Brameld, *Toward a Reconstructed Philosophy of Education* (New York: Holt, Rinehart and Winston, 1956).

Existentialists view life in a very personal way.[13] Existentialism conveys a feeling of desperation about the human condition, but it also brings forth a feeling of hope because it sees human beings as having the capacity to achieve true personal freedom. The word *feeling* is important for Existentialists as it conveys the total human experience. Life is emotional and affective as well as intellectual. To achieve true personal freedom and authenticity, Existentialist educators emphasize personal reflection and commitment on life's significant choices.

Jean-Paul Sartre, the Existentialist thinker, wrote that "existence precedes essence." For Sartre, human beings are born into a world that is without an intrinsic purpose. They simply appear in the world at birth, and as they become conscious, they are faced with choices. While some choices are inconsequential, others reach to the very meaning of life and lead to personal self-definition. Human beings create their own definition or, as Sartre would have it, make their own essence. They are what they choose to be.

The more traditional philosophical systems of Idealism, Realism, and Thomism hold that we inhabit an orderly and purposeful universe. For them, human life draws its meaning from the very purpose that God or reality assigns to it. In contrast, most Existentialists assert that individuals live in a purposeless world and must create their own meaning in life. Christian Existentialists recognize that they live in a purposeful world, but they also assert that the individual person ultimately must make a decision to identify with God's purpose for humankind.

The Existentialist, conceiving the human being as an "essence creator," differs from the Idealists and Realists, who see the person as a universal category. A categorical definition is a precondition that circumscribes human freedom. Since human freedom is total, the Existentialists claim that the individual has a total responsibility for choice.

Angst, or the feeling of pervasive dread, is an important Existentialist concept. Each person lives with the knowledge that his or her destiny is inevitable—death and disappearance. He or she knows that his or her presence in the world is but temporary. The individual bears this knowledge of ultimate demise and disappearance during every conscious moment. It is with this sense of dread that each person must make the choices that define him or her as a human being. In making the important decisions of life, only the choice maker knows how the choice affects the meaning of his or her life. As indicated, Existentialism believes that human life carries with it feelings of both desperation and hope. Human beings are desperate creatures who know that their life is temporary and their disappearance inevitable. They live in a world in which they are constantly encountering others—persons, institutions, and agencies—that are obstacles to choice and freedom. It is easy to pretend to abandon choice to other persons or institutions. Such abandonment is merely a pretense to escape from responsibility. Those who claim to be following orders have to choose to do so. Ultimately, the real question is, "Do I choose to be self-determined, or do I choose to let others define me?" Every person can choose to be inner directed and authentic if he or she has the consciousness and courage to be such a person. An authentic person, who is free and aware of freedom, realizes that

13. George F. Kneller, *Existentialism and Education* (New York: John Wiley, 1958).

every choice is a personal decision. The authentic person is aware that self-definition is a personal responsibility.[14]

Existentialist Educational Implications

Existentialism has many implications for teachers and students. It seeks to create a certain consciousness and attitude about learning. The Existentialists know that physical reality exists; they also know that science is a necessary and useful part of the curriculum. However, many significant choices are personal and nonscientific. Existentialists contend that our most important knowledge is about the human condition and personal choice. Education is a way of developing consciousness about the human condition, the freedom to choose, and the personal responsibilities that authenticity brings to persons who seek to be free. An Existentialist education seeks to raise consciousness by examining choice making in its many human dimensions.

Existentialist educators encourage students to philosophize about the meaning of the human experiences of life, love, and death. An Existentialist teacher poses questions to stimulate self-consciousness. Such questioning, it is hoped, will grow into a dialogue among the students. The answers to these questions are personal and subjective. For questions of personal meaning, no single answer is correct for everyone.

An Existentialist curriculum would emphasize philosophizing, or dialogue, among students and between students and teacher. It would examine individual choice making. Because Existentialism is so personal and subjective, it vivifies life's emotional, aesthetic, and poetic dimensions. In an Existentialist curriculum, literature and biography are important means of examining personal choice.[15] Drama and film that portray the human condition and dilemma would be discussed by students. To create their own modes of self-expression, students would experiment with artistic media to dramatize their emotions, feelings, and insights. In the Existentialist school, teachers and students would be free to engage in dialogue and discussion about their own lives, choices, and identities. Subjects would be studied that illuminate choice making by examining the human condition as presented in literature, drama, biography, and history.

Philosophical Analysis

Philosophical Analysis, a philosophical technique for analyzing language, was developed in the early twentieth century by philosophers who were dissatisfied with speculative philosophical systems.[16] G. E. Moore and Bertrand Russell were two pioneering theorists in developing the methods used by Analytical Philosophers. Russell, who sought to identify the logical structures underlying language usage, saw the task of philosophy as that of formulating the logical rules upon which language is based. The ideas of Russell and Moore were developed by other Philosophical Analysts, such as Ludwig Wittgenstein and his Vienna Circle.

---

14. Van Cleve Morris, *Existentialism in Education: What It Means* (New York: Harper & Row, 1966).
15. Maxine Greene, *Existential Encounters for Teachers* (New York: Random House, 1967).
16. D. J. O'Connor, *An Introduction to Philosophy of Education* (New York: Random House, 1957).

Philosophical Analysis rejects the metaphysical bases of Idealism, Realism, Thomism, and other traditional philosophies that claim to be complete philosophical systems. For Analysts, metaphysical systems are pure speculation without verifiable meaning. They contend that metaphysics cannot be verified or tested in human experience. Analysts are also critical of some of the more recently developed contemporary philosophies. Existentialism, for example, is regarded as being too subjective, emotional, and poetical to be used as a basis for making educational policy decisions. Existentialist subjectivism obscures meaning rather than clarifying it. Social Reconstructionism, too, is regarded as another ideology that is merely contesting in political fashion against competing ideologies. Although Pragmatism is somewhat more acceptable because it relies on the scientific method, the language used by some Pragmatists in education is regarded as unclear. Terms like *growth*, *democracy*, *consensus*, and *the whole child*, for example, commonly used by Experimentalist educators, are regarded by Analysts as jargon-ridden and in need of further clarification.

Philosophical Analysis is designed to analyze the language used in everyday discourse, as well as in the technical. In particular, it is used by educational theorists who believe that our communication about education has grown confused, polemical, and jargon-ridden. To establish meaning, Analysts seek to render educational statements into empirical terms that are verifiable. Rather than being a systematic philosophy like Realism or an ideology like Social Reconstructionism, Philosophical Analysis provides a method for clarifying educational issues. This clarifying process is regarded as a first step in resolving educational controversies and in explaining educational policies.

In clarifying the way in which we express ideas, the Analysts begin with the sentences used to express our propositions about reality. They regard only some sentences as candidates for meaningful expression. Meaningful sentences are valid either analytically or empirically.[17] The following kinds of sentences illustrate the procedures used by Analysts to clarify language.

Analytical Propositions

Analytical propositions are statements in which the subject of the sentence is accepted as true and in which the predicate expresses the same thing as or carries identical value to that of the subject. Analytical propositions are often mathematical, for example:

8 = 4 + 4
(The number 8 is accepted as valid; 4 + 4 means the same thing as 8. Note that 4 + 4 tells us the same thing as is expressed by 8.)

Empirically Verifiable Statements

Empirically verifiable statements are candidates for presenting new information or knowledge to use. These statements are meaningful if they can be tested and verified. For example:

17. Albert J. Taylor, *An Introduction to the Philosophy of Education* (Dubuque, Iowa: Kendall/ Hunt, 1978), pp. 142–148.

Paris is the capital city of France. (We can establish that Paris is a city, that France is a nation-state, and that Paris is its capital.)

John Brown weighs 185 pounds. (We can identify a person named John Brown, place him on an accurate scale, and determine his weight.)

Only analytical and empirically verifiable statements convey meaning; other statements that appear to carry meaning are really subjective or emotional expressions. For example, the Idealist statement that "the world is spirit" and the Existentialist statement that "existence precedes essence" appear to be meaningful, but they are only statements affirming their authors' commitment to believe that they are true. The Analysts would most likely assert that "the world is spirit" is not analytically valid, and "existence precedes essence" is not empirically valid. The Analysts caution us to observe that many statements made in politics, philosophy, and education that purport to be factual are in reality merely preferences expressed by their authors.

Philosophical Analysis is a response to the knowledge and communications explosions of the twentieth century. Human occupations, professions, and specializations have grown increasingly technical and complicated. Each specialty has developed its own language to be used by the experts in that field. The growing use of highly specialized terminologies has made it difficult to communicate across areas of specialization. By clarifying the language used in a complex technological society, the Philosophical Analysts seek to make our communication more meaningful.

Because education is simultaneously a public and a technical matter, it, too, is beset by the same problems of communication and meaning found in other areas of life. Public education in the United States involves national, state, and local politics; it is subject to the demands and particular programs of competing special interest groups. Much that claims to be sound education upon examination can be found to mask special interests. The close examination of the language used in educational policy statements can serve to clarify and explain the true intent of the individuals and groups making these statements.

As a profession, education involves many areas of specialization. It involves social workers, psychologists, administrators, curriculum makers, sociologists, historians, philosophers, teachers, subject matter experts, and many other specialists. Each of these areas of specialization has brought its own specialized language into the field of education. It often becomes difficult for the various experts within education to communicate in a meaningful dialogue with each other. Language analysis can help those who work in education to understand and to communicate with each other.

Conclusion

Philosophy of education is one of the most basic and fundamental concerns of teachers. Although those beginning to teach will face many urgent problems in the early stages of their careers, they will eventually come to consider the purpose of what they are doing with their life. Questions of basic purpose and meaning are never easy to deal with because they involve large and often seemingly overwhelming decisions and commitments. Philosophical thinking involves the difficult undertaking of trying to see one's life and the lives of others in the most general terms. The abstract thought that philosophical thinking requires is reflective and eventually calls for judgments to be made. If you do not now have a philosophy of education, you will eventually develop one. As you philosophize about education and your role in it, consider the following questions:

1. What do I believe is ultimately real in life, in the world, and in my existence? How does my conception of reality influence what I teach children?
2. How do we know what we claim to know? What is the process by which we know? Is my conception of knowledge and knowing reflected in my teaching?
3. What is it that I hold to be valuable and beautiful? What are my values, ethics, and perceptions of beauty? How do values enter into my teaching and into the lives of those I encounter? What is the basis for my standards of conduct, behavior, and performance for myself and for others?
4. What are the principles by which I organize my life, my time, my modes of instruction?
5. Most important, what is the basis for my interaction with other human beings? What is my perception of human personality and human dignity?

DISCUSSION QUESTIONS

1. Prepare and present to the class short biographical sketches of Charles Peirce, William James, and John Dewey. Attempt to establish how their experiences contributed to the formulation of Pragmatism.
2. Read one of John Dewey's books and review it for class discussion.
3. Define the following terms: Pragmatism, Experimentalism, Instrumentalism, scientific method, Progressivism, Social Reconstructionism.
4. Describe the Progressive orientation to life and education.
5. Identify and examine the difference between a child-centered Progressive view of education and a Social Reconstructionist view.
6. Reflect on and discuss the possibilities of creating an Existentialist school.
7. Describe the functions of Philosophical Analysis.

FIELD EXERCISES

1. Invite a philosopher of education at your college or university to visit your class to present his or her philosophy of education.
2. Visit a nontraditional school and report to the class on that school's underlying philosophy.
3. Design an activity for use in the classroom based on Dewey's "Complete Act of Thought."
4. Design an activity for classroom use based on Kilpatrick's project method.
5. Debate the proposition: Resolved, the school should build a new social order.
6. Identify a drama or book in which individuals face significant choice-making situations; then lead a class discussion that examines these choices.

7. Select a paragraph from a textbook used in an education course. Analyze the paragraph according to the procedures used by Philosophical Analysts.

SUGGESTED READINGS

BAYLES, ERNEST E. *Pragmatism in Education.* New York: Harper & Row, 1966.

BRAMELD, THEODORE. *Toward a Reconstructed Philosophy of Education.* New York: Holt, Rinehart & Winston, 1956.

COUNTS, GEORGE S. *Dare the School Build a New Social Order?* New York: John Day, 1932.

CREMIN, LAWRENCE. *The Transformation of the School: Progressivism in American Education, 1876–1957.* New York: Knopf, 1961.

CRUNDEN, ROBERT M. *Ministers of Reform: The Progressives' Achievement in American Civilization 1889–1920.* Urbana: University of Illinois Press, 1984.

DENNIS, LAWRENCE J. *George S. Counts and Charles A. Beard: Collaborators for Change.* Albany: State University of New York Press, 1989.

Dewey, John. *The Child and the Curriculum.* Chicago: University of Chicago Press, 1902.

———. *Democracy and Education.* New York: Macmillan, 1916.

———. *The School and Society.* Chicago: University of Chicago Press, 1923.

———. *Experience and Education.* New York: Macmillan, 1938.

FEINBERG, WALTER. *Understanding Education: Toward a Reconstruction of Educational Inquiry.* New York: Cambridge University Press, 1983.

FITZGIBBONS, ROBERT E. *Making Educational Decisions: An Introduction to Philosophy of Education.* New York: Harcourt Brace Jovanovich, 1981.

GRAHAM, PATRICIA A. *Progressive Education: From Arcady to Academe.* New York: Teachers College Press, Columbia University, 1967.

GREENE, MAXINE. *Existential Encounters for Teachers.* New York: Random House, 1967.

GUTEK, GERALD L. *The Educational Theory of George S. Counts.* Columbus: Ohio State University Press, 1970.

———. *George S. Counts and American Civilization: The Educator as Social Theorist.* Macon, Ga.: Mercer University Press, 1984.

GUTMANN, AMY. *Democratic Schooling.* Princeton, N.J.: Princeton University Press, 1987.

KILPATRICK, WILLIAM H. *The Project Method.* New York: Teachers College Press, Columbia University, 1921.

KNELLER, GEORGE F. *Existentialism and Education.* New York: John Wiley, 1964.

———. *Movements of Thought in Modern Education.* New York: John Wiley, 1984.

MORRIS, VAN CLEVE. *Existentialism in Education: What It Means.* New York: Harper & Row, 1966.

POWER, EDWARD J. *Philosophy of Education: Studies in Philosophies, Schooling, and Educational Policies.* Englewood Cliffs, N.J.: Prentice-Hall, 1982.

RUGG, HAROLD O., AND SCHUMAKER, ANN. *The Child-Centered School.* New York: World Book, 1928.

SCHEFFLER, ISRAEL. *Conditions of Knowledge.* Glenview, Ill.: Scott, Foresman, 1965.

SOLTIS, JONAS F. *An Introduction to the Analysis of Educational Concepts.* Reading, Mass.: Addison-Wesley, 1968.

———, ED. *Philosophy of Education Since Mid-Century.* New York: Teachers College, Columbia University, 1981.

VANDENBERG, DONALD. *Human Rights in Education.* New York: Philosophical Library, 1983.

WIRTH, ARTHUR. *John Dewey and Education: His Design for Work in Education, 1894–1904.* New York: John Wiley, 1966.

_7_

Multicultural Education

In recent years, educators have given attention to the multicultural dimension of American society. This emphasis is based on the growing realization that the United States is composed of a variety of religious, ethnic, social, and linguistic groups and that each of these groups has a unique contribution to make to the still unfinished American social fabric. The respect for ethnic and social diversity, know as *multiculturalism*, reverses the patterns of earlier years when public schooling was conceived of as an agency for cultural assimilation or homogenization. Chapter 7 examines the rise of multicultural education and explores its impact on American education.

The general focusing questions that will be answered as you read this chapter include the following:

1. How were the theories of Americanization, the "melting pot," and cultural pluralism responses to ethnicity in American society?
2. What have been the major trends in the education of African Americans?
3. What have been the major trends in the education of Hispanic Americans?
4. What have been the major trends in the education of Asian Americans?
5. What have been the major trends in the education of Native Americans?
6. What have been the major trends in women's education?

Public Schooling and Ethnicity

As every child learns in social studies and history, the United States is a nation of immigrants. With the exception of Native Americans, all — Europeans, Africans, Hispanics, and Oriental Americans — were once newcomers to the United States. The patterns of immigration from the founding of the British colonies in North America until the mid-nineteenth century were basically from northern Europe, with English-speaking peoples predominating. Although there were Dutch, French, Spanish, Swedes, and Germans, the population of the 13 original colonies was dominated by English, Scots, and Scottish-Irish from the British Isles. The major religious creeds were Protestant.

In the nineteenth century, especially from the 1840s to the Civil War, two social and educational trends developed and converged almost simultaneously: (1) the origin and implementation of the common school system and (2) the beginning of a shift in immigration patterns from Protestant English-speaking groups to Catholic and non-English-speaking groups. Famine in Ireland caused thousands of Irish Catholics to immigrate to the United States and to locate in what was then Protestant New England. Political turmoil, particularly the Revolution of 1848, brought large numbers of Germans to the United States. From 1870 to 1920 the pattern of immigration was to shift again as immigrants came from southern and eastern Europe. The historical convergence of the origin of the common school and the new immigration pattern worked to fix an assimilationist, or Americanization, policy upon American public education. The common-school leaders saw that institution as an agency of assimilating immigrants by the Americanization process. In the mid-nineteenth century, Americanization meant the following:

1. The language of instruction in the public schools was English. Non-English-speaking children had to learn English to succeed in public schools.
2. Although the public school was not a religious institution, the generalized value attitude and formal exercises—such as Bible reading and opening prayers—followed a non-denominational Protestantism.

By the late 1840s and 1850s, the Americanization ideology dominated many common-school systems. Restive Roman Catholics who feared that Americanization would mean the Protestantization of their children began to establish their own parochial schools. While Irish Catholics used English in their schools, Germans and other non-English-speaking groups established bilingual and bicultural schools.

During the long period from 1870 to 1920, millions of immigrants came to the United States from eastern and southern Europe. Italians, Poles, Czechs, Slovaks, Russians, Jews, Greeks, Hungarians, and Roumanians came to work in mines, factories, and farms. In many large northern and eastern cities such as New York, Chicago, and Pittsburgh, the ethnic ghetto, known as little Italy, little Warsaw, and so on, developed. The immigrant and "first-generation" children who attended public schools encountered and had to yield to an unbending assimilationist ideology that professed that a person became a "good American" by being ashamed of and forgetting his or her ethnic heritage.

According to the "melting pot" theory advanced in the early twentieth century, the various ethnic groups would lose their ethnicity through assimilation and eventually become one people, an American race. Although the term *melting pot* was used widely in the first half of the twentieth century as an accomplished fact, a new wave of sociologists in the 1960s called the "melting pot" a myth. They discovered that many ethnics had not melted into one homogeneous people and that ethnicity was alive and flourishing in the United States. A renaissance of ethnic consciousness contributed to multicultural education in the 1980s.

Since the 1970s, the assimilationist ideology has been under attack and largely discarded by American educators. In place of cultural homogenization, the public schools have incorporated a multiethnic perspective into the curriculum based on the following principles:

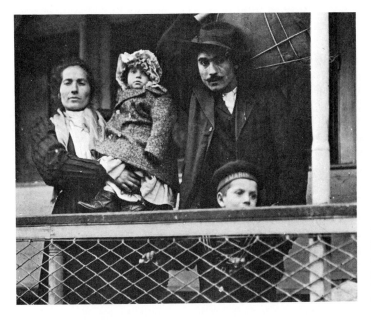

This family, part of the massive immigration from southern and eastern Europe in the late nineteenth century, contributed to making the United States into a multicultural nation.

1. Public schooling should emphasize the common, unifying, and integrative dimensions of American life in a manner that respects and encourages ethnic diversity and expression.
2. The American social and cultural experience is perceived as an "open," rather than "closed," society. Rather than being a monolithic social fabric, the American cultural experience is a mosaic in which each ethnic group has a contribution to make.
3. Educators should recognize that Americans live in an ethnically and culturally pluralistic society. The curriculum should include topics or units that provide insights into the contribution of the various ethnic groups to American culture and life.

Schooling and the African-American Experience

As indicated, the American public school followed an assimilationist ideology toward ethnic groups throughout much of its history. Although some parallels exist between the ethnic and African-American experience in the public schools, black Americans encountered different attitudes because of different historical circumstances. The entry of African Americans into the New World occurred in the early colonial years as blacks were transported to North America to work as slaves on the tobacco, rice, indigo, and cotton plantations of the South. Slavery, that peculiar and cruel American institution, had the effect of inducing "cultural shock" on its victims. The Africans were literally torn out of their own culture and society by force, packed on slave ships, and sold as chattel to plantation owners. Often, members of a particular language or tribal group were isolated from each other to prevent communication and revolt.

The African slaves experienced cultural shock in that they were uprooted from their homeland, their culture, their traditions and values, and their tribes and kinship groups. Such a complete uprooting often was disorienting and anxiety generating. In time, Africans established an African-American culture in the New World.

Although there were free blacks living in the United States throughout its history, the vast majority were slaves—primarily in the southern and border states—until the Civil War, the Emancipation Proclamation, and the Thirteenth Amendment ended slavery. Prior to black emancipation, the official policy and law in the slave states made it illegal to instruct slaves in reading and writing. Although some blacks learned to read and write, the majority were illiterate when the Civil War ended in 1865. The federal government, through the Freedmen's Bureau, inaugurated a literacy campaign among blacks by establishing schools and bringing northern teachers to the South as instructors. In addition to federal efforts, the legislatures of the southern states in the reconstruction period, 1865–1877, enacted laws that established common or public schools—supported by public taxation. It should be pointed out that many of these legislatures had substantial black representation in the Reconstruction decade and that the establishment of public schools in the South was a major achievement.

When Reconstruction ended, racial segregation was established in the South with the force of law. Although racially segregated schools were allegedly "separate but equal," the schools attended by black children were usually underfinanced and educationally inferior. Blacks generally suffered political, economic, social, and educational discrimination. The response of black leaders to racial segregation and discrimination has been illustrated frequently by the conflicting educational philosophies of Booker T. Washington and W. E. B. DuBois.

The Washington–DuBois Controversy

Booker T. Washington (1856–1915), a former slave who made his way to a position of national leadership, is today a controversial figure. As head of Tuskegee Institute in Alabama, Washington became the recognized leader of and spokesperson for black Americans. Following a conservative and often paternalistic educational ideology, Washington asserted the following:

1. Blacks should avoid political agitation for civil and legal rights and instead make themselves economically indispensable as farmers, craftsworkers, and artisans to the American, particularly southern, economy.
2. The appropriate education for blacks was not professional study of law, medicine, or higher education, but vocational training for agriculture and occupational trades.

In his "Atlanta Compromise" address, Washington advocated a symbiotic racial relationship between blacks and whites. Both races, he asserted, could live separate social lives but be mutually supporting in economic affairs. Today, Washington is frequently criticized as a compromiser who failed to advance the cause of his race and who said what the "white power structure" wanted to hear. Defenders of Washington claim that he was a survivor who was making the best of a "bad situation."

W. E. B. DuBois (1868–1963), a founder
of the NAACP, was a sociologist and
historian who fought for civil rights for
African Americans and racial integration
for American society.

Booker T. Washington (1856–1915) was president of
Tuskegee Institute and the proponent of the "Atlanta
Compromise."

Washington and DuBois—Black educational leaders who debated the purposes of education for black
Americans. While Washington advocated basic skill training, DuBois urged higher and professional
education.

Washington's educational ideology was challenged by the historian and sociologist W. E. B. DuBois (1868–1963), who argued that the progress of black Americans required action in many areas: educational, political, economic, and social. DuBois, a founder of the National Association for the Advancement of Colored People (NAACP), asserted that

1. Blacks should organize to gain the civil rights promised in the U.S. Constitution.
2. Blacks should not restrict themselves to vocational training; they should pursue degrees in higher education and careers in law, medicine, politics, science, and research.

Whereas Washington believed that black progress would come slowly in short, gradual, and noncontroversial steps, DuBois did not fear controversy. Rather, DuBois believed that a black leadership elite, a "talented tenth," should be identified and lead the black people of America. This talented tenth would bring about progress for their race from the top downward.

African Americans and the School Ideology

In the century from emancipation to the civil rights activism of the mid-1960s, the attitudes of public school educators toward black Americans experienced several changes. The common-school leaders, many of whom were from the northeastern states, were generally sympathetic to the educational needs of the former slaves in the Reconstruction era after the Civil War. In some respects, the crusade for common schools and the Abolitionist movement to abolish slavery had originated in the northeastern states and then spread throughout the northern states. Political and educational leaders such as Horace Mann, Henry Barnard, Horace Greeley, Thaddeus Stevens, and others endorsed public education and also opposed slavery. In the post–Civil War Reconstruction decade, they aided efforts to educate the former slaves in the South.

From 1865 to 1900, the vast majority of African Americans were located in the South. There was also a small but growing black population in the North. In the South, a dual school system existed, with students separated according to race. Like black educators such as Washington and DuBois, white educational leaders had differing perspectives on black education.

William T. Harris, the U.S. commissioner of education and former superintendent in St. Louis, believed that black children needed the same basic literary and mathematical skills as whites. Harris also believed that all students needed to be introduced to the classics and to the sources of Western civilization. The general attitude to black education was that black children should learn the basics — reading, writing, arithmetic — and be introduced to white, Anglo-Saxon American culture. As was true of the schooling of immigrant children, black students were presented with a monolithic view of American culture. The African-American experience and contribution to American life was not incorporated into the curriculum. While the dominant ideology of American education predicted that the children of European ethnics would become part of a melting pot, such was not true of black children. African Americans were to be inculcated with the ideas and values of white America. They were to read and study about white Americans and accept white heroes as value models, but they were also being prepared to accept a "second-class" role in American society.

In the early decades of the twentieth century, like the ethnic contribution to American culture, the black experience was portrayed narrowly in the literary and historical parts of the school curriculum. The treatment of slavery and the Reconstruction era in history textbooks illustrated the new official ideology. This historical version took the following lines:

1. African-American slaves were generally well treated and were content with their lot on the plantations of the South. Although slavery was a social evil, many white plantation owners were well-meaning persons who provided kindly care to their slaves.
2. After the Civil War, unscrupulous northern "carpetbaggers" and southern "scalawags" misled blacks by convincing them to take political power in the southern states. Once in power, black politicians and their white "radical allies" inflicted corrupt regimes on the former Confederate states.

3. After federal troops were withdrawn from the South, white political leadership was restored in the South, and honest government was reasserted.

4. The African-American path to progress would be slow and gradual. It would come from patience, hard work, and industriousness, not from political agitation. Booker T. Washington and scientist George Washington Carver were cited frequently as examples of hardworking black leaders whose achievements were based on a willingness to help others.

This distorted and incomplete version of the African-American experience was challenged by John Hope Franklin, Rayford Logan, and other historians, who condemned slavery as an evil institution that had personally and socially debilitating effects on both black slaves and white slave-owners. The Reconstruction legislatures in the South—composed of a substantial number of black representatives—brought reforms and progressive policies to the southern states. For example, political participation was broadened and uniform systems of taxation were created. Political corruption existed in the northern cities and states as well and often to a larger extent than in the South. When federal troops left the South, segregation was established by the new legislatures. "Jim Crow" laws, poll taxes, and disenfranchisement followed. It was not until the mid-twentieth century that more adequate and historically accurate interpretations appeared.

Emergence of a New Black Consciousness

The period from World War I to the civil rights movement of the 1950s and 1960s marked the emergence of a new black consciousness. Although many black and white scholars and educators had rejected the standard textbook version of the African-American experience, it persisted until it was challenged academically and publicly in mid-twentieth century. Civil rights leaders such as Martin Luther King and historians such as John Hope Franklin called for a more complete and accurate interpretation of the black experience in America.

The Supreme Court decision in the *Brown* case in 1954 marked the beginning of the end of racially segregated schools in the United States. The incorporation of the African-American contribution in a multicultural society was not merely a matter of judicial decision making, however. It involved reexamination of the cultural heritage, discovering hitherto neglected evidence, and creating a more adequate interpretation of the African-American past and contributions to the school curriculum. For black Americans, this often meant a painstaking search to discover their roots, to celebrate the uniqueness of their heritage, and eventually to create a synthesis with a multicultural context.

In educational institutions, especially at the college and secondary level, the first wave of the renascent black consciousness took the form of separate courses on black culture, literature, and history. Colleges often established Black Studies departments. The first wave of activity tended to emphasize the uniqueness and separateness of the black experience. Black heroes and heroines were identified as models for black children to imitate. Black pride, expressed in the slogan "Black is Beautiful," was frequently a dominant theme. Neglected sources were found and incorporated into older versions of the black experience. Importantly, the perspectives on black culture in American were broadened in this first wave. For example:

1. The African culture roots of the African-American experience were identified and examined for linkage and insight.
2. The emphasis on blacks in industry and politics was broadened to include the black contribution to art, literature, music, poetry, and science.

The first wave of black consciousness as it was felt in schools and in the curriculum had a positive effect of identifying a unique African-American experience for many black children. It had several negative consequences, however.

Where it concentrated on the separateness of the black experience, it lacked a multicultural dimension. The same phenomenon was true, however, of early ethnic studies programs that concentrated on a particular ethnic group in isolation from other groups. Although a beneficial addition to American education, black or ethnic studies tended to suffer from cultural and educational isolation. Another defect was that, in the haste to prepare curriculum guides, textbooks, and other instructional materials, the treatment was sometimes superficial and uncritical.

The second wave of black consciousness, as well as ethnic consciousness, was to incorporate both African-American and European ethnic studies into the context of multicultural education. This new and broader context seeks to treat both the uniqueness of the particular group's experience and to examine its relationships and interactions with other social and ethnic groups and with the total society. Its purpose is to create a sense of racial or ethnic identity that recognizes uniqueness and also encourages transracial and transethnic understanding for all participants of American society.

Schooling and the African-American Experience

African Americans, now representing about 12 percent of the total U.S. population, number some 26.5 million persons. The largest number of African Americans live in the southern states and in the large urban areas of northern states. For example, African Americans constitute more than 20 percent of the total population in Mississippi, South Carolina, Louisiana, Georgia, Alabama, Maryland, and North Carolina. Among the large northern cities, New York has an African-American population of 1,784,337; followed by Chicago, with 1,197,000; Detroit, with 758,939; Philadelphia, with 636,878; and Los Angeles, with 505,210.[1]

School attendance districts, based on residence, reflect the segregated pattern of the neighborhoods served by the particular school. In the 1980s, the national migration of African Americans became a two-way movement, both to and from the South. The African-American population in the southern states has been stable since the late 1970s and stands at about 53 percent of the total African-American population.[2] While the African-American population in the large northern cities is

---

1. U.S. Department of Commerce, Bureau of the Census, *America's Black Population: 1970–1982: A Statistical View* (Washington, D.C.: U.S. Government Printing Office, 1983), p. 1.
2. Ibid.

FIGURE 7-1   Distribution of the Black Population by Metropolitan
and Nonmetropolitan Residence, 1970 and 1980

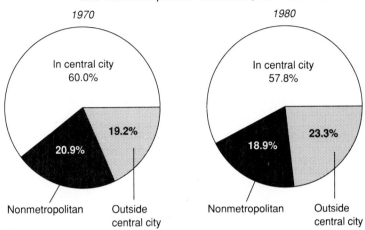

1970

In central city
60.0%

19.2%

20.9%

Nonmetropolitan   Outside
central city

1980

In central city
57.8%

23.3%

18.9%

Nonmetropolitan   Outside
central city

SOURCE: From William C. Matney and Dwight L. Johnson, *America's Black Population:*
1870 to 1982: A Statistical View (Washington, D.C.: U.S. Government Printing Office,
1983), p. 5.

still highly concentrated in the central core areas, there has been a small but steady
movement of African Americans to the outer-city and suburban areas. (See Figure
7-1 for metropolitan and nonmetropolitan distribution of African-American
populations.)

In terms of educational enrollment, attendance, and attainment, the picture
for the African Americans is mixed. From 1970 to 1981, the number of African
Americans attending school increased from 7.8 to 8.4 million. During the 1980s,
there was a decline in attendance that paralleled the decreasing enrollments of whites
during the same period because of declining birth rates. The long-standing disparity
in the number of African American and white students in school attendance,
between the ages of 7 and 15, ended, although the high school drop-out rate of
African Americans after age 15 remained higher than that for whites. Finally,
African-American attendance in colleges and universities increased from 7 percent
of the college population in 1970 to 11 percent by the end of the 1980s.[3] See Table
7-1 and Figure 7-2 for enrollments by race and ethnicity.

Schooling and the Hispanic Experience

In the same decades that European ethnics and African Americans were experiencing a revived cultural identity and consciousness, a similar phenomenon was taking
place among Spanish-speaking Hispanic Americans. Again, the Hispanic experience
resembles but bears differences from the black and European ethnic experience. It
shares the similarity of being generally neglected in American public education. It
differs in that the Hispanic experience arises from unique historical circumstances.

3. Ibid., p. 16.

TABLE 7–1 Enrollment in Public Elementary and Secondary Schools, by Race or Ethnicity and State, Fall 1986

State	Percent of Enrollment, by Race or Ethnicity					
	Total	White[1]	African American[1]	Hispanic	Asian or Pacific Islander	Native American
United States	**100.0**	**70.4**	**16.1**	**9.9**	**2.8**	**0.9**
Alabama	100.0	62.0	37.0	0.1	0.4	0.5
Alaska	100.0	65.7	4.3	1.7	3.3	25.1
Arizona	100.0	62.2	4.0	26.4	1.3	6.1
Arkansas	100.0	74.7	24.2	0.4	0.6	0.2
California	100.0	53.7	9.0	27.5	9.1	0.7
Colorado	100.0	78.7	4.5	13.7	2.0	1.0
Connecticut	100.0	77.2	12.1	8.9	1.5	0.2
Delaware	100.0	68.3	27.7	2.5	1.4	0.2
District of Columbia	100.0	4.0	91.1	3.9	0.9	0.1
Florida	100.0	65.4	23.7	9.5	1.2	0.2
Georgia	100.0	60.7	37.9	0.6	0.8	(2)
Hawaii	100.0	23.5	2.3	2.2	71.7	0.3
Idaho	100.0	92.6	0.3	4.9	0.8	1.3
Illinois	100.0	69.8	18.7	9.2	2.3	0.1
Indiana	100.0	88.7	9.0	1.7	0.5	0.1
Iowa	100.0	94.6	3.0	0.9	1.2	0.3
Kansas	100.0	85.6	7.6	4.4	1.9	0.6
Kentucky	100.0	89.2	10.2	0.1	0.5	0.0
Louisiana	100.0	56.5	41.3	0.8	1.1	0.3
Maine	100.0	98.3	0.5	0.2	0.8	0.2
Maryland	100.0	59.7	35.3	1.7	3.1	0.2
Massachusetts	100.0	83.7	7.4	6.0	2.8	0.1
Michigan	100.0	76.4	19.8	1.8	1.2	0.8
Minnesota	100.0	93.9	2.1	0.9	1.7	1.5
Mississippi	100.0	43.9	55.5	0.1	0.4	0.1

State						
Missouri	100.0	83.4	14.9	0.7	0.8	0.2
Montana	100.0	92.7	0.3	0.9	0.5	5.5
Nebraska	100.0	91.4	4.4	2.4	0.8	1.0
Nevada	100.0	77.4	9.6	7.5	3.2	2.3
New Hampshire	100.0	98.0	0.7	0.5	0.8	0.1
New Jersey	100.0	69.1	17.4	10.7	2.7	0.1
New Mexico	100.0	43.1	2.3	45.1	0.8	8.7
New York	100.0	68.4	16.5	12.3	2.7	0.2
North Carolina	100.0	68.4	28.9	0.4	0.6	1.7
North Dakota	100.0	92.4	0.6	1.1	0.8	5.0
Ohio	100.0	83.1	15.0	1.0	0.7	0.1
Oklahoma	100.0	79.0	7.8	1.6	1.0	10.6
Oregon	100.0	89.8	2.2	3.9	2.4	1.7
Pennsylvania	100.0	84.4	12.6	1.8	1.2	0.1
Rhode Island	100.0	87.9	5.6	3.7	2.4	0.3
South Carolina	100.0	54.6	44.5	0.2	0.6	0.1
South Dakota	100.0	90.6	0.5	0.6	0.7	7.6
Tennessee	100.0	76.5	22.6	0.2	0.6	(2)
Texas	100.0	51.0	14.4	32.5	2.0	0.2
Utah	100.0	93.7	0.4	3.0	1.5	1.5
Vermont	100.0	98.4	0.3	0.2	0.6	0.6
Virginia	100.0	72.6	23.7	1.0	2.6	0.1
Washington	100.0	84.5	4.2	3.8	5.1	2.3
West Virginia	100.0	95.9	3.7	0.1	0.3	0.0
Wisconsin	100.0	86.6	8.9	1.9	1.7	1.0
Wyoming	100.0	90.7	0.9	5.9	0.6	1.9

SOURCE: From National Center for Education Statistics, *Digest of Education Statistics 1989*, I (Washington, D.C.: U.S. Government Printing Office, 1989), p. 56.
NOTE: The tabulation was derived from a sample survey of public school districts from the 1986 Elementary and Secondary School Civil Rights Survey. State estimates may differ from other data sources because of variations in survey methodology. Because of rounding, details may not add to totals.
[1]Excludes persons of Hispanic origin.
[2]Less than 0.05 percent.

FIGURE 7–2   Enrollment in Public Elementary and Secondary Schools, by Race and Ethnicity, Fall 1976, 1984, and 1986

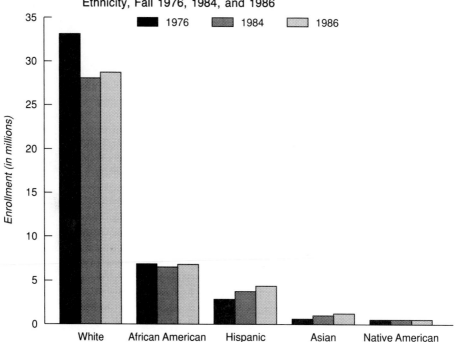

SOURCE: From Curtis O. Baker, ed., *The Condition of Education 1989* (Washington, D.C.: U.S. Government Printing Office, 1989), p. 55

Further, the term *Hispanic* as a general category for Spanish-speaking must be used carefully. While Mexican Americans, Cuban Americans, and Puerto Rican Americans share a common mother tongue, their heritages are based on differing cultural contexts. The Hispanics share certain characteristics with the European ethnics because they share a common European cultural origin. But, whereas most immigrants from southern and eastern Europe came directly to the United States from their native lands, the Spanish-speaking immigrants first settled and lived for centuries in other American countries such as Cuba, Mexico, or Puerto Rico before entering the United States. An exception to this generalization is seen in the many Hispanics in the southwestern or western United States who are descended from the Spanish colonists. A second very important difference is that the Hispanics are Spanish-speaking; they share a common language, whereas the European immigrants lacked a common language to link them to other ethnic groups. While European ethnics have sometimes argued for bilingual instruction in public schools, they have not done so in a forceful or concerted fashion. Bilingual and bicultural education has been a generally successful demand of Hispanic Americans.

Examining the Hispanic Generalization

The Hispanic population is the most rapidly growing ethnic group in the United States. In 1982 there were 15.8 million Hispanics in the United States; that population is expected to reach 31 million in 2010.[4] (See Table 7–2.) However, while "Hispanic American" is a convenient category, it is also an overgeneralization. A genuine program of multicultural education needs to begin not only with the similarities but also with an explanation of the differences between Spanish-speaking groups.

Mexican Americans, or Chicanos, for example, present an historical and cultural experience that differs from the experience of other Hispanics. The Mexican-American experience can be examined from two perspectives: that of the older Mexican-American stock, whose inclusion in the United States dates from the Mexican–American War (1846–1848), and that of the more recent immigrants from Mexico to the United States. The history of the older Mexican-American stock goes back to the Spanish colonial period when what are now the states of California, Texas, and New Mexico were parts of New Spain. The descendants of the early Spanish settlers established *encomiendas*, agricultural estates, cities, and schools. Spanish Roman Catholic missionary orders met the religious and educational needs of the Spanish colonists and their descendants and worked to convert the Indians to Catholicism. A number of missions were established by the Franciscan friars to provide religious, craft, and agricultural education to the Indians and to protect them from exploitation.

As a result of the Mexican–American War, Mexico, which had earlier won its independence from Spain, was forced to cede large areas of land to the United States. The Spanish-speaking Mexican population of these lost areas became a "conquered people." With annexation, the English language became the official language of government and schooling. When public schools were established in the southwestern states, the standardized Anglo-centered curriculum was also imposed on Mexican-American children. Little was done to relate instruction to the language and culture of the Mexican American. Indeed, many school districts required that only English be used in instruction.

In the twentieth century, there has been considerable immigration from Mexico to the United States. These more recent immigrants have been employed as migrant agricultural workers or as unskilled laborers. Entering the United States as illegal aliens, some migrant workers have been underpaid and exploited. Since mid-twentieth century, the Mexican-American population of the large cities has increased.

As has been typical of other ethnic groups, Mexican Americans have experienced a rise in consciousness. The educational demands of the two groups of Mexican Americans are somewhat similar but also different. They are similar in wanting the Mexican-American heritage and contributions recognized in the school curriculum. Both groups also favor bilingual and bicultural education in Spanish and English. One major difference between the groups is that the more recent Mexican-American immigrants, particularly the children of migrant workers, often require compensatory educational programs.

Puerto Rican migrants to the continental United States are citizens as Puerto Rico is an American commonwealth. Puerto Rico passed directly from Spanish to

---

4. Gregory Spencer, *Projections of the Hispanic Population: 1983–2080.* (Washington, D.C.: U.S. Government Printing Office, 1986), p. 2.

TABLE 7-2 Percent Distribution of the Population, by Age, Race, and Spanish Origin; 1982–2080*

Year	Total	Under 5	5–13	14–17	18–24	25–34	35–44	45–64	65 and Over	85 and Over
						Age (years)				
Total										
1982	100.0	7.5	13.1	6.4	13.1	17.0	12.1	19.2	11.6	1.1
1985	100.0	7.7	12.4	6.2	12.0	17.5	13.4	18.7	12.0	1.1
1990	100.0	7.7	12.9	5.2	10.3	17.4	15.2	18.6	12.7	1.3
1995	100.0	7.2	13.3	5.4	9.1	15.6	16.2	20.2	13.1	1.6
2000	100.0	6.6	12.8	5.7	9.2	13.6	16.3	22.7	13.0	1.8
2010	100.0	6.3	11.3	5.3	9.8	13.1	13.0	27.5	13.8	2.3
2020	100.0	6.2	11.2	4.9	8.6	13.4	12.6	25.8	17.3	2.4
2030	100.0	5.8	10.8	5.0	8.6	12.2	13.2	23.2	21.2	2.8
2050	100.0	5.7	10.5	4.7	8.3	12.4	12.6	24.0	21.8	5.2
2080	100.0	5.5	10.2	4.6	8.1	12.0	12.3	23.7	23.5	5.9
Spanish origin										
1982	100.0	11.1	18.0	7.9	14.8	18.2	11.4	13.7	4.9	0.3
1985	100.0	11.6	17.3	7.4	13.6	18.8	12.3	13.8	5.1	0.4
1990	100.0	11.5	17.5	6.8	12.0	18.2	14.0	14.3	5.7	0.5
1995	100.0	10.7	17.9	6.7	11.1	16.5	15.2	15.5	6.3	0.6
2000	100.0	9.9	17.4	7.2	11.0	15.1	15.1	17.6	6.8	0.7
2010	100.0	9.3	15.5	6.7	11.7	14.7	12.9	21.1	8.0	0.9
2020	100.0	8.6	15.0	6.3	10.7	15.2	12.9	20.9	10.6	1.2
2030	100.0	7.8	14.0	6.2	10.5	14.3	13.6	20.3	13.3	1.5
2050	100.0	6.6	12.2	5.5	9.8	14.2	13.5	22.6	15.6	3.0
2080	100.0	5.8	10.6	4.8	8.6	12.6	13.0	24.2	20.4	4.4
White non-Hispanic										
1982	100.0	6.8	12.1	6.1	12.7	16.8	12.4	20.3	12.8	1.2
1985	100.0	6.9	11.5	5.9	11.6	17.3	13.7	19.8	13.4	1.3
1990	100.0	6.9	11.8	4.8	9.9	17.1	15.4	19.7	14.3	1.5
1995	100.0	6.4	12.1	5.1	8.6	15.2	16.4	21.4	14.8	1.8

	Total									
2000	100.0	5.8	11.7	5.3	8.6	13.1	16.5	24.2	14.8	2.2
2010	100.0	5.5	10.0	4.9	9.2	12.5	12.8	29.3	15.8	2.8
2020	100.0	5.4	10.0	4.4	7.9	12.8	12.4	27.2	19.9	2.8
2030	100.0	5.1	9.7	4.5	7.9	11.4	12.9	24.1	24.4	3.4
2050	100.0	5.3	9.7	4.3	7.6	11.6	12.1	24.6	24.7	6.3
2080	100.0	5.4	9.9	4.5	7.9	11.6	11.9	23.5	25.3	6.7
African American										
1982	100.0	9.8	16.3	8.0	15.0	17.0	10.6	15.3	7.9	0.6
1985	100.0	10.5	15.3	7.4	14.2	17.9	11.7	14.9	8.0	0.7
1990	100.0	10.2	16.2	6.2	12.1	18.7	13.7	14.7	8.2	0.8
1995	100.0	9.4	17.0	6.4	10.5	17.1	15.4	15.9	8.3	1.0
2000	100.0	8.6	16.2	7.1	10.6	14.9	16.3	18.1	8.3	1.2
2010	100.0	8.2	14.1	6.4	11.5	14.3	13.2	23.4	8.9	1.4
2020	100.0	7.7	13.8	5.9	10.0	14.9	12.9	23.2	11.6	1.5
2030	100.0	7.1	12.9	5.8	10.0	13.5	13.8	21.6	15.3	1.7
2050	100.0	6.3	11.7	5.3	9.2	13.4	13.2	23.3	17.6	3.8
2080	100.0	5.7	10.5	4.8	8.4	12.2	12.5	23.9	22.0	5.1
Other races										
1982	100.0	9.9	15.8	6.8	13.1	19.7	13.6	15.1	5.9	0.4
1985	100.0	9.0	15.2	6.7	12.2	19.5	15.2	15.9	6.3	0.5
1990	100.0	8.0	14.9	6.2	11.1	18.5	16.9	17.4	7.0	0.5
1995	100.0	7.7	13.7	6.4	10.5	17.0	17.1	19.9	7.8	0.6
2000	100.0	7.4	13.1	5.5	10.7	15.8	16.5	22.4	8.6	0.7
2010	100.0	6.9	12.4	5.4	9.4	15.0	14.6	25.5	10.8	1.1
2020	100.0	6.5	11.8	5.2	9.2	13.9	14.2	24.8	14.4	1.5
2030	100.0	6.3	11.4	5.0	8.9	13.6	13.5	24.1	17.2	2.1
2050	100.0	6.1	11.0	4.9	8.7	13.1	13.2	23.7	19.3	3.7
2080	100.0	5.9	10.7	4.8	8.5	12.7	12.8	23.6	21.0	4.7

SOURCE: From Gregory Spencer, *Projections of the Hispanic Population: 1983 to 2080* (Washington, D.C.: U.S. Government Printing Office, 1986), p. 15.

*As of July 1. Includes Armed Forces overseas. Data from the middle series.

American control as a result of Spain's defeat in the Spanish–American War of 1898. The relationship between Puerto Rico and the United States has been mixed. Some Puerto Ricans seek independence; others prefer to continue some form of relationship with the United States. Puerto Ricans in the United States have tended to settle in large northern cities. As with other Hispanics, Puerto Ricans generally have endorsed bilingual and bicultural education. They also advocate the incorporation of appropriate units of Puerto Rican culture and contributions into the public school program.

A third major Hispanic ethnic group in the United States are Cuban Americans, many of whom are exiles from the Castro regime. The Cuban immigration to the United States has centered in Florida and from that state to other locations. The Cuban immigrants included many of middle-class origin — physicians, lawyers, educators, and other professionals. Like other Hispanic Americans, they advocate bilingual, bicultural education and the recognition of the Cuban cultural contribution.

Bilingual, Bicultural Education

As indicated, Hispanic Americans generally are strong advocates of bilingual and bicultural education programs. Bilingual education means that instruction should be conducted in two languages, for example, Spanish and English. Bicultural education is more comprehensive in that it includes not only instruction in two languages but also learning about two cultures. Although bilingual education is well established in public schools in many areas of the country, there is controversy over whether such programs should be for transition or for maintenance. Transitional programs are designed to help Spanish-speaking children learn English by a series of gradual phases in which an initially large amount of instruction in Spanish is slowly replaced by English. Maintenance programs, in contrast, are designed to preserve and cultivate Spanish-speaking ability and also to make the students proficient in English. Bilingual and bicultural programs require preparation of instructional materials and teachers in both languages.

Schooling and the Asian-American Experience

Although much of the discussion about the European ethnic experience in the United States applies to Asian Americans, there are several obvious but noteworthy differences. The major Oriental-American ethnic groups are the Chinese, Japanese, Filipino, Indian, and Korean. More recent immigrants are groups from Southeast Asia, such as the Cambodians, Laotians, Vietnamese, and Thais. The cultural and linguistic background of the Asian ethnics differs from those of the European ethnics. China, Japan, and India, in particular, represent ancient and complex civilizations. A genuine explanation of these highly developed civilizations is a major but necessary undertaking for a true multicultural educational program.

In the late-nineteenth and early-twentieth centuries, nativist sentiment was generally anti-Asiatic. Chinese workers who were brought to the United States to work in the mines and on railroad construction in the West were feared as cheap laborers who were a threat to the more highly paid white workers. Federal legislation at first limited and then excluded the entry of Chinese immigrants to the United States. The general attitude to Chinese Americans has experienced several shifts in the twentieth century. During World War II, when China was an ally of the United States, Chinese were portrayed sympathetically in the press and in motion pictures. American missionaries and business interests that were active in China also encouraged American involvement and support for China. After mainland China adopted communism, relations with China cooled, particularly during the Korean conflict. Today, there is renewed interest among American political, business, and educational leaders in China. The Chinese government has also become more interested in improving relations with the United States in order to modernize the country. Despite the changing circumstances of international relations, the general public attitude in the United States has often been simplistic and stereotypic regarding China, the Chinese, and Chinese Americans.

The prevalent popular attitudes to Japanese Americans have been similar to those pertaining to Chinese Americans. However, while the Chinese enjoyed popularity during World War II, the reverse was true of Japanese Americans. After the bombing of Pearl Harbor in 1941, there was an almost hysterical suspicion toward Japanese Americans. The Roosevelt administration, contrary to its general stance on behalf of civil liberties, reacted by confining Japanese Americans to resettlement or internment camps, often without regard to their personal and property rights. The action by the U.S. government denied civil rights to Japanese Americans. During World War II, U.S. propaganda depicted the Japanese in stereotypic fashion.

Until the mid-1950s, the American public school curriculum generally ignored serious treatment of Asian cultures and civilizations. Courses in world history and world culture up to that time concentrated on Europe and North America. When Asia was discussed, the treatment was peripheral at best. (The same was generally true of the textbook coverage of Africa and South America.) When they were included, Asian civilizations were treated as outposts of Western nations. Generally, there was a passing reference to the "American open-door policy" toward Asia or to the European colonization of Asia. The mid-1950s marked a change in the place that Asia had in the public school curriculum. World history and world culture courses, particularly at the secondary level, were broadened to include a treatment of Asia in terms of its own civilizations. At the elementary level, the entry of anthropology and sociology units into the social studies contributed to an examination of stereotypic thinking and of the Asian contribution to world civilization.

Schooling and the Native-American Experience

The Native-American experience has often been neglected, distorted, or romanticized in both schools and in the public mind. Since the time of the Leatherstocking Tales of James Fenimore Cooper, the Native American has been portrayed as either a noble savage or a cruel adversary rather than as a member of a particular cultural group with its own traditions and life-styles. From the Atlantic to the Pacific, the variety of Native American cultures is complex and varied; to refer to Native Americans as a single group is to oversimplify.

Relationships between Native Americans and whites were influenced by the impact of the frontier in American history. For the westward-moving white fur traders, miners, and settlers, the frontier meant the extension of culture and civilization into the western territories of the United States. For the Native Americans, however, the frontier marked an invasion into ancestral lands and an attack on a way of life that was in harmony with, rather than a conquest of, the natural environment.

Robert M. Utley, a distinguished historian, has written that, despite their physical contact on the frontier, whites and Native Americans lived in "a great cultural chasm" that made each people incomprehensible to the other.[5] Recent efforts of historians, social scientists, and multicultural educators have attempted to reduce this cultural chasm.

The general educational philosophy and program pursued by the U.S. Bureau of Indian Affairs, private philanthropic groups, and religious societies was to assimilate Native Americans into white culture by eradicating tribal traditions, customs, and values. Schools for Native Americans — both off and on reservations —

Sioux Indian children at the Rosebud Reservation School in the 1890s.

5. Robert M. Utley, *The Indian Frontier of the American West 1846–1890* (Albuquerque: University of New Mexico Press, 1984), p. xix. Also see Margaret Connell Szasz, *Education and the American Indian: The Road to Self-Determination since 1928* (Albuquerque: University of New Mexico Press, 1977).

followed a program of Americanization that was to "de-Indianize" in much the same way that public schools eroded ethnic languages and values. The curriculum in these Native American schools stressed the English language and American patriotism. Boys were to learn farming, blacksmithing, and carpentry. Girls were to learn sewing, cooking, and housekeeping.

Supported by federal funds channeled through the Bureau of Indian Affairs, a system of contract schools, conducted under religious auspices, and government schools arose on Native-American reservations. Some schools were day schools that taught reading, writing, arithmetic, and Americanism to students. Boarding schools, in which the students lived away from home and away from tribal influences, were agencies of industrial training and assimilation into white culture and values.[6] A well-known model of the boarding school was the Carlisle Indian School, established in 1879 by Richard Henry Pratt, a former U.S. Army officer, who sought to eradicate Native-American culture by a process of total immersion in white culture far from the students' tribal homes.

The 1970s and 1980s witnessed efforts by historians and other scholars to create a more accurate understanding of the Native American in American life and culture. The D'Arcy McNickle Center for the History of the American Indian, aided by the National Endowment for the Humanities, made a concerted effort to encourage the diffusion of a more accurate portrayal of Native-American history in the writing and teaching of United States history.[7]

Despite these recent efforts, many textbooks continue to present stereotyped images of the Native American as irrational primitives who clung tenaciously to a doomed way of life.[8] Frederick Hoxie, a leader in the effort to develop a more accurate assessment of the Native American in American history and culture, argues for textbooks and curriculum materials that (1) present a coherent view of Indian cultures and behavior, (2) examine the impact of tribal interaction, and (3) present a "broader, more complex" appraisal of the Native-American experience and contribution to American life.[9]

The richness and variety of the Native-American experience is still a mystery to many Americans. Although efforts have been made to include realistic and accurate units of Native-American life and culture into the curriculum, these have been minimal and peripheral even in multiethnic or multicultural education programs. A genuine multicultural program will explore and illustrate the uniqueness of the Native-American contribution to American life. It should illustrate the commonalities of the Native-American experience but also point out the cultural differences that exist between the various tribal and regional groupings.

In the twentieth century, the number and conditions of Native Americans changed considerably. The Native-American population experienced considerable growth. More Native Americans had left their historic reservations, areas set aside by treaty with the federal government for settlement by a particular tribe.

6. Utley, *The Indian Frontier of the American West,* pp. 217–218.
7. *The Impact of Indian History on the Teaching of United States History* (Chicago: Newberry Library, 1985).
8. Frederick E. Hoxie, *The Indians Versus the Textbooks: Is There Any Way Out?* (Chicago: Newberry Library, 1984), p. 16.
9. Ibid., pp. 18–21.

A group of Native-American children in Alaska involved in an educational discussion.

Estimates of the Native-American population at the time of entry of Europeans on the North American continent vary greatly. While some scholars have estimated the number of Native Americans to have been quite large, others contend that their numbers never exceeded 1 million. It was not until 1890 that a census of the Native American population was made. The 1890 census identified the Native-American population as 248,000. During the next 60 years, the slowly growing Native-American population showed only a slight increase, reaching 357,000 in 1950. During the next 30 years, from 1950 to 1980, however, the Native-American population showed a phenomenal increase. By 1980, the number of Native Americans had increased to 1,364,000. (See Figure 7–3.) In its distribution, 50 percent of the Native-American population lives in the western states, 27 percent in the South, 18 percent in the Midwest, and 6 percent in the Northeast.[10]

Demographics highlight some problems faced by the Native-American population in regard to education. Although around 44 percent of the Native-American population is of school age, under 20 years old (nationally, this figure is 32 percent), the educational attainment level of the Native-American population is below that of the general population. For example, the drop-out rate of Native-American high school students is high; the number of Native Americans completing high school is 67 percent below that of the total U.S. population. Only about 8 percent of the Native-American population is likely to complete four years of college.[11]

10. U.S. Department of Commerce, Bureau of the Census, *We, the First Americans* (Washington, D.C.: U.S. Government Printing Office, 1988), p. 3.

11. Ibid., pp. 4–5.

FIGURE 7–3   Native American Population, 1890–1980
(Numbers in Thousands)

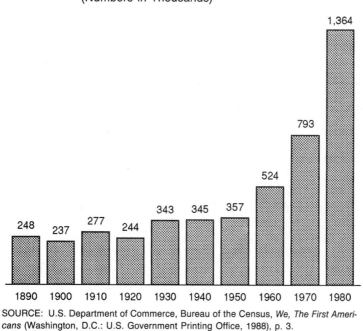

SOURCE: U.S. Department of Commerce, Bureau of the Census, *We, The First Americans* (Washington, D.C.: U.S. Government Printing Office, 1988), p. 3.

The number of unemployed persons in the Native-American population is higher than in the general U.S. population. Among a variety of factors, the high drop-out rate for high school students and the low participation rate of Native Americans in higher education contribute to their unemployment. For those reasons, too, the income level of the Native-American population is considerably lower than the national average. A disproportionate number of Native Americans live at or below the poverty level.

The Native Americans' heritage is inextricably interwoven in the multicultural American experience. The stereotypes of Native Americans need to be replaced by an accurate portrayal of their cultural diversity and contributions. The serious economic and educational problems they face still remain to be addressed by American society.

Schooling and American Women's Experience

In its long history, the women's rights, or feminist, movement has struggled for equal political, social, economic, and educational opportunities in a male-dominated society. Initially, the women's rights movement grew out of the crucible of reform that characterized New England in the 1830s, especially the Abolitionist crusade. In the 1840s, Lucretia Mott and Elizabeth Cady Stanton organized a movement for women's rights that, at its convention in Seneca Falls, New York, in

1848, demanded that women be given the right to vote and freed from discriminatory laws that gave men control of their property.

In 1869, Susan B. Anthony and Elizabeth Cady Stanton organized the National Women Suffrage Association, which was committed to ratification of a constitutional amendment that would give women the vote. It was not until 1919, 50 years later, that the Nineteenth Amendment enfranchised American women.

In the 1960s, a revitalized women's liberation movement organized to gain equal educational, employment, and political opportunities. Although the feminist movement was not new to American life, it developed new strategies during that time.[12] Although members of the movement differed on specific objectives, one of the most important goals of the feminist movement was to end discriminatory employment practices that had relegated women to low-paying and low-status stereotypic occupations. Feminist spokespersons challenged the traditional attitude that women should be confined to housekeeping, cooking, and child-rearing.

The drive for women's equality in employment accelerated as lawsuits were filed to end discrimination in hiring. The Civil Rights Act of 1964 had made it illegal to discriminate in employment on the basis of sex. In 1972, Congress sent the Equal Rights Amendment (ERA) to the states for ratification, but it failed to secure the needed number of states required to make the ERA part of the Constitution.

However, the women's liberation movement produced significant changes in American education. It weakened the traditional concept that there was an "appropriate" gender-based education for men and another for women. For example, a gender-based curriculum held that manual training, technical courses, and medical,

Susan B. Anthony was a nineteenth-century leader of the movement for women's rights and an organizer of the National Woman Suffrage Association.

12. For more on the women's movement, see Vivian Gornick and Barbara K. Moran, eds., *Woman in Sexist Society: Studies in Power and Powerlessness* (New York: Basic Books, 1971), and Aileen S. Kraditor, ed., *Up from the Pedestal: Selected Documents from the History of American Feminism* (Chicago: Quadrangle Books, 1968).

engineering, and legal studies were appropriate studies for males. Home economics, domestic science, nursing, elementary school teaching, and secretarial programs were appropriate programs for women. With the weakening of gender-based education, women enrolled in ever-larger numbers in training programs in medicine, law, engineering, journalism, and other professions.

As had been true of blacks, Hispanics, and other ethnic minorities, women wanted to have their role in American life and culture reexamined so that the contribution of women in science, law, education, politics, and other areas would be included in textbooks and in courses of study.

The Feminist Curriculum

As with black and other minority group studies, women's studies programs have experienced extensive development since the early 1970s. It is estimated that 600 women's studies programs exist in American colleges and universities.[13]

Women's studies generally incorporate the following curricular goals: (1) encouraging a reassessment of cultural attitudes and values to correct gender discrimination, (2) encouraging a more accurate and realistic examination of the role of women and their contributions to American life, and (3) encouraging social, political, and economic change by generating a more egalitarian perspective. As with black, Hispanic, and ethnic studies programs, there is debate over the issue of maintaining separate women's studies programs or infusing content and issues related to feminist education throughout the curriculum. Journals such as the *Women's Studies Quarterly* examine the theories and issues related to feminist education.

Although most women's studies programs are found in colleges and universities, recent scholarship in feminist perspectives and education has also affected elementary and secondary schooling. Textbooks and course content, especially in history and the social studies, have been revised to include discussions of women's contributions and issues. In analyzing the "gender-balanced classroom," Frances Muher has called for the transformation of content in a way that "takes equal note of female experiences of and viewpoints on the world."[14] Instructional planning delivery should recognize the differences in student experiences produced by gender as well as race and socioeconomic status.

Whither the Multicultural Dimension of American Education: A Summary View

Multiculturalism is a new and also ill-defined phenomenon in American education. Today, many state departments of education, state legislatures, and accrediting agencies require units or courses on multiculturalism in the school curriculum and in

13. Paula R. Holleran, "The Feminist Curriculum: Issues for Survival in Academe," in Barbara Hillyer Davis, ed., *Feminist Education*, Special Topic Edition of the *Journal of Thought*, 30, No. 3 (Fall 1985) (Norman: University of Oklahoma, 1985), p. 25.
14. Frances Muher, "Pedagogies for the Gender-Balanced Curriculum," in Barbara Hillyer Davis, ed., *Feminist Education*, Special Topic Edition of the *Journal of Thought*, 30, No. 3 (Fall 1985), (Norman: University of Oklahoma, 1985), p. 49.

teacher training programs. Ethnic and racial groups and organizations have argued for the recognition of their particular group's contribution to American culture. In many respects, this is as it should be. A portrayal of the American experience that omits or neglects the contributions of the racial and ethnic groups that are part of American life is distorted and incomplete. It is also time that racial, ethnic, and sexual stereotyping ends in our schools. At the same time, it is important that multicultural education not be just another fad that will be discarded. The various books, articles, and materials that are being produced on multicultural education must be written accurately, organized carefully, and follow the best canons of scholarship.

The public school philosophy in regard to multicultural education also must be developed carefully. It was always a distortion of American life to portray the American experience as exclusively white, male, Anglo-Saxon, and Protestant. Multicultural education can correct this narrow view of American life. On the other hand, public schooling also needs to emphasize the commonalities of American culture. The term *common school* means that there is something in common that all Americans share. The public school philosophy—as it develops its multicultural dimensions—will need to reflect the commonalities or consensus of American life and also the cultural differences that enrich that common life.

DISCUSSION QUESTIONS

1. Define and distinguish among *Americanization*, *the melting pot theory*, and *cultural pluralism*.
2. Examine the various changes that have occurred in the public school ideology toward African Americans.
3. Analyze the Hispanic-American cultural experience as it relates to education.
4. Analyze the educational experience of a particular Asian-American group.
5. Analyze the educational experience of a particular Native-American group.
6. Define *multicultural education*.
7. Examine the general educational experience of American women in terms of historical trends, sexual stereotyping, and the feminist curriculum.

FIELD EXERCISES

1. Invite the director of the African-American studies program at your college or university to describe the program to your class.
2. Invite representatives of Hispanic-American organizations to visit your class to present their educational objectives.
3. Invite representatives of Asian-American organizations to visit your class to present their educational objectives.
4. Prepare a directory of multicultural resources in your community, such as ethnic and racial museums, organizations, and cultural centers.
5. Examine several textbooks used in elementary and secondary schools. Identify examples of ethnic or racial stereotyping.

6. Examine selected secondary school history textbooks and analyze their treatment of Native Americans.

7. Compare and contrast selected secondary school textbooks published in the 1950s with books published in the 1990s.

SUGGESTED READINGS

BANKS, JAMES A. *Multiethnic Education: Theory and Practice*. Boston: Allyn & Bacon, 1981.

BENNETT, CHRISTINE I. *Comprehensive Multicultural Education: Theory and Practice*. Boston: Allyn & Bacon, 1986.

BERRY, MARY F., AND BLASSINGAME, JOHN W. *Long Memory: The Black Experience in America*. New York: Oxford University Press, 1982.

BULLOCK, HENRY A. *A History of Negro Education in the South: From 1619 to the Present*. Cambridge, Mass.: Harvard University Press, 1967.

DAVIS, BARBARA HILLYER, ED. *Feminist Education*. Special Topic Edition of the *Journal of Thought*, 30, No. 3 (Fall 1985). Norman: University of Oklahoma, 1985.

EDMUNDS, R. DAVID. *American Indian Leaders: Studies in Diversity*. Lincoln: University of Nebraska Press, 1980.

FRANKLIN, JOHN HOPE. *From Slavery to Freedom*. New York: Knopf, 1967.

FUCHS, ESTELLE, AND HAVIGHURST, ROBERT J. *To Live on This Earth: American Indian Education*. Garden City, N.Y.: Doubleday, 1973.

GERBER, DAVID A. *The Making of an American Pluralism: Buffalo, New York, 1825–60*. Urbana: University of Illinois Press, 1989.

GILLIGAN, CAROL. *In a Different Voice: Psychological Theory and Women's Development*. Cambridge, Mass.: Harvard University Press, 1982.

GOLDFIELD, DAVID R. *Black, White, and Southern: Race Relations and Southern Culture, 1940 to the Present*. Baton Rouge: Louisiana State University Press, 1990.

GOLLNICK, DONNA M., AND CHINN, PHILIP C. *Multicultural Education in a Pluralistic Society*. St. Louis: C. W. Mosby, 1983.

HARVEY, KAREN D., HARJO, LISA D., AND JACKSON, JANE K. *Teaching About Native Americans*. Washington, D.C.: National Council for the Social Studies, 1990.

IRVINE, JACQUELINE JORDAN. *Black Students and School Failure: Policies, Practices, and Prescriptions*. New York: Greenwood Press, 1990.

JOHNSTON, BASIL H. *Indian School Days*. Norman: University of Oklahoma Press, 1989.

KEHOE, ALICE B. *North American Indians: A Comprehensive Account*. Englewood Cliffs, N.J.: Prentice-Hall, 1981.

KENNEDY, JOHN F. *A Nation of Immigrants*. New York: Harper & Row, 1964.

KINCHELOE, JOE L., KINCHELOE, THERESA S., AND STALEY, GEORGE H., EDS. *Indian Education: 1984*. Special Topic Edition of the *Journal of Thought*, 19, No. 3, (Fall 1984). Norman: University of Oklahoma, 1984.

KRUG, MARK M. *The Melting of the Ethnics— Education of the Immigrants, 1880–1914*. Bloomington, Ind.: Phi Delta Kappa Educational Foundation, 1976.

NASH, GARY B. *Red, White and Black: The Peoples of Early America*. Englewood Cliffs, N.J.: Prentice-Hall, 1982.

SIKKEMA, MILDRED AND NIVEKAWA, AGMES. *Design for Cross-Cultural Learning*. Yarmouth, Me.: Intercultural Press, 1987.

STEINER, STAN. *Fusang: The Chinese Who Built America*. New York: Harper & Row, 1979.

SZASZ, MARGARET CONNELL. *Education and the American Indian: The Road to Self-Determination Since 1928*. Albuquerque: University of New Mexico Press, 1977.

TIEDT, PAMELA L., AND TIEDT, IRIS M. *Multicultural Teaching: A Handbook of Activities, Information and Resources*. Boston: Allyn & Bacon, 1989.

UTLEY, ROBERT M. *The Indian Frontier of the American West 1846–1890*. Albuquerque: University of New Mexico Press, 1984.

8

International Education and the Teacher

Chapter 8 examines the international dimension of education; it is intended to build a bridge between education, schooling, and teaching in American society and the larger world community. The chapter will also include a brief foray into comparative education and compare Soviet and Japanese education to American education. The general focusing questions that will be answered as you read this chapter include the following:

1. What are the dimensions of international education?
2. What are the major trends affecting world education?
3. How has education served as an agency of modernization and development?
4. In comparative terms, what similarities and differences exist among Soviet, Japanese, and American education?

The Dimensions of International Education

International education is not a new subject, but it is often neglected. Throughout its history, education has had an international dimension. In the seventeenth century, Comenius sought to create a *Pansophist* philosophy of education—one that incorporated all knowledge—as a means of bringing conflicting religious and national groups together in a commonly shared peace. In the nineteenth century, Horace Mann, Henry Barnard, and other American educators traveled to Europe to find and import innovative educational methods such as Pestalozzi's and Froebel's to the United States. In the 1960s, both Peace Corps volunteers, many of whom were teachers, and development educators worked in overseas assignments where they introduced American educational concepts and methods to the schools of developing countries. The 1970s saw American educators interested in the idea of "open education," which was based on the British Primary School. The national reports on education of the 1980s, such as *A Nation at Risk*, warned that American schools and students are academically deficient in mathematics, science, and other areas in comparison to their counterparts in foreign countries, especially Germany and Japan. American education, then, does not exist in isolation but is influenced by events and forces of a global nature.

America's International Frontier: An Imperative

While there have been many advocates of international education in the past, the call for a more concerted effort to educate Americans internationally gained momentum in the late 1980s. Historically, arguments for incorporating international education into the school curriculum and into teacher education generally came from advocates who sought to develop "worldmindness," intercultural understanding, and a rather generalized global perspective.[1] During the late 1980s, the arguments for international education gained a new group of proponents. Political leaders, among them the nation's governors, and business leaders became advocates of international education. These new proponents of internationalizing the curriculum were most concerned about the growing economic interdependence of the world and the role that the United States would play in the new economic configurations that were rapidly emerging. Many state governors were so concerned that they commissioned a task force to study and make recommendations to improve international education. Business leaders, too, shared the concern about the nation's economic productivity and position in the world marketplace. Addressing the imperative for international education, Governor Gerald Baliles of Virginia stated:

The international frontier is no longer the future — a new age has arrived. The evidence abounds. A common market in Western Europe will be finalized in 1992. The United States and Canada are on a ten-year path toward free trade. World output is shifting dramatically to Japan and the Pacific Rim. And, in an attempt to encourage trade and foreign investment, the People's Republic of China and the Soviet Union are experimenting with capitalism. By the beginning of the 21st century, the economic terrain will be one of large trading blocs, instead of individual countries, trying to maximize their growth through trade.[2]

The Task Force on International Education of the National Governor's Association identified several weaknesses that have a limiting effect on America's role in the emerging new economic order. American students and adults are often geographically illiterate. Many are unable to locate countries on a map. For example, one-half of American adults polled in a national survey could not locate South Africa on a map and could not identify at least one South American country. In addition, Americans are unprepared linguistically for the international communication that an emerging world economy requires. Most Americans speak English exclusively, and only a minority of elementary and secondary students is studying a

---

1. For example, see Robert G. Hanvey, *An Attainable Global Perspective* (New York: Global Perspectives in Education, 1982). For an historical overview, see Willard M. Kniep, *A Critical Review of the Short History of Global Education: Preparing for New Opportunities* (New York: Global Perspectives in Education, 1985).
2. Task Force on International Education, *America in Transition: The International Frontier* (Washington, D.C.: National Governor's Association, 1989), p. iv.

foreign language. The task force noted that, in a 1987 study, "only one in five American high school graduates" were found to have completed two years foreign language study.[3]

To infuse international education into their state elementary, secondary, and higher education programs, the governors' task force developed a state action agenda that included the following recommendations:

1. Incorporating international education throughout the curriculum so that it becomes part of the basic education of all elementary and secondary students
2. Developing the proficiency of elementary and secondary students in foreign languages by beginning such study as early as first grade and by developing second language summer- and after-school programs
3. Improving classroom teachers' knowledge about international education through inservice programs and curriculum development
4. Disseminating information about resources and materials available to schools and teachers for the purpose of international education
5. Ensuring that college and university graduates are "knowledgeable about the broader world and conversant in another language"
6. Calling upon the business community "to support international education" in the nation's schools and colleges
7. Providing the business community with access to international education, especially information about "export markets, trade regulations, and overseas cultures"[4]

Guidelines on Internationalizing Teacher Education

Although many educators have advocated international education, world consciousness, and a global perspective, the concept of international education, while meaningful, has often eluded precise definition. A working definition has been developed by the International Council on Education for Teaching (ICET), which is associated with the American Association of Colleges for Teacher Education (AACTE):

> *International education is the process by which people acquire a global perspective to explain events in recognition of the increasing interdependence of nations and cultures. This understanding is essential for effective citizenship as well as, ultimately, human survival.*[5]

To encourage a global perspective in teacher education programs, the AACTE in collaboration with the ICET and the National Council for Foreign Language and International Studies has prepared *Guidelines for International Teacher Education*. According to these guidelines, "International Education is a fundamental part of general and professional studies" and is the "preparation for social, political, and economic realities that humans experience in a culturally diverse and interdependent

---

3. Ibid., pp. 2–4.
4. Ibid., pp. 15–20. These recommendations have been reorganized by the author to incorporate the task force's major objectives and subobjectives.
5. American Association of Colleges for Teacher Education, *A Global Perspective for Teacher Education* (Washington, D.C.: AACTE, 1983), p. 1.

world." Students preparing for careers as teachers should be provided with the knowledge that makes it possible to understand the meaning and impact of global events. This knowledge base should facilitate their intelligent and responsible participation in global foreign policy decisions as individuals and citizens. Teacher education programs should be infused with a global knowledge base designed to develop "competencies and sensitivities for perceiving, believing, evaluating, and participating in the complex human and ecological interactions that characterize the globe." Such an internationalized curriculum should cultivate

1. A sensitivity that other people may view the world differently.
2. An awareness of prevailing and emergent world conditions, developments, and trends.
3. An awareness of the interdependency of local economic and social patterns with global systems.
4. A realization that developments in other countries may have an impact on one's profession or business.
5. A knowledge of the social movements that have created goals and values that "transcend national cultures and ideologies."
6. A knowledge of and sensitivity to the ethical issues that arise from an awareness of global conditions.[6]

Types of International Education

This section identifies some of the major types or categories of international education that can be found in American schools and colleges. In terms of curricular development, two basic strategies for internationalizing the curriculum are used: separate courses and/or programs, or infusion throughout the curriculum.

Foreign Policy, or *Foreign Relations Studies*, is a program or course that is usually offered in colleges and universities. At the secondary level, it is generally a part of the American history or social studies curriculum. Its major focus is to educate Americans about the world role of the United States in terms of national interests, commitments, policies, and treaties.[7]

World Culture Education, sometimes called *Intercultural Education*, is designed to increase knowledge, understanding, and appreciation for peoples who have cultures that are different from our own. Often it relies heavily on anthropology and sociology. As a broad field study, it can be used to facilitate linkages between multicultural examinations of American domestic society and cultures in the world context. Although often not identified specifically as a course, world culture concepts and materials have been infused into the social studies curriculum at the elementary and secondary levels.

---

6. American Association of Colleges for Teacher Education, *Guidelines for International Teacher Education* (Washington, D.C.: AACTE, 1989), p. 6. The author has condensed some of the curriculum objectives.
7. See, for example, Robert Wesson, *International Relations in Transition* (Englewood Cliffs, N.J.: Prentice Hall, 1990).

Peace Education is an old and continuing form of international education.[8] It often assumes that international tensions, terrorism, and wars are the consequences of racial or ethnic stereotyping, economic exploitation, or extreme nationalism. By examining these tension-generating conditions, it assumes that they can be defused. It also assumes that knowledge of differing peoples and their cultures will contribute to international understanding, appreciation, and peace. It often suggests that the therapeutic techniques used to resolve interpersonal tensions can be applied internationally.

Regional Area Studies generally are found in colleges or universities, but they have also had an impact on elementary and secondary schools. They provide an interdisciplinary examination of a particular region of the world, such as the Soviet Union and Eastern Europe, Latin America, India, Southeast Asia, or Africa. Rather than relying on a single academic discipline, regional or area studies involve an interdisciplinary approach in which historians, economists, political scientists, sociologists, and anthropologists use their disciplines to examine a particular region.

Development Education refers to strategies, primarily educational, that are used to assist underdeveloped nations—often characterized by a subsistence economy, with concomitant illiteracy, poverty, and endemic disease—to solve these problems. A general assumption is that developing countries can selectively borrow techniques from developed nations and apply them to improve their agricultural, industrial, and educational structures. Recent trends in development education will be examined in more detail later in this chapter.

International Exchange Programs and *Foreign Study Programs* exist for elementary, secondary, and college students, as well as for teachers, administrators, and college professors. These programs have enabled Americans to study abroad and have brought foreign students and teachers to the United States. A number of federal laws—the Fulbright Act of 1946, the U.S. Information and Exchange Act of 1948, the Agricultural Trade Development and Assistance Act of 1954, and the Mutual Educational and Cultural Exchange Act of 1961—provided the funds for scholarly and educational exchange. Today, local school districts send American students abroad and act as host institutions for visiting students from foreign countries. Many American colleges and universities also offer a "junior year abroad" and other programs.

Global Education is the most recent development that relates to internationalizing American education. Alger and Harf, two leading proponents of global education, have defined it as "education that enables people to make decisions while taking into account the ways in which they are affected by a diversity of economic, social, political, military, and natural phenomena that link together peoples of the world."[9] In contrast to approaches that construe international education to be the study of relations between nations, global education emphasizes the study of economic, educational, social, political, and military transactions between peoples on a worldwide basis.

8. An eloquent commentary on peace education can be found in Lawrence E. Metcalf, *Peace Education Within a War System* (Society of Professors of Education, 1985).
9. Chadwick F. Alger and James E. Harf, "Global Education: Why? For Whom? About What?" Unpublished typescript. (Columbus: Ohio State University, 1984), p. 1.

Worldwide Educational Trends

In the 1980s, several global trends had an impact on education in both the developed Western nations, such as the United States, and in developing third-world nations in Africa and Asia. These trends were products of the massive educational expansions that had occurred in the 1960s and 1970s. The emerging nations of Africa and Asia had made large investments in education as an instrument of national development. Simultaneously, the developed industrial nations of Western Europe and the United States had also expanded their educational systems to democratize educational opportunity by including groups that had limited access to schools in the past.[10]

The expansion of education that had reduced illiteracy in the developing nations also had the effect of creating greater demands for education. However, the inflation of the 1980s had reduced the financial resources available for investments in more educational facilities, schools, and teachers. In some cases, many secondary school and college graduates were unable to find employment because of sluggish economies.

In developed countries, such as the United States and the United Kingdom, technological change caused the stagnation of the industrial sector and the expansion of low-paying jobs in service areas. New jobs, for a small number of highly trained people, developed in the high-tech industries. The result in both developing and developed countries was to weaken the creditability of formal education as the appropriate pathway to economic security and social status.

The late 1970s and the early 1980s also saw dramatically different rates of population increase between the developed and the developing countries. The number of children of school age either remained stable or decreased in the developed nations. Declining enrollments in these countries limited the quantitative expansion of schooling. In contrast, the school-age population in the developing countries of Asia and Africa increased at a rate that exceeded their capacity to provide educational facilities and services. Although the rates of population growth differed, both developed and developing countries shifted their educational priorities from quantitative expansion to a reconsideration of issues of quality.

Changing Conceptions of Development Education

In the 1960s, American educators and universities were both involved in development education programs designed to aid underdeveloped countries to solve their social, economic, health, and educational problems.[11] Among these problems were large population increases that exceeded economic resources, poor sanitation and health services, low food intake per person despite labor-intensive agriculture, high rates of illiteracy, and wealth concentrated in a small elite class. The development theories of the 1960s assumed that Western technology, methods, and education

10. Philip H. Coombs, *The World Crisis in Education: The View from the Eighties* (New York: Oxford University Press, 1985), pp. 3–5.
11. For a discussion of development education, see Don Adams and Robert M. Bjork, *Education in Developing Areas* (New York: David McKay, 1969), pp. 20–46.

could be used to improve the economic condition of these underdeveloped lands. Because the underdeveloped nations of Asia and Africa were traditional rural and agricultural societies, development education was often seen as an agency of their modernization.

In the 1960s and in some instances in the 1980s, development education followed a "top-down" strategy. Development programs were designed by planners in the central government who were aided by Western experts. Modernization projects for industrialization, transportation, and agriculture were often large scale, with little or no involvement of the people living in the poorer rural areas. The strategies generally involved industrial development in urban areas and the introduction of export agriculture in rural areas. Educationally, agricultural extension centers were used to encourage modern farming techniques, and vocational training programs were established to provide trained personnel for industrial modernization.

The top-down, or linear, models of development education had some limited successes. For example, the "green revolution" in India enabled that country to improve its output of food through the introduction of high-yield hybrid rice and wheat. In 1983, the government of the People's Republic of China inaugurated concerted efforts to modernize service technology and education. China's modernization efforts involve sending educators, scientists, and engineers to American and other Western universities for up-to-date training in their fields. American educators are also teaching and advising in China. Like many efforts at modernization, the process had results that the Chinese Communist government and party wanted and also consequences they did not anticipate. As Chinese educators and students interacted more freely with the West, they also wanted to encourage greater freedoms in the People's Republic of China. University students in Beijing organized a prodemocracy movement to encourage reforms aimed at liberalizing Chinese society and higher education. However, the leaders of the Communist government used the army to brutally suppress the movement, and a massacre of prodemocracy students and their supporters occurred in Tienanmen Square in the Chinese capital on June 4, 1989.

The linear development or modernization programs of the 1960s also had some unanticipated consequences. In some countries, the gap between urban and rural areas widened. In the rural areas of many developing countries, less than 10 percent of the school-age population completed school. The trend to grow crops for export also created numbers of landless peasants whose lands were expropriated by large corporations.[12]

In the 1980s, a more humanistic, grassroots concept of development education emerged that challenged the older linear, top-down approach. Emphasizing rural development, the grassroots approach relies on the people of the local community to define their needs and establish their projects.[13] Instead of large-scale development

---

12. Coombs, *World Crisis in Education*, pp. 15–17.

13. An example of the humanistic approach to development education is Pierre Pradervand, *Development Education: The 20th Century Survival and Fulfillment Skill* (Bern: Swiss Federal Department of Foreign Affairs, 1982). Also, see InterFaith Hunger Appeal, *Education for Development* (New York: InterFaith Hunger Appeal, 1989).

projects, the local projects are smaller and less expensive. They are directed to improving sanitation, health care, and education at the local level. Such local projects have often relied more on "nonformal" education than on formal schooling.

Nonformal education is an educational activity "carried on outside" the formal system that provides "selected types of learning." It may include agricultural training, adult literacy, occupational training, health instruction, and other educational activities.[14]

The Comparative View

This section of the chapter provides a brief introduction to *comparative education*. Comparative analysis examines education in different countries in its historical, social, political, economic, and cultural contexts. It seeks to identify similarities and differences between educational systems. Essentially, school organization and structures exhibit some similarities throughout the world in that they are age-specific to children and adolescents, are organized hierarchically, and have a curriculum that is sequential. However, these structural similarities of schooling are given substance and philosophical and ideological direction by the cultural context in which they operate. It is this contextual area of language, politics, tradition, religion, and society that creates the differences between systems.

Comparative education has many uses for American teachers. It is a means of broadening perspectives so that teachers understand that they are participants in a global undertaking. Comparisons between education in the United States and other nations also provide a perspective for examining one's own educational system in terms of the systems of other nations. Although American education can be compared with that of many other nations, our focus here is on Japan and the Soviet Union.

Japanese Education

When Americans look abroad for educational models that can be used to improve the performance of American schools and students, they are often intrigued and challenged by Japan's economic and educational success. For example, an editorial in the *Chicago Tribune* asked, "Are Japanese children smarter than American youngsters? Have the Japanese found a way to produce not only high quality cars and stereos but brighter people?"[15] After calling attention to the social and cultural differences between Japan and the United States, another *Tribune* editorial identified the following areas in which American educators could learn from Japan:

1. Considering the high level of Japanese academic achievement, Americans "should raise their assumptions of what children are capable of learning, especially in math and science."
2. American youngsters "should spend more time" both in and out of school on academic learning.

14. Coombs, *World Crisis in Education*, pp. 20–25.
15. "How Japan Builds Brains," *Chicago Tribune*, November 24, 1985, sec. 2, p. 12.

3. "The Japanese emphasis on teaching productive work habits—concentration, attention to detail, order, diligence—can be a model for American schools."

4. Americans could emulate the Japanese by teaching teachers to accept responsibility for the quality of their schools and for their students' academic progress.[16]

While educational borrowing among nations has gone on throughout history, it needs to be recognized that the imported idea, structure, method, or innovation works to the degree that it fits the cultural context into which it is transplanted. When the Japanese developed their educational system in the late nineteenth and early twentieth centuries, they borrowed heavily from the United Kingdom, France, Germany, and the United States; however, they made sure that the transplanted ideas did not affect the basic Japanese core of culture, attitudes, and values.

Japanese and American cultures are very different. First, Japan's culture is highly homogeneous, while that of the United States is highly diverse and multi-ethnic. Second, the United States is a much larger nation in land area and population. Third, Japan is much more limited than the United States in natural resources, including food supply. Because of the differences in resources, the Japanese outlook has been shaped by a fear of economic fragility. Fourth, the Japanese system of schools is highly centralized and more easily controlled than is the diverse, locally controlled American system.[17] With these differences in mind, we can consider the basic outlines of education in Japan.

Modern education began in Japan with the issuance of the Education System Order in 1872 following the Meiji Restoration. Designed to end feudalism and to modernize Japan, the Meiji government looked to education as an important means of national development. The new educational system was organized into elementary schools, middle schools, and universities. By 1900, the educational system was extended to include vocational schools, girls' high schools, normal schools, and university preparatory schools. In 1908, the elementary school program was extended from four to six years, and attendance was made compulsory.

The leaders who developed Japan's educational system were Shimpei Eto, the first minister of education, and Yukichi Fukuzawa, the country's leading educational theorist. Under their guidance, Japan's new schools embarked on a defensive modernization program to build a strong nation able to preserve its integrity against the colonial designs of the major Western powers. The Japanese educators used a two-pronged strategy of educational development: (1) They were determined to preserve and transmit the basic core values of traditional Japanese culture, and (2) they were prepared to adopt specific Western techniques, especially scientific and technological ones, and apply them to Japan's modernization.[18]

After Japan's defeat in World War II, the Fundamental Law of Education, enacted in 1947, set Japanese schools on a democratic course that had as its primary aim the education of "self-reliant citizens of a peaceful and democratic state and

16. "Japanese Lessons for the U.S." *Chicago Tribune*, September 21, 1985, sec. 1, p. 12.
17. A highly readable and useful examination of Japanese education is provided by Merry White, *The Japanese Educational Challenge: A Commitment to Children* (New York: Free Press, 1987).
18. Cynthia Hearn Dorfman, ed., *Japanese Education Today* (Washington, D.C.: U.S. Government Printing Office, 1987), pp. 77–79.

A Japanese elementary school science class.

community with a respect for human values."[19] The series of educational laws that followed the Fundamental Law of 1947 established the present-day system of schools: a six-year elementary school, a three-year lower secondary school, a three-year upper secondary school, and a four-year university.

All Japanese children between the ages of 6 and 15 are required to attend the six-year elementary schools and three-year lower secondary schools, which are state supported, or their private equivalents. As of 1985, Japan had 25,040 elementary schools staffed by 468,200 teachers and a student enrollment of 11,095,372; there were 11,131 lower secondary schools staffed by 278,900 teachers and a student enrollment of 5,990,183.[20] The elementary and lower secondary school curricula are centralized and standardized by the Ministry of Education, which in its "Course of Study" prescribes the subjects and the time allotted to teaching them. The elementary curriculum consists of Japanese language, social studies, arithmetic, science, music, art and handicrafts, homemaking, physical education, moral education, and special activities. The lower secondary school curriculum continues most of these subjects but at a more advanced level. For example, arithmetic now becomes mathematics; physical education is broadened to include health; and handicrafts become industrial arts.

The three-year upper secondary school offers the following curricula: general academic, technical, commercial, domestic arts, and other specialties. Japan's 5,453

19. *Facts About Japan: Educational System* (Tokyo: Ministry of Foreign Affairs, 1985), p. 2.
20. Ibid., p. 4.

upper secondary schools employ 258,600 teachers and enroll 5,177,681 students.[21] The required subjects, prescribed by the Ministry of Education, are Japanese language, social studies, mathematics, science, health and physical education, and fine arts.

At the higher education level, there are junior colleges, technical colleges, and universities. The 460 universities, with a combined faculty of 110,700 teachers, enroll 1,848,698 students. The university admission process, based largely on the "Joint Achievement Test"—a unified examination—is highly selective. Japanese students spend much of their study, time, and effort in preparing for this difficult examination, which determines if they will be admitted to university study. For the elite group who passes the examination, a university education provides entry into preferred business and government positions. Although frequently criticized by educators, the university entrance examination system appears to be a durable and dominant part of the Japanese educational system.

A Nation at Risk and other national reports on education have attributed Japan's success as a leader in the world economy to its high rate of academic achievement, particularly in mathematics, science, and technology. At times, it has been recommended that American schools imitate certain features of Japanese education. However, this is not feasible. Besides the cultural and geographical differences noted above, the organization and control of Japanese and American education are very different. Whereas American schools are locally organized and controlled, Japan has a highly centralized national system that is directed by the Ministry of Education. Unlike the many local options that prevail in decentralized American schools, the curriculum content, textbook selection, school organization, and teacher assignment in Japan are centrally determined. This tendency toward centralization is designed to ensure that Japan's schools fulfill the following goals: (1) to transmit a common and unified body of knowledge and values conducive to cultural unity and cohesion and (2) to develop the specific scientific and technological skills that promote the nation's economy and security.[22]

Instruction in Japanese schools is more teacher-controlled and prescribed than in American schools. Japanese education is more goal-specific but provides fewer opportunities than in American schools for creativity and problem solving. Japanese students spend more time in school and in studying than do their American counterparts. They attend five-and-a-half days per week in a longer school year. Japanese instruction is geared to the highly selective examinations that admit only a small percentage of students to universities. American schools have emphasized equality of educational opportunity throughout the educational ladder, up to and including college and university education.

Soviet Education

During the long Cold War that began in 1947 and ended in 1988, the United States and the Union of Soviet Socialist Republics were global adversaries. American and

---

21. Ibid.
22. William B. Boyd, "Education in Japan," *The Wingspread Journal*, Special Section, Summer 1984, p. 1.

Soviet interests and policies clashed in eastern Europe, where the Soviets had established satellite Communist states; in Asia, Mao Zedong had established the People's Republic of China; and even in the Western Hemisphere, in Castro's Cuba, where Soviet missiles were located. It was only the withdrawal of these missiles from Cuba that prevented armed conflict and perhaps nuclear war between the giant adversaries. According to the American version of Cold War rhetoric, the United States was a modern-day Athens, the defender of democracy in the world. In contrast, the Soviet Union was depicted as the modern Sparta, run by a rugged military oligarchy bent on spreading the totalitarian Communist ideology throughout the world. During the cold war, education and schools in the two rival countries were frequently compared. In 1957, for example, when the Soviets succeeded in orbiting the artificial satellite Sputnik around the earth, American schools were blamed for failing to educate a scientific elite that could match the Soviet performance in space. These comparisons of Soviet and American schools led to educational reforms in the United States that included enacting the National Defense Education Act to bolster American efforts in mathematics and science education.

Changes began to occur in the Soviet Union and in Soviet–American relations after 1985, when Mikhail Gorbachev became the general secretary of the Commu-

A photograph of a poster glorifying Lenin. The translation of the slogan reads, "The accomplishments of the Soviet people continue the cause of the October Revolution; a realization of the ideas of the great Lenin. Let us carry the recommendations of the 25th Congress into life." Today, the cult of Lenin is being downgraded in the Soviet Union.

nist Party Union and then later became the Soviet president. With Gorbachev's rise to power, momentous and unexpected changes occurred in the Soviet Union, especially in its domestic and foreign policies. Upon assuming power, Gorbachev found that the Soviet Union's economy had become stagnant and that policy-making was taking place at a snail's pace due to rigid bureaucratic centralization. In the late 1980s, Gorbachev developed new policy guidelines: *perestroika* (restructuring, or transformation), *glasnost* (public openness), *demokratizatsiia* (democratization), and *novoe myshlenie* (new strategy in foreign policy). As a result of these policies, phenomenal changes have occurred in central and eastern Europe.[23] Former satellite nations—Czechoslovakia, Poland, Hungary—established non-Communist governments. In 1989, the Berlin Wall, erected early in the Cold War to separate East and West Berlin, was torn down, and in 1990 East and West Germany were reunited as one nation. At the same time that these highly important developments occurred, the progress of Gorbachev's policies in bringing about change in the Soviet economic and political system was slow and uneven.

In describing education in the Soviet Union, it is necessary to consider the ideological structures that developed after the Communist seizure of power in 1917 until the inauguration of the Gorbachev era in 1986. Recent developments of the Gorbachev reform era can then be placed in their historical and political context. When the legacy of over 70 years of Communist rule is considered along with the recent, brief era of reform, a more realistic assessment emerges.

In the Soviet Union, as in the United States or in any other country, it must be remembered, schooling reflects society's history, culture, ideology, politics, language, economy, and values. Comparisons of educational systems need to recognize that schooling exemplifies the life-style and value expectations of particular countries. Educational systems reflect different historical and socioeconomic contexts.

After V. I. Lenin's Bolsheviks seized power and established a Communist state in 1917, Soviet leaders defined education as a total ideological process of creating the new "Soviet man and woman."[24] Basing educational philosophy and policies on Marxist-Leninist ideology, the Central Committee of the Communist Party was the key agency in determining educational priorities and the programs to achieve them. The major goal that the Central Committee sought to achieve was to eradicate old loyalties and create a new ideological conformity to the Soviet system. Equally important in the educational priorities of the various five-year plans was the transformation of the backward agricultural economy that the Communists inherited from their tsarist predecessors into a modern industrial, technological giant.

Lenin, the founder of the Soviet state, and his successors, especially Joseph Stalin and Leonid Brezhnev, regarded the radio, motion picture, press, books, art, television, and even the circus as nonformal education agencies to shape the ideological outlook of the Soviet people. The term *upbringing* was used to refer to the total attitudinal shaping of Soviet children and youth. In addition to the school, Commu-

---

23. Ben Eklof, *Soviet Briefing: Gorbachev and the Reform Period* (Boulder, Colo.: Westview Press, 1989), p. 1.

24. George S. Counts, *The Challenge of Soviet Education* (New York: McGraw-Hill, 1957), is still an excellent analysis of Soviet education as a total system of ideological formation.

nist Party youth organizations were used to provide recreational and educational activities. From ages 9 to 14, most Soviet children were members of the Young Pioneers. Older Soviet youth, from ages 14 to 26, were enrolled in the Komsolmol, the All-Union Leninist Communist Union of Youth. These organizations offered crafts, sports, music, dancing, and recreation, and they also built ideological commitment to the Communist Party through a continuous program of indoctrination.

When the 1980s began, Soviet schools, reflecting the Marxist-Leninist philosophy, had a definite political character. Nearly every classroom had a centrally and prominently displayed picture of Lenin. School bulletin boards carried Communist Party slogans calling upon children and youth to put forth their best effort in building a strong and modern Soviet nation. In ceremonies and exhibitions about the "Great Patriotic War," as World War II is called in the Soviet Union, Soviet children were imbued with a patriotic love for their motherland. In and out of school, evidence of the cult of Lenin could be seen. Daily, thousands of Soviets waited patiently in long lines to view, for a moment, Lenin's body in the mausoleum shrine in Red Square near the Kremlin's walls.

In the 1980s when Gorbachev came to power, the ideological uniformity that had marked Soviet society and education began to change. To encourage innovation, he sought to remove the stifling centralized bureaucracy of entrenched party officials. To revitalize the stagnating economy, he made the first efforts to introduce a market economy. The educational system, which had shaped Soviet society under Communist Party control and direction, had to be reformed so that it could be an agency of change rather than one of conformity and indoctrination. However, many of the ills of Soviet society—indifference, low-quality standards, social passivity, and bureaucratization—were also present in the school system.

In the spirit of *perestroika* and *glasnost*, the schools, which had once been used to create the conformist "new Soviet man and woman," were now called upon to educate the young generation with "nontraditional attitudes and values" and a risk-taking willingness to innovate.[25] In the spirit of *glasnost*, a number of critics within the Soviet Union argued that the schools themselves needed to be reformed before they could contribute effectively to the national restructuring. Critics claimed that the centralized educational bureaucracy and administrative rigidity made it difficult, if not impossible, to restructure the administration and curriculum of the school system. While there have been arguments for decentralizing the system, decision-making may have become more centralized. For example, in 1988, the Ministry of Education, the Ministry of Higher and Specialized Secondary Education, and the Committee on Public Education were merged into one All-Union Committee on Public Education.[26] While overlapping duplication of agency jurisdiction may be reduced by this merger, more policy-making power has been lodged in a single agency.

Another major challenge for Soviet education lies in the writing, publishing, and disseminating of textbooks and instructional materials that are free of the

---

25. Gerald Howard Read, "Education in the Soviet Union: Has *Perestroika* Met Its Match?" *Phi Delta Kappan*, 70 (April 1989), p. 606.

26. Ibid., p. 610.

censorship and ideological restraints of the past. Calling for "radical and immediate changes" in social science research, in textbook writing, and in introducing creative teaching methods, Gorbachev stated that these areas had "suffered the most from the personality cult, from bureaucratic methods of management, from dogmatism and incompetent meddling."[27]

An example of a new Soviet textbook that presents a more accurate historical portrayal is *The History of the USSR*, published in 1990. This new version of Soviet history no longer praises Stalin as a hero of the Soviet people, but tells about his forced labor camps, purges, and responsibility for the deaths of 20 million of his own people. Students reading the text found that the Communist Party had a diminished role in Soviet history. The Soviet decision to send soldiers into the war in Afghanistan, in which 15,000 died, is interpreted as "considerably undermining the credibility of the Soviet Union and its peaceful intentions."[28]

Gorbachev's efforts to reform Soviet political, economic, and educational structures have also had a consequence that he did not anticipate: the rekindling of nationalism among the various ethnic and language groups that comprise the Soviet Union. The Baltic states of Latvia, Lithuania, and Estonia are seeking independence from the Soviet Union. Demands for greater autonomy have developed among the Ukrainians, Belorussians, Azerbaijanis, and other groups. The rekindling of nationalism among the various peoples of the Soviet Union will be felt in the schools of the various republics of the Union. There will be greater demands that the school curricula in these republics reflect the local culture, language, and traditions.

The future also presents economic uncertainty for the Soviet people. In the midst of social unrest, the basic educational institution remains the 11-year unified school, which enrolls students ranging in ages from 6 to 17. The unified school is a single institution, in contrast to the variety of organizational forms in the United States, such as kindergarten and eight-year elementary school, four-year high school, two-year junior high school, and three-year middle school. Although the control of schools in the Soviet Union is undergoing change, it is highly centralized in comparison to the American pattern, where policies are determined by local school boards.

The 11-year school, which is officially designated the General and Polytechnical School with Vocational Training, is the main link in the Soviet educational system. Its goals are to (1) establish sound foundations in the basic academic skills and subjects, (2) cultivate a receptive attitude in students for socially useful work, and (3) instill a patriotic commitment to the Soviet system and state. It is estimated that the 190,000 11-year schools educate approximately 50 million students. In addition to the general 11-year school, there are also specialized schools for gifted students in science, foreign languages, art, music, and dance.

The curriculum of the 11-year schools is generally uniform throughout the Soviet Union. In elementary grades 1 through 3, the subjects studied are Russian

27. "Mikhail Gorbachev's Address at the 19th All-Union Party Conference," *Moscow News*, No. 27 (1988), p. 2, as quoted in Read, "Education in the Soviet Union," p. 611.

28. Vincent J. Schodolski, "New Soviet History Book Describes Stalin's Blunders," *Chicago Tribune*, September 30, 1990, sec. 1, p. 3.

Schoolchildren in an eleven-year school in the Soviet Union.

language (in non-Russian-speaking regions, youngsters begin to study Russian in the second grade); mathematics, which includes basic arithmetic, weights and measures, and elements of algebra and geometry; natural science, which includes geography and the study of plant and animal life; craft and vocational training; art and music; and physical education.

In grades 4 through 10, Soviet students pursue a highly structured and academically based subject-matter curriculum that includes the following:

> *Russian-language* studies
> *Russian, Soviet, and foreign literature* that emphasizes themes congenial to the Communist perspective
> *History* that follows a chronological organization
> *Social science* that examines the goals and problems of socialism
> *Mathematics*, a strongly emphasized subject that includes algebra, geometry, and trigonometry
> *Chemistry* and *physics*, priority subjects, along with other sciences, such as astronomy, biology, and geography
> *Vocational education*, taught for a polytechnic orientation
> *Foreign languages*, such as English, French, German, and Spanish, in which instruction begins in the fifth grade and continues through grade 10
> *Music, art*, and *physical training*

Upon completion of the 11-year school, graduates may enter institutions of higher education or the work force, depending upon their academic record, success on examinations, and the personnel needs of the Soviet state and economy. Institutions of higher education in the USSR include universities, pedagogical institutes for teacher preparation, technical institutes to train engineers and technicians, agricultural institutes, and schools of fine arts.

In contrast to the curricular uniformity of Soviet schools, curriculum and instruction in the United States assume a variety of organizational patterns and exhibit a diversity of teaching methods. In the Soviet Union, where curriculum and instruction are characterized by uniformity, emphasis is placed on the systematic study and mastery of the basic subjects, especially of mathematics, science, chemistry, physics, and native and foreign languages. Recitation, in which a student carefully answers the teacher's questions, is the common method of instruction.

Soviet schools place major emphasis on the basic sciences of chemistry and physics, subjects that contribute to the nation's goal of industrial and technological development. There is also a major emphasis on foreign languages, especially English, German, and, more recently, Spanish. Children in the USSR begin to study foreign languages in the fourth form, or grade, and continue to study that language for six years as students in the 11-year school. Those who continue into higher education may continue to study the language. This sustained effort contributes to mastery of a foreign language. In foreign-language instruction, another sharp contrast can be made between American and Soviet education. In the United States, foreign-language instruction is much more limited than in the USSR.

Soviet and American schools also present a striking paradox in the emphasis given to competition. In theory, Marxist-Leninist philosophy emphasizes the cooperation of co-workers in a classless society. In reality, however, academic competition is stressed, as are examinations and grades. Academic achievement is the means by which a student enters higher education and gains some choice of careers. Academic competitions, or marathons, are used to identify and reward able students. Although academic competition is also a part of American education, the various educational alternatives that exist reduce the acute sense of competition in American schools.

Conclusion

This chapter has introduced and examined the international and comparative dimensions of education. By identifying and defining the general categories of international education, it is hoped that the outlook of American teachers will be broadened to include the global or worldwide perspective. Because the United States is a nation of immigrants, some connections can be made between multicultural and international education. Finally, comparative education helps one to analyze one's own system of education.

DISCUSSION QUESTIONS

1. Analyze and evaluate the goals and objectives of international education.
2. Define the major types or categories of international education.

3. Identify and examine the arguments for and against the inclusion of international education in the curriculum.

4. Examine the changing conceptions of development education.

5. Compare and contrast Japanese and American education.

6. Compare and contrast education in the Soviet Union and education in the United States.

7. Examine the relationships between multicultural and international education.

FIELD EXERCISES

1. Conduct a panel discussion among those members of the class who have participated in foreign study or travel. Ask them to analyze their experiences in terms of impressions and awareness of other peoples from other countries and cultures.

2. Conduct a survey and prepare a guide to programs related to international education at your college or university.

3. In an informal survey of class members, identify the products of foreign origin that they own or have used on a specific day.

4. Conduct a survey and provide a guide to agencies in your community that have an international dimension.

5. Invite an international student attending your college or university to speak to the class on comparisons between education in her or his country and that in the United States.

6. Have a committee of students enrolled in the course prepare a questionnaire that surveys the class's knowledge of world affairs and events.

7. By reviewing the philosophy, programs, and courses offered by your department or school of education, determine how well it is internationalizing prospective teachers.

SUGGESTED READINGS

ADVISORY COUNCIL ON INTERNATIONAL EDUCATION. *International Education: Cornerstone of Competition: Innovative Programs from the States*. Washington, D.C.: Southern Governor's Association, 1987.

ADVISORY COUNCIL FOR INTERNATIONAL EDUCATIONAL EXCHANGE. *Educating for Global Competence: The Report of the Advisory Council for International Educational Exchange*. New York: Council on International Educational Exchange, 1988.

AMERICAN ASSOCIATION OF COLLEGES FOR TEACHER EDUCATION. *A Global Perspective for Teacher Education*. Washington, D.C.: AACTE, 1983.

———. *Guidelines for International Teacher Education*. Washington, D.C.: AACTE, 1989.

ANDERSON, CHARLES J. *International Studies for Undergraduates, 1987 Operations and Opinions*. Washington, D.C.: American Council on Education, 1988.

ASO, MAKOTO, AND AMANO, IKUO. *Education and Japan's Modernization*. Tokyo: Japan Times, 1983.

COGAN, JOHN J., AND SCHNEIDER, DONALD O., EDS. *Perspectives on Japan: A Guide for Teachers*. Washington, D.C.: National Council for the Social Studies, 1983.

COOMBS, PHILIP H. *The World Crisis in Education: The View from the Eighties*. New York: Oxford University Press, 1985.

CUMMINGS, WILLIAM K. *Education and Equality in Japan*. Princeton, N.J.: Princeton University Press, 1980.

GUMBERT, EDGAR B., ED. *A World of Strangers: International Education in the United Sates, Russia, Britain, and India*. Atlanta: Center for Cross Cultural Education, College of Education, Georgia State University, 1985.

——. *Fit to Teach: Teacher Education in International Perspective*. Atlanta: Center for Cross Cultural Education, College of Education, Georgia State University, 1990.

HAMILTON, JOHN MAXWELL. *Main Street America and the Third World*. Cabin John, Md.: Seven Locks Press, 1986.

INTERFAITH HUNGER APPEAL. *Education For Development*. New York: InterFaith Hunger Appeal, 1989.

JACOBY, SUSAN. *Inside Soviet Schools*. New York: Schocken Books, 1974.

KNIEP, WILLARD M. *A Critical Review of the Short History of Global Education: Preparing for New Opportunities*. New York: Global Perspectives in Education, 1985.

KOBAYASHI, TETSUYA. *Society, Schools and Progress in Japan*. New York: Pergamon Press, 1976.

LEVINE, ROBERT A. *Still the Arms Debate*. Brookfield, Vt.: Dartmouth, 1990.

MEDISH, VADIM. *The Soviet Union*. Englewood Cliffs, N.J.: Prentice-Hall, 1985.

NATIONAL GOVERNORS' ASSOCIATION. *Educating Americans for Tomorrow's World: State Initiatives in International Education*. Washington, D.C.: National Governors' Association, 1987.

PRADERVAND, PIERRE. *Development Education: The 20th Century Survival and Fulfillment Skill*. Bern: Swiss Federal Department of Foreign Affairs, 1982.

TASK FORCE ON INTERNATIONAL EDUCATION. *America in Transition: The International Frontier*. Washington, D.C.: National Governors' Association, 1989.

ROHLEN, THOMAS P. *Japan's High Schools*. Berkeley: University of California Press, 1983.

SHIELDS, JAMES J., ED. *Japanese Schooling: Patterns of Socialization, Equality, and Political Control*. University Park: Pennsylvania State University Press, 1989.

STUDY COMMISSION ON GLOBAL EDUCATION. *The United States Prepares for its Future: Global Perspectives in Education*. New York: Global Perspectives in Education, 1988.

U.S. DEPARTMENT OF EDUCATION JAPANESE STUDY TEAM. *Japanese Education Today*. Washington, D.C.: U.S. Government Printing Office, 1987.

WHITE, MERRY. *The Japanese Educational Challenge: A Commitment to Children*. New York: Free Press, 1987.

9

The Federal Role
in Education

As indicated in earlier chapters, after the American Revolution and during the early national period, organized education (or schooling) in the United States was related to the general civic welfare. In the American political system, each division of government plays an educational role. In the United States, educational authority was retained primarily by each of the states. Following the early New England precedents of local school control, the states, in turn, delegated important educational responsibilities to local school boards. Over the years, the once-limited federal role in education has grown. Chapter 9 examines the historical development and contemporary role of the federal government in American education.

The general focusing questions that will be answered as you read this chapter include the following:

1. Historically, what has been the educational role of the federal government?
2. What are some of the recent federal programs designed to aid education?
3. How have federal court decisions produced educational change?
4. What is the contemporary educational role of the federal government?
5. How has the federal government stimulated educational change?

An Historical Perspective of the Federal Role in Education

Earlier chapters examined the importance that the early American colonists gave to education and to establishing schools. A frequently cited historical example of this dedication to education is found in the Massachusetts Bay Colony Acts of 1642 and 1647, which required towns to provide instruction to children. Although differing educational patterns existed in the various states, the northern states generally imitated New England's decentralized pattern. The U.S. Constitution, ratified in 1789, did not refer specifically to education. According to the "reserved powers" clause of the Tenth Amendment, education was recognized as a state prerogative.

The federal government was responsible for administering the western territories before they were organized as states and admitted into the Union. The federal

174   Chapter 9

government encouraged and promoted education in the western territories with the greatest single resource available at the time—the land grant. Because land in the West was plentiful, the federal government used this resource to encourage internal improvements conducive to national development. Congress appropriated grants of federal land to stimulate road, canal, and later railroad construction. These internal improvements connected the various regions of the country, stimulated economic development, and promoted national unity. The establishment of schools in the western territories not only promoted the general welfare by facilitating popular education but also represented an internal improvement that spurred national development.

The precedents for the land grant system of aid to education occurred even before the Constitution's ratification. For example, the Land Ordinance of 1785, passed by Congress under the Articles of Confederation, provided that the Northwest Territories, the vast area of federal land bordered by the Ohio River and the Great Lakes, were to be divided into townships of 36 sections. The revenue earned from the sale of one of these sections was used to support education. A provision of the Northwest Ordinance of 1787 stated, "Religion, morality and knowledge being necessary to good government and the happiness of mankind, schools and the means of education shall forever be encouraged," affirming the federal government's early commitment to educational development.

Throughout much of the nineteenth century, the federal government used land grants to aid public education. From the time of the Ohio Enabling Act of 1802, the federal government granted land to each new state admitted to the Union. Throughout the history of the land grant mechanism, the federal government granted a total of 98.5 million acres to the states for public schools.[1]

Federal Aid After the Civil War

In 1862, Congress passed and President Lincoln signed the First Morrill Act, which provided the states with federal land grants to establish colleges for agricultural and industrial education. During Reconstruction, from 1865 to 1877, the federal government supported the education of the newly freed slaves.

During the Civil War, federal aid supported schools for a small number of liberated blacks on Virginia's offshore islands. When the Civil War ended, severe educational as well as economic and political problems plagued the devastated former Confederate states. Because of restrictions imposed by their previous condition of servitude, the vast majority of the 2.7 million freed blacks were illiterate. The federally funded Freedman's Bureau, under the leadership of General O. O. Howard, established and staffed schools for blacks in the South.

In the great majority of nations, education is a national function that is subject to central control. In many countries, a minister of education or secretary of education is a member of the national cabinet. In contrast, the United States has followed a policy of decentralized rather than centralized educational control.

1. Sidney Tiedt, *The Role of the Federal Government in Education* (New York: Oxford University Press, 1966), pp. 14–17.

Because of the tradition of decentralization, the United States did not have a secretary of education at cabinet level until the creation of the Department of Education by the Carter administration in 1979. There were, however, earlier departments of education and commissioners of education at the federal level.

For example, the first federal Department of Education was established in 1867 to (1) collect educational statistics in the states and territories and (2) promote education throughout the United States. The department, headed by Henry Barnard, existed at subcabinet level. It later became a bureau of the Interior Department, with a small staff and limited budget. Its function was not to frame national policies but to provide information on American education.

Nineteenth-Century Debates over Federal Aid

In the late nineteenth century, attempts to bring about greater federal involvement caused considerable controversy. In 1870, Representative George Hoar of Maine introduced a bill to establish a national system of education by setting federal standards that the states would be required to meet. In states failing to meet these standards, the federal government was to intervene by appointing a federal superintendent of state schools who would correct the deficiencies.[2] Hoar's bill, designed to improve educational opportunities for blacks in the southern states, encountered strong opposition. States rights advocates saw it encroaching on the reserved rights of states. Some public school organizations opposed it as an attempt to undermine local control. Roman Catholics condemned it as an attempt to create a vast monolithic public school system designed to destroy private schools. While Hoar's proposal failed, it outlined the kind of opposition that federal aid to education would encounter until well into the twentieth century.

In the 1880s, Senator Henry Blair of New Hampshire introduced federal aid legislation on five occasions. The Blair bill passed the Senate in 1884, 1886, and 1888 but failed in the House of Representatives.[3] Among the provisions of the Blair bill were the following:

1. Rather than using land grants, federal aid would be distributed as direct money grants based on the illiteracy rate.
2. States were to match the amount of federal funding in their own educational outlays.
3. States were to distribute school revenues without distinction of race or color.

The Blair bill was not enacted, but its major provisions anticipated the direction of federal assistance in the twentieth century. The move from land to cash grants marked a significant departure from earlier precedents for aid. While the Blair bill did not call for the ending of segregated schools, it did require an equitable distribution of funds to schools regardless of race. By requiring the states to match funds, the Blair bill was designed to encourage greater initiatives by state governments.

---

2. Gordon Lee, *The Struggle for Federal Aid: First Phase, 1870–1890* (New York: Teachers College Press, Columbia University, 1949), pp. 42–44.
3. Ibid., pp. 88–98.

As the nineteenth century ended, the essential arguments of the opponents and proponents of federal aid to and involvement in education were clear. The opponents argued that

1. There was no need for the federal government to support education as state and local funding were adequate.
2. Federal aid violated the long-standing principles of local educational control and initiative.
3. Federal aid would end the safeguard of educational decentralization and create a federally controlled monopoly over schools.

The proponents of federal aid used the following arguments:

1. Both the quantity and quality of education varies so greatly from state to state that children do not really enjoy equality of educational opportunity. Only the federal government can equalize state-to-state disparities.
2. Because education relates to the national interest, the federal government has an educational role to promote the general welfare.
3. Because of the mobility of the American population, the educational deficiencies of one state are likely to impact other states.
4. Some states have denied educational opportunity to certain of its citizens, particularly blacks in southern states, and the federal government should correct these inequalities.

Federally Assisted Vocational Education

In the twentieth century, the federal government encouraged vocational education. The movement for aid to vocational education illustrates the effect that special-interest groups can have on behalf of specific educational programs. When particular special-interest groups have educational objectives, they can be particularly effective in securing the passage of specific aid programs and often mandates at either the federal or state levels. General aid that requires a more integrated but less concentrated effort is more difficult to secure.

In the early twentieth century, the vocational education lobby was particularly strong. In 1917, the Smith–Hughes Act was passed to provide federal funding for agricultural, industrial and home economics education in secondary schools. The Smith–Hughes Act provided for (1) grants to states, on a matching basis, for teachers' salaries, curriculum development, and administrative costs in the specified vocational subjects and (2) establishment of the federal Board of Vocational Education to administer the program.

Throughout the twentieth century, vocational education received additional funding. In particular, the George–Barden Act of 1946 expanded vocational education programs and transferred their administration to the U.S. Office of Education.

Recent Federal Aid Programs

From the 1930s to the 1950s, the history of the federal role in education was one of controversy and debate and also of inaction. During the Depression of the 1930s, a number of Franklin Roosevelt's New Deal programs had an indirect rather than a direct educational impact.[4] For example, the Reconstruction Finance Act provided loans to school districts to aid in paying teachers' salaries, some school construction projects were financed by the Public Works Administration, the Civilian Conservation Corps provided instruction to its members, and the National Youth Administration also conducted some educational projects. During World War II, the Lanham Act (1941) aided school districts that were impacted by military mobilization with funds for school construction and provided auxiliary educational services, such as nursery schools.

In the post–World War II era, from 1945 until the enactment of the National Defense Education Act (NDEA) in 1958, federal aid to education opponents and often temporary coalitions came together to defeat federal aid proposals. During this period, southern conservative Democrats opposed federal aid to education on the grounds that it violated states' rights and would be used to end segregated, dual school systems.

Roman Catholic opposition was strong to any provision that denied federal aid to private and parochial schools. Equally determined, a number of organizations condemned aid to religious schools as a violation of the doctrine of separation of church and state. Fiscal conservatives believed that federal aid to schools would open the federal coffers to an unending demand for more money once the initial grants were made.

The National Defense Education Act

As the 1950s neared their end, the continuing debate over federal aid to education was interrupted by fears that the United States was losing its scientific, technological, and educational superiority to the Soviet Union. The Soviet success in orbiting the Sputnik space satellite and well-publicized American space failures at that time engendered a feeling that "something was wrong with American schools." Although this mood was grossly exaggerated by cold war fears, it brought contentious parties together in Congress to enact the National Defense Education Act in 1958. The NDEA was based upon congressional affirmation that

1. National security required the "fullest development of the mental resources and technical skills" of America's young men and women.
2. The national interest required that the federal government "give assistance to education for programs which are important to our national defense."[5]

The NDEA provided federal assistance to programs designed to improve instruction in mathematics, science, and foreign language—three curricular areas related to national defense. Mathematics and science were related to basic research and the development of technologies for the space age. Critics of foreign language

4. David Tyack, Robert Lowe, and Elisabeth Hansot, *Public Schools in Hard Times; The Great Depression and Recent Years* (Cambridge, Mass.: Harvard University Press, 1984), pp. 92–138.
5. Advisory Commission on Intergovernmental Relations, *The Federal Role in the Federal System: The Dynamics of Growth; Intergovernmentalizing the Classroom: Federal Involvement in Elementary and Secondary Education* (Washington, D.C.: U.S. Government Printing Office, 1981), p. 25.

instruction in the United States had charged that Americans were generally un-prepared to cope with an international multilingual reality. The NDEA also pro-vided grants on a matching basis to the states to improve guidance and counseling in secondary schools. It should be noted that the NDEA provided specific assistance to defense-related areas rather than general aid to all educational areas.

The Elementary and Secondary Education Act

The enactment of the Elementary and Secondary Education Act (ESEA) in 1965, under the Johnson administration, began a new era of federal aid to education. Unlike previous specific aid programs, ESEA provided general aid to elementary and secondary schools. By the mid-1960s, civil rights activism, racial unrest in large cities, and President Johnson's War on Poverty had identified new national priori-ties. As part of the War on Poverty, Johnson wanted to aid those who were disadvantaged economically, socially, racially, and educationally to enter the main-stream of what he termed the Great Society.

To avoid the religious controversies that had impeded federal aid programs in the past, the ESEA legislation followed the "child benefit" theory. Federal aid would be available to educationally disadvantaged children in both public and parochial schools; it would assist the child rather than the school. Among the major catego-ries, or titles, of aid provided by ESEA were the following:

1. Grants to the states to improve school library resources and to purchase textbooks and other instructional materials
2. Funds to establish educational centers to provide educational services and encourage innovative programs
3. Educational research and training grants for universities to conduct and disseminate educational research
4. Grants to state educational agencies to improve the planning, the collection of data, and the training of personnel

The enactment of the ESEA set the basic directions in education that the federal government was to follow in the ensuing decade. Its major focus was educational reform and innovation, with a special concern for the education of the disadvantaged. The federal government was to encourage new programs to improve the education of the handicapped, those in poverty-impacted areas, bilingual educa-tion, and the education of Indian children. Table 9–1 summarizes federal programs for elementary and secondary education and related activities for the years 1787–1988.

The Federal Courts and Education

The federal government is divided into three major branches: executive, legislative, and judicial. In the area of federal aid, the primary initiatives are with the executive branch, particularly with the president, and with the legislative branch, the Congress.

TABLE 9–1 Federal Programs for Education and Related Activities

1787 **Northwest Ordinance** authorized land grants for the establishment of educational institutions.

1802 **An act fixing the military peace establishment of the United States** established the U.S. Military Academy. (The U.S. Naval Academy was established in 1845 by the secretary of the navy.)

1862 **First Morrill Act** authorized public land grants to the states for the establishment and maintenance of agricultural and mechanical colleges.

1867 **Department of Education Act** authorized the establishment of the Department of Education.

1890 **Second Morrill Act** provided for money grants for support of instruction in the agricultural and mechanical colleges.

1917 **Smith–Hughes Act** provided for grants to states for support of vocational education.

1935 **Bankhead–Jones Act** (Public Law 74–182) authorized grants to states for agricultural experiment stations.

1941 **Amendment to Lanham Act of 1940** authorized federal aid for construction, maintenance, and operation of schools in federally impacted areas. Such assistance was continued under Public Law 815 and Public Law 874, 81st Congress, in 1950.

1943 **Vocational Rehabilitation Act** (Public Law 78–16) provided assistance to disabled veterans.

School Lunch Indemnity Plan (Public Law 78–129) provided funds for local lunch food purchases.

1944 **Servicemen's Readjustment Act** (Public Law 78–346) provided assistance for education to veterans.

1946 **National School Lunch Act** (Public Law 79–396) authorized assistance through grants-in-aid and other means to states to assist in providing adequate foods and facilities for the establishment, maintenance, operation, and expansion of nonprofit school lunch programs.

George–Barden Act (Public Law 80–402) expanded federal support of vocational education.

1948 **United States Information and Educational Exchange Act** (Public Law 80–402) provided for the interchange of persons, knowledge, and skills between the United States and other countries.

1954 **An act for the establishment of the United States Air Force Academy and other purposes** (Public Law 83–325) established the U.S. Air Force Academy.

National Advisory Committee on Education Act (Public Law 83–532) established a National Advisory Committee on Education to recommend needed studies of national concern in the field of education and to propose appropriate action indicated by such studies.

School Milk Program Act (Public Law 83–597) provided funds for purchase of milk for school lunch programs.

1958 **National Defense Education Act** (Public Law 85–865) provided assistance to state and local school systems for strengthening instruction in science, mathematics, modern foreign languages, and other critical subjects; improvement of state statistical services; guidance, counseling, and testing services and training institutes; higher education student loans and fellowships; foreign language study and training provided by colleges and universities; experimentation and dissemination of information on more effective utilization of television, motion pictures, and related media for educational purposes; and vocational education for technical occupations necessary to the national defense.

Education of Mentally Retarded Children Act (Public Law 85–926) authorized federal assistance for training teachers of the handicapped.

1963 **Higher Education Facilities Act of 1963** (Public Law 88–204) authorized grants and loans for classrooms, libraries, and laboratories in public community colleges and technical institutes, as well as undergraduate and graduate facilities in other institutions of higher education.

1964 **Civil Rights Act of 1964** (Public Law 88–352) authorized the commissioner of education to arrange for support for institutions of higher education and school districts to provide in-service programs for assisting instructional staff in dealing with problems caused by desegregation.

Economic Opportunity Act of 1964 (Public Law 88–452) authorized grants for college work-study programs for students from low-income families; established a Job Corps program and authorized support for work-training programs to provide education and vocational

TABLE 9-1 *Continued*

training and work experience opportunities in welfare programs; authorized support of education and training activities and of community action programs, including Head Start, Follow Through, and Upward Bound; and authorized the establishment of Volunteers In Service To America (VISTA).

1965 **Elementary and Secondary Education Act** (Public Law 89–10) authorized grants for elementary and secondary school programs for children of low-income families; school library resources, textbooks, and other instructional materials for school children; supplementary educational centers and services; strengthening state education agencies; and educational research and research training.

Higher Education Act of 1965 (Public Law 89–329) provided grants for university community service programs, college library assistance, library training and research, strengthening developing institutions, teacher training programs, and undergraduate instructional equipment. It authorized insured student loans, established a National Teacher Corps, and provided for graduate teacher training fellowships.

National Foundation on the Arts and the Humanities Act (Public Law 89–209) authorized grants and loans for projects in the creative and performing arts and for research, training, and scholarly publications in the humanities.

National Technical Institute for the Deaf Act (Public Law 89–36) provided for the establishment, construction, equipping, and operation of a residential school for postsecondary education and technical training of the deaf.

National Vocational Student Loan Insurance Act (Public Law 89–287) encouraged state and nonprofit private institutions and organizations to establish adequate loan insurance programs to assist students to attend post-secondary business, trade, technical, and other vocational schools.

1966 **International Education Act** (Public Law 89–698) provided grants to institutions of higher education for the establishment, strengthening, and operation of centers for research and training in international studies and the international aspects of other fields of study.

Adult Education Act (Public Law 89–750) authorized grants to states for the encouragement and expansion of educational programs for

adults, including training of teachers of adults and demonstrations in adult education (previously part of Economic Opportunity Act of 1964).

Elementary and Secondary Education Amendments of 1966 (Public Law 89–750), in addition to modifying existing programs, authorized grants to assist states in the initiation, expansion, and improvement of programs and projects for the education of handicapped children.

1967 **Education Professions Development Act** (Public Law 90–35) amended the Higher Education Act of 1965 for the purpose of improving the quality of teaching and to help meet critical shortages of adequately trained educational personnel.

1968 **Elementary and Secondary Education Amendments of 1967** (Public Law 90–247) modified existing programs, authorized support of regional centers for education of handicapped children, model centers and services for deaf and/or blind children, recruitment of personnel and dissemination of information on education of the handicapped; technical assistance in education to rural areas; support of dropout prevention projects; and support of bilingual education programs.

1970 **Environmental Education Act** (Public Law 91–516) established an Office of Environmental Education to develop curriculum and initiate and maintain environmental education programs at the elementary and secondary levels; disseminate information; provide training programs for teachers and other educational, public, community, labor, and industrial leaders and employees; provide community education programs; and distribute material dealing with environment and ecology.

Drug Abuse Education Act of 1970 (Public Law 9–527) provided for development, demonstration, and evaluation of curriculums on the problems of drug abuse.

1972 **Drug Abuse Office and Treatment Act of 1972** (Public Law 92–255) established a Special Action Office for Drug Abuse Prevention to provide overall planning and policy for all federal drug abuse prevention functions; a National Advisory Council for Drug Abuse Prevention; community assistance grants for com-

TABLE 9–1 Continued

munity mental health centers for the treatment and rehabilitation of persons with drug abuse problems, and, in December 1974, a National Institute on Drug Abuse.

Education Amendments of 1972 (Public Law 92–318) established the Education Division and the National Institute of Education; general aid for institutions of higher education; federal matching grants for state student incentive grants; a National Commission on Financing Postsecondary Education; State Advisory Councils on Community Colleges; a Bureau of Occupational and Adult Education and state grants for the design, establishment, and conduct of postsecondary occupational education; and a bureau-level Office of Indian Education. Prohibited sex bias in admission to vocational, professional, and graduate schools, and public institutions of undergraduate higher education.

1975 **Indian Self-Determination and Education Assistance Act** (Public Law 93–638) provided for increased participation of Indians in the establishment and conduct of their education programs and services.

Indochina Migration and Refugee Assistance Act of 1975 (Public Law 94–23) authorized funds to be used for education and training of aliens who have fled from Cambodia or Vietnam.

Education of All Handicapped Children Act (Public Law 94–142) provided that all handicapped children (5 to 18 years old) have available to them a free appropriate education designed to meet their unique needs.

1979 **Department of Education Organization Act** (Public Law 96–88) established a Department of Education containing functions from the Education Division of the Department of Health, Education, and Welfare, along with other selected education programs from HEW, the Department of Justice, the Department of Labor, and the National Science Foundation.

1980 **Asbestos School Hazard Protection and Control Act of 1980** (Public Law 96–270) established a program for the inspection of schools for the detection of hazardous asbestos materials and provided loans to assist educational agencies to contain or remove and replace such materials.

1984 **Education for Economic Security Act** (Public Law 98–377) added new science and mathematics programs for elementary, secondary, and postsecondary education. The new programs include magnet schools, excellence in education, and equal access.

1986 **Handicapped Children's Protection Act** (Public Law 99–372) allowed parents of handicapped children to collect attorney's fees in cases brought under the Education of the Handicapped Act and provided that the Education of the Handicapped Act would not preempt other laws, such as Section 504 of the Rehabilitation Act.

Reauthorization of the Education of the Handicapped Act Amendments (Public Law 99–457) reauthorized for three years the discretionary programs under the Education of the Handicapped Act and required education services for all handicapped three- to five-year-olds. Included were programs to provide demonstration projects for severely disabled individuals, research and technology activities, early childhood education, and a state grant program to provide early intervention services for handicapped children from birth through age two.

The Drug-Free Schools and Communities Act of 1986 (Public Law 99–570), part of the Anti-Drug Abuse Act of 1986, authorized funding for fiscal years 1987 to 1989. Established programs for drug abuse education and prevention, coordinated with related community efforts and resources, through the use of federal financial assistance.

1988 **The Omnibus Trade and Competitiveness Act of 1988** (Public Law 100–418) authorized new and expanded education programs. Title VI of the Act, Education and Training for American Competitiveness, authorized new programs in literacy, math-science, foreign language, vocational training, international education, technology training, and technology transfer.

The Omnibus Drug Abuse Prevention Act of 1988 (Public Law 100–690) authorized a new teacher training program under the Drug-Free Schools and Communities Act, an early childhood education program to be administered jointly by the departments of Health and Hu-

TABLE 9–1   *Continued*

man Services and Education, and a pilot program for the children of alcoholics. **Stewart B. McKinney Homeless Assistance Act** (Public Law 100–628) extended for two ad-	ditional years programs providing assistance to the homeless, including literacy training for the homeless adults and education for homeless youths.

This table is based on National Center for Education Statistics, "Federal Programs for Education and Related Activities," *Digest of Education Statistics 1989* (Washington, D.C.: U.S. Government Printing Office, 1989), pp. 325–332. It has been abridged and edited by the author to identify the most significant programs that impact education.

Since the mid-twentieth century, the federal judiciary has exerted an ever-growing impact on education. Some commentators on the federal role have called the U.S. Supreme Court "the national school board." While this may be an overstatement, decisions of the federal judiciary have changed substantially the course of American education. The following section examines the impact of the federal courts on American education.

Brown v. Board of Education

One of the most momentous events to bring the federal courts into education occurred in 1954, with the Supreme Court's decision in *Brown* v. *Board of Education of Topeka*. Overturning the "separate but equal" doctrine established in *Plessy* v. *Ferguson* in 1896, the Supreme Court in the *Brown* decision ruled segregated schools to be "inherently unequal" and in violation of the Fourteenth Amendment of the Constitution. Using sociological and psychological evidence, Chief Justice Earl Warren stated:

> *Segregation of white and colored children in public schools has a detrimental effect upon the colored children. The impact is greater when it has the sanction of the law; for the policy of separating the races is usually interpreted as denoting the inferiority of the Negro group. A sense of inferiority affects the motivation of a child to learn. Segregation with the sanction of law, therefore, has a tendency to retard the education and mental development of Negro children and to deprive them of some of the benefits they would receive in a racially integrated school system.*[6]

The desegregation ruling had its first impact on the dual school systems of southern and border states, where segregation was de jure, with the force of state law as well as custom. Later, desegregation efforts had an impact on the school systems of the large northern cities, where racial segregation was de facto in that it was based on residential housing patterns and local attendance areas rather than by force of law.

The Civil Rights Act of 1964

In breaking the hold of segregation on American schools, judicial action went hand-in-hand with congressional legislation and civil rights enforcement by the executive branch, especially the Justice Department. A key element in the desegregation

6. *Brown* v. *The Board of Education*, 347 U.S. 483 (1954).

machinery and process was the Civil Rights Act of 1964, which prohibited discrimination in public accommodations, employment practices, and education and provided for federal enforcement through the courts. Of particular importance in education was the provision that prohibited discrimination in federally funded programs. School districts and educational institutions that violated the non-discriminatory provisions of the act could lose federal funds.

"With All Deliberate Speed"

The Supreme Court and the federal judiciary sought to implement its decision that school desegregation should proceed "with all deliberate speed." In 1968, in the *Green* v. *County School Board* and *Monroe* v. *Board of Commissioners* decisions, the Supreme Court ruled unconstitutional local plans that allowed students the option of transfer to avoid desegregation. In *Alexander* v. *Holmes City Board of Education*, the Court declared that districts were obligated "to terminate dual school systems at once." In its 1971 decision in *Swann* v. *Charlotte-Mecklenburg*, the Supreme Court upheld the use of citywide busing to achieve integration.[7]

The decisions of the Supreme Court and other federal courts in desegregation and civil rights matters had a decided impact on American education and resulted in legal requirements with which school districts and other educational institutions must comply. Although this body of legal requirements is growing, it is also continually being reviewed. It is clear that racially segregated, dual school systems are unconstitutional and that, to achieve desegregation, the courts will redress grievances that come from racially motivated assignments of students, organization of attendance areas, construction of facilities, and teacher assignments that maintain segregated patterns of schooling.

The Federal Judiciary and the Handicapped

Following the precedents that ended racial discrimination, the courts heard cases in which parents challenged local school practices that excluded the handicapped. A federal district court in Pennsylvania heard a suit brought by the Pennsylvania Association for Retarded Children (PARC) against the Commonwealth of Pennsylvania in 1971. The court's decision was that handicapped children had a constitutional claim to free education as did nonhandicapped children. *Mills* v. *Board of Education of the District of Columbia* in 1972 extended the right to an education to all handicapped children and guaranteed them the right to due process protection.[8]

The decisions of the federal district courts to guarantee the rights of handicapped children to an education anticipated the legislation that followed. The

---

7. *Green* v. *County School Board* 391 U.S. 430 (1968); *Monroe* v. *Board of Commissioners*, 391 U.S. 377 (1968); *Alexander* v. *Holmes City Board of Education*, 396 U.S. 19 (1969); *Swann* v. *Charlotte-Mecklenburg*, 402 U.S. 1 (1971).
8. *Pennsylvania Association for Retarded Children (PARC)* v. *Commonwealth of Pennsylvania*, 243 F. Supp. 279 (E.D. PA 1972); *Mills* v. *Board of Education of the District of Columbia*, 348 F. Supp. 866 (D.D.C. 1972).

Rehabilitation Services Act of 1973 and the Education of All Handicapped Children Act of 1975 were far-reaching laws that are examined in Chapter 20.

In the 1970s, the Supreme Court also rendered a decision regarding bilingual education in *Lau* v. *Nichols*.[9] In the *Lau* decision, the Supreme Court ruled that the City of San Francisco violated the Civil Rights Act by failing to make appropriate educational provisions for non-English-speaking children of Chinese descent. The Court's decision in the *Lau* case has been interpreted to mean that schools receiving federal aid are to provide special instruction to non-English-speaking children.

Religion and the Schools

Activity by the federal courts continues in the issue of separation of church and state. The First Amendment of the Constitution, stating that "Congress shall make no law respecting an establishment of religion, or prohibiting the free exercise thereof," led to a series of cases dealing with aid to parochial schools and religious observance and prayer in the public schools.

In the matter of federal aid to parochial schools, the Supreme Court has consistently ruled direct aid to parochial schools to be unconstitutional. However, in several specific cases, the Court has allowed indirect aid. In the *Everson* case in 1947, the Court upheld a New Jersey law that provided public transportation reimbursements to parents of both public and parochial school children. In *Walz* v. *Tax Commission* in 1970, the Court granted tax-exempt status to property used only for religious purposes. In *Board of Education* v. *Allen* in 1971, the Court upheld the lending of state-approved textbooks to children attending parochial schools.[10]

In addition to cases related to public aid to religious schools, the federal judiciary also has heard cases relating to religion and the curriculum. In 1920, the Supreme Court, in *Pierce* v. *Society of Sisters*, upheld the right of parents to send their children to private schools—including religious schools—providing that these schools met minimum state standards. In *Zorach* v. *Clauson* in 1952, the Court upheld "released-time" programs in which children attending public schools were allowed to attend religious instruction in facilities other than the public schools. In *Engel* v. *Vitale* in 1962, the Court ruled that state laws requiring prayer in the public schools violated separation of church and state.[11] In other decisions, the Supreme Court has ruled that it is permissible for public schools to teach about religion as an objective study but not to provide denominational religious education.

The Contemporary Federal Role in Education

By the 1970s, the principle of federal assistance to education appeared to have general acceptance. The administration of Presidents Ford and Carter continued the assistance programs of previous administrations. A major tendency that occurred

9. *Lau* v. *Nichols*, 414 U.S. 563 (1974).
10. *Walz* v. *Tax Commission*, 397 U.S. 644 (1970); *Board of Education* v. *Allen*, 392 U.S. 371 (1971).
11. *Pierce* v. *Society of Sisters*, 268 U.S. 310 (1920); *Zorach* v. *Clauson*, 343 U.S. 306 (1952); *Engel* v. *Vitale*, 370 U.S. 421 (1962).

throughout the 1970s was the growing complexity of federal guidelines and regulations governing the application for and the receiving of federal aid. Complaints were frequently heard, however, from both educators and administrators about the time and energy required to deal with the federal bureaucracy.

The Federal Department of Education

In his campaign for the presidency in 1976, Jimmy Carter urged creation of a separate Department of Education, at cabinet level, to focus national attention on educational issues and to identify a national agency to speak for education. The issue of the creation of a federal Department of Education provoked considerable controversy. Conservative political groups generally opposed the Department of Education as another example of federal expansion into areas reserved to local and state governments. Although many of the nation's educational associations favored the creation of a federal department, there was also opposition among some educational groups. The National Education Association led a strong campaign for the department. The American Federation of Teachers and the National Catholic Education Association were opposed. After considerable debate, Congress created the federal Department of Education in 1979. Headed by Shirley M. Hufstedler, the new department administered programs that had previously been scattered throughout several federal agencies. It assumed responsibilities for administering federal programs for overseas dependents, special education and rehabilitation services, elementary and secondary education, vocational and adult education, higher education, bilingual and minority language affairs, and educational research. Figure 9–1 illustrates the organization of the U.S. Department of Education.

FIGURE 9–1   U.S. Department of Education

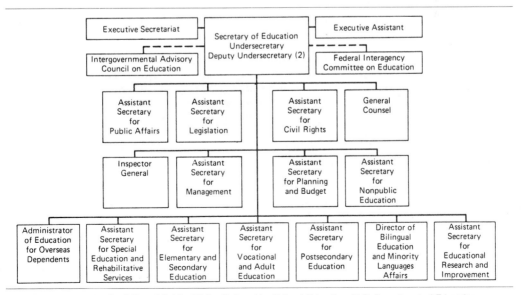

SOURCE: Published by the Office of Public Affairs, National Institute of Education, U.S. Department of Education

The Federal Role in Stimulating Education Change

As indicated throughout this chapter, the federal government has used a variety of strategies to bring about educational change. Among them have been federal funding for specific programs such as the NDEA, special requirements regarding the education of handicapped and bilingual, bicultural children, and federal court decisions affecting racial integration and the separation of church and state. In addition, federal officials have sought to stimulate educational change and reform through their speeches and activities and through the reports of national commissions.

The educational policies of the Reagan administration provide an excellent illustration of the role of the federal government as an initiator of educational change. Terrel H. Bell, secretary of education from 1981 to 1984, stimulated sweeping educational reforms by using a threefold strategy: First, he appointed a National Commission on Excellence in Education whose report, *A Nation at Risk*, warned that the academic standards and quality of American elementary and secondary education had seriously declined; second, through a series of federally sponsored forums and conferences, the concerns and recommendations of the National Commission received nationwide publicity; third, the call for educational reform, initiated by the federal government, stimulated state governments to enact legislation and local school districts to enact policies that incorporated many of the recommendations of the National Commission.

A Nation at Risk

The role of both the National Commission on Excellence in Education and the national report as agents of educational change can be illustrated by examining the recommendations of *A Nation at Risk: The Imperative for Educational Reform*, which appeared in 1983. Finding the United States to be "at risk," the report of the National Commission on Excellence warned:

> . . . the educational foundations of our society are presently being eroded by a rising tide of mediocrity that threatens our very future as a nation and a people.
>
> If an unfriendly foreign power had attempted to impose on America the mediocre educational performance that exists today, we might well have viewed it as an act of war. As it stands, we have allowed this to happen to ourselves. We have even squandered the gains in student achievement made in the wake of the Sputnik challenge. Moreover, we have dismantled essential support systems which helped make those gains possible. We have, in effect, been committing an act of unthinking, unilateral disarmament.[12]

The report, which compared American education achievement to that of other countries, particularly Germany and Japan, found the academic performance of American students to be inferior. The Commission on Excellence in Education found the following:

---

12. National Commission on Excellence in Education, *A Nation at Risk: The Imperative for Educational Reform* (Washington, D.C.: U.S. Government Printing Office, 1983), p. 5.

1. There was a high rate of functional illiteracy among young people and adults, with "13 per cent of all 17-year olds," "some 23 million" adults, and an estimated "40 per cent" of minority youth that could be classified as functional illiterates.
2. There had been a general decline of performance of American students on standardized achievement tests as evidenced by "a virtually unbroken decline from 1963 to 1980" on the College Board's Scholastic Aptitude Tests (SAT) and consistent declines in English, mathematics, and science.
3. Colleges had to establish remedial mathematics courses and that business and military leaders had complained "that they are required to spend millions of dollars on costly remedial education and training programs in such basic skills as reading, writing, spelling and computation."[13]

The Commission on Excellence issued recommendations that urged the reform of the school curriculum, the raising of academic standards and expectations, more effective use of institutional time, and improved teacher competency and effectiveness. Among its recommendations were

> . . . *that state and local high school graduation requirements be strengthened and that, at a minimum, all students seeking a diploma be required to lay the foundations in the Five New Basics by taking the following curriculum during their four years of high school: (1) 4 years of English; (2) 3 years of mathematics; (3) 3 years of science; (4) 3 years of social studies; and (5) one-half year of computer science. For the college bound, 2 years of foreign language in high school are strongly recommended in addition to those taken earlier.*
>
> . . . *that schools, colleges, and universities adopt more rigorous and measurable standards, and higher expectations, for academic performance and student conduct, and that 4-year colleges and universities raise their requirements for admission. This will help students do their best educationally with challenging materials in an environment that supports learning and authentic accomplishment.*
>
> . . . *that significantly more time be devoted to learning the New Basics. This will require more effective use of the existing school day, a longer school day, or a lengthened school year.*
>
> . . . *that citizens across the nation hold educators and elected officials responsible for providing the leadership necessary to achieve these reforms, and that citizens provide the fiscal support and stability required to bring about the reforms we propose.*[14]

To improve teacher effectiveness, the Commission on Excellence in Education recommended (1) that admission standards to teacher education programs be raised and that prospective teachers demonstrate aptitude for teaching and competence in an academic discipline, (2) that teachers' salaries be raised but that increases reflect effective performance evaluation, (3) that school boards adopt an 11-month contract for teachers, (4) that career ladders be established for teachers distinguishing between beginning, experienced, and master teachers, (5) that efforts be made to solve teacher shortages in mathematics and science by using nonschool personnel, (6) that financial incentives, such as loans and scholarship grants, be used to attract more capable students to teaching, and (7) that master teachers exercise a role in

13. Ibid., pp. 8–9.
14. Ibid., pp. 23–31.

designing teacher education programs and in supervising teachers during probationary service.

What Works

William J. Bennett, who succeeded Terrel Bell as secretary of the U.S. Department of Education, continued his predecessor's efforts to shape public opinion on behalf of specific educational reform. Bennett, in *What Works: Research About Teaching and Learning*, published in 1986, outlined his conception of the role of the Department of Education:

> *The first and fundamental responsibility of the federal government in the field of education is to supply accurate and reliable information about education to the American people.*[15]

In an effort to "demystify" educational research, *What Works*, in a series of clear and concise statements, described essential findings in three broad categories that affect children's education: the home, the classroom, and the school.

Recent Federal Initiatives

The inauguration of George Bush as president in 1989 appeared to mark a continuation of many of the educational initiatives and activities of the Reagan administration. President Bush, who announced his desire to be known as the "Education President," has addressed the general issue of educational reform and encouraged greater state initiatives to improve elementary and secondary education. He has also supported a greater federal initiative in supporting day care and early childhood education programs.

In 1991, President Bush proposed that educators, business leaders, and scholars work together to reform American education by developing innovative schools. Bush's proposal urges that national tests be developed to assess students' achievement in English, science, mathematics, history, and geography. Bush also endorsed, as did the previous Reagan administration, greater freedom for parents to choose the school that their children would attend.[16]

Recently enacted education legislation has been directed in three directions: the continued support of programs directed to the education of handicapped persons, efforts to improve the United States' economic position internationally by supporting science and mathematics education, and efforts at drug abuse education linked to the "war on drugs." The Reauthorization of the Education of the Handicapped Act Amendments in 1986 reestablished the discretionary programs supported under the Education of the Handicapped Act and required educational services for three- to five-year-old children with handicaps. The Omnibus Trade and

---

15. *What Works: Research About Teaching and Learning* (Washington, D.C.: U.S. Department of Education, 1986), p. v.

16. Thomas J. DeLoughry, "Bush Proposes 'Populist Crusade' to Reform Education; Colleges Would Help to Develop Schools, Train Adults," *The Chronicle of Higher Education*, Vol. XXXVII, No. 32 (April 24, 1991), pp. A21, A23.

Competitiveness Act of 1988 authorized new and expanded education programs in literacy, mathematics, science, foreign languages, occupational training, international education, and technological training. The Omnibus Drug Abuse Prevention Act of 1988 authorized a new teacher education program to be administered jointly by the departments of Health and Human Services and Education.

During the period 1980–1988, federal funding of education decreased. In 1980, total federal education appropriations were $79,607,500; in 1988, they were $71,216,700. From fiscal year 1980 to fiscal year 1989, funds for elementary and secondary education declined by 17 percent, and those for higher education by 27 percent. However, research funding increased by 36 percent, and other program funding by 38 percent.[17]

Conclusion

Ever since the establishment of the American Republic, the federal government has very gradually increased its involvement in education through programs of federal funding and assistance. The federal role in education has always been controversial, particularly in such areas as local initiative, states' rights, and separation of church and state.

Since the 1950s, the federal role increased dramatically, especially as a result of the Supreme Court decision in the *Brown* case. The enactment of the NDEA and the ESEA provided substantial assistance to schools. Federal involvement and assistance is unpredictable, however, because it depends on the public mood and the changing circumstances of American political life.

DISCUSSION QUESTIONS

1. Analyze the federal role in education until the Civil War.
2. Identify the organizations and groups that opposed federal aid to education in the century from the Civil War to the enactment of the NDEA. Analyze the motives of these groups in opposing federal aid.
3. Using the enactment of the Smith–Hughes Act for aid to vocational education as a case study, examine the role of special-interest groups in obtaining federal aid.
4. Describe the climate that led to the enactment of the NDEA.
5. Analyze the policy implications of *A Nation at Risk* and *What Works*.
6. Describe the provisions of the ESEA.
7. Analyze the reasoning of the Supreme Court in the *Brown* case of 1954.
8. Describe the role of the federal government in desegregation of American schools.
9. Comment on the role of the federal government in bilingual education and the education of the handicapped.
10. Comment on the decisions of the U.S. Supreme Court regarding separation of church and state that have a relevance to education.

17. *Digest of Education Statistics 1989* (Washington, D.C.: U.S. Government Printing Office, 1989), pp. 232–234.

FIELD EXERCISES

1. Identify a particular U.S. senator or member of the House of Representatives. Examine his or her record on federal aid to education.

2. Keep a log of the articles that appear in major newspapers or news magazines on the role of the federal government in education.

3. Invite a member of the administration of your college or university to visit your class to discuss the various areas of institutional involvement with the federal government.

4. Invite an elementary or secondary school administrator to visit your class to discuss his or her district's involvement with the federal government.

5. Debate the proposition: Resolved, federal aid to public schools should be increased.

6. Debate the proposition: Resolved, the federal government should provide tuition tax credits to the parents of private school children.

7. Interview or write to your state representative and attempt to determine how national reports like *A Nation at Risk* have influenced state legislation related to schools.

SUGGESTED READINGS

ADVISORY COMMISSION ON INTERGOVERNMENTAL RELATIONS. *The Federal Role in the Federal System: The Dynamics of Growth; Intergovernmentalizing the Classroom: Federal Involvement in Elementary and Secondary Education.* Washington, D.C.: U.S. Government Printing Office, 1981.

BAILEY, STEPHEN K., AND MOSHER, EDITH K. *ESEA: The Office of Education Administers a Law.* Syracuse, N.Y.: Syracuse University Press, 1968.

BELL, TERREL H. *The Thirteenth Man: A Reagan Cabinet Memoir.* New York: Free Press, 1988.

BENNETT, WILLIAM J. *Our Children and Our Country: Improving America's Schools and Affirming the Common Culture.* New York: Simon and Schuster, 1989.

FINN, CHESTER E., JR. *Education and the Presidency.* Lexington, Mass.: D. C. Heath, 1977.

GRAHAM, HUGH D. *The Uncertain Triumph: Federal Education Policy in the Kennedy and Johnson Years.* Chapel Hill: University of North Carolina Press, 1984.

HOGAN, JOHN C. *The Schools, the Courts, and the Public Interest.* Lexington, Mass.: D. C. Heath, 1985.

NATIONAL COMMISSION ON EXCELLENCE IN EDUCATION. *A Nation at Risk: The Imperative for Educational Reform.* Washington, D.C.: U.S. Government Printing Office, 1983.

The Nation Responds: Recent Efforts to Improve Education. Washington, D.C.: U.S. Government Printing Office, 1984.

REBELL, MICHAEL A., AND BLOCK, ARTHUR R. *Equality and Education: Federal Civil Rights Enforcement in the New York City School System.* Princeton, N.J.: Princeton University Press, 1985.

THOMAS, NORMAN C. *Education in National Politics.* New York: David McKay, 1975.

WARREN, DONALD R. *To Enforce Education.* Detroit: Wayne State University Press, 1974.

What Works: Research About Teaching and Learning. Washington, D.C.: U.S. Department of Education, 1986.

10

The State Role in Education

Unlike many of the nations of the world, the United States does not have a national school system. It has 50 state public school systems. Since the authority for education rests with each state, it is historically and legally accurate to speak of the Illinois, Texas, or Massachusetts systems of public schools, say, rather than the American school system. The underlying reasons for the absence of a national school system and the existence of 50 state systems can be explained in part by the historical and social forces that have shaped American educational patterns.

The general focusing questions that will be answered as you read this chapter include the following:

1. What are the historic origins of state authority in education?
2. What are the educational responsibilities of state governments?
3. What are the areas of state control of education?
4. What are the major state initiatives in education?

Historical Perspective on State Authority

Although debate ensued about a federal system of education in the early national period, the U.S. Constitution did not specifically address education. The Tenth Amendment, ratified in 1791, states: "The powers not delegated to the United States by the Constitution, nor prohibited by it to the States, are reserved to the States, respectively, or to the people." Under the "reserved powers" clause, each of the states has the power to organize, administer, and support education.

In their own constitutions, the various states made some statement or provision concerning education. In each state, the legislature enacts laws, including those governing education and schools. Legally, then, the legislature of each state is the supreme policymaking body in that state. The state legislature enacts the laws that govern school organization, administration, and financing. From the initial statement of educational responsibility in the state constitution, each state evolved the historical patterns that shaped its schools.

Common Schools and the States

In the various states of the Union, it was the common-school movement of the early nineteenth century that made the state constitutional provisions an institutional reality that culminated in the present-day public school. In its origins, a common school was an elementary school that was supported by public taxation, governed by elected officials, and served the educational needs of the children living in the area in which it was located. The common school, or school for all children, offered a curriculum that stressed the basic skills of reading, writing, and arithmetic, often along with history, geography, music, art, and health.

In each of the states in the early nineteenth century, there were those who wanted common schools and those who opposed them. Essentially, however, in the history of the state role in education, the crusade for common schools was a major episode in the emergence of state educational control. Although the actual historical events differed somewhat from state to state, a general pattern emerged.

First, the state legislature enacted permissive legislation that made it possible for the residents of the various sections of the state to organize school districts. Generally, the majority of voters who lived within the boundary lines of the proposed district would have to vote to establish a district. In most of the northern states, the district pattern of organization was based on that of New England, especially Massachusetts, which had established school districts as far back as the colonial period. The establishment of school districts was an important first step in that the state legislature was using the district as the basic unit for state control. The essential definition of a school district, framed in the early nineteenth century, has remained much the same.

A school district is an instrument or agency of the state that operates under state laws and is intended to execute the state's policy for the administration of public education. The school district, internally, is governed by an elected board that is responsible for the establishment, maintenance, organization, and support of the school or schools within its jurisdiction. The geographical jurisdiction of the school district is determined by boundary lines that designate the area whose population it serves and whose population will support it.

After permitting the organization of districts in the state, the legislature then encouraged districts to organize and levy taxes for support of common, or public, schools. The state usually encouraged public education by giving funds as grants-in-aid to districts that were taxing themselves for school support. It did not, however, mandate or make publicly supported common schooling compulsory. Several important characteristics of the emergent public school system appeared at this stage. The local district would raise most of the money needed to support schools through local taxes, usually a property tax. Local funds would then be supplemented by state aid.

The third stage in the development of the state system of schools came with a state mandate that made public or common schooling compulsory. In effect, the state now was requiring that school districts organize to provide public education to the children of the state. Also as a result of this historical experience, two kinds of state laws concerning education emerged: mandatory and permissive. While mandatory laws were to be followed uniformly throughout the state, permissive laws gave local school districts the option to use discretionary powers in certain limited situations.

In terms of chronology, the movement for common schools occurred first in New England, where Massachusetts was a leading state, then in the states of the old Northwest Territory, followed by the Middle Atlantic states. States in the South generally did not enact effective common school legislation until Reconstruction.

In the campaigns that were launched on behalf of common schools, certain major educational leaders emerged. Among them were Horace Mann in Massachusetts, Henry Barnard in Connecticut, and Calvin Wiley in New York. These individuals frequently popularized the idea of common schooling and led the campaign for it in the state legislatures. To illustrate the role played by such leaders of the common-school movement, we will look at the career of Horace Mann.

Horace Mann as a Common-School Leader

Horace Mann (1796–1859), often called the Father of American Public Education, led the movement for common schools in Massachusetts. His public career shows him to be a leader who helped to define the concept of public education and who contributed to the state role in public education. A native of Massachusetts, Mann was educated in the town school of Franklin, graduated from Brown University in 1819, and entered the legal profession.[1] He was elected to the Massachusetts state legislature in 1827, where he served for six years. From 1833 to 1837, he served in the

Horace Mann (1796–1859), the "Father of the American Common School," was secretary of the Massachusetts Board of Education and a national leader of the public school movement.

1. For the definitive biography of Mann, see Jonathan Messerli, *Horace Mann: A Biography* (New York: Knopf, 1972).

Massachusetts Senate. As a leading member of the Massachusetts legislature, Mann was concerned with education. In this regard, he was not unlike other political leaders who recognized the need of improving public education in their states. As a result of the efforts of Mann and other like-minded legislators, Massachusetts passed An Act Relating to Common Schools in 1837.

When the Massachusetts Board of Education was established, Mann was appointed its secretary. Mann's function was to collect school statistics, make information available about the condition of schools, and encourage the improvement of schools and teaching. To accomplish these tasks, he visited schools throughout the state so that he could determine directly the condition of education.

From 1837 to 1848, as secretary of the State Board of Education, Mann worked to increase support for common schools, to improve teacher preparation in normal schools, and to improve instruction. To publicize the cause of public education, Mann edited the *Common School Journal* and wrote annual reports to the Board of Education, classic statements about the role and purposes of American public education. Mann's *Twelfth Annual Report,* in 1848, summed up his thoughts on public education: the "Common School . . . may become the most effective and benignant of all forces of civilization."[2]

As a result of the pioneering efforts of Mann, state governments began to exercise a minimal supervisory function through a state board of education, state superintendent, or commissioner of education. The state superintendent became identified as the chief official for public education in the state. As the functions of the office developed in the nineteenth century, the state superintendent was responsible for (1) collecting educational statistics and data, (2) making recommendations for improving common schools, (3) preparing reports to inform the public, and (4) overseeing the distribution of school funds from the state to the local districts. Near the end of the nineteenth century, state superintendents also assumed the responsibility of registering teachers' certificates and presenting minimal certification requirements.

Educational Responsibilities within State Government

The authority of each of the states to provide and maintain schools is a broad responsibility that is subdivided among the various branches of the state government. Essentially, the state legislature enacts the laws governing education, and the executive branch of state government (the governor) enforces them. State courts often render decisions regarding litigation over school matters. It is important to note that the state government has delegated significant responsibilities to school boards (boards of education) in local school districts.

Responsibilities of the Legislature

In most states, the state constitution charges the state legislature with the responsibility of establishing and maintaining a system of free public, or common, schools.

2. Horace Mann, *Lectures and Annual Reports on Education* (Cambridge, Mass.: Cornhill Press, 1867), p. 80.

Within this general area of responsibility, local school boards are part of state government and serve as its agent in performing its educational functions. Although local school boards have considerable powers, their authority is delegated to them and is exercised at the pleasure of the state legislature.

Legislation affecting schools enters a range of complex areas, especially that of establishing the foundation formula that allocates state funds to local school districts. Although the state legislature must enact the laws governing schools, legislators are guided by recommendations from the state department of education and special committees and task forces on educational matters. In enacting school legislation, the members of the legislature have to deal with the conflicting arguments and demands of various educational lobbies, such as the school boards' association, teachers' unions and organizations, citizens groups, and other special-interest groups.

Much of the work preliminary to the enactment of legislation is done by committees of the senate and house of the state legislature, particularly those on finance and education. Committee recommendations are then brought to each house of the legislature for action. Bills that pass both houses are then sent to the governor for signature or veto.

The School Code

The state legislature enacts the laws that govern the establishment, organization, administration, and financing of schools, minimum standards, minimum curriculum requirements, and other matters affecting public schools. The state school laws are collected and published in a document called the state *school code*. The typical school code is a comprehensive and detailed compendium of the state's laws affecting education. Among the topics found in a school code are school board elections, child labor laws, transportation, conduct of school board meetings, school construction, education of handicapped children, budgets, tax rates, bonds, compulsory attendance, school holidays, and safety provisions. Teachers are affected directly by the provisions in school codes that relate to their employment, tenure, and duties and to curriculum and instructional material. For example, the school code of Illinois states:

> *History of the United States shall be taught in all public schools and in all other educational institutions in this State, supported or maintained, in whole or in part, by public funds. The teaching of history shall have as one of its objectives the imparting to pupils of a comprehensive idea of our democratic form of government and the principles for which our government stands as regards other nations including the studying of the place of our government in world-wide movements and the leaders thereof, with particular stress upon the basic principles and ideals of our representative form of government. The teaching of history shall include a study of the role and contributions of American Negroes and other ethnic groups including, but not restricted to, Polish, Lithuanian, German, Hungarian, Irish, Bohemian, Russian, Albanian, Italian, Czechoslovakian, French, Scots, etc., in the history of this country and this state. No pupil shall be graduated from the eighth grade of any public school unless he has received such instruction in the history of the United States and gives evidence of having a comprehensive knowledge thereof.*[3]

3. *The School Code of Illinois 1981* (St. Paul, Minn.: West, 1981), pp. 165–166.

The school codes are technical and detailed, setting forth the statutes governing education in each state. Final legal authority in each state over the constitutionality of a state law is held by that state's court of highest appeal, usually the state supreme court. In many instances decisions have been appealed to the U.S. Supreme Court.

Executive Responsibilities

At the executive level of state government, responsibility for education is lodged with the governor, the chief state school officer (usually the state superintendent of public instruction or school commissioner), and the state board of education and its staff. The governor is charged with enforcing school laws. As a political leader in the state, the governor influences party members in the legislature to support or to oppose particular bills affecting education. The governor's budget recommendations are crucial for school support in that they indicate the amount of state aid that schools will receive in a given year, provided that the legislature agrees. It is the governor who either signs the bills, creating law, or vetoes them. Of significance is the governor's power of appointment. In states where the state board of education is appointed, the governor has this important function. Through the power of appointments, the governor influences policymaking that has an impact on schools.

State Board of Education

Although the legal authority for education rests in the legislature, the various states have established state boards of education to set educational policies for the state. Although variations exist from state to state, the state board generally has authority over elementary and secondary school districts. For example, 48 states give authority to a board of education over elementary and secondary school districts in that state.

Membership on state boards of education also varies from state to state. Membership is by appointment, election, or some combination of election and appointment. In 30 states, members are appointed by the governor; 9 states have elected boards; 11 states use a combination of election and appointment. The number of members on a state board of education also varies. Texas is the largest, with 21 members; Mississippi has only 3 members. The usual number ranges between 7 and 11.

The role of the state board of education can be understood best by examining its functions. Its general functions are to carry out the educational responsibilities that must be administered at the state level. As a policymaking body, the state board formulates the educational policies that relate to the implementation, control, and supervision of education throughout the state. Frequently, the state board appoints or elects the chief state school officer, designates the term of appointment, defines the duties, and fixes the salary.

State School Officers

One of the major responsibilities of the state board of education is to select the chief school officer of the state, whose title is usually state superintendent of public instruction or commissioner of education. In 24 states, the chief state school officer is appointed by the state board of education. In five states this official is appointed by the governor. Twenty-one states continue to elect their superintendents of public instruction.

The chief state educational officer and staff constitute the state department of education. The functions of the state department of education, again, vary from state to state. However, some of the common functions can be identified. First, the state department enforces the school codes by making certain that the local school districts are in compliance with their provisions. Second, the state department is the agency for the distribution of state and federal funds to local school districts; it also distributes funds allocated to the state by the federal government for specific purposes, such as vocational education, special education, and school lunch programs. Third, the state department is the principal agency for teacher certification, establishing and enforcing certification requirements for teachers at the various levels and in the various subject matters. Fourth, the state department establishes task forces to investigate and propose solutions to specific problems, such as declining enrollments, school vandalism, and other issues, and publishes reports to aid local school districts in dealing with their own special problems.

The state department of education exercises its greatest control over local school districts by establishing and enforcing minimum standards, which are designed to provide pupils with a basic standard of education regardless of their location within a state. Minimum standards include (1) making sure that teachers possess the minimum qualifications needed for state certification, (2) requiring that students be in attendance for a minimum number of days each year, (3) requiring that the curriculum include such subjects as English language, American history, health education, and physical education, and (4) ensuring that school buildings meet certain standards of construction, heating, lighting, and ventilation that protect students' health and safety. If local districts fail to meet the minimum standards established by the state board of education, they face penalties, such as reduction in state financial aid.

The State and Local Control of Schools

While the state legislature and executive branch of state government are charged with establishing and maintaining public schools, they have delegated much of the day-to-day operation of these schools to local boards of education. Although delegated responsibilities are extensive, the powers of the local school board are prescribed and delimited by the state legislature and are recorded in the state school code. A detailed account of the role of the local school district and board of education appears in Chapter 11. Chapter 12, on finance, examines state and local school support.

Areas of State Control

Considerable variation exists among the states regarding the specific areas they reserve to themselves and those they delegate to local districts. The following sections examine some of the major areas that are subject to direct state prescription.

Curriculum and Instruction

The states are responsible for identifying certain basic curriculum areas that must be offered in the public elementary and secondary schools of the state. Such basic curriculum areas often include the study of the English language, American and in some instances local history, the study of the U.S. and state constitutions, health, and physical education. The states may also require certain minimal standards or levels of competency in these mandated curriculum areas. Many states allow broad discretionary powers to local boards of education in curricular and instructional matters. A recent trend has been for some states to require minimal competency tests as part of the graduation requirement for students.

Most states allow the local school boards to select and purchase textbooks and other instructional materials, but some state boards of education identify and distribute the textbooks used in the public schools.

Compulsory Attendance

Each of the states has enacted legislation requiring compulsory school attendance. Although there are variations from state to state, most states require children to attend school from age 6 or 7 until age 16 or 17. To illustrate some of the variations among the states, Virginia requires compulsory attendance from ages 5 to 17; California, from 6 to 16; Minnesota, from 7 to 16; Mississippi, from 6 to 14; and Utah, from 6 to 18.[4] The states also specify a minimum school year that requires schools to be in session for a prescribed number of days. The national average for the number of days per school year is 178.[5] The states also specify certain state holidays on which schools are not to be in session.

Requirements for High School Graduation

The states set the minimum requirements for high school graduation. These requirements are measured by the completion of Carnegie units, a standard measurement that represents one credit for the completion of a one-year course. The general trend during the 1980s, which continues in the 1990s, was for the states to increase the number of units required, especially in mathematics, science, and English courses. This trend reversed the tendency of the late 1960s to permit more course electives. Since more courses are now required or mandated, the freedom to elect nonrequired courses has been severely reduced for high school students in many states. For example, the required units in Alabama increased from 20 in 1980 to 22 in 1987; in

4. National Center for Education Statistics, *Digest of Education Statistics 1989* (Washington, D.C.: U.S. Government Printing Office, 1989), p. 138.
5. Ibid., p. 139.

Kansas, they increased from 17 to 21; in Minnesota, from 15 to 20; in New York, from 16 to 18.5.[6]

Minimum Competency Testing

Another trend of the 1980s was the involvement of many of the states in requiring minimum competency testing of students in elementary and secondary schools. Minimal competency testing generally refers to testing programs used to measure student achievement for grade promotion or high school graduation.[7] Such testing programs are based on the setting of minimum standards. Students are required to demonstrate skills or proficiencies that meet or exceed the minimum standards. Generally, students are required to demonstrate acceptable performance in basic skills, such as reading, English composition, and mathematics, at specified grade levels. In some states, satisfactory performance on the tests is required for promotion to the next higher grade or for high school graduation. In other states, the tests are advisory to local school districts. Once again, marked differences exist in state minimum competency testing requirements. In 23 states, the state establishes the performance standards. In five states, the state and the local school district share responsibility for setting performance standards. Eleven states have delegated the responsibility to the local districts. The remaining states have not enacted legislation requiring minimum competency testing. The grade levels when minimum competency testing is required also vary from state to state. Texas requires testing at grades 1, 3, 5, 7, 9, 11, and 12; Maryland requires it at grades 7 and 9; Colorado, at grades 9 and 12.[8]

Certification of School Personnel

The states have established specific requirements and regulations that govern the certification of school teachers, administrators, counselors, social workers, psychologists, and other educational personnel. Designed to ensure that those who hold a certificate have the appropriate academic background and experience, certification refers to the general process by which a state, or its authorized agency, such as the teacher certification board, provides a credential to an individual.

Many state boards of education have established teacher certification boards that issue certificates to teachers, administrators, and other educational personnel. These certification boards also recognize or approve college and university preparation programs and grant certificates to graduates of approved programs. They also permit individuals to present their credentials to the state certification board and to request the issuance of a certificate.

---

6. Ibid., pp. 140–144.
7. For the literature on minimal competency testing, see Rodney Riegle and Ned Lovell, *Minimum Competency Testing* (Bloomington, Ind.: Phi Delta Kappa Educational Foundation, 1980); R. M. Jaeger and C. K. Tittle, eds. *Minimum Competency Achievement Testing* (Berkeley, Calif.: McCutchan, 1980).
8. *Digest of Education Statistics 1989,* p. 145.

In the late 1980s and early 90s states increasingly required state-administered tests for the initial certification for teachers. Forty-three states require some kind of testing for the initial certificate. Among the tests used are the National Teacher Examination (NTE), the California Basic Education Skills Test, and examinations developed by the state education agency.

Facilities Standards and Requirements

Most states' school codes have provisions relating to the specifications of school buildings and other physical plant facilities. Designed to ensure the life safety of the students, they set standards for school construction, ventilation, heating, lighting, recreation areas, and other matters connected with buildings and maintenance.

Financial Support

Because the state is responsible for establishing and maintaining public schools, formulas for public taxation must be designed, approved, and implemented. The bulk of the financial support for schools comes from the local property tax and state aid. The states generally have been specific as to the taxing powers and rates that local school districts can levy. The states have developed foundation programs to determine the distribution of state aid.

Most states have established a ceiling on the taxation rate that a local school district can levy. They prescribe the format for the local school budget and the assessment and collection of school funds, especially through the local property tax, by county or other units of government.

Recent State Educational Initiatives

As indicated earlier in this chapter, education in the United States historically has been and remains a prerogative and responsibility of each of the 50 states. Though each state maintains its autonomy in education, the 1980s witnessed some coordination efforts at educational reform, especially by the Education Commission of the States' Task Force on Education for Economic Growth.

Action for Excellence

The report of the Task Force on Education for Economic Growth, *Action for Excellence,* appeared in 1983. Chaired by James B. Hunt, Jr., the governor of North Carolina, the task force assembled a prestigious panel that included 13 governors, 14 leaders from major business corporations, and various educational and organizational leaders. Concerned with declining U.S. economic growth and productivity in the face of growing international competition, the task force sought to encourage "partnership" between business and schools and to make American education more effective and responsive to economic needs. In defining the challenge facing American education, the task force stated that, "Technological change and global competition make it imperative to equip students in public schools with skills that go beyond the basics."[9]

The authors of *Action for Excellence* saw American schools weakened by lowered standards, educational deficits, and "blurred goals," with the result that other nations, especially Japan and Germany, were challenging America's prominence as a scientific and technological leader. To regain America's threatened technological supremacy, the task force identified two imperatives; (1) expanding and upgrading the definition of basic skills beyond reading, writing, and arithmetic and (2) mobilizing the educational system to teach the required new skills effectively.

In analyzing the causes of America's educational crisis, the Task Force on Education for Economic Growth, like the Commission on Excellence, catalogued a list of educational deficits that included

1. Problems in student achievement, such as inadequate reading, writing, comprehension, and mathematical skills.
2. Serious educational deficiencies in mathematics and science, the specific areas most closely related to technological progress, manifested by "a lack of general scientific and mathematical literacy" and by projected shortages of skilled scientists and engineers. This educational liability was aggravated by an obsolete science curriculum.
3. A "teacher gap" resulting in shortages of "qualified teachers in critical subjects like mathematics and science.
4. Low salaries—paying teachers according to "rigid salary schedules" rather than rewarding superior performance.[10]

The task force developed an action plan to stimulate each state to work to improve its educational quality. Its chief recommendation was that the governor of each state—working with that state's legislature, state and local boards of education, and business and other leaders—should develop and implement an action plan to improve the state's schools, from kindergarten through grade 12.[11] Each state plan would incorporate the objectives of preparing a "well-educated work force" with the "changing skills" needed for economic growth. It would also establish alliances among community, business, labor, government and education leaders to improve education for economic growth.

The task force's second recommendation urged the creation of broad and effective "partnerships between businesses and schools" (1) to encourage business leaders to share "their expertise in planning, budgeting, and management" with school administrators, (2) to customize job-training efforts between businesses and schools, and (3) to train students and teachers in the skills, techniques, and equipment actually used in businesses.

The task force's third recommendation, namely, the marshaling of resources essential for improving public schools, urged the states and the local districts "to assign higher budget priority" to educational improvement and to ensure that existing fiscal resources would be used more effectively and efficiently, by being "selectively invested" to promote educational quality.

9. Task Force on Education for Economic Growth, *Action for Excellence* (Denver: Education Commission of the States, 1983), p. 9.
10. Ibid., pp. 22–30.
11. Ibid., pp. 34–41.

In action recommendation four, the task force dealt with the need to improve teachers' recruitment, preparation, status, and salaries. It endorsed the career ladder concept by which responsibility, pay, and status would change as teachers advanced through various career stages or steps, rather than the rigid adherence to the increments of the conventional teachers' salary schedule.

The task force's fifth recommendation sought to make students' academic experience more rigorous and productive by urging local school districts to establish "firm, explicit and demanding requirements concerning discipline, attendance, homework, grades and other essentials of effective schooling." The academic rigor of the curriculum would be strengthened by eliminating nonessential, academically "soft" courses. Moreover, eliminating nonessentials and lengthening the school year would ensure more effective use of the existing school day and school year.

In its sixth recommendation, the task force urged state boards of education to provide "quality assurance in education" by establishing objective systems to measure and reward teacher effectiveness and performance. Designed to reward effective teachers, quality assurance was also to lead to the dismissal of those teachers judged ineffective. Public school systems were advised to institute the "periodic testing of general achievement and specific skills" and colleges and universities were to "upgrade their entrance requirements."

Recommendation seven, improving leadership and management in the schools, emphasized the school principal as the chief instructional leader and a crucial agent in bringing about successful school reform.

The eighth recommendation urged schools to improve services to students who were currently "unserved or underserved." It specifically encouraged increased enrollment by women and minority students in mathematics and science courses and professions. Moreover, the task force called for the identification of academically gifted students and for the development of curricula sufficiently rigorous and enriching to challenge and develop students' talents.

Stimulated by the general climate of educational reform of the 1980s, many states developed comprehensive action plans to improve public elementary and secondary schooling. Representative of the various comprehensive state plans were "A Plan for Excellence: Alabama's Public Schools," "Better Education for Michigan Citizens: A Blueprint for Action," and "Reaching for Excellence: An Action Plan for Educational Reform in Missouri." These plans generally incorporated strategies designed to improve teacher effectiveness and competency, integrate technology into instruction, emphasize the academic components of the curriculum, strengthen graduation requirements, raise teacher certification requirements, and find additional and new sources for financing of public education.[12]

Conclusion

The American educational system is comprised of 50 different state school systems. In each state, the legislature is responsible for establishing, organizing, and financing public schools. The states, in turn, have delegated substantial educational

---

12. Task Force on Education for Economic Growth, *Action in the States* (Denver: Education Commission of the States, 1984), pp. 5–6.

responsibility to local school districts. Among the major responsibilities of state government to education is the financing of schools. To this end, state legislatures have established foundation formulas for state aid to schools. The governor of the state has the responsibility for implementing the state laws governing education. The state superintendent of instruction or school commissioner has the responsibility for making recommendations to the legislature, governor, and other state officials. The state board of education exercises a variety of educational functions, including the certification of teachers.

DISCUSSION QUESTIONS

1. Do research on education in France and the United States. Briefly compare and contrast the role of the national government in each country.
2. What is the constitutional basis for the states' role in education?
3. Trace the effects of the common-school movement in developing the states' educational role.
4. Read a biography of a leader in the common-school system, such as Horace Mann or Henry Barnard. From your reading, ascertain the growing role of the state in educational affairs.
5. Examine your state's school code. Identify the major areas covered in the code.
6. Describe the functions of the state board of education in your state.
7. Enumerate the functions of the state department of education in your state.
8. What is your state's policy on textbook selection?
9. Identify the subjects that are mandated in your state.

FIELD EXERCISES

1. Invite a member of the state legislature to your class to discuss your state's educational role.
2. Maintain a log on newspaper articles dealing with state actions in education.
3. Invite a local school board member to your class to discuss his or her conception of the state's educational role.
4. Invite a member of a local teachers' union or association to your class to discuss his or her conception of the state's educational role.
5. Analyze your governor's statements on education and see if you can identify his or her basic educational policy.
6. Identify your state superintendent of public instruction and the members of the state board of education. Prepare short biographical statements for each.
7. Prepare a newsletter for members of your class that identifies and describes pending legislation affecting education in your state.

SUGGESTED READINGS

CAMPBELL, ROALD F., CUNNINGHAM, LUVERN L., USDAN, MICHAEL D., AND NYSTRAND, RAPHAEL O. *The Organization and Control of American Schools.* Columbus, Ohio: Charles E. Merrill, 1980.

CAMPBELL, ROALD F., AND MAZZONI, TIM I., JR. *State Policy Making for the Public Schools.* Berkeley, Calif.; McCutchan, 1976.

DOYLE, DENNIS P. AND HARTLE, TERRY W. *Excellence in Education: The States Take Charge.* Washington, D.C.: American Enterprise Institute for Public Policy Research, 1985.

HARRIS, SAM P. *State Departments of Education, State Boards of Education and Chief State School Officers.* Washington, D.C.: U.S. Government Printing Office, 1973.

KATZ, MICHAEL S. *A History of Compulsory Education Laws.* Bloomington, Ind.: Phi Delta Kappa Educational Foundation, 1976.

MESSERLI, JONATHAN. *Horace Mann: A Biography.* New York: Knopf, 1972.

MUELLER, VAN D., AND MCKEOWN, MARY P. *The Fiscal, Legal, and Political Aspects of State Reform of Elementary and Secondary Education.* Cambridge, Mass.: Ballinger, 1986.

TASK FORCE ON EDUCATION FOR ECONOMIC GROWTH. *Action for Excellence.* Denver: Education Commission of the States, 1983.

———. *Action in the States.* Denver: Education Commission of the States, 1984.

WIRT, FREDERICK M., AND KIRST, MICHAEL W. *The Political Web of American Schools.* Boston: Little, Brown, 1972.

__11__

The Local Role
in Education

Although the constitutional authority for education is the state government, American educational patterns historically have been decentralized, with important responsibilities being vested in local school districts. Instead of a national system of education, the decentralized pattern of American education takes the form of thousands of local school districts throughout the United States. In these school districts, boards of education make the policies that govern public schools and levy the taxes that pay for them. Chapter 11 examines the historical origins of local control of education and discusses the contemporary forces and trends that shape educational policies in the local school districts of the nation.

The general focusing questions that will be answered as you read this chapter include the following:

1. What are the historical origins of local control?
2. What is the nature and function of the local school district?
3. What is the role of the local board of education?
4. How can schools have effective relationships with the communities they serve?

Historical Origins of Local Control

The origins for the local control of American education date back to the seventeenth century. In New England, particularly in Massachusetts, religious, economic, and social forces made the town the basic social, political, and educational unit. An area of from 20 to 40 square miles, the town was settled by members of a particular religious congregation. The congregation would petition the General Court, the colonial legislature, for permission to organize a new town. When the General Court granted the petition, the town as a corporate entity was entitled to hold town meetings, elect selectmen or trustees, and send representatives to the General Court.[1] In addition to their attachment to local government, the New England

---

1. Newton Edwards and Herman G. Richey, *The School in the American Social Order* (Boston: Houghton Mifflin, 1963), pp. 41–43.

Puritans also were strongly committed to schooling as a means of bringing up a literate and religiously orthodox population. These two factors of town control and a commitment to education were important forces in originating the American concept of local control of education.

Laws that reflected the Puritan commitment to civil control of education were those of 1642 and 1647 enacted by the General Court of Massachusetts. The General Court's action originated the principle that the state government had the authority to control schools. The civil or political authority was to supervise and control schools and to require that children be educated through the expenditure of public funds. In Massachusetts, the laws placed responsibility for education on local town boards of selectmen or trustees who were to (1) examine, commission, and certify the schoolmaster, (2) establish and maintain the school, and (3) levy taxes for the support of the school. As the towns became more heavily populated, colonial legislatures gave towns the right to divide into smaller local districts to direct, conduct, and administer schools. Each district within a township was a separate and independent entity for school governance. In the late eighteenth and early nineteenth centuries, each district, with its own elected board of trustees, often administered a single school.

Local Control in the Nineteenth Century

After the American Revolution and in the first half of the nineteenth century during the common-school movement, the general pattern of school control that emerged remained localized and decentralized in most of the northern states. The school district, with its own elected board, became the most immediate unit of organization and administration of public education. As the midwestern and other northern states entered the Union, they adopted the New England pattern of township or district control. The southern states used the county as their unit of educational organization.

Although the states made the local districts responsible for implementing their educational policies, school districts are creatures of and derive their powers from the state. Only by permission of the state legislatures or through powers delegated to it can the local school district control its own affairs.

Contemporary School Districts

The local school district is the basic unit of educational governance, administration, organization, and support for elementary and secondary schools in the United States. A school district can be defined as an entity, created by the state, to provide public education for the children residing in its service area. Its typical governing body is an elected board of citizens that usually hires a professional educator, a superintendent, to administer the public school system under its jurisdiction. School districts have their own taxing power to generate revenue to support the local schools.

Relying on historical precedents, the states have created a variety of local districts to educate the children who live in that district. The types of school districts vary in that there are elementary, secondary, and unit districts that combine both elementary and secondary schools. Some local districts are township units; others are county units. There are rural, urban, and suburban districts. Despite these variations, local school districts share some common features.

First, a local school district is a quasi-corporation because, while it operates like a corporation, it does not have articles of incorporation. As a state instrument, it operates under state laws and is designed to execute the state's educational policy and to facilitate the administration of public education within that state. The state's authority is executed through an elected board of education that is responsible to the state government. Second, a local school district has the responsibility of educating the children who live within that district, as identified by district boundary lines. Third, a local school district is also a unit for the financial support of schools, through taxes on its residents' property. Fourth, within the local district, citizens, through their elected board of education, establish educational policies to govern the administration, organization, financing, and maintenance of schools.

Before describing the functions of the board of education that governs each local school district, it is useful to examine the number and types of school districts and the relationships existing between school districts and other governmental units.

Number of School Districts

The history of school districts in the United States shows a steady decrease in their number. In 1938, there were 119,001 local school districts. Succeeding decades reveal the decline. In 1948, there were 94,426; in 1958, 47,594; in 1968, 22,010; in 1978, 16,014; and in 1988, 15,577.[2] This trend has largely been due to the consolidation of smaller rural districts into larger ones. In some states, the decrease can be attributed to the consolidation of elementary and secondary school districts into unit districts that combine both educational levels. Despite their decreasing number, however, importance of local school districts in the American educational process has not diminished. They remain the basic agency for governing and financing public education.

The trend to consolidate school districts has met resistance from those who believe that smaller districts are more closely controlled by and more responsive to the people of the district; however, the advocates of consolidation have generally prevailed. The arguments for consolidation have generally been as follows:

1. Larger districts eliminate the duplication of administrative and support services and result in cost saving.
2. A larger district has a more diverse social, economic, ethnic, and racial population, with greater opportunities for a genuinely integrated school population.
3. A larger district has a greater tax base that provides more revenue for educational purposes.
4. The larger tax base and administrative efficiency enable more resources to be devoted to increasing the program diversity in the curriculum.

2. *Digest of Education Statistics 1989* (Washington, D.C.: U.S. Government Printing Office, 1989), p. 50. The number of districts found in individual states varies greatly, ranging from more than 1,000 (California, Illinois, Nebraska, and Texas) to fewer than 50 local districts (Delaware, Hawaii, Maryland, Nevada, Rhode Island, and Utah).

A divergent pattern of relationships exists between school districts and other units of government. In 29 states, the school districts are independent of other government units; in 4 states, the school district has a dependent relationship with the political division in which it is located; the remaining 17 states present a mixed pattern of relationships, with varying degrees of dependency to the other governmental units.

The general argument for making school districts independent of other governmental units is that it provides them with greater freedom from partisan politics, political control, and political patronage. In addition, the following advantages are cited frequently: (1) The boundaries of school districts can be defined logically rather than being drawn on the historical and political accidents that have shaped other governmental units, and (2) taxation for school purposes may be viewed more favorably by voters when it is not tied to other government expenditures and budgets. Several disadvantages arise from independent school districts, as when a school district overlaps with several other units of government (for example, municipalities, townships, and park districts), such that school planning, construction, and use of facilities may have to be coordinated with several agencies of government. Obviously, in these cases, school boards and administrators have to spend more time and effort in working cooperatively with multiple governmental agencies.

Population Areas Served by School Districts

Another important factor is that of the student population and residential area served by the local school district. The following illustrates student populations/ districts:

Number of Students	Districts
≥ 25,000	173
10,000–24,999	447
5,000– 9,999	915
2,500– 4,999	1,823
1,000– 2,499	3,504
< 1,000	8,851

The range in student enrollment among local districts reveals the great variety of size and complexity that exists in American education at the local level.

Despite the variations that exist, it is possible to distinguish four types of population and residential patterns: the large city, or urban; the suburban; the small town; and the rural or agricultural. Each of these population patterns presents unique opportunities and problems.

The Urban School District In terms of student enrollments, the largest school district in the United States is New York City, with a student population of 939,000. It is followed by Los Angeles, with 568,000; Chicago, with 419,000; Dade County, Florida, with 253,000; and Philadelphia, with 194,000.[3] Fifty-six other urban school districts have enrollments that exceed 50,000.

3. Ibid., p. 92.

The problems of education in the larger cities are complex and stem from complicated demographic, sociological, and economic forces. The large-city district has historically been the location of America's greatest social mobility and change. In the late nineteenth and early twentieth centuries, the large-city districts included thousands of immigrant children in their school populations. At that time, the major problems were related to the assimilation of immigrant children. Today, the large-city district is the residence of many members of disadvantaged minority groups. The so-called inner city is the area in which the African-American, Chicano, and Appalachian populations are clustered; the residential areas of the white or advantaged social and economical groups are found in the outer edges. Residential patterns found in most of the large cities have contributed to de facto segregation.

Not only do the large-city districts have problems in achieving racial integration, but they also have generally experienced a decreasing tax base as businesses and industries move to suburban areas or to other parts of the country.

The Suburban School District   Another demographic and sociological phenomenon that has affected American Society and education since World War II has been the growth and development of the suburb. The large city, with its equally large single school district, is ringed by numerous suburbs, each having its own form of municipal government and its own school district or districts. Of the great variation among suburbs, some are old and exhibit conditions that are similar to the cities they surround; others are new and are experiencing population growth. School districts found in the newer suburbs often have a wealthy tax base, growing housing and population developments, and newer school physical plants.

The Smaller-City or Town District   School districts located in smaller towns and cities serve various populations, from a few thousand people to over a hundred thousand. They differ from the suburbs in that the residents of the smaller city usually work in that city rather than commute to the larger city. The small cities may have one or more school districts at the elementary level and enlarged districts at the secondary level. Some also have unified elementary and secondary districts.

The school populations of the small city, especially in the secondary or high school district, may be more heterogeneous in social background than those of the suburb or large city, however, as large cities are composed of neighborhoods populated by persons of similar social, racial, ethnic, or economic backgrounds. Because schools are attended by children who live in the neighborhoods, the student population reflects that of the particular neighborhood.

Rural, or Agricultural, Districts   In the past when the majority of the American population lived on farms and earned their livelihoods in agriculture, the small, often single-school, district was the dominant pattern of school organization in the United States. The one-room schoolhouse, with a single teacher and administered by its own school board, characterized elementary education in the rural United States. Since the Civil War, there has been a steady movement of population from rural to urban areas. Except in the most sparsely populated regions of the United States, the trend in rural districts has been to consolidate small districts into larger ones, to bring about more efficient operations and provide a wider range of opportunities to students.

Local Board of Education

The local board of education, or school board, is the legal agent specified by the state legislature with the responsibility for conducting education. For convenience, the local board will simply be referred to as the school board in the remainder of this chapter.

A school board can be defined as the body that is responsible for the general governance of a public school district. Its general responsibilities include authorizing, financing, and evaluating the educational activities in a given school system of the district for which it is responsible. Although its members are generally elected locally, in legal reality, the school board is a state agency rather than an adjunct to or a subsidiary of local government.

School boards are generally granted large latitude by the state in governing their schools and have authority to act in many areas unless they are specifically prohibited from doing so. Despite these broad powers, school boards are subject to numerous state laws and regulations that are specified in the school codes of the various states.

Election or Selection of Board Members

About 85 percent of school board members are elected to their positions by the voters of the district; the remaining 15 percent are appointed to their positions by some other governmental agency. In many of the large-city districts, for example, school board members are appointed by the mayor, with the approval of the city council. Because of many intrusions of partisan politics into school matters in the past, reforms were enacted that made the election or appointment of school board members nonpartisan. This means that school board candidates are not the formal nominees of regular or existing political parties. In a real sense, however, many school board members may be supported for election by partisan political groups or may have close ties to them.

Although candidates for school board may simply file the needed petitions to secure a place on the ballot, many districts use some sort of initial screening to identify qualified nominees. Some kind of screening committee or district caucus approves a slate of endorsed nominees to be presented to the voters at the school board elections.

Qualification of Board Members

The legal requirements for candidacy to a board of education are generally few and simple. The candidate must be a qualified voter and a resident of the school district. However, a number of factors or characteristics are desirable for members of school boards. Among them are the following:

1. Board members should be generally knowledgeable about educational needs, problems, issues, and resources. Although they are not expected to be professional educators, they need to demonstrate a sincere and sustained interest in education.
2. They should be able to understand the nature and role of a school board.
3. They should be able to understand and direct the financial and business affairs of the school district.
4. They should know how to cooperate with their colleagues on the board, and desire to do so.
5. They should see educational issues in broad, general terms that enable them to rise above special interests.
6. Because membership on a school board is time-consuming, members should have enough time and energy to devote to the office.

Ideally, members of school boards should try to see the broad issues facing education in the nation and state as well as in their district so that the policies that they enact will serve the general interests of all the children of the district. However, in the realities of policymaking, individual board members often represent specific as well as general interests. Board members may often find themselves exercising a transactive role as they mediate between the specific interests present in the district without losing sight of the goal of general policymaking.

The term of office for school board members varies from state to state, but it is generally believed that board members should serve for terms of three to five years so that they become familiar with their duties and responsibilities. To provide continuity in board matters, the terms of office for board members are staggered.

The number of members of a board of education varies from state to state. The size of a large-city board often exceeds that of a smaller district. In Illinois, for example, most school boards consist of 7 members. Although opinions vary as to the desired size of a board of education, it is generally argued that a board should be large enough to be representative but not so large that it is inefficient in conducting its business. Most board members are not paid for their service, but a few city and county boards offer some compensation.

Socioeconomic Background of Board Members

The backgrounds of school board members tend to reflect the social and economic status of their districts. Although the number of women who serve on boards is increasing, males still predominate. In 1984, 61.7 percent of board members nationally were men and 38.3 percent women. In terms of racial composition, the percentage of whites serving on boards of education was 86.8 percent; African Americans, 2.6 percent; Hispanics, 2.6 percent; Asian Americans, 2.6 percent; and Native Americans, 1.8 percent. In addition, 43.3 percent of board members were in the age range 41–50.[4] As has been the case historically, the majority of board members are from higher-income and higher-status groups, with a large number coming from

4. "Seventh Annual Survey of Board Members – Heads Up: Professionally and Financially You're Better off Than Ever Before," *The American School Board Journal,* 172, No. 1 (January 1985), pp. 29–31.

business and professional backgrounds. Members of minority and lower-income groups are generally underrepresented.

Functions of a Board of Education

Primarily, a school board establishes educational goals and develops the policies by which these goals are attained efficiently. While it is the superintendent's responsibility to operate the schools according to these policies on a day-to-day basis, the board is responsible for seeing that the schools in the district are functioning according to their general policies.

As a policymaking body, school boards may act only at authorized, public meetings as a board. Individual board members may not make decisions that are binding on the district. It is important that both the public and the board members understand that board members should not assume the tasks of the superintendent and professional staff.[5]

As a policymaking body, the decision of a local school board should occur at public meetings that are held at time and places convenient to the general public and open to the news media. All board actions should be recorded in accurate minutes that are open to the public. For the board to be effective, it should adopt and follow procedures that contribute to its efficient operations. The following is a sample agenda that many local school boards follow:

1. A call to order by the president of the board
2. A roll call of the board members
3. Approval of minutes of the previous meeting
4. The recognition of visitors, delegations, and the receipt of petitions from the public
5. Financial matters, such as the approval of pay orders, the acceptance of invoices, and a review of receipts and expenditures
6. The superintendent's report
7. Old business that remains from previous meetings
8. New business
9. Adjournment

Although the board has the general functions of establishing a district philosophy and general policies for education within the district, it also has to attend to many specific matters. Among the most important of the board's functions is that of employing a professional educational staff that includes a superintendent, associate or assistant superintendent, a business manager, teachers, custodians, secretaries, clerks, and other support personnel. The key appointment is that of the superintendent, who recommends the hiring of staff members who are in subordinate positions. When it employs a superintendent, the board delegates executive functions to that individual.

The school board also has the function of supporting the schools and the educational program financially. To do so, it must levy taxes, approve budgets, establish salary schedules, and keep account of the funds spent. While it relies on the

5. *Guidelines for Effective School Board Membership: A Handbook* (Springfield: Illinois Association of School Boards, 1976), p. 7.

superintendent, business manager, and other professional staff for advice, it alone has the responsibility for keeping the schools financially solvent.

Within the prescriptions of the state-mandated subjects, the board approves the overall educational program or the curriculum to be followed in the district. In this important function, it has the benefit of the professional staff's expertise. However, the final decision over the choice of instructional programs and materials, again, rests with the school board.

The school board is also responsible for providing that the children of the district have schools that are physically safe and conducive to learning. School codes establish the basic requirements for the life safety of students, but the school board is responsible for maintaining heating, lighting, and ventilation that safeguard the health and physical well-being of the students who attend the district's schools. School boards, upon the recommendation of the superintendent and professional staff, also have the responsibility for approving the school calendar and the district transportation policy and establishing the boundaries of school attendance areas.

In addition to their general policymaking functions, the school board acts as a mediating agency between the public and the professional staff. It provides the public with information regarding the educational progress and problems of the school district. It also sorts out and discusses the problems that concern the public.

As teacher organization, such as the NEA and the AFT, have become more action oriented in achieving their goals, school boards have spent more time and energy in negotiations with the bargaining agencies that represent teachers. Usually, these negotiations are conducted through well-defined procedures. Negotiations between school boards and teacher bargaining agents usually involve such matters as salary schedules, sick leaves, fringe benefits, and teaching conditions.

Board–Administrator–Staff Relationships

Although more will be said about the organization of the professional staff in Chapter 18, it is important to make some general observations about board, administrator, and staff relationships in terms of the operations of the local school district.

In any discussion of board and administrator relationships, it should be remembered that the board is the policymaking and governing body of the district and that the superintendent of schools is the chief administrative officer. When these roles become confused, the district is likely to experience unnecessary controversy and difficulty. That is, the superintendent should not try to make policy, and the board members should not usurp the superintendent's professional role. Both public and staff confidence in the district's school system can be undermined when there is either lack of trust or a breakdown of communications between the board and the administrator. Within these general guidelines, it is possible to explore board–staff relationships in greater depth.

If the local school district is to fulfill its major function of providing optimum education, there must be a clearly defined and harmonious working relationship among the board, the superintendent, and the other administrators and staff. Once a board has adopted its policies, it becomes the responsibility of administrators to implement them. The methods used to implement policies should be defined in a handbook of rules and regulations that also contains the job descriptions of all persons employed by the district. This handbook should be available to all employees of the district.

As the chief administrator of the district, the superintendent is charged with the enforcement of board-adopted policies. This means that administrative decisions should be consistent with these policies. Administrative assignments of principals, assistant principals, and other personnel should be recommended by the superintendent and approved by the board of education. While each administrator should have sufficient autonomy to function in his or her area of responsibility, the board members and the administrators of the district need to realize that a complete educational program requires mutual trust, respect, and a team effort to succeed.

School–Community Relations

Ever since common schools were established in the early decades of the nineteenth century, astute leaders of public education have realized that the school's success depends on favorable relationships with the local community. Historically, local communities have taken pride in and supported their public school systems. By the late 1970s, there were signs that the traditional mutuality of support between school and community was in danger of eroding. Many communities resisted efforts to increase local taxes for education. Voters in some states, such as California, with Proposition 13, abolished local discretion on property tax rates. The erosion of the close relationship between schools and communities was also influenced by the lack of direct contact that many residents had with the local schools. It is estimated that 30 percent of all households in the United States are made up either of childless couples, older couples with grown children, or young couples who have deferred having children to a later stage in their marriage. When added to the 23 percent of those who live alone, households without children comprise the majority of households in the United States. It is obvious that the household without children enrolled in the local schools has only an indirect involvement in local education. The task then is for schools to try to reach and involve both parents and nonparents in the issues and problems of local education.[6]

In the 1980s, concerted efforts have been directed to repairing and to strengthening school–community relationships by creating a wide range of partnerships. For example, The Task Force on Education for Economic Growth recommended the creation of "broader and more effective partnerships for improving education in the states and communities of the nation." Specifically, the task force urged business leaders to establish partnerships between business and the schools.[7]

Business leaders have become increasingly visible on committees to improve public schooling and to advise school boards and educational administrators. Busi-

6. Mary Lou Fuller, "The American Family: What Does It Look Like? How Does It Act?" *PTA Today,* 11, No. 3 (December 1985–January 1986), pp. 5–6.
7. Task Force on Education for Economic Growth. *Action for Excellence* (Denver: Education Commission of the States, 1983), p. 35.

ness firms, through adopt-a-school and other collaborative efforts, have participated directly in the programs of specific schools.[8]

One of the traditional community partners in supporting public schools has been the home and family. Home–school partnerships contribute to the improvement of local education in that they (1) encourage parents to focus their time and energy to foster the education of larger groups of children, (2) encourage teachers to know their students in a broader context, and (3) contribute to the community's involvement in the schools.[9]

Most local schools have a home–school organization such as the parents' club, booster club, or a unit of the Parent-Teacher Association (PTA). The PTA, founded in 1897, has a membership of 5.6 million and is involved in a wide range of projects, programs, and publications to support local schools.

School board members, administrators, and teachers, especially at the local district and local school level, need to work at building partnerships with the local community.[10] Improving community relationships between educators and the public is a necessary means of winning and sustaining confidence in and support for public education.

Conclusion

Prospective teachers become employees of a local board of education when they secure a teaching position. After initial employment, teachers will be affected by the policies made by a local board of education. There will be many occasions when a teacher, often as a member of a committee, will meet with members of a board of education. Whether one teaches in a large or a small district, one needs a clear idea of the role and functions of the local board of education.

DISCUSSION QUESTIONS

1. To a degree, contemporary institutions are a product of historical circumstances. To what degree does this statement apply to public schools?

2. What is the definition of a local school district? What is the impact of local control on American public education?

3. What are the social, economic, political, and educational advantages and disadvantages of larger consolidated school districts?

4. Describe the type of school district in which you live. Is it urban, suburban, small-town, or rural? What is the district's socioeconomic and ethnic composition?

5. As a teacher, describe the type of school district in which you would prefer to be employed.

8. Michael Timpane, "Business Has Rediscovered the Public Schools," *Phi Delta Kappan,* 65, No. 6 (February 1984), pp. 389–392.

9. Annette Lareau and Charles Benson, "The Economics of Home/School Relationships: A Cautionary Note," *Phi Delta Kappan,* 65, No. 6, (February 1984), pp. 401–404.

10. Richard W. Saxe, *School-Community Relations in Transition* (Berkeley, Calif.: McCutchan, 1984), provides a thorough examination of this subject.

6. Read a newspaper published in a larger city and a newspaper published in a suburb or a small town. Make a list of the educational issues reported in these newspapers. Compare and contrast the problems that public schools face in these different settings.

7. What is a local school board? What are its powers, responsibilities, and functions?

8. What are the desirable characteristics of school board members?

9. Describe the proper relationship that should exist between a superintendent and a school board.

FIELD EXERCISES

1. You are seeking a teaching position in a particular small-town school district. Identify and do some basic research about that district. What is its population? What is the socioeconomic, ethnic, and racial composition of the district? Who are the members of the local school board? What is the condition of the schools? What are the educational issues in that district? After having developed a profile of the district based on your research, visit the district. Spend some time in its business district and its neighborhoods. Visit a school. Based upon the information that you have gathered, would you want to accept a teaching position in that district?

2. You are seeking a teaching position in a large-city (urban) school system. Refer to and use the same questions asked in Field Exercise 1, but adapt them to a subdivision, a district, within that system so that your research has a manageable base.

3. You are a newspaper reporter covering a school board meeting. Attend a school board meeting and note the following: (a) Where is the meeting held? (b) Who is in attendance? (c) What items are on the agenda? (d) What decisions are reached? (e) What issues are raised by the public? (f) What are the interactions among board members and among board members and the superintendent and other administrators present?

4. Interview several school board members and through your questions attempt to determine how they perceive their roles and responsibilities.

5. Interview several teachers and through your questions attempt to determine how they perceive the impact that a school board has on their professional roles and responsibilities.

6. Interview the president of a parent–teacher organization in a local school and through your questions determine that person's perceptions of school–community relations.

7. Visit a school that has an adopt-a-school program. Report your observations of that program to the class.

SUGGESTED READINGS

BORMAN, KATHRYN M., AND SPRING, JOEL H. *Schools in Central Cities: Structure and Process.* New York: Longman, 1984.

BOWERS, C. A., ED. *Education and Social Policy: Local Control of Education.* New York: Random House, 1970.

BRODINSKY, BEN. *How a School Board Operates.* Bloomington, Ind.: Phi Delta Kappa Educational Foundation, 1977.

BURKE, FRED G. *Public Education: Who's in Charge?* New York: Praeger, 1990.

CAMPBELL, ROALD F., CUNNINGHAM, LUVERN

L., USDAN, MICHAEL D., AND NYSTRAND, RAPHAEL O. *The Organization and Control of American Schools.* Columbus, Ohio: Charles E. Merrill, 1980.

CISTONE, PETER J., ED. *Understanding School Boards.* Lexington, Mass.: Lexington Books, 1975.

CRONIN, JOSEPH M. *The Control of Urban Schools.* New York: Free Press, 1973.

FULLER, WAYNE E. *The Old Country School: The Story of Rural Education in the Middle West.* Chicago: University of Chicago Press, 1982.

KIRST, MICHAEL W. *Who Controls Our Schools? American Values in Conflict.* New York: W. H. Freeman, 1984.

MACLEOD, FORA, ED. *Parents and Schools: The Contemporary Challenge.* New York: Falmer Press, 1989.

MASTORS, CHARLOTTE. *School Volunteers: Who Needs Them?* Bloomington, Ind.: Phi Delta Kappa Educational Foundation, 1975.

OAKES, JEANNIE, AND LIPTON, MARTIN. *Making the Best of Schools: A Handbook for Parents, Teachers, and Policymakers.* New Haven, Conn.: Yale University Press, 1990.

SAXE, RICHARD W. *School–Community Relations in Transition.* Berkeley, Calif.: McCutchan, 1984.

SHARMAN, CHARLES C. *Decision Making in Educational Settings.* Bloomington, Ind.: Phi Delta Kappa Educational Foundation, 1984.

VITERITTI, JOSEPH P. *Across the River: Politics and Education in the City.* New York: Holmes and Meier, 1983.

12

Financing Public Education

The subject of school finance may not seem exciting to a person preparing for a teaching career. But it becomes apparent that school finance is of basic importance to citizens, teachers, administrators, and students. The quality of education depends upon the willingness of citizens to support schools. The availability of teaching positions and salaries, educational programs and services, and facilities depends upon the willingness and ability of communities to support them.

The general focusing questions that will be answered as you read this chapter include the following:

1. What is the condition of contemporary school financing?
2. What is the local role in funding education?
3. What is the state role in funding education?
4. What is the federal role in funding education?
5. What political factors influence financing schools?
6. What is the budgeting process at the local district level?
7. What current developments are reshaping educational financing?
8. How has the private sector entered the area of financially supporting schools?

Contemporary School Financing

In the late 1970s and early 1980s, it became increasingly difficult to provide adequate funding for public elementary and secondary schools. Because most state financial aid is based on average daily pupil attendance, declining enrollments reduced the amount of money received by local school districts. The dramatic inflationary cycle of the period and the economic recession, especially in northern industrial states, simultaneously inflated school expenditures but also reduced revenues. In addition, well-organized taxpayer groups, hard-pressed by the twin forces of recession and inflation, organized to defeat referenda to raise tax rates for school support.

By the mid-1980s, however, there were indications of a greater willingness to fund public education, particularly at the state level. This improved outlook for school financing was produced by a significantly lower rate of inflation, improved economic conditions in most states, and renewed interest in educational reform stimulated by national reports such as *A Nation at Risk* and *Education for Excellence*. Whereas support for public schools has increased since 1980, the economics of school support remain tied to many factors beyond the control of educational administrators; these include fluctuating energy costs and the international balance of trade. However, in the last analysis, school financing rests largely on the willingness of communities to support their educational systems.

The three major sources of financial support for public schools are the local, state, and federal governments, which distribute tax money to school districts. Throughout most of America's educational history, the bulk of school income has been generated by local taxes, primarily the property tax. Locally generated revenues have decreased from approximately 83 percent in 1920 to the current level of about 43.9 percent. During the same period, state support for schools has increased slowly but steadily from 17 percent to 49.8 percent. It is expected that the states' share will increase as school districts experience problems in raising needed school revenues locally. The federal government's support of education has grown from less than 1 percent in 1920 to the current level of 6.4 percent. These percentages are based on national averages; the revenues actually generated from each funding source vary from state to state.

In dollar amounts, the real revenues for public schools generated in 1980 from local government sources were $35.3 billion (42 percent of total support), the amount from state government was $41.1 billion (48.9 percent), and the amount from the federal government was $7.7 billion (9.2 percent), for a total of $84 billion. Two years later, in 1982, total revenues had decreased by $1.5 billion, to $82.5 billion, of which local governments contributed $35.4 billion (43.2 percent), state government $40.3 billion (49.1 percent), and the federal government $6.7 billion (7.7 percent). By 1984, total revenues had increased to $89.3 billion, breaking the cycle of declining support of the early 1980s. The amounts contributed by local governments, $39.7 billion (44.5 percent), and state government, $43.8 billion (49.1 percent), had increased. This increase offset the continued declining support of the federal government, which in 1984 was $5.7 billion (6.4 percent).[1] As of 1986, local districts were contributing $65 billion, or 43.8 percent of the total expenditures of public elementary and secondary schools; the states were contributing $73.2 billion (49.3 percent). The federal contribution of $9.9 billion was 6.7 percent of the total expenditures.[2]

While the dollar amounts of expenditures for elementary and secondary schools have increased dramatically over the past two decades, the percent of the gross national product (GNP) that Americans invest in elementary and secondary schooling has remained consistent at the level of slightly more than four percent. In 1967, 4.3 percent of the GNP was spent on public elementary and secondary

1. Task Force on Education for Economic Growth, *Action in the States: Progress Toward Education Renewal* (Denver: Education Commission of States, 1984), p. 19.
2. *Digest of Education Statistics 1989* (Washington, D.C.: U.S. Government Printing Office, 1989), p. 32.

education. In 1977, the same percentage was being used. As of 1987, however, the percentage had declined slightly, to 4.1 percent.[3]

Local Educational Funding

The property tax can be defined as a tax levied on land and its improvement. Based on the assessed value of real estate and personal property, it generates approximately 98 percent of local school revenue. Real estate includes residential and commercial land and buildings. Personal property includes items such as automobiles, furs, jewelry, and stocks and bonds. The property tax originated in America's frontier past, when wealth was measured primarily in land. It remains a widely used tax for historic reasons and because it produces a stable rate of collection since it is difficult to evade.

Appraisals of property to establish its assessed valuation include such factors as location, structure, condition, and use. The value of real property is reviewed at regular intervals, usually in a quadrennial assessment, to establish current market value. Although continuing efforts have been made to assess property close to its market value, the assessed value is usually fixed at a percentage of the market value. Underassessment may result from such factors as obsolete assessment practices, lack of expertise on the part of assessors, and political reasons.

Multiple local government units use the property tax to support varied services, such as police and fire protection, mosquito abatement, park and library districts, and highway and bridge maintenance. Because the taxable property wealth of communities within a state varies, inequalities of educational opportunity have resulted from a primary reliance on property taxes.

Most of the states specify by law the basic minimum property tax rate that local school districts can levy. Increases in the tax rate beyond this minimum usually require approval by the voters of the district. Since the mid-1970s, local school districts have had difficulty in raising the property tax as voters continue to defeat referenda for that purpose.

When the local property tax is considered without relationship to state and federal aid, there are great inequalities in the income that can be generated by a local school district. A district that has a high assessed valuation of property can generate more income for schools than can one with a low assessed valuation.

A simple example illustrates the relationship of the property tax to the education of children in two local school districts. The income generated by the property tax can be divided by the number of pupils in average daily attendance. For example, if school district A has an assessed valuation of $100 million and 1,000 pupils and school district B has an assessed valuation of $50 million for 1,000 pupils, a tax rate of $2 per $100 of assessed valuation would produce $2 million for school support in district A and $1 million in district B. District A would have $2,000 to spend per pupil, as compared with $1,000 in district B. Thus, an equal number of students—1,000 in each district—would be likely to receive an unequal education, since the amount of revenue generated in the poorer district would only be half of

3. Ibid., p. 29.

that of the wealthier district. It should be remembered, however, that state aid—depending upon the particular state formula—would tend to equalize the funds available.

Legal Challenges to the Property Tax

In the 1970s, litigation in several states challenged the primary reliance on property taxes to finance public education. The most often cited of these cases occurred in 1971 in *Serrano v. Priest*, when California's Supreme Court heard a case alleging that the heavy reliance on local property taxes in financing California public schools violated the Fourteenth Amendment. Specifically, the plaintiffs, several parents of public school children in Los Angeles County, contended:

> *The California public financing law with its primary reliance on local property taxes created large disparities among local school districts in the amount of revenue generated to finance public education. This resulted in gross financial and educational inequalities. Further, this condition violated the equal protection clause of the Fourteenth Amendment to the U.S. Constitution and the California Constitution.*[4]

In a 6-to-1 vote that agreed essentially with the plaintiffs, the California Supreme Court ruled:

> *The commercial and industrial property which augments a district's tax base is distributed unevenly throughout the state. To allot more educational dollars to the children of one district than to those of another merely because of the fortuitous presence of such property is to make the quality of the child's education dependent upon the location of private commercial and industrial establishments. Surely, this is to rely on the most irrelevant of factors as the basis of educational financing. . . . We find that such financing system as presently constituted is not necessary to the attainment of any compelling state interest. Since it does not withstand the requisite "strict scrutiny," it denies to the plaintiffs and others similarly situated the equal protection of the laws. If the allegations of the complaint are sustained, the financial system must fall and the statutes comprising it must be found unconstitutional.*[5]

Following upon the *Serrano* decision, state courts in Minnesota, Texas, New Jersey, Wyoming, and Arizona issued similar decisions. In 1973, however, the U.S. Supreme Court, in *San Antonio Independent School District v. Rodriguez*, upheld reliance on the property tax by a 5-to-4 decision.[6] In the *Rodriguez* case, the Court ruled that (1) while public school finance was chaotic, it was not unconstitutional, and (2) the property tax was not necessarily discriminatory, since poor people were not necessarily concentrated in poor districts. The Court did urge fundamental reform, however, in school finance.

Since the 1970s, a great deal of litigation regarding school finance has occurred in the courts. In California, Connecticut, New Jersey, Washington, and Wyoming, for example, existing systems of school finance were found unconstitutional. In

4. Charles S. Benson, *The Economics of Public Education* (Boston: Houghton Mifflin, 1978), pp. 339–342.
5. *Serrano v. Priest*, California Supreme Court, 96 *California Reporter*, (1971), pp. 601–626.
6. *San Antonio Independent School District v. Rodriguez*, 36 Law. Ed. 2d 16 (1973).

Idaho, Ohio, and Oregon, existing financial patterns were upheld. Although reliance on the property tax appears to be continuing, more legal challenges can be expected.

The impact of the judicial decisions on primary reliance on the local property tax to finance public elementary and secondary education is not yet clear. The trend seems to be that the use of alternative taxes will increase in the future and that the state will assume a larger share of the responsibility for financing public schools.

Criticisms of the Property Tax

Although the property tax is the oldest means of generating revenues for public schools, it is criticized as inadequate to meet today's economic needs. Criticisms of the property tax include the following:

1. It places a disproportionate tax burden on the homeowner.
2. It is easy for voters to strike out against higher taxes by defeating referenda to raise school rates. Such voter action forces school boards to eliminate needed programs and services.
3. A broader tax base is needed to raise needed school revenue and to create a more equitable distribution of the tax burden.
4. The assessment of property and the collection and administration of the property tax has been inequitable and inefficient in many communities.
5. Because there are vast differences in property wealth among local districts, financial inequalities have led to educational inequalities.

State Educational Funding

Subject to continuing legislative revision, state methods for financing public schools are extremely varied and complex. Since the state is the unit of government that has primary responsibility for and jurisdiction over education, it is important that citizens, in general, and teachers, in particular, have a basic understanding of state school finance. Although the states have delegated certain powers and responsibilities to local school districts, the state remains responsible for educating its citizens. It appears likely that, as local school districts experience greater difficulties in financing their schools through the property tax, the state will assume more financial responsibility.

State Revenue Sources

The major sources of state revenues come from taxes on sales and gross receipts, income, licenses, and other miscellaneous categories. A general breakdown of items included in these taxes is as follows:

Sales and gross receipts taxes on general sales, motor fuels, alcohol and tobacco, insurance, and amusements
Income taxes on individual and corporate income
Licenses on motor vehicles and their operators, corporations, occupations, and hunting and fishing

Miscellaneous taxes on property, mineral extractions, inheritance, and gifts

Every state uses some form of sales tax to generate more than half its revenue; almost 30 percent of state revenue comes from income taxes, and the remainder from other taxing categories.

Sales taxes are levied by all the states and occasionally by other government units. State sales taxes range from 2 to 6 percent. The sales tax is collected by the vendor (the seller) who is responsible for accounting and payment of the tax to the state. Although the collection of the sales tax is relatively easy, the amount of revenue generated depends on economic fluctuations. The sales tax has been attacked as a regressive tax that falls most heavily on lower-income persons, especially when such essential items as food, clothing, and medicines are taxed.

The state income tax is based on personal and corporate income. It can be withheld from wages. Income taxes can be a flat percentage or graduated according to income. With a graduated income tax, individuals in higher income brackets pay at a correspondingly higher rate.

State Aid

In addition to local revenues generated largely through the property tax, the state provides financial assistance—state aid—to local school districts. Often a complicated matter, the distribution of state aid varies considerably among the states. The rationale for state aid is partially historical and partially a product of current economic factors. In the era of the common-school movement in the nineteenth century, the state sometimes used grants-in-aid to encourage local school districts to organize and to levy a certain minimum taxation rate. It became apparent that local districts within a state varied greatly in their wealth and correspondingly in their financial ability to support schools. As a result, states have devised aid formulas to equalize per-pupil expenditures.

In terms of its use, state aid is classified as either *general* or *categorical* aid. General aid is given to the local district to use as it determines. Categorical aid is distributed to local districts to finance state-determined programs. For example, the use of categorical aid may be restricted to transportation, vocational education, driver training, and special education. Often, the state establishes categorical aid as an incentive to districts to establish specific programs.

General State Aid and Foundation Programs   General aid rests on the assumption that each child in the state should have basic educational opportunities. To equalize these opportunities, the states have devised foundation programs to distribute that aid to pupils. A foundation program refers to the procedure by which state funds are used to supplement local district revenues to support public elementary and secondary education. State foundation programs generally guarantee a "minimum foundation," an amount of financial support, from state sources to local school districts regardless of their ability to fund elementary and secondary education.

The following elements are involved in establishing the foundation program:

1. Determining the dollar value of the foundation effort in a state, usually on a per-pupil basis
2. Determining the minimum standard of local effort, usually based on revenues generated by the property tax
3. Determining a means of distributing funds to school districts based on their school population and their local wealth as indicated by assessed valuation of property

Flat Grant Model   The flat grant model is the oldest and simplest but also the most unequal method of allocating state aid to local school districts. State allocations to local school districts are determined by a flat grant, usually a fixed amount that is multiplied by the number of pupils enrolled in the district's schools. State aid supplements the revenue generated by local taxes, usually on property. Although the flat grant approach is simple, it means that wealthier districts have more funds at their disposal than poorer districts. Thus, the education received by a child in one part of the state may be unequal to that in another part of the state.

The Foundation Model   Some form of the foundation model is used in about two-thirds of the states to equalize per pupil expenditures across districts. Guaranteeing an equal minimum of aid per pupil, the foundation model provides the amount of state aid needed to supplement a minimum required local tax effort. Generally, the state's contribution is inversely related to local property tax wealth. With the foundation model, each local school district in the state is required to put forth the same minimum local effort to finance its schools. This local minimum tax rate produces the local district's share of the foundation level. Because this tax rate will produce more revenue in a wealthy district than in a poorer district, the poorer district will receive more aid from the state than will the wealthier district.

In the foundation model, two crucial and often controversial elements are (1) the degree of local tax effort required and (2) the amount of local leeway permitted. Local leeway permits wealthier districts to use surplus revenues from local taxes to finance schools above the foundation level. At the same time that local leeway has perpetuated inequalities in per-pupil expenditure, it has enabled some districts to develop high-quality and often innovative education programs.

Equalized Percentage Grants   Some states have attempted both to provide fiscal equality between children of different districts and to encourage local districts on their own initiative to levy higher tax rates for school support. Equalization refers to state funding formulas to supplement local funding among districts within a state. The general purpose of equalized funding is to adjust for variations in the local tax bases and to provide greater equity among school districts. State supplemental funds are provided to poorer districts so that they can achieve a minimal per-pupil support level. In the equalized percentage model, the local school district determines its own rate of expenditure—often with limits set by the state—beyond the required minimum. The local district determines a local property tax rate, and the state guarantees equal levels of expenditure for equal tax effort.

Recent Trends in State School Financing

By the late 1980s, the following major trends in school financing by the states were discernible:

1. The strengthening of general equalization aid programs
2. The design of new strategies to find additional revenues for local school districts
3. Expanded state aid for programs to strengthen basic, special, and gifted education programs
4. Increasing use of the sales tax to generate additional revenues
5. Efforts generally to upgrade teachers' salaries and establish career ladders as alternatives to the conventional salary schedule[7]

The climate of school reform of the 1980s also stimulated state action to increase support for public education. For example, Arkansas, in 1983, and South Carolina, in 1984, increased their sales taxes to generate more revenues for public schools. Other states are likely to follow their examples. Several states have taken specific actions to fund improved teachers' salaries. The Idaho School Improvement Act of 1984 provided $20.3 million to raise the salaries of certified teachers. Minnesota appropriated $6 million in 1984 to integrate educational technology in the school curricula.[8] These efforts to provide increased support for public education generally and for specific program improvement point to a greater state contribution to financing education. (See Fig. 12-1.)

FIGURE 12-1   Trends in Revenue Sources for Public Elementary and Secondary Education, 1970–1987

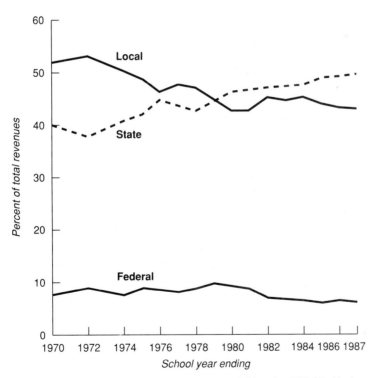

SOURCE: From Curtis O. Baker, ed. *The Condition of Education 1989* (Washington, D.C.: U.S. Government Printing Office, 1989), p. 35.

7. Allan Odden and John Augenblick, *School Finance Reform in the States: 1980* (Denver: Education Commission of the States, 1980), pp. 3–6.
8. Task Force on Education for Economic Growth, *Action in the States*, pp. 16–17.

Federal Educational Funding

Although the U.S. Constitution reserved education to the states, the federal government has historically provided some financial support for public elementary and secondary education. Always controversial, this support has sometimes been enthusiastic but more often reluctant. Federal aid has usually been categorical and for specific purposes rather than general.

A major change in the federal policy toward the financing of education came in 1965 with the Elementary and Secondary Education Act (ESEA). Although still categorical, the ESEA was broad in scope. As part of President Lyndon Johnson's War on Poverty, the major thrust of the ESEA sought to equalize educational opportunities, particularly in inner-city and rural poverty areas. Local education agencies that wished to participate in the ESEA had to prepare proposals within the guidelines of the act's various titles. In the 1970s, federal revenue sharing provided for the return of some revenues to the states. Some of the states used these funds for educational programs.

Until the Johnson programs of the Great Society, the limited amount of federal aid was for specific programs and categories. Among the categories of federal support have been vocational education, manpower development, special education, national defense, aid to areas impacted by poverty, veterans' education, school lunches, educational television, school libraries, economic opportunity programs, and others. While these categories of special aid have benefited particular programs, they frequently have had negative side effects in increased bureaucracy and red tape. Federal aid—in the form of assistance to particular educational categories—often has been short-lived and poorly planned.

At the same time that basic programs of regular education have languished due to the inability of many local districts to support them adequately, federal programs have tended to overemphasize isolated new and innovative programs. Federal grants have also been superimposed on state and local districts. In their eagerness to tap the source of the federal funds, states and local districts have sometimes devised programs that really do not meet or benefit local needs.

Educators who argue for increased federal aid would prefer to have it without the bureaucracy and confusion that often accompanies it. They argue that federal assistance should be reformed so that (1) the many categories of aid to special programs are condensed into a few large and comprehensive categories and (2) revenue sharing with the states would permit federal assistance to be given directly to the local school districts for general programs support.

Politics of School Financing

At the bottom line, the financial support of the public schools rests on the willingness of citizens to support them. Schools are supported at the local level primarily through the property tax, at the state level by aid allocated according to various foundation formulas, and at the federal level through categorical aid programs. A general population trend for the 1980s and 90s strongly indicates a continued increase in the 65-and-over age group. This means a decrease in the number of people who have a direct interest — children enrolled — in schools. Unless local school boards and administrators develop strategies to enlist the support of those who are not directly related to schools, the number of voters favorable to increased support is likely to decrease.

Proposition 13

In the late 1970s, signs of a taxpayers' revolt against increased taxation emerged. The most dramatic example of a growing fiscal conservatism occurred when a large majority of California voters supported Proposition 13, an initiated referendum to freeze property tax rates and assessments.

Proposition 13 decreased local revenues in California. Of local government units, school districts suffered the greatest loss of revenue in that they lost over 50 percent of their property tax revenue. The immediate effects of Proposition 13 were blunted somewhat by the use of a state surplus for local government finance.

Special Interests

The rise of special-interest groups is another trend that has affected school financing, as well as other areas of American life. Special-interest groups for special, vocational, or bilingual education, for example, may lobby for mandated programs and categorical funding at the state level. Teacher organizations and unions often pursue their own specific "bread and butter" programs for their membership. An unfortunate result is that the ranks of those who argue for general school aid are badly fractured. A properly functioning school system needs adequately supported regular education programs upon which to base special programs to meet particular needs.

A Greater State Role

A very significant trend in financing public elementary and secondary education has been the steady increase in the states' contribution. In 1979, a noteworthy historic shift occurred: The states' contribution exceeded that of the local school districts for the first time in the history of American education. Between the 1969–1970 and 1986–1987 school years, the state contribution increased from approximately 40 percent to about 50 percent. During the same period, the contributions by local districts decreased from 52 to 44 percent, and the federal government's contribution declined from 8 to 6 percent.[9] Dislike of and rebellion against the property tax, judicial litigation, and state finance reform are likely to increase further the states' share in financing schools. It seems likely that federal aid will decrease.

A rising state role in financing public schools suggests strongly that many crucial decisions affecting school support will take place in the legislative chambers and governors' offices of the state capitals.

9. Curtis, O. Baker, ed., *The Condition of Education 1989* (Washington, D.C.: U.S. Government Printing Office, 1989), p. 34.

Education Budgeting Process

In the broadest sense, a local school district's budget is a planning instrument that establishes educational priorities and allocates the financial resources to achieve its goals. More specifically, a budget expresses the financial plan of the local school district and its educational program in dollar amounts. The states, in their school codes, generally prescribe the forms and procedures to be used by local school districts in preparing, adapting, administering, and auditing their budgets. School budgets are usually prepared on an annual basis, and they project income and expenditures for a given fiscal year.

The school budgeting process involves three elements:

1. Establishing the priorities of the school district, expressed as goals and objectives, and specifying the programs, staff, facilities, and support needed to achieve them. The setting of educational priorities involves continuing long-range and short-range planning on the part of the members of the community, the board of education, and school administrators and staff.
2. Estimating the revenues available to finance the costs of the total educational program, broken down into its specific components.
3. Ascertaining the financial plan, or expenditures, needed to meet the costs of the educational plan.

A local school district's budgeting process may be divided into four major steps: (1) preparation, (2) presentation and adoption, (3) administration, and (4) appraisal. The district superintendent, assisted by a staff, usually prepares the budget.[10]

Preparation of the Budget

Budget preparation is a continuous process in that the financial plan for a given year cannot be isolated from the budgets that have preceded and are likely to follow it. The initial point of budgeting involves both the philosophy and the politics of education. The philosophy shared by the community determines in large part the priorities of the local school district. The willingness of the community to support implementation of that philosophy is expressed in concrete school programs, physical facilities, professional staff, and support services.

After the board of education has established educational priorities—really a sense of educational direction—in terms of goals and objectives, the superintendent and staff have the difficult task of making the abstract goals operational in terms of specific programs and the necessary staff and support services. This operationalizing is accomplished by balancing the revenue available with the anticipated expenditures of the program. A key factor in the process is having the professional staff—principals, department heads, and teachers—prepare and submit budgetary requests to the superintendent.

---

10. For treatments of the budgeting process, see Robert D. Lee and Ronald W. Johnson, *Public Budgeting Systems* (Baltimore: University Park Press, 1977); Aaron Wildevsky, *The Politics of the Budgetary Process* (Boston: Little, Brown, 1984); John Greenhalgh, *School Site Budgeting* (Lanham, Md.: University Press of America, 1984).

Presentation and Adoption of the Budget

The school administration—the superintendent, business manager, and their staffs, which depend on the size of the school district—prepares the budget in tentative form. It is then presented to the board of education and to interested citizens and groups for explanation and perhaps modification. After discussion, the budget is drafted in final form and presented for public hearing. It is then ratified by the board of education or other appropriate legal bodies. Although in most states the appropriate legal body to ratify the budget is the board of education, a few states require approval by other bodies, such as the city council or the voters of the district.

Administration of the Budget

After the estimated revenues have been transferred to the school accounting ledgers as initial entries, the budget is ready to be implemented. The terms *cost-effective* and *fiscally responsible* are used to identify carefully administered school financing. In the long run, it is crucial that expenditures not exceed income, that purchases be carefully made, and that spending be monitored carefully.

Appraisal

Most directly, appraisal means that educational results are used to measure the degree to which the planning objectives have been accomplished. The appraisal involves an audit of expenditures and educational results.

Classification of Budgetary Items

The classification of budgetary items varies from state to state and from local district to local district, depending upon the approved budgetary format. The U.S. Office of Education has developed a general format that classifies educational expenditures under three major headings: current operating expenses, capital outlay, and debt services. Current operating expenses include expenditures for operations and maintenance. In nearly all school district budgets, the largest amount of revenue is spent on expenses related to instruction, such as teachers' salaries, books, and supplies. Capital outlay items include expenditures for land, buildings, physical facilities, and equipment. Debt service includes repayment of borrowed money and the interest on debt.

The following outline indicates the various items that may appear in these three categories:

I. Current Operating Expenses
   A. Instruction: teachers' salaries, textbooks, supplies, in-service training and workshops
   B. Administration: superintendent, central office staff, principals, other administrative staff, clerical and support personnel
   C. Pupil personnel and auxiliary support services: student health services, guidance, cafeteria and food service

   D. Transportation services: bus drivers, buses, vehicle leasing, vehicle maintenance

   E. Operation and maintenance: utilities, fuel, cleaning supplies, maintenance personnel

   F. Student activities: athletics, student organizations, clubs

   G. Fixed charges: contributions to retirement plans, social security, health insurance, fringe benefits

   H. Intersystem and cooperative payments: payments to other school districts for shared facilities or projects; contributions to consortia or cooperatives

  II. Capital Expenses: building construction, remodeling, landscaping, paving (permanent improvements to be paid for on a long-term basis)

  III. Debt Services: Redemption of bonds and interest on money owed by the district

Rather than using the traditional budgetary category of instruction or education, some school districts use planned program budgeting that classifies expenditures by programs, such as the reading, the mathematics, or the industrial arts program. In this way, the costs of a particular program are separated from the costs of other programs. The rationale for planned program budgeting is that it operationalizes accountability so that the costs of a particular program can be related specifically to educational achievements.

Planning Programming Budgeting Systems (PPBS) is a sophisticated version of program budgeting. It requires department heads or program directors to identify specific objectives, develop means to measure output, calculate total costs over the long run, prepare multiyear fiscal plans, and analyze the costs and savings of alternative programs.

Current Issues in Educational Financing

The recent history of the United States has been marked by economic unrest and anxiety. The major economic trends of this period have been inflation and sporadic recession, spiraling energy costs, and a large federal deficit. Paralleling this, the demographic conditions affecting public education have also changed. The number of individuals not related directly to the public schools, especially childless couples and senior citizens, has increased. Tax-conscious citizens groups have charged that the costs of maintaining public schools have not been equalled by educational results. From various and often unrelated sources have come demands for retrenchment and greater accountability on the part of public school officials and teachers.

Accountability

The term *accountability* is applied to educational financing and outcomes.[11] Accountability implies a direct relationship between educational spending and educational results and asserts that dollars spent on education should be measured by

---

11. For discussions of accountability in American education, see T. Martin, George E. Overholt, et al., *Accountability in American Education: A Critique* (Princeton, N.J.: Princeton, 1976); Maurice Kogan, *Education Accountability: An Analytic Overview* (Dover, N.H.: Hutchinson Education, 1986).

pupil achievement. Proponents of accountability want schools to be judged by their output in terms of their students' educational accomplishments.

The demand for accountability was stimulated by such recent trends as the rising cost of financing schools, a widely held public assumption that students' achievement has declined, and a growing loss of credibility in public education.

As is true of most public services, the costs of public schooling have increased because of greater demands being placed on schools and because of the high cost of financing schools in an inflationary era. Energy and fuel costs, teacher's salaries, building maintenance, and the cost of support services have risen. When called upon to provide additional support for public schools, taxpayers have demanded specific justification for added taxes for schools.

In addition to increased costs of schooling, there is a widely held assumption that students' basic competencies in reading, writing, comprehension, and mathematics have declined. Critics of the achievements of the public schools have charged that, although more money is spent on education today, academic achievement of American students has declined.

In operational terms, the movement for accountability has caused many schools to define their general educational goals in specific objectives. First, the schools must identify their goals; then, they must translate them into specific instructional performance objectives for students. Such goals as reading or mathematical competency must be indicated in specific objectives for each grade level.

Accountability can also be implemented through the budgeting process if the accounting system records expenditures by educational programs. For example, what is the cost of the reading, the mathematics, or the physical education program? What are the measurable results of the particular program in terms of student achievement? When indicated by program, the costs of the program can be determined by the accomplishments of the program's stated performance objectives. In other words, accountability places the responsibility for educational outcomes—for student achievement—directly on administrators and teachers.

Educational Vouchers

Educational voucher plans have been proposed to give parents public funds or tax credits to pay the cost of educating their children at the school of their choice, be it public or private. The proponents of the voucher system claim that it is unfair for the public schools to exist as a tax-supported educational monopoly. The voucher system, they contend, would bring greater competition to the educational arena. Public schools would have to compete with private schools. This competition would raise the quality of education in both sectors by forcing the mediocre schools out of the educational business. Vouchers, they insist, would result in greater freedom of educational choice.

Critics of the voucher plans contend that they would weaken the public schools as a common-school system. Public schools might become the refuge of the economically disadvantaged and of minority groups as more affluent groups abandoned them for private schools. They also charge that vouchers would encourage racial segregation and encourage expensive duplication of schools and lead to many of marginal quality. Aid to parochial schools, they contend, would violate the principle of separation of church and state.

Private-Sector Support

A recent trend in financing public schools is indirect or direct grant support from the private sector, especially from philanthropic foundations or from business corporations.[12] *A Nation at Risk, Education for Excellence* and other national reports on education have encouraged business involvement in assisting public schools. The U.S. Chamber of Commerce through its Business Education Action Plan has developed strategies to involve business firms and corporations in education in their local association. Many school systems, particularly in large urban areas, have established adopt-a-school programs, in which business firms and other private-sector agencies are paired with local schools and work with them on specific projects.

The school–business partnerships provide limited but indirect financial assistance to public schools. The cost of certain materials are borne by the private sector. Also, corporate aid to schools may take the form of computers, video systems, and other expensive items useful in integrating technology into the school curriculum.

A more direct kind of aid from the private sector has been grants to school districts from corporations, philanthropic agencies, and endowment funds in the private sector. Such private-sector initiatives were a noteworthy trend of the 1980s. For example, the Bank of Boston established a permanent endowment fund of $1.5 million to award grants for projects to improve teaching effectiveness. Several large corporations in California established the California Educational Initiatives Trend to award grants to school districts in that state.[13] Similar examples of private-sector assistance can be found in other states.

Although private-sector assistance holds significant possibilities for assisting public education in the United States, the amount — around $50 million annually — is small in terms of total costs. Further, private-sector aid, which is often temporary, is subject to changing economic conditions. It has also been directed to initiating specific new programs rather than to sustaining basic programs. There are important questions to be answered: Will the various private-sector initiatives be sustained in the long run? Will they move from specific programs to more general assistance?

Conclusion

This chapter has examined the complex but vitally important subject of school finance. The ability and the willingness of Americans to pay for their schools has long-range social, political, and educational consequences. Poor schools will mean a poorly educated citizenry that will be poorly equipped to maintain the quality of American life.

12. Research and Policy Committee of the Committee for Economic Development, *Investing in our Children: Business and the Public Schools* (New York: Committee for Economic Development, 1985), offers a useful treatment of school–business partnerships.
13. Task Force on Education for Economic Growth, *Action in the States*, pp. 11–12.

As an educator, your understanding of the general bases of school finance will help you to recognize the various constituents that contribute to educational financing at the local, state, and federal levels.

DISCUSSION QUESTIONS

1. Prepare an analysis of public financing of education in your state showing the proportion of local, state, and federal funding.
2. Examine the rationale and implementation of state efforts to equalize educational opportunities.
3. Debate the advantages and disadvantages of various taxes used to generate revenue for public schools.
4. Do you agree with the concepts of "accountability" and "school vouchers"?
5. Describe the general procedures for preparing and administering a local school district budget.
6. Identify and analyze recent trends in educational financing.

FIELD EXERCISES

1. Invite a local school district superintendent or business manager to speak to your class on the budgeting process.
2. Interview several members of local boards of education on school finance issues and problems. Report to the class on the trends that you discerned in your interviews.
3. Attend a budget hearing in a local school district and report to the class on your reactions to the hearing process.
4. Research the attempt of a local school district to pass a referendum to increase its tax rate. Was the effort successful? If so, why? If not, why not?
5. Arrange a debate on the issue of school vouchers.
6. Survey private-sector corporations in your locality to determine if they have programs designed to support schools.

SUGGESTED READINGS

ALEXANDER, KERN, AND MONK, DAVID H., EDS. *Attracting and Compensating America's Teachers.* Cambridge, Mass.: Ballinger, 1988.

BURRUP, PERCY E., BRIMLEY, VERN, JR., AND GARFIELD, RULON R. *Financing Education in a Climate of Change.* Boston: Allyn & Bacon, 1988.

BOWLES, SAMUEL, AND GINTIS, HERBERT. *Schooling in Capitalist America.* New York: Basic Books, 1976.

CATTERALL, JAMES S. *Education Vouchers.* Bloomington, Ind.: Phi Delta Kappa Educational Foundation, 1984.

COHN, ELCHANAN. *The Economics of Education.* Cambridge, Mass.: Ballinger, 1975.

DUKE, DANIEL L. *Decision Making in an Era of Fiscal Instability.* Bloomington, Ind.: Phi Delta Kappa Educational Foundation, 1984.

DYER, HENRY S. *How to Achieve Accountability in the Public Schools.* Bloomington, Ind.:

Phi Delta Kappa Educational Foundation, 1973.

GARMS, WALTER, FUTHRIE, JAMES, AND PIERCE, LAWRENCE. *School Finance: The Economics and Politics of Public Schools.* Englewood Cliffs, N.J.: Prentice-Hall, 1977.

GOERTZ, MARGARET. *Money and Education: How Far Have We Come?* Princeton, N.J.: Education Policy Research Institute, Educational Testing Service, 1979.

GOLDSTEIN, WILLIAM. *Selling School Budgets in Hard Times.* Bloomington, Ind.: Phi Delta Kappa Educational Foundation, 1984.

GRAHAM, GLENN T., WISE, GORDON L., AND BACHMAN, DUANE L. *Successful Strategies for Marketing School Levies.* Bloomington, Ind.: Phi Delta Kappa Educational Foundation, 1990.

LEWIS, ANNE C. *Partnerships Connecting School and Community.* Arlington, Va.: American Association of School Administrators, 1986.

MANNING, ALTON C. *Adopt a School—Adopt a Business.* Bloomington, Ind.: Phi Delta Kappa Educational Foundation, 1987.

MONK, DAVID H. *Educational Finance: An Economic Approach.* New York: Random House, 1990.

ODDEN, ALLAN, AND AUGENBLICK, JOHN. *School Finance Reform in the States: 1980.* Denver: Educational Commission of the States, 1980.

OTTERBOURG, SUSAN D. *School Partnerships Handbook.* Englewood Cliffs, N.J.: Prentice-Hall, 1986.

RESEARCH AND POLICY COMMITTEE FOR ECONOMIC DEVELOPMENT. *Investing in Our Children: Business and the Public Schools.* New York: Committee for Economic Development, 1985.

TASK FORCE ON EDUCATION FOR ECONOMIC GROWTH. *Action in the States: Progress Toward Education Renewal.* Denver: Education Commission of the States, 1984.

_13_

Early Childhood Education

Chapter 13 examines the major theories that have shaped current practices and institutions in early childhood education. It identifies leading pioneers of early childhood education, such as Rousseau, Pestalozzi, Froebel, Montessori, Piaget, and Erikson, and it examines the structures and organization of nursery and kindergarten education. The pioneering work of the early childhood theorists has implications for all stages of human growth and development as well as early childhood. The treatment of nursery and kindergarten education should be considered as an institutional prelude to elementary education, which is examined in Chapter 14.

The general focusing questions that will be answered as you read this chapter include the following:

1. What conceptions of children's nature and education were developed by leading early childhood educators?
2. What are the current early childhood institutions and practices?

Child Nature

It is difficult to treat the rich and complex history of early childhood education in a single chapter. But it is possible to examine some of the major conceptions of childhood that have developed throughout our history and to consider some of the important educators who shaped our changing conceptions of childhood and early childhood education.[1]

Children are born into the human group that reproduces itself biologically, but children do not inherit biologically the knowledge and values of the human group of which they are members. Knowledge and values, customs and beliefs, manners and

---

1. For the definitive treatment of childhood in Western civilization, see Philippe Aries, *Centuries of Childhood: A Social History of Family Life* (New York: Vintage Books, 1962); the changing perspectives of childhood in American culture are examined in Philip J. Greven, Jr., *Child Rearing Concepts, 1628–1861* (Itasca, Ill.: F. E. Peacock, 1973), and N. Ray Hiner and Joseph M. Hawes, *Growing Up in America: Children in Historical Perspective* (Urbana: University of Illinois Press, 1986).

mores are learned by processes of socialization and enculturation in which the immature members of the group, the children, acquire the culture of the group. The socialization process contains many variables that may alter the intended result. That is, children may not turn out exactly as adults would have them.

A basic cultural tension that has emerged in the education of children and that is reflected in the various theories of early childhood education involves the relationship of the child to the group. This tension is not unique to early childhood but occurs throughout the life cycle.

Throughout history, most of the patterns of early childhood education that developed were designed to bring children into group life in a deliberate and specifically defined manner that encouraged little or no diversity. Children were trained in the mores, folkways, knowledge, and values of the group by parents, elders, or guardians. Usually, the leader of the group and/or head of the family acted as the guardian of the cultural traditions that were imposed on children. Basically, children were to acquire the standards or norms of behavior of the group into which they were born. Once these standards were learned, the child became a participant in the group's cultural processes. As an adult, he or she was expected to transmit the heritage to his or her offspring. Such a pattern of cultural transmission and imposition on children was to safeguard the heritage by reproducing it culturally in the offspring of the group. This basic pattern of cultural reproduction through imposing the cultural heritage on children was true in the time before recorded history, in ancient Greece and Rome, during the medieval period, and throughout most of human history.

The theory of cultural imposition — that is, giving the cultural heritage to the young so that it might be perpetuated — is a continuing characteristic of early childhood and indeed of all education. The theory of cultural imposition rests on a strategy of determining what knowledge and values are appropriate for a child to acquire. You might consider the various meanings of appropriate education as it affects childhood.

There is appropriateness in terms of socioeconomic conditions. In an agricultural society, the children of farmers would be expected to acquire the knowledge appropriate to land tenure and the production of farm products. The same conditions of appropriateness would apply to children born into a seafaring culture or a mining society. Moreover, there is appropriateness in terms of politics and nationality. Children born in the United States are expected to acquire the political concepts and practices through political socialization or civic education that will enable them to share and participate in American political life and institutions.

In addition to social, economic, and political appropriateness, there are other forms of what is regarded as appropriate learning for children. Such forms of appropriateness are based on the norms required for membership in a particular socioeconomic class or religious, linguistic, or ethnic group. Historically, there were also strongly enforced expectations of what was gender appropriate to boys and girls. For example, boys were to be wage earners, soldiers, businessmen, politicians, lawyers, physicians, and engineers. Girls were to be wives, mothers, cooks, laundresses, and elementary school teachers. Today, sexual stereotyping based on predetermined career roles has been challenged, and career goals and orientations are no longer proscribed because of one's sex. However, much education is based on the expectations that society holds as appropriate for its future members.

If you consider your own upbringing and early education, you will discover the degree to which cultural imposition according to appropriate group norms has shaped your life and attitudes. For example, as a child you learned to speak the language of your parents or guardians. You really had no conscious choice in the matter. Your being born into a certain family meant that you would learn the family's language. At the same time that this language was imposed upon you, learning it also gave you an immense amount of power that enabled you to express your needs and to communicate with those around you. Being born in a particular country meant that you would be a citizen of that nation, with all its privileges and duties.

Although cultural imposition occurs in everyone's life and education, the important factor is the degree to which that imposition allows for alternative behavior and choice. Some groups and their cultures permit few alternatives; other cultures permit a variety of choices within a basic context of cultural consensus. All education, and early childhood education in particular, is shaped by the society and the social, cultural, economic, and political expectations that it has for its young.

The Individual Child

While childhood has been imposed upon by social norms and by what the adult members of society have defined as appropriate learning and behavior for children, a number of important educational reformers have sought to liberate childhood from the prescriptions of adult-imposed social control. These advocates of child freedom have ranged from those who sought to free children from social imposition such as Rousseau to those who wanted to enlarge child freedom within a framework of social consensus as did Dewey and many of the progressive educators. Basically, those who sought to liberate the child believed that childhood was an important time of human growth and development that has its own intrinsic patterns. Some early childhood educators had a new vision of society and wanted to liberate children from the norms of the old society so that they could build a new society. Others were interested in children and child nature and culture so that they could develop a more adequate method of child rearing. Regardless of their motivation, the pioneer figures of early childhood education challenged many of the social preconceptions that were imposed upon children.

What the pioneers of early childhood education did was to define appropriateness in a new way. As a reference point, they rejected what adults had defined as appropriate to childhood. For Froebel, Montessori, and Piaget, what was regarded as appropriate to a child's education came from developmental and growth patterns of childhood itself. These pioneers of early childhood education used various means of research that ranged from introspection about their own childhood experiences, to the observation of children, to philosophical and historical inquiry, to clinical studies. They identified stages of child development and sought to develop educational activities and experiences appropriate to them. In varying degrees, the criterion of appropriateness was defined as what was necessary to the child's stage of development and readiness, rather than what was expected by society. The following sections identify and examine some of these major contributors to early childhood education.

Jean Jacques Rousseau

Jean Jacques Rousseau (1712–1778) was an iconoclast who challenged the conventional wisdom of his day on religious, social, economic, political and educational matters; in this section, we focus on his vision of the child's education. In his didactic novel *Emile,* published in 1762, Rousseau imagined himself the tutor of Emile, the son of a wealthy family.[2] In *Emile* and his other works, Rousseau attacked the two widely held educational doctrines of *child depravity* and *social imposition*.

The doctrine of child depravity, often ascribed to Calvinist Puritanism, perceived human nature to be innately evil. Because of the sin of Adam and Eve, human beings had inherited the afflictive corruption of Original Sin. While some people were chosen by God for salvation, the vast majority of human beings were doomed to hell. To overcome their inherited corruption, which inclined them to idleness and mischief, children needed discipline and moral training. Play and games, now regarded as desirable children's activities, were then considered to be a nonsensical, childish waste of time. The "good child" was one who looked, dressed, spoke, and behaved like a miniature adult.

Jean Jacques Rousseau (1712–1778) wrote *Emile,* an influential novel advocating permissive, naturalistic education.

2. William Boyd, ed., *The Emile of Jean Jacques Rousseau: Selections* (New York: Teachers College Press, Columbia University, 1966).

Rejecting the concept, Rousseau proclaimed children to be naturally good, "noble savages." Because they are born good, children's needs, impulses, and desires are also naturally good. The child's senses and feelings were seen as the best guide to his or her education. The wise educator, personified by Emile's tutor, did not interfere with a pupil's impulses and emotions.

Rousseau also abandoned the theory of social and cultural imposition. Arguing that there was no evil in the infant at birth, Rousseau said that evil came from a corruptive society. Not knowing how to lie, cheat, or steal at birth, children were taught these vices by adults. If free to follow their natural inclinations and escape the corruption of the society about them, children could grow up as natural men and women. Socially isolated in his early childhood, Emile's growing up is done in natural surroundings, exploring the environment, and discovering nature's ways. Only after becoming a genuinely authentic natural person does Emile enter society.

Rousseau also discarded the venerable tradition that acquiring knowledge from the liberal arts and sciences was educationally desirable. Rather, he believed that verbal and literary information, organized in encyclopedic form, was useless and pernicious in that it produced artificial rather than natural men and women. Opposed to vicarious learning in early childhood, Rousseau believed that premature instruction in reading and writing harmed rather than benefited children because it stuffed their young minds with disconnected, often meaningless words. Only after enjoying a wide range of direct experience should children begin to read and write.

From his challenge to conventional education, Rousseau developed several ideas that influenced early childhood education:

1. *Follow nature.* Born innocent and without guile, children should not be governed by social conventions and artificialities. Human instincts, impulses, emotions, and feelings come from nature itself and are trustworthy. It is undesirable and unhealthy to force children to repress their natural inclinations.

2. *Learn from the environment.* Nature, again, provides the ideal setting for learning. Rather than acquiring secondhand, indirect bookish information, children should learn directly from the environment. Rousseau emphasized sense experience in learning; our ideas, he believed, resulted from the objects sensed in the environment. Rousseau's admonition that children learned most effectively from their environment stimulated other educational theorists, such as Froebel, Montessori, and Dewey, to emphasize the environment's educative role and assert that environmental manipulation was the key to learning.

3. *Develop permissive teacher–learner relationships.* As indicated, the Puritanical conception of child depravity contributed to the psychological and physical coercion of children. Rousseau recognized that adult coercion caused children to repress their interests and emotions. Repressed children tended to become artificial adults. Contrary to the adage that children should be seen but not heard, Rousseau recommended permissive child–adult relationships, in which children, acting on impulse, experienced either success or failure. Children thus learned that their actions had consequences. As the natural and direct consequences of action, rewards and punishments were not bestowed artificially at the pleasure or displeasure of adults.

4. *Divide childhood into stages of human growth and development.* Rousseau did not consider childhood to be of one piece but rather divided it into developmental stages. Infancy, the first developmental stage, from birth until the age of five, was a time when almost everything had to be done for the virtually dependent child. Attention was given to physical growth and development and to building strong, healthy bodies. The infant's diet was to consist of simple country food. Rousseau was opposed to confining children to playpens. He wanted them to have freedom to develop and exercise muscles. In terms of moral development, Rousseau did not believe that infants were moral beings. Arguing that good and evil had relevance only for those who could reason, Rousseau believed that children—in infancy—were governed only by their feelings of pleasure and pain. In terms of language development, Rousseau stated that the child's first words should be few, simple, and clear and should be names for the objects found in the immediate environment.

Rousseau's second developmental stage was boyhood, from ages 5 to 12. At this stage, Emile was physically stronger and was able to do more for himself. The tutor who was to avoid trying to teach virtue by moral preachment was also to keep the environment free of social corruption and vice. The boy's experience was still essentially nonsocial. The emphasis in learning was on physical and sensory training in which Emile observed objects in the environment and their relationships to each other. Sensory training—using one sense to check another sense—involved measuring, counting, weighing, and comparing objects.

Rousseau's third developmental stage, from ages 12 to 15, could be termed early adolescence. Now Emile learned the concept of utility, that is, that objects and actions have purposes and consequences. He learned a manual skill, such as carpentry or gardening, that contributed to the correct combination of mental and physical labor. Emile's continuing interaction with the natural environment led slowly, at this stage, to the forming of ideas about science and geography. He also read his first book, *Robinson Crusoe,* where he learned of a man's survival on an isolated island.

Rousseau's fourth stage, that of later adolescence, from ages 15 to 18, is the time when Emile developed social relationships with others. Emile's questions about sexual development and relationships are answered directly by his tutor, with neither mysteriousness nor coarseness.

The fifth and last stage treated in *Emile* is from ages 18 to 20, called by Rousseau the age of humanity. Emile now studied history and languages and traveled. He met and fell in love with Sophie, whom he married.

The most important fact about Rousseau's developmental stages is that during them the learner—because of physical and psychological maturation—has a readiness to learn certain things. The teacher's task is to recognize this readiness and to create a situation that provides for the exercise of this readiness.

Johann Heinrich Pestalozzi

Johann Heinrich Pestalozzi (1746–1827) was a Swiss educator whose theory and practice influenced both early childhood and elementary education. A shy, introspective, and occasionally eccentric but consistently humane individual, Pestalozzi attempted religious, legal, and agricultural careers before deciding to devote his life to education.[3] An eager and receptive reader of *Emile,* Pestalozzi endeavored to make Rousseau's novel an educational reality. He also saw education, particularly that of children, as an instrument of human regeneration and social reformation.

As was true for Montessori and other early childhood educators, Pestalozzi's educational work began with socially and economically disadvantaged children.

---

3. For a systematic treatment of Pestalozzi's life and ideas, see Kate Silber, *Pestalozzi: The Man and His Work* (London: Routledge and Kegan Paul, 1960).

Johann Heinrich Pestalozzi engaged in teaching students at his institute in Switzerland; note the wall charts used for teaching arithmetic.

From 1774 to 1779, he conducted a farm school at Neuhof for poor children. For a short time he was headmaster of an orphanage at Stans. He then established well-known educational institutes at Burgdorf and Yverdon, where he developed and perfected his insights into early childhood education.

Pestalozzi also wrote on educational themes. Like Rousseau, he was an educational novelist. His *Leonard and Gertrude,* published in 1781, told of the moral, social, and economic revitalization of a fictional Swiss village that had implemented educational reforms. Pestalozzi's *How Gertrude Teaches Her Children,* published in 1801, was a treatise of his philosophy and method of education.

As an early childhood educator, Pestalozzi emphasized the total development of the child. Anticipating what later-day progressives would call the education of the whole child, Pestalozzi gave importance to emotional as well as cognitive development. Conventional schooling, he believed, had often been one-sided in that it stressed cognitive development but minimized or ignored emotional and physical development.

Pestalozzi's educational strategies were based on his concepts of children's growth and development. In the wholesome mother–infant relationship, the infant had basic needs for food, warmth, and affection. The good mother responded to and satisfied her child's basic needs. The child, in turn, responded with a growing love and affection to the mother. From this elemental but crucial mother–infant relationship, the child experienced emotional security and love. Once established firmly in the psyche of the child, the initial feelings of love could be extended outward to others in what Pestalozzi called the widening circles of humanity. The child extended his or her love to other members of the family circle—to the father, brothers, and sisters. Such a loving family situation built an emotionally secure household. Once the child experienced an emotionally healthy and secure family life, he or she could then extend trust and love the neighbors and other members of the community. Still growing ever outward, the feelings of love could be extended to one's fellow citizens, to all members of the human race, and ultimately to God.

Pestalozzi's view of the growth and development of emotionally secure children had several important educational implications. First, his theory of emotional security was based on the child's immediate needs and their satisfaction in the very intimate mother–child relationship. He avoided treating emotional development in abstract terms. Second, at Neuhof and Stans, Pestalozzi attempted to educate emotionally scarred, frightened, and often suspicious children who distrusted adults. Discovering that his initial efforts accomplished little cognitive learning among such emotionally disadvantaged children, Pestalozzi then sought to reshape the school environment into a climate of love, trust, and emotional security. Once the children trusted and loved their teachers, effective instruction could take place. Pestalozzi's stress on the need for creating an educational climate of love and emotional security became known as his *General Method,* which had to be established prior to physical and cognitive learning. For effective instruction to take place, the emotional security of the General Method had to be maintained.

Once the General Method had been used to cultivate emotional security and growth, Pestalozzi's *Special Method* could be employed as an instrument of physical and cognitive development.[4] The Special Method was based on the principle of *Anschauung,* the German word for "a viewpoint," which Pestalozzi used to signify the process of concept formation. As did Locke and Rousseau, Pestalozzi also believed that human knowledge was based on sense impressions of the environment. Again, as did Rousseau, Pestalozzi attacked the verbalism and memorization of conventional schooling, which he believed was miseducation. Pestalozzi's Special Method was designed to make the direct sensation of objects systematic, effective, and efficient. Known as the object lesson, Pestalozzi's Special Method consisted of form, number, and name lessons that he claimed should be taught prior to traditional schooling's reading and writing.

According to Pestalozzi, human beings encounter objects in their environment. These objects have a form, a shape, a design. Children should learn to recognize and distinguish the forms of particular objects. They can trace the shapes of smaller objects or can draw larger objects. From drawing would slowly come the process of writing. Objects also have quantity. Children can learn to count real objects, such as beans, peas, stones, or marbles. They can learn to subtract, multiply, and divide these objects. Only after extensive practice with real objects should children be introduced to the number that signify the various quantities. The sound or name lessons are to give children practice in using the words used to identify various objects.

---

4. Gerald L. Gutek, *Pestalozzi and Education* (New York: Random House, 1968), pp. 80–128.

The Special Method included a number of instructional strategies that teachers were to observe. Among them were the following:

1. Begin instruction with something that is related directly to the child's experience and environment; do not introduce concepts or ideas that are remote or foreign to the child's experience.
2. Base instruction on concrete objects and proceed gradually to more abstract concepts.
3. Learning should begin with the simplest and easiest element of a particular skill, which should be mastered before the child advances to more complicated learning.
4. Emphasize simple ideas and concepts before going on to those that are more sophisticated and complex.

Pestalozzi's contribution to early childhood education was to recognize and stress the importance of well-rounded emotional, cognitive, and physical development. His attention to the creation of an environment of love and emotional security encouraged more permissive attitudes that recognized the dignity of the child.

Friedrich Froebel

Friedrich Froebel (1782–1852), a German educator, developed the early childhood school known as the *kindergarten,* or "child's garden." Froebel, whose mother died when he was nine months old, was the victim of a strict and unhappy childhood. After several starts in such varied careers as forester, mineralogist, and museum curator, Froebel turned to education.[5] To gain teaching experience, he went to Switzerland to study with Pestalozzi, whose methods he found useful but not completely satisfactory. Froebel reasoned that Pestalozzi's method needed a more systematic and complete philosophical base.

Froebel established schools at Griesheim in 1816, at Keilhau in 1818, and at Blankenburg in 1837, where he and his colleagues educated children between ages

Friedrich Froebel (1782–1852) founded the kindergarten, which stressed the unfolding nature of the child and play.

5. Robert B. Downs, *Frederick Froebel* (Boston: Twayne, 1975), pp. 11–33.

three and eight in programs featuring games, stories, play, gifts, and occupations. These early preschools were designed to stimulate the child's growth and development by self-activity. As did Pestalozzi, Froebel wrote several books explaining his educational theory and practice. *The Education of Man,* published in 1826, expressed his highly mystical educational philosophy. Related most directly to early childhood education were Froebel's *Outline of a Plan for Founding and Developing a Kindergarten,* in 1840, and *Mother and Play Songs,* in 1843.

Froebel's philosophy of early childhood education, a form of Idealism, came from several sources. Among them were (1) introspection into his own unhappy and melancholy childhood, (2) beliefs and symbolism related to the Lutheran Church, of which his father was a minister, (3) the reading of various German Idealist philosophers, and (4) his own impressionistic forays into the natural sciences. From these diverse sources came Froebel's views of human nature, childhood, and education.

For Froebel, all creation had a spiritual origin and destiny in that it originated in God, a supernatural and spiritual Being. Humankind came from and was destined to return to God. In every human being, there was, Froebel said, a spiritual essence, a life force, that moved the person to self-activity. Throughout life, this Divinely implanted spiritual force sought externalization. For Froebel, then, the Divine essence in every person endowed human nature with spiritual worth and dignity. Froebel's view of human nature differed radically from the Puritanical doctrine of human depravity. It also varied from Rousseau's naturalistic doctrine of innate human benevolence. While Froebel concurred with Rousseau that the human infant was innately good, he did so for far different reasons.

Froebel's view of the child was based on his conception of human nature. Children possessed an intrinsic spiritual force that motivated and moved them to

SECOND GIFT

Friedrich Froebel's second gift in the series of educational materials.

self-activity. Using the analogy of plant life, Froebel believed that all that the child was to be was already present within him or her at birth in the same way that the entire plant was already present in the seed. Just as the capable gardener provides plants with sunlight, water, and suitable soil, the good teacher is to provide children with an educational environment that encourages their growth and development. To this end, Froebel developed his kindergarten.

Giving credence to the cultural recapitulation theory, Froebel believed that childhood's stages represented the child's propensity to act out and portray by play the history of the human race in a short time span. Among examples of cultural recapitulation were the following: Children may draw on walls to recapitulate that period of human history in which primitive people decorated their cave dwellings; boys who play at hunting or tent-making were reenacting the nomadic life-style of their ancestors. Although largely rejected today, Froebel's acceptance of cultural recapitulation shaped his kindergarten practices. Many kindergarten songs, stories, and games were intended to unite the individual child with other children. These activities not only socialized children but also introduced them to the stories and songs of their culture.

One of Froebel's significant contributions to early childhood education was his legitimizing of play. Regarding it as the means by which children externalized their interior nature, Froebel saw play as a means by which children could imitate and "try out" adult roles and behavior.

To prepare the kindergarten's environment for learning, Froebel designed a series of gifts and occupations. Gifts were items or objects given to children in completed form. For example, the ball—representing a spherical shape—and the cube were gifts with which children could play. As they used the gifts, children came to understand the concepts of shape, dimension, size, and their relationships. The occupations were malleable items, such as clay, paints, paper, wood, and cardboard, upon which children could imprint their own designs. They could make the figures of animals from clay or externalize their thoughts and emotions with paints, brush, and paper. Through the occupations, children externalized the concepts within their minds.

Maria Montessori

Maria Montessori (1870–1952) was born in Italy to well-educated, upper-middle-class parents. Unlike the typical girl of her social class, she attended a technical rather than a finishing school. Admitted to the University of Rome, she first studied mathematics, physics, and natural sciences and then medicine. In 1894, she was the first Italian woman to receive a medical degree from the University of Rome.[6]

Montessori was appointed to the staff of the Psychiatric Clinic of the University of Rome, where she specialized in the educational problems of mentally retarded children. At this time, she read and was influenced by the work of Edouard Seguin, a French physician who was a pioneer in special education. Believing that every child

6. E. M. Standing, *Maria Montessori: Her Life and Work* (New York: New American Library, 1962).

had the right to education, Seguin devised instructional materials to stimulate the learning of children labeled mentally defective.

As did Pestalozzi in his early career, Montessori worked first with disadvantaged children. From 1899 to 1901, she directed the State Orthophrenic School in Rome, where she worked with mentally handicapped children and trained teachers. In 1907, she founded the Casa dei Bambini, the Children's House, for socially disadvantaged children who lived in the slums of Rome's San Lorenzo district. As a result of her careful observation of these children and her anthropological and psychological research, Montessori devised her method, which consisted of using learning exercises and didactic materials in a prepared environment. Children, she concluded, preferred meaningful tasks to play, enjoyed order rather than disorder, and were capable of sustained concentration. Her method was so successful that Montessori schools opened throughout Italy. The Montessori method gained international recognition as schools were established throughout the world.

Montessori was also a prolific writer. Among her works were *The Montessori Method, The Secret of Childhood, The Discovery of the Child, Spontaneous Activity in Education, Education for a New World,* and *The Absorbent Mind.*

Assuming that children possessed a tremendous potential for self-development, Montessori identified a series of crucial transitory periods of special sensitivity to particular learning that children experienced.[7] From birth to age six, children's major work was to absorb and organize environmental stimuli. It was important that the child learn the appropriate skill at the time of greatest sensitivity for that learning.

As did Froebel, Montessori reasoned that self-development occurred most expeditiously when children used the sequential didactic materials and exercises of a prepared environment. In such an environment, the directress, or teacher, was an observer who assisted indirectly in the child's perceptual, motor, intellectual, emotional, and social development.

Among Montessori's instructional strategies were the exercises of practical life and those based on manipulating didactic materials. The practical exercises involved everyday activities, such as washing hands, serving lunch, lacing and buttoning, and dressing, designed to cultivate both motor skills and self-reliance. Montessori warned that adults who performed these activities for children denied them needed practice and stifled their "spontaneous" urge to self-accomplishment.

Montessori's didactic materials consisted of self-corrective and graded items that facilitated sensory awareness and muscular coordination. For example, Montessori devised sets of cylinders of varying diameters that could be arranged according to decreasing height or decreasing diameter. The didactic materials were to be used in a prescribed manner so that the child would master the specified skill.

The Montessori method enjoys widespread popularity in the United States and elsewhere. It is acclaimed by those who prefer a structured and ordered environment for early childhood education. Although it is an organized environment, it also permits children to work at their own readiness and rates of learning.

7. Maria Montessori, *The Discovery of the Child* (New York: Ballantine Books, 1972).

The critics of the Montessori method, particularly progressive educators, contend that it is too rigid and overly structured. They criticize it for prematurely stressing academic development to the neglect of children's socialization.

Jean Piaget

Contemporary early childhood education owes much to Jean Piaget's research. Like those two historical giants of educational theory, Rousseau and Pestalozzi, Piaget (1896–1980) was a native of Switzerland. From 1921 on, he was associated with the Rousseau Institute in Geneva, becoming its co-director in 1932. Piaget was variously a professor at the universities of Neuchatel, Geneva, and Lausanne. He also founded the International Center of Genetic Epistemology in Geneva.

Piaget made significant contributions to the literature on early childhood education and developmental psychology. Among his important works are *The Language and Thought of the Child, The Child's Conception of the World, The Origins of Intelligence in Children, The Construction of Reality in the Child,* and *Structuralism.* Among the topics of Piaget's research and writing on early childhood are those dealing with children's conceptions of physical causality, moral judgment, number, space, logic, and geometry.

Piaget's major contribution to early childhood education—that children are the primary agents in their own education and development—is based on his developmental psychology. In identifying the changes in cognitive structure occurring during human development, Piaget discovered that mental development takes place through a complex and continuous interactive process between the child and the environment. Human behavior, he asserted, is an adaptation of the person to the environment. Adaptation is a two-way process in which the individual (1) assimilates the factors of the environment and (2) accommodates to the requirements of the environment. Cognitive development is a process in which the individual arrives at a balance between assimilation and accommodation that is accompanied by a growing ability to generalize, differentiate, and coordinate cognitive schemata. In other words, children form mental structures that correspond to their experience of the external world and continually modify these structures because of new experiences.

Piaget discerned that human intelligence develops in stages and in sequence. His theory emphasizes that because of their mental structures and organization of experience, children are ready to learn certain things at specific times and that there are appropriate things for them to learn. Children proceed from one developmental stage to another because of their own activity. Learning is a continuous process in which a person assimilates the external facts of experience and integrates them into his or her own internal mental structures. Each stage, based on a particular organization of cognitive structures, flows from the preceding into the following stage.

Piaget identified four major stages in the development of human intelligence: (1) sensorimotor, from age 18 months to 2 years; (2) preoperational representation, from 2 to 7 years; (3) concrete operations, from 7 to 11 years; and (4) formal operations, from 11 to 15 years.

In the *sensorimotor stage,* initially infants conduct a series of isolated explorations of their environment by using their mouth, eyes, and hands independently of each other.[8] Later, they coordinate these actions for a more concerted and thorough exploration. For Piaget, this exploratory activity is the means that children use to construct an organized view of the world. In the Piagetian mode, this activity proceeds thus:

1. An action is represented in the brain by a plan, which Piaget called a scheme; the child sees and acts upon an object. This interactive experience — a visual configuration — is incorporated into the scheme.
2. Each time the child manipulates a given object in a different way, a new scheme is added to the original one. A compound schema is created, composed of the various ways that the object can be acted upon.
3. The various compound schema become part of a coordinated whole.

The *preoperational representation stage* occurs between the ages of 2 and 7 as the child continues to bring order to the environment. Objects are now gradually seen as entities, classified into related groups, and named. The child's organization and classification only approximate that of adults. During the preoperational stage, children continue to build on the schema developed in the preceding, sensorimotor stage. They are building on objects to form concepts and on concepts to form classes of concepts. Although their thinking differs from that of adults in many respects, children are beginning to use logical relationships.

The development of logical thought patterns proceeds as children begin to develop a series of hunches about reality. They have difficulty in explaining causal and chronological relationships. Their speech patterns can be both communicative and egocentric. Their egocentric speech is self-satisfying and consists of monologue and mimicry. In their play, children prefer simple and direct games without a great many rules.

Piaget's third stage, *concrete operations,* takes place between the ages of 7 to 11, as children use schemes involving classes of objects and people. They isolate the general characteristics of objects and people, such as size, duration, length, and use them in more complex mental operations. While the child's cognitive operations are still rooted in concrete objects, they are becoming more and more abstract.

At this stage, children can comprehend number signs, processes, and relationships. They can carry out operations mentally but while so doing visualize these operations in concrete terms. They have difficulty in comprehending adequately abstract concepts such as love, honor, dignity, and freedom. They tend to argue with each other but not with adults. Although appearing to accept adult authority, they question it in their own minds. They begin to use reason in structuring their arguments. They prefer games and play with rules. More socially inclined, they form clubs and groups.

The *stage of formal operations,* from ages 11 to 15, is characterized by the individual's independence of concrete objects in generating abstract, formal conclusions. The person at this stage functions at a high level of generality and comprehends and uses the properties of objects such as numbers, quantity, and weight. Because individuals at this stage understand cause-and-effect relationships, they can

8. Jean Piaget, *The Origins of Intelligence in Children,* trans. Margaret Cook (New York: W. W. Norton, 1952), pp. 23–42.

use the scientific method in explaining reality. For example, they are ready to relate concepts such as mass and number, and they can conjecture cause-and-effect relationships and apply them to hypothetical situations.

At this stage, individuals enjoy using abstract ideas and are influenced by formal concepts, ideas, classifications, relationships, and logical structures. They are capable of learning complex mathematical, linguistic, mechanical, and scientific processes. They can use moral standards that can be applied fairly. They also enjoy examining and discussing attitudes, customs, and life-styles that differ from their own.

Piaget's cognitive theory has important implications for both early childhood and elementary education. As had Rousseau and Pestalozzi, Piaget suggested strongly that human development occurs in sequential stages and that certain states of readiness and activities are appropriate to each stage. Because the learning cycles are sequential and cumulative, teacher-assisted learning should begin at an early age. What is to be learned and how it is to be learned should be matched with the child's stage of development.

For Piaget, the role of the teacher is to assist children in their learning processes.[9] Learning cannot be forced until the individual child is ready to learn, nor should it be delayed when the child is ready to learn. Teaching is to create situations in the environment where children can actually discover structures; it does not mean attempting to transmit structures verbally to children. As Pestalozzi admonished more than a century ago, Piaget believed that verbal instruction is likely to stay at this level and be neither understood nor internalized by children. In the Piagetian environment, the following takes place:

1. Teachers should arrange situations that encourage children to explore and experiment.
2. Instruction should be individualized so that children can learn at their own readiness and pace.
3. Children should be provided with concrete materials to touch, manipulate, and use.

Erik Erikson

Erik Erikson, the eminent psychoanalytical theorist, was born in Frankfort am Main, Germany, in 1902. His early educational career began in 1927, when he taught in the Burlingham School, a private school with a psychoanalytical orientation in Vienna. He also was familiar with the work of the Vienna Psychoanalytic Institute. Erikson's involvement in the anthropological study of simple cultures facilitated his understanding of the interrelationships among culture, family, and children.[10] For a time, Erikson was a psychology professor at the University of California. In 1950, Erikson's major work, *Childhood and Society,* developed his cycle theory. Among his other works are *Young Man Luther: A Study in Psychoanalysis and History* (1958), *Gandhi's Truth* (1969), *Dimensions of the New Identity* (1974), and *Toys and Reasons* (1977).

9. For the application of Piaget's theory to teaching, see Hans G. Furth, *Piaget for Teachers* (Englewood Cliffs, N.J.: Prentice-Hall, 1970).

10. Maria W. Piers and Genevieve M. Landau, "Erik H. Erikson," in David Sills, ed., *International Encyclopedia of the Social Sciences,* vol. 18 (New York: Free Press, 1979), pp. 172–176.

Erikson's major theory is that stages of human psychosocial development are to a large extent determined biologically. As biological entities, human beings are products of and guided by genetic and environmental factors. As participants in human history, individuals interact with and change their environment and themselves. Erikson also developed the concept of *identity crisis,* in which a conflict may occur when a person experiences traumatic situations that impede sequential development.

According to Erikson's life-cycle theory, the human race, over time, has always experienced the same sequence of developmental stages. The human life cycle goes through the following succession of eight developmental stages:

1. Trust versus mistrust — birth to 18 months
2. Autonomy versus shame and doubt — 18 months to 3 years
3. Initiative versus guilt — 3 to 6 years
4. Industry versus inferiority — 6 to 12 years
5. Identity versus role confusion — adolescence
6. Intimacy versus isolation — youth
7. Generativity versus stagnation — mature adulthood
8. Ego integrity versus despair — old age

As can be noted, each stage presents a specific conflict to the person. If the individual succeeds in resolving the conflict positively, he or she reaches the next higher stage of human development.

In *trust versus mistrust,* tendencies to trusting or mistrusting influence the person's social relationships. Regarding basic trust as the foundation of a healthy personality, Erikson believes that trust facilitates the person's social encounters with others and interactions with the environment. Conversely, mistrust impedes these relationships. The infant's trust grows out of the feeling that there always will be someone present who can be trusted. Erikson's first stage resembles Pestalozzi's circle of love and trust between mother and child. In the case of both theorists, the initial relationship of trust fosters more general feelings of emotional security.

In Erikson's second stage, *autonomy versus shame and doubt,* at around 18 months, the sense of the self becomes clear as children exhibit tendencies to independent action in wanting to do things for themselves rather than having things done for them. However, children at the "toddler" stage have feelings of doubt that they will be able to accomplish control over their toilet habits and walking on their own. In some respects, the so-called terrible twos represent a series of conflicts between parents who must put limits on the child's behavior and the child who wants to have his or her own way. Independent action can foster a sense of autonomy if the child's actions are successful. In large measure, successful consequences depend upon adult approval or disapproval. When adults approve of and encourage a child's behavior, it leads to a greater sense of self-confidence than when such behavior elicits adult disapproval and punishment that brings about self-doubt and shame.

In *initiative versus guilt,* the child's sense of autonomy, if developed supportively, has reached a high state of evolution. Along with the sense of autonomy comes benign aggressiveness in which children actively explore their environment, experimenting with new and different objects and situations. At times, children may experience guilt feelings that their curiosity has caused them to go too far. To nourish initiative, children need encouragement to explore their environment actively. Again, it is important that parents, teachers, and other adults encourage rather than impede the child's initiative. If overly controlled or punished for their explorations, children may develop guilt feelings that plague them throughout life.

In *industry versus inferiority,* children enjoy and experience new powers. Their bodies are developed and coordinated better physically; they are interacting socially with their peers in both cooperative and competitive activities. Children now use advanced language patterns and intellectualize their experiences by using rational thought processes.

To develop a sense of industry, children need to channel their growing energies in constructive, task-oriented directions. The sense of industry stimulates feelings of competence, pride in work well done, and a joy in crafts skills. Once again, adult disapproval, rejection, and punishment can stifle initiative and create inferiority feelings. It is crucial that individuals in this preadolescent period develop strong feelings of self-worth. Erikson's fourth stage coincides with elementary schooling. Teachers can stimulate industriousness by developing and encouraging children in activities and projects that cultivate a sense of purpose, work, and accomplishment.

In *identity versus role confusion,* childhood ends and adulthood begins. During these storm-and-stress years, adolescents experience feelings of inferiority, self-doubt, and incompetence. Simultaneously, they experience feelings of power, might, independence, and freedom. This is a crucial stage in making the determinations and clarifications that lead to a sense of personal identity. Diverse attitudes, feelings, roles, and experiences are either integrated into a positive self-concept or disintegrated. During this period, adolescents search for, find, and experiment with a variety of models and life-styles, ranging among those provided by parents, media figures, and peer group members. The exploratory period of adolescence is simultaneously exciting, painful, and joyful. As adolescents seek their own self-identity and self-definition, it is important that junior and senior high school teachers understand the dynamics of their students' psychological and emotional development.

Erikson's concept of sequential development of personal identity has had significant implications for early childhood education, as well as for other periods of human development. It is a statement of the need for the positive reinforcement of the concepts of self-worth and self-esteem in children.

Current Early Childhood Institutions and Practices

Thus far we have identified several of the major contributors to early childhood education. We turn now to some of the institutions and trends in the early education of American children. In particular, we focus on nursery schools and the kindergarten.

The Home in Early Childhood Education

Successful educational efforts at any level depend upon cooperative relationships between the home and the school or educational agency. In recent years, a growing attention and literature have developed on the subject of responsible parenting. Of the many areas of deliberate instruction, education to prepare persons for parental roles and responsibilities has been most neglected.

As stressed by pioneers of early childhood, learning begins in the home environment. A good learning environment is provided by the home that is emotionally secure and has the material requirements needed to foster positive growth and development. Professional educators have recognized that a great deal of important learning takes place in the home before the child enters school and encounters teachers. For example, children learn behavior patterns based on adult norms; they begin to develop patterns of social interaction based on their relationships to siblings and peers; they acquire a conversational command of language that permits them to communicate; they begin to internalize the value syndrome of parents as they acquire preferences for certain foods, dress, words, and actions.

In home–school relationships, particularly those of early childhood, it is desirable that the values of the home and the school be compatible. Later educational efforts are more likely to succeed when children already possess the value predispositions that are conducive to learning.

Most early childhood educators emphasize the role that direct experience exercises in human learning, particularly that of children. These educators stress that children should have opportunities for direct experience, especially with the world of persons and objects. Family excursions, trips to parks, zoos, and museums, and family projects involving making and doing things all provide children with a network of direct experience.

Because early childhood is crucial in establishing the directions for later learning, recent efforts have been made to identify psychological or physical problems before children enter school. Preschool screenings are used so that children can be examined and tested to identify potential learning disabilities. Remedial programs involve (1) medical and psychological diagnosis, (2) special activities, and (3) parental discretion.

Parental and Family Education

Children's first teachers are their parents; thus, parents need to be prepared for their responsibilities and duties. Parenting education may be offered to students before they marry and have children; more often, parenting education is studied by parents or prospective parents. Hospitals, medical centers, and public and private agencies have courses on child care for expectant parents.

Parental and family-life education programs are often provided by voluntary organizations, churches, and social agencies; they are not generally offered in a concerted manner by the public schools. Topics that might be discussed in a family-life education program include the role of parents and children as a family unit; the impact of family relationships and attitudes on early childhood education and development; family stress and problems; effective parenting; and parents' and children's needs and expectations.

Impact of Television on Early Childhood Education

The entry of television into American homes after World War II has had a continuing and profound impact on American education in general and on early childhood education in particular. As with other media, television is a neutral instrument that can be used for good or for ill. While it has been educative in bringing into American homes programs of national and international significance, television can be mis-educative, particularly when it is grossly commercial.

It is estimated that 97 percent of American homes have television sets. It is further estimated that the average child watches 4,000 hours of television programs before entering school. Undoubtedly, television can facilitate learning by giving children a "head start" as in the case of "Sesame Street," but it should be remembered that the programs that children view present values and models that they tend to imitate in their play. It is also true that television viewing is sedentary and provides indirect experience that is conducive to passive rather than active learning.

Because television has easy entry into the overwhelming majority of American homes, educators should reflect on the learning style that it encourages. Television programs rely on the quick and dramatic, and television news programs may treat events of major significance in one or two minutes. The kind of learning style fostered by television is superficial rather than in-depth. It is noisy rather than quiet. Some educators think that school-based learning should imitate the quickness and drama of television; others argue that the school should stress the more reflective and in-depth learning associated with print rather than the television screen.

Head Start Programs

During the Johnson administration, attention was given to educational programs for minority groups and for poverty-impacted areas. The Economic Opportunity Act of 1965 created a number of early childhood educational programs, known collectively as Operation Head Start. As the name implies, these programs were designed to give economically and culturally disadvantaged children an early educational opportunity before entering school.

Head Start programs are designed to provide cultural stimulus and educational experiences to lower-income children that are generally common to middle-class children. They provide story telling; field trips to museums, zoos, and parks; group games, songs, and play; and activities that stimulate learning readiness, such as drawing, coloring, and painting. Dental and physical examinations are included. Head Start staff members seek to enlist parents in the educational program so that the learning activities will be continued at home.

The results of Head Start programs have been mixed and often controversial. Some observers feel that the programs provide an initial start, as intended, but need to have better designed follow-up strategies to continue this initial impetus when children enter regular school programs. Critics of the program claim that the initial achievement is lost by the time the child enters the third grade and that other instructional strategies need to be designed for children from disadvantaged groups.

Early Childhood Education Principles

Specialists in the education of young children distinguish between preschool education programs, which generally focus on nursery schools, enrolling children between two to five years of age, and early childhood education programs, which generally encompass grades kindergarten through three, or ages five through eight.

At the present, many preschool teachers are prepared in community colleges or in departments of home economics and do not have the required certification to teach in public schools. Early childhood certification, necessary for teaching in the public schools, usually encompasses kindergarten through grades three or six, depending upon the particular state. In some states, proposals are being considered to enroll four-year-olds in the public schools. If the entering age of children is lowered, changes in early childhood programs and certification are likely to follow.

Although differences exist between preschool and early childhood education programs because of variations in the stages of child growth and development, many guiding principles are appropriate for both. Early childhood education programs, following the principles of the pioneers in the field, emphasize the development of the whole child — physically, psychologically, socially, intellectually, and creatively. In order to encourage children's total development, early childhood educators generally have used a flexible program that builds on the child's interests and needs as advocated by such American progressive educators as John Dewey and the British primary school educators. Although philosophical and methodological differences may exist between early childhood educators, there is a general agreement on the following principles:

1. In the early years, encourage learning that grows out of and is oriented to play, which is the child's natural way to learn.
2. Create learning environments that are rich in materials that stimulate curiosity and encourage exploratory learning.
3. Develop a readiness for later learning by helping children to build a positive self-image and confidence for entering group activities.

Nursery School Education

Nursery school education is one of the most rapidly growing educational sectors today, as a result of numerous social, economic, and educational factors, including the recent favorable findings of psychological and educational research and the entry of more women into the job force. Although nursery schools and day-care centers are gaining popularity in the United States, other countries, especially Israel, the Soviet Union, and the Scandinavian countries, have a long and concerted experience in nursery school education.

Scope of Nursery School Education   The two most common forms of nursery education are day-care centers and nursery schools. Often, the services provided by both agencies are so similar that it is difficult to differentiate functionally between them.

The day-care center is a custodial, recreational, and educational agency that is designed to provide care for prekindergarten children of working parents. It also provides meals, play, socialization, and educational activities for children enrolled in the day-care facility. Today, more than half the married women in the United States are employed; there are approximately six million working mothers with children under six years of age. As more women enter the working force, the need for trained day-care personnel will increase.

The nursery school can be defined as a separately organized and administered preschool for children during the years preceding kindergarten. ~~Some nursery~~ schools have well-developed educational programs designed and staffed by trained early childhood educators. The quality of nursery schools varies greatly, however. Parents should investigate the kind of services provided, especially those of an educational nature, before enrolling their children in a particular nursery school. While some nursery schools provide a carefully designed educational environment, others really perform a strictly custodial, baby-sitting service for working parents. Some nursery schools will accept children as young as two; others at age three or four. Some operate a full-day schedule; others a half-day cycle.

Depending upon the state, day-care centers and nursery schools may be inspected and licensed by state welfare departments or by state departments of education.

Types of Nursery Schools   More than half the nursery schools in the United States function independently of public school or other educational systems. The typical nursery school is sponsored, supported, and conducted by independent organizations, social welfare agencies, churches, philanthropic organizations, or parent associations. In a few situations, nursery schools are part of the public school system. They can also be found as demonstration and observation laboratories for colleges and universities that offer specialization in early childhood education. (See Figure 13–1 for the distribution of preprimary enrollments).

Nursery schools conducted under the auspices of churches often have curricula that include religious stories, lessons, and experiences. In addition to the usual range

FIGURE 13–1   Distribution of Preprimary Enrollments

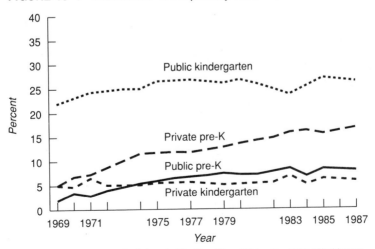

SOURCE: From Laurence T. Ogle, ed., *The Condition of Education 1990* (Washington, D.C.: U.S. Government Printing Office, 1990), p. 58.

of preschool learning activities, children are introduced to the beliefs and practices of the particular religious denomination supporting the school.

Enrollments and Control   Since the 1970s, preprimary education (encompassing nursery schools and kindergartens) has experienced considerable growth in enrollments. From 1970 to 1983, preprimary enrollments in private and public schools rose from 4.3 million to 5.7 million, an increase of 33 percent. In 1989, preprimary enrollments had reached 6 million. By 1993, the number of enrollments is expected to reach 7 million.[11] A significant trend of the increasing enrollment of children in preprimary schools is the high proportion of those enrolled in full-day programs. In 1980, 32 percent were enrolled in full-day programs; as of 1987, 35 percent were enrolled.[12]

This surge in preprimary enrollments is due to (1) the increasing entry of mothers into the work force, (2) a greater public and parental sensitivity to the importance of early education, (3) a greater availability of nursery and kindergarten programs, and (4) significant contemporary changes in the structure of American families. Between 1970 and 1988, major changes occurred in the composition of families. In 1970, 50 percent of families were married-couple families with children under age 18; in 1988, the percentage of married-couple families in this category had decreased to 38 percent. During this 18-year period, the proportion of single-parent families headed by women, with no husband present in the household, rose from 6 to 10 percent. In 1987, the total number of families with children under 18 years of age was estimated at 64,491,000. Of these families, 51,537,000 were married-couple families, 2,510,000 were headed by a male householder with no spouse present, and 10,445,000 were headed by a female householder with no spouse present. In 1987, more than one out of every five children under 18 lived in a household headed by a single parent.[13]

Most nursery schools are privately controlled and supported. Some, particularly those serving low-income families, receive support from government agencies, especially at the federal level through the Department of Education, the Office of Child Development, and the Social and Rehabilitation Service. Some private businesses operate day-care and nursery schools for their employees. Finally, there is a demand for public school systems to include preschooling efforts beyond the kindergarten.

The majority of nursery schools are privately controlled and supported. In 1987, 1,736,000 children were enrolled in private and 819,000 in public nursery schools.[14]

Staff   Nursery schools staffs vary considerably in professional preparation. Day-

11. Valena White Plisko and Joyce D. Stern, eds., *The Condition of Education: 1985 Edition* (Washington, D.C.: U.S. Government Printing Office, 1985), p. 4.
12. National Center for Education Statistics, *Digest of Education Statistics 1989* (Washington, D.C.: U.S. Government Printing Office, 1989). p. 40.
13. Ibid., pp. 4, 24.
14. Ibid., p. 57.

care centers and nursery schools that perform primarily custodial functions are unlikely to have a highly trained staff of professionals. Nursery schools that emphasize the educational development of children require a staff professionally prepared in early childhood education. Such preparation involves study and experience in child growth and development, educational instructional methods suited to young learners, and a knowledge of children's literature, music, and art. It is important, as Pestalozzi and Froebel noted, that those who work with young children be emotionally secure, patient, and warm. It is also important that early childhood educators be able to relate to parents as well as to students.

Kindergarten Education

The kindergarten, developed in the mid-nineteenth century by Friedrich Froebel, was brought to the United States initially by immigrants who left Germany after the failure of the Revolution of 1848. Margaretha Mayer Shurz (1834–1879) is credited with opening the first kindergarten for German-speaking children in Watertown, Wisconsin, in 1856. Caroline Louise Frankenburg, who had been trained by Froebel, also established a number of kindergartens in Ohio and Pennsylvania that served German-speaking communities. In cities such as Milwaukee and St. Louis, where the German-American population was concentrated, Froebel's kindergarten

A teacher reads to kindergarten students to develop reading interest and readiness.

principles were used as part of the curriculum for the younger children who attended bilingual schools.

Henry Barnard, who popularized Pestalozzian education in his *American Journal of Education,* enthusiastically advocated Froebel's kindergarten. While attending the International Exhibit of Educational Systems in London in 1854, Barnard saw a display of kindergarten materials. He afterward praised Froebel's principles for their usefulness in early childhood education.[15]

Elizabeth Peabody (1804–1894), a pioneer in kindergarten education in the United States, established an English-language kindergarten in Boston in 1860. After studying Froebelian pedagogy in Europe, she dedicated her life to advancing kindergarten principles through lecturing, writing, and editing the *Kindergarten Messenger.*

William T. Harris (1835–1909), the superintendent of schools in St. Louis, was attracted to the Froebelian method on both philosophical and educational grounds. Harris, like Froebel, was a philosophical Idealist who believed that the kindergarten was the ideal institution to externalize the child's potentialities. Because of his advocacy of Froebelian education, the kindergarten became part of the St. Louis public school system in 1873. Susan Blow (1843–1916) worked with Harris in St. Louis, where she prepared teachers in kindergarten methods. By the turn of the century, other school systems followed St. Louis and incorporated the kindergarten as part of the public school. By 1900, approximately 5,000 kindergartens were functioning throughout the United States.[16]

The kindergarten is the institution of early childhood education with which most Americans have had some experience. Today, the kindergarten is an important part of the American public school system. Although not compulsory, many American children enter the kindergarten at age five, their first introduction to formal schooling. The conventional kindergarten pattern enrolls children for half a day, five days a week, for the school year, usually nine months.

A recent trend in some states and local school districts has been to extend kindergarten programs from half-day to full-day sessions. Advocates argue that full-day kindergartens (1) provide a broader range of educational activities than do half-day programs, (2) can be more cost-effective, and (3) encourage a heightened academic, social, and developmental readiness.[17]

Kindergarten Programs   Although kindergarten practices have changed since the founding of the institution by Friedrich Froebel in the nineteenth century, certain essential features have been maintained. Rather than serving as an institution for academic development, kindergarten programs seek to develop a general readiness

15. Evelyn Weber, *The Kindergarten: Its Encounter with Educational Thought in America* (New York: Teachers College Press, Columbia University, 1969), p. 24.
16. Nina C. Vandewalker, *The Kindergarten in American Education* (New York: Arno Press and The New York Times, 1971), p. 195.
17. Carol G. Harding, *Full-Day Kindergarten: Does Time Make A Difference?* (Chicago: Center for Educational Leadership and Policy Studies, School of Education, Loyola University of Chicago, 1987), pp. 2–6.

for learning that emphasizes well-rounded, physical, emotional, social, and mental development.

Activities that kindergartens stress include the following:

1. Introducing children to a larger social environment in which they encounter children other than siblings and an adult other than parents or relatives — the teacher
2. Introducing patterns of regularity and a sense of time that is conducive to children's entry into the primary grades
3. Enriching children's experiences through projects, activities, and field trips
4. Enriching children's vocabulary, speech, and reading readiness by books and stories
5. Stimulating mathematical readiness by introducing arithmetic concepts, numbers, and counting exercises
6. Developing writing readiness by drawing, cutting, and other activities that encourage eye-hand and muscular coordination
7. Developing aesthetic readiness and creativity through painting, dancing, singing, and dramatic plays
8. Developing muscular coordination and physical stamina through games, play, and activities
9. Developing a readiness for science by nature studies, studying nature, plants, and animals

In addition to cultivating readiness for later learning, the kindergarten is a major agency of socialization. It introduces children to the concepts of respect for private and group property, to taking turns in using books and equipment, to respect for others, and to listening to the teachers and to other children.

Although most kindergartens continue to emphasize socialization and learning readiness as primary goals, kindergarten programs have been experiencing change. Factors that have stimulated this change are social, economic, and educational. As more children are enrolled in nursery schools, they will encounter at an earlier age many of the experiences and activities that used to occur initially in the kindergarten. Television, particularly educational television programs such as "Sesame Street," introduce many youngsters to word and number concepts before such exposure occurs in kindergarten. Finally, some parents and parent groups have pressed school districts to begin basic skill development in the kindergarten.

Conclusion

This chapter has introduced several major theories of early childhood education, along with the institutions designed for early childhood education. Although this introduction has been necessarily brief, it provides an overview of the theoretical richness of early childhood education. The various theories treated in the chapter have implications for early childhood practice. They are also relevant for elementary education, the subject of the next chapter.

The second section of the chapter described the institutions of early childhood education in the United States. Early childhood education is a growing area. Socioeconomic changes have increased the need for day-care and nursery services. In the future, the demand for trained professionals will accelerate.

DISCUSSION QUESTIONS

1. Read a biography of one of the early childhood educators discussed in the chapter and trace the development of the educator's theory.
2. Analyze the issue of social imposition versus child freedom.
3. Examine the meaning of *appropriateness* in a child's education.
4. Examine the impact of television on early childhood education.
5. Analyze the factors that have contributed to the growth of day-care centers and nursery schools.
6. What are the purposes of the kindergarten?
7. Project the future trends in early childhood education.

FIELD EXERCISES

1. Using the method of recalling early childhood educational experiences, arrange a panel discussion in which the participants examine, share, and analyze their own impressions of their childhood experiences.
2. Arrange visits to private, church-related, and, if possible, public nursery schools. Observe the children and their programs and report your observations to the class.
3. Read a book on the Montessori method of education and then arrange a visit to a Montessori school. Note the extent to which the method is being followed. Report your observations to the class.
4. Visit a kindergarten. Observe the program and report your observations to the class.
5. Watch several television programs intended for children's viewing. Include programs that appear on educational and on commercial television. Note (a) the particular learning strategy being used, (b) the value models being cultivated, and (c) the degree to which the program seeks to shape the child's attitudes.
6. If you are especially interested in exploring early childhood education as a career, volunteer to act as a part-time aide in a nursery school, kindergarten, or other children's program.

SUGGESTED READINGS

AYERS, WILLIAM *The Good Preschool Teacher: Six Teachers Reflect on Their Lives.* New York: Teachers College Press, Columbia University, 1989.

BEARD, RUTH M. *An Outline of Piaget's Developmental Psychology for Students and Teachers.* New York: Basic Books, 1969.

BERK, HULDA G. *Early Childhood Education: An Introduction Bridging the Gap.* Buffalo, N.Y.: Prometheus Books, 1988.

BERRCUTA-CLEMENT, J. R. *Changed Lives: The Effects of the Perry Preschool Program on Youths Through Age 19.* Ypsilanti, Mich.: High Scope Press, 1984.

BOYD, WILLIAM. *The Emile of Jean Jacques Rousseau: Selections.* New York: Teachers College Press, Columbia University, 1966.

DOWNS, ROBERT B. *Heinrich Pestalozzi: Father of Modern Pedagogy.* Boston: Twayne, 1975.

FEENEY, STEPHANIE, CHRISTENSEN, DORIS AND MORAVCIK, EVA. *Who Am I in the Lives of Children? An Introduction to Teaching Young Children.* Columbus, Ohio: Merrill, 1987.

FROEBEL, FRIEDRICH. *The Education of Man,* trans. W. N. Hailman. New York: Appleton, 1896.

FURTH, HANS G. *Piaget for Teachers.* Englewood Cliffs, N.J.: Prentice-Hall, 1970.

GUTEK, GERALD L. *Pestalozzi and Education.* New York: Random House, 1968.

———. *Joseph Neef: The Americanization of Pestalozzianism.* University: University of Alabama Press, 1978.

HILDEBRAND, VERNA. *Building Young Children.* New York: Macmillan, 1990.

HINER, N. RAY, AND HAWES, JOSEPH M. *Growing Up in America: Children in Historical Perspective.* Urbana: University of Illinois Press, 1986.

JENSEN, MARY A., AND CHEVALIER, ZELDA. *Issues and Advocacy in Early Education.* Boston: Allyn & Bacon, 1990.

KILPATRICK, WILLIAM H. *The Montessori System Examined.* Boston: Houghton Mifflin, 1914.

———. *Froebel's Kindergarten Principles: Critically Examined.* New York: Macmillan, 1916.

LILLARD, PAULA P. *Montessori: A Modern Approach.* New York: Schocken Books, 1973.

LILLY, IRENE M. *Friedrich Froebel: A Selection from His Writings.* Cambridge: Cambridge University Press, 1967.

MCNULTY, BRIAN, SMITH, DAVID, AND SOPER, ELIZABETH. *Effectiveness of Early Education.* Denver: Colorado Department of Education, 1983.

MITCHELL, ANNE W., SELIGSON, MICHELLE, AND MARX, FERN. *Early Childhood Programs and the Public Schools: Between Promise and Practice.* Dover, Mass.: Auburn House, 1989.

MONTESSORI, MARIA. *The Discovery of the Child.* New York: Ballantine Books, 1972.

———. *The Secret of Childhood.* New York: Ballantine Books, 1972.

OREM, R. C. *Montessori Today.* New York: Capricorn Books, 1971.

PENROSE, WILLIAM O. *A Primer on Piaget.* Bloomington, Ind.: Phi Delta Kappa Educational Foundation, 1979.

PESTALOZZI, JOHANN H. *How Gertrude Teaches Her Children,* trans. Lucy E. Holland and Francis Turner. London: Swan Sonnenschein, 1907.

———. *Leonard and Gertrude,* trans. Eva Channing. Lexington, Mass.: D. C. Heath, 1907.

PIAGET, JEAN. *The Origins of Intelligence in Children,* trans. Margaret Cook. New York: W. W. Norton, 1952.

———. *The Grasp of Consciousness: Action and Concept in the Young Child.* Cambridge, Mass.: Harvard University Press, 1976.

READ, KATHERINE H., GARDNER, PAT, AND MAHLER, BARBARA CHILD. *Early Childhood Programs: Human Relationships and Learning.* New York: Holt, Rinehart, and Winston, 1987.

SEEFELDT, CAROL, ed. *The Early Childhood Curriculum: A Review of Current Research.* New York: Teachers College Press, Columbia University, 1987.

SHAPIRO, MICHAEL S. *Child's Garden: The Kindergarten Movement from Froebel to Dewey.* University Park: Pennsylvania State University Press, 1983.

SPODEK, BERNARD, ed. *Today's Kindergarten: Exploring the Knowledge Base, Expanding the Curriculum.* New York: Teachers College Press, Columbia University, 1986.

STANDING, E. M. *Maria Montessori: Her Life and Work.* New York: New American Library, 1962.

VANDEWALKER, NINA C. *The Kindergarten in American Education.* New York: Arno Press and The New York Times, 1971.

WEBER, EVELYN. *The Kindergarten: Its Encounter with Educational Thought in America.* New York: Teachers College Press, Columbia University, 1969.

———. *The English Infant School and Informal Education.* Englewood Cliffs, N.J.: Prentice-Hall, 1971.

WEIKART, DAVID P. *Quality Preschool Programs: A Long-Term Social Investment.* New York: Ford Foundation, 1989.

_14_

Elementary Education

Chapter 14 presents a brief historical overview of elementary education and examines the goals of elementary education. It then discusses the elementary school program and patterns of organization and analyzes recent trends in elementary education.

The general focusing questions that will be answered as you read this chapter include the following:

1. Historically, what have been the major purposes of elementary education?
2. What are the continuing goals of elementary education?
3. What are the basic features of the elementary school program?
4. How are elementary schools organized?
5. What are some recent trends in elementary education?

Historical Overview of Elementary Schooling

Throughout history, adults have prepared children to participate in and contribute to their society by giving them the skills and knowledge that they regard as needed for the group's survival. In its oldest sense, elementary education is the means by which the mature members of a society transmit their knowledge, beliefs, methods, and values to the immature members of the society. When this transmission takes place, the group's heritage is preserved in the life of the next generation. The transmission process can range from a static indoctrination designed to perpetuate the status quo to one that encourages change and progress.

In preliterate societies, elementary education of a utilitarian sort was done in families or kinship groups, where children learned hunting, fishing, farming, and cooking. Religious values—usually the group's ethical core—were transmitted by tribal priests or elders.

In literate societies, such as those of ancient Greece and Rome, elementary education stressed the process of becoming literate by learning to read and write the language and becoming familiar with its literature. In the school of the "grammatist," the young Athenian boy living in the fifth century B.C. learned his letters, reading, writing, counting, poetry, music, drama, and gymnastics. By the end of the third century B.C., Roman boys were attending an elementary school called the *ludus*, where they learned reading, grammar, and literature. These Greek and

Roman elementary schools were private, and a teacher taught pupils for a fee. The important historical development is that elementary education in a literate society became identified with schooling that stressed the learning of language. In the thirteenth and fourteenth centuries, a variety of parish, chantry, guild, and monastic schools provided instruction in reading, writing, arithmetic, and religion under the auspices of the Christian church.

The Protestant Reformation of the early sixteenth century exercised a decided influence on elementary education. Believing that reformed Christians should read the Bible in their own language, Calvin, Luther, and other leaders of the Reformation encouraged the establishment of elementary or vernacular schools in which children learned to read and write so that they would know the Scriptures and the principles of their religion.

At the time of the settlement of North America, the purposes and function of elementary schooling were shaped heavily by the imprint of the Protestant reformers. In Puritan New England, in particular, the town schools incorporated the conventional pattern of elementary education—the learning of the language by reading and writing it. Closely related to the process of becoming literate was a thorough program of religious education, or indoctrination, literally the internalization of the doctrines of the church so that one could defend it against those who held contrary creeds. Along with reading, writing, spelling, and religion, arithmetic was taught. The typical methods of instruction were the recitation of memorized lessons and the answering of questions contained in the catechism. Discipline was harsh, and corporal punishment was administered freely by the teacher.

The most direct institutional ancestor of today's elementary school was the common school of nineteenth-century America. The common school was so called because it sought to be the educational institution that was open to all the children, educating them in common without class distinctions. It also was to provide the children who attended it with a common body of skills, knowledge, and values. Because Americans held differing religious beliefs and because the Constitution prohibited the establishment of religion, the common school was nondenominational. While it did not teach the tenets of a particular religion, it did emphasize the values of hard work, industriousness, thrift, and punctuality, which had been prized by the Puritans. In secular form, these values were impressed on thousands of children who learned to read with the help of McGuffey's readers.

By the mid- and late nineteenth century, elementary school teachers prepared for teaching careers in normal schools, where they reviewed the general elementary curriculum, practiced the methods of teaching, and studied principles of pedagogy. It was during this time that multitudes of women embarked on careers as elementary teachers. Revisionist historians assert that, in an industrializing country, women were employed because they were a cheap labor force that could be paid low salaries and were willing to teach under restricted conditions. One could also contend, however, that elementary teaching made it possible for women to leave the home and enter the career world. Perhaps, the entry of women into elementary teaching careers was an early step in the womens' liberation movement.

The common schools of the nineteenth century varied from the little one-room schoolhouse of rural America to the large, factorylike buildings in the large cities. It was in the urban schools that served large numbers of children that the graded pattern of organization was developed by which children were assigned in classes according to their age. This pattern of organization caused many elementary schools to be called grade schools.

By the beginning of the twentieth century, American elementary schooling was well established and tending to become overly formal. The rote instruction and emphasis on routine sparked the Progressive Movement in American education, in which educators such as Francis Parker, John Dewey, and William H. Kilpatrick criticized traditional schooling for being overly literary and formal and too removed from the real needs of children.[1] The impact of progressive education was to introduce activities, projects, problem solving, field trips, and "hands-on" laboratory learning into elementary schools.

Today's elementary school is largely a result of the impact of historical forces. Still emphasizing the need for basic, foundational skills and knowledge, modern elementary schools seek to cultivate both the cognitive and affective development of the children whom they educate.

Goals of Elementary Education

As have most educational institutions, American elementary schools have experienced change. Elementary education has been changed by a number of forces, such as the findings of research into child growth and development, an evolving sensitivity to the needs of children, and the rising expectations that society has for its children. In the section that follows, some of the continuing goals of American elementary education are identified and examined.[2]

Preparation in Fundamental Skills and Knowledge

Since the establishing of the earliest schools, elementary education has sought to provide children with the fundamental skills and basic knowledge necessary to function as members of society. In literate societies, this means that organized elementary education prepares children to use language by teaching reading, writing, and comprehension. In the elementary curriculum, the language arts are designed to cultivate this ability to use language.

1. For a treatment of progressive reform, see the definitive work by Lawrence A. Cremin, *The Transformation of the School: Progressivism in American Education, 1876–1957* (New York: Knopf, 1962).
2. From time to time, individuals and organizations have sought to identify the goals of elementary education. For examples of such identifications, see Educational Policies Commission, *The Purpose of Education in American Democracy* (Washington, D.C.: National Education Association, 1938); Educational Policies Commission, *Education for All American Youth* (Washington, D.C.: National Education Association, 1953), pp. 2–4; William J. Bennett, *First Lessons: A Report on Elementary Education in America* (Washington, D.C.: U.S. Government Printing Office, 1986), pp. 1–2; Nolan C. Kearney, *Elementary School Objectives* (New York: Russell Sage Foundation, 1953), pp. 52–120; George Manolakes, *The Elementary School We Need* (Washington, D.C.: Association for Supervision and Curriculum Development, National Education Association, 1965), pp. 20–21.

In a literate society — especially in an industrialized and technological one — the ability to understand information and to communicate effectively is needed for personal development, for social interaction, for participation, for ongoing education, and for employment. In the language arts, reading instruction occupies much of early elementary education, particularly in the primary and intermediate grades. The reading materials used in school convey the values that the society has for its children. For example, an examination of the various readers used in elementary schools will indicate social change, expectations, and values. *The New England Primer* used in the town schools of colonial New England emphasized religious precepts, stern admonitions against the child's tendency to idleness and sin, and the need to practice the virtues of frugality, hard work, and perseverance. The readers and spelling books written by Noah Webster stressed many of the same values but also added themes of American cultural nationalism and patriotism. *McGuffey's Readers,* which enjoyed a long-lasting and wide popularity, reiterated the values of the Protestant ethic and promised children that honesty, patience, diligence, punctuality, and effort would bring them success in life as well as in school. The readers of the late 1940s and early 1950s that featured "Dick, Jane, and Baby Sally" and their parents depicted an American middle-class family that lived in a white frame house and in which the father took a briefcase to his office rather than a lunch pail to a factory. The stories in current readers are about a multicultural and pluralistic society in which children live in cities as well as suburbs, in apartments as well as

LESSON XI.

ĭ'ron (ī'urn)
eȳe' lĭd̦;
fŏr̄ge
in tĕnse'

elĭŋ'ker ty
shrĭŋk
lā'bor
hăm'mer

THE BLACKSMITH.

1. Clink, clink, clinkerty clink!
    We begin to hammer at morning's blink,
        And hammer away
        Till the busy day,
    Like us, aweary, to rest shall sink.

2. Clink, clink, clinkerty clink!
    From labor and care we never will shrink;
        But our fires we'll blow
        Till our forges glow
    With light intense, while our eyelids wink.

Sally said, "Oh, oh, oh.

Come here, Dick.

See what I see.

See my little blue boat now.

See who wants my boat.

My little blue boat.

See who wants it now."

McGuffey's Readers of the late nineteenth century and the "Dick and Jane" series of the mid-twentieth century. These readers were used widely in American elementary schools.

houses, in which the family may be a single-parent one, and in which the characters are African American, Chicano, and Asian Americans, as well as white. A discerning analysis of elementary reading materials will often illuminate not only the purposes of elementary education but also those of American society.

Along with the fundamental skills of reading, writing, spelling, and listening, elementary education prepares children in basic mathematics—in counting, number systems, and fundamental processes. The foundations of science, social science, art, music, and physical education are also established in the elementary school years. A continuing goal of American elementary education, then, has been to cultivate fundamental skills and processes.

While most educators concur on the need to emphasize fundamental skills and knowledge in the elementary school, many of the controversies among elementary teachers are about the most effective methods for accomplishing this goal. Essentialists and "Basic" educators call for what they refer to as a no-nonsense, structured, teacher-directed learning environment, characterized by drill and practice in the basic skills. More progressive educators, influenced by the tradition of Francis Parker, John Dewey, and William Kilpatrick, believe that a hands-on, learning-by-doing, child-centered approach is not only more humane but also more effective educationally. Progressives argue that meeting children's interests is the best way to begin teaching fundamental skills. In most elementary schools, teachers have created a synthesis that incorporates both fundamental skills and experiential activities.

Entrance into a Larger World

Elementary education has personal and social goals as well as academic ones. It has the general goal of expanding the child's perceptions that are based on the home, family, and neighborhood into a world view. To accomplish this goal, elementary education needs to articulate with and relate the early childhood and kindergarten experience that precede with the secondary school experience that follows it. No part of the school sequence can be treated in isolation from its related components. As part of a child's education, elementary education seeks to introduce children to the diversity and also to the commonness of human experience. It seeks to develop a sense of personal integrity, of cooperation with others, and a respect for human values. This means that the child's world needs to be expanded into new dimensions.

Recognizing the Health and Physical Development of Children

The years from 6 to 11, when most American children are attending elementary school, are an important time of physical, mental, emotional, and social development. Programs of health, safety, and physical education that are incorporated in the formal elementary school curriculum are designed to aid the child's development. However, much that occurs in elementary education is of an informal or extracurricular nature. As children learn with other children in groups, intricate patterns of social interaction, friendship, rivalry, competition, and cooperation develop. In addition to academic learning, children are acquiring and practicing the skills that will lead to social success or frustration. The ability to make a series of personal adjustments to different persons and situations is an important learning goal in elementary education. Children learn that other individuals are like them in many ways but also different from them. In a multicultural society, children need to learn to respect racial and ethnic groups other than their own and also to understand at the same time the commonness of human experience.

Teachers need to be sensitive to the problems that all children have as they are growing up. At times, however, some children may have serious mental and emotional problems that teachers need to recognize and refer to specialists.

Extending the Horizons of Space and Time

The elementary school child often begins school with limited concepts of space and time that are based on his or her small world of family and neighborhood. In the early nineteenth century, Pestalozzi urged teachers to begin instruction with what was close, near, and immediate to the child's experience and then to lead the child outward to the larger world by a series of carefully planned but short steps. In his classic work, *Democracy and Education*, John Dewey wrote that the elementary curriculum should begin with "making and doing" activities that involved children actively in socially significant projects and problems based on their interests and needs.[3] From making and doing, Dewey stated, the second level of curriculum

A scene of a social studies discussion in an elementary classroom.

3. John Dewey, *Democracy and Education* (New York: Macmillan, 1916), pp. 228–270.

involved history that helped to create a sense of time and geography that extended the sense of space.

Elementary education has a major role in broadening the child's horizons into time and space. Teachers should be aware that today's elementary children may well bring a different perspective of time and place with them to school because of their exposure to television. For example, from an astronaut's perspective, photographs of planet Earth taken from the moon give a much different orientation to space than that which children had in earlier times. In the formal elementary curriculum, the social studies, particularly when they include materials from history and geography, give children a sense of their particular time in relationship to the past and of their particular place in relationship to a global society.

Developing Democratic Values

Since the founding of the American republic, elementary education has stressed the cultivation of citizenship and the processes of participating in a democratic society. In their arguments for common schooling, Horace Mann, Henry Barnard, and others saw public education as a necessary instrument in providing the knowledge and values needed for effective citizenship. Today, there has been a strong revival of interest in the role that elementary education plays in developing the values needed for life in a democratic society.

Once again, the social studies have an important role in citizenship education.[4] This role is supplemented by the milieu of the elementary classroom as children learn the process of sharing, discussing, and reaching decisions in a peaceful and representative manner.

Liberating Creative Impulses

Since the time of Comenius and Froebel, educators have viewed the years of elementary education as a time for children to liberate their creative impulses. Music, art, drama, dance, and writing are ways that children can portray and vivify these impulses through artistry in various media. While the fundamental skills contribute to cognitive development, the arts contribute to affective expression. The arts in the elementary curriculum provide a means by which the child can take an idea, a mood, or a feeling and embody it in a picture, drawing, or song. The elementary school program should provide experiences that stimulate creativity, inventiveness, and originality. In the broad sense, it should cultivate both aesthetic appreciation and creativity.

Definition of Elementary Education

In terms of a curricular definition, elementary education educates children in the fundamental skills and primary areas of knowledge. It can be defined broadly but

---

4. James P. Shaver, ed., *Building Rationales for Citizenship Education* (Arlington, Va.: National Council for the Social Studies, 1977).

vaguely as that education that takes place before secondary education. The age range of the children who attend elementary schools is from 6 to 12, 13, or 14, depending upon the particular pattern of organization. In many school districts throughout the United States, elementary education includes grades one through six. Some school districts still retain the more traditional pattern of grades one through eight.

Within most school districts and in many teacher preparation programs, elementary education is organized into the following subdivisions: *primary*: grades one to three (kindergarten may also be included); *intermediate*: grades four, five, and six; and *upper*: grades seven and eight. It should be noted that grades seven and eight are designated as junior high schools in still other patterns of organization. Where junior high school patterns of organization are used, grades seven and eight are frequently identified with secondary education. The discussion in this chapter is limited to grades one through six.

Elementary School Program

The educational program or curriculum in the elementary school is designed to provide the fundamental skills and areas of knowledge needed for participation in society, for personal growth and development, and for ongoing education. In the early years, the program is more generalized and then becomes gradually more specialized in the intermediate and upper grades. To some extent, the curricula of the lower schools have been influenced by that of the higher institutions. For example, graduate and professional schools have influenced the college curriculum, which has influenced the high school curriculum, which in turn has influenced the elementary school curriculum. However, elementary schools generally have been influenced less directly by higher institutions. As a result, elementary schools frequently have been more innovative and experimental than secondary and higher institutions.

Because the curriculum at the primary and intermediate levels of the elementary school is general rather than specific, there is also a greater stress on methodology than in secondary and higher institutions. Although content is important, the methodology of instruction is vitally important at the elementary level. For example, children need to learn to read, and teachers must be able to teach them to read, before it is possible to proceed to other curricular areas.

The typical elementary school curriculum, which emphasizes general education, is organized around the theme of "broad fields," or general areas.

Broad Field	Includes
Language arts	Reading, handwriting, listening, literature, spelling, speech, creative writing, drama
Social studies	Concepts and materials from history, geography, political science, economics, anthropology, environmental studies
Mathematics	
Science	Concepts and materials from natural and physical sciences, introduction to the scientific method, environmental studies

Health and physical education	Health concepts and practices, physical fitness and motor skills, safety, recreation
Music and art	

The Primary Grades

The primary division of the elementary school generally consists of kindergarten and grades one, two, and three. Today, the first introduction of schooling for most children occurs in preschools and in private or public kindergartens. For some children, however, first grade may be the initial introduction to organized education. In any event, the primary grades build on the work of the family and home and extend the child's experience into the skills and subjects that comprise the broad fields of the elementary school curriculum.

In the primary grades, the most fundamental and foundational activity is reading, because so much of the school's program depends upon it. The major objectives of elementary reading programs are

1. To begin, develop, and improve reading skills.
2. To develop the skill of gaining information through the printed medium.
3. To cultivate the value of reading for enrichment, enjoyment, and recreation.

Contemporary reading programs are related to and often integrated with the other broad fields of the elementary curriculum. Much of the progress that the

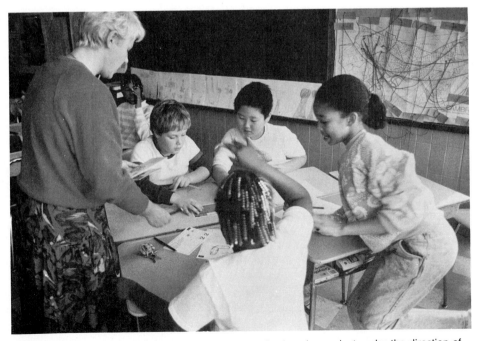

A group of elementary students involved in a cooperative learning project under the direction of a teacher.

children are expected to make in social studies, mathematics, and science depends upon their ability to read. In addition to reading, children are introduced to concepts in the other broad fields of the curriculum. The primary grades continue the socialization process in which children acquire and develop their skills of interacting with others and of participating in group activities.

The Intermediate Grades

In most elementary schools, the intermediate grades are grades four, five, and six. The emphasis on reading continues in the intermediate grades, but the informational and enjoyment functions of reading receive greater emphasis than do the mechanics and comprehension stressed in the primary grades. The broad fields of the curriculum—social studies, mathematics, and science—also are pursued in greater depth.

The Upper Grades

The upper grades in the elementary school are grades seven and eight. While some school districts continue to locate the upper grades in the same buildings with the primary and intermediate grades, other districts have created upper-grade centers. Throughout the country, many districts use the junior high school or the middle school as the institution for educating children in these grades. Since the junior high and middle school are treated elsewhere, the upper grades receive only a brief discussion here. In the upper grades, pupils are entering adolescence and are in a transitional stage of development. The broad fields that characterized the primary and intermediate grades are often differentiated into more specialized subjects, such as English, literature, social studies, history, natural and physical sciences, and mathematics. Of special importance in these grades are vocational, industrial, home arts, career, sex, and drug abuse prevention education.

Elementary School Organization

Elementary schools, and other schools as well, are organized vertically and horizontally. Vertical organization relates to the movement of students in time, usually by grade, through the various levels of the school system. Vertical organization can be viewed as a ladder, with each level being a rung on the ladder and the students climbing from rung to rung until they reach the top. Horizontal organization, to be discussed later, is a lateral form of organization in which students are classified, grouped, and assigned at given educational levels.

The Grade School

Historically, the common school—the early nineteenth-century public elementary school—was often a one-room building staffed by a single teacher. Within this one-room school, the teacher divided the pupils into groups for instructional purposes, often according to their age.

The graded school, a mid-nineteenth-century innovation, was introduced by Francis Parker, in Quincy, Massachusetts. This pattern, which organized elementary schools into grades, was followed throughout the country, first, in large urban districts and then in smaller districts. In the grade school, children were assigned to a given grade on an age-specific basis. For example, all six-year-olds were placed in the first grade, seven-year-olds in the second grade, and so on. Teachers were assigned to a specific grade level and identified with the grade level they taught. A specific body of skills and subjects was assigned to each grade. At the end of the school year, students who completed the requirements of a given grade were promoted to the next grade. Those who failed were retained. Thus, the following typical graded elementary school pattern emerged:

Grade 1	Age	6
Grade 2	Age	7
Grade 3	Age	8
Grade 4	Age	9
Grade 5	Age	10
Grade 6	Age	11
Grade 7	Age	12
Grade 8	Age	13

At a time when testing and evaluation were at a primitive stage of development, the graded system, based on pupil ages, was a simple and specific means of classifying and assigning children and of organizing the instructional program. Unfortunately, as with many educational innovations, the graded system became overly formal and routinized. In many schools, elementary education became a lockstep system in which armies of children moved at an inflexible and rigid cadence. A system based solely on age is indifferent to children's individual differences and needs. Although they might have been born within the same year, important differences exist among children of the same age in terms of psychological and emotional development and learning readiness. The traditional graded system did not recognize the need of gifted children to move at an accelerated pace or that of slower learners for more time than that allotted by the prescribed syllabus and time schedule.

Because the children assigned to a given grade were heterogeneous in everything except age, creative teachers turned to grouping—a simple form of horizontal organization—within a grade level. To group children of similar readiness and ability together, homogeneous small groups are used. Children within a given grade are grouped according to their ability within a skill or subjects. For example, those who are progressing in reading at a similar rate may be organized into a particular reading group. Although progressive educators have attacked the rigidity of the graded system over the years, it is still a common pattern of elementary school organization.

Because of dissatisfaction with the inflexibility of the graded system, the multigraded pattern—a fairly recent modification of the more traditional graded school pattern—was introduced. Although grade level designations may still be used, the multigraded patterns combine several grades so that more homogeneous groupings can be organized from the larger number of students. An individual child, then, has the opportunity to work in several ability groups in different subjects. In a fourth and fifth grade combination, for example, a child might be working with a fifth grade mathematics group and a fourth grade social studies group.

The Ungraded School and Individualized Instruction

The nongraded, or ungraded school, plan is designed to eliminate completely the rigidity of the graded system. Because it uses age-specific assignments, instruction in the graded school is often directed to learners of average ability. The nongraded organization emphasizes that there is no average child and that a good elementary school should meet the individual needs of every learner. The nongraded philosophy stresses:

1. Children are unique and have their own readiness for and rate of learning.
2. Specific learning tasks need to be developed for each child.
3. Pupil progress is determined not by the years spent sitting in a classroom but by an individual's achievement.

The theme of the nongraded school is flexible scheduling of children so that they can move at their own pace from module to module or unit to unit within a given skill or subject. This generally means that individual classroom teachers must be reorganized into teaching teams. The curriculum also must be reorganized. The continuous progress curriculum, found in nongraded schools, is organized into smaller and often more diverse units to permit children to move at intervals of a few weeks and to work with other children who are functioning at their ability level. Ability levels, too, will vary for the same child according to the particular subject or skill. Since small groupings are used, children can be assigned to several groups according to their individual needs, interests, and abilities in a particular subject. The children may move to another group when they are ready to do so rather than be required to spend the entire school year with a single class as in the conventional graded school.

Individually guided education (IGE), another innovation in school organization, is used as the instructional program and method in some nongraded schools. Since the mid-1960s, a number of elementary schools were reorganized to implement IGE as the instructional pattern. The IGE system individualizes instruction by designing and programming specific learning tasks so that individual learners can progress through the program at their own level of readiness and own learning rate. The implementation of highly individualized instructional programs such as IGE requires a staffing pattern that encourages a team effort by teachers. It also requires a curricular design that permits the continuous evaluation and assignment of pupils.

In the late 1970s, nongraded schools and highly individualized instructional programs came under criticism from some educators and parents. Advocates of basic education were especially disenchanted with these innovations, which they claimed lacked specific academic standards and requirements for pupil promotion. The critics contended that highly individualized instruction also neglected proper order and sequence in the curriculum.

Horizontal Organization of the Elementary School

Elementary schools are also organized horizontally; that is, children within the same educational level may be assigned to a variety of groups at that level. If, for example, there are 100 children at the third grade level in a given elementary school, these children might be divided horizontally into four classes of 25 pupils. Within a particular classroom, the teacher may divide the children further into five reading groups of five pupils. The following diagram illustrates the interrelationship of vertical and horizontal organization:

Vertical Organization　　　　　　　**Horizontal Organization**

Grades 6

     5

     4　　　　100 pupils

     3　　————————————　Four sections of third grade,

     2　　　　　　　　　　　　25 pupils per section

     1

     K

The conventional unit of horizontal organization in the elementary school is the self-contained classroom in which pupils of a given age level are instructed by a teacher assigned to that classroom. In the self-contained classroom, a single teacher instructs the entire class of pupils for the whole school day. Despite criticism over the years, the self-contained classroom remains a widely used pattern of horizontal organization, for it enables the teacher to become familiar with the needs of the whole child and to make sure that the children's instruction is integrated into a total educational pattern. The successful self-contained classroom teacher needs to be a generalist in elementary education but must also be competent in providing instruction in particular skill and subject areas. The weakness in the self-contained pattern is that particular subjects and skills may be neglected if the teacher is unable to integrate them all into a total learning experience for the children.

In many elementary schools, the self-contained pattern has been modified so that the teacher is assisted by specialist or resource teachers in art, music, physical, and special education. The following illustrates the typical self-contained classroom pattern that uses specialist and resource teachers:

Self-Contained Classroom

Classroom teacher provides instruction	in	Reading Language Arts Mathematics Social Studies Science Health	to Pupils
Specialist teachers provide instruction	in	Art Music Physical Education Special Education	to Pupils

While the self-contained classroom is found in many elementary schools, the departmentalized pattern of horizontal organization is also used. In the departmentalized model, specialist teachers are assigned to teach a particular curricular field or area. For example, reading and language arts may be assigned to specialist teachers in those subjects. Mathematics, science, social studies, physical education, and art also would be taught by specialists.

Some elementary schools also use a combination of the self-contained and departmentalized models. For example, kindergarten and grades one to three may be self-contained, and grades four, five, and six departmentalized.

Horizontal organization can also be arranged on the readiness and ability grouping of children. Children are assigned to heterogeneous groups according to age and other factors such as readiness, ability, and achievement. Proponents of heterogeneous grouping claim that it is a more realistic and democratic arrangement since children are not segregated on any basis other than age. Children of high ability as well as those of lower ability learn to work together and to appreciate individual differences.

In homogeneous grouping, children with similar problems, needs, and, most frequently, ability levels are grouped together for instructional purposes. Advocates of homogeneous groupings contend that instruction can be planned and delivered more efficiently when the pupils who are being instructed are in a similar ability range. Gifted and high-ability learners can move at an accelerated rate and use more advanced materials and not be held back by slower children when they are grouped homogeneously. Pupils who are progressing at a slower learning rate or who may be experiencing learning difficulties also can be grouped so that teachers can address their particular needs.

While there are purists who will argue for either homogeneous or heterogeneous grouping, a sound educational approach often takes a middle ground and uses both patterns of horizontal organization. Pupils can be grouped on the basis of readiness and ability in some skills and subjects, such as reading, language arts, and mathematics, and then be in heterogeneous groups for social studies, music, art, and physical education. Thus, they can learn with students of the same ability in certain subjects and still share experiences with classmates of differing abilities in other subjects.

Contemporary Trends in Elementary Education

During the past several decades, important trends have emerged in elementary education. In curriculum, the trend in the early 1960s was to "inquire" into the "structure of disciplines" and away from the conventional patterns of cumulative sequence. In the 1980s, there was a strong trend to curricular programs that stressed basic skills and subjects, organized in a sequential pattern. This section examines several contemporary trends in elementary education.

Instructional and Organizational Trends

Team teaching, an "effort to improve instruction by the reorganization of personnel," is a form of cooperative teaching in which two or more teachers plan and work together to instruct the same group of students.[5] Team teaching requires organizing the school staff into a close working group in which team leaders, cooperating teachers, and instructional aides form a coordinated instructional team.

While every teacher is not expected to be expert in all subjects, teachers involved in team teaching need a thorough understanding of the entire educational process. Members of the teaching team need to work cooperatively with their colleagues in planning, organizing, presenting, and evaluating instruction. Team teaching tends to reduce the isolation of teachers from their colleagues that often occurs in the self-contained classroom. It also permits and encourages teachers to develop special areas of expertise.

Team teaching requires a more flexible pattern of organization, scheduling, and staffing. In the elementary school, for example, pupils would be assigned to (1) large groups for demonstrations, presentations, films, television, and field excursions, (2) small groups for discussion, projects, experiments, and group work, and (3) independent reading and study. Because of the flexibility that team teaching requires, it is more often found in ungraded schools and in situations that encourage individualized instruction. Flexible scheduling provides for modules of 20 to 30 minutes of instruction, rather than the longer periods found in conventional arrangements.

While team teaching encouraged a number of changes in elementary schools, such as flexible scheduling of pupils and differential staffing of teachers, it did not have the revolutionary impact that some of its proponents predicted. At times, it was introduced by administrators who did not understand that its successful implementation required a thorough reorganization of the school program. In other cases, teachers were expected to become part of a teaching team without having the necessary commitment or in-service preparation. Merely assigning two teachers to the same group of students is not team teaching.

Programmed Learning and Computer-Assisted Instruction

In recent years, programmed learning and computer-assisted instruction have been introduced into elementary as well as secondary schools. Programmed learning is a companion innovation to the ungraded school, team teaching, and individualized instruction. It is designed to bring pupils to concept formation or skill acquisition through a series of carefully graduated sequences that provide them with a means of instant self-evaluation. Because pupils are given instant feedback, they recognize their correct and incorrect responses as rapidly as they make them and can progress at their own learning rate. Although the principles of programmed learning can be applied to most skills and subjects, it is particularly adaptable to those that can be reduced easily to elemental steps, such as spelling, language development, and mathematics. Initially, programmed learning was introduced with the teaching machines that are still used widely in elementary schools, especially in learning

---

5. Judson T. Shaplin, "Team Teaching," in Ronald Gross and Judith Murphy, eds., *The Revolution in the Schools* (New York: Harcourt Brace, 1964), p. 93.

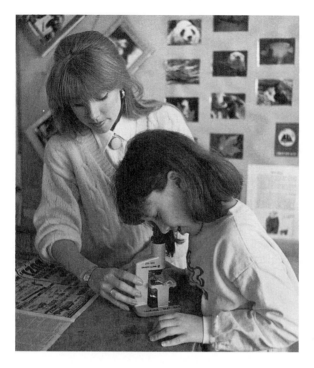

A teacher guides a student in using a microscope in a science class.

centers. Textbooks, workbooks, and other printed materials are now available that incorporate the principles of programmed learning.

Another contemporary instructional innovation involves computers. Since the early 1970s, computers have entered the mainstream of American life, especially in science, business, and industry, where they make it possible to store, classify, record, and retrieve vast amounts of information. Computer-assisted instruction is used in elementary schools to (1) individualize instruction so that it relates to pupil needs and skill levels and (2) bring about computer literacy—familiarity with and facility in using computers—in much the same way that literacy is developed in reading, writing, and understanding language.

From Open Learning to "Back to Basics"

Many of the curricular innovations of the early 1960s were designed by university professors in mathematics, the sciences, and other academic disciplines who developed new programs, such as the "new mathematics," the "new physics," and the "new social studies." Underlying these innovations in curriculum could often be found Jerome Bruner's learning theory, which emphasized identifying the structure of disciplines and using the inquiry or discovery method.[6]

The movement for curriculum revision began first in the sciences and then extended into language arts and social studies. The new curricula were designed to

6. Jerome Bruner, *The Process of Education* (Cambridge, Mass.: Harvard University Press, 1960).

replace the emphasis on facts with the key concepts needed to understand a field. Stressing the inquiry or discovery method, the new curricula sought to introduce students to the methods of investigation used by scientists and other scholars in their research. Rather than the direct presentation of factual information in textbooks or by teachers, the students were to investigate topics or problems and reach their own conclusions.

The curricular innovations of the 1960s were supported by the federal government, which funded special institutes and workshops for teachers through the National Defense Education Act. The Carnegie Corporation, the Ford Foundation, and other private philanthropic organizations also encouraged the new curricula. Commercial publishers promoted the movement by designing and marketing "learning packages" featuring the new programs.

Although professors of education were sometimes involved in designing new programs, the major impact came from professors in academic disciplines. Frequently, the academic innovators were unaware of or neglected already existing research on learning. In some instances, the new curricula were introduced without sufficient attention to the experience of classroom teachers. Some critics contended that the apparent sophistication of the new curricular programs masked a superficiality that neglected needed information and skills. Nevertheless, the concerted efforts of the private corporations, the federal government, and the commercial publishers brought about the introduction of the new curricula into many elementary schools.

In the early 1970s, a group of educational critics emerged who wanted to reform elementary education according to a child-centered philosophy that emphasized the liberation of children's impulses. The new critics argued that many elementary schools were too formal, bureaucratic, and inflexible. A series of books by educational critics such as Herbert Kohl, Jonathan Kozol, George Dennison, and John Holt argued for informal and open learning.[7] As did some of the progressive educators before them, these critics urged that children should be free to follow their own curiosity, interests, and needs. Teachers were to guide the learning process in an enthusiastic, informal, interesting, and exciting way.

The cause of informal and open learning gained a major impetus with the publication of Charles E. Silberman's *Crisis in the Classroom* in 1970.[8] Silberman contended that American public schools had become overly formal. Excessive routine and formality had devitalized schools, which practiced a mindless routine. For Silberman, the remedy was to create more open, informal, and humanistic schools. He argued that the model of the British primary school, or integrated day school, could be adapted to American elementary education. Informal open classrooms would encourage teachers to follow and guide learners' interests.

---

7. Among the representative critics are George Dennison, *The Lives of Children* (New York: Random House, 1969); James Herndon, *The Way It Spozed to Be* (New York: Simon & Schuster, 1968); John Holt, *How Children Learn* (New York: Pitman, 1967); Jonathan Kozol, *Death at an Early Age* (Boston: Houghton Mifflin, 1967).
8. Charles E. Silberman, *Crisis in the Classroom: The Remaking of American Education* (New York: Random House, 1970).

Silberman's work, as well as that of other educators, promoted an American enthusiasm for the British primary school.[9] In its various forms, the British primary school rested on the philosophy that children learned most effectively when they were directly involved with the immediate environment in which they pursued their interests with the guidance of teachers. Rather than following the scheduled time sequences of more traditional schools, the British primary school stressed longer blocks of time in which the children worked individually or in small groups at a wide range of activities. The British primary school gained a following among enthusiastic American educators, who began to implement it as open-space education.

During the late 1960s and early 1970s, the open-education movement gained ground steadily in the United States. A noteworthy example of the implementation of open education occurred in North Dakota, where a number of small schools were converted into informal or open schools. Throughout the country, school districts inaugurated open classrooms or open-space schools.

By the mid-1970s, the pendulum of educational change had begun to swing away from curricular innovation and open education to basic education. The "Back to Basics" movement was inaugurated by parents and nonprofessionals and then began to influence professional educators. Essentially, advocates argued that the school curriculum should emphasize basic skills and subjects. There was a fear that essential skills of reading, writing, and arithmetic were being neglected. Along with the attention to the basic skills and subjects, advocates urged a return to discipline and order in a structured classroom in which the teacher was the center of authority.

A leading force in the Back to Basics movement is the Council for Basic Education, which was organized in 1956 to work for an increased emphasis on the fundamental intellectual disciplines in the public schools. The council has urged that students receive adequate instruction in the basic intellectual disciplines of English, mathematics, science, history, foreign languages, and the arts.[10]

In the 1980s, the emphasis in elementary education has been on creating "effective schools." The characteristics of effective schools have been identified as

1. Strong educational leadership on the part of the school principal.
2. The maintenance of a safe and orderly school environment that is conducive to learning.
3. A curriculum that facilitates achievement in learning basic skills and subjects.
4. Teachers who work collegially to foster student achievement.[11]

---

9. The major source on the British primary school is Lady Bridget Plowden and others, *Children and Their Primary Schools: A Report of the Central Advisory Council in Education* (London: Her Majesty's Stationery Office, 1966). Other works on open education are John Blackie, *Inside the Primary School* (London: Her Majesty's Stationery Office, 1967); Mary Brown and Normal Precious, *The Integrated Day in the Primary School* (New York: Agathon Press, 1970); Lillian S. Stephens, *The Teachers Guide to Open Education* (New York: Holt, Rinehart & Winston, 1974).

10. For the theory of basic education, see James D. Koerner, ed., *The Case for Basic Education* (Boston: Little, Brown, 1959).

11. William J. Bennett, *What Works: Research About Teaching and Learning* (Washington, D.C.: U.S. Department of Education, 1986), p. 45.

Conclusion

In discussing elementary education, Chapter 14 has examined its role as an agency of cultural transmission. In the United States, the common school of the early nineteenth century was the prototype of today's public school. The elementary school has been designed to cultivate fundamental skills and knowledge in the young. While an instrument of cognitive development, it also serves to cultivate social, personal, and aesthetic sensibilities in children. The elementary school is the institution that prepares youngsters for entry to the junior high or middle school, which is the subject of Chapter 15.

DISCUSSION QUESTIONS

1. Debate the proposition that elementary education's major purpose is to transmit the cultural heritage from adults to children.
2. Prepare your own list of goals for elementary education and provide a rationale defending your statement of goals.
3. Examine the various books that have been used to teach reading at a particular level in elementary schools over a given historical period. Identify the values that are emphasized in these books.
4. Debate the proposition that elementary schools tend to be more innovative than secondary schools.
5. Why is the elementary school curriculum generally arranged into broad fields?
6. Distinguish between vertical and horizontal patterns of organization and provide examples of each.
7. Compare and contrast homogeneous and heterogeneous groupings.
8. Compare and contrast the graded and nongraded elementary school.
9. Identify and analyze the "open education" and "basic education" philosophies. Compare and contrast these educational perspectives.

FIELD EXERCISES

1. Invite an elementary teacher to visit your class to describe a typical school day.
2. Visit an elementary school and observe classes at the primary and intermediate levels. Note the similarities and differences between these levels. Report your observations to the class.
3. Invite an elementary school principal to visit your class to describe the way in which his or her school is organized.
4. If possible, visit both a graded and an ungraded elementary school. Compare and contrast them. Decide in which school you would prefer to teach.
5. Interview several elementary teachers on their reactions to recent curricular changes. Try to elicit their opinions about the new mathematics, new social studies, and other curricular innovations.
6. Visit an elementary school in which team teaching is used. Report your observations to the class.

7. Read a book written by an advocate of informal, or open, education. Identify the author's critique of elementary education and analyze it for the class.

8. If there is a group in your community that advocates basic education, invite its representatives to speak to your class on the organization's purposes.

SUGGESTED READINGS

BENNETT, WILLIAM J. *First Lessons: A Report on Elementary Education in America*. Washington, D.C.: U.S. Government Printing Office, 1986.

BLOOM, BENJAMIN. *All Our Children Learning: A Primer for Parents, Teachers, and Other Educators*. New York: McGraw-Hill, 1980.

BRUNER, JEROME. *The Process of Education*. Cambridge, Mass: Harvard University Press, 1960.

FEATHERSTONE, JOSEPH. *Schools Where Children Learn*. New York: Liveright, 1971.

GEGA, PETER C. *Science in Elementary Education*. New York: Macmillan, 1990.

GOODLAD, JOHN. *A Place Called School*. New York: McGraw-Hill, 1984.

———, AND ANDERSON, ROBERT H. *The Nongraded Elementary School*. New York: Teachers College Press, Columbia University, 1987.

GUTEK, GERALD L. *Basic Education: A Historical Perspective*. Bloomington, Ind.: Phi Delta Kappa Educational Foundation, 1981.

HOLT, JOHN. *How Children Fail*. New York: Pitman, 1964.

———. *How Children Learn*. New York: Pitman, 1967.

HUNTER, ROBERT, AND SCHEIRER, ELINOR A. *The Organic Curriculum: Organizing for Learning 7–12*. New York: Falmer Press, 1988.

KELLY, JAMES L., AND KELLY, MARY JEAN. *The Successful Elementary Teacher*. Lanham, Md.: University Press of America, 1985.

LEMLECH, JOHANNA KASIN. *Curriculum and Instructional Methods for the Elementary School*. New York: Macmillan, 1990.

McCULLOCH, LOU W. *Children's Books of the 19th Century*. Des Moines, Iowa: Wallace–Homestead, 1979.

PERRONE, VITO. *Open Education: Promise and Problems*. Bloomington, Ind.: Phi Delta Kappa Educational Foundation, 1972.

SEWALL, GILBERT T. *Necessary Lessons: Decline and Renewal in American Schools*. New York: Free Press—Macmillan, 1983.

SHAVER, JAMES P., ED. *Building Rationales for Citizenship Education*. Arlington, Va.: National Council for the Social Studies, 1977.

SILBERMAN, CHARLES E. *Crisis in the Classroom: The Remaking of American Education*. New York: Random House, 1970.

STEPHENS, LILLIAN S. *The Teacher's Guide to Open Education*. New York: Holt, Rinehart & Winston, 1974.

What Works: Research About Teaching and Learning. Washington, D.C.: U.S. Department of Education, 1986.

15

The Junior High and Middle School

Chapter 15 examines the origins, development, and contemporary condition of the American junior high school. In most instances, the junior high school, which did not appear until the early twentieth century, is a three-year institution that consists of grades seven, eight, and nine; less frequently, it is a two-year school that includes grades seven and eight. There are also variations on these patterns. Within this general framework, it enrolls adolescents ranging in age from 12 through 14 or 15.

The general focusing questions that will be answered as you read this chapter include the following:

1. What historical forces contributed to the organization of the junior high school?
2. What are the goals and curricular patterns of the contemporary junior high school?
3. What is the educational rationale for the middle school?

Historical Development of the Junior High School

The period from 1900 to 1920, the era in which the junior high school appeared and took shape, was influenced by (1) massive immigration from southern and eastern Europe to the large cities of the United States, (2) the continuing industrialization of the United States, which was marked by the emergence of a technological society, (3) the recognition, caused by the Spanish–American War and World War I, that the United States was a world power, (4) the growing impact of behavioral research and science on education and society, and (5) the impact of progressive education and pragmatic philosophy on American schools. These trends, which would eventually result in the reorganization of American life and society, also stimulated reorganization in the way in which Americans ran their schools.

An important source of discontent with the "8–4" school system came from advocates of industrial education, who believed that traditional schooling had failed to provide the skilled workers and technicians needed for an America that had become one of the world's leading industrial nations. These critics believed that American schools needed to update and modernize their system of organization, curriculum, and instruction. They contended that the eight-year elementary, or graded, school still reflected rural, nineteenth-century America; they also believed that the high school was still overly oriented to the traditional college preparatory curriculum. The proponents of industrial education were impressed by the role that technical-industrial education had in German schools. They felt that a modernized and industrially competent American economic and productive system also required an economically and socially efficient school system.

In 1907, the proponents of industrial education organized the National Society for the Promotion of Industrial Education (NSPIE) to promote their cause in the schools. NSPIE worked to reorganize the school system to create units or institutions that offered programs distinct from the basic literary and mathematical preparation of the elementary schools and also different from the traditional college preparatory secondary school.

While the proponents of industrial education were promoting educational reorganization, some professional educators were also questioning the traditional 8–4 system, for example, Frank Spaulding and Franklin Bobbitt, who urged the application of scientific management to education. They believed that the curriculum should be constructed according to measurable outcomes that had social or economic results. As did the industrialists who wanted an educational institution to respond to economic needs, social efficiency educators wanted schools to be economically and socially justifiable.

The proponents of industrial education were active at the state and national levels. Using the argument that industrial training would open to American youth a wide range of useful occupations, this group and their allies in Congress secured the passage of the Smith–Hughes Act in 1917 to promote vocational education.

While the entry of industrial education was a major goal of certain advocates of educational reorganization, other educators wanted to create new structures to facilitate the transition from elementary to secondary schooling. The major question was the appropriate time at which to begin the transition from elementary to secondary school. They were concerned that the upper years of the elementary schools, particularly the seventh and eighth grades, were too repetitious of the preceding grades. They wanted to replace the repetitious reviews of reading, arithmetic, spelling, and vocabulary exercises with different kinds of educational experiences. While they might agree that different experiences were needed, they could not always agree if these experiences should be the earlier introduction of secondary courses or increased vocational education.

For still other educators, the movement for reorganization developed a new perspective about the nature of adolescence and the need to adapt educational institutions to patterns of human growth and development. Educational psychologists such as G. Stanley Hall (1846–1924) had developed the pioneering studies of adolescent psychology. Hall's two-volume work *Adolescence* (1904) and *Educational Problems* (1911) outlined the educational implications of his theories of adolescent growth and development. While these theorists saw the high school as an institution for adolescents, they also believed that an educational institution was needed for the early adolescent period. They also believed that the years of early adolescence were sufficiently distinct from those of childhood.

Early Junior High Schools

Just as a variety of reorganized school patterns developed throughout the country, there were also different kinds of reorganized intermediate schools. In 1910, the Cleveland, Ohio, system had established an "intermediate industrial school" for 14- to 16-year-old boys and girls. The Cleveland curriculum was modified to include vocational work for boys and home arts for girls.

A prototype of today's junior high school was created in 1910 by Superintendent Frank Bunker in Berkeley, California, where grades seven through nine were organized into an "introductory high school." Bunker's concept for this new school was based on (1) the characteristics of adolescence, (2) the need for a more "gradual transition" between elementary school and work, (3) the need to alleviate overcrowded central schools, and (4) the need to develop a curriculum that reflected the future occupational needs of students.[1] The curriculum of the Berkeley "introductory high school" was revised to emphasize vocational courses, such as typewriting, bookkeeping, stenography, commercial law, elementary banking, manual training, domestic science, business arithmetic, and business English.[2]

In addition to the early junior high schools in Cleveland and Berkeley, there were others throughout the country. However, there was little agreement as to the scope of instruction or to the grades to be included in a reorganized school plan. Some districts marked off the seventh and eighth grades as the years for junior high school instruction. In other localities, arrangements were based on 6–6, 7–4, 6–2–4, and 6–3–3 plans. While there was diversity throughout the country, the general trend was for a six-year elementary school, a three-year senior high school, and an intermediate school—the junior high school composed of the seventh, eighth, and ninth grades.[3]

By 1920, several educators had written authoritative books about the junior high school.[4] Leonard Koos, in particular, described the major functions of the junior high school that had emerged in the first two decades of its existence. According to Koos, the junior high school was to

1. Retain students in school by reducing the dropout rate and by easing the transition from elementary to high school.
2. Economize instructional time by the earlier introduction of certain secondary-level subjects and by eliminating unnecessary repetition and review of subjects studied in the elementary school.
3. Recognize and provide for individual differences in students' ability, interests, environment, age, and development.

1. Frank P. Bunker, *Reorganization of the Public School System* (Washington, D.C.: U.S. Government Printing Office, 1916), pp. 108–109.
2. W. Richard Stephens, "The Junior High School: A Product of Reform Values, 1890–1920," paper presented at the Midwest History of Education Society, Chicago, October 27–28, 1967, p. 16.
3. Francis T. Spaulding, O. L. Frederick, and Leonard V. Koos, *The Reorganization of Secondary Education*, National Survey of Secondary Education, Monograph 5, United States Office of Education Bulletin 17, 1932 (Washington, D.C.: U.S. Government Printing Office, 1935), pp. 27–29, 38–44.
4. Noteworthy examples are Leonard Koos, *The Junior High School* (New York: Harcourt Brace, 1920); Thomas H. Briggs, *The Junior High School* (Boston: Houghton Mifflin, 1920).

4. Provide more extensive guidance, especially about careers and occupations.
5. Initiate vocational education by providing a range of vocational activities, training, and experiences.
6. Recognize the nature of adolescence and its impact on education.
7. Begin subject matter departmentalization and thereby increase teacher specialization.
8. Increase students' educational and socialization opportunities by providing a variety of physical, social, recreational, athletic, and educational activities.[5]

The trend to school reorganization, including an increase in the number of junior high schools, is demonstrated by the following statistics. In 1930, there were 16,460 regular high schools, 1,842 junior high schools, and 3,287 junior-senior high schools. In 1952, there were 10,168 four-year high schools, 3,227 junior high schools, 1,760 senior high schools, and 8,591 junior-senior high schools. In 1959, there were 6,044 high schools on the 8–4 system, 1,407 high schools on the 6–2–4 system, 1,651 senior high schools on the 6–3–3 system, 5,027 junior high schools on the 6–2–4 and 6–3–3 systems, and 10,155 junior-senior high schools on the 6–6 system.[6] By the mid-twentieth century, the junior high school was an important and widely acknowledged part of the American educational ladder. Although there were still school systems based on the 8–4 pattern, the majority of school systems had been reorganized to incorporate the junior high school.

The Contemporary Junior High School

Now that the historical development of the American junior high school has been examined, we describe its general goals and curriculum.

Goals

As indicated, the junior high school's origins were diverse. The following goals still reflect this diversity, namely, (1) to provide a transition from elementary to secondary education, (2) to introduce learners to separate subject matters and disciplines, (3) to recognize and provide for the physical, physiological, emotional, and social changes that are taking place in adolescent students, (4) to introduce students to the range of careers and occupations, (5) to provide opportunities for social and physical, as well as educational, development, and (6) to provide articulation with the senior high school.

Junior High School Curriculum

Unlike the typical elementary school curriculum, the junior high school curriculum is usually differentiated into specific subject matter courses. Similar to senior high school teachers, those in junior high schools are expected to be specialists in the content of and in the teaching of their subjects. Educators who work to construct curricula for junior high schools must answer questions such as these:

5. Koos, *The Junior High School*, pp. 13–85.
6. Robert E. Potter, *The Stream of American Education* (New York: American Book, 1967), p. 376.

This scene from a junior high school shows a more departmentalized learning situation.

How can the junior high school curriculum build on skills and subjects learned in the primary and intermediate grades of the elementary school?

What academic skills and subjects are appropriate to and needed by junior high school students?

What physical, social, recreational, athletic, and educational experiences and activities are appropriate to and needed by adolescents enrolled in junior high schools?

What skills, subjects, and experiences are mandated by state authorities?

How does the curriculum and extracurricular program relate to the social and economic realities—including career or occupational possibilities—of the community served by the junior high school?

To what extent should the junior high school curriculum articulate with that of the senior high school? How well does it prepare students to meet the academic expectations of the high school?

What should be the scope (the breadth) and the sequence (the arrangement) of subjects, experiences, and activities that have been included in the junior high school curriculum?

What instruments should be developed and used to evaluate the progress of junior high school students?

Junior high school administrators, teachers, parents, and students have considered and answered these questions in the past. As this curriculum is revised, they will need to address these questions in the future. Today's junior high school curriculum represents a combination of recommended or required and elective courses. Required courses generally are English, or language arts, mathematics, social studies, science, health, and physical education. Elective courses are likely to be art, music, home and industrial arts, and foreign languages. Required and elective courses may vary from school district to school district.

The following descriptions provide an overview of a "typical" junior high school curriculum.

English, or Language Arts   English, often called language arts, represents a continuation of certain skill-building activities from the elementary level and an introduction to more specialized subject matter content. The techniques and skills of reading may be continued. The study of literature is used to introduce the concepts of genre or type, subject, form, interpretation, and appreciation in prose and poetry. The study of the English language as written and oral expression may be subdivided into units on language structure, grammar, and usage. Basic research skills involving the use of the dictionary, reference books, and the library are also stressed.

Mathematics   Since the early 1960s, when the "new math" was incorporated into the junior high curriculum, mathematics instruction has been in a state of change. The "new math" emphasized the process of mathematical reasoning. In the late 1970s, declines in computational skills and scores on achievement tests caused many school districts to rethink their mathematics programs. Recently, junior high school mathematics curricula have reflected an emphasis on basic computation and application. Units included in the mathematics curriculum at the junior high school include basic computation, fractions, percentages, ratios, decimals, metrics, measurement, graphing, practical problem solving, and an introduction to algebra and geometry.

Social Studies   As is true in both the elementary and senior high school, the social studies or social science curriculum represents a wide variety of subjects and courses. If the curriculum is organized as separate subjects, the most frequently offered courses are geography, world history, American history (which is typically mandated by the state), local and state history (which, again, may be mandated), and civics. In many junior high schools, social science courses are multi- or interdisciplinary. Such integrated courses include selected concepts from history, geography, economics, sociology, psychology, and anthropology.

Science   While the pattern of science instruction was found in the general science course at most junior high schools until the late 1950s, a great deal of experiment, revision, and development took place in the 1960s and 1970s. The development was stimulated by funds provided by the National Defense Education Act (NDEA) in 1958 and by the National Science Foundation. Among the various projects that stimulated change in the junior high school science curriculum were the Elementary Science Study (ESS), Science Curriculum Improvement Study (SCIS), Intermediate Science Curriculum Study (ISCS), Introductory Physical Science Study (IPSS), Biological Science Curriculum Study (BSCS), Earth Science Curriculum Project (ESCP), and Secondary School Science Project (SSSP). The major impact of these projects was in the stimulation of revisions in existing science curricula and in the creation of new courses in earth, biological, and physical sciences and chemistry.

Along with content that reflects the structure of the parent scientific discipline, the new science programs generally emphasized the research and investigative processes used by scientists in laboratory situations.

Health   Although it may be incorporated into the science or physical education curriculum, most junior high schools teach health as a separate subject. Health education at this level includes units on nutrition, hygiene, cleanliness, disease, dental care, and the organs of the body. Special units, often reflecting state mandates, and local community concerns, are often included on preventing the use of tobacco, alcohol, and drugs. Units on the use of tobacco present information about the harmful effects of tobacco smoking on the human body. Units on the use of alcohol tend to discuss the physiological, psychological, sociological, and economic consequences of drinking. The impact of alcoholism on the individual and his or her family may also be discussed. Units on drugs are generally intended to create an awareness in students of the effects of drug abuse on human beings and on society. Such topics may be treated as (1) the names and characteristics of certain drugs, (2) drug abuse, (3) legal aspects and penalties of drug abuse, and (4) the availability of medical and psychological rehabilitation for drug users. Health units also include instruction in sex education that describes the physiology of the reproductive organs and may explore sexual decision making. AIDS education may also be included as a unit.

Physical Education   The junior high school curriculum includes organized physical education activities. The major objectives of junior high school physical education programs generally are (1) development of physical fitness and the acquisition of useful body skills, (2) development of a desire to participate in and enjoy recreational activities as leisure-time activities, and (3) provision of experiences in a variety of skills, games, and fitness activities. Activities that may be included in a junior high school physical education program are badminton, basketball, rhythmic exercises, bowling, cross-country racing, football, hockey, gymnastic stunts and tumbling, soccer, softball, square dancing, swimming, tennis, volleyball, weight lifting, and wrestling.

Industrial Arts   As was indicated, demands for increased industrial and vocational training were a major force in stimulating the junior high school movement. Today's junior high industrial arts program is rarely designed to prepare students for an immediate entry into the work force. Social attitudes, economic realities, and child labor laws have deferred vocational preparation until senior high school. Contemporary junior high school industrial arts seek to (1) stimulate interest and skills in industrial arts, (2) introduce students to the range of industrial careers, (3) encourage a sense of design and expert technique, and (4) encourage safety habits in using machines and materials. Units included in industrial arts are woodwork, metalwork, plastics, graphic arts, electronics, design, printing, photography, and leather and textile work. Whereas only boys were enrolled in industrial arts in the past, the contemporary junior high school enrolls girls as well as boys.

Home Economics   Home economics, or home arts, is a co-educational subject in today's junior high school. The general objectives of home economics are to (1) introduce concepts and practices needed for family life and home management, (2) develop the basic functional skills needed in home management, (3) examine the responsibilities and roles of family members, and (4) examine the impact of socio-economic change on family life. Home economics courses may include units in food preparation, sewing, money management, child care, clothing design and construction, grooming, and etiquette.

Foreign Languages   In the mid-1960s, foreign language instruction in the junior high schools experienced growth. Since the late 1960s, foreign language offerings have declined seriously. Where they remain at the junior high school level, they are typically elective courses. The most common foreign language offered is Spanish. Other languages are French, German, Italian, and Portuguese. If a particular foreign language is spoken by large numbers of people in a community, it may find a place in the junior high school curriculum.

Music   Most junior high schools provide a variety of courses and activities in music, such as instrumental music, vocal music, and music appreciation. Students have the opportunity to participate in band, orchestra, choir, and glee club. They may perform in school and in public musical performances.

Art   As with music, courses and junior high school activities in art are designed to promote artistic appreciation and creation. While some junior high schools may require art, it is often an elective. Units include art history, art appreciation, painting, crafts, design, weaving, macramé, and sculpture. Junior high schools may sponsor exhibitions where students' work is displayed for other students, parents, and the public.

As can be seen from the discussion about the origins, purposes, and curriculum of the junior high school, teaching junior high school students is challenging and exciting. Junior high school teachers need to understand the physical and psychological transitions that young people experience upon entering adolescence. In many respects, junior high school teachers need to be "bridge builders" between the basic educational skills and subjects of the elementary school and the more complex and differentiated subjects of high school. They need to be expert in adolescent psychology and in organizing instruction to meet the social and educational needs of students entering the early stages of young adulthood. An important feature of such teaching is that of being a leader in exploratory education.

Junior high school students are introduced to new subjects and experiences. They are consciously and seriously beginning to ponder career choices as they are introduced to business, home economics, agriculture, and various vocations. In addition to academic instruction, junior high school students need counseling about their interests, problems, aptitudes, and educational and career goals and choices.

Emergence of the Middle School

In the mid- and late 1960s, the middle school concept was developed as a new approach at school reorganization. The concept gained popularity in the decade between 1967 and 1977, and the number of institutions designated as middle schools increased from 1,101 to 4,060.[7] Middle schools seek to incorporate the intermediate grades—fifth and sixth—with the upper grades—seventh and eighth—into a separate institution. Proponents of middle schools have argued that the social and educational needs of the 10- to 14-year-old population can be met more adequately in such a reorganized institution than in either the elementary or junior high school arrangement. In the section that follows, the definition and rationale of one of America's newest educational institutions—the middle school—is examined.

Although definitions of the middle school vary, it is usually agreed to be a school that is intermediate between elementary and high school that combines grades five through eight or six through eight into one organization and facility.[8] Middle schools are also often characterized by team teaching, flexible scheduling, and interdisciplinary institutionalized programs. The proponents of the middle school have tended to view junior high schools as overly imitative of the senior high school and of failing to fulfill its original promise of creating an educational climate and program to meet the needs of youngsters in their early adolescent years. Among the arguments given for the middle school are the following:

1. The middle school is designed to meet the unique requirements of adolescent learners, who need the security of the elementary school while gaining confidence and skill through a broad exploratory learning.
2. Because of its unique combination of grade levels, the middle school can serve as a socially and racially comprehensive institution.
3. The middle school facilitates a great deal of individualization in the instructional program to meet the needs of a heterogeneous student population that includes pre-adolescents, early adolescents, and older adolescents.

Middle school proponents frequently identify the institution's primary function as being related to the developmental needs of early adolescence. They contend that early adolescence is an important definitional stage in human development during which the person shapes his or her value system, behavior code, and self-esteem. Because of its important formative effects on early adolescent development, middle school educators agree that, while linking elementary and secondary education, it is a unique institution, distinct from both elementary and high school.[9]

---

7. William M. Alexander and Paul S. George, *The Exemplary Middle School* (New York: Holt, Rinehart & Winston, 1980), p. 13.
8. For the various definitions of the middle school, see William E. Klingele, *Teaching in Middle Schools* (Boston: Allyn & Bacon, 1979), pp. 6–8.
9. Tedd Levy, "Making a Difference in the Middle," *Social Education*, 52 (February 1988), pp. 104–106.

In 1977, the National Middle School Association (NMSA) developed the following priority goals for shaping the middle school's direction:

1. Each student should be well known as a person by at least one adult in the school who accepts responsibility for his or her guidance.
2. Every student should be assisted in achieving optimum mastery of the skills of continued learning, together with a commitment to using and improving them.
3. Every student should have ample experiences designed to develop decision-making and problem-solving skills.
4. Every student should acquire a functional core of fundamental knowledge.
5. Every student should have opportunities to explore and develop interests in aesthetic, leisure, career, and other aspects of life.[10]

Based on these directional goals, middle school educators contend that the curriculum should be developmentally appropriate to the needs of early adolescence. However, they recognize that the students in this age range exhibit significant differences in their physical, social, psychological, and intellectual development. Therefore, a developmentally appropriate curriculum needs to provide a range of varied learning experiences. An effective curriculum needs to be sensitive to students' needs for self-identification and socialization, as well as promoting academic learning.[11]

A 1987 task force report, *Caught in the Middle: Educational Reform for Young Adolescents in California Public Schools,* stresses that the most effective schooling for middle school students emphasizes the academic integrity of instruction while maintaining a strong emotional connection with students. Middle schools in the 1990s will need to meet three important challenges: (1) preparing students for academic success in high school, (2) ensuring that students are connected to the goals and purposes of their schools, and (3) providing ample opportunities for students to develop and increase their self-esteem.[12]

Exaggeration of the differences between junior high and middle schools should be avoided, but certain philosophical differences should be mentioned. Middle schools are supposed to be more student oriented, more open to a process-oriented curriculum, more likely to use flexible scheduling and to individualize instruction. Junior high schools are likely to emphasize departmentalization, a subject matter curriculum, more teacher-directed instruction, and a standard six-period instructional day. Despite these philosophical differences, junior high and middle schools may be more similar than different operationally.

Conclusion

Junior high and middle schools represent a recent refinement of the American educational ladder. Designed to meet the educational, social, and vocational needs

---

10. "Report of the NMSA Committee on Future Goals and Directions," *Middle School Journal,* 8 (November 1977), p. 16, as cited in William H. Alexander, "Schools in the Middle: Rhetoric and Reality," *Social Education,* 52 (February 1988), pp. 107–109.
11. Levy, "Making a Difference in the Middle."
12. Bill Honig, "Middle Grade Reform," *Social Education,* 52 (February 1988), pp. 119–120.

of the early years of adolescence, the junior high school resulted from demands to reorganize the traditional 8–4 pattern of organization.

Today's junior high and middle schools are transitional institutions that are subject to pressures and demands that come upward from the elementary school and downward from the high school. At the same time that they have eased the transition from elementary to high school, these intermediate educational institutions have also maintained articulation with the high school. While providing articulation and transition, junior high and middle schools have become unique educational institutions that serve the educational and social needs of American young people in the early stages of their adolescence.

DISCUSSION QUESTIONS

1. Identify and examine the major social, political, economic, and educational trends that contributed to the development of the junior high school.
2. Identify and examine the major functions of junior high schools.
3. If you attended a junior high school, reflect on your experiences. Then write a short educational biography about your experiences as a junior high school student.
4. Examine the transitional function of the junior high school in terms of its implications for students, curriculum, and educational institutions.
5. Compare and contrast the concepts of the junior high school and middle schools.
6. Read a book on either the junior high or middle school and review its content for the class.
7. Identify the characteristics of an effective middle school.

FIELD EXERCISES

1. Interview a junior high school principal or teacher and ask the following questions:
   a. How does the junior high school curriculum build on skills and subjects learned in the elementary school?
   b. What academic skills and subjects are appropriate and needed by junior high students?
   c. What extra- or co-curricular activities are appropriate to junior high school students?
   d. How does the junior high school relate to the senior high school?

   After obtaining answers to these questions, report and discuss your information with members of your class.
2. Obtain a copy of a junior high school student or parent handbook. Examine its content and answer the questions raised in Field Exercise 1.
3. Interview several junior high school students and try to determine (a) the transitional problems they experienced in going from the elementary to the junior high school and (b) what they enjoy or dislike about their experiences as junior high school students.
4. Visit a junior high school and record your impressions of (a) teachers, (b) students, (c) classroom instruction, and (d) activities.

5. Visit a middle school and record your impressions of (a) teachers, (b) students, (c) classroom instruction, and (d) activities.

6. Prepare a summary of recommendations of recent reports on improving middle school education.

7. Based on your reading of several books on adolescent psychology, determine the characteristics of this period of human development that should be addressed in junior high and middle school education.

SUGGESTED READINGS

ALEXANDER, WILLIAM M., AND GEORGE, PAUL S. *The Exemplary Middle School.* New York: Holt, Rinehart & Winston, 1981.

BRIGGS, THOMAS H. *The Junior High School.* Boston: Houghton Mifflin, 1920.

BROOKS, KENNETH, AND EDWARDS, FRANCINE. *The Middle School in Transition: A Research Report on the Status of the Middle School Movement.* Lexington: College of Education, University of Kentucky, 1978.

GEORGE, PAUL S., AND OLDAKER, LYNN L. *Evidence for the Middle School.* Columbus, Ohio: National Middle School Association, 1985.

HAMBURG, DAVID A. *Preparing for Life: The Critical Transition of Adolescence.* New York: Carnegie Corporation, 1986.

HONIG, BILL. *Caught in the Middle: Educational Reform for Young Adolescents in California Public Schools.* Sacramento: California State Department of Education, 1987.

JOHNSON, MAURITZ, ED. *Toward Adolescence: The Middle School Years.* Seventy-Ninth Yearbook of the National Society for the Study of Adolescence. Part 1. Chicago: University of Chicago Press, 1980.

JOHNSTON, J. HOWARD, AND MARKLE, GLENN C. *What Research Says to the Middle Level Practitioner.* Columbus, Ohio: National Middle School Association, 1986.

KINDRED, LESLIE W., WOLOTKIEWICZ, RITA J., MICKELSON, JOHN M., COPLEIN, LEONARD E., AND DYSON, ERNEST. *The Middle School Curriculum.* Boston: Allyn & Bacon, 1976.

KLINGELE, WILLIAM E. *Teaching in Middle Schools.* Boston: Allyn & Bacon, 1979.

KOOS, LEONARD. *The Junior High School.* New York: Harcourt Brace, 1920.

NASSP's COUNCIL ON MIDDLE LEVEL EDUCATION. *Assessing Excellence: A Guide for Studying the Middle Level School.* Reston, Va.: National Association of Secondary School Principals, 1988.

———. *Middle Education's Responsibility for Intellectual Development.* Reston, Va.: National Association of Secondary School Principals, 1989.

TASK FORCE ON EDUCATION OF YOUNG ADOLESCENTS. *Turning Points: Preparing Youth for the 21st Century: The Report of the Task Force on Education of Young Adolescents.* Washington, D.C.: Carnegie Council of Adolescent Development, 1989.

VARS, GORDON F., ED. *Guidelines for Junior High and Middle School Education: A Summary of Positions.* Washington, D.C.: National Association of Secondary School Principals, 1969.

16

American
Secondary Education

Although generally agreed that elementary schools should prepare children in basic literary, computational, and social skills, the purposes of secondary education are often debated. Elementary school controversies often deal with methodological issues about the most efficient way to teach a skill, for example, reading. At the secondary level, controversies are generally curricular and relate to the essential purposes of secondary schooling.

The following generalizations are useful to establish a frame of reference for discussing American secondary education:

1. Secondary education refers to schooling that follows elementary but precedes higher education. In terms of levels of learning and institutional articulation, secondary schooling is transitional between elementary and higher education.
2. Institutionally, in the United States, secondary education generally occurs in the high school. In some instances, however, it may take place in academies and institutes.
3. In the United States, secondary education generally is age specific to adolescence.

Apart from these basic generalizations about secondary education, there are few other areas of agreement.

The general focusing questions that will be answered as you read this chapter include the following:

1. How was American secondary education shaped by transplanted European concepts?
2. What were the major developments in the history of American secondary education?
3. What is the nature and function of the contemporary high school?
4. What recent changes have occurred in the American high school student population?
5. What are some current plans to reform secondary schools?

European Concepts of Secondary Education

The European colonists in North America brought with them preconceptions about secondary education as they did about other matters. Traditionally, European schools were organized according to the inherited socioeconomic class structure. By the Renaissance and Reformation, two separate and distinct educational tracks had been developed: primary schools for the children of the masses and classical humanist schools for the offspring of the upper socioeconomic and political classes.

The classical humanist schools of the Renaissance that gave an elitist preparatory education to the sons of the ruling class prepared young men for leadership positions in church and state. Graduates of humanist schools would enter higher education, government service, or other leadership positions. Because they catered to an elite, the European classical humanist schools were exclusive and selective. To be a teacher or a student in a humanist school carried prestige and status.

European humanist schools have flourished since their Renaissance origins. In Italy, the schools of Vittorino da Feltre and Guarino da Farrara educated the scions of aristocratic houses to be courtiers, rulers, and diplomats. Their schools became the prototype of the Italian *liceo*. In France, the academic preparatory school was the *lycée*, frequently conducted by religious teaching orders such as the Jesuits. In England, the famous *public schools*, really private schools, such as Rugby, St. Paul's, Eton, and Harrow, educated young English gentlemen to serve king and country. For the Germans, the classical preparatory school was the *Gymnasium*. During the Protestant Reformation, leading reformers such as Luther, Melanchthon, and Calvin endorsed classical humanist education as most effective for preparing young men for college and the ministry.

Certain institutional characteristics of the European classical humanist school have shaped our conventional conception of secondary schooling. When the British settled in North America, they imported the Latin Grammar school that embodied the following characteristics:

1. Secondary schooling should be preparatory for more advanced or higher learning. For students who ended their education with secondary school, the classical curriculum would benefit them as much as those students who continued their education.
2. A good preparatory education was based almost exclusively on mastering the classical Greek and Latin languages and literature. This conception persisted until the early twentieth century; knowledge of Latin was frequently required for college entry.
3. Because it focused on the classical languages, knowledge was thought of as originating in the past and was construed in verbal or literary terms. Even when Latin was dethroned as the language of the educated person, learning was still thought of as language mastery. For example, science might be included in the curriculum, but instruction was based on reading scientific books rather than using experimental laboratory processes.
4. Secondary schooling was to be restricted to a small group of students — to a socioeconomic or academic elite. It was not thought necessary to provide secondary education for most of the age-specific population.

These prevailing attitudes were brought to North America in the sixteenth and seventeenth centuries; they would be reshaped by time and by the social and educational change caused by living in a new land. To plot these changes, we turn to the historical development of American secondary education.

The History of American Secondary Education

Two major developments stand out as greatly significant in the history of American secondary education: (1) the emergence and public acceptance of the comprehensive high school and (2) the role of the high school in completing the American educational ladder. The comprehensive high school resulted from gradual historical processes that defined it as the basic institution of American secondary education. This process of institutional development began when the English colonists imported the Latin Grammar school in the seventeenth century, continued with the appearance of the academy in the nineteenth century, and culminated with the comprehensive high school in the late nineteenth and early twentieth centuries.

Although many states had established common or elementary schools by the Civil War, the public high school did not appear until later in the nineteenth century. When the public high school became the major institution of American secondary education, the well-known American educational ladder was completed. This meant that American youngsters could proceed from the kindergarten, through the common elementary school, to the high school and eventually enter the state college or university. The development and public acceptance of the high school marked a crucial phase in American educational history for it established the basic institutional framework of the American public school system.

The concept of the "educational ladder" refers to the single, articulated, and sequential school system that characterizes public education in the United States. In contrast to the educational ladder, the traditional European dual system differentiated students into separate tracks, with some schools educating the elite and others preparing the children of the masses. While the American educational ladder provides for upward movement through elementary, secondary, and higher institutions, it should be remembered that this movement is often limited by social and economic variables, such as family background, income, degree of tax support, and community attitudes, that may limit genuine equality of educational opportunity.

To review the development of the educational ladder, three major periods in the history of American secondary schooling can be identified: (1) that of the Latin Grammar school of the colonial period, (2) that of the academy of the nineteenth century, and (3) that of the public high school of the late nineteenth and twentieth centuries.

Latin Grammar School

The Latin Grammar school, the major preparatory institution, was attended by the sons of the social, economic, and political elite who were intended for leadership positions in Britain's North American colonies. Students in the Latin Grammar school had already learned to read and write in English and knew some mathematics prior to their admission. Entering the school at age eight, they usually remained another eight years. The Latin Grammar school curriculum formed a direct cultural link between the New and the Old Worlds. Its emphasis on the Latin and Greek classics was inherited from the Renaissance classical humanist tradition, and a strong denominational religious influence came from the Protestant Reformation.

Students studied Latin classical authors, such as Cicero, Terence, Caesar, Livy, Vergil, and Horace. Advanced students read Greek authors, such as Aesop, Hesiod, Homer, and Isocrates. Little attention was given to utilitarian subjects such as mathematics, science, and modern languages.

By the eighteenth century, the Latin Grammar school—losing much of the intellectual vitality of its Renaissance origins—had become increasingly formalized and sterile. When it was established in North America, the Latin Grammar school curriculum narrowly emphasized mastery of grammatical and stylistic mechanics.

Even before the American Revolution, critics of the Latin Grammar school, such as Benjamin Franklin, objected to the limited curriculum. There were also a number of private-venture schools that offered a more utilitarian educational alternative. Usually conducted by a single teacher, these schools offered modern languages, navigation, bookkeeping, and surveying in trade locations such as New York, Philadelphia, and Charleston. The political impact of the American Revolution and the economic impact of the Industrial Revolution contributed to the decline of the Latin Grammar school. The public began to demand a more utilitarian education that would prepare young people for citizenship in the new nation and for the more practical skills needed in industrial society. The academy was the educational institution that appeared to fill these needs of a changing society.

The Academy

Although appearing in the late eighteenth century, academies enjoyed their greatest popularity in the period of nation building in the nineteenth century in the decades between the Revolution and the Civil War. In the Jacksonian era of individualism, mobility, and expansion, the academy seemed ideally suited as the institution that would provide the needed educational opportunities through its easy admission requirements and unstructured curricula. In that time of "free enterprise" entrepreneurship and economic growth, the privately controlled academy extended the competitive spirit into education.

The academy either replaced or absorbed the Latin Grammar school. In many respects, it combined the functions of the Latin Grammar school and the private-venture school. As did the former, it provided the classical Greek and Latin preparation needed for college entry. As did the private-venture school, it offered such practical subjects as bookkeeping, navigation, surveying, and modern languages. The academies attracted as students the sons and daughters of the middle-class business people, professionals, and entrepreneurs. The popularity of the academy was demonstrated by its growth. Theodore Sizer, an historian of the academy movement, reports that by 1855 more than 263,000 students were enrolled in 6,185 academies.[1]

The academies met three major needs: (1) They made it possible for more people to attain more formal schooling, (2) they satisfied the industrial and commercial demand for individuals with utilitarian skills, and (3) they continued to exercise

---

1. Theodore R. Sizer, *The Age of Academies* (New York: Teachers College Press, Columbia University, 1964), p. 12.

the college preparatory function that was traditional to secondary education. The American academies satisfied these needs by their wide course offerings that were usually fashioned into three basic curricula: the classical (college preparatory); English (terminal); and the normal (teacher preparation). Within these three major curricula, a number of curricular hybrids such as the English-classical, English-scientific, English-commercial, and English-normal could be found. The course listings in the prospectuses of the academies included these:

Classical languages: Greek and Latin and their literatures
English language: English grammar and composition, English and American literature, rhetoric, composition, oratory, declamation
Modern languages: French, Spanish, Portuguese, German, Italian
Mathematics: arithmetic, algebra, geometry, trigonometry
Sciences: geology, biology, botany, chemistry, physics, natural philosophy, optics, astronomy, phrenology
Commercial subjects: bookkeeping, accounting
Geography and history: English history, American history, ancient history, regional geographies
Philosophy: moral philosophy, political philosophy, logic
Agriculture
Domestic sciences and needlework
Art and music
Pedagogy: art of teaching, principles of teaching, review of common-school subjects
Military drill and tactics

The attempt to offer such a wide range of courses often exhausted the academies' energies. While some academies sought to offer as many courses as possible, others were satisfied with a restricted curriculum. As the curriculum varied, so did the quality of instruction. Some of the academy "professors" were well trained and highly competent scholars and teachers; others were superficially prepared and diffused their energies by trying to teach all subjects. Methodology, based on mental discipline, stressed the acquisition of factual information by drill, memorization, recitation, and repetition. Because no recognized standards existed for certifying teachers or accrediting academies, the quality of secondary education was uneven at best. A chaotic proliferation of courses resulted, and some of the weaknesses in the academies were later inherited by their institutional successor, the high school.

Because they were private institutions, academies were controlled by independent boards of trustees. Although a few academies received state subsidies at their inception, the trustees usually were responsible for building the academy, hiring the staff, and attracting students. Most of the financial support came from the students' tuition fees.

The academy was often maintained by particular religious denominations. Methodists, Episcopalians, Baptists, Roman Catholics, Presbyterians, Congregationalists, and other denominations established academies to teach the principles of their faith and prepare students for college. Many small denominational colleges existing today were originally chartered as academies.

Some academies were also downward extensions of colleges and universities. When colleges found that applicants were inadequately prepared, they sometimes established preparatory branches, or academies, to prepare students for admission to their undergraduate programs.

By the 1870s, academies were being replaced by public high schools. The trend to the high school was partially a product of urbanization. Large cities were often able to support an extensive public secondary school system because of their larger tax base. In addition, a more technically inclined industrial society also needed more systematically organized secondary education than that provided by the loosely structured academy.

Emergence of the High School

Although high schools had existed in the United States since the early nineteenth century, it was in the latter half of that century that the high school replaced the academy as the dominant institution of American secondary education. In 1889–1890, the U.S. commissioner of education reported that the 2,526 public high schools enrolled 202,063 students, in contrast to the 94,391 enrolled in the 1,632 private secondary schools and academies.[2]

The emergence of the comprehensive high school as the dominant form of secondary education can be attributed to a number of factors, some of which related to socioeconomic, political, and educational change. Perhaps the most obvious factor was that the United States was ready for a more extensive secondary school system. The expressed political philosophy emphasized the responsibility of the individual to participate in political life. If America was truly the land of opportunity, then its educational institutions should further that opportunity by being open to larger numbers of people. The country was also ready economically to support a more extensive school system. Industrialization, with its attendant urbanization, had created a larger and more concentrated tax base — a wealth — that could be used to pay for high schools. While industrialists had come to see the need for more highly trained workers, labor leaders saw the high school as providing greater opportunity to the children of working men and women.

If the nation was ready politically and economically for the high school, it was also entering a state of educational and psychological readiness that was receptive to the institution. The system of elementary schools, generally kindergarten through grade eight, was recognized as necessary to the national well-being. Elementary schools, flourishing throughout the states, were preparing thousands of children for continuing and more extensive schooling. Furthermore, professors in normal schools and university departments of education were developing a science of education to rationalize the educational process. Psychologists, such as G. Stanley Hall, had developed a theory of adolescence that pointed to the need for an education designed to meet the needs of adolescents. In many respects, then, the United States was ready for the public high school.

At the same time that the country was generally ready for the high school, many groups were unable, unwilling, or unprepared to attend the high school. Those

---

2. Edward Krug, *The Shaping of the American High School*, Vol. I (New York: Harper & Row, 1964), p. 5.

who would attend the high school in the first two decades of the twentieth century generally came from the more economically and socially favored groups; they were the children of business people, professionals, and wealthy farmers. The sons and daughters of immigrants, especially those from southern and eastern Europe, frequently dropped out of school as soon as legally possible. The children of immigrants often went to work in factories, mines, and small family-owned shops to earn money to augment the family's income. African-American children, too, went to work rather than to high school. The rural poor were also usually not among those attending the high school.

The *Kalamazoo* Case

If the country was ready for the high schools generally, there were still some who challenged its legitimacy as a tax-supported institution. Although several court cases are applicable to legally establishing public taxation for high schools, the decision of Justice Thomas C. Cooley in the *Kalamazoo* case of 1874 is cited as precedent making.[3] A taxpayer's group sued to prevent the Kalamazoo, Michigan, board of education from levying a tax to finance a high school. Arguing that the primarily college preparatory high school curriculum benefited only a small minority, the claimants contended that the majority was being taxed to support the education of the college-bound minority.

Upholding the right of the Kalamazoo school district to tax for high school support, Justice Cooley found that the state was obligated to provide not only elementary education but also to maintain equal educational opportunity for all. Because public funds were already supporting elementary schools and colleges, Cooley ruled it inconsistent to fail to provide the transitional stage whereby students could move from elementary to higher education. He affirmed the right of the school board to tax for the support of high school, the transitional institution. The *Kalamazoo* and similar cases made it possible for students to attend a complete sequence of tax-supported and publicly controlled educational institutions from kindergarten, through elementary and high school, to the university.

The Committee of Ten

The basic identity of the American comprehensive high school was shaped from 1880 to 1920 when many issues related to the high school were debated. Was it a college preparatory institution as had been true traditionally of secondary education? Or was the high school a terminal institution for those completing their formal education? Should it stress traditional college preparatory subjects, or should it offer industrial, commercial, vocational, and agricultural education?

Initially, the high school inherited some of the curricular weaknesses of its predecessor, the academy. It offered a multiplicity of ill-defined curricula bearing names such as ancient classical, business-commercial, shorter commercial, English-terminal, English-science, and scientific. College and university administrators, in

3. *Stuart v. School District No. 1 of Village of Kalamazoo*, 30 Mich. 69 (1874).

particular, wanted to standardize the high school curriculum to facilitate the evaluation of the transcripts of high school graduates.

To resolve the problems of curricular standardization, the National Education Association (NEA) established the Committee of Ten in 1892. Composed of five college representatives, one public school principal, two private school headmasters, and William T. Harris (the U.S. commissioner of education), the committee's chairman was Charles Eliot, Harvard's influential president.[4] Known for introducing the elective principle at Harvard, Eliot wanted to improve the efficiency and the quality of high school instruction. The committee developed its policies around two of Eliot's basic concepts: (1) the early introduction of the fundamentals of subjects into the upper elementary grades and (2) standardization of subject matter for all high school students.[5]

The Committee of Ten recommended an eight-year elementary and a four-year high school. Directing its report to the issues in secondary education, the committee sought to end the proliferation of courses that had weakened the quality of instruction in the academies. It recommended that the high school offer a small number of subjects and that each subject be studied intensively for a longer period of time. Further, each subject should have the same content and be taught in the same way for both terminal and college preparatory students. The committee's recommended list of courses was significant in that it shaped the basic outlines of the high school curriculum:

1. English language and literature
2. Foreign language, such as Greek, Latin, German, French, and Spanish
3. Mathematics, such as algebra, geometry, and trigonometry
4. Natural sciences, such as astronomy, meteorology, botany, zoology, physiology, geology, and physical geography
5. Physical sciences, such as physics and chemistry

The report of the Committee of Ten demonstrates the tendency of the higher institution, the college, to dominate the lower, the high school. Although the committee claimed that the high school was not exclusively a college preparatory institution, it emphasized the subjects needed for college entrance. Justifying its orientation on the mental discipline theory, it claimed that its recommended subjects were well suited to the needs of terminal and college preparatory students because it trained their powers of observation, memory, expression, concentration, and thinking.

High School Accreditation

In the 1890s, one of the major problems facing high schools was to establish curricula that satisfied college admission requirements. To deal with accreditation issues, the North Central Association was established in 1895, with a combined

---

4. *Report of the Committee on Secondary School Studies* (Washington, D.C.: U.S. Government Printing Office, 1893).
5. Krug, *The Shaping of the American High School*, p. 17.

membership of secondary schools and colleges in the north-central states.[6] In 1899, the NEA's Committee on College Entrance Requirements proposed a set of constant subjects as a core of courses for all high school students, without regard to their educational destination. The constants recommended in the core were four units of foreign languages, two of mathematics, two of English, one of history, and one of science. The remainder of the courses was to be elected by the student. A unit was defined as a subject studied for four or five periods of at least 45 minutes per week. Furthermore, all high school curricula were to include as constants three units of English and two units of mathematics.[7]

In addition to the North Central Association, other regional accreditation agencies were established: the New England Association, the Middle States Association, the Northwest Association, the Western Association, and the Southern Association. Historically, the accreditation associations developed two patterns for admitting students to college: by examination, such as that of the College Entrance Examination Boards, or by graduation from an accredited high school.

Commission on the Reorganization of Secondary Education

In 1918, the NEA established the Commission on the Reorganization of Secondary Education to reexamine the function of the high school. Under the leadership of its chairman, Clarence Kingsley, the commission issued the "Cardinal Principles of Secondary Education," which proclaimed objectives of health, command of fundamental processes, worthy home membership, vocational preparation, citizenship, worthy use of leisure, and ethical character.

The commission saw the high school as both an academic institution and an agency of social integration. The comprehensive public high school would bring students of different racial, religious, ethnic, and economic backgrounds together in the same institution. A comparison of the reports of the Committee of Ten and the Commission on the Reorganization of Secondary Education reveals some of the major changes in social and educational attitudes between 1893 and 1918. In this short span of 25 years, significant social and economic changes in American life and education had affected the high school curriculum. Whereas college professors of academic disciplines had dominated the Committee of Ten, the Commission on the Reorganization of Secondary Education was influenced by professors of education and educational administrators. Whereas the academic professors saw the high school as a college preparatory institution, the members of the commission saw it in a larger social, economic, and political perspective. The commission members regarded the high school as an institution in which a diverse adolescent population would define its goals and interests.

---

6. Calvin O. Davis, *A History of the North Central Association of Colleges and Secondary Schools* (Ann Arbor, Mich.: The North Central Association of Colleges and Secondary Schools, 1945), p. 7.
7. Ibid., p. 49.

Contemporary Secondary Education

By the 1880s, the vast majority of Americans had attended the common elementary school. One hundred years later the education of most Americans had extended upward to the high school. Although many factors contributed to this phenomenal increase in high school attendance, the most compelling ones were social and economic. Modernization and its attendant need for persons who possessed more sophisticated knowledge and technical competencies made at least a high school education a necessity for most jobs. Furthermore, state laws that set a minimum age for beginning employment and that required compulsory school attendance also worked to keep most of the appropriate age group enrolled in school. At the beginning of the 1980s, more than 95 percent of the population between the ages of 14 and 17 were enrolled in school. Although the number of high school dropouts continues to be a serious problem among some groups in some communities, more than 80 percent of students who begin secondary school will graduate. In contrast to the high level of attendance in American secondary schools, the average attendance at the secondary level in many European nations is less than 20 percent. It is clearly apparent that a major characteristic of American secondary education is mass attendance.

The Comprehensive High School

As a multifunctional institution serving a widely diverse adolescent population, the comprehensive American public high school (1) provides a general education for all students, (2) prepares some students for college entry, (3) prepares some students for jobs, and (4) acts as an agency for civic, social, and personal development and integration. In the vast majority of communities, the comprehensive high school strives to satisfy the needs of all youth of secondary school age. The curricular pattern in most comprehensive high schools is to (1) enroll all students in a common core of general education courses so that individuals of varying interests and career goals have the opportunity for common association and learning, (2) provide parallel curricular tracks, such as the college preparatory, industrial-vocational, commercial, general, and, in rural areas, the agricultural, to satisfy the special needs of students, and (3) provide elective courses to permit students to exercise freedom of choice in satisfying particular interests. Comprehensive in a social as well as an educational sense, the comprehensive high school brings students of varying social, economic, religious, racial, and ethnic backgrounds together in a single institution. The important principle regarding the comprehensive high school is to avoid segregating students on either academic or nonacademic grounds into separate, specialized schools.

The Conant Reports

Although the comprehensiveness of the high school has long been a guiding principle of American secondary education, observers such as James B. Conant have

James B. Conant, a former president of Harvard University, conducted extensive research on the nature and purpose of the American comprehensive high school.

warned that its force as an integrating agency in American society is being weakened.

In *The American High School Today*, Conant, a former university president, scientist, and diplomat, made a number of recommendations to restore the vitality of the comprehensive high school.[8] Public schools, he wrote, should educate all of the nation's children regardless of their social and economic class. They should both provide a common core of learning for all students and also meet individual academic and vocational needs.

For Conant, the comprehensive high school is the secondary institution that best meets the needs of American democracy. He used the term *comprehensive* in two ways. First, a public high school should be socially comprehensive so that it enrolls students from a wide range of social, family, ethnic, economic, and racial backgrounds. The comprehensive school should neither segregate nor isolate any group, but bring students together in an institution that satisfies common social as well as institutional needs. Second, a public high school should be large enough to provide broad curricular possibilities that encompass programs to meet the vocational needs of terminal students as well as those of academically oriented, college-bound students.

In Conant's conception, the American comprehensive high school serves three broad purposes:

8. James B. Conant, *The American High School Today* (New York: McGraw-Hill, 1959).

1. It should provide a sound general education for all future citizens, regardless of socioeconomic background and career expectations. Such a general curriculum should consist of English, social studies, mathematics, and science.
2. It should provide a rigorous program for academically talented students who are likely to enter college.
3. It should offer a range of elective programs to meet the needs of terminal students. Based upon their appropriateness to the economic realities of each local community, vocational programs should be diversified enough to encompass training in agriculture, business, trade, and industry.

Thus, Conant sought to preserve and to strengthen the comprehensive high school as the basic institution of American secondary education.

Conant's *Slums and Suburbs*, appearing in 1961, correctly predicted the coming of a crisis that would have a pronounced impact on urban schools.[9] He feared that "social dynamite" was building up in the large cities as unresolved social, economic, and racial tensions accumulated and festered as white families fled to the suburbs and were replaced by African-American and Hispanic families.

Urban high schools were unprepared to meet the educational and economic needs of minority group students. The high school curriculum was often irrelevant to preparing students for jobs. Unemployed and underemployed youths would become not only economically disadvantaged but also socially alienated. Conant's call for the infusion of funds to support special programs for minority youth was prophetic of what would become "compensatory education" later in the decade. Unless concerted efforts were made to restore the social and educational comprehensiveness of the public high school, Conant predicted, a dual school system would develop, with suburban schools catering to an affluent elite and urban schools being used by a segregated and disadvantaged minority.

Goals of Secondary Education

As indicated in the discussion of the origins and development of American secondary education, the high school as a multifunctional institution has been subject to conflicting interpretations about its role and function—its mission—in American society. Some critics, such as Arthur Bestor and Admiral Rickover in the 1950s and Back to Basics advocates, have argued that the high school should be a strictly academic institution that emphasizes the learning of academic skills and subjects. Others, such as those associated with the life-adjustment education movement of the late 1940s and early 1950s, de-emphasized the academic role of the high school and argued that it should meet the personal and social needs of adolescents. Still others want the high school to be an institution for career development and vocational preparation that will provide graduates with immediately useful and salable skills in the economic marketplace. It is difficult to specify the general goals of American secondary education because of these varied voices that plead for the satisfaction of their special interests.

9. James B. Conant, *Slums and Suburbs: A Commentary on Schools in Metropolitan Areas* (New York: McGraw-Hill, 1961).

The Three- and Four-Year High School

The traditional organizational pattern of American public secondary education has been the four-year high school with its well-known freshman, sophomore, junior, and senior years—grades 9, 10, 11, and 12. In some states, particularly California, Illinois, and New Jersey, the four-year high school remains the basic organizational pattern. In these states, the high school district may function as a separate entity with its own board of education and is distinct from the elementary district. There is a trend to combine elementary and secondary schools into a combined or unit district. Large urban systems typically combine elementary and secondary schools into a unified district.

In other states, the senior high school follows a three-year pattern of organization that includes grades 10, 11, and 12. Three-year senior high schools are linked institutionally to junior high, grades eight and nine. Because the junior high school has become an increasingly important institution in American education, it is treated more fully in Chapter 15.

The Comprehensive Curriculum

The three- or four-year comprehensive high school provides a range of courses designed to satisfy the general education, college preparatory, and vocational needs of students. The following curriculum areas offered by the high school also indicates the areas in which prospective high school teachers may prepare.

English   Courses in English language and literature are required of all high school students. While some high schools may require students to enroll in English courses each year, other high schools may require two or three years of study in the subject. Instruction in English is subdivided into such courses as practical English, reading skills, grammar, composition, creative writing, expository writing, journalism, American literature, English literature, world literature, business English, speech, and drama.

Mathematics   The majority of American high schools require two or more years of mathematics. The range of courses includes general mathematics, algebra, advanced algebra, plane geometry, analytical geometry, trigonometry, and calculus. Some high schools may also offer statistics and computer mathematics.

Social Science   The area of social science, also known as social studies or social education, may consist of courses in the separate disciplines of history and other social sciences or various interdisciplinary courses combining elements from several of the social sciences. Social science courses in the high school curriculum are American history (usually a required subject), world history, African or Asian history, state history (required in certain states), geography, regional geography, physical geography, government, economics, sociology, psychology, personal development, anthropology, peace studies, and international studies.

Natural Science   Courses in the natural sciences, like those in the social sciences, range from interdisciplinary introductory courses to advanced courses in particular disciplines. Among the courses offered are natural science, physical science, general science, earth science, biology, botany, chemistry, and physics. Certain high schools, particularly large schools, may also offer courses in physiology, geology, and zoology.

Health   Most high schools require a course in health education that includes such topics as general hygiene, diet and nutrition, sex education, dental care, and drug abuse and provides information about the health problems that may be caused by using tobacco and alcohol. Units on AIDS education may also be included.

Physical Education   Physical education, a required subject, includes a range of experiences, such as team sports, physical fitness activities, and recreational activities. Among the areas offered are football, baseball, basketball, soccer, tennis, swimming, dance, body building, bowling, rhythmic activities, weight lifting, gymnastics, wrestling, and track and field.

Business Education   Business education may also be called commercial education in some high schools. A concentration of courses in this area may form the program of students enrolled in specialized career preparation. Students enrolled in other programs may elect courses in this area. Among the courses that the large high school may offer in business education are general business principles, business mathematics, business law, business English, typing, shorthand, bookkeeping, office management and organization, consumer education, career education, data processing, word processing, and key punch and office machines.

Industrial Arts   Industrial arts courses originated in the manual arts in the early years of this century. In some schools, industrial arts may be a separate area or may be combined with the larger and more encompassing area of vocational education. Course offerings include woodworking, metalwork, plastics, automobile mechanics, drafting, mechanical drawing, graphic arts, manufacturing, construction and architectural home planning.

Vocational Education   This area of instruction often combines organized in-school training with on-the-job experiences. The following areas may be offered: machine shop, electricity, food preparation and service, carpentry, nursing, child care, plumbing, painting, sheet metal and welding, cosmetology, drafting, automobile maintenance, printing, television repair, building construction, retailing, refrigeration and air conditioning, distributive education, and marketing.

Agriculture   In rural high schools, courses in vocational agriculture are an important part of the curriculum. This area provides instruction in farming, ranching, animal husbandry, forestry, landscape gardening, horticulture, and maintenance of farming implements and equipment.

Foreign Language   As indicated earlier, foreign language instruction has long been a part of the secondary school curriculum. When it was required for college entry, foreign language enrollments were large. In recent years, enrollments in foreign language courses have responded to international trends. Enrollments accelerated in the Sputnik era and then declined in the late 1960s and 1970s.

Traditionally, the classical languages of Greek and Latin formed the core of foreign language instruction. By the turn of the century, Greek had largely disappeared. Although still offered, Latin has suffered a substantial decline. Among the modern languages, Spanish and French have enjoyed sustained popularity, followed by German and Italian. Today, some high schools also offer courses in Russian and Chinese.

Music   High school music courses are generally elective. Offerings may include orchestra, marching band, piano, choir, chorus, glee club, general music, and music theory appreciation. Students in music education are often involved in extra- or co-curricular activities, such as concerts, band, and orchestra, performing at school and civic activities.

Art   Art or fine arts education forms another area of elective courses. Among the offerings are design, art appreciation, drawing, painting, weaving, crafts, leather work, ceramics, photography, commercial art, illustrating, jewelry, and cartooning.

Driver Education   The driver education course involves classroom instruction and street driving.

The areas indicated constitute the formal curriculum of the three- or four-year comprehensive high school; a great deal of learning also occurs in the extra-curricular or co-curricular activities. As well as being an academic institution, the comprehensive high school is an agency for the socialization of American adolescents. Students can participate in activities such as student government, intramural and interscholastic athletics, drama, debate, the school newspaper and yearbook production, dances, and a wide range of clubs and organizations that reflect their academic and career interests.

Public Vocational, Technical, and Specialized High Schools

In addition to the three- or four-year general or comprehensive public high school, there are public vocational, technical, and specialized high schools. These schools, usually found in large urban systems, offer programs for students who will enter the labor force upon graduation or preparatory study that leads to advanced technical education.

While they include general education courses, the curricula in vocational, technical, and specialized high schools prepares students for particular occupations as clerical workers, technicians, and tradespersons. Often the curricula are based on local labor needs. For example, a commercial high school will have a curriculum that specifically prepares students for clerical, secretarial, data processing, bookkeeping, and office work; a technical school's curriculum may emphasize design, drafting, and related courses. Trade schools may prepare students in appliance repair, automobile mechanics, machine-shop operation, radio and television servicing, welding, and refrigeration and heating maintenance and repair. Among the newer areas being offered in specialized high schools are chemical technology, marketing, computer technology, and practical nursing.

Periodically, the federal government has stimulated vocational education by aid through legislation, for example, the Smith–Hughes Act of 1917, the National Defense Education Act of 1958, and the Vocational Education Act of 1963. Vocational education appeals to students because it provides specific training that may have an immediate economic payoff for those who are not interested in entering college.

At the same time that vocational technical schools have their defenders, they also have their critics. Those opposed allege that they erode the comprehensive high school's role as an agency of academic and social integration. They also contend that job-related training at the secondary level is premature and may actually restrict the student's later range of career choices. Critics also allege that specific vocational and technical training tends to become obsolete very quickly, whereas general education provides the knowledge base and intellectual skills that can be used in a variety of occupational, technical, and vocational situations in later life.

Private Secondary Schools

As indicated in the historical sections of this chapter, the antecedents of today's private secondary school can be traced to the colonial Latin grammar school and the nineteenth-century academy. The general types of private secondary schools are (1) those operated under the auspices and control of religious denominations, (2) those operated under independent boards of trustees of a nonreligious or nondenominational nature, and (3) various private trade, technical, and commercial schools.

Private high schools that are controlled and operated by religious denominations may be parochial or nonparochial. A parochial high school is related to a particular parish or church. While an occasional Roman Catholic parish may maintain a high school, it is more usual for private religious high schools to enroll students from a number of parishes. Such schools are better termed independent religious high schools, rather than parochial high schools.

High schools, supported by religious denominations, constitute the largest sector of private secondary schooling, enrolling 75 percent of nonpublic secondary schools. The largest number of these schools are Roman Catholic, and their enrollment is about 85 percent of those attending private secondary schools. Roman Catholic secondary schools are usually operated by religious teaching orders, such as the Dominicans, Franciscans, Sisters of Mercy, Sisters of Charity, or Christian Brothers. While Roman Catholic high schools continue to be operated by religious communities, they now include large numbers of lay teachers who are not members of religious communities. In addition to the Roman Catholic secondary schools, there are Lutheran, Jewish, Episcopal, and Christian independent schools. The number of schools operated by these religious groups is much lower than that of the Catholics. It should be noted, however, that the number of Christian schools has increased rapidly. A Christian high school may be maintained by a number of religious denominations, usually of a fundamentalist persuasion, who oppose the secular orientation of the public schools and prefer a more strictly disciplined atmosphere for their children.

Private independent high schools of a nonreligious type may reflect a wide diversity of educational philosophies. They may range from very traditional, well-endowed, prestigious preparatory schools, such as Phillips, Groton, Andover, Exeter, and Choate, which generally adhere to a highly structured curriculum, to independent schools that are very progressive and feature experimental programs. Still others are military academies.

Among the private secondary schools are technical, trade, and career schools. Usually, they do not offer a complete curriculum of general studies but rather concentrate on a particular specialty. Examples of such schools are business, modeling, dancing, acting, beauty, and computer programming schools. These profit-making institutions charge tuition.

Contemporary Efforts to Reform Secondary Education

Throughout its history, American secondary education has experienced controversy and periodic efforts to bring about change and reform. In the 1980s, *A Nation at Risk* and the reports of various national commissions focused attention on a range of concerns related to the quality of the American high school. The criticisms of the high school could be grouped into two broad categories: declining academic standards and deteriorating moral and social values. Critics alleged that a general erosion of educational standards and competencies and a weakening and partial displacement of such rigorous academic subjects as mathematics and science had lowered the scholastic achievement of American high school graduates. Symptoms of this academic malaise were grade inflation, widespread social promotion, and a continued declined in SAT scores. In addition to their concerns about declining academic achievement, critics also pointed to an apparent deterioration of social and moral values among high school youth. Symptoms of this decline were increased truancy and absenteeism, a lack of discipline, vandalism and crime in schools, higher incidence of drug and alcohol abuse, and rising teenage pregnancy and suicide rates.

Reexamination of American Secondary Education

The 1980s witnessed the reexamination of the objectives, organization, curriculum, and outcomes of American secondary education. The reforms proposed for the high school were part of a continuing cycle of efforts to restructure American secondary education. For example, the Committee of Ten in 1873, the Commission on the Reorganization of Secondary Education in 1918, and the Conant report of 1959 were national examinations of secondary education that led to a significant reshaping of the high school. Among the reports that examined the condition of American secondary education were *High School: A Report on Secondary Education in*

America, sponsored by the Carnegie Foundation for the Advancement of Teaching, and *Horace's Compromise: The Dilemma of the American High School,* co-sponsored by the National Association of Secondary School Principals and the Commission on Educational Issues of the National Association of Independent Schools.[10]

Ernest L. Boyer, in *High School: A Report on Secondary Education in America,* examined the high schools of the 1980s. Using a method that resembled James B. Conant's monumental study of American secondary education in the 1950s, Boyer, president of the Carnegie Foundation for the Advancement of Teaching and a former U.S. commissioner of education, based his report on the findings of a research team of educators who studied the philosophy, administration, organization, curricula, instruction, teaching staff, and students in 15 public high schools located in various parts of the country. The schools represented a cross section of American secondary education and varied in size and socioeconomic composition.[11]

Boyer found that the high schools were philosophically adrift in that they lacked a "clear and vital" vision of their mission. Secondary school educators had been unable to formulate broad-based "common purposes" and to establish "educational priorities." To create a unifying philosophy, Boyer proposed that high schools follow four thematic goals designed to assist students to:

1. Develop critical thinking and effective communication skills by mastering language.
2. "Learn about themselves, the human heritage," and their "interdependent world" through a core curriculum based on "consequential" and "common" human experiences.
3. Prepare "for work and further education" through an elective program that develops "individual aptitudes and interests."
4. Fulfill "social and civic obligations through school and community services."[12]

Core of Common Learning

Boyer's proposed secondary curriculum, the "core of common learning," consisted of the following academic units:

Language . . . . 5 units
    (including the writing of basic English, speech, literature, foreign language, and
    the arts)
History . . . . 2½ units
    (including American history, Western civilization, and non-Western studies)
Civics . . . . 1 unit
    (consisting of classic political ideas and the structure and functions of contemporary
    government)

10. For reports on secondary education, see Ernest L. Boyer, *High School: A Report on Secondary Education in America* (New York: Harper & Row, 1983); Theodore R. Sizer, *Horace's Compromise: The Dilemma of the American High School* (Boston: Houghton Mifflin, 1984); Daniel Tanner, "The American High School at the Crossroads," *Educational Leadership,* 41, No. 6 (March 1984).
11. Boyer, *High School,* p. 11.
12. Ibid., pp. 66–77.

Science .... 2 units
    (including both physical and biological sciences)
Mathematics .... 2 units
Technology and health .... 2 units
Seminar on work and .... ½ unit each
    independent project

Although the proposed curriculum core was organized into separate courses, Boyer stressed that students be exposed to a commonly shared, interdisciplinary body of knowledge. To achieve this common ground of knowledge and understanding, students were to pursue a senior independent research project that examined a significant contemporary issue.[13] Critics of Boyer's proposed core curriculum argued that it reduces the multipurpose comprehensive high school to a single college preparatory function and that it neglects vocational preparation.[14]

Horace's Compromise: The Dilemma of the American High School

Theodore R. Sizer's *Horace's Compromise*, a report based on a study of high schools, also focused on the condition of American secondary education. In his report, Sizer, a one-time headmaster of Phillips Academy and a former dean of Harvard's Graduate School of Education, advocated a synthesis that fused a humanistic orientation with renewal of academic competency. Unlike some of the other national reports on education, such as *A Nation at Risk*, *Horace's Compromise* was not a call for basic education. Like Boyer's study and the earlier Conant report, Sizer's research design used intensive field study and observation of selected, representative high schools. Sizer's educational research team examined a triad of students, teachers, and curricula.[15] From the case studies of the high schools visited, Sizer offered the following recommendations to improve American secondary education:

1. Too many high schools underestimated their students' potential by overemphasizing adolescent vulnerability and inexperience; to correct this attitude, schools should respect students by raising their expectations and standards of accountability.
2. The high school diploma should be earned when students demonstrate an "agreed-on level of mastery" rather than an accumulation of credits earned by taking a long list of unrelated subjects.
3. Using the premise that "less is more," high school curricula and instruction should emphasize important concepts and methods of inquiry rather than extensive coverage of detailed information of subjects taught in isolation from each other.[16]

In contrast to other national reports, Sizer did not advocate that a prescribed curriculum of mandated subjects be studied for specific periods of time. He and Boyer did concur on the need to encourage interdisciplinary curricular and learning outcomes, however. Avoiding an emphasis on covering subject matter, Sizer instead

---

13. Ibid., p. 117.
14. Tanner, "The American High School at the Crossroads," p. 11.
15. Sizer, *Horace's Compromise*, p. 5.
16. Ibid., pp. 33–34, 89.

posed three basic questions that high schools were to answer in terms of their graduates:

1. Are students capable of self-instruction that enables them to "observe and analyze a situation or problem" by understanding, criticizing, rejecting, or accepting it?
2. Are they decent persons?
3. Can they effectively use the modes of observation and inquiry found in the major academic discipline?[17]

Instead of advocating the "one best" prescribed secondary school curriculum, Sizer used these focusing questions to create a model for organizing high schools into four departments:

1. Inquiry and Expression
2. Mathematics and Science
3. Literature and the Arts
4. Philosophy and History

Sizer's proposed high school model also designed learning spheres to advance students' educational achievement. The first sphere of learning was to develop the essential skills of reading, writing, speaking, listening, measuring, estimating, calculating, and seeing as the "staple of all schooling," including that of high schools. These skills, according to Sizer, were taught most effectively by coaching, in which teachers constructively guided students' work to improve student performance.[18]

In acquisition of knowledge, the second learning sphere, the primary instructional strategy was narration or explanation by lecture, textbooks, films, and other means of transmitting knowledge. In acquiring knowledge, the basic guidelines were as follows:

1. Students who were deficient in the essential "standards of literacy, numeracy, and civic understanding" were to work exclusively on these necessary intellectual skills.
2. Curricular decision making depended on the priorities that students, teachers, families, and communities established.
3. Subject matter should relate to, support, and develop skill learning.
4. Subject matter should relate to students' interests, lead to a destination, and be integrated with other subjects and learning experiences.

The cultivation of understanding and the powers of discrimination and judgment by provocative questioning was Sizer's third learning sphere. For effective questioning, small seminar discussions were judged as the appropriate pedagogical method and situation.[19]

Sizer's *Horace's Compromise* did not mandate more prescribed subjects in the curriculum but was directed to raising students' expectations and achievement in a more flexible environment.

Conclusion

The comprehensive public high school is a unique product of American education. Attempting to serve a diverse adolescent population, the history of the high school has been marked by debate, conflict, and frequent attempts to redefine and restruc-

17. Ibid., p. 131.
18. Ibid., p. 99.
19. Ibid., pp. 109–119.

ture. The challenges that face secondary school teachers and administrators in the future are not unlike the issues that were raised in the past. Namely, is it possible to have a single institution that can do the following?

Provide an education for the vast majority of American adolescents
Provide programs of academic excellence for talented American youth
Provide the practical training needed for useful and productive vocations and occupations
Provide an atmosphere that will encourage worthwhile personal and social development

DISCUSSION QUESTIONS

1. Identify and describe the major traditional functions of secondary education.
2. Trace the historical development of American secondary education from the Latin Grammar school to the academy to the high school.
3. To what degree is the American educational ladder fact or fiction?
4. Compare and contrast the function of the high school as viewed by the Committee of Ten and the Commission on the Reorganization of Secondary Education.
5. Reflect on your high school education. To what degree was your education comprehensive?
6. Identify and analyze the current proposals to reform high school education. What appears to be their basic direction?

FIELD EXERCISES

1. Interview an experienced high school teacher and attempt to get his or her views of (a) the changes that have taken place in his or her subject matter specialty and (b) the changes that have occurred in student aspirations and attitudes.
2. Visit a high school in your community and report your observations to the class.
3. Read a novel or see a motion picture that has a high school as a setting. Describe and analyze the author's perception of the high school environment.
4. Interview several high school students and elicit their perceptions of (a) their curriculum, (b) their teachers, and (c) their peers.
5. Consult the classified section (Yellow Pages) of your phone directory. Identify the types of for-profit private schools.
6. Organize a panel discussion in which participants assess the current efforts to reform American secondary education.

SUGGESTED READINGS

ARMSTRONG, DAVID G., AND SAVAGE, TOM V. *Secondary Education: An Introduction.* New York: Macmillan, 1990.

BOYER, ERNEST L. *High School: A Report on Secondary Education in America.* New York: Harper & Row, 1983.

BUNZEL, JOHN H., ED. *Challenge to American Schools: The Case for Standards and Values.* New York: Oxford University Press, 1985.

COLEMAN, JAMES, AND HOFFER, THOMAS. *Public and Private High Schools.* New York: Basic Books, 1987.

CONANT, JAMES B. *The American High School Today*. New York: McGraw-Hill, 1959.

———. *Slums and Suburbs: A Commentary on Schools in Metropolitan Areas*. New York: McGraw-Hill, 1961.

EMMER, EDMUND T. *Classroom Management for Secondary Teachers*. Englewood Cliffs, N.J.: Prentice Hall, 1989.

EKSTROM, RUTH B., GOERTZ, MARGARET E., AND ROCK, DONALD A. *Education and the American Youth: The Impact of the High School Experience*. New York: Falmer Press, 1988.

FETTERS, WILLIAM B., BROWN, GEORGE H., AND OWINGS, JEFFREY A. *High School Seniors: A Comparative Study of the Classes of 1972 and 1980*. Washington, D.C.: National Center for Education Statistics, 1984.

GRANT, GERALD. *The World We Created at Hamilton High*. Cambridge, Mass.: Harvard University Press, 1988.

HAMPEL, ROBERT. *The Last Little Citadel: American High Schools Since 1940*. Boston: Houghton Mifflin, 1986.

KAUFMAN, BEL. *Up the Down Staircase*. Englewood Cliffs, N.J.: Prentice-Hall, 1964.

KRUG, EDWARD A. *The Shaping of the American High School*. New York: Harper & Row, 1964.

———. *The Shaping of the American High School, 1920–1941*. Madison: University of Wisconsin Press, 1972.

LIGHTFOOT, SARA LAWRENCE. *The Good High School: Portraits of Character and Culture*. New York: Basic Books, 1983.

LOWE, ROY, ED. *The Changing Secondary School*. New York: Falmer Press, 1989.

PERRONE, VITO. *Portraits of High Schools: A Supplement to High School: A Report on Secondary Education in America*. Princeton, N.J.: Carnegie Foundations for the Advancement of Teaching, 1985.

POWELL, ARTHUR G., FARRAR, ELEANOR, AND COHEN, DAVID K. *The Shopping Mall High School*. Boston: Houghton Mifflin, 1985.

SIZER, THEODORE R. *The Age of Academies*. New York: Teachers College Press, Columbia University, 1964.

———. *Horace's Compromise: The Dilemma of the American High School*. Boston: Houghton Mifflin, 1984.

TASK FORCE ON EDUCATION OF YOUNG ADOLESCENTS. *Turning Points: Preparing American Youth for the 21st Century: The Report of the Task Force on Education of Young Adolescents*. Washington, D.C.: Carnegie Council on Adolescent Development, 1989.

WILSON, BRUCE L., AND CORCORAN, THOMAS B. *Successful Secondary Schools: Visions of Excellence in American Public Education*. New York: Falmer Press, 1989.

17

Patterns of American Higher Education

Chapter 17 examines the origins, development, and patterns of American higher education, the major aim being to provide an overview of American colleges and universities. The general focusing questions that will be answered as you read this chapter include the following:

1. What were the significant trends in the history of American higher education?
2. What types of institutions provide higher education in the United States?
3. How are colleges and universities governed and financed?
4. What are the current enrollment trends in higher education?

The Historical Development

The conceptions of higher education in the colonial period were primarily European and were brought to the New World by the English colonists. The major European influences that shaped the early American colleges were (1) the scholasticism of the medieval university, (2) Renaissance classical humanism, and (3) the denominationalism of the Protestant Reformation.

In the colonies, collegiate education was modeled on Oxford and Cambridge, the leading English universities, which offered the liberal arts and professional curricula in law, medicine, and theology. The institutional structures of Oxford and Cambridge were inherited from the medieval universities of Paris, Salerno, and Bologna.[1] The traditional liberal arts curriculum consisted of the *trivium* (grammar, rhetoric, and logic) and the *quadrivium* (music, astronomy, geometry, and mathematics). Catering to the educational needs of England's wealthy families, Oxford and Cambridge sought to "train up" cultured, well-rounded gentlemen who would be comfortable and adept in drawingroom and playing field. In addition to educating gentlemen for service to king and country, the English universities prepared

---

1. Allan B. Cobban, *The Medieval English Universities: Oxford and Cambridge to c. 1500* (Berkeley: University of California Press, 1988.

classically educated scholars, theologians, lawyers, and physicians. English higher education was designed for a favored elite, not for the masses.

After completing the liberal studies, medieval students might enter professional study in theology, law, or medicine. Instruction in the medieval university was the scholastic method developed by Abelard and Thomas Aquinas. Latin was the language of educated discourse and instruction.

The fourteenth- and fifteenth-century Renaissance period revitalized humanistic studies. Classical humanist educators stressed Greek and Ciceronian Latin as the languages of the educated person. With the Protestant Reformation, religious studies dominated higher education as various churches sought to build doctrinal loyalty and prepare educated ministers.

Almost as soon as they had arrived in Massachusetts, the Puritans established a college to prepare ministers for their churches. On October 28, 1636, the Massachusetts General Court created Harvard College and appropriated an endowment for its support. Harvard's curriculum followed the traditional liberal arts model of the medieval universities. True to its task of preparing an educated clergy, the college emphasized Hebrew, Greek, and Latin, which were useful for scriptural study. As good Congregationalists, the Harvard professors were to adhere to John

Harvard College, chartered by the Massachusetts General Court in 1636, was modeled on the English conception of liberal education.

Calvin's theology.[2] When Harvard's faculty appeared to be liberalizing their theological persuasion, more traditional Congregationalists established Yale at New Haven in 1701 to preserve religious orthodoxy.

The plantation-owning southern gentry at first sent their sons to England for collegiate education. When Virginians demanded their own college, a royal charter was granted in 1693 for the establishing of William and Mary. In 1779, Thomas Jefferson stimulated reorganization of William and Mary's curriculum to include the more secular subjects of science, mathematics, law, anatomy, medicine, moral philosophy, fine arts, and modern languages.

In the Middle Atlantic colonies, Presbyterians chartered Princeton in 1746 in New Jersey. King's College, later Columbia, was chartered in 1754 to serve New York's Anglicans. By the outbreak of the Revolutionary War, Dartmouth had been established in New Hampshire and Brown in Rhode Island. The University of Pennsylvania received its charter in 1799.

The following generalizations characterize the colonial colleges: (1) They resembled their European institutional counterparts, (2) they were founded by religious denominations, and (3) they offered a liberal arts curriculum. Although it varied from institution to institution, the colonial college curriculum had the following general sequence:

Year 1:   Latin, Greek, logic, Hebrew, and rhetoric
Year 2:   Greek, Hebrew, logic, and natural philosophy
Year 3:   Natural philosophy, metaphysics, and moral philosophy
Year 4:   Mathematics and review in Latin, Greek, logic, and natural philosophy[3]

The colonial colleges were small institutions that were attended by the sons of the wealthier classes. Young women were excluded from the male-dominated institutions. The presidents of these early colleges, usually well-known ministers, acted as father figures for both faculty and students. Despite the generally paternalistic atmosphere, the students occasionally complained about lodging, food, and the quality of instruction.

The Scottish University Influence

Whereas the most direct influence on the colonial colleges came from the English universities of Oxford and Cambridge, the Scottish universities also influenced American higher education.[4] Immediately prior to the American Revolution, large numbers of Scots and Scottish-Irish immigrated to North America. The Presbyterian ministers who accompanied these immigrants wanted to establish colleges modeled on such universities as Saint Andrew, Glasgow, Aberdeen, and Edinburgh

2. For the history of Harvard, see Samuel Eliot Morison, *The Founding of Harvard College* (Cambridge, Mass.: Harvard University Press, 1935), and *Three Centuries of Harvard* (Cambridge, Mass.: Harvard University Press, 1936).
3. Frederick Rudolph, *The American College and University: A History* (New York: Knopf, 1962), pp. 25–26.
4. Douglass Sloan, *The Scottish Enlightenment and the American College Ideal* (New York: Teachers College Press, Columbia University, 1971).

in Scotland. The Scottish universities, which stressed utilitarianism and science, attracted American students, such as Benjamin Rush, a founder of American medical education. Rush, who studied medicine at Edinburgh, introduced the new learning at the College of Philadelphia and the University of Pennsylvania.

The College of New Jersey, founded in 1742, particularly reflected the educational ideas of the Scottish universities. While retaining the classics and theology, New Jersey's curriculum included mathematical and scientific studies. The methods of instruction also emphasized experimentation. The major contribution of the Scottish universities to American higher education was that the college was viewed as a center for scientific and applied research.

The Early National Period

During the Constitutional Convention, establishment of a national university was proposed. Although supported by Washington, Jefferson, and Madison, the proposal failed. In the early national period, state colleges were chartered. Among the new state colleges were the University of Georgia, established in 1785, the University of North Carolina, in 1789, the University of Tennessee, in 1794, and South Carolina College, in 1801.

The University of Virginia, established in 1825, was one of the first major American institutions of higher learning to deviate in organization, control, and curriculum from the pattern found in the older colonial colleges. Conceived of by Thomas Jefferson, the University of Virginia was free of religious domination and was to promote scientific progress. The University of Virginia exemplified several characteristics of the new state universities: (1) It was publicly controlled and supported, (2) it had a scientific rather than a classical curriculum, (3) it had several curricula rather than a single one prescribed for all students, and (4) it was a nonsectarian institution.[5] These factors were found in other state-established and state-maintained universities, such as Indiana, founded in 1820, Michigan, in 1837, and Wisconsin, in 1848.

In addition to the newly established state universities, church-related colleges were established as the various denominations followed the path of westward migration. Presbyterians, Congregationalists, Roman Catholics, Methodists, Lutherans, Christian Disciples, Baptists, Episcopalians, Quakers, and Mormons were among the churches that established colleges. Several factors involved religious denominations in higher education: (1) It was already part of the American tradition since the days of the colonial college, (2) the great majority of the churches valued a well-educated ministry, (3) the proliferation of religious sects during the great revivals of the nineteenth century stimulated a competition that was also felt in education, and (4) the churches had assumed a social service as well as a religious role that extended into education.

5. John S. Brubacher, "A Century of the State University," in William Brickman and Stanley Lehrer, eds., *A Century of Higher Education: Classical Citadel to Collegiate Colossus* (New York: Society for the Advancement of Education, 1962), pp. 70–71.

The *Dartmouth College* Case

By the early national period, it was clear that the United States was developing two parallel systems of higher education: state and private. The *Dartmouth College* case of 1819 reinforced the existence of these two approaches to higher education. The *Dartmouth* case resulted from a controversy over the control of Dartmouth College. In 1816, the New Hampshire legislature attempted to take control of Dartmouth by changing its charter and establishing a new institution called the University of New Hampshire. The Dartmouth board of trustees contended that the state's action was unconstitutional. Arguing before the U.S. Supreme Court, Daniel Webster won a decision that affirmed the original charter, restored the college to the board of trustees, and returned it to its earlier status as a private educational institution.

The *Dartmouth College* decision protected the existence of the independent, privately controlled college and ended state efforts to establish control over such institutions by legislative action. It sanctioned the duality of higher education in the United States, which has since produced two great academic systems, one private and the other state supported.

Land-Grant Colleges and Universities

As western areas such as the Northwest Territories and the Louisiana Purchase were organized and then admitted as states, the state governments established their own state universities. State initiatives were encouraged by the federal policy of granting land from the national domain for education. The use of federal land grants for education dates back to the Ordinances of 1785 and 1787 by the Continental Congress. The Ordinance of 1785 reserved the sixteenth section of each township of the Northwest Territory for education; the Ordinance of 1787 expressed a federal commitment to encourage "schools and the means of education." The use of abundant frontier land as a source of financial aid to education was an obvious step for the federal government because it did not require increased taxation. The establishment of state universities was also encouraged by the federal land-grant policy that granted land for founding institutions of higher learning to each state as it entered the Union.

In addition to the land-grant provisions contained in the enabling acts under which states were admitted to the Union, there were contributions to several projects by the federal government to achieve specific objectives rather than to provide general aid to higher education.[6] For example, the military academies at West Point and Annapolis were established to train army and naval officers, respectively. In 1857, the Columbia Institute for the Deaf, later named Gallaudet College, was established with federal assistance. After the Civil War, Howard University was established to provide higher education for the former black slaves. By the 1850s, a

---

6. For additional reading related to the federal government's role in education, see Hollis P. Allen, *The Federal Government and Education* (New York: McGraw-Hill, 1950); Richard G. Axt, *The Federal Government and Financing Higher Education* (New York: Columbia University Press, 1952); Homer D. Babbidge and Robert M. Rosenzweig, *The Federal Interest in Higher Education* (New York: Columbia University Press, 1962).

strong demand had been generated, particularly in the western states, for federal assistance in establishing agricultural and mechanical colleges and universities. Finding the existing liberal arts colleges unresponsive to their needs, a number of agricultural and industrial organizations wanted a new institution of higher education.

Justin S. Morrill, a Vermont representative, introduced a land-grant act to encourage the establishment of agricultural and mechanical institutions. The enactment of the Morrill Act of 1862 granted each state 30,000 acres of public land for each senator and representative it had in Congress according to the census of 1860.[7] The income from this land was to support at least one college whose primary purpose was agricultural and mechanical instruction. In states lacking adequate acreage of public land, the grant was given in federal scrip (that is, certificates based upon the public domain that could be sold by the state). The proceeds that accrued were then used to establish the land-grant college. The Second Morrill Act, passed in 1890, provided a direct cash grant of $15,000, to be increased annually to a maximum of $25,000, to support land-grant colleges and universities. This act also provided aid to institutions for black students in states that prohibited their enrollment in existing land-grant institutions. The federal government required that land-grant colleges provide instruction in agricultural and mechanical subjects and in military training. The Morrill acts were a response to the rapid industrial and agricultural growth of the United States in the nineteenth century.

Since the passage of the First Morrill Act, land-grant institutions have been established throughout the United States. In a number of states, these agricultural and mechanical schools are part of the state university.

U.S. Representative Justin S. Morrill, who introduced legislation leading to federal support for agricultural and mechanical land grant universities.

7. Benjamin F. Andrews, *The Land Grant of 1862 and the Land-Grant College* (Washington, D.C.: U.S. Government Printing Office, 1918), pp. 7–8.

Examples of such universities are Maine, founded in 1865, Illinois and West Virginia, in 1867, California, in 1868, Nebraska, in 1869, Ohio State in 1870, and Arkansas in 1871. A more recent example is the University of Hawaii, founded in 1907. In still other states, agricultural and mechanical colleges were established as separate institutions, such as Purdue University, founded in 1869, the Agricultural and Mechanical College of Texas, in 1871, and the Alaska Agricultural College and School of Mines, in 1922. Seventeen southern states established separate land-grant colleges for black students under the provisions of the Second Morrill Act.

Land-grant colleges emphasize agriculture as a blending of science and practice. They also provide research and teaching in areas closely related to agriculture, such as home economics and veterinary medicine. Maintaining their commitment to industrial development, they stress technology, engineering, and applied science. In addition to agricultural and industrial education and research, they offer liberal arts and teacher education programs. Many land-grant universities also maintain large extension and continuing education programs.[8]

The German Research Influence

German universities, which emphasized specialized scholarly and scientific research, had a significant impact on American higher education in the late nineteenth century. Universities such as Berlin, Halle, Gottingen, Bonn, and Munich encouraged scholarship by having a graduate faculty guide the research of students by the seminar method. American professors who had studied at German universities sought to introduce the German model into American higher education. For example, Daniel Coit Gilman made Johns Hopkins University a center of graduate study and research by imitating its German counterpart. Johns Hopkins used the seminar method, in which a professor and a select group of graduate students research specific topics in a given scholarly discipline. The methods of Johns Hopkins were emulated by the graduate schools at Harvard, Yale, Columbia, Princeton, and Chicago.[9] The German emphasis on scholarship and research came to dominate American universities as graduate faculties devoted themselves to the pursuit of truth and advancement of knowledge.

The American university reached its basic pattern in the late nineteenth century. The focal point of the university was the undergraduate college of liberal arts and sciences, which eventually was surrounded by the graduate college and the professional schools of law, medicine, agriculture, education, nursing, social work, theology, dentistry, commerce, and engineering.

Types of Higher Education

As the historical section indicated, American higher education has taken a variety of institutional forms. American colleges and universities include (1) two-year junior or

8. Hugh S. Brown and Lewis B. Mayhew, *American Higher Education* (New York: Center for Applied Research in Education, 1965), pp. 26–27.
9. Abraham Flexner, *Universities: American, English, German* (New York: Oxford University Press, 1930), pp. 73–74.

community colleges, (2) four-year private liberal arts colleges, (3) four-year multi-purpose institutions that often originated as teachers colleges, (4) state land-grant universities, and (5) a variety of professional schools and institutes. Although many states recently have established boards of higher education to coordinate higher education planning, development, and financing, the development of American higher education was virtually unplanned. This section examines the major types of institutions.

Junior and Community Colleges

The junior college concept originated in the late nineteenth century when several university presidents suggested that the first two years of undergraduate education be provided in an institution other than the four-year college or university. Henry Tappan of Michigan, William Follwell of Minnesota, and William Rainey Harper of Chicago believed that junior colleges would free university professors from teaching basic undergraduate courses and allow them to concentrate on scholarly research.

The junior college concept won support slowly. The first junior college was established in 1901 in Joliet, Illinois. Directed by Superintendent J. Stanley Brown, the Joliet Junior College enrolled high school graduates in postgraduate courses without additional tuition.[10] Brown's experiment at Joliet was imitated elsewhere throughout the country. During the 1920s, 1930s, and 1940s, the number of junior colleges increased steadily.

As a new institution, the junior college faced the problem of establishing an institutional identity. According to the university presidents who proposed it, the junior college would offer general liberal arts courses to students who were planning to enter four-year institutions. In 1925, the American Association of Junior Colleges expanded its institutional definition by stating that its members would offer two years of collegiate instruction of a quality equivalent to the first two years of a four-year college and also serve the social, civic, and vocational needs of the surrounding community.[11]

During the 1930s and 1940s, junior colleges gave greater emphasis to vocational and technical training programs for students who were not college bound. For example, the Los Angeles Junior College introduced extensive semiprofessional curricula that included 14 separate terminal programs in 1929, its inaugural year. Junior colleges throughout the country increased their offering of terminal programs.

Today, the junior or community college is the fastest-growing sector in American education. Although the terms *junior* and *community* college are often interchanged, they describe the same institution but illustrate differing institutional conceptions. The term *junior college*, based on the institution's historic origins, signifies that the institution provides the first two years of undergraduate education, after which the student who has earned an associate of arts or science degree

---

10. Elbert K. Fretwell, Jr., *Founding Public Junior Colleges* (New York: Teachers College Press, Columbia University, 1954), pp. 11–12.
11. James W. Thornton, *The Community Junior College* (New York: Wiley, 1966), p. 51.

transfers to a four-year college. When viewed as a junior college, the institution is a downward extension of the four-year college. In the 1960s, many junior colleges were transformed into community colleges. While they remained two-year institutions, the term *community college* designates a broader range of educational activities, such as postsecondary terminal education, technical training, community service, and noncredit continuing education.[12] In many ways, the community college resembles the "people's college" that was urged by some of the nineteenth-century advocates of popular education. As such, it becomes an upward extension of the public elementary and secondary school systems.

Today, the junior college is an important link in the educational systems of many of the states. California is an example of a state that has established an extensive junior college system. In 1907, its legislature authorized high school districts to offer postgraduate courses. Ten years later, in 1917, state financial aid was provided for such programs. Then, in 1921, the California legislature authorized the formation of junior college districts. In planning for higher education, California has provided an extensive community college system that serves a large student population. The presence of this system has enabled the state to provide the opportunity for higher education for many students and also maintain a selective university admissions policy.

The increase in enrollment in community and other two-year colleges has been one of the striking phenomena of American education. In 1960, approximately a half-million students were attending such institutions. Five years later, in 1965, enrollment had more than doubled, with 1,152,086 students on the rolls of two-year colleges. In 1975, enrollments had reached 3,970,119, and 1985 marked a further enrollment increase to 4,531,077 students.[13]

More than an academic institution offering the first two years of liberal arts courses for transfer into four-year colleges, the contemporary junior college is a comprehensive, multipurpose institution. While continuing to offer basic undergraduate liberal arts and science courses, it also provides a wide range of vocational, technical, and adult education programs, among them data processing, communications, electronics, medical technology, recreation, food preparation, and dental hygiene.

As one of the most recent additions to the American educational ladder, the community college is still in the process of institutional self-definition. As time goes on, it will probably cease to be either an upward extension of the secondary school or a downward extension of the college and will define its own unique institutional identity. The major purposes of the community college have been defined as providing

1. Academic programs for students planning to transfer to four-year colleges.
2. Technical and preprofessional programs for postsecondary students.
3. General education for all students.

12. Steven Brint and Jerome Karabel, *The Diverted Dream: Community Colleges and the Promise of Educational Opportunity in America, 1900–1985* (New York: Oxford University Press, 1989).
13. National Center for Education Statistics, *Digest of Education Statistics 1989* (Washington, D.C.: U.S. Government Printing Office, 1989), p. 168.

4. Continuing education in general, cultural, and vocational education for adults.
5. Part-time education.
6. Community service.
7. Counseling and guidance of students.[14]

State Colleges and Universities

Although a few four-year colleges may be municipal, most public colleges and universities are state supported and controlled. While most states have a number of state colleges, every state has at least one state college or university. State colleges and universities have had a variety of origins. Some state colleges began in the nineteenth century as two-year normal schools for teacher education and were later transformed into four-year state teachers colleges. Most of these institutions have now become multipurpose state colleges that offer a broad range of degree programs. Other state institutions were established originally as four-year liberal arts and science colleges. Still other four-year colleges and universities resulted from the Morrill Act of 1862 that provided land grants to the states to establish agricultural and mechanical colleges. Today, state universities have established graduate and professional schools and colleges.

Historically, state colleges and universities have been governed by individual and autonomous boards of trustees that serve as policymaking bodies. While this is still true in some states, the most recent trend has been to establish a state board of higher education that acts as a statewide coordinating agency to establish policies, coordinate development, and allocate finances to its colleges and universities. In some states, each university or college is fairly autonomous; in other states, the colleges and universities are integral units of a single system. For example, New York state represents an example of an integrated and coordinated state university system. In New York, the community colleges, state colleges of arts and sciences, agricultural and technical institutes, university centers, and professional schools are governed by a single board of trustees.

Land-grant institutions refer to the 69 state colleges and universities that were established with funds from the Morrill Act. Some land-grant institutions are state universities, as in Minnesota, Illinois, Arizona, and Nebraska. Other land-grant institutions still retain their agricultural and mechanical arts designations, such as the Alabama Agricultural and Mechanical College. In a few instances, such as Cornell University, a land-grant institution is part of a private university.

Private Colleges and Universities

As indicated, the American system of higher education originated in the privately established religious institutions of the colonial era. During the nineteenth century, religious denominations established colleges—often four-year liberal arts institu-

14. Thornton, *The Community Junior College*, p. 59.

tions—to provide higher education within a religious context. Today, there are approximately 800 private church-related institutions of higher education. In addition, approximately 500 private liberal arts colleges operate under independent but nonreligious auspices.

Like their public counterparts, private colleges and universities exist in a variety of institutional forms. Although many of these colleges and universities have received federal aid in the form of specific grants or state aid in scholarships to individual students, they are governed by self-perpetuating boards of trustees. Among the various private and religious institutions of higher education, one can find

1. The small four-year liberal arts college. In the past, some of these institutions enrolled either men or women; today, most of them are coeducational. Their curriculum is designed to educate undergraduate students.
2. The technical or specialized institute or college that prepares persons in engineering, the performing arts, music, art, nursing, or other fields.
3. The private university that offers a full range of higher education programs, from the liberal arts to graduate and professional education. Some of these institutions, such as the University of Chicago and Johns Hopkins University, have distinguished reputations for scholarship and research. Other universities, often associated with religious denominations, particularly the Roman Catholic Church, provide higher and professional education in urban settings.

Throughout the 1980s, the cost of attending college rose steadily. Rising college costs caused by increased expenditures for salaries, maintenance, energy, and supplies have had an impact on private institutions. These costs, partially borne by higher tuitions, have made it more difficult for private colleges and universities to compete with publicly supported institutions. For example, the average tuition, room, and board at a private institution in 1987 was $11,501 for an academic year, compared to $4,442 at public institutions.[15] For an illustration of the impact of college costs on family income, see Figure 17-1. In terms of enrollments at four-year institutions, 5,543,987 students were attending public institutions in 1988 compared to 2,631,021 in private institutions.[16]

Because of rising expenses, some private institutions have been forced to close. Other institutions have joined consortia or merged to create larger and more cost-effective operations. Unless private institutions receive greater support through grant programs or extended state scholarships to students, more of them will cease to exist. Advocates of private education argue that a variety of institutions of higher education provides a desirable diversity that would be lacking should the surviving institutions of higher education be exclusively state supported.

15. Nabeel Alalam, ed., *The Condition of Education 1990*, II (Washington, D.C.: U.S. Government Printing Office, 1990), p. 15.
16. National Center for Education Statistics, *Digest of Education Statistics 1990* (Washington, D.C.: U.S. Government Printing Office, 1990), p. 189.

FIGURE 17–1   Tuition, Room, and Board as a Percent of Family
Income

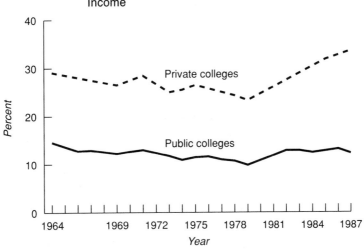

SOURCE: From Nabeel Alalam, ed., *The Condition of Education 1990,* II. (Washington,
D.C.: U.S. Government Printing Office, 1990), p. 23.

Proprietary Institutions

Proprietary institutions are private schools operated for profit. Proprietary postsecondary schools prepare persons for specialized careers in such fields as business,
performing arts, commercial art, music, fine arts, computer technology, electronics,
refrigeration, and many other fields. Historically, these institutions developed from
the tradition of the private-venture schools of the colonial and later eras, which
offered instruction neglected by more academic institutions. They fill an educational
need in that they are usually able to respond to the changing supply-and-demand
relationships of the marketplace. If in a technical area, they may be more responsive
to innovation; if in the fine arts area, they may engage professionals as part-time or
adjunct instructors to offer training that directly relates the aspiring performer to
the stage or concert hall.

Graduate and Professional Schools

Since the Middle Ages, universities have offered professional study. Although the
patterns vary from institution to institution, most universities offer both undergraduate and graduate programs. The major universities have a college, or school of
liberal arts and sciences that provides undergraduate education — usually in a four-
year program leading to the bachelor's degree. Upon completing undergraduate
study, certain students — usually of high academic potential — continue their education in professional schools. Originally, the three professional schools were theology, law, and medicine. Over the course of time, the number of professional schools
has multiplied because of the impact of social and technological change on higher

education. Today, the modern university includes undergraduate education in liberal arts and sciences and in professional areas at both the undergraduate and graduate levels. Large universities have professional schools in medicine, law, education, business, social work, veterinary medicine, agriculture, journalism, architecture, fine arts, nursing, engineering, music, and library science. Some of the professional schools offer both undergraduate and graduate programs. For example, the typical college or school of education offers undergraduate instruction leading to the bachelor's degree and graduate programs leading to the master's and doctoral degrees. Schools of business administration, nursing, and social work also provide both undergraduate and graduate education. In medicine, law, and dentistry, the pattern differs in that students admitted to these schools typically must already possess the bachelor's degree as a prerequisite to professional study.

The relationship between undergraduate and professional study has been enriched further and made more sophisticated but also more complicated by the evolution of graduate education. By way of illustration, a college of liberal arts and sciences in a university contained departments of English, history, and chemistry. In the late nineteenth and early twentieth centuries, universities began to offer postbaccalaureate work that led to the master's or doctoral degree, usually the Ph.D. (doctor of philosophy), in these academic areas. To develop, coordinate, and maintain the quality of these advanced academic programs, graduate schools — with graduate deans at their head — were established within universities. At the same time that academic departments were developing graduate programs, professional schools, for example, in law, medicine, and education, were offering programs beyond the undergraduate or baccalaureate level. From this development came graduate programs and degrees, such as the Ed.D (doctor of education), M.D. (doctor of medicine), and M.S.W. (master of social work), among others. The coordination, development, quality control, and articulation of professional programs at the graduate level brought about a variety of administrative arrangements in universities. They may be administered through the dean of the professional school involved, the dean of the graduate school, or cooperatively by both deans.

Examination of the catalogues of various institutions indicates the bewildering variety of graduate and professional degree requirements that exist from institution to institution. Several factors must be considered by institutions that develop professional or graduate programs. Among them are the following:

1. The general education requirements at the undergraduate level that are a necessary preparation for entering such study.
2. The areas of professional or graduate study regarded as necessary components by the disciplines or professions involved. For example, what does the American Medical Association regard as the necessary preparation of the physician? What does the American Library Association regard as necessary for the librarian? What do political scientists regard as appropriate preparation in their field? Frequently, these components of a professional degree program are specified by accreditation bodies that represent the profession. In professional education, the National Council for the

Accreditation of Teacher Education (NCATE) establishes standards for both undergraduate and graduate preparation.

3. Entry into professions such as medicine, law, architecture, teaching, and nursing is also governed by state certification requirements and examinations. Programs of professional preparation should meet certification requirements and prepare students to sustain state certification examinations.

4. In addition, there may be requirements pertinent to the particular institution offering the degree. A private or religious institution offering graduate and professional programs may have requirements based on the educational philosophy that is unique to it.

Because of the complexity and variety of degree programs, it is difficult to generalize about them. However, the general outlines of the master's degrees (M.A. and M.S.) and the doctorate (Ph.D.) will illustrate degree requirements. The typical master's degree program includes (1) completion of an undergraduate degree, with appropriate courses relating to the subject of graduate study and an academic average that promises success in graduate work in the field, required for admission, (2) completion of a specified number of graduate courses—typically 30 semester hours of graduate credit—in the area of study requiring at least a year, the fifth year, beyond the bachelor's degree, (3) comprehensive examinations, which may be written or oral or a combination of both, and (4) completion of a field experience, a research project, or a thesis. In professional education, for example, the degrees commonly awarded at the master's level are the master of arts or master of science in education (M.A. or M.S.), the master of education (M.Ed.), or the master of arts in teaching (M.A.T.).

The doctor of philosophy (Ph.D.) or equivalent professional degree, such as the doctor of education (Ed.D.) or doctor of science (Sci.D.), is the highest degree awarded by American universities. Although it is called the doctor of philosophy because of medieval origins, the recipient may have studied any number of academic areas other than philosophy. The typical doctoral program involves (1) completion of an undergraduate degree program and usually, but not always, a master's program for admission, (2) an academic record that promises success at the doctoral level, (3) completion of 75 to 90 semester hours of graduate course work, depending upon the particular program and institution, (4) passing written and oral examinations, or a combination of both, that admit the student to doctoral candidacy, (5) the research and writing of a doctoral dissertation on an original topic, and (6) the successful defense of the dissertation before a committee of professors. Doctoral work is a challenging undertaking requiring the ability to do independent research. The completion of doctoral study may take from three to five years, depending upon the student's time and ability and the institution's requirements. In professional education, many institutions may award either the Ph.D. or the Ed.D. degree. Distinctions between the two degrees have become blurred over time. Generally, the Ph.D. degree is preferred by students seeking to become professors of education or educational researchers, as its focus is often specialized on a particular discipline in education, such as educational history, philosophy, or psychology. The Ed.D. frequently exposes students to the various fields of education and includes field work or applied research. The Ed.D. is often preferred by students preparing for careers in educational administration, supervision, or curriculum development.[17]

Governance of Higher Education

Although the role and structure of the state governance of higher education is a highly complex matter that varies from state to state, two general patterns emerge: (1) There is the single university pattern in which all the institutions of higher education are part of one system governed by a single board of higher education, usually appointed by the governor, and (2) there is a more decentralized pattern that provides for a state board of higher education that acts as the planning and coordinating agency for all institutions of higher education in the state but that allows considerable autonomy to boards of trustees of each of the colleges and universities in the statewide system. In both patterns, state boards of higher education (1) review requests for capital budget outlay of the colleges and universities within the system, (2) provide general reviews of institutional budgets, (3) interpret functional differences between various institutions, (4) approve new programs and modifications of existing programs, and (5) plan for the orderly growth of higher education and make recommendations concerning needs and locations of new facilities. In performing these functions, the state board of higher education exercises a general role of being a statewide planning and coordinating body for higher education.

Although state boards of higher education have sought a larger role in private higher education, their functions remain generally limited. They may grant charters to private institutions and approve programs relating to professional licensure and certification.

Boards of Trustees

Private institutions and many state institutions are governed by their boards of trustees. These boards of trustees are generally self-perpetuating; that is, as a board, they appoint their own successors. Their functions are to (1) exercise ceremonial roles connected to university observances, commencements, and events, (2) establish and approve general governing policies, (3) approve operating and capital budgets, and (4) appoint the president of the institution. In addition, the board of trustees also facilitates communications between the institution and the communities or publics that it serves. Boards of trustees of state or public institutions provide a vehicle of communications for the general public, taxpayers, citizens groups, and alumni. Those of private institutions can facilitate communications with foundations, benefactors, and alumni. Boards of trustees of private institutions are active in fund raising. In both state and private institutions, boards of trustees generally confine their activities to general policymaking and delegate implementation of policies to the president and other university administrators.

---

17. For a rationale for the Ed.D., see Geraldine Joncich Clifford and James W. Guthrie, *ED SCHOOL: A Brief for Professional Education* (Chicago: University of Chicago Press, 1988), pp. 358–359.

Administrators

Appointed by the board of trustees, the college or university president is the institution's chief executive officer. His or her powers depend upon the nature of the institution and its governing policies. The president is the chief institutional spokesperson to the public, the faculty, the students, the state legislature, and the alumni. Depending upon the style of the administrator and the institutional traditions and policies, the president may be the chief educational leader, the principal manager, or the agent by which consensus is established. Frequently, contemporary institutional presidents have found themselves in the difficult role of the chief adjudicator of conflicts.

Although the specific functions of the university president are not well defined, the general responsibilities include (1) enforcement of corporate rules and regulations governing the institution, (2) appointment and removal of executive, administrative, and academic officers of the institution, (3) approval or disapproval of policies and procedures of institutional committees, (4) communication between the board of trustees and the university community, and (5) preparation of reports on the university.

The changing role of the university presidency can be illustrated by comparing the perspectives that two university presidents have provided on their role. Charles Eliot, Harvard's president in the late nineteenth century, and Clark Kerr, president of the University of California in the mid-twentieth century, provide two models that illustrate the chancing nature of the university presidency.

Charles Eliot   The career of Charles Eliot, president of Harvard from 1869 to 1909, reveals how one major American university was transformed from a classically dominated institution into one that met the needs of a modern and technological society.[18] Eliot, a Harvard graduate, was trained in the classics, mathematics, and chemistry. On a European tour in 1863, Eliot visited French and German universities and polytechnic institutes. Returning to the United States, he urged the selective adaption of certain aspects of European higher education. However, he also believed that American universities should grow out of their own unique environment and respond to their own changing society.

During his 40-year presidency at Harvard, Eliot's leadership influenced both his own institution and American higher education as well. Traditionally, college and university presidents had been distinguished churchmen, who conducted their offices in a higher ministerial or paternalistic fashion. Eliot, in contrast, saw himself as the manager of a highly complex educational corporation. He gave equal attention to undergraduate, graduate, and professional education and sought to achieve more efficiency, higher standards, and greater freedom.

Committed to freedom of choice in higher education, Eliot introduced the "elective principle" at Harvard in the 1870s. Students were to be free to choose, or "elect," a certain number of courses rather than follow a totally prescribed curricu-

18. Hugh Hawkins, *Between Harvard and America: The Educational Leadership of Charles W. Eliot* (New York: Oxford University Press, 1972), pp. 30–32.

Charles W. Eliot, president of Harvard University from 1869–1909, transformed the role of the university president from paternalistic figure into skilled executive leader and manager of a complex institution.

lum. The elective principle, Eliot believed, would encourage undergraduate specialization. It would stimulate new fields of specialized study by freeing professors to teach in their areas of expertise rather than in mandatory general courses.

Because a technological society requires highly trained specialists, Eliot saw the university's role to be that of efficiently preparing well-educated and highly trained specialists. Regarded as one of America's leading educational representatives, Eliot helped to make American higher education more responsive to the needs of a modernizing nation.

Clark Kerr In the 1960s, Clark Kerr, then president of the University of California, commented on the difficult and complex role that had to be exercised by a president of a large university. Kerr said it was no longer possible to speak of a university governed by a single person. In fact, the modern university had become a "multiversity" composed of often conflicting special-interest groups.

Writing in 1963, Kerr described the University of California as an institution with a total operating budget of nearly a half-billion dollars, spending nearly $100 million for construction, employing over 40,000 persons, maintaining operations in over 100 locations, conducting projects in more than 50 foreign nations, listing 10,000 courses in its catalogues, and anticipating an enrollment of 100,000 students. Such an institution, Kerr said, could no longer be described as a single community of scholars and students. It was rather a loose collection of subcommunities united only by a common name and governing board. Coining the term *multiversity*, Kerr said:

> *The multiversity is an inconsistent institution. It is not one community but several—the community of the undergraduate and the community of the graduate; the community of the humanist, the community of the social scientist, and the community of the scientist; the communities of the professional schools; the community of all the nonacademic personnel; the community of the administrators. Its edges are fuzzy—it reaches out to alumni, legislators, farmers, businessmen, who are all related to one or more of these internal communities. As an institution, it looks far into the past and far into the future, and is often at odds with the present. It serves society almost slavishly—a society it also criticizes, sometimes unmercifully. Devoted to equality of opportunity, it is itself a class society. A community, like the medieval communities of masters and students, should have common interests; in the multiversity, they are quite varied, even conflicting. A community should have a soul, a single animating principle; the multiversity has several—some of them quite good, although there is much debate on which souls really deserve salvation.*[19]

Composed of a number of often conflicting special interest subcommunities, the multiversity is difficult to govern. As California's president, Kerr found several competitors for power in the multiversity: first, the students who, through the elective system, determine which disciplines the university will develop; second, the faculty who have achieved some control over admissions, programs, examinations, degree granting, appointments, and academic freedom; third, public authorities, such as the board of trustees, the state department of finance, the governor, and the legislature, who scrutinize organization and expenditures; fourth, special interests that exert pressures on the multiversity, such as agriculture and business organizations, trade unions, public school groups, and mass media; and, fifth, the administration, which has become a prominent feature of the multiversity.

In the modern university, the president's office is often the place of collision between the conflicting demands of students, trustees, alumni, faculty, and deans. Today's college or university president has the difficult assignment of developing consensus among the various interest groups comprising the institutional community and of providing leadership and direction for the university as a whole.

As with the modern corporation, college and university administration also has become more elaborate, functional, and bureaucratized. Universities have an array of vice-presidents who are responsible for various administrative, service, and

---

19. Clark Kerr, *The Uses of the University* (Cambridge, Mass.: Harvard University Press, 1963), pp. 18–19.

academic functions. Usually directly responsible to the president, the academic vice-president is responsible for faculty appointment and dismissal, academic programs, and the operations and coordination of general instructional activities. Indirectly, he or she may also be responsible for the supervision of admissions, registrations, records, and other academic functions. The vice-president for finance has general jurisdiction over the institution's financial and budgetary affairs. The vice-president for student services is responsible for nonacademic matters relating to students, such as counseling services, residence halls, and student activities and organizations. The vice-president for development works with public relations, alumni, and benefactors and with fund-raising activities. The vice-president for personnel is responsible for administrators with nonfaculty appointments, secretarial and clerical staff, grounds and maintenance staff, and other nonacademic personnel. He or she is responsible for hiring, promoting, and dismissing nonacademic staff.

Academic Deans

The academic deans are the chief executives and administrators of the various colleges and schools of the university. For example, the College of Liberal Arts and Sciences, the College of Education, the College of Fine Arts, the School of Medicine, and other colleges are each headed by a dean who is appointed by the president of the institution. As the chief executive officer of the college that provides academic instruction, the deans perform such functions as (1) executing universitywide policies established by the board of trustees and the president within their school or college, (2) preparing the budgets for their school or college and the direction and supervision of the expenditure of approved funds, (3) supervising the quality of instruction within the school or college, (4) chairing of meetings of chairpersons and faculty of the school or college, and (5) recommending faculty in their school or college for appointment, promotion, tenure, and termination.

Department Chairpersons

The chief administrative officer for organizing instruction at the departmental level is the chairperson. Chairpersons are generally appointed by the academic vice-president or president upon the recommendation of the dean of the unit in which the department is located. They report to the dean, who in turn reports to the academic vice-president. Among the responsibilities of department chairpersons are (1) organizing the schedules of courses within their departments and assigning faculty to teach them, (2) evaluating faculty within their department and recommending them for tenure, promotion, salary increments, and termination, (3) executing university, college, or school policies within their departments, and (4) calling and presiding over meetings of the members of their department.

Faculty

College and university faculty members are usually members of departments within a college or school. They are usually holders of a Ph.D. degree. The initial appointment may be at the rank of instructor or assistant professor. Upon the completion of a specified number of years at the rank of assistant professor, the faculty member may be promoted to associate professor. With appointment to associate professor, the faculty member is usually granted tenure, depending upon the particular institutional policies. The highest rank, which is awarded to senior members of departments, is professor.

The granting of tenure and promotion through the various professional ranks is earned by faculty members who have distinguished themselves by scholarly contributions to their discipline and by excellence in instruction. Tenure means that a faculty member is a member of the faculty of the college or university for an indefinite period of time, generally from the time tenure is awarded until retirement, unless the specialty that the tenured faculty members teaches is no longer offered by the university. Tenure gives the faculty member who receives it a great deal of independence and security because dismissal of tenured faculty members rarely occurs. Tenure was designed to protect academic freedom and to free the faculty member from the vicissitudes of changing administrations and public pressures. Critics of tenure allege that tenured faculty members may not maintain the same degree of scholarly and instructional activity throughout their careers; they also charge that large numbers of tenured faculty limit entry of younger scholars into teaching positions at the college or university levels.

Promotion through the various academic ranks of the university depends upon factors such as scholarship, teaching competence, and service to the profession and the university. An important element in both promotion and tenure is "peer review," in which already tenured faculty members review the accomplishments of colleagues who seek tenure and promotion. These review committees then recommend tenure and promotion to appropriate university committees or administrators.

In the modern university or college, tenure and promotion depend largely on scholarly productivity. University faculty members are expected to do research and to publish the results of this research in scholarly journals and books. These publications are then reviewed by other experts in the discipline. Competency in teaching is another factor affecting tenure and promotion decisions. Here student and peer evaluation of the faculty member's teaching skill is important. Criteria used to verify teaching competency are subject to more debate and discussion because they are not as precise as those that relate to scholarship and publication. Service to the profession and the university usually means that the faculty member has contributed to professional associations and university committees.

Financing Higher Education

Institutions of higher education are supported financially by various sources. All colleges and universities derive a part of their income from student tuition and fees. It is estimated that private colleges rely on tuition to pay 60 percent of their expenditures. Tuition-generated income is, however, generally inadequate to support an institution of higher education. At state institutions, student tuitions and fees cover about 20 percent of the costs. Public institutions—community colleges, colleges, universities, and professional schools—receive a substantial amount of their support from public tax monies. Junior and community colleges, depending upon the state, are supported by a combination of local tax support and state

FIGURE 17–2   Trends in College and University Enrollment, by Type and Control; Fall of Selected Years, 1970–1988

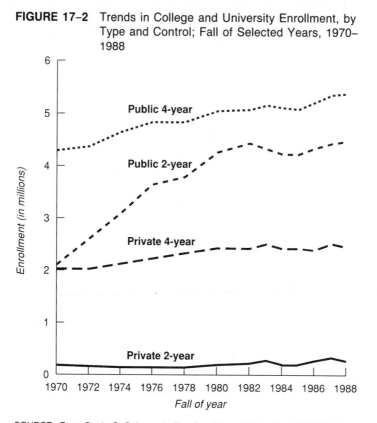

SOURCE: From Curtis O. Baker, ed., *The Condition of Education 1989* (Washington, D.C.: U.S. Government Printing Office, 1989), p. 115.

funding. State colleges and universities are supported by funding at the state level, generally by appropriations by the state legislature. Private and independent institutions of higher education are supported by foundations, alumni donations, and other philanthropic funding. The federal government has aided both state and private institutions to some degree by the funding of special programs.

Throughout the 1980s, the expenditures of colleges and universities increased dramatically. The increase in expenditures was matched by continuous increases in students' tuition and fees. Between 1975 and 1985, expenditures for institutions of higher education increased by 23 percent. For private institutions, the rate of increase was 32 percent. Public institutions' expenditures rose at a rate of 16 percent. Much of the rise in expenditures was due to increases in administrative and faculty salaries and other operating expenses. Faculty salaries in the 1970s and early 1980s failed to keep pace with inflation, with the result that university and college faculty suffered a 17 percent loss of purchasing power. Between 1980 and 1987, salary increases of 16 percent largely offset the losses of the preceding decade. In addition, inflationary trends, such as higher fuel costs, also impacted the expenditures of colleges and universities.

Between 1977 and 1988, tuition, fees, and room and board increased by 110 percent at public colleges and universities and by 150 percent at private institutions.

For the academic year 1990–1991, undergraduate charges for tuition, fees, and room and board were estimated at $4,970 at four-year public institutions and at $13,544 at four-year private colleges and universities.[20] The increasing costs of a college education have raised serious concerns about the opportunity to attend college. As the costs of attending four-year institutions increase, two-year public community colleges, whose costs in 1990–1991 averaged $841, can be expected to attract increased student enrollments. Also, the number of students enrolled on a part-time basis is likely to increase. For trends in enrollment, see Figure 17–2; note the dramatic increase in two-year college enrollments.

Enrollment Trends in Higher Education

Between 1970 and 1980, college enrollments increased by more than 40 percent. This increase was primarily due to the large number of college-age persons in the U.S. population. Since 1980, enrollments have continued to increase, but at a slower rate. Between 1980 and 1987, enrollments increased from 12.1 to 12.8 million, an increase of 6 percent. During this seven-year period, the percentage of males enrolled remained static, while the percentage of women students increased by 10 percent. In addition, there was a steady increase in the number of part-time students.

Although many experts in higher education predicted a significant decrease in college enrollments, this did not occur. The experts' predictions were based on a declining cohort of college-age students. However, the projected decline of these traditional students was offset by the increasing numbers of nontraditional students. For example, the number of older students grew more rapidly than the number of younger students. In the period from 1970 to 1985, the enrollment of students under age 25 increased by 15 percent, while the enrollment of those over age 25 rose by 114 percent.

Between 1976 and 1980, the number of minority students attending colleges and universities increased. In 1976, 15.4 percent of the total enrollment was identified as students from minority groups, such as African Americans, Asian Americans, Native Americans, and Hispanics. By 1986, the percentage of minority students had increased to 17.9. While the number of Asian-American students was increasing, the percentage of African-American students showed a slight decline, from 9.4 percent in 1976 to 8.7 percent in 1986.[21]

Conclusion

The American system of higher education is unique among those of the world in that it has attempted to provide mass education on both a quantitative and qualitative basis. While the basic institutional structures of American higher education devel-

20. National Center for Education Statistics, *Digest of Education Statistics 1989*, p. 161; *Chicago Tribune*, September 27, 1990, p. 16.
21. Ibid., pp. 159–160.

oped without a great deal of planning in the past, the future will not permit Americans the luxury of unplanned college and university growth. The future of American higher education will require the careful setting of educational priorities and the judicious allocation of financial resources.

The college student of the future is also likely to be different from the stereotypical carefree sophomore of the 1920s, the G.I. of the late 1940s, and the political activist of the 1960s. The college campus of the 1990s will have more women attending professional schools, more members of minority groups enrolled, and more older students preparing for second careers or for the pure pursuit of knowledge.

DISCUSSION QUESTIONS

1. Identify and examine the major factors shaping American higher education in the colonial and early national periods.
2. What was the First Morrill Act and how did this legislation shape American higher education?
3. Identify a college or university of your choice and write a brief history of that institution.
4. Read an autobiography or a biography of a college or university president and prepare an analysis of his or her style of administration.
5. How do the entry requirements for graduate and professional study have an impact on undergraduate education?
6. Identify the major problems facing your college or university. Arrange them in priority and speculate on possible solutions.
7. Assess the impact of increased fees for tuition and room and board on the opportunity to attend college.
8. What are the enrollment patterns at your college or university in terms of nontraditional and minority students?

FIELD EXERCISES

1. Identify a community college in your locality. Obtain a copy of its catalogue. Arrange a visit to the institution and report to the class on the various programs offered by the college.
2. Arrange a debate on the issue: "Resolved: The first two years of undergraduate education should take place in a community college."
3. Invite a professor of one of the arts and science disciplines to speak to your class on his or her preparation for a career in higher education.
4. Invite a chairperson or dean in your college or university to speak to your class on his or her perceptions of the problems facing higher education.
5. Examine your local phone directory and identify the postsecondary proprietary schools in your area.
6. Identify the various degrees offered by the institution that you are attending.

7. Consult the catalogue of a college or school of education. Identify the requirements for master's and doctoral programs of that college.

8. Interview several nontraditional students who are attending your college or university. Determine their choice of an area of specialization or major. Report your findings to the class.

SUGGESTED READINGS

APPS, JEROLD W. *Higher Education in a Learning Society: Meeting New Demands for Education and Training.* San Francisco: Jossey-Bass, 1989.

ASTIN, ALEXANDER W. *Achieving Educational Excellence: A Critical Assessment of Priorities and Practices in Higher Education.* San Francisco: Jossey-Bass, 1985.

BLITS, JAN, ED. *The American University: Problems, Prospects and Trends.* Buffalo, N.Y.: Prometheus Books, 1985.

BLOOM, ALLAN. *The Closing of the American Mind: How Higher Education Has Failed Democracy and Impoverished the Souls of Today's Students.* New York: Simon and Schuster, 1987.

BRINT, STEVEN, AND KARABEL, JEROME. *The Diverted Dream: Community Colleges and the Promise of Educational Opportunity in America, 1900–1985.* New York: Oxford University Press, 1989.

COBBAN, ALAN B. *The Medieval English Universities: Oxford and Cambridge to c. 1500.* Berkeley: University of California Press, 1988.

COHEN, ARTHUR M., AND BRAWER, FLORENCE B. *The American Community College.* San Francisco: Jossey-Bass, 1984.

DIENER, THOMAS. *Growth of an American Invention: A Documentary History of the Junior and Community College Movement.* Westport, Conn.: Greenwood Press, 1986.

ELAM, ADA M. *The Status of Blacks in Higher Education.* Lanham, Md.: University Press of America, 1989.

GREEN, MADELEINE F., ED. *Leaders for a New Era: Strategies for Higher Education.* New York: American Council on Education and Macmillan, 1988.

HOENACK, STEPHEN A., AND COLLINS, EILEEN B., EDS. *The Economics of American Universities: Management, Operations, and Fiscal Environment.* Albany: State University of New York Press, 1989.

HOROWITZ, HELEN LEFKOWITZ. *Campus Life: Undergraduate Cultures from the End of the Eighteenth Century to the Present.* Chicago: University of Chicago Press, 1987.

OLIVAS, MICHAEL A., ED. *Latino College Students.* New York: Columbia University, Teachers College Press, 1986.

PAZANDAK, CAROL H. *Improving Undergraduate Education in Large Universities.* San Francisco: Jossey-Bass, 1989.

SCHUSTER, JACK H. *Governing Tomorrow's Campus: Perspectives and Agendas.* New York: American Council on Education and Macmillan, 1989.

SLAUGHTER, SHEILA. *The Higher Learning and High Technology: Dynamics of Higher Education Policy Formation.* Albany: State University of New York Press, 1989.

TIERNEY, WILLIAM G. *Curricular Landscapes, Democratic Vistas: Transformative Leadership in Higher Education.* New York: Praeger, 1989.

18

The School System and Staff

Chapter 18 examines the school system by identifying its major staff components: the school board, administrators, teachers, and other personnel. Preliminary to this discussion, a brief review of certain basic principles governing American education is useful:

1. Education, when defined in its organized sense as schooling, is a state prerogative.
2. States have delegated substantial authority in organizing and administering schools to local boards of education (that is, the local school board).
3. Local school boards establish the general policies governing schools and their employees and engage professional educators such as superintendents, principals, and teachers to provide instruction to the students residing in the school district.

Although they are state agents, local school board members are also responsible to the public, the community members residing in the school district. Because school policies are a community concern, school issues are discussed and debated publicly. Local control of schools is designed to encourage community involvement and participation in the public schools.

Although the local district is the immediate location and focus of school governance, the matter is not so simple. The state—through its school code and through legislation—exerts many controls over education, ranging from mandated curriculum areas to statutes regulating teacher tenure, employment, and dismissal. Although education is a state function, the federal government, over time, has assumed an educational role through legislation such as PL 94–142, which establishes guidelines for educating the handicapped, and through court decisions, such as the *Brown* case of 1954, which outlawed de jure racial segregation in public schools. These factors should be kept in mind when considering the nature of a school system. While the structural components of a school system can be identified, such a system does not exist in isolation from other social, political, and economic systems and variables.[1]

1. For an analysis of schooling in the United States from the perspective of critical social theory, see Kathleen P. Bennett and Margaret D. LeCompte, *How Schools Work: A Sociological Analysis of Education* (New York: Longman, 1990).

Although political scientists and sociologists have developed extended analyses of "systems," Chapter 18 uses a limited and necessarily simplified view of a system. Our discussion concentrates on the staffing pattern found in most school systems.

A major purpose of the chapter is to identify the staff members with whom prospective teachers will work. The basic orientation is that teachers are part of a system that requires the cooperative efforts of all its members if it is to succeed in performing its primary educational mission.

The general focusing questions that will be answered as you read this chapter include the following:

1. What are the role and functions of the district superintendent?
2. How does the school system function?
3. What are the role and functions of the principal?
4. What are the role and functions of teachers as members of the school system?
5. Who are the other members of a school staff, and how do they contribute to the educational system?
6. What are effective schools?

Superintendent of Schools

Each school district in the United States employs a general superintendent of schools as its chief executive officer. The local board of education is responsible for creating the policies governing the district schools, and the superintendent is responsible for implementing those policies. The general superintendent's position can be defined by the following major responsibilities that he or she performs for the board of education:

1. Implementing and supervising of the district's educational program.
2. Preparing the annual budget and managing the district's finances.
3. Recommending the employment of teachers, administrators, and custodial, secretarial, and other support staff.
4. Preparing reports and recommendations on the district's relationships to state, federal, and other educational authorities.
5. Supervising the general operations and physical facilities of the district.

In small, usually rural, school districts, the superintendent may perform all these duties and also serve as a building principal. In districts of an intermediate size, the superintendent generally works directly with the school building principals and a small number of central office personnel. In large, usually big-city, districts, the superintendent heads a large central office staff and often has deputy superintendents as administrative subordinates in the various regions of the district. Regardless of the district's size and complexity, the superintendent heads the administrative hierarchy and is responsible for implementing the policies enacted by the board of education.

Historically, the position of the superintendent appeared first in the urban areas of the United States, especially in the large eastern and midwestern cities. When the management of a number of schools became too difficult and demanding for a citizen board of laypersons, it was determined that a professional educator was needed to coordinate the administrative functions of the schools. By the end of the nineteenth century, large school districts typically employed a general superintendent.[2] As the rural school district consolidation proceeded in the twentieth century, superintendents were also hired in these areas. Three phases occurred in the historical development of the general superintendency:

1. Initially, the superintendency was essentially a clerical and information office that dealt with the minor but detailed administrative tasks assigned by the board of education.
2. Gradually, the superintendent emerged as the district's educational leader and expert. As educational issues and problems became more complex, boards of education came to recognize and value the expert professional opinions of the superintendents who prepared policy recommendations for them.
3. In the third stage, the superintendent, who was now recognized as the district's educational leader, was given the added responsibility of managing its financial and business affairs. The superintendent was now responsible not only for curriculum and instruction but also for the management of the district's property, finances, investments, and budget.

As a result of this historical evolution of the superintendency and because of the complexity of contemporary American education, the modern superintendent is expected to fill many demanding roles and complete many difficult assignments. In a national survey, superintendents identified, in rank order, the challenges and issues they considered most significant in their role as the school district's chief executive officer: financing education; planning and goal setting; assessing educational outcomes; maintaining credible accountability; evaluating administrators and staff; maintaining cooperation among board members; administering special education programs; obtaining accurate and current information for decision making; conducting negotiations with teachers' bargaining units; dealing with either rapidly increasing or decreasing enrollments; gaining greater visibility for the office of superintendent; efficiently managing personal time; dealing with parental apathy and irresponsibility, including child abuse; complying with state and federal record-keeping requirements; administering student discipline; selecting and recruiting staff; dealing with changes in values and norms of behavior; and dealing with the use of drugs and alcohol in schools.[3]

The superintendent is expected to be an educational leader, a political leader, a business manager, and a human-relations expert. The following paragraphs examine these demanding dimensions of the superintendency.

2. For an historical analysis of the development of superintendent-board relations, see David B. Tyack, *The One Best System: A History of American Urban Education* (Cambridge, Mass.: Harvard University Press, 1974), pp. 126–176.
3. Luvern L. Cunningham and Joseph T. Hentges, *The American School Superintendency 1982: A Summary Report* (Arlington, Va.: American Association of School Administrators, 1982), p. 38.

Educational Leadership

As an educational leader, the superintendent is expected to have knowledge and skill in curricular design, development, and implementation.[4] While many curricular matters must be delegated to the professional staff, the superintendent has final responsibility and is accountable for the success or failure of the school district's educational program. The superintendent is expected to assist the board of education in developing policies that govern the district's educational program. As the foremost educator in the district, the superintendent is accountable for the performance of the district's building principals and teachers.

Political Leadership

Effective superintendents need to be skilled in political leadership and public relations. It is often the superintendent who explains policies and decisions to the professional staff, the public, and the news media. It is the superintendent who has to reconcile the interests of conflicting groups without jeopardizing the primary educational mission of the schools. The modern superintendent needs political and human-relation skills of tact, diplomacy, and patience in implementing an educational program for the children of the school district. If the superintendent lacks these skills, conflicts with the board, staff, and public may develop that will affect the district's educational mission.

Business Management

The superintendent is responsible not only for educational leadership but also for managing and monitoring the financial affairs of the district. The superintendent is expected to be an expert on tax rates, the state funding formula, investments, and bonds. It is the superintendent's responsibility to prepare and present the annual budget to the school board. Often, the superintendent is involved in negotiations with the teachers' organization on teachers' salaries and fringe benefits. Further, the superintendent is responsible for maintaining the physical facilities of the district.

Personal and Personnel Relations Expert

In any institution, problems will occur involving the individuals employed to perform the functions of that organization. These problems often relate to the interpersonal relationships of administrators, teachers, and other personnel employed by the school district. These time-consuming problems often come to the desk of the superintendent for solution. The superintendent needs to have the skills in stimulating teachers and other staff members to work at their optimum levels. To a large extent, the educational and working environment of the district is shaped by the superintendent's attitudes.

---

4. For a discussion of the issue of education leadership, see Stephen L. Jacobson and James A. Conway, eds., *Educational Leadership in an Age of Reform* (New York: Longman, 1990).

The Superintendent's Functions   The district superintendent has a direct influence on the teacher's professional career. As the district's chief executive officer and educational leader, the superintendent has a crucial role to play in staff hiring, supervision, and development. If teachers are to be granted tenure, it is on the superintendent's recommendation. If they are to be dismissed, it is also with his or her recommendation. It is important, therefore, for the classroom teacher to be aware of the various specific functions that the superintendent exercises in the school district:

1. Meetings with community groups, parents of pupils, representatives of the media, and agents of companies doing business with the district
2. Planning and attending board of education meetings
3. Meetings with the professional staff, subordinate administrators, teachers, and non-instructional personnel
4. Attending to instructional matters, such as program objectives, curriculum and instruction, organization and scheduling, and materials and equipment
5. Supervising pupil personnel matters, such as guidance, health, and discipline and related legal items
6. Dealing with staff personnel matters, such as recruitment, assignment, records, welfare, policies, and in-service education
7. Attending to school physical plant facilities matters, such as construction, maintenance, repair, heating, lighting, ventilation, and energy conservation
8. Conducting the financial and business affairs, such as budgeting, purchasing, and accounting
9. Attending to school–community relations and services of a public-relations nature, such as appearing at public events, making speeches, and participating in public-service activities and organizations
10. Involvement with professional activities and organization.[5]

The School System Hierarchy

The roles and responsibilities of various staff members of the school system are discussed in the sections that follow. However, it is important to consider first the flow of authority within the school system. In terms of authority, the school staff is organized in a hierarchy, in which positions and their attendant responsibilities are arranged so that those exercising the greater and more general authority are placed higher in the staffing pattern.[6] Because the superintendent is accountable to the school board for all the district's operations, he or she ranks highest in the school system hierarchy. The flow of authority is downward in a line from the superintendent to subordinate administrators. If the district is large enough to have area or regional deputy superintendents, they occupy the next rung in the administrative hierarchy. In terms of line authority, the building principal comes next. As a teacher, your most frequent encounters will be with the principal, who has line authority and responsibility for the operations in a school. Teachers are next in the

---

5. Roald F. Campbell, Luvern L. Cunningham, Michael D. Usdan, and Raphael O. Nystrand, *The Organization and Control of Schools*, 4th ed. (Columbus, Ohio: Charles E. Merrill, 1980), pp. 217–220; 233–246.
6. For a discussion of the school system hierarchy, see ibid., pp. 251–274.

flow of authority and responsibility in that they are accountable for implementing the district's educational program in their classrooms. The hierarchical pattern should not be viewed by teachers as a coercive bureaucracy. It is a means of identifying and clarifying areas of responsibility within a school system. It simply means that someone is responsible for particular functions in the school system. The following diagram is intended to illustrate hierarchical line patterns in the school system:

Line Authority In a School System

Board of Education
(makes policy for entire district)

Superintendent
(implements policy for entire district)

Deputy Superintendents
(in large districts)
(implement policy in subdivisions of the district)

Building Principals
(implement policy in a single school of the district)

Teachers
(implement policy — the educational program
in a particular classroom of a school)

In addition to and supportive of the line positions in the administrative hierarchy of the school, there is also staff personnel, such as program directors, special service personnel, and curriculum specialists, who report to, assist, and advise administrators, such as the superintendent and principal who hold line positions. The recommendations of staff personnel must be accepted by line administrators before they are implemented. Personnel in staff positions are specialists who provide expert opinion to the line administrators, who are accountable for operating the schools and implementing the district's educational program. Figure 18–1 illustrates line–staff relationships in the school system hierarchy.

FIGURE 18–1 School System Line–Staff Relationships: Large District Model

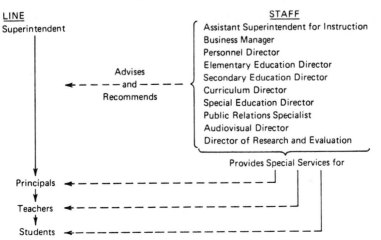

Central Office Staff

Subordinate to the superintendent in the administrative hierarchy of the school system is a central office staff that assists in the operations of the district. The success or failure of the superintendent in achieving district goals depends on his or her ability to select capable subordinates and to organize them into an effective administrative team. The school district's size determines to a large extent the number and functions of subordinate central office administrators and personnel. In a very small district, the central office might consist of only the superintendent and a secretary. In the large urban district, it might consist of a large number of subordinate administrators, such as deputy superintendents, administrative assistants, managers, program directors, and curriculum specialists.

For example, the central office staff of a large urban school district might include the following:

> Assistant superintendent for instruction
> Assistant superintendent for business
> Assistant superintendent for personnel
> Assistant superintendent for pupil personnel services
> Director of elementary education
> Director of curriculum
> Director of special education
> Director of audiovisual and media services
> Public relations and information specialist
> Director of research and evaluation
> Director of buildings, grounds, and maintenance services
> Director of health services
> Director of cafeteria and food services
> Director of transportation
> Specialists, supervisors, and consultants for elementary education, music, art, physical education, mathematics, science, social science, foreign language instruction, and other special subjects

Most central office personnel are in staff positions insofar as they perform specific tasks assigned by the superintendent in their area of specialized expertise. They also advise the superintendent on the recommendations to be made to the board of education.

The Building Principal

A school district is subdivided into attendance areas, with a particular building designated as the school serving the educational needs of students who live within the boundaries designated by the board of education. The typical pattern is to have a principal designated as the administrative officer of that building. The principal is the administrative head and educational leader of a school who has been delegated the major responsibility for coordinating and directing the programs and activities of the school. Depending upon the size of the building and its enrollment, the principal may have a number of assistant principals to aid in administering the school. Junior high and high schools may also have a registrar, director of guidance, and department chairpersons for various subject matter areas. Figure 18-2 illustrates the division of a district into attendance areas.

Historically, the position of building principal evolved from the concept of the principal teacher of the school. Regarded as a school's most knowledgeable and experienced teacher, the principal teacher was a master educator who could assist, advise, and often supervise less experienced or beginning teachers. In Europe, the master teacher who administered the school was called a *headmaster* or *headmistress*. Private schools, particularly academies, in the United States still use the titles of headmaster or headmistress to designate the chief administrator. As the principalship evolved in American public education, the principal, while still being regarded as the educational leader of the school, also was assigned many other responsibilities of an indirectly educational nature. As public schools assumed more social services, such as providing transportation, meals, and health services, the principal was expected to administer these added assignments.

In most elementary schools, the building principal is the administrator with whom teachers have the greatest contact. Just as the district or general superintendent plays many roles and performs many functions in the school district, the principal exercises a wide range of functions within the attendance area served by the

FIGURE 18-2   Attendance Areas and Schools Within a District

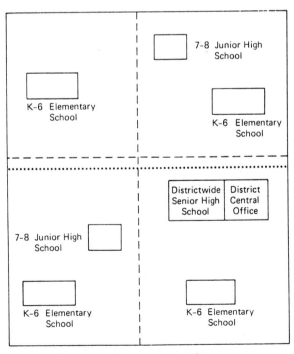

— — — — Elementary attendance area boundary.
•••••••••••• Junior high attendance area boundary.

school under his or her jurisdiction.[7] It is the principal's duty to implement district policies and administer the instructional program for children attending the school. School planning, staff development, and supervision are also areas of responsibility that the principal is expected to perform. The principal maintains student records, schedules sections of grades or subjects, and deals with staff and student problems.

Much of the research of the 1980s identified the building principal as the key agent in bringing about educational change and in implementing policies that facilitate effective instruction by creating an orderly learning environment and using resources wisely. According to *What Works*, published by the U.S. Department of Education:

> *Effective principals have a vision of what a good school is and systematically strive to bring that vision to life in their schools. School improvement is their constant theme. They scrutinize existing practices to assure that all activities and procedures contribute to the quality of the time available for learning. They make sure teachers participate actively in this process. Effective principals, for example, make opportunities available for faculty to improve their own teaching and classroom management skills.*[8]

Teachers

The school system of a district exists to educate children. Empowered to do so by the state, a board of education develops the general policies needed to perform this primary function and employs a superintendent to implement its policies. In the hierarchical structure of the school system, the building principal executes policy decisions in his or her particular school. However, the key to a successful educational program is the classroom teacher who actually instructs the students assigned to him or her.[9]

Teachers' Instructional Role in the School System

In performing their instructional responsibilities, the teachers' role and functions in the school system are diverse, demanding, and complex. Although the teacher has the district's curriculum guides and instructional handbooks that accompany particular programs and textbook series, much of the planning, organizing, and delivering of instruction is a responsibility that only the teacher can perform. Within the school system as a whole and within the classroom in particular, competent instruction requires the teacher to perform as follows:

1. *Determining Learning Objectives.* Precisely what is it that the teacher is attempting to teach and the children are expected to learn? Learning objectives provide the teacher with a focused rationale for instruction, as opposed to unfocused, scattered dissemination of infor-

---

7. For a well-done examination of the role of the principal in contemporary schools, see Lawrence F. Rossow, *The Principalship: Dimensions in Instructional Leadership* (Englewood Cliffs, N.J.: Prentice Hall, 1990). Also see Terrence E. Deal and Kent D. Peterson, *The Principal's Role in Shaping School Culture* (Washington, D.C.: U.S. Government Printing Office, 1990).

8. *What Works: Research About Teaching and Learning* (Washington, D.C.: U.S. Department of Education, 1986), p. 50.

9. A broad-based analysis of the teacher's role is provided in Dan Lortie, *School Teacher: A Sociological Study* (Chicago: University of Chicago Press, 1975).

mation. In focusing instruction, objectives help the teacher and the learners to define what is the subject of instruction and to include what is necessary and exclude what is unnecessary and often extraneous and confusing.

Consciously identified learning objectives are useful in determining if instruction has been effective and if the desired learning has taken place. If the objectives are not fulfilled, the teacher can determine if another approach or method should be used or if more time is needed by students. If learning objectives are met, the teacher can go on to the next phase of instruction.

2. *Identifying Learners' Needs, Interests, and Readiness.* At the same time that the teacher is determining the objectives of a particular instructional phase, it is necessary to diagnose the particular needs, interests, and readiness of the children who will receive that instruction. This means that the teacher must first know the students in order to design instruction for them. The questions to be asked in getting to know learners include these: (a) Are there children who might have particular emotional, physical, or psychological problems in dealing with the material being planned for instruction? (b) Are the children educationally ready—are they prepared by previous instruction—for the new learning that is planned?

Because the children's education is cumulative, the entire school system has a role to play in identifying learners' needs, problems, and readiness. The results of previous instruction, at earlier grade levels, the comments of former teachers, and the diagnosis of guidance and special education staff members are especially useful in assessing the learner's readiness.

3. *Planning Instruction.* When objectives have been framed and learners diagnosed, the teacher can plan the actual instruction that is to occur. The questions to be answered in planning instruction include these: (a) What am I going to teach? (b) To whom will I teach it? (c) How will I teach it? (d) How will I know if my teaching has resulted in learning? The following instructional flowchart is helpful in planning instruction:

Instructional Planning Chart

What?	*To Whom?*	*How?*	*Assessment?*
What is the subject or skill?	Who are the learners?	What method will I use? Or what combination of methods will I use?	How will I evaluate my instruction and my students' performance?
What is its relationship to previous or following units of instruction?	What is their level of readiness and previous experience?	What materials will I use?	
	What are their problems?	What instructional aides or resource materials are available?	
	What are their interests?		

Instructional planning, while it centers on and is the responsibility of the individual classroom teacher, requires the assistance of various components of the school system. The identification of the subject or skill that will be taught needs to be integrated into the school district's curriculum plan. The materials and the resources that will be used depend upon the school board's allocation of funds for their purchase and efforts of the administrative staff to provide them for classroom instruction.

4. *Implementing Instruction.* To a considerable extent, successful instruction depends on the care with which preparatory planning is done. Teaching and learning, however, are an intensely human encounter that is subject to the "unplanned" elements that are part of human experience. Skillful teaching depends both on planning and on the ability to improvise when necessary. Obvious examples of the need to improvise occur when the bulb in the projector burns out or the tape recorder malfunctions. Although most successful teaching appears to be done by the experienced teacher with ease, instruction requires knowledge, method, and effort. Implementing instruction means that the teacher is actually teaching and the children are actually learning. It means that something is taking place—a transaction among teacher, learners, and subject matter is occurring. It means that the theory involved in planning is being put into practice.

   5. *Evaluation.* It is obviously important for teachers to determine if the students in the classroom have learned some knowledge, skill, or attitude as a result of instruction. In this last stage of the instructional task, the teacher returns to the learning objectives that were framed to focus and guide the lesson. Were the objectives fulfilled? Teachers have a variety of means to evaluate students' learning. Among them are formal examinations or tests, teacher observation of performance, and student demonstration of a skill or operation. In the evaluation process, teachers should be sensitive both to the learning of the overtly stated objectives and to the more subtle concomitant learning that may occur. For example, learning to share books or playthings is important concomitant learning in the kindergarten and primary grades. The acquiring of social skills and using democratic decision-making processes are desired concomitant learnings throughout school.

   Evaluation is meant not only for students but also for teachers. The teacher should be prepared to use student performance outcomes as a guide to revising instructional objectives and instruction.

   In addition to instructional responsibilities, teachers have a number of other related roles to play in the school system. For example, the teacher often is an informal counselor and academic advisor to students. The teacher may be assigned to perform certain administrative and supervisory tasks and to participate on curriculum committees. Because they have direct responsibility for instruction, teachers also become public-relations persons for the school district as they meet with parents and other community members. The following sections explore the noninstructional roles that teachers exercise in the school system.

Teachers' Noninstructional Role in the School System

The Teacher as Counselor   In addition to the immediate role of instructing children, the teacher who truly knows his or her students becomes a person who assists their learning, growth, and development as individuals and as members of society. Students not only have a cognitive side to their personalities; they also have emotional, physical, and social needs. For successful learning to take place, the teacher needs to be aware of the physical condition, mental health, and emotional needs of his or her students. Frequently, the gaining of such insights takes the teacher out of the classroom and into the community, for many of the factors affecting a child's learning originate in the home. For example, sickness, illness, or death in the child's family will affect that child's school behavior and learning. Children who have a drug- or alcohol-abuse problem need to be identified and given help. In addition to the serious problems that children face in today's pressure-ridden society, there are always the important but common problems that arise as a child grows and develops: shyness, lack of acceptance in a social group, and peer-group conflicts. To recognize and deal with children's emotional and interpersonal problems, teachers need an academic preparation in educational psychology, human growth and development, and interpersonal relations and communication and also on-site observation of children and experience in working with them prior to teaching.

In dealing with the emotional, psychological, and social problems of children and adolescents, teachers need to establish some guidelines to govern their counseling responsibilities. Probably the most important function that the teacher can exercise is to recognize problems and to know to whom to refer serious problems in the school system. Although it is often tempting for teachers to assume the role of psychiatrist or therapist, that is an inappropriate response. It is inappropriate because teachers may become involved in situations in which they lack professional competence. Most junior high, middle, and high schools have professionally trained counselors on their staff. In many elementary and secondary school systems, the school district employs school psychologists and social workers to deal with severe problems.

The most important aspect of informal counseling that the teacher can exercise is that of being sensitive to children's and adolescent's needs and being available to listen to and talk with them. Teachers have always played the role of a helper in the "growing up" process. They can be an important source of help, advice, and information about how to deal with personal problems, peer-group relations, and career decisions.

Teachers' Role in Administration   In many popular novels and motion pictures about teaching, the hero or heroine is portrayed as a humane and concerned young teacher whose efforts are thwarted by an unfeeling and rigid bureaucratic administration. Although there are examples of heavy-handed school officials sapping the energy and initiative of creative teachers, the reverse is often true. At times, individual teachers neglect to follow the policies and guidelines established to govern the school system to create a functioning educational environment for learners. For any system, it is necessary for its various components to function cooperatively in an atmosphere of mutual support. Just as superintendents, principals, and department chairpersons are responsible for allocating instructional resources and materials, teachers have a responsibility to perform certain semiadministrative tasks that the system requires. For instruction to take place, it is important that these delegated administrative tasks do not overwhelm teachers and prevent them from performing their primary function, however.

The following are some of the semiadministrative tasks that teachers may be called upon to perform within the school system:

1. Maintaining and completing records for the students assigned to his or her class
2. Ordering instructional materials, films, tapes, and other classroom aids
3. Maintaining accurate daily attendance records (state aid formulas are based on the average daily student attendance)
4. Developing and maintaining an accurate reporting system of students' academic progress
5. Adding health data, test scores, grades, and other necessary information to the students' cumulative file

While the paperwork may not seem related directly to day-to-day instruction, it is needed to record the child's educational progress as well as for legal and administrative purposes. Just imagine how difficult it would be for the teacher to "get to know" the children in her or his classroom if their previous teachers had not provided information relating to their learning readiness, academic progress, and special problems.

The Teacher as Curriculum Maker

The curriculum — its content, activities, and experiences — constitute the heart of the school's learning process. In terms of the formal school structure, the school board approves the curriculum that is presented to it by the superintendent. The superintendent, in turn, arrives at his or her curricular recommendations through the combined efforts of the curriculum specialists and consultants and the advice of the classroom teachers. Once a curriculum is approved, it is expected that teachers will implement it in the instruction they provide to students.

The preceding is a brief and formal statement of the curriculum adoption and implementation process; it tells only part of the story of curriculum making. Much of the important work is often done by teachers in curriculum committees that examine and revise existing instructional programs or develop new ones. These committees also identify and recommend the textbooks, materials, and learning resources needed to implement the instructional programs that are approved by the school board.

Service on a curriculum committee for the school district can be challenging, exciting, time-consuming, and occasionally frustrating. Such service assumes as a prerequisite that the teacher has acquired in her or his professional preparation and ongoing experience a general knowledge of the nature and organization of the curriculum and of the particular subject or grade level that she or he is teaching. The following represents questions that teachers assigned to curriculum committees need to consider:

> **The Curriculum Committee Process**
> 1. *A Review of the General Curriculum*
>   What is the general nature of the curriculum?
>   What is the particular curriculum that exists in the school district?
> 2. *The Particular Subject or Skill*
>   What is the particular subject or skill that is being reviewed by the committee?
>   What grade level?
>   What is the subject's or skill's sequence?
>   How does it relate to preceding and subsequent grade levels, courses, or units?
> 3. *Students*
>   Who are the students who will receive instruction in the subject or skill?
>   What is their age range, ability, and grade level?
>   What is their previous educational experience in this subject and skill or in related subjects or skills?
> 4. *Availability of Materials*
>   What materials are available in the subject or skill in terms of textbooks, workbooks, and audiovisual materials?
>   What materials are suited best to the curricular philosophy of the school district, its students, and its staff?

What is the expected cost of the materials?

5. *Teachers*

What are the particular strengths and weaknesses of the professional staff in instruction in the particular subject or skill?

What are the staff preferences and professional judgments about the particular curricular area under consideration?

What in-service training will be needed should a given program be adopted?

The curriculum committee is generally composed of teachers in the field under review, curriculum consultants and specialists, and often an administrator from the central office staff. As the committee meets, it investigates, researches, and discusses the curricular area under review. During the review process, the teacher involved will need to consider and often reconcile differing perspectives among the committee members. Such a sharing of professional opinion contributes to the individual teacher's professional growth, self-knowledge, and knowledge of colleagues. Once the committee has completed its report, it is reviewed by the superintendent, who suggests modifications, if necessary, before presenting it to the board of education for action. At this point, members of the curriculum committee may appear before the board of education to provide further information or to explain its recommendations. As can be seen, the teacher's role as a curriculum maker relates to the school system as a whole.

The following are some of the ways in which teachers can be effective spokespersons for the school system:

1. Become familiar with the community the school serves. Know its racial, ethnic, social, and economic composition so that you can relate to and listen to parents and other community members.
2. Attend meetings of the Parent–Teacher Association (PTA) or Parent–Teacher Organization (PTO) and work to build constructive relationships with their members.
3. Develop a systematic but informal means of communicating with parents about their children's progress through notes or brief messages that tell about the child's progress and achievements, as well as problems.
4. Be aware of your own social, economic, ethnic, racial, and class biases and do not let them prevent you from relating to the community and the children you serve.

Other Staff Members

The superintendent, building principals, and teachers are key members of the school system. There are other members of the school system who exercise important supportive roles to those key members. Some of these positions are identified now. The size of the particular school district determines how many of these significant others will be present in the system. It is useful for prospective teachers to have an idea of the role and function of these staff colleagues. Figure 18–3 illustrates the percentage of teachers to other staff and shows how staffing has changed in the recent past.

Counselors

School counselors are found in most secondary schools, in both junior and senior high schools. Less frequently, counselors are members of the professional staff of

FIGURE 18–3   Classroom Teachers as a Proportion of Total
Public School Staff, Selected School Years
(Ending 1960, 1970, 1981, and 1985–1988)

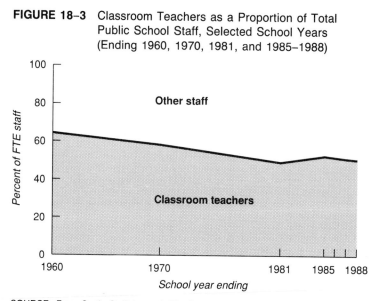

SOURCE: From Curtis O. Baker, ed. *The Condition of Education 1989* (Washington,
D.C.: U.S. Government Printing Office, 1989), p. 41.

elementary schools. Unlike the classroom teacher, who is usually instructing groups
of students, the school counselor works with the individual student on a variety of
matters, ranging from career choice and academic decision making to solving
personal and behavioral problems:

1. Providing information and guidance about careers, vocations, and colleges
2. Providing advice about elective courses
3. Listening to and helping students to deal with parental, peer-group or teacher-related
   problems
4. Listening to and helping students to recognize and cope with a range of emotional,
   psychological, or behavioral problems

Often the school counselor is the member of the school staff to whom teachers
refer students who have persistent and serious behavior problems that lead to
violations of classroom discipline. While counselors seek to alleviate immediate
discipline problems, they also work toward long-range solutions to these problems.
The school counselor, usually an experienced teacher who has a master's degree in
school guidance and counseling, needs to have a background in educational and
counseling psychology and possess a wide repertoire of counseling skills and techniques. When the counselor identifies a student with a severe emotional or psychological problem, the student should be referred to an appropriate specialist, such as
a clinical psychologist or psychiatrist.

School Psychologist

In recent years, school psychologists have joined the staffs of many school districts,
especially those of intermediate or large size. Usually assigned to the central office

staff, school psychologists have a districtwide assignment rather than a location within a single school. The school psychologist's role in the school district is to provide psychological diagnoses of students. The functions performed by the school psychologist include the following:

1. Administration and interpretation of tests used in assessing intelligence and identification of students for gifted, mentally retarded, and educationally handicapped programs.
2. Diagnosing students' emotional or psychological problems and suggesting remediation and therapy for these problems.
3. Preparing diagnostic profiles for students requiring special assistance or remedial work. Although some school psychologists are experienced classroom teachers, many are not. They frequently hold a master's or a doctoral degree in psychology.

School Social Worker

The school social worker, who possesses a master's degree in school social work, works closely with staff members who are responsible for guidance and student personnel services within the school district. Specifically, the school social worker, who works cooperatively with counselors and the school psychologist, is frequently involved in case work with parents and students at the home and family level. For example, if it seems that home factors or conditions are causing a student's problems, the school counselor or psychologist will refer the matter to the school social worker. The social worker then arranges to visit the home and seeks to work closely with family members to resolve the problem.

School Librarian

Over recent decades, the functions of the school librarian have been enlarged and expanded in most school districts. Whereas in the past, the school librarian was in charge of identifying, ordering, and cataloguing books, periodicals, and other printed materials, the modern librarian's assignment has become more complex as libraries have been converted into learning resource centers, with tapes, filmstrips, cassettes, tape recorders, computers, learning machines, and programmed learning materials that can be used independently by students. As a learning resource center specialist, the librarian both provides materials and helps students to learn to use these resources in independent study. The school librarian also serves as a resource person for teachers who may need books, periodicals, and other materials in developing their instructional plans and to supplement in-class textbooks and materials.

The school librarian, or learning resource director, is usually certified, with training in research, organizing and using reference materials, and organizing card catalogues and library collections. The school librarian is an important participant in the school system and its staff because the learning resources that he or she provides are a necessary support and supplement of classroom instruction.

Curriculum Specialists and Consultants

In districts that range from intermediate to large, curriculum specialists are generally employed. While attached to the central office, they also provide specialized service to the various schools in the district. Depending upon the particular practice in the district, curriculum specialists have the following designations: curriculum coordinator, curriculum director, or curriculum consultant. Depending on the size and complexity of the school district, curriculum specialists may have the following assignments at various grade levels or subject matters or a combination of both factors:

> *Specialists for curriculum at grade levels*, such as director of primary education, director of intermediate education, director of junior high school education, director of senior high school education
>
> *Subject matter curriculum specialists*, such as consultants for social studies, mathematics, reading, science, language arts, music, physical education, art, and so on

The number and the function of curriculum specialists vary greatly from school district to school district. The district's size and its financial ability to support a staff of specialists are key factors in determining the number of curriculum specialists. In very small districts, curriculum review and development may be assigned to the superintendent. In medium-sized districts, an assistant superintendent may be assigned to curricular matters. In small districts, certain experienced classroom teachers may be given reduced teaching loads to serve as curriculum consultants. In large urban districts, a large department of curriculum specialists may work at reviewing, designing, and constructing the district's curriculum.

The following are activities carried out by curriculum specialists:

1. Reviewing, redesigning, and constructing the curriculum in cooperation with central office administrators and teachers' curriculum committees
2. Visiting schools to supplement or advise teachers in particular curricular areas
3. Planning institute days and in-service workshops for teachers in particular curricular areas

Within the school system, curriculum specialists play an advisory and consultative role for administrators and teachers. Curriculum specialists are typically experienced teachers who have earned advanced degrees, masters or doctorates, in curriculum, often with a specialization in a particular subject matter.

Media Specialists

Intermediate and large school districts often employ media specialists, who are trained in the educational uses of various kinds of media, such as television, motion pictures, audiovisuals, filmstrips, overhead projectors, record players, transparency makers, cameras, photocopy machines, and other instructional "hardware." Many districts have discovered that it is more efficient to provide a central location for the storage of hardware when it is not in use or is being repaired and to allocate particular items to schools on the basis of need and frequency of use. The functions performed by media specialists include these:

1. Identify and advise the administration on the hardware that should be purchased to augment district instructional programs.
2. Assist teachers in using media by providing in-service training sessions and demonstrations.

3. Organize, catalogue, and maintain equipment. In small school districts that cannot afford to employ a media specialist, this work often falls on the building principals or teachers as a special assignment. This sort of arrangement often causes problems in coordinating the use of media and in maintaining equipment with the result that it sometimes goes unused. To overcome these problems, small districts have joined together to employ a specialist to provide services for the various affiliated districts.

Regardless of the availability of a media specialist, it is important that classroom teachers be aware of, know how to operate, and can integrate media instruction. Since the advent of television, educators have used increasingly multimedia aids to enhance instruction. The media specialist performs services that, like those of the librarian, complement and support the classroom teacher's work.

School Nurse

The school nurse, a health care professional, is found in many elementary and secondary schools. Although schools provide limited health service to students, the primary responsibility for health care remains with parents. The school nurse usually administers hearing and vision tests at regular intervals. He or she also is alert to observing symptoms of contagious diseases or problems of a physical nature among students. In cases of emergency or illness at school, the school nurse performs such duties as taking students' temperatures, cleansing wounds, and giving first aid. The school nurse generally has an office or station in which students who are ill may rest until they recuperate, are taken home, or are attended by a physician.

The kinds of services that a school nurse can provide are defined by law and often by school district policies. Districts have developed specific guidelines and regulations governing the school nurse's activities to avoid litigation and legal suits. Generally, the school nurse may not dispense medications to students unless directed to do so by a physician, with the express consent of parents.

The school nurse provides educational as well as health care services. She or he may give instruction on hygiene and health education to students and may serve as a resource person to teachers who are providing instruction in these areas.

Paraprofessionals

The paraprofessional, also often referred to as a teacher aide or assistant, assists teachers in performing routine work and clerical tasks or provides tutorial instruction to individuals or small groups. This assistance enables the teacher to concentrate on the major phases of instruction. The tasks performed by paraprofessionals include the following:

1. Readying instructional materials for use by the teacher and students.
2. Assisting teachers in using audiovisual equipment.
3. Serving as an assistant in art, science, vocational, or home arts and other subjects involving laboratory work.
4. Assisting the teacher in working with children who may have learning deficits in reading, mathematics, and other subjects where individual instruction is of special help.
5. Assisting on field trips.

6. Assisting teachers with examinations and in record keeping.
7. Serving as supervisors in libraries, cafeterias, playgrounds, and hallways.

The qualifications for paraprofessionals vary from state to state and from district to district within a state. In some districts, the aides hired may be parents or others who assist on a part-time basis. Other districts employ only those who have had two years of college and some work in professional education.

Support Staff

A school system, as with any other system, depends on the support services of individuals who are not charged directly with the primary function of the system. Without their efforts, however, the system would not be able to function. Among members of the support staff are clerical, food service, custodial and maintenance, and security personnel.

Clerical personnel include secretaries, receptionists, clerks, and typists who prepare reports, make arrangements, handle appointments and schedules, and attend to the other office details. Within a school system, clerical personnel are found in a variety of offices, such as the central office.

The principal's secretary is one of the key persons in managing the noninstructional side of the school. An efficient secretary is indispensable to a principal in operating a well-run school. Among the tasks performed by the principal's secretary are serving as an office manager, organizing and maintaining school records, scheduling appointments and meetings, ordering supplies and materials, preparing reports, and answering the questions of teachers and parents.

Food service personnel staff the cafeteria, plan menus, prepare food, and serve meals to students and teachers. Some large districts employ a chief dietician or director of food services who coordinates the activities of the division. Because the .school curriculum emphasizes the importance of a healthy and well-balanced diet, it is important that the food served in the school cafeteria meet the standards stressed in instruction. Attention needs to be paid to providing students with nutritious and balanced meals, particularly in the current era of "fast food" and "junk food."

Food service patterns vary. Despite the general trend for school districts to provide hot meals to students, some small districts merely provide a place for students to eat a sack lunch brought from home. In larger school districts, food is often prepared in a central location and is then distributed to cafeterias in the various schools in the district. Another recent trend is for the school district to contract with commercial food service corporations that prepare food for students.

Custodial and maintenance personnel are key persons in doing the housekeeping, cleaning, and repair work that is vital to keeping a school in operation. An attractive and well-maintained school presents not only a pleasing appearance to the public but is also important to the comfort of students, teachers, and staff members. Often, custodial work and maintenance is taken for granted until a problem occurs, such as a leaking roof, a breakdown of the heating plant, or a failure of the electrical system. When these events take place, little or no instruction can occur until damage is repaired. A good deal of the board of education's time and the taxpayer's money are spent on building or maintaining facilities. Once again, the size of the district determines the number and specialization of maintenance and custodial workers. In the small school district, the school custodian may be a "jack-of-all-trades" whose singular efforts keep the building in operating condition. Large school districts may employ a range of custodial and maintenance personnel, such as carpenters, electricians, plumbers, painters, heating and ventilation experts, and gardeners.

Security personnel are a recent addition to the school system. In the past several decades, violence and vandalism have plagued school systems, particularly those in large urban areas. Certain schools have had epidemics of gang warfare, and other schools have had isolated break-ins in which property has been stolen or damaged. Violence in schools is a serious and debilitating force that erodes public confidence and creates severe stress and anxiety for administrators, teachers, and students. An environment in which persons fear for their safety is not a place in which teachers can teach and students can learn. Of the various threats to academic freedom, violence is one of the most pernicious. Vandalism, too, has weakened schools in recent decades. Money that could be spent on teachers, books, and instructional materials has been diverted to repairing the damage to buildings and facilities. Large-city school systems have spent considerable sums on the continual task of replacing broken windows that are smashed not by the occasional baseball, but by vandals.

To offset violence and vandalism, some school systems have employed security forces, off-duty police officers, and nighttime guards. When security personnel are added to the school staff, it is important that school board policy be framed carefully to specify their duties and responsibilities. It is equally important that security personnel not intrude on the instructional and educational environment of the school and that they be trained to perform their responsibilities without infringing upon the privacy and rights of either teachers or students. On the other hand, unless the tendency to violence and vandalism ends, more school districts are likely to use security persons to "police" schools so that violent persons are not allowed to destroy the school as an environment for teaching and learning.

Effective Schools

The current educational reform climate has focused attention on strategies designed to create and sustain effective schools. Indeed, all of the members of the school staff—superintendent, principals, teachers, and support persons—have as their mission the efficient use of resources to achieve the effective education of students. Educational research has determined that schools with the highest student academic achievement and morale are characterized by (1) strong and vigorous educational leadership, (2) principals whose decisions are made clearly, consistently, and objectively, (3) a safe and orderly learning environment with clearly defined and consistent discipline policies and practices, (4) instructional practices and a curriculum that emphasize basic academic skills and achievement, (5) a teaching staff that works cooperatively as an instructional team and that holds high achievement expectations for their students, and (6) established processes for the frequent and consistent review and assessment of student progress.[10]

To achieve effective education, the school system and its staff need to establish and implement priorities that focus on achieving academic excellence. As the policy-making authority for the school district, the board of education should formulate a working philosophy and clearly defined policies to emphasize academic achievement. To make the implementation of the general policies possible, the board of education must also ensure that financial resources are used effectively.

As the educational leader of the school district, the superintendent needs to make sure that district policies are known, understood, and implemented by building principals. Effective principals implement policies and encourage teacher initiatives that contribute to an orderly learning environment that supports and rewards effective instruction.

Teachers, in effective school systems, avoid the isolation that traditionally comes from working within the self-contained classroom or within the particular subject matter specialty. Isolation weakens instructional effectiveness because it reduces the collegial sharing of ideas, methods, materials, problems, and experiences. Effective schools exhibit high teacher morale and a sense of shared responsibility for the success or failure of the instructional program. A climate of teacher collegiality, characterized by faculty interaction and communication, contributes an element of mutual support that reduces isolation and fosters both instructional effectiveness and a humane learning environment.

Students, in effective school systems, know that their teachers have high academic and personal expectations for them as individuals and that they do not assign them to impersonal categories. High expectations and their achievement are related to fair, objective, and consistent discipline policies that create the order in the school that is necessary for instruction and learning to take place. Effective discipline policies that cultivate an academic learning environment encourage regular attendance, respect for self, fellow students, and teachers, and the recognition that academic achievement is the primary mission of the school. Effective discipline policies have been identified as (1) reflecting community values, (2) having been shaped by all members of the school community, (3) clearly defining acceptable and unacceptable behavior and its consequences, and (4) being administered fairly and consistently.[11]

Conclusion

This chapter has identified the key persons involved in staffing a school system. It is important that prospective teachers have the information to define their own job requirements and responsibilities in relationship to the other professionals in the school system. Teachers do not work in isolation; they are members of a staff that is

10. *What Works: Research About Teaching and Learning*, p. 45. See also R. Kyle, ed. *Reaching for Excellence: An Effective Schools Sourcebook* (Washington, D.C.: U.S. Government Printing Office, 1985), pp. 39–53, 71–97.
11. *What Works: Research About Teaching and Learning*, p. 47.

engaged in the common purpose of educating students. To fulfill this major function, they need to unite their efforts with those of their co-workers.

DISCUSSION QUESTIONS

1. Describe the role and functions of the district superintendent of schools.
2. Distinguish between line and staff authority in a school system.
3. Describe the functions of a school district central office.
4. Describe the role and functions of a school building principal.
5. Analyze the teacher's role and functions in the school system.
6. Define the role and functions of the following members of the school system: counselor, school psychologist, school social worker, librarian, curriculum specialist, media specialist, school nurse.
7. Identify the functions of the paraprofessional.

FIELD EXERCISES

1. Invite a superintendent of schools to visit your class to describe his or her functions in the school system.
2. Invite a building principal to visit your class to discuss his or her work with the building staff and students.
3. Invite the following members of a school system to visit your class to discuss their roles and functions with you: counselor, school psychologist, school social worker, librarian, curriculum specialist, media specialist, school nurse.
4. Invite several elementary or secondary students to visit your class to discuss their relationship to the school system.
5. Visit an elementary or secondary school; identify the various members of the school system and observe their functions.
6. Invite a professor of school administration to visit your class to discuss the characteristics of an effective school.

SUGGESTED READINGS

BACHARACH, SAMUEL B. *Education Reform: Making Sense of It All.* Needham Heights, Mass.: Allyn & Bacon, 1990.

BENJAMIN, ROBERT. *Making Schools Work: A Reporter's Journey Through Some of America's Most Remarkable Classrooms.* New York: Continuum, 1981.

BENNETT, KATHLEEN P., AND LECOMPTE, MARGARET D. *How Schools Work: A Sociological Analysis of Education.* New York: Longman, 1990.

BLUMBERG, ARTHUR, AND GREENFIELD, WILLIAM. *The Effective Principal: Perspective on School Leadership.* Needham Heights, Mass.: Allyn & Bacon, 1986.

CAMPBELL, ROALD F., CUNNINGHAM, LUVERN L., USDAN, MICHAEL D., AND NYSTRAND, RAPHAEL O. *The Organization and Control of Schools,* 4th ed. Columbus, Ohio: Charles E. Merrill, 1980.

CLEMMER, ELWIN F. *The School Policy Handbook: A Primer for Administrators and School Board Members.* Needham Heights, Mass.: Allyn & Bacon, 1991.

COPPOCK, NAN, AND TEMPLETON, IAN. *Paraprofessionals.* Arlington, Va.: National Association of Elementary School Principals, 1974.

CUERVO, AMALIA G. *Toward Better and Safer Schools.* Alexandria, Va.: National School Boards Association, 1984.

DEAL, TERRENCE E., AND PETERSON, KENT D. *The Principal's Role in Shaping School Culture.* Washington, D.C.: U.S. Government Printing Office, 1990.

GOODLAD, JOHN. *A Place Called School.* New York: McGraw-Hill, 1984.

GUTHRIE, JAMES W., AND REED, RODNEY J. *Educational Administration and Policy: Effective Leadership for American Education.* Englewood Cliffs, N.J.: Prentice-Hall, 1986.

HOSFORD, PHILIP L., ED. *Using What We Know About Teaching.* Alexandria, Va.: Association for Supervision and Curriculum Development, 1984.

JACOBSON, STEPHEN L., AND CONWAY, JAMES A., EDS. *Educational Leadership in an Age of Reform.* New York: Longman, 1990.

LEVIN, HENRY, AND CARNOY, MARTIN. *Schooling and Work in the Democratic State.* Stanford, Calif.: Stanford University Press, 1985.

LORTIE, DAN. *School Teacher: A Sociological Study.* Chicago: University of Chicago Press, 1975.

MORRIS, VAN CLEVE, CROWSON, ROBERT L., PORTER-GEHRIE, CYNTHIA, AND HURWITZ, EMANUEL, JR. *Principals in Action: The Reality of Managing Schools.* Columbus, Ohio: Charles E. Merrill, 1984.

ROSSOW, LAWRENCE F. *The Principalship: Dimensions in Instructional Leadership.* Englewood Cliffs, N.J. Prentice Hall, 1990.

SERGIOVANNI, THOMAS J. *The Principalship: A Reflective Practice Perspective.* Newton, Mass.: Allyn & Bacon, 1987.

SERGIOVANNI, THOMAS J., AND MOORE, JOHN H. *Schooling for Tomorrow: Directing Reform to Issues That Count.* Needham Heights, Mass.: Allyn & Bacon, 1989.

SQUIRES, DAVID A., HUITT, WILLIAM G., AND SEGARS, JOHN K. *Effective Schools and Classrooms: A Research-Based Perspective.* Alexandria, Va.: Association for Supervision and Curriculum Development, 1983.

TYACK, DAVID B. *The One Best System: A History of American Urban Education.* Cambridge, Mass.: Harvard University Press, 1974.

UBBEN, GERALD C., AND HUGHES, LARRY W. *The Principal: Creative Leadership for Effective Schools.* Newton, Mass.: Allyn & Bacon, 1987.

WALKER, STEPHEN. *Changing Policies, Changing Teachers: New Directions for Schooling.* New York: Taylor and Francis, 1987.

What Works: Research About Teaching and Learning. Washington, D.C.: U.S. Department of Education, 1986.

_19_
Curriculum and Instruction

Chapter 19 identifies and describes the major instructional areas found in American schools. Specifically, it deals with the skills and subjects that you may be preparing to teach as a prospective elementary or secondary teacher. In reading this chapter, you should focus attention on the following questions:

1. What are the major components of the elementary and secondary school curriculum?
2. What are some recent curricular trends?
3. What is the relationship between curricular and co-curricular activities?
4. How do teachers function as curriculum decision makers?

Language Arts and English

Most generally, language arts are designed to assist children to become literate, to communicate effectively, and to appreciate literature. In the contemporary elementary school, language arts are fused into an integrated core that interrelates the various language skills rather than treats them in isolation as was frequently done in the past. The elementary language arts curriculum seeks to develop the essential modes of communication of speaking, listening, reading, and writing. It is generally agreed that the elementary school program in language arts should provide

1. Systematic instruction in listening necessary for both academic success and effective lifelong communication.
2. Instruction and opportunities for effective speaking to enable students to express and to share ideas and experiences.
3. An introduction to the structures and patterns of the English language.
4. Experiences to develop both functional and creative writing skills.
5. Opportunities to become familiar with and to use basic research tools such as libraries, dictionaries, encyclopedias, and reference books.
6. An introduction to literature and poetry that develops a critical sensitivity and sense of appreciation.[1]

1. William W. Joyce, Robert G. Oana, and W. Robert Houston, *Elementary Education in the Seventies; Implications for Theory and Practice* (New York: Holt, Rinehart and Winston, 1970), pp. 367–368.

The language arts program in the elementary school prepares students for and leads them to the high school English curriculum. It also develops the ability to locate, read, and use printed information needed for academic, economic, and social success both as a student and as an adult. The skills acquired in the language arts curriculum are highly related to developing competency in all the other areas of the curriculum. A well-developed elementary school language arts program and high school English program should provide experiences appropriate to the learners' readiness and interests at a given stage of development and also prepare them for the next higher level of instruction. This means that there must be articulation, planning, and coordination among grade levels within a school and among the elementary, junior, and senior high schools.

The outline that follows identifies the skills and subjects usually found as areas of instruction at the elementary and junior and senior high school levels. As you examine this outline, notice how the skills and subjects in the elementary school lead to and relate to those at the secondary level.

Elementary School Language Arts Curriculum
(typically grades kindergarten through six)

The skills and subjects are taught as an integrated core and generally are not separated into specific subject matters.

> Listening and oral communication skills
> Reading: word recognition, oral reading, silent reading, narrative and expository reading
> Handwriting: Printing in primary grades and cursive in intermediate grades
> Spelling: integrated with reading and writing
> Composition: sentence building, capitalization, punctuation, expository creative writing
> Literature: integrated with reading, introduction to basic literary forms such as stories, myths, plays
> Research skills: use of libraries and reference sources such as dictionaries and encyclopedias

Junior High School Language Arts Curriculum
(typically grades seven and eight; a middle school may also include grade six)

The skills and subjects of the junior high or middle school language arts curriculum are transitional between the elementary and senior high school. They continue the skill development begun in the elementary grades and prepare students for the more specialized and departmentalized high school program.

> Reading: emphasis on either remedial or accelerated reading, depending on needs of student
> Speech and dramatics: introduction to forms and style of speech such as discussion and debate

Literature: further elaboration of literary themes and types. Emphasis on appreciation of literature
Writing: more extensive report, research, narrative, and creative writing
Grammar: structure of the English language
Research skills: further experience in using reference sources

High School Curriculum
(typically grades nine, ten, eleven, and twelve, although variations exist)

The high school English curriculum is more specialized than the elementary school language arts curriculum. It is organized into subject matter courses. In general, there is a continuing emphasis on grammar, writing, and literature. The courses offered include the following:

Basic and remedial English
American, English, and world literatures
Business English
Composition
Journalism
Creative writing
Speech
Drama
Radio and television scriptwriting and broadcasting

Reading

In defining reading as "the process of constructing meaning from written texts," the Commission on Reading calls it a "complex skill" requiring "coordination of a number of interrelated sources of information." The commission described skilled reading as

1. A "constructive process" in which readers integrate new knowledge from the text with that they already possess.
2. A fluent process in which readers construct meaning by decoding words "quickly and accurately."
3. A process in which readers use a strategy of flexible skills.
4. A process stimulated by the reader's motivation and recognition that reading is informative and interesting.
5. A "life long pursuit" that improves with use.[2]

It has long been recognized that good reading skills are needed for both academic achievement and success in life. Throughout history, primary or elementary schooling has stressed reading and writing, and recent trends have not lessened

---

2. R. C. Anderson, E. H. Heibert, E. H. Scott, and I. A. Wilkinson, *Becoming a Nation of Readers: The Report of the Commission on Reading* (1985), as cited in Marilyn R. Binkley, *Becoming a Nation of Readers: Implications for Teachers* (Washington, D.C.: U.S. Department of Education, 1986), pp. 3–4.

This photograph of a school scene from the 1940s illustrates the continuing importance of reading.

this emphasis. Both professional educators and the public have recognized that the United States has a national reading problem. According to the National Commission on Excellence in Education, approximately 13 percent of all 17-year-olds in the United States can be considered to be functionally illiterate. The commission also estimates that 23 million adults are functionally illiterate.[3] Reading improvement programs range from those initiated by local school districts to the federally funded National Reading Improvement Program. Figure 19–1 illustrates reading proficiency scores by race and ethnicity at selected grade levels.

Reading instruction has long been controversial. In the United States, reading experts are divided between advocates of phonics, in which students associate the spoken sounds of letters with printed symbols, and the "look-say" method, in which students recognize whole words through association with pictures, context clues, or intuition. Some reading programs combine both phonics and word recognition.

Psycholinguistic research into the teaching of reading argues that reading is a holistic process.[4] Focusing on establishing meaning, the reading act involves predict-

3. The National Commission on Excellence in Education, *A Nation at Risk: The Imperative for Educational Reform* (Washington, D.C.: U.S. Department of Education, 1983), p. 8.

4. Bernice J. Wolfson, "Psychological Theory and Curricular Thinking," in Alex Molnar, ed., *Current Thought on Curriculum: 1985 ASCD Yearbook* (Washington, D.C.: Association for Supervision and Curriculum Development, 1985), pp. 63–64.

FIGURE 19–1   Average Reading Proficiency, by Race and
Ethnicity: 1986

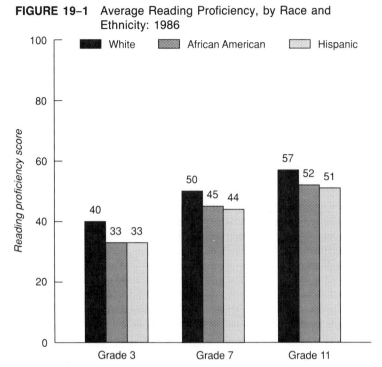

SOURCE: From Curtis O. Baker, ed. *The Condition of Education 1989* (Washington,
D.C.: U.S. Government Printing Office, 1989), p. 9.

NOTE: The range of the reading proficiency scale was from 0 to 100. The average
scores by grade were 38.1 for grade 3, 48.9 for grade 7, and 56.1 for grade 11.

ing and verifying the text. A psycholinguistic approach to reading involves *semantics*
to establish the meaning of the text, *syntax* to discern language patterns, and
phonetics to use speech sounds as a means of textual deciphering. Rather than
reducing reading instruction into separate skill activities, the psycholinguistic perspective takes an integrative approach.

In the past decade, many developments have occurred in reading instruction.
For example, more sophisticated techniques have been developed to identify, diagnose, and remedy reading problems that result from physical or psychological
disabilities. School districts employ reading specialists to assist classroom teachers in
dealing with reading problems. Several of the states have also increased the course
preparation in reading methods for both elementary and secondary school teachers.

Recent research on teaching reading emphasizes the need for a carefully
articulated program of instruction. Parent and kindergarten components should
emphasize reading readiness activities that build on oral language. Such activities
include

1. Reading aloud to children for entertainment and also to develop comprehension skills
   on how language is used and how stories are structured.
2. Having the class as a group create collaborative stories that are recorded.
3. Providing daily individual writing experiences that link writing and reading.

4. Providing an immersion in print through books and magazines.
5. Providing thoughtful discussion of events in children's lives.[5]

In beginning reading instruction, phonics should be systematically emphasized as an instructional strategy. Phonics should be related to the meaning of text and not used as an isolated skill, however. Phonics and comprehension skills can be developed in directed reading lessons, stressed in the primary grades. The directed reading lesson has three stages:

1. *Preparation:* The teachers and students discuss vocabulary and background information related to the story.
2. *Reading:* Students read the selection, which may be subdivided into smaller segments, each section of which is "preceded and succeeded by discussion, questions, or both."
3. *Discussion:* By responding to the teacher's questions, students review the entire story and extract its implications.[6]

Recent Perspectives on English Education

Language arts and English remain a crucial component in the American school curriculum. The national reports on education reform universally emphasized the centrality of language learning to success in other curricular subjects. In *A Nation at Risk*, the National Commission on Excellence in Education, in recommending that four years of English be required of all high school students, stated:

> The teaching of English in high school should equip graduates to: (a) comprehend, interpret, evaluate, and use what they read; (b) write well-organized, effective papers; (c) listen effectively and discuss ideas intelligently; and (d) know our literary heritage and how it enhances imagination and ethical understanding, and how it relates to the customs, and ideas, of today's life and culture.[7]

In *High School: A Report on Secondary Education in America*, sponsored by the Carnegie Foundation, Ernest Boyer, recognizing language as the first priority, recommended that high schools help all students to develop critical thinking and effective communication skills through the written and spoken word.

In discussing literacy and language as essential learning tools, Boyer developed an articulate set of recommendations that linked the elementary and secondary school curricula. He recommended that elementary school instruction in language arts should (1) build on the children's "own language experience" and "build confidence" by actively involving them in "writing and reading their own thoughts," (2) equip students to read and comprehend the main ideas of a written work and to use "standard English sentences with correct structure, verb forms, punctuation, word choices and spelling," and (3) equip students to organize their thoughts around a topic.[8]

---

5. Binkley, *Becoming a Nation of Readers*, pp. 5–6.
6. Ibid., p. 11.
7. The National Commission on Excellence in Education, *A Nation at Risk*, p. 25.
8. Ernest L. Boyer, *High School: A Report on Secondary Education in America* (New York: Harper & Row, 1983), pp. 86–87.

So that language learning is continuous between elementary and secondary schooling, Boyer urged that each student's language development be monitored and documented. Students who needed remedial work were to receive it rather than being promoted for social reasons.

English language instruction in the high school, Boyer insisted, should develop competencies of clear written expression, reading with improved comprehension, listening with discrimination, speaking precisely, and being skilled in the application of knowledge. To develop these competencies, a basic English course, with emphasis on writing, should be required of all freshmen students.[9]

Mathematics

Mathematics instruction seeks to develop an awareness of arithmetical and computational relationships in a logical manner. Mathematics instruction and materials should integrate understanding, computation, and application. A basic goal of mathematics instruction is to develop facility in the four basic arithmetical operations—addition, subtraction, multiplication, and division—and to cultivate an understanding of their interrelatedness.[10]

Mathematics at the elementary level of instruction seeks to achieve the following general objectives: (1) to develop readiness for mathematics, followed by concept acquisition and the development of computational procedures and problem-solving skills, (2) to provide practice whereby children learn to estimate and compute with accuracy, and (3) to develop a mathematical sensitivity that can be a basis for further study. The mathematics curriculum follows careful sequencing so that the skills and knowledge acquired by students are cumulative. Throughout the various levels of the curriculum, problem-solving skills and logical thinking should be emphasized.

Elementary School Mathematics Curriculum
(typically grades kindergarten through six)

The following listing of units is an example of program sequencing in the elementary school mathematics curriculum:

> Counting and developing facility with the real number system
> Experiences with grouping to establish the concept of place value numerals
> Developing the concepts of set, set membership, and set combinations
> Developing the concept of inequalities and the symbols > and <
> Developing basic skills of addition, subtraction, multiplication, and division
> Using fractions and decimals
> Measuring units: length, area, volume, weight, time, money, and temperature

9. Ibid., pp. 89–90.
10. Calhoun, C. Collier and Harold H. Lerch, *Teaching Mathematics in the Modern Elementary School* (New York: Macmillan, 1969).

Developing skills of estimation and approximation
Introduction to simple algebra and geometry

Junior High School Mathematics Curriculum
(typically grades seven and eight; a middle school may also include grade six)

The junior high school mathematics curriculum is transitional between the elementary and the high school programs in that it develops skills begun at the lower level and prepares students for more advanced and specialized work at the higher level. Skills and subjects include the following:

General mathematics, with special emphasis on fractions, decimals, percentages, and graphs
Introduction to algebra and geometry

High School Curriculum
(typically grades nine, ten, eleven, and twelve, although variations exist)

The high school mathematics curriculum is more specialized and arranged into separate courses. Most high schools require at least two courses, or credit units, in mathematics. Students may enroll in general mathematics or algebra, which leads to further work in mathematics. The courses offered include the following:

General mathematics: dealing with percentages, ratios, proportions, graphs, insurance, banking, investing, consumer purchasing, and taxation
Algebra: factoring, powers and roots, polynomials, fractional expressions, quadratic equations, and linear equations
Advanced general mathematics
Advanced algebra
Geometry: plane and solid
Trigonometry
Introduction to elementary data analysis and statistics
Computer science and its application

Trends in Mathematics Education

Since the early 1950s, mathematics education has experienced dramatic changes. At that time, scholars in the liberal arts and sciences, education, and engineering devised new mathematics courses and trained teachers in new methods of instruction. By the mid-1950s, "new math" programs were introduced in schools throughout the country. Generally, the "new math" programs stressed the understanding of mathematical concepts and processes through the use of the discovery method. An explicit objective of the "new math" was to have students understand the processes that they were using.

By the late 1960s, a concerted reaction set in as some parents and teachers became disenchanted with the "new math." A generation gap had developed as parents experienced difficulty in relating to their children's work in mathematics.

Critics also charged that an emphasis on abstract reasoning had detracted from learning basic mathematical skills.

The contemporary mathematics curriculum exhibits a synthesis of certain concepts of the new mathematics with some of the more traditional approaches, and with computer applications. A trend has been to introduce topics and techniques from statistics and probability and computer science and programming into the mathematics curriculum.

Attention is being directed to improving mathematics instruction at all grade levels of elementary, middle, and secondary schools. The National Science Board Commission on Precollege Education in Mathematics, Science, and Technology has recommended the following innovations in elementary and middle school mathematics instruction:

1. The introduction of calculators and computers at the earliest practicable grade to enhance the understanding of arithmetic and geometry and provide problem-solving skills
2. Placing more emphasis on developing skills in mental arithmetic, estimation, and approximation and less on paper-and-pencil operations
3. Providing more direct experience in data collection and analysis.[11]

Academic Preparation for College, a report by the College Board, stated that secondary school graduates in college preparatory programs should (1) be able to apply mathematical technique in solving real-life problems, (2) be familiar with the language, notation, and deductive nature of mathematics, (3) be able to express quantitative ideas with precision, (4) be able to use calculators and computers, (5) be familiar with the basic concepts of statistics and statistical reasoning, and (6) have an in-depth and functional knowledge of algebra and geometry.[12]

Science

The modern science curriculum emerged from what was called "natural philosophy" in the early nineteenth century. Today, both a knowledge of scientific concepts and an understanding and ability to use the scientific method are of vital importance in living in a modern, technological civilization. A knowledge and an appreciation of science is not only important as part of the general education of the educated person, but is also of practical necessity in preparing for careers in engineering and the health fields of medicine, nursing, and dentistry. It is generally accepted that the science curriculum should

1. As a part of general education, provide students with an understanding of the natural and physical universe in which they live.
2. Acquaint students with the scientific method of problem solving and provide experience in using that method both in solving science-related and general life problems.

11. Henry O. Pollak, "The Mathematical Sciences Curriculum K–12. What Is Still Fundamental and What Is Not," in National Science Board Commission on Precollege Education in Mathematics, Science, and Technology, *Educating Americans for the 21st Century: Source Materials* (Washington, D.C.: National Science Foundation, 1983), p. 1.
12. The College Board, *Academic Preparation for College: What Students Need to Know and Be Able to Do* (New York: The College Board, 1983), pp. 19–20.

3. Develop both a humanistic and a technical understanding of science as an instrument for dealing with national and world problems, such as environmental pollution, disease, famine, and poverty.

4. Provide knowledge of basic scientific concepts and methods in the various natural and physical sciences, such as botany, biology, chemistry, physics, astronomy, and zoology.

5. Acquaint students with the applications of basic science in the applied sciences and professions, such as engineering, medicine, nursing, and dentistry, as well as other fields.[13]

In the primary and intermediate grades of the elementary school, science is usually taught in an integrated and undifferentiated manner. Elementary science instruction integrates concepts and materials from the biological, earth, and physical sciences. The general emphasis is to create an awareness of the interactions of animal, vegetable, and human life with the environment. Plants and animals are usually used to demonstrate these interrelationships. In the junior high and middle school, the science curriculum generally exhibits greater differentiation into life and earth sciences. The high school science curriculum shows still further differentiation into well-defined subject matter areas, such as biology, botany, chemistry, physics, and astronomy. There are also programs in high school science that represent a fusion of concepts and materials from the various sciences. In various states, the science curriculum at the junior and senior high school levels also includes units on the effects of using tobacco, alcohol, and drugs. The following outline of the science curriculum at the elementary, junior high, and high school levels indicates some of the skills and knowledge areas related to this area of instruction.

Elementary School Science Curriculum
(typically grades kindergarten through six)

Until the 1950s, science instruction at the elementary school level was generally underdeveloped. Since that time, the elementary science curriculum has developed but has also remained integrated and undifferentiated. Among the frequent themes found in elementary science programs are living things, the earth and the universe, energy, and the seasons. Although science programs vary, the following representative units illustrate scope and sequence in elementary science instruction:

> Growing plants, such as beans and peas
> Observing animals in the classroom, such as gerbils, hamsters, fish, and lizards
> Measuring lengths, areas, and volumes
> Observing and recording changes caused by natural processes, such as rusting, melting, molding, and decaying

13. These general objectives of the science curriculum represent the views of the author. Other representative statements of objectives can be found in Paul E. Blackwood, "Science Teaching in the Elementary School: A Survey of Practices," *Journal of Research in Science Teaching*, 3 (September 1965), p. 180; National Science Teachers Association Curriculum Committee, *Theory into Action in Science Curriculum Development* (Washington, D.C.: National Science Teachers Association, 1964); Eugene C. Lee, *New Dimensions in Science Teaching* (Belmont, Calif.: Wadsworth, 1967).

Collecting and classifying rocks and minerals
Using the microscope and other scientific apparatus
Studying electricity and magnetism
Observational astronomy relating to the earth, sun, moon, and other planets
Preparing and collecting gases to discover their properties

Junior High School Science Curriculum
(typically grades seven and eight;
a middle school may also include grade six)

As is true in the case of most junior high school curricula, the science program is transitional between the elementary and high school. In some schools, the science course is called general science; in other schools, it is differentiated into several science areas. The following course listing illustrates the kind of program arrangement found in junior high schools:

General science: a core curriculum that integrates concepts and materials from various sciences
Biological science
Introductory physical science
Life science
Earth science

High School Science Curriculum
(typically grades nine, ten, eleven,
and twelve, although variations exist)

Once again, the secondary school curriculum is differentiated into specific subject matter courses. For example, the following might be found at the high school level:

General science
Biology
Chemistry
Physics
Applied science
Physiology
Geology
Advanced chemistry and physics
Botany
Zoology
Physiology

Trends in Science Education

Since the 1950s, important changes have occurred in science education. New programs were stimulated by the National Science Foundation, a federal agency created "to develop and encourage the pursuit of a national policy for the promotion of basic research and education in the sciences." The foundation encouraged the reorganization of the science curriculum and instruction. Grants from the National Science Foundation and the National Defense Education Act were used for research, institutes, development of materials, and improvement of school and college laboratory facilities.

The reorganization of the science curriculum produced new programs that were styled the "new physics" or the "new chemistry" in imitation of the "new math." These various new scientific programs emphasized the structure of the various sciences by identifying their key, or "necessary," concepts. Through the use of the discovery method, students were to approach their study in the same way that a scientist used the scientific method. The objective was to have students actively involved in the processes and methods of science rather than to be passive memorizers of scientific terminologies and information. The result of these curricular innovations encouraged science instruction to be more process oriented, with much of the learning being laboratory or experimentally based. Those who see these curricular changes in positive terms claim that the process-oriented approach to science instruction has contributed to a more exciting, more unified, and better coordinated program. The criticisms of those who have reservations about the new science programs are similar to the attacks on the "new math." They allege that an overreliance on process has neglected scientific content. They further charge that much of what appears to be an inquiry approach in science is superficial and neglects building a basic foundation that rests on scientific principles.

Science Education Concerns

In the 1980s, numerous commentators agreed that science education was in a state of crisis. Several of the national reports, such as *A Nation at Risk* and *Education for Excellence*, warned of the decline in scientific knowledge and competency among American students. Concern was expressed that, in comparison with other developed nations such as Japan and the Soviet Union, American secondary students enrolled in fewer science courses for a shorter period of time. In addition, the shortage of qualified science and mathematics teachers was a major source of concern.[14]

Many states have responded to the science education crisis by requiring more science units, usually three to four years, for high school graduation.

The education reform climate focused on improving science curricula and instruction. For example, the Conference on Goals for Science and Technology Education recommended "A Revised and Intensified Science and Technology Curriculum" for the elementary and secondary schools. This curriculum was to include (1) a balanced physical and biological science program for grades K–6 that emphasized phenomena in the natural environment and afforded experience in collecting and processing data, (2) emphasis in grades 7–8 on the biological, chemical, and physical aspects of life and the development of quantitative analytical skills, (3) emphasis in grades 9–11 on applying science and technology to the improvement

14. Roger E. Yager and Vincent N. Lunetta, "New Foci for Science Teacher Education," *Journal of Teacher Education*, (November/December 1984), pp. 37–42.

of the local and national community life, and (4) providing options in grades 11–12 for discipline-oriented career preparation courses in science.[15]

In *Academic Preparation for College*, the College Board, like other national commissions, called for an upgrading of the scientific competencies of college-bound high school students. The board recommended four major areas of competency:

> *Fundamental concepts* to provide an in-depth understanding of such unifying concepts from the life and physical sciences as "cell theory, geological evolution, organic evolution, atomic structure, chemical bonding, and transformation of energy"
>
> *Detailed knowledge* of at least one scientific field—biology, chemistry, or physics, or an interdisciplinary approach
>
> *Mathematical skills* to ensure a quantitative understanding of at least one field of science in order to interpret and apply data to scientific problems
>
> *Laboratory and field work* involving experimentation, observation, and the organizing and communication of scientific information.[16]

Innovative Science Programs

In response to the national concern over the quality of instruction in science, several innovative science education programs have been recognized by the National Diffusion Network as exemplary programs. These newly developed programs have originated primarily in actual classroom settings and integrate the learning of scientific concepts and processes in a thematic fashion. They also emphasize the students' direct involvement in using the scientific method of problem solving. New programs that are likely to have an impact on science education in the 1990s include the following.

"Conservation for Children"   This program for grades 1–6, integrated around environmental conservation, emphasizes the "interdependence of plants and animals, requirements of life, energy sources and use, pollution problems, recycling, and other conservation concepts based on scientific principles." Curriculum and instruction in this program combines basic skills in language arts, mathematics, social studies, and science with the conservation concept. The program reflects and provides a scientific basis for dealing with the contemporary problem of environmental pollution.

"Foundational Approaches in Science Teaching" (FAST)   A course for grades 6, 7, and 8 of the junior high and middle school, FAST emphasizes concepts and methods of the biological, physical, and earth sciences in relationship to the environment. The course is organized around three strands—physical science, ecology, and relational study—that students study concurrently. "The physical science strand intro-

---

15. Earle L. Lomon, "A Revised and Intensified Science and Technology Curriculum Grades K–12 Urgently Needed for Our Future," in National Science Board Commission on Precollege Education in Mathematics, Science, and Technology, *Educating Americans for the 21st Century: Source Materials*, p. 35.
16. College Board, *Academic Preparation for College*, pp. 23–24.

duces such concepts as mass, volume, density, buoyancy, physical and chemical properties of matter, pressure, vacuum, heat, temperature and energy; the ecology strand such concepts as ecology, plant and animal growth and development, weather and climate, field mapping and population sampling; the relational study strand such concepts as resource management, technology, environment use, energy use and conservation."

"Hands-On Elementary Science"   Designed for grades 1–5, this program is intended to provide elementary students with direct involvement with scientific processes and problem solving. Science instruction is organized at each grade level around three basic units. In first grade, observation skills are developed by units dealing with seeds, patterns, and magnetism; in second grade, classification skills are developed by units on insects, sinking or floating, and measurement; in third grade, experimentation skills are developed by units on flight, measuring, and plants; in fourth grade, analytical skills are developed by units on biocommunities, electricity, and chemistry; in fifth grade, application skills are developed by units on earth science, soil analysis, and small animals. The development of each skill area brings students to increasingly higher levels of processes appropriate to scientific problem solving.

"Physics — Teach to Learn"   This is a highly innovative physics program designed for secondary school students. It uses teacher-controlled computer stimulations to explore and illustrate selected physics events. The selected events are those most frequently misunderstood by students and the most difficult for teachers to illustrate in the classroom. The computer simulations require the students to make a judgment about each physical event illustrated.[17]

Social Studies

The nature, scope, and sequence of the social studies curriculum have always been difficult to define.[18] Generally, the social studies, or social sciences, encompass the disciplines that explain the interactions of human beings and groups with the social, political, and economic environments. Because the social experience of the human race can be examined from a variety of perspectives, the social studies curriculum embraces a multidisciplinary, interdisciplinary, and even a transdisciplinary approach. Among the problems of definition that social studies educators face are the following:

1. What is the nature of the social studies? How should they be defined?
2. Of the various social sciences, which are most significant for inclusion in the elementary and secondary curriculum?

17. These and other innovative science education programs are described in Mary G. Lewis, *Science Education Programs That Work: A Collection of Proven Exemplary Education Programs and Practices in the National Diffusion Network* (Washington, D.C.: Office of Education Research and Improvement, U.S. Department of Education, 1988), pp. 3, 4, 6, 11.
18. For an effort to define the social studies, see Robert D. Barr, James L. Barth, and S. Samuel Shermis, *Defining the Social Studies* (Washington, D.C.: National Council for the Social Studies, 1977).

3. How should the social studies be organized for program and instructional purposes? What should be the sequence of social studies instruction?

4. What is the appropriate relationship between content and values in the social studies?

A brief historical examination of the evolution of the social studies curriculum illustrates the often-changing definition and rationale of the social studies. In the early nineteenth century, the social studies that emerged as common school subjects were history and geography. History was organized primarily as the study of the American past, with an orientation that was political, military, and literary. At the secondary level, there were courses in ancient and medieval history. By the early twentieth century, history as the dominant social studies subject was represented by courses in American and world history. World history was viewed as the historical experience of the Western European nations, primarily England, France, and Germany. Geography was the standard companion course to history. Instruction usually emphasized the geography of the United States and world regional geography.

By the 1920s, the dominance of history and geography was challenged by other curricular approaches in the social studies. Because social studies were regarded as instruments of building citizenship, civics and American problems courses were introduced that focused on political, economic, and social issues. These courses included materials from political science, economics, and social psychology as well as history and geography. At times, the interdisciplinary approach was referred to as "social education." As new programs evolved, the traditional courses that relied solely on history and geography began to decline.

After World War II, social studies became still more interdisciplinary. Concepts, materials, and strategies from political science, economics, sociology, social psychology, anthropology, and law have been incorporated into the curriculum. In addition, more attention has also been given to international, multicultural, minority, ethnic, African-American, and Hispanic studies. The scope of the social studies has also broadened from an emphasis on American and Western societies to include Asian, African, and Latin American cultures. Since the post-Watergate period, some educators have called on social studies experts to stimulate a renewal of civic education and values. A long-standing controversy in social studies education has been the degree to which this area should reflect social values or seek to change or reconstruct these values.

The Curriculum Task Force of the National Commission on Social Studies has identified the characteristics of the social studies curriculum needed for the twenty-first century. The following characteristics suggest a rationale for organizing the social studies curriculum in the future:

1. The social studies curriculum should develop a "clear understanding of the roles of citizenship in a democracy and provide opportunities for active, engaged participation in civic, cultural, and volunteer activities" that enhance the quality of community and national life.

2. It should provide for "consistent and cumulative learning from kindergarten through 12th grade."

3. While history and geography, which develop "perspectives of time and place," should be the curricular framework, "concepts and understandings from political science, economics, and the other social sciences" should be integrated throughout the social

studies curriculum to provide students with a "firm understanding of their principles and methodologies."

4. "Selective studies of the history, geography, government and economic systems of the major civilizations and societies should together receive attention at least equal to the study of the history, geography, government, economics and society of the United States."

5. Since they provide an "obvious connection between the humanities and the natural and physical sciences, the integration of the social studies with other subjects should be encouraged.

6. Rather than being merely accepted and memorized, content from the social studies should be the means by which open and vital contemporary questions are examined and confronted.[19]

Although the scope and sequence of the social studies curriculum vary greatly across the nation's school systems, the following outline represents some of the topics and units that might be found in the social studies curriculum.

Elementary School Social Studies Curriculum
(typically grades kindergarten through six)

At the elementary level, there is a variation from school district to school district and from state to state in social studies curriculum. The curriculum is highly undifferentiated and includes materials from a number of the social sciences. The general focusing themes found in many elementary social studies programs are the following: From history, what has been the human past? From anthropology, how did human beings become what they are? From economics, how do people earn a living? From sociology, how do people relate to each other? From psychology, why do people behave as they do? From political science, how are people governed? From geography, how do people interact and live in their environment? In answering such thematic questions, elementary social studies programs often include such units or topics as

> Family life
> Home and school
> Neighborhood and community
> Community workers and services
> Concepts of culture, social organizations, and social processes
> Environment, society, and economics
> Political organization and processes
> The American political system: local, state, and federal governments
> American history
> Technology and modernization
> Rural and urban life
> People of other countries

19. National Commission on Social Studies in the Schools, *Charting a Course: Social Studies for the 21st Century* (Washington, D.C.: National Commission on Social Studies in the Schools, 1989), p. 3. For an in-depth assessment of the social studies, see David Jenness, *Making Sense of Social Studies* (New York: Macmillan, 1990).

Junior High School Social Studies Curriculum
(typically grades seven and eight; a middle school may also include grade six)

Although the social studies curriculum is transitional at the junior high school to the elementary and high school, it varies in sequence from school district to school district and from state to state. No definite pattern emerges. The following courses may be found at the junior high level:

> Social studies: a continuation of themes from the elementary school
> World geography: an introduction
> United States history
> Regional studies, such as Latin America, Asia, Europe, Africa
> State and local history (may be required in certain states)

High School Social Studies Curriculum
(typically grades nine, ten, eleven, and twelve, although variations exist)

As is usual at the high school level, the curriculum in social studies becomes more differentiated into specific subjects. Most schools require from one to three courses in social studies, one of which must be in American history. The most frequently offered courses are American history, American government, and economics. Among the courses offered in social studies at the secondary level are the following:

> American history
> World history
> Modern history
> Ancient and medieval history
> Civics
> World geography
> Economics
> American government
> Problems of democracy
> Sociology
> Psychology
> State and local history (may be required in certain states)
> International relations, global education, development education
> Anthropology
> Current events
> Ethnic history
> African-American studies
> Hispanic studies
> Personal development (may incorporate career choices and drug abuse, alcohol abuse, and other state-mandated units)
> Law-related education

Trends in Social Studies

The 1980s witnessed a trend to reemphasize history in the curriculum. Proponents for the revival of history in the curriculum, especially in the high school, included those who warned that American students had become increasingly uninformed about the history of their own country and lacked historical perspective on Western culture and institutions.[20] For an illustration of how high school students responded to history test items, see Table 19–1. The emphasis on history has also been part of the effort to reassert the role of the humanities in American education.[21]

The Bradley Commission on History in the Schools was established in 1987 to examine the inadequacies of history instruction in elementary and secondary schools. In providing a rationale for the revitalization of historical study in the schools, the commission stated that all students should study history, regardless of their academic ability and standing and career plans. The study of history, said the commission, "is vital for all citizens in a democracy, because it provides the only avenue we have to reach an understanding of ourselves and of our society, in relation to the human condition over time, and of how some things change and others continue." The commission further outlined two important aims: (1) using history as the central humanistic discipline for personal growth, and (2) cultivating an "active and intelligent citizenship" that provides a "wide range of models and alternatives for political choice in a complicated world."[22] The Bradley Commission's recommendations included the following:

1. History should be required for all students since the "knowledge and habits of mind" that it cultivates are indispensable for democratic citizenship.
2. "To develop judgment and perspective, historical study must often focus upon broad, significant themes and questions rather than short-lived memorizations of facts without context."
3. Increased curricular and instructional time for historical study is needed in American schools to develop students' genuine understanding and engagement.
4. The kindergarten through sixth grade social studies curriculum should be history centered.
5. Local school districts and states should require at least four years of history during grades 7 through 12.
6. Every student should have an understanding of the history of Africa, the Americas, Asia, and Europe.
7. To develop an understanding of the constituent parts of society, the history of women, racial and ethnic minorities, and people of all classes should be integrated into historical instruction.

20. For the way in which history has been taught in the schools, see Frances FitzGerald, *America Revised: History Schoolbooks in the Twentieth Century* (New York: Vintage Books, 1980).
21. Clair W. Keller, "Improving High School History Teaching," in Chester E. Finn, Jr., Diane Ravitch, and Robert R. Fancher, eds., *Against Mediocrity: The Humanities in America's High Schools* (New York: Holmes & Meier, 1984), pp. 79–91.
22. Bradley Commission on History in Schools, *Building a History Curriculum: Guidelines for Teaching History in Schools* (Washington, D.C.: Educational Excellence Network, 1988), p. 5. Also, see Bradley Commission on History in Schools, *The Future of the Past: The Plight of History in American Education* (New York: Macmillan, 1989).

TABLE 19–1 U.S. History Item Responses, 1986

More than 80 Percent Answered Correctly	Percent Correct	Less Than 30 Percent Answered Correctly	Percent Correct
Thomas Edison invented the light bulb	95.2	Andrew Jackson was president between 1820 and 1840	29.9
Location of the Soviet Union on a map	92.1	The Reformation led to the establishment of Protestant groups	29.8
Alexander Graham Bell invented the telephone	91.1		
George Washington was president between 1780 and 1800	87.9	The United Nations was founded between 1934 and 1947	25.9
Location of Italy on a map	87.7	The Seneca Falls Declaration was concerned with women's rights	25.8
The Underground Railroad was a network for helping slaves escape	87.5	Abraham Lincoln was president between 1860 and 1880	24.7
Adolph Hitler was the leader of Germany when the United States entered World War II	87.4	Medicare and the Voting Act were passed under Lyndon Johnson's Great Society	23.9
Thomas Jefferson was the primary author of the Declaration of Independence	87.4	Betty Friedan and Gloria Steinem are leaders in the women's movement	22.8
The assembly line was introduced in the U.S. automobile industry	87.2	Progressive movement refers to the period after World War I	22.6
Location of the area representing the 13 original states on a map	84.8	Reconstruction refers to the readmission of the Confederate States	21.4
The Ku Klux Klan used violence to oppose equality for minorities	83.9	John Winthrop and the Puritans founded a colony at Boston	19.5
Harriet Tubman was a leader in helping slaves escape to the North	83.8		
Bill of Rights guarantees freedom of speech and religion	81.3		
Location of the Rocky Mountains on a map	81.3		
The Japanese attack on Pearl Harbor led the United States into World War II	80.0		

SOURCE: From Curtis O. Baker, ed. *The Condition of Education 1989* (Washington, D.C.: U.S. Government Printing Office, 1989), p. 148.

8. Teachers of the social studies in middle and high schools should complete a substantial program in history at the college or university level as part of certification requirements.
9. College and university departments of history should review the structure and content of their major programs with reference to their appropriateness to teachers.[23]

Foreign Language

Historically, foreign language instruction has occupied a prominent place in the curriculum, especially in secondary and higher education. Until the end of the

23. Ibid., pp. 7–8.

nineteenth century, Latin and Greek were required for admission to many colleges. The curricula of the Latin Grammar schools of the eighteenth century, the academies of the nineteenth century, and the high schools of the early twentieth century emphasized Latin as both a college-entry requirement and as an area of general culture. By the end of the nineteenth century, modern foreign languages, such as French, Spanish, and German, entered the secondary school curriculum. Correspondingly, Greek virtually disappeared. Although it has lost its dominating position, Latin continues as a subject in the foreign language curriculum. Today, many high schools offer instruction in such languages as Latin, French, Spanish, Russian, and Italian.

The presence of certain foreign languages in the curriculum has been based, to some degree, on the ethnic composition of the communities served by the school. In several instances, bilingual programs existed in German and English in the St. Louis and Milwaukee school systems. Today the largest bilingual programs are in Spanish and English. These programs are found in areas of the country that have large Spanish-speaking populations, such as the western and southwestern states and the urban centers. While the Spanish-English programs are most evident, programs also exist in other languages.

Although foreign language instruction has been found traditionally in secondary and higher education, there have been efforts periodically to introduce it to the elementary school. The American tendency to reserve foreign language instruction to secondary education contrasts sharply to that of other countries, particularly those of Europe, where it begins much earlier. In the late 1950s and early 1960s, the federal government encouraged foreign language instruction in the elementary school curriculum. A study group of the Modern Language Association known as Foreign Languages in Elementary School (FLES) argued that younger children have fewer inhibitions in learning and using a foreign language than do older students and adults. Also, an early beginning would facilitate more sustained study in a given language. In the 1960s, there was an increase in foreign language study in elementary schools. Throughout the 1970s, however, the trend to foreign language study in elementary school was reversed dramatically. Because of financial retrenchment and a declining interest among the public, many programs were eliminated. An exception to this general trend has been in bilingual programs where Spanish is the first language of many children. In some schools with a large bilingual population, English may actually be taught as a second language.

In contrast to other countries, American efforts in foreign language instruction have been rather weak and sporadic. At several crucial periods in the country's history, it was recognized that American competency in foreign languages was sadly deficient. This weakness has become more and more apparent as the United States assumed a greater international involvement.[24]

In foreign language study in secondary and higher education, the quality of instruction has generally improved in recent years. The stress on grammar that often dominated foreign language instruction in the past has yielded to more informal methods that maximize conversational skills. Multimedia instruction, including the

24. Paul Simon, *The Tongue-Tied American* (New York: Continuum Books, 1980).

use of sophisticated language laboratories, is also more common. Some high schools also include opportunities for field study in a foreign country to provide immersion of the student in the language. Many colleges maintain overseas centers where students can live in a foreign country, assimilate the culture, and use the language that they are studying. It is hoped that we will see a greater awareness of the need for more American involvement in foreign language study.

Based upon these trends, the following outline identifies the pattern of foreign language instruction in American elementary, junior high, and high schools.

Elementary and Junior High School Foreign Language Curriculum
(typically grades kindergarten to eight)

Because foreign language instruction is not common to many elementary schools, it is included here with the junior high and middle school. In some instances, instruction may be found at the kindergarten through eighth grade level in the following languages:

Spanish
French
German
Russian
Italian
Others

High School Foreign Language Curriculum
(typically grades nine, ten, eleven, and twelve)

In American high schools, the leading foreign language courses traditionally have been Latin, French, and Spanish. Latin, however, has declined steadily in favor of modern foreign languages. The languages that may be offered include the following:

Latin	Swedish
Spanish	Greek
French	Polish
German	Norwegian
Russian	Italian
Chinese	Czech
Japanese	African languages
Hebrew	Native-American
Arabic	(in some western states)
Portuguese	

Trends in Foreign Language Study

The educational reform climate also generated renewed interest in strengthening foreign language study. Some colleges are again requiring units in foreign language for admission and as degree requirements. In addressing the subject of foreign language instruction, the National Commission on Excellence in Education called for two years of foreign language in high school for college preparatory students. The commission also recommended that foreign language instruction begin in the elementary grades and continue for four to six years.[25] It appears, however, that foreign language instruction has been overshadowed by the urgency given to mathematics and science education.

Physical Education and Health

Since the early nineteenth-century common-school movement, American schools have given attention to health and physical education. In the modern elementary school, physical education programs have these general goals:

1. Promoting proper growth and development with physical activity
2. Developing physical skills and coordination for work and leisure
3. Developing the proper attitudes toward play, exercise, recreation, and relaxation
4. Improving balance, rhythm, and posture
5. Providing opportunities for participation in various activities and sports

In some small elementary schools, the regular teacher in the self-contained classroom may be responsible for the physical education and health program. The trend in most districts, however, is to employ specialist teachers for instruction in these areas.

Because the objectives and activities of the physical education program are diverse, a selective listing illustrates the scope and sequence in this curricular area: understanding instructions and rules of simple games; appreciating the need for group success and teamwork; learning to take turns; developing an improved sense of balance, basic physical movements, and coordination; developing rhythmical patterns in running, walking, skipping, and hopping; learning to accept both defeat and victory; developing self-control to overcome awkwardness and self-consciousness; and learning that guided practice improves performance. Activities undertaken to achieve these objectives include games, folk dancing, square dancing, ballroom dancing, tumbling, track and field events, softball, basketball, volleyball, soccer, tennis, swimming, badminton, football, and calisthenics.

Many of the skills and attitudes that are introduced at the elementary level are developed and refined further at the secondary level, and individual and team sports become more diverse. Activities such as dancing, golf, tennis, skiing, swimming, boating, bowling, yoga, and bait and fly casting may be offered, as well as the conventional team sports of field and track, basketball, football, baseball, and soccer. The enrichment of the physical education curriculum seeks to develop interest and skills in recreational and leisure activities that will continue throughout life rather than be limited to the school years. The major goal is that of preparing individuals who will be interested in maximizing their recreational and physical fitness potentialities.

25. National Commission on Excellence in Education, *A Nation at Risk*, pp. 25–26. Also, for a reasoned argument for restoring foreign language instruction, see Carlos R. Hortas, "Foreign Languages and Humane Learning," in Finn, Ravitch, and Fancher, *Against Mediocrity*, pp. 70–78.

Often closely related to the formal curriculum in physical education are the co- or extracurricular interscholastic athletics and sports. It is a long-standing tradition in American education that the football, baseball, and basketball teams are often focal points for school pride and morale.

A recent development has been the efforts to provide equal opportunity and service to both boys and girls in the physical education curriculum. Title IX of the Education Amendments of 1972 prohibits discrimination on the basis of sex in schools and colleges. Schools and colleges are to provide instructors and equipment for female teams. As a result of the impetus of Title IX, coeducational physical education classes are common in many schools.

Health education is often related to the physical education curriculum. The scope of health education includes physical fitness, nature of disease, awareness of environmental hazards, prevention of accidents, safety, first aid, knowledge of community health services, recreation, mental health, sex education, AIDS education, and an understanding of the health risks that may result from the use of tobacco, alcohol, drugs, and narcotics. Driver education is also often included in the secondary school health and physical education curriculum. The outline that follows is intended to illustrate the physical education and health curriculum.

Elementary School Physical Education and Health Curriculum
(typically grades kindergarten through six)

In the elementary school, physical education and health programs often include the following:

    Games
    Rhythm and coordination activities
    Balancing, running, skipping, and hopping
    Dancing
    Calisthenics
    Sports
    Safety and accident prevention
    Health and diet

Junior High and High School Physical Education and Health Curriculum
(typically grades seven through twelve; a middle school may also include grade six)

Many of the physical education activities and individual and team sports that are begun in the junior high school are continued through the high school. These activities and health education units include the following:

Physical Education
Dancing: square, folk, ballroom, and disco
Track and field events
Softball, baseball, basketball, and football

Volleyball
Soccer
Tennis
Swimming
Badminton
Camping
Golf
Bait and fly casting

Health Education
Nutrition
Dental care
Sex education
AIDS education
Drug and alcohol abuse education
First aid
Safety and accident prevention
General health and health services

AIDS Education

In 1980, the first cases of acquired immunodeficiency syndrome (AIDS) were identified in the United States. Physicians treating these patients found that even the most aggressive treatment was ineffective in controlling unusually virulent infections that were eventually fatal. Kaposi's sarcoma, ordinarily a benign skin lesion, was common and overwhelmingly malignant in AIDS cases. Other patients had *Pneumocystis carinii* pneumonia, a rare lung disease. Some patients had both infections. In all cases, the disease did not respond to treatment, and the patient died. As of 1988, 64,506 cases of AIDS had been reported to the Centers for Disease Control. As a result of concerted research, the human immunodeficiency virus (HIV) has been identified as causing the disease. It is estimated that the number of persons in the United States infected with HIV is from 1 million to 1.5 million.[26] HIV can be transmitted by sexual contact with an infected person, by using needles or other injection equipment that an infected person has used, or from an infected mother to her infant before or during birth. In addition, the virus has been transmitted to persons who have received transfusions of infected blood. Although research continues, there is at present no cure for this disease, nor vaccine to prevent it.

By the late 1980s, AIDS reached epidemic proportions not only in the United States, but throughout the world. One of the measures to prevent the spread of the disease is education, both nonformally, through the media and other means, and through schools. Since the HIV is transmitted largely by behavior that persons can modify and control, educational programs that provide knowledge about the disease and how it is spread and the means by which individuals can avoid transmitting the virus have been developed. In this section, guidelines for an AIDS education program are discussed. This section is included with health education since many experts see AIDS education as part of a comprehensive health education curriculum.

26. *Report of the Presidential Commission on the Human Immunodeficiency Virus Epidemic* (Washington, D.C.: U.S. Government Printing Office, 1988), pp. 1–2.

Ideally, it can also be related to and integrated with the biological sciences and the social studies. It also is related to sex education and drug abuse prevention programs.

Among its recommendations, the Presidential Commission on the Human Immunodeficiency Virus Epidemic has called for widely disseminated programs of nonformal and formal education, the distribution of clearly stated factual information, and the development of curricula appropriate to local value systems. According to the Presidential Commission:

> *HIV-related education needs to take place in all locations, both within and outside of society's mainstream. Education about HIV needs to occur both inside and outside of our nation's schools and workplaces. No corner of society can be neglected as educational programs about the HIV epidemic are developed and implemented.*
>
> *. . . HIV education programs . . . should discourage promiscuous sexual activity and recognize the benefits of abstinence and monogamy; however, they need to be explicit in nature so that there is no confusion about how to avoid acquiring or transmitting the virus.*
>
> *. . . the federal, state, and local governments should convey the current medical and scientific facts to the American public and they, in turn, will build curricula suited to their own community value system.*[27]

The Presidential Commission has identified three components as vital elements in AIDS education programs: (1) education that is part of school-based curriculum and instruction, (2) local and state policies that support the knowledge, skills, and values that are developed in such education, and (3) government policies and legislation that reinforce such programs. In its recommendations, the Presidential Commission called for both a near-term immediate response based on the urgency of the AIDS epidemic and a long-term response that involves developing a comprehensive health education curriculum.

The Presidential Commission strongly recommended establishment of an age-appropriate comprehensive health education curriculum that encompasses grades K–12. According to the Presidential Commission, the problems that afflict youth today, "such as sexually transmitted diseases including HIV infection, drug abuse, school-aged pregnancy, and decisions to drop-out or run away—are all inseparably intertwined. The HIV epidemic provides a unique impetus to address these problems in total rather than continue the piecemeal, fractured, and largely ineffective approach that is being undertaken today."[28] The Presidential Commission further recommended that such a comprehensive health education curriculum be taught through the life sciences curriculum, with an emphasis on developing an early interest in science that relates to matters of deep human concern. A truly comprehensive program should integrate concepts in the biological and behavioral sciences and the application of decision-making and problem-solving skills in "the context of real-life individual and social issues."

The U.S. Department of Health and Human Services has developed guidelines for health education programs to prevent the spread of AIDS. Instruction in the early elementary grades should be designed "to allay excessive fears of the epidemic

---

27. Ibid., p. 83.
28. Ibid., pp. 89–90.

and of being infected." In late elementary, junior high/middle, and high school, education about AIDS should include information on the following:

> The nature of viruses and their transmission
>
> The fact that AIDS "is caused by a virus that weakens the ability of infected individuals to fight off disease"
>
> The fact that about 1 million to 1.5 million people in the United States are infected with the AIDS virus and consequently are capable of infecting others
>
> The fact that "People who are infected with the AIDS virus live in every state in the United States and in most other countries of the world, infected people live in cities as well as in suburbs, small towns, and rural areas. Although most infected people are adults, teenagers can also become infected. Females as well as males are infected. People of every race are infected, including whites, blacks, Hispanics, Native Americans, and Asian/Pacific Islanders."
>
> The fact that the AIDS virus can be transmitted by sexual contact with an infected person, by using needles and injection equipment that an infected person has used, and from an infected mother to her infant before or during birth
>
> The fact that it sometimes takes several years after infection by the AIDS virus for the symptoms of the disease to appear
>
> The fact that most infected persons who develop symptoms of AIDS live only two years after being diagnosed
>
> The fact that "the risk of being infected with HIV can be virtually eliminated by not engaging in sexual activities and by not using illegal intravenous drugs"
>
> The fact that "sexual transmission of HIV is not a threat to those uninfected individuals who engage in mutually monogamous sexual relations."[29]

Home Arts

The home arts curriculum, also called *home economics* or *domestic science*, is generally offered at the junior high or secondary school level as either a required or an elective course. Although some educational experiences relating to home arts occur in the elementary school, most of the structured courses are offered and more organized learning takes place in secondary schools. At the end of the nineteenth century and the beginning of the twentieth, home arts—then termed *domestic science*—was designed exclusively to prepare girls to be homemakers. The early domestic science courses stressed household management, cooking, sewing, and child care. The Smith–Hughes Act of 1917, which provided federal funds on a matching basis to the states, stimulated the concerted entry of home economics courses in the high schools. Contemporary home arts programs assist both boys and girls in understanding and solving the problems of personal, social, and family life.

---

29. U.S. Department of Health and Human Services, *Guidelines for Effective School Health Education to Prevent the Spread of AIDS* (Atlanta, Ga.: Public Health Service, Centers for Disease Control, Center for Health Promotion and Education, 1988), pp. 5–6. These guidelines have been excerpted by the author. The full document, with its detailed guidelines, is highly recommended for those involved in developing and implementing AIDS Education programs. Also recommended is the succinct and highly readable publication by William L. Yarber, *AIDS Education: Curriculum and Health Policy* (Bloomington, Ind.: Phi Delta Kappa Educational Foundation, 1987).

Although the units treated vary from program to program, home arts courses typically include the following:

Clothing design, sewing, and textiles
Food preparation and serving
Career choice and planning
Home and family management
Preparation for marriage
Housing and interior decoration and design
Social and community relations
Child development and care
Consumer economics
Clothing selection and grooming
Personal and family income management
Time management

Industrial, Vocational, and Technical Education

The contemporary curriculum in industrial, vocational, and technical education evolved from the manual training programs of the early twentieth century. When apprenticeship training failed to keep pace with the needs of an increasingly industrialized society, manual and industrial training programs were introduced. In 1917, the federally enacted Smith–Hughes Act aided the growth of vocational education by providing matching funds to the states for such programs.

The contemporary industrial arts curriculum emphasizes the processes of industrial design and creation as well as the end product. Among the objectives of the modern industrial arts curriculum are the following:

1. To develop an understanding and appreciation of the role of industry and technology in modern society
2. To develop safety techniques in using machines, equipment, and materials
3. To develop an understanding of the application of mathematics and science to industrial and technological processes
4. To develop a sense of appreciation and pride for design, crafts, and careful work
5. To develop planning skills to understand and cope with industrial and technological change

The scope of industrial and vocational education curricula varies from school system to school system. One can find conventional courses in printing, woodworking, metalworking, and clerical-secretarial skills. In addition, some schools provide training in cosmetology, television repair, automobile maintenance, and the operation of sophisticated business machines. In recent years, there have been demands that high schools should provide training in saleable skills to enable graduates to compete successfully in the job market.

Although they deal with related subject matter, important distinctions generally exist between the junior high school industrial arts curriculum and vocational and industrial education at the high school level. In the junior high school, grades seven and eight, industrial arts education is intended to be an exploratory introduction to industrial courses. Of a general nature, programs in industrial education in junior high schools are nonvocational in that they do not provide specific career training.

Junior High School Industrial Arts Curriculum
(grades seven and eight)

The junior high school industrial arts curriculum provides a general introduction to industry and technology rather than specific vocational training. General areas included in industrial education at this level are introductory shopwork, mechanical drawing and drafting, graphic arts and printing, handicrafts, and an introduction to careers. The following listing of units indicates the curricular possibilities at the junior high school level:

> Drafting procedures and equipment
> Organization of manufacturing industries
> Introduction to manufacturing careers
> Use of hand and power tools
> Introduction to the construction industry
> Introduction to transportation
> Power and energy resources
> Engines, turbines, rockets
> Electricity
> Electronics
> Leather, jewelry, metal, ceramics, textiles, wood, weaving

High School Vocational and Industrial Education Curriculum
(grades nine, ten, eleven, and twelve)

At the high school level, vocational and industrial education is intended primarily for specific career preparation, but it may also provide experiences that are introductory to the general area of vocational and industrial careers. Despite the usual curricular variations characteristic of American schools, the following broad areas can be found in the vocational programs at the secondary level:

> Clerical, secretarial, and business office preparation
> Technical education
> Agricultural education: animal husbandry, forestry, gardening, horticulture, landscaping
> Allied health education
> Trade and industrial education: air conditioning, auto mechanics, bricklaying, cabinetmaking, carpentry, drafting, electricity, food trades, machine shop, printing, sheetmetal, welding
> Distributive education: marketing, sales promotion, advertising

The problems of industrial and vocational education have grown with the increasing complexity of American technological society. The modernization process has caused greater specialization; it is difficult for schools to provide sufficient specialized training to keep pace with technological change. The shops, equipment, and laboratories needed for industrial education are expensive and become outdated quickly. To offset the obsolescence of equipment, many schools are making a greater use of business, industry, and community facilities to provide practical work experience and on-the-job training for students.

A major impetus was given to career education when the U.S. Office of Education established a Center for Career Education. The rationale for career education emphasizes that schools should (1) identify the various careers and provide students with information about career preparation and entry and (2) develop comprehensive career development programs that include work observation, work experience, and skill development. Career education, while related to vocational and industrial education, is generally seen as a broad and integrated program in career preparation rather than as a specialized vocational course.

Arts Education

In elementary and secondary schools, arts education generally has emphasized art and music. In recent years, the conception of arts education has grown, however, to include a wide variety of plastic, dramatic, and graphic art forms. There has been a greater recognition that a broadly conceived conception of art education will enable students to realize their creative potentialities.

Toward Civilization: A Report on Arts Education, issued by the National Endowment for the Arts, seeks to define arts education and to identify the goals for instruction in this area of the curriculum. According to this report:

Basic arts education aims to provide all students, not only the gifted and talented, with knowledge of, and skills in, the arts. Basic arts education must give students the essence of our civilization, the civilizations which have contributed to ours, and the more distant civilizations which enrich world civilization as a whole. It must also give students tools for creating, for communicating and understanding others' communications, and for making informed and critical choices.[30]

Taking a broad perspective, the National Endowment report includes the following in the arts curriculum:

Literature—from the art of writing
Visual art and design—from the arts of painting, sculpture, photography, video, crafts, architecture, landscape and interior design, and product and graphic design
Performing art—from the arts of dance, music, opera, musical theater, and theater
Media art—from the arts of film, television, and radio.[31]

Emphasizing the importance of arts education, the authors of *Toward Civilization* have identified four major reasons for including it in the school curriculum:

30. National Endowment for the Arts, *Toward Civilization: Overview from A Report on Arts Education* (Washington, D.C.: National Endowment for the Arts, 1988), p. 1. The full report is National Endowment for the Arts, *Toward Civilization: A Report on Arts Education* (Washington, D.C.: National Endowment for the Arts, 1988.)
31. Ibid.

Education in the arts; a class in music instruction.

1. To provide students with a sense and an understanding of civilization
2. To encourage creativity
3. To teach effective communication in the language of the arts
4. To provide the models and standards that make it possible to assess critically what one reads, sees, and hears.[32]

Music Education

Since the time of the ancient Greeks, music has been an integral part of the curriculum. Today, it is an important means of enjoyment, appreciation, and communication. As a part of general education, it is important that all students enjoy worthwhile experiences in music and be provided with opportunities to develop skills for musical expression. In school settings, the curriculum should introduce students to their musical heritage and also provide the means for artistic expression through vocal and instrumental music. Among the general objectives of music education are (1) introducing students to a range of music that enables them to appreciate the role of this art form in human culture, (2) providing musical activities, such as the development of vocal and instrumental skills, that correspond to the stages of human growth and development, and (3) developing sensitivity in singing, playing, and listening.

Music education is a recognized component of elementary and secondary schooling. At the primary and intermediate levels, music instruction is the respon-

32. Ibid., pp. 2–6.

sibility of the classroom teacher or special teacher. From the junior high school years upward, music instruction becomes the responsibility of specialist teachers of music, who are often located in music or fine arts departments.

The following sample of units in music is intended to illustrate the scope and sequence of the elementary school music curriculum:

recognizing basic types of music
recognizing the direction of melodic movements
becoming aware of rhythm, harmony, and tone patterns
singing songs of different types
clapping or playing simple instruments
developing meaning and sensitivity for music concepts such as melody, rhythm, harmony, form, and dynamics
becoming aware of basic differences and similarities in various musical styles
becoming familiar with a variety of musical compositions, such as symphonies, operas, and ballets
having a familiarity with folk dances

Music education in the junior and senior high school often relates the curricular to the co- or extracurricular. Students may participate in musical and vocal groups, choruses and glee clubs, marching bands, jazz bands, and orchestras. Contemporary trends in music education emphasize techniques that encourage students to play compositions early in their study. This approach avoids many of the often tedious exercises that discourage students from continuing with music. There is also a greater emphasis on creativity that encourages students to write and perform their own musical compositions.

Art Education

As with music education, the fine arts curriculum is designed to encourage both aesthetic appreciation and creativity. It introduces learners to the role of art as a means of human expression in the cultural heritage and also encourages students to express themselves creatively in art forms and objects. Among the general objectives embodied in the art curriculum are (1) to provide opportunities that encourage students to think, feel, and act creatively with art forms and materials and (2) to introduce students to the art works of the past and present to cultivate aesthetic sensitivity and appreciation. The traditional concepts and media of the fine arts have broadened from the conventional coloring and water and oil painting to include sculpture, ceramics, plastics, carving, block and silk-screen printing, and photography.

The following list of topics serves to illustrate the scope and sequence of the art curriculum:

noting details and distinguishing relationships pictorially
using tempera paint, crayon, chalk, and pencils
using and arranging shapes imaginatively
combining threads, yarns, and fibers
using clay to explore texture and shapes

developing construction, cutting, and pasting skills
making prints by cutting out designs from linoleum or vinyl tile
carving objects in wood or clay
portrait drawing
becoming familiar with and using the concepts of abstraction and realism
and painting from nature and still life.

Other Humanities and Arts

Although music and art continue to occupy a major position in the humanities and fine arts curriculum, some contemporary humanities programs extend beyond these two areas. Expressive dancing, ballet, and modern and folk dancing are also important forms of individual and group expression. Drama in its various forms should also have a place in the fine arts curriculum. Many high schools have courses in theater and film to provide opportunities for creative expression.

Toward Civilization: Recommendations

The National Endowment for the Arts in its major national report, *Toward Civilization*, has developed a number of recommendations for creating a strong curriculum for arts education:

1. "Arts education should provide all students with a sense of the arts in civilization, of creativity in the artistic process, of the vocabularies of artistic communication, and of the critical elements necessary for making informed choices about the products of the arts."
2. State and local educational agencies should develop and implement "explicit policies" that make "arts education a sequential part of the basic curriculum for all students in grades K–12." The curriculum defined by these agencies should "include each of the arts (dance, design, literature and creative writing, the media arts, music, opera and musical theater, theater, and the visual arts) and provide for instruction in history and critical analysis as well as production and performance." Further, these policies "should define a core of subject content and skills in the arts which all students would be required to achieve, and provide for a selection of required courses in relation to optional courses in the basic curriculum."
3. State teacher certification requirements should strengthen requirements for those who teach the arts. The training of elementary teachers, specialist art teachers, and teachers of subjects in which the arts are relevant should include (a) "study of important works of art (their craft, history, and significance to the civilizations which they symbolize)" and (b) the "study of techniques for creating or performing one of the arts."[33]

New Curricular Movements

In the preceding sections of this chapter, the major components of the conventional curriculum were identified and examined. The curriculum, however, is not a static body of skills and subjects. It is subject to forces of change. Some of these pressures

---

33. Ibid., pp. 23–25.

for change come from forces that are internal to the school and others are stimulated by external social, economic, and political factors. In this section, some of the recent tendencies for curricular change are identified and examined.

Ethnic and Bilingual Education

Since the late 1960s, programs emphasizing the ethnic, racial, and linguistic diversity of the United States have been incorporated into the curriculum. Chapter 7 examined these developments in multicultural education. Multicultural education encourages students to develop an attitude of cultural pluralism that respects their own ethnic group as well as members of other ethnic groups.

The Bilingual Education Act of 1968 provided federal funds to aid local school districts in meeting the needs of students of limited English-speaking ability. Approximately three million children between the ages of 3 and 18 are members of non-English-speaking families. Stimulated by either federal initiatives or responding to their own needs, most states have required bilingual programs.

Bilingual education is usually defined as instruction that involves using two languages for part or all of the school day. The study of the history and culture associated with a student's mother tongue is also regarded as part of bilingual education. Although the definition of bilingual education is clear, there has been considerable controversy regarding the general goal of these programs. Some educators have argued that bilingual instruction should be transitional; that is, instruction in the student's mother tongue should be carried on to the point that the student can use English effectively. Others argue that bilingual education should maintain facility in the mother tongue and also provide for the learning of English.

Bilingual education programs exist in many languages, depending upon the language composition of the school population. They range from Native American languages to Chinese, Japanese, Greek, and Spanish. The largest group participating in bilingual programs are students whose mother tongue is Spanish. California and the southwestern states have traditionally had large Spanish-speaking populations, primarily Mexican American. The major urban areas also have large Hispanic communities, particularly Puerto Rican and Cuban.

In the 1960s and 1970s, the elementary and secondary school curriculum, as well as that of higher education, experienced the addition of units or courses relating to black and ethnic studies. Black studies, designed to correct the traditional neglect and stereotyping of the African-American experience, emphasized the antecedents of blacks in Africa and their contributions to the American experience. These programs gave black students a greater awareness into their cultural heritage and also introduced white students to the African-American experience.

Stimulated by a growing consciousness that the United States is a multicultural nation, Congress passed the Ethnic Heritage Studies Act in 1973, which provided funds for program development. New curriculum materials were prepared and disseminated that illustrated the traditions of ethnic groups in the United States. For example, curriculum materials were prepared that dealt with Polish Americans, Italian Americans, Chinese Americans, Mexican Americans, and other ethnic groups.

Environmental Education

Since the 1960s, there has been pronounced concern about the dangers of environmental pollution. This concern was stimulated by scientific research and a growing public awareness that the environment was being adversely affected by the misuse of natural resources and by the pollution of air and water. Not only was the quality of human life being harmed but species of certain plants and animals were also threatened with extinction.

The general concern for the protection and preservation of the natural environment led educators to develop courses and curricular materials for environmental education. Although environmental education received a new impetus in the 1960s, curriculum units have existed on conservation education since the early 1900s. Current environmental education programs generally are more comprehensive and multidisciplinary, however. In its broadest perspective, environmental education views the earth as an ecosphere, a total life system. The problems of environmental pollution are then regarded as global concerns that affect the whole planet and its inhabitants. Because of its nature, environmental education is interdisciplinary and draws its materials from the various physical, natural, life, and social sciences.

Although some school systems have developed specialized courses in environmental education, the general trend is to integrate environmental study into the established curriculum by means of units that can be incorporated into the natural and social sciences courses. In addition to classroom instruction, environmental education programs include learning through direct observation of the environment and by having students involved in field study projects that enable them to work in actually restoring or protecting the natural environment.

Sex Education

Sex education is often subject to controversy for it relates to basic human drives and values that have personal, social, and moral significance. Sex education also is connected to the family and to the home.

The presence of sex education in the elementary and secondary school curriculum relates to social changes in modern society. Once reserved to the family or the church, sex education is now regarded by many to be appropriate for the school. The increase in premarital pregnancies, venereal disease, and abortions among teenagers was a major factor that prompted the development of sex education programs.

Sex education is an interdisciplinary subject that involves the integration of materials from a number of academic disciplines, such as biology, physiology, sociology, and medicine. In the elementary and secondary school curriculum, it can be taught as a separate subject, or it can be correlated with health education.

Because it includes materials that are not only physiological but also value laden, the curriculum in sex education should be planned carefully and involve cooperation between the school, the home, and community health agencies. It is particularly important that both teachers and communities are prepared for the introduction of sex education into the curriculum and that there is cooperation among all interested groups in developing the curriculum.

Substance Abuse Prevention Education

Of the world's industrialized nations, the United States has the highest rates of substance abuse. The incidence of substance abuse is especially high among teenagers and young adults. See Figure 19-2 for trends in drug and alcohol use. To combat drug abuse, the federal government in 1989 launched a "war on drugs" that aims to stop the supply of illegal drugs, such as cocaine, that enter the United States from foreign sources and to stop the domestic consumption of such drugs. Education in the form of a substance or drug abuse prevention curriculum and instruction is a crucial component of the war on drugs.[34]

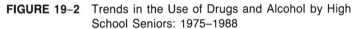

FIGURE 19-2 Trends in the Use of Drugs and Alcohol by High School Seniors: 1975–1988

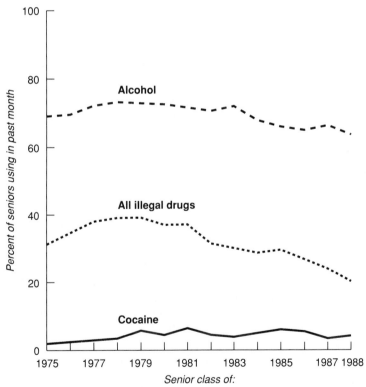

SOURCE: From Curtis O. Baker, ed., *The Condition of Education 1989* (Washington, D.C.: U.S. Government Printing Office, 1989), p. 61.

34. A practical guide that educators can use to deal with substance abuse is U.S. Department of Education, *What Works: Schools Without Drugs* (Washington, D.C.: U.S. Department of Education, 1986).

Substance prevention education essentially deals with three types of substances: those, such as marijuana, cocaine, and heroin, commonly called drugs; alcoholic beverages; and tobacco products. While using certain drugs is illegal for everyone, the use of alcohol and tobacco by adults is legal. In every state, the age when a person can legally consume alcoholic beverages is 21. In 44 states and the District of Columbia, the sale of tobacco to minors is illegal.

Substance abuse in the United States has reached such large proportions that it has had a significant negative impact on social welfare, economic productivity, and personal well-being and health. Drug abuse is not limited to certain socioeconomic or age groups; it is a national problem. The following indicators of substance abuse among the school-age population provide evidence of the magnitude of the nation's drug abuse problem:

1. Drug abuse is no longer a "big city" problem. By graduation from high school, 32 percent of rural and 39 percent of urban youth have used drugs.
2. Drug abuse rates are comparable for male (38 percent) and female (34 percent) students.
3. Elementary and junior high school students, as well as high school students, are experiencing serious drug abuse pressures and problems. Pressure to use illegal drugs begins in many schools in fourth grade. Between fourth and sixth grade, the use of alcohol by children increases from 6 percent to 17 percent; 2 percent of sixth-graders have experimented with marijuana; 5 percent of the junior high students are daily alcohol users.
4. "By high school graduation, one-quarter of American students are frequent users of illegal drugs, two-thirds are frequent users of alcohol, and one-fifth (19 percent) are daily tobacco users. Over 50 percent have used marijuana, over 10 percent hallucinogens, such as LSD and PCP; and over 90 percent have used alcoholic beverages."[35]

Efforts to deal with the problem of substance abuse have involved the federal, state, and local governments. In an effort to marshal education as one element in the war on drugs, 39 states, as of 1988, have mandated education about substance abuse. Thirty-two states have developed minimum substance abuse curricula standards. Evidence of substance abuse education is required for teacher certification in 11 states. See Table 19–2 for state requirements (p. 400). Seventy-three percent of the local school districts have established policies against substance abuse that generally require notification of parents and police about policy violations, may lead to the suspension of violators, and provide counseling services. Some districts have established substance prevention education programs at all grade levels and throughout the curriculum.[36] For these federal, state and local efforts to be effective, they must enlist the support of the entire community. They need to have the understanding, commitment, and support of parents and community leaders and agencies, as well as of teachers and school administrators.

A crucial element in organizing, implementing, and sustaining drug prevention education is a clear policy statement by the school district. According to the Office

---

35. Office of Educational Research and Improvement, *Drug Prevention Curricula: A Guide to Selection and Implementation* (Washington, D.C.: U.S. Department of Education, 1988), p. 1.
36. Ibid., p. 3.

of Educational Research and Improvement of the U.S. Department of Education, such a policy should contain the following:

1. A "clear definition, based on state law, of what types of drugs and drug use are covered by the policy (making clear, for example, that prescribed medication is not covered, but that drinking alcohol is)"
2. A "clear statement that the defined drugs and drug use are prohibited on school grounds, at school-sponsored functions, and while students are representing the school"
3. A "description of the consequences to be expected upon violating the policy"
4. An "explanation of the process for referral for treatment — with a guarantee that self-referral will be treated in confidence, and will not result in punishment"[37]

In identifying the themes of an effective drug prevention curriculum, the Office of Educational Research and Improvement has identified the following:

"A clear and consistent message that the use of alcohol, tobacco, and other illicit drugs is unhealthy and harmful"

"Knowledge of all types of drugs, including what medicines are, why they are used, and who should (or should not) administer them"

"The social consequences of substance abuse"

"Respect for the laws and values of society"

"Promotion of healthy, safe, and responsible attitudes and behavior by correcting mistaken beliefs and assumptions, disarming the sense of personal invulnerability, and building resistance to influences which encourage substance abuse"

"Strategies to involve parents, family members, and community in the effort to prevent use of illicit substances"

"Appropriate information on intervention and referral services, plus similar information on contacting responsible adults when help is needed in emergencies"

"Sensitivity to the specific needs of the local school and community in terms of cultural appropriateness and local substance-abuse problems.[38]

Since the most effective drug abuse prevention curricula are systematic, comprehensive, cumulative and sequential, the knowledge base and value orientation should articulate at each level of instruction. In grades K–3, the program should emphasize "wellness." It should provide structured experiences that stress the positive benefits of being healthy and acting safely. Health, wellness, and safety can be the key concepts in developing a desire and determination to avoid using drugs and provide the knowledge and value base for later drug prevention education.

Since fourth grade has been identified as the time in which students begin to experience pressures to experiment with drugs, alcohol, and tobacco, substance abuse prevention education needs to provide fourth-graders with more information and content and work to develop a stronger value commitment to avoid substance abuse. Ideally, health education and social studies education can be integrated in such a way that a person's desire for health, wellness, and safety can be related to society's need to protect people from dangerous substances and behavior. The enactment of legislation by government to prevent drug abuse and the need to

37. Ibid., p. 7.
38. Ibid., p. 10.

TABLE 19-2 States Requiring Education, Minimum Curriculum Standards, and Teacher Certification on Substance Abuse Education, by State: 1986–1987

State	State Requires Substance Abuse Education	Minimum Curriculum Standards Provided	Certification Requirement for all Teachers
Total number with requirement	39	32	11
Alabama	X	X	
Alaska		X	
Arizona	X	X	
Arkansas	X	X	X
California	X	X	
Colorado	X	X	
Connecticut	X		
Delaware	X	X	
District of Columbia	X	X	X
Florida	X	X	
Georgia	X	X	
Hawaii		X	
Idaho	X		
Illinois	X	X	X
Indiana	X		X
Iowa	X	X	
Kansas			
Kentucky	X	X	X
Louisiana	X	X	
Maine	X	X	
Maryland	X	X	
Massachusetts	X		
Michigan		X	
Minnesota	X	X	X
Mississippi			
Missouri			X
Montana			
Nebraska	X		
Nevada	X	X	X
New Hampshire	X		
New Jersey	X		X
New Mexico	X	X	
New York	X	X	X
North Carolina			
North Dakota	X		
Ohio	X		X
Oklahoma			
Oregon	X		
Pennsylvania	X	X	
Rhode Island	X	X	
South Carolina	X		
South Dakota			
Tennessee		X	
Texas	X	X	
Utah	X	X	
Vermont	X	X	

TABLE 19–2 *Continued*

State	State Requires Substance Abuse Education	Minimum Curriculum Standards Provided	Certification Requirement for all Teachers
Virginia	X	X	
Washington	X	X	
West Virginia	X	X	
Wisconsin	X	X	
Wyoming			

SOURCE: From National Center for Education Statistics, *Digest of Education Statistics 1989* (Washington, D.C.: U.S. Government Printing Office, 1989), p. 147.

develop personal but socially linked value systems can be examined. Presentations by community members who are directly involved in substance abuse prevention and treatment, such as physicians, nurses, counselors, and police provide a useful instructional supplement to the curriculum and provide community support for the school program.

Substance abuse curricula at the middle and junior high school level (grades seven, eight, and often nine) need to recognize that the onset of adolescence presents new and greater challenges to students to avoid experimenting with and using drugs. Learning objectives and content need to arm students with the knowledge and values to respond to the pressures and threats they encounter to use drugs. Students need to know the "hard facts" about the effects that drugs can have on them physically, psychologically, and socially. Emphasis should be placed on "how alcohol, tobacco, and other drug use can immediately affect their appearance, coordination, thinking, and behavior." The curriculum should also emphasize the need for personal responsibility and an awareness of the law and of the penalties for violating it.

The secondary level (grades nine or ten through twelve) should provide the culminating experiences in the school's substance abuse prevention education program. While high school students can obtain licenses to drive and may have entered the work force on a part-time basis, they are still minors under the laws of most states. Substance abuse education programs need to continue to motivate high school students to continue personally to resist using illicit substances and to assume the broader social responsibility of combating drug abuse in the larger society. At this level, substance abuse education can provide information about the consequences of drug abuse on individuals and their families and friends and also about the social and economic costs that such abuse brings to the nation. It is important that the knowledge and values acquired in the school program be transferred to adult life and situations that take place after graduation.[39]

Technology Education and Computer-Assisted Instruction

Two recent trends have been the infusion of technology education into the curriculum and the widespread diffusion of computers throughout schools. The national

39. Ibid., pp. 14–25.

reports of the 1980s that warned that the economic productivity of the United States had been declining called for educational reforms. The Task Force on Education for Economic Growth stated that many American communities were experiencing technological or structural unemployment because "our workers, our factories and our techniques are suddenly obsolete. To many Americans, technological change today seems a dark and threatening force, rather than a bright confirmation of our national genius."[40] A report to the National Science Board Commission, which recommended strategies to improve technological literacy, used the following definitions to explain the emerging field:

> *Technology consists of the tools, devices and techniques that have been created to implement ideas borne of science and engineering. Technology exists to manage and modify the physical and biological world in a constructive way and relies on a foundation of mathematics. Technological systems result from engineering design and development. Technological literacy is the possession of a reasonable understanding of the behavior of technological systems and required knowledge of scientific and mathematical concepts. Along with this must go an understanding of certain underlying concepts that are unique to engineering.*[41]

The general strategy recommended for introducing technology education into the curriculum is to infuse technology units into the elementary and middle school curriculum and to develop specialized courses at the secondary level. The goals of technology education are to develop understanding of (1) the historical role of technology in human development, (2) the relationship between technological decisions and human ethics and values, (3) the strategies for choosing among various technologies, (4) the role and impact of technological innovation, and (5) the impact of technology on present and future social and cultural change.[42]

One of the sweeping innovations of the 1980s was the massive introduction of microcomputers and use of computer-assisted instruction in public schools. In 1981, only 18.2 percent of the public schools were using microcomputers. Only three years later, in 1984, 85.1 percent of schools were using them. For elementary schools, from 1981 to 1984, the percentage jumped from 11.1 percent to 82.2 percent, for junior high and middle schools it rose from 25.6 percent to 93.1 percent, and for senior high schools, from 42.7 percent to 94.6 percent.[43] By 1987, 95 percent of public schools had computers for use in instruction. It is estimated that there are now between 1.2 and 1.7 million computers in the public schools.[44] For an illustration of the distribution of computers, see Figure 19–3.

The widespread use of computers in education is part of the integration of technology into the classroom, but computer use is more comprehensive than other

40. Task Force on Education for Economic Growth, *Action for Excellence* (Denver: Education Commission of the States, 1984), p. 13.

41. John G. Truxal, "Fundamentals in Precollege Technology Education," in National Science Board Commission on Precollege Education in Mathematics, Science, and Technology, *Educating Americans for the 21st Century: Source Materials*, pp. 73–74.

42. Ibid., p. 74.

43. Valena White Plisko and Joyce D. Stern, eds., *The Condition of Education: 1985* (Washington, D.C.: U.S. Government Printing Office, 1985), p. 44.

44. Office of Technology Assessment, *Power On! New Tools for Teaching and Learning: Summary* (Washington, D.C.: U.S. Government Printing Office, 1988), p. 4.

FIGURE 19–3   Distribution of Computers in U.S. Public Schools, 1988

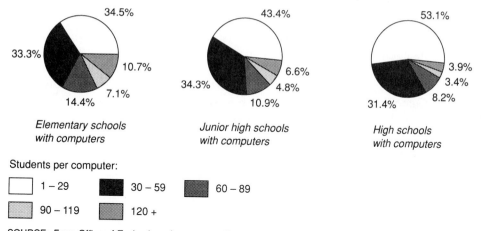

Elementary schools
with computers

Junior high schools
with computers

High schools
with computers

Students per computer:

	1 – 29	■	30 – 59	▓	60 – 89
▒	90 – 119	▒	120 +		

SOURCE: From Office of Technology Assessment, *Power On! New Tools for Teaching and Learning: Summary* (Washington, D.C.: U.S. Government Printing Office, 1989), p. 5.

technologies in that computers affect virtually every area of curriculum and instruction. The entry of computers into education has coincided with the rise of the "information society," which is characterized by the collection, storage, and retrieval of data for scientific, technological, and other purposes.[45] Harold Shane, in analyzing the impact of the microelectronic and information explosions on the schools, predicts profound changes in American education. He calls for an integrative approach in which the new technologies of information and instruction will be considered in terms of larger issues of social change and values.[46]

The National Commission of Excellence in Education has recommended that all high school students be required to complete a half-year of computer science as one of the "new basics," in addition to the traditional English, mathematics, science, and social studies courses. The National Commission stated that the study of computer science should equip graduates to "(a) understand the computer as an information, computation, and communication device; (b) use the computer in the study of the other basics and for personal and work-related purposes; and (c) understand the world of computers, electronics, and related technologies."[47]

The Commission on Excellence in Education addressed computer science in secondary schooling; computer-assisted instruction is also a major innovation in elementary and junior high schools. Thus, teachers at all grade levels and in all subject areas need to be computer literate. Teachers who are computer literate should be able to (1) identify and describe the functions of the various components of a computer system, (2) interact with, evaluate, and use educational software

---

45. For interpretations of the rise of the postindustrial information society, see John Naisbitt, *Megatrends* (New York: Warner Books, 1982), and Yoseji Masuda, *The Information Society as Post-Industrial Society* (Tokyo: Institute for the Information Society, 1980).

46. Harold G. Shane, "The Silicon Age II: Living and Learning in an Information Epoch," *Phi Delta Kappan*, 65 (October 1983), pp. 126–129.

47. National Commission on Excellence in Education, *A Nation at Risk*, p. 26.

effectively, (3) read and write computer programs, and (4) understand the impact of computers on socioeconomic change.[48]

Despite the wide distribution of computers, the Office of Technology Assessment, sponsored by the U.S. Congress, found that "the vast majority of schools still do not have enough of them to make the computer a central element of instruction." It is estimated that the students who use computers in school average slightly more than one hour per week on the computer, about 4 percent of their total instructional time.[49]

The use of computers, videodiscs, and other electronic means of instruction is referred to collectively as "interactive technologies." The interaction can be between a person and a machine, as in computer-assisted instruction, or between people by means of long-distance transmission and reception equipment, as in distance learning.[50] In a recent report, the Office of Technology concluded:

> . . . although new interactive technologies cannot alone solve the problems of American education, they have already contributed to important improvements in learning. These tools can play an even greater role in advancing the substance and process of

Computer-assisted instruction exemplifies a growing use of educational technology.

48. Mindy Pantiel and Becky Petersen, *Kids, Teachers, and Computers: A Guide to Computers in the Elementary School* (Englewood Cliffs, N.J.: Prentice-Hall, 1985), p. 12. For a collection of articles on the theme of "High Technology and Computers in Teacher Education," see *Journal of Teacher Education,* 34 (September/October 1983).
49. Office of Technology Assessment, *Power On!*, p. 4.
50. Ibid., p. 1.

education, both by helping children acquire basic skills and by endowing them with more sophisticated skills so they can acquire and apply knowledge over their lifetimes.[51]

According to the Office of Technology Assessment, the greatest asset of interactive technologies for instruction lies in their flexibility for use in a variety of situations. The most promising uses include the following:

1. Providing drill and practice for basic mastery in subjects such as mathematics and reading as a supplement but not a substitute for conventional teacher-directed classroom instruction.
2. Developing writing skills by providing students with an efficient means of reading, critiquing, and revising their written work.
3. Developing problem-solving and higher-order thinking skills by using computer simulations, data bases, and other software programs that "train students to break down problems into their component parts and set strategies for their solution."
4. Using computer simulations to develop the understanding of abstract mathematical and scientific concepts and situations.
5. Developing the skills of data manipulation through data base management systems that encourage students to define and reduce problems into their component parts.
6. Developing computer and related skills to prepare students for life and careers in an increasingly technological world.
7. Providing access and communication for students with special needs, such as those with handicaps. For example, students who cannot hold pencils are enabled to write by word processors, speech-impaired students are enabled to communicate orally by speech synthesizers.
8. Using distance education, which involves television satellite and electronic networks to provide information and lessons for teachers and students in remote locations.
9. Using computer-based technology for individualized instruction that is related to each student's prior knowledge, rate of learning, and style of response.
10. Encouraging cooperative learning through telecommunications and electronic networks, which facilitate information and data collection from diverse sources and people.
11. Making the management of classroom activities, recordkeeping, and materials preparation efficient by using computer programs with spreadsheets, data base managers, and desktop publishing.[52]

Co- and Extracurricular Activities

The preceding sections have examined the nature, organization, content, and issues of the formal curriculum. Now, we examine briefly co- or extracurricular programs. Teachers will often find that, although instruction in a formal area of the curriculum is their major responsibility, they also are involved in co- or extracurricular activities. The words *co-curricular* and *extracurricular* are often used interchangeably; in fact, *co-curricular* means that the activity, although not part of the formal program of instruction, is related to and enhances it, whereas *extracurricular* refers to activities that may be sponsored by the school but are not required by it. To simplify

51. Ibid., p. 2.
52. Ibid., pp. 10–12.

the discussion, only the term *co-curricular* will be used. The participation of students in co-curricular programs is usually voluntary.

In the United States, athletics and sports are prominent and popular co-curricular activities. Football, baseball, basketball, hockey, swimming, soccer, tennis, track and field, wrestling, and fencing are some of the co-curricular activities of an athletic nature that are found in most American high schools. These activities are related closely to physical education programs.

While music is part of the formal curriculum, it is also co-curricular in those schools that sponsor and organize a wide variety of musical groups, such as glee clubs, choruses, bands, orchestras, and jazz and rock groups. These groups perform in programs in the school or community. Music is an area in which the curricular and co-curricular are mutually reinforcing.

Speech clubs and societies are also a popular form of co-curricular activity. Since the colonial period, debating societies have existed in American schools. In addition to debating, panel discussions, extemporaneous speaking, and orations, newer types of speech activities are radio broadcasting and telecasting. Drama clubs stage and present plays as school and community events. In preparing plays, dramatics clubs are responsible for preparing stage settings, costumes, lighting, advertising, and selling tickets.

Literary societies and journalism clubs represent co-curricular organizations that relate to the formal curriculum by providing opportunities for improving literary and writing skills. Student organizations often prepare and disseminate the school newspaper, yearbook, and literary magazine.

There are also various forms of student government. These include class officers, such as a class president, vice-president, secretary, and treasurer, who conduct class meetings and plan social events. Most schools, especially high schools, have student governments, student councils, and student courts. Student governments often establish policies governing student organizations and conduct. Participation in student government provides students with experience in democratic processes and procedures.

In addition to the general kinds of extracurricular activities identified in the previous sections, there are student organizations that relate to a wide variety of interests and vocations. Representative organizations are the Future Teachers, Future Farmers, 4-H, photography clubs, Student Education Association, various language clubs, and ethnic societies.

Many reasons exist for schools to sponsor and encourage co-curricular activities and organizations. They may stimulate interests that are not satisfied by the formal curriculum or may reinforce and expand interests that are related to the formal curriculum. They provide occasions and experiences for developing friendships and social skills. They promote a sense of cooperation among students that often goes beyond that found in the classroom. Finally, the co-curricular dimension fulfills recreational and leisure needs that may grow into avocations in adult years.

The Teacher and the Curriculum

Now that we have examined curriculum and instruction, you may want to consider some direct curricular responsibilities that you may have as a teacher. As a teacher, you are responsible for implementing the curriculum guide or syllabus of your school district. Therefore, it is important that teachers be familiar with the general curriculum guide of the school district and also with those dealing specifically to the subject or grade level of immediate responsibility.

Teachers also serve on committees when particular subjects are being reviewed. Chapter 18 provided a detailed discussion of the teacher's role in the curriculum process as a member of the school system's professional staff.

Curriculum revision and implementation involves important cost factors. What will it cost to purchase the textbooks, workbooks, films, tapes, and in-service training to implement or revise a curriculum? While it is a crucial factor in determining the educational quality in a given school district, curriculum revision is also expensive and time-consuming. In most instances, curriculum development and adoption of materials is a responsibility of the local school district. In a few cases, for example, in Texas, state committees recommend statewide adoptions of textbooks. The state purchases large quantities of approved textbooks and stores them in book depositories. Local districts in these states receive the books from the state and, in turn, lend them to students.

The teachers and administrators who serve on curriculum committees then examine the textbooks and materials that are provided for review by publishers. Often the curriculum materials are part of a series designed to maintain sequential continuity from grade to grade. The shaping of the curriculum is, then, also influenced heavily by the publishing companies involved in preparing and marketing educational materials. It may also be necessary for curriculum committees and curriculum specialists to design and prepare their supplementary materials.

Conclusion

The process of curriculum making is long and involved, but, it is crucial to the educational mission of the school. It involves theoretical questions of great cultural, intellectual, philosophical, and moral significance. It also requires a skilled plan and procedure for practical implementation. The professional educator needs to be both a skilled theoretician and a practitioner in dealing with the curriculum of the schools.

DISCUSSION QUESTIONS

1. Examine recent curricular trends in language arts, mathematics, science, social studies, foreign language, physical education, home and industrial arts, vocational and technical education, art, and music.

2. Examine how curriculum and instruction relates to social and health issues found in the larger social context.

3. Should bilingual education be used for maintenance or for transition?

4. How has curriculum change resulted from attempts to integrate technology into the classroom?

5. Examine the recent trend to include such interdisciplinary studies as environmental education, sex education, and drug abuse education in the curriculum. What social

problems have led to this trend? Why are these new curriculum areas interdisciplinary rather than disciplinary?

6. Examine the relationship between curricular and co-curricular activities.

FIELD EXERCISES

1. Study the curricular organization of a particular elementary school and determine how articulation is achieved from grade level to grade level.

2. Interview an elementary and a secondary school principal. In each interview, attempt to determine how articulation is achieved between the higher and lower institutions.

3. Examine the curriculum guides and then observe classroom instruction in a particular school district or system in one of the following: language arts, mathematics, science, social studies, foreign languages, physical education, home and industrial arts, and music.

4. Interview a classroom teacher and through questioning attempt to discern how the curriculum in his or her area of specialization has changed.

5. Interview several high school students and attempt to discern the degree to which they participate in co-curricular activities. Give special attention to their motivations for participation and the relationships they perceive between the curriculum and co-curricular activities.

SUGGESTED READINGS

ALLIANCE FOR ARTS EDUCATION, JOHN F. KENNEDY CENTER FOR THE PERFORMING ARTS, AND AMERICAN ASSOCIATION OF SCHOOL ADMINISTRATORS. *Performing Together: The Arts and Education*. Washington, D.C.: American Association of School Administrators, 1985.

AMERICAN ASSOCIATION FOR THE ADVANCEMENT OF SCIENCE. *Project 2061: Science for All Americans*. Washington, D.C.: American Association for the Advancement of Science, 1989.

APPLEBEE, ARTHUR N. *Tradition and Reform in the Teaching of English: A History*. Urbana, Ill.: National Council of Teachers of English, 1974.

ATWOOD, VIRGINIA A. ED., *Elementary School Social Studies: Research As a Guide to Practice*. Washington, D.C.: National Council for the Social Studies, 1986.

BANKS, JAMES A. *Multiethnic Education: Theory and Practice*. Boston: Allyn & Bacon, 1981.

BARR, ROBERT D., BARTH, JAMES L., AND SHERMIS, S. SAMUEL. *Defining the Social Studies*. Washington, D.C.: National Council for the Social Studies, 1977.

BEARDSLEE, EDWARD C., AND DAVIS, GEOFFREY L. *Interactive Videodisc and the Teaching-Learning Process*. Bloomington, Ind.: Phi Delta Kappa Educational Foundation, 1989.

BEGLE, EDWARD G., ED. *Mathematics Education*. The Sixty-ninth Yearbook of the National Society for the Study of Education. Chicago: University of Chicago Press, 1970.

BINKLEY, MARILYN R. *Becoming a Nation of Readers: Implications for Teachers*. Washington, D.C.: U.S. Department of Education, 1986.

BRADLEY COMMISSION ON HISTORY IN SCHOOLS. *Building a History Curriculum: Guidelines for Teaching History in Schools*. Washington, D.C.: Educational Excellence Network, 1988.

————. *The Future of the Past: The Plight of History in American Education*. New York: Macmillan, 1989.

CAISSY, GAIL A. *Microcomputers and the Classroom Teacher*. Bloomington, Ind.: Phi Delta Kappa Educational Foundation, 1987.

CHALL, JEANNE. *Learning to Read: The Great Debate*. New York: McGraw-Hill, 1968.

CHENEY, LYNN V. *American Memory: A Report on the Humanities in the Nation's Public Schools*. Washington, D.C.: National Endowment for the Humanities, 1987.

COMMAGER, HENRY STEELE, AND MUESSING, RAYMOND H. *The Study and Teaching of History*. Columbus, Ohio: Charles E. Merrill, 1980.

COMMITTEE ON THE MATHEMATICAL SCIENCES IN THE YEAR 2000. *Everybody Counts: A Report to the Nation on the Future of Mathematics Education*. Washington, D.C.: National Academy Press, 1989.

CORNBLETH, CATHERINE, ED., *An Invitation to Research in Social Education*. Washington, D.C.: National Council for the Social Studies, 1986.

DOWNEY, MATTHEW T., ED. *Teaching American History: New Directions*. Washington, D.C.: National Council for the Social Studies, 1982.

FINN, CHESTER E., JR., RAVITCH, DIANE, AND FANCHER, ROBERT T., EDS. *Against Mediocrity: The Humanities in America's High Schools*. New York: Holmes & Meier, 1984.

GETTY CENTER FOR EDUCATION IN THE ARTS. *Beyond Creating: The Place for Art in America's Schools*. Los Angeles, Calif.: Getty Center for Education in the Arts, 1985.

HALL, JANICE K. *Evaluating and Improving Written Expression: A Practical Guide for Teachers*. Needham Heights, Mass.: Allyn & Bacon, 1988.

HAWLEY, RICHARD A., PETERSON, ROBERT C., AND MASON, MARGARET C. *Curriculum for Building Drug Free Schools*. Rockville, Md.: American Council for Drug Education, 1986.

HERTZBERG, HAZEL WHITMAN. *Social Studies Reform 1890–1980*. Boulder, Colo.: Social Science Education Consortium, 1983.

HIRSCH, E. D., JR. *Cultural Literacy: What Every American Needs to Know*. Boston: Houghton Mifflin, 1987.

HUFSTEDLER, S. M., AND LAGNENBERG, D. N. *Science and Engineering Education for the 1980s and Beyond*. Washington, D.C.: U.S. Government Printing Office, 1980.

HURD, PAUL DEHART. *Reforming Science Education: The Search for a New Vision*. Washington, D.C.: Council for Basic Education, 1984.

JENNESS, DAVID. *Making Sense of Social Studies*. New York: Macmillan, 1990.

KOOP, C. EVERETT. *Surgeon General's Report on Acquired Immune Deficiency Syndrome*. Washington, D.C.: Public Health Service, U.S. Department of Health and Human Services, 1986.

LEHMAN, P. R. *Music in Today's Schools: Rationale and Commentary*. Reston, Va.: The Music Educators National Conference, 1987.

LEWIS, MARY G. *Science Education Programs That Work: A Collection of Proven Exemplary Programs and Practices in the National Diffusion Network*. Washington, D.C.: Office of Education Research and Improvement, U.S. Department of Education, 1988.

MACDONALD, DONALD I. *Adolescent Drug and Alcohol Abuse*. Chicago: Year Book, 1984.

MASUDA, YOSEJI. *The Information Society as Post-Industrial Society*. Tokyo: Institute for the Information Society, 1980.

NAISBITT, JOHN. *Megatrends*. New York: Warner Books, 1982.

NATIONAL COMMISSION ON SOCIAL STUDIES IN THE SCHOOLS. *Charting a Course: Social Studies for the 21st Century*. Washington, D.C.: National Commission on Social Studies in the Schools, 1989.

NATIONAL ENDOWMENT FOR THE ARTS. *Toward Civilization: A Report on Arts Education*. Washington, D.C.: National Endowment for the Arts, 1988.

———. *Toward Civilization: Overview from A Report on Arts Education*. Washington, D.C.: National Endowment for the Arts, 1988.

NATIONAL SCIENCE BOARD COMMISSION ON PRE-COLLEGE EDUCATION IN MATHEMATICS, SCIENCE, AND TECHNOLOGY. *Educating Americans for the 21st Century: A plan of action for improving mathematics, science, and technology education for all American elementary and secondary students so that their achievement is the best in the world by 1995*. Washington, D.C.: National Science Foundation, 1983.

OFFICE OF EDUCATIONAL RESEARCH AND IMPROVEMENT. *Drug Prevention Curricula: A Guide to Selection and Implementation*. Washington, D.C.: U.S. Department of Education, 1988.

OFFICE OF TECHNOLOGY ASSESSMENT. *Informational Technology and Its Impact on American Education*. Washington, D.C.: U.S. Government Printing Office, 1982.

———. *Power On! New Tools for Teaching and Learning: Summary*. Washington, D.C.: U.S. Government Printing Office, 1988.

PANTIEL, MINDY, AND PETERSEN, BECKY. *Kids, Teachers, and Computers: A Guide to Computers in the Elementary School*. Englewood Cliffs, N.J.: Prentice-Hall, 1985.

Report of the Presidential Commission on the Human Immunodeficiency Virus Epidemic. Washington, D.C.: U.S. Government Printing Office, 1988.

STEEN, ARTHUR LYNN, ED. *On the Shoulders of Giants: New Approaches to Numeracy*. Washington, D.C.: National Academy Press, 1990.

TAYLOR, ROBERT P., ED. *The Computer in the School: Tutor, Tool, Tutee*. New York: Teachers College Press, 1980.

TOBIAS, JOYCE. *Kids and Drugs: A Handbook for Parents and Professionals*. Annandale, Va.: PANDA Press, 1986.

TOFFLER, ALVIN, ED. *Learning for Tomorrow: The Role of the Future in Education*. New York: Random House, 1974.

U.S. DEPARTMENT OF EDUCATION. *What Works: Schools Without Drugs*. Washington, D.C.: U.S. Department of Education, 1986.

U.S. DEPARTMENT OF HEALTH AND HUMAN SERVICES. *Guidelines for Effective School Health Education to Prevent the Spread of AIDS*. Atlanta, Ga.: Public Health Service, Centers for Disease Control, Center for Health Promotion and Education, 1988.

YARBER, WILLIAM L. *AIDS Education: Curriculum and Health Policy*. Bloomington, Ind.: Phi Delta Kappa Educational Foundation, 1987.

———. *AIDS: What Young Adults Should Know*. Reston, Va.: American Alliance, 1987.

20

The Education of Special Learners

In recent years, both the general public and professional educators have directed greater attention to the education of special learners. This new direction was stimulated by several national trends. The civil rights activism and judicial decisions of the 1960s to foster racial integration drew attention to the rights of people in other categories who had been denied equal educational opportunities. Among these groups were persons with handicaps.

In schools, the segregation of children on the basis of race and handicap was sometimes interrelated. Large numbers of children from minority groups were labeled as handicapped and were placed in isolated special schools and classes.

The medical and psychological professions had advanced further in studying physiological and behavioral problems; their discoveries were translated into educational practice. Persons especially interested in the problems of the handicapped, such as parents, guardians, and others, had organized strong advocacy groups to identify and promote educational opportunities for children with handicaps.

It was in this context of greater attention to the rights of children with handicaps that a U.S. district court decision in 1971 ordered Pennsylvania school districts to educate all retarded learners between the ages of 4 and 21. The concept of the "right to education" was now expanded to include learners with mental and emotional handicaps.

The general focusing questions that will be answered as you read this chapter include the following:

1. How has federal legislation advanced the education of learners with handicaps?
2. What is *mainstreaming* and how does it affect education?
3. What are the basic terms used in describing *exceptionality*?
4. What educational programs have been designed to serve gifted and talented learners?

Federal Legislation

Congressional legislation complemented the action of the courts regarding the education of persons with handicaps, with two federal laws being especially relevant: the Vocational Rehabilitation Act of 1973 (PL 93–516) and the Education of

All Handicapped Children Act of 1975 (PL 94–142). These laws had far-reaching implications for education at all levels.

The intention of federal legislation was to remove restrictions that prevented individuals with handicaps from participating in the opportunities of American education. The Vocational Rehabilitation Act of 1973, especially Section 504, provided for (1) vocational training in mainstream settings, (2) the promotion and expansion of employment opportunities, and (3) the removal of architectural and transportation barriers. This legislation was designed specifically to encourage the entry of more persons with handicaps into the job force and to eliminate unnecessary obstacles to their hiring and in their job performance.

The 1975 Education of All Handicapped Children Act established a national policy that the nation's children with handicaps (individuals between the ages of 3 and 21) would be assured of a "free, appropriate public education" designed to meet their unique needs. PL 94–142 has had far-reaching consequences in that it directly affects the approximately eight million children with handicaps in the United States. It defines handicapped children as "mentally retarded, hard of hearing, seriously disturbed, orthopedically impaired, or children with specific learning disabilities, who by reason thereof require special education and related services." The law, particularly its provisions for mainstreaming, affects virtually every child, teacher, and school in the United States. Because PL 94–142 has had such pervasive ramifications for American education, it is useful to identify its key provisions and requirements:

1. Each state is to identify and locate all its children with handicaps and to provide a curriculum responsive to the needs of each child.
2. Each state is to establish an advisory board—composed of handicapped individuals, teachers, and parents of handicapped children—to advise and comment on needs, regulations, and evaluative procedure.
3. Children with handicaps are to be mainstreamed, that is, educated whenever possible in the least restrictive environment, preferably a regular classroom, with nonhandicapped children. Children with handicaps are to be placed in the more restrictive environment of special or separate classes only when their exceptionality makes it impossible to educate them in regular classrooms.
4. Due process provisions are to be observed to protect children with handicaps against improper placement and to give their parents or guardians the right to access to pertinent records. According to due process provisions, parents or guardians have the right to participate in the placement of their children and to protest and appeal decisions by school officials.
5. School personnel are to prepare an individualized educational plan (IEP) for each handicapped child. The plan is to be developed by a support team that includes a school representative, usually the building principal, the teacher, and the child's parent or guardian. Whenever appropriate, the child is to be included. The plan, which is to be reviewed and revised annually according to the child's growth and development, is to specify long- and short-term educational goals and needed services.
6. Instruments and methods used to test and evaluate children with handicaps must be racially and culturally nondiscriminatory and must be in the child's primary language or "mode of communication." Also, no single test or evaluative procedure is to be used as the exclusive basis for determining a child's educational program.

FIGURE 20-1   Special Education Enrollment in Federally
Supported Programs

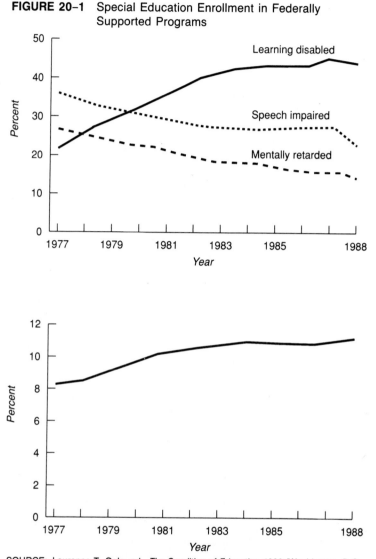

SOURCE: Laurence T. Ogle, ed., *The Condition of Education 1990* (Washington, D.C.
U.S. Government Printing Office, 1990), p. 47.

7. Related transportation and developmental, corrective, and supportive services are to be
provided to children with handicaps. These include speech pathology, audiology,
psychological seminars, physical and occupational therapy, recreation, and counseling
and medical services needed for diagnosis and evaluative purposes.

8. If children with handicaps cannot be educated with other children, then they must be
educated in their homes, hospitals, or other institutions. The placement of children in
private institutions is to be done at no cost to parents. Private school programs must
meet the same standards the law requires of public school programs.

9. If states fail to comply with the law, federal funds can be withheld after a reasonable notice and hearing.

10. If local school districts are unable or unwilling to comply with the law, the state can suspend payments to them. The state must then use the funds to provide direct service to the children.

In the 1980s, Congress enacted legislation that reaffirmed and extended the basic policies established by PL 94–142. The Education of the Handicapped Act of 1983 (PL 98–199) provided for the establishment of a national advisory committee on special education, gave permission to use federal funds for children under the age of three, provided grants to the states to develop comprehensive early childhood services, expanded postsecondary vocational and training programs, established grants for parent education, and encouraged research to improve curriculum and instruction. The Education of the Handicapped Act of 1986 (PL 99–457) expanded the federal government's role in the education of pre-school-age children with handicaps. Its major direction was on the education of children from the ages of three to five and on providing early intervention services for children from birth to age two. For special education enrollments in federally supported programs, see Figure 20-1.

The federal legislation had a pronounced impact on American public education. It meant that regular classroom teaching had to be redesigned to meet the needs of learners with handicaps. Not only did the new responsibility fall on teachers who were already in service, but it also fell on teacher education departments and colleges, which needed to redesign many of their teacher-preparation programs.[1] In the sections that follow, attention will be given to the concept of "mainstreaming" and to identifying the various categories of handicapped learners.

Special Education and Regular Education

Before discussing "exceptionality," it is useful to examine the relationships of *special* and *regular* education. First, it should be remembered that public schools were established and are supported to educate all American children. The general guidelines that relate to teaching and learning are applicable to all children. Those who decide to pursue careers in special education should be knowledgeable about the curriculum and methods of instruction that apply to schooling in general so that their work is integrated with the general instructional program. Second, it also should be remembered that each individual child has unique as well as general needs. Teachers, both regular and special, need to know and to be alert to the unique needs of individual boys and girls. Teachers who are sensitive to the economic, social, racial, and ethnic diversity of students will be better prepared to meet both their general and their specific needs. Multicultural education attempts to prepare teachers to recognize and deal with racial and ethnic differences. In much the same way, regular classroom teachers need to recognize the various kinds of physical,

---

1. *A Common Body of Practice for Teachers: The Challenge of Public Law 94–142 to Teacher Education* (Washington, D.C.: American Association of Colleges for Teacher Education, 1980), pp. 3–5.

psychological, and emotional needs of children so that they can benefit from a public education. In other words, just as children should not be isolated because of race or handicap, neither should teachers work in educational isolation from each other—regardless of their specialization.

In examining the relationship between regular and special education, the term *exceptional children* is often used. The exceptional child has been defined as differing from the normal child in mental characteristics, sensory abilities, neuromuscular or physical characteristics, social or emotional behavior, communication abilities, or a combination of these characteristics and abilities such that a modification of regular school practices or special education services is required. By definition, exceptional children are those, who because of certain atypical characteristics, have been identified by professionally trained specialists as requiring special educational planning and services. Exceptionality may be identified on the basis of (1) physical, health, or sensory handicaps, (2) behavioral problems or emotional handicaps, (3) observable variations in mental abilities, such as those of gifted individuals or of mentally retarded individuals. Some exceptional children may have more than one type of exceptionality.[2]

The degree of exceptionality determines the degree to which the individual child will be educated by regular classroom teachers or special education teachers. Mildly handicapped children, for example, are likely to have more contact with the regular classroom teacher than with the special education teacher; conversely, profoundly handicapped children are likely to have more contact with the special education teacher than with the regular classroom teacher. The majority of exceptional children, falling midway between the poles of mildly and profoundly handicapped, will have contact with both regular and special education teachers.

Special education refers to direct instruction, planned learning experiences, and consultative activities designed primarily to meet the needs of exceptional children and students. Special education programs are usually designed for students with the following exceptionalities: (1) physical handicaps, (2) emotional disturbances, (3) cultural differences, including compensatory educational needs, (4) mental retardation, (5) learning disabilities, and (6) mental gifts and talents. When referring to instructional programs for students identified as handicapped and needing services not provided by the regular curriculum, *special education* implies that the curriculum has been adapted or modified to meet the identified needs of the individual pupil.[3]

Those responsible for designing and implementing this instruction are special educators who have been prepared and certificated to carry out their specific functions in educating students with handicaps. Special educators include teachers,

2. For a discussion of exceptionality, see Daniel P. Hallahan and James M. Kauffman, *Exceptional Children: Introduction to Special Education* (Englewood Cliffs, N.J.: Prentice-Hall, 1988).
3. For the development of special education, see Jay G. Chambers and William T. Hartman, eds. *Special Education Policies: Their History, Implementation, and Finance* (Philadelphia: Temple University Press, 1982). For highly useful information on special education, see Kenneth Shore, *The Special Education Handbook: A Comprehensive Guide for Parents and Educators* (New York: Teachers College Press, 1986).

counselors, teacher educators, and administrators, such as special education directors, who possess training and competencies for educating certain categories of exceptional children.

In addition to the professional personnel responsible for the education of exceptional children, the term *special education* also has relevance for curriculum, methodology, and materials. Some exceptional children may require a curriculum that differs from the regular curriculum; that is, deaf learners may require speechreading and blind learners may need braille. The instructor of certain categories of exceptional children may also require particular methods of instruction; for example, behavior modification techniques are often used with students who have severe learning disabilities. Exceptional children may also need instructional materials that are designed specifically to meet their needs. Among the instruments and materials that are available are braille and large-type books for the visually impaired and special typewriters for the physically handicapped.

School Programs for Exceptional Children

School programs for exceptional children (learners with handicaps) generally consist of three major and related components: identification, evaluation, and remediation.[4]

Identification

The usual methods of identifying exceptional children are screening and teacher referrals. Many school districts conduct comprehensive preschool screening programs that seek an early identification of cognitive, motor, and communicative problems. Early in the school year, special education personnel may interview or observe children to identify those who have possible problems. Regular classroom teachers, in daily contact with children, are able to observe and assess the child's behavior in various social and academic situations. Of course, obvious and known disabilities are referred to school personnel by parents and physicians.

Evaluation

Interdisciplinary teams that include psychologists, special educators, medical personnel, administrators, social workers, and classroom teachers help in the process of evaluation. The major purpose of evaluation is to compile information about the child that can be used to develop remedial plans and IEPs. Comprehensive evaluations require the collection and coordination of data obtained through (1) the child's case history, (2) specialized standardized tests and procedures, and (3) the observation of the child's behavior.

4. This discussion is adapted from Gerald G. Freeman, *Speech and Language Services and the Classroom Teacher* (Reston, Va.: Council for Exceptional Children, 1977), pp. 25–48.

Remediation

Specific strategies designed to modify behavior and improve performance will vary with the nature and degree of the handicap or disability. A general program of remediation is likely to involve (1) establishing a success level for the child in terms of specific skills or learning, (2) identifying target behaviors for modifications, (3) outlining plans to develop the recommended behavior or learning, (4) implementing the plans, and (5) revising the plans to meet the child's changing needs as development and learning take place.

Educators of exceptional children have tended to use behavior modification or management as an instructional strategy. Because behavior modification stresses specific skills and behaviors, general goals are reduced to specific learning. The careful working out of sequence is important so that the learning of a skill grows out of one learned previously and leads to one that is slightly more complex and cumulative. The following techniques of behavioral management are often used in remediation and in teaching handicapped children: (1) identifying the desired behavior, (2) isolating the behavior, (3) mastering the isolated behavior, (4) transferring the skill to the classroom setting, and (5) fixing or stabilizing the use of the skill in a variety of life situations.

The remediation of disabilities caused by handicaps requires an interdisciplinary team approach. Such a team may include medical personnel, special educators, learning specialists, psychologists, social workers, administrators, parents, and the classroom teacher. The effective interdisciplinary team should (1) coordinate their roles, responsibilities, and functions; (2) integrate the competencies of each member into a remedial program; and (3) relate the child's needs to the educator who is best able to satisfy them.

Mainstreaming

It will be recalled that PL 94–142 required that children with handicaps be educated in the least restrictive environment and that each handicapped child have an individualized education plan, or IEP, prepared by a support team that includes regular and special educators, as well as other professionals. Although regular and special educators need to cooperate throughout the entire process of schooling, it has been mainstreaming—the integration of handicapped learners—into the regular classroom that has made such cooperation imperative. For the distribution of special education students in various educational settings, see Table 20-1.

In describing mainstreaming, Maynard C. Reynolds says:

> . . . *mainstreaming is based on the principle of educating most children in the same classrooms and providing special education on the basis of learning needs rather than categories of handicaps. Thus, under mainstreaming, children with learning problems can receive the expert help of special education teachers without being labeled or excluded from association with their peers. Furthermore, under mainstreaming conditions, regular and special classroom teachers share their skills and knowledge to teach the same children. Indeed, mainstreaming is distinguished by the amalgamation of*

TABLE 20–1 Percentage Distribution of Handicapped Persons 3 to 21 Years Old Receiving Special Education Services, by Educational Environment: 1985–1986

Type of Handicap	All Environments	Regular Class	Resource Room	Separate Class	Public Separate School Facility	Private Separate School Facility	Public Residential Facility	Private Residential Facility	Correction Facility	Homebound/Hospital Environment
All conditions	**100.0**	**26.4**	**41.5**	**24.5**	**3.6**	**1.6**	**1.0**	**0.4**	**0.3**	**0.7**
Learning disabled	100.0	15.3	61.7	21.1	0.9	0.5	(¹)	(¹)	(¹)	(¹)
Speech impaired	100.0	66.3	25.6	5.5	0.8	1.5	(¹)	(¹)	(¹)	(¹)
Mentally retarded	100.0	3.0	24.9	56.5	9.8	1.9	2.9	(¹)	(¹)	(¹)
Seriously emotionally disturbed	100.0	8.8	33.8	35.8	8.8	4.5	1.8	2.3	1.7	2.3
Hard of hearing and deaf	100.0	19.4	21.5	34.5	7.9	4.0	11.0	1.1	(¹)	0.6
Orthopedically handicapped	100.0	26.4	16.6	33.2	10.6	4.0	0.6	(¹)	(¹)	8.1
Other health impaired	100.0	26.3	19.0	26.1	4.3	2.6	3.1	0.8	(¹)	17.8
Visually handicapped	100.0	34.2	25.4	20.7	4.1	2.2	10.8	1.0	(¹)	1.4
Multihandicapped	100.0	4.1	15.6	44.3	19.3	9.5	3.0	2.1	(¹)	1.7
Deaf-blind	100.0	6.8	17.4	23.9	12.3	3.3	26.3	8.8	(¹)	1.2

SOURCE: From National Center for Education Statistics, *Digest of Education Statistics 1989* (Washington, D.C.: U.S. Government Printing Office, 1989), p. 60.
NOTE: This table reflects a compilation of data reported by the states. There are some reporting variations, e.g., estimated or incomplete data and nonstandard definitions, from state to state. Data exclude U.S. Territories and schools operated by the Bureau of Indian Affairs. Because of rounding, details may not add to totals.
¹Less than 0.05 percent.

regular and special education into one system to provide a spectrum of services for all children according to their learning needs. Consequently, special education is a re-source for the entire school population rather than an isolated body of skills and knowledge.[5]

In some respects, mainstreaming is not a new concept. Prior to the professional development of special education, handicapped children were often included in the regular classrooms in the nineteenth and early twentieth centuries. Unfortunately, these children, who usually received no special attention, were classified as "problem children" or "dullards" by teachers who lacked sufficient expertise. As special education developed in the twentieth century, many children with handicaps were identified and placed in special classes or institutions that isolated them from students and experiences in regular classrooms. Although they received a "special education" in these special environments, they were segregated because of their exceptionality. By the 1960s, serious questions were raised about the isolation of exceptional children in special classrooms.

1. If a child with a handicap is given a special education in a socially and educationally segregated environment, does that situation provide for equality of educational opportunity?
2. Does not the isolation of persons with handicaps foster many of the same social attitudes that racial segregation promotes? By the 1970s, mainstreaming was promoted to provide for the education of the children with handicaps in regular classrooms to avoid not only social and educational isolation but also to meet the child's special needs.[6]

In addition to the legal mandate for mainstreaming, social and educational developments have also contributed to the development of the concept. Jack Birch, an early advocate and expert in mainstreaming, has identified the major social and educational reasons that support the concept of mainstreaming:

1. The improvement of the capability to deliver special education services to exceptional children in regular classrooms.
2. Parental demands that exceptional children be provided high-quality special education in regular classrooms.
3. The general public and professional rejection of the notion that children needing special education should be socially and educationally isolated because of labeling. Mainstreaming minimizes the need for labeling and eliminates many of its undesirable effects on children.
4. The legal recognition that the courts have given to the right of all children to have a full and free education regardless of handicap.
5. Historically, psychological tests of intelligence and achievement were major determinants in identifying children for special education classes and special schools. Today, spokespersons for minority children have challenged the application and appropriateness of such tests in placing children in special educational arrangements.

5. Maynard C. Reynolds, "Foreword," in Jack W. Birch, *Mainstreaming: Educable Mentally Retarded Children in Regular Classes* (Reston, Va.: Council for Exceptional Children, 1974), p. iii.
6. John G. Herlihy and Myra T. Herlihy, "Why Mainstreaming?" in *Mainstreaming in the Social Studies* (Washington, D.C.: National Council for the Social Studies, 1980), pp. 2–7.

6. A general recognition that nonhandicapped children are deprived of important educational experiences if they do not associate with handicapped children.
7. The compatibility of the concept of mainstreaming with the American belief in equality of educational opportunity for all children.[7]

Mainstreaming Procedures

Most teachers will be involved in mainstreaming, so the following general procedures that help explain the process are useful:

1. Mainstreaming can be done at any grade level.
2. Students with handicaps should be selected for mainstreaming in terms of their educational needs and capabilities rather than on the basis of clinical categories or diagnostic labels.
3. Exceptional (handicapped) children are assigned to regular classes, and special educational services are provided for them while they remain in the regular classroom for as much of the day as possible; mainstreamed students with handicaps leave the regular classroom only for essential small-group or individual special instruction or assessment.
4. Regular and special education teachers and educational administrators and supervisors need to cooperate in educational planning and programming so that children with

An illustration of a mainstreamed learning environment.

7. Birch, *Mainstreaming*, pp. 2–7.

handicaps — as well as nonhandicapped children — can benefit academically and socially from participation in the regular classroom.

5. Regular and special education teachers work together to plan individual schedules and assignments needed by students with handicaps; the regular classroom teacher or subject matter teacher is responsible for the grading and reporting of children with handicaps in consultation with the special education teachers.

6. Mainstreaming needs should be considered by school boards, educational cooperatives, and administrators in planning and organizing instruction, allocating space, providing materials, and designing facilities.

Individual Education Program

While PL 94–142 mandates the mainstreaming of most children with handicaps into the regular classroom, it also requires that their instruction be individualized. The law requires that an IEP be prepared at least annually for each child by a support staff or committee composed of regular and special teachers, administrators, ancillary professional personnel, and the child's parents or guardian. Directly stated, an IEP is "a written statement about the objectives, content, implementation and evaluation of a child's educational program."[8]

In its most general terms, an IEP includes such information as, What is to be taught to the child? Who is to do the teaching? How is the material to be taught? How will the effectiveness of the child's instructional program be evaluated? More specifically, an IEP involves the following:

1. A *description and analysis of the student's educational status*, which includes formal and standardized test data, informal school reports, physical and medical data, and other related information. From this information, a status report is compiled in performance terms that identify the child's academic, physical, and psychological strengths and weaknesses. The status report is used to identify needs so that appropriate instructional strategies can be devised.

2. A *statement of annual goals*, which are behavioral outcomes that reflect the skills and content of the grade level or subject matter.

3. A *statement of instructional objectives*, which describes the particular schedule and process for achieving the stated annual goals. The objectives may relate to skills, content, or remediation of the handicapping condition. The instructional objectives are derived from the statement of annual goals and represent short-term and specific ways of achieving them.

4. A *statement of instructional and service requirements*, which describes the various support services and professional personnel needed to educate the child with handicaps. This may involve the special education teacher and the use of special equipment and facilities.

5. A statement indicating the *degree, time*, and *nature of the mainstreaming and support service*, which specifies the time that the child with handicaps will require special education services.

6. An *evaluation*, which is used to measure the student's success in achieving stated program goals. The evaluation should be formative so that it can contribute to needed modifications of instruction designed to achieve goals more effectively.

8. Maynard C. Reynolds and Jack W. Birch, *Teaching Exceptional Children in All America's Schools* (Reston, Va.: Council for Exceptional Children, 1977), p. 157.

7. *Due process* is interwoven into the design and execution of the IEP. Students and their parents have the right to review and to monitor the IEP. They also have the right to legal action if they believe that the system is failing to achieve stated goals. School administrators and teachers also have the right to due process.[9]

The IEP represents an effort to solve an old educational problem. How can teachers provide for the child's individual needs and differences in a group institutional setting? On the one hand, the homogeneous group that is composed of students of the same abilities, achievement levels, or interests is often an effective and efficient vehicle for instruction. The group is also an agency for socialization as well as for specific learning. While group instruction has these advantages, it often sacrifices individual needs for the good of the majority. Individualized instruction — long a goal of many educators — provides for the unique needs of each child. Unfortunately, it may isolate children from the social relationships and developments that they need. The IEP is designed to satisfy both the individual and social needs of the exceptional learner.

As an essentially cooperative educational effort, mainstreaming requires the participation of school administrators, regular classroom teachers, and the special education staff. Its central theme is that regular classroom teachers can educate exceptional children in the regular classroom with the support and consultative services of special education personnel. Mainstreaming requires partnership on the part of all teachers — both regular and special — in educating all children.

Toward a Terminology of Exceptionality

Experts in special education have developed a terminology to identify and define the various categories of exceptionality. Because special education has been a rapidly developing field, its expanding terminology has been subject to frequent redefinition and change. The terminology that has been devised is designed to describe more accurately and precisely the various forms of exceptionality. In using the terminology that follows, be aware that changes and redefinition are likely.

Learning Disabilities

Although the term *learning disabled* (LD) is used frequently in special education, its definition is subject to controversy. Historically, the term was used to identify learners with perceptual disorders caused by neurological impairment.[10] Today, it

9. This description of an IEP is based on John C. Herlihy and Myra T. Herlihy, "The IEP — Individualization of an Institution," in *Mainstreaming in the Social Studies*, pp. 23–25. Useful information on mainstreaming is provided by Maynard C. Reynolds and Jack W. Birch, *Adaptive Mainstreaming: A Primer for Teachers and Principals* (New York: Longman, 1988); also see Ann P. Turnbull and Jane B. Schulz, *Mainstreaming Handicapped Students: A Guide for the Classroom Teacher* (Boston: Allyn & Bacon, 1979), and Colleen Blankenship and Lilly M. Stephen, *Mainstreaming Students with Learning and Behavior Problems: Techniques for the Classroom Teacher* (New York: Holt, Rinehart and Winston, 1981).

10. For a discussion of learning disabilities, see Daniel P. Hallahan, James M. Kauffman, and John W. Lloyd, *Introduction to Learning Disabilities* (Englewood Cliffs, N.J.: Prentice-Hall, 1985).

refers to a wide range of learning deficits or disabilities. In PL 94–142, a "specific learning disability" refers to

> *a disorder in one or more of the basic psychological processes involved in understanding or using language spoken or written, which may manifest itself in an imperfect ability to listen, think, speak, read, write, spell or to do mathematical calculations.*

According to the law the term *learning disability* includes perceptual handicaps, brain injury, minimal brain dysfunction, dyslexia, and developmental aphasia. It excludes learning problems resulting primarily from visual, hearing, or motor handicaps, from mental retardation, or from environmental, cultural, or economic disadvantages.

It is important to distinguish between learners who are neurologically handicapped and those who are mentally retarded. The learner with a neurological handicap may be intellectually capable of normal academic progress; the mentally retarded is not. Thus, it is imperative that neurologically impaired students be diagnosed correctly so that they receive an appropriate education.

The term *neurologically handicapped* refers to persons with an impairment of the central nervous system. This impairment can be congenital or caused by accident; it may be mild or severe. Among the causes of neurological dysfunction are injury to the fetus, injury or oxygen deprivation during pregnancy or birth, malnutrition, chemical or blood irregularities, genetic aberration, and illness of the mother during pregnancy. Often, the symptoms of neurological handicap may not become apparent until the child enters school. It is important that the regular classroom teacher be alert to the following symptoms of neurological impairment:

1. Erratic performance in schoolwork
2. Easy distractibility
3. Swift mood changes
4. Clumsy psychomotor skills
5. Ineptness in play activities

Mental Retardation

The term *mental retardation* describes significantly subaverage general intellectual ability and cognitive functioning, existing concurrently with defects in adaptive behavior and manifested during the child's developmental period, which adversely impact educational performance.[11] Mental retardation may result from such causes as German measles during pregnancy, poor prenatal or postnatal care, oxygen deprivation at birth, physical injury, or genetic-chromosomal disorder. Mental retardation is a permanent condition that adversely impacts a learner's cognitive abilities such as association, comparison, comprehension, generalization, and symbolization. Among the general learning problems of the retarded child are the following:

11. For a discussion of the education of the mentally retarded, see Cecil D. Mercer and Martha E. Snell, *Learning Theory Research in Mental Retardation: Implications for Teaching* (Columbus, Ohio: Charles E. Merrill, 1977).

1. A limited vocabulary and reading ability that impedes learning in other basic subjects
2. Short attention span and limited retention
3. Difficulty in learning from experience
4. Less capability for making social adjustments

Retarded learners can be aided by proper diagnosis and appropriate instruction that often involves behavior modification and programmed instruction. Behavior modification is based on the strategy that rewards will reinforce desirable behaviors and that the failure to reward undesirable behaviors will reduce them. Programmed instruction in which lessons are reduced to small, sequential steps is also used with retarded as well as other learners. The general educational goal is to assist retarded learners to develop adaptive behaviors that will make them as self-sufficient as possible.

There are three general categories of mentally retarded persons; educable mentally retarded (EMR), with IQs of between 50 and 75; trainable mentally retarded (TMR), with IQs below 50, who are capable of learning some academic skills; and custodial, with IQs below 30, who are capable of only the rudimentary learning of nonacademic skills. The Children's Bureau has estimated that 30 out of every 1,000 persons are retarded. Of these 30, it is estimated that 25 are educable, four are trainable, and one is custodial.

Educable mentally retarded children are capable of learning academic skills, but with limited facility. They are increasingly being mainstreamed into regular classrooms rather than kept in special education classes. Teachers who are instructing EMR children should be certain that

1. Content and materials are within the child's capacity to learn
2. Materials relate directly to the child's environment and experiences
3. Assignments are within the child's ability range
4. Visual aids are used to illustrate more abstract concepts

Trainable learners are children who are unable to benefit from regular classroom experience but do not need to spend their lives in special institutions. With appropriate instruction, trainable children can learn to take care of themselves, to make a reasonable social adjustment, and to learn simple occupational skills. They may or may not become economically self-sufficient. Some public school systems have provided special ungraded classrooms for trainable youngsters; others may be placed in residential schools.

Custodial children have a very limited range of intelligence and require close supervision and care at home or in residential institutions. They can be subdivided into the severely retarded and the profoundly retarded. The severely retarded are capable of learning only rudimentary self-care skills and elementary speech. They may perform simple tasks at home or in sheltered workshops. The profoundly retarded are incapable of speaking and need permanent nursing care.

Behavioral Disabilities

Behavioral disabled (BD), a general term that has not been defined precisely, includes the psychologically disordered and the socially maladjusted. Among the behaviors exhibited by BD youngsters are conduct disorders; hyperactivity; extreme physical and verbal aggression; extreme fear, anxiety, and feelings of inadequacy; and social delinquency. Behaviorally disabled youngsters exhibit atypical and extreme forms of behavior.

The Physically Handicapped

Physical handicaps range from congenital birth defects to injuries caused by accidents. Because it is beyond the scope of this book to classify the various categories of physical handicaps in detail, we will discuss only the most common types that have a general impact on education.

Speech and Language Impairment   Learners with speech and language impairments constitute the largest group of physically handicapped children.[12] Speech impairment refers to any acoustic variation from an accepted speech standard that is so extreme as to be conspicuous in the speaker and confusing to the listener. A speech impairment can be defined as a disorder in the mechanics of speech, such as articulation, voice, and fluency. Among the common kinds of speech defects are stuttering, lisping, cluttering, nasality, thick speech, baby talk, hoarseness, and impairments caused by organic difficulties such as cleft palate and cerebral palsy. Language impairment refers to a student's inability to understand, express, and use language.

Voice problems can be caused by physical abnormalities or from vocal misuse. School speech pathologists and speech-language therapists should refer students with voice problems to medical personnel, usually with a specialty in otolaryngology, for diagnosis and treatment before initiating a remedial program. In cooperation with the speech pathologist or therapist, the regular classroom teacher should plan a program to remediate the speech or language difficulty. Although specific objectives should be tailored to the individual child's needs, teachers should observe the following general guidelines:

1. Enter into full cooperation with the speech pathologist and interdisciplinary support team.
2. Enlist the assistance of parents in implementing the program of remediation and in-class participation.
3. Encourage children to speak and to participate in speech activities despite their disability.
4. Refrain from threatening or ridiculing students who are speech or language impaired.

Hearing Impairment   Hearing impairment, a very broad and general term, encompasses hearing problems (auditory or acoustical) that interfere with learning. Hearing-impaired children may be deaf or hard of hearing.

Deafness refers to the absence of hearing in both ears. A major educational problem in the instruction of the deaf is that they may have never heard speech and

---

12. For a discussion of recent developments, see Freeman, *Speech and Language Services and the Classroom Teacher*.

may lack the normal use of language as a means of communication. The difficulty with language development is likely to extend to the learning of basic skills and may adversely affect academic learning. The absence of a normal language foundation means that deaf children require special education services. Often, one or more of the following special educators may be involved in providing services to deaf children: hearing clinician, speech therapist, and teacher of the deaf or hearing impaired.

The term *hard of hearing* refers to individuals who once had sufficient hearing to acquire the basic foundations of language with special teaching but who later lost part or all of their hearing.[13] Hard-of-hearing children may experience distortion in language development and have difficulties in acquiring additional communication skills. While hard-of-hearing children have significant hearing losses, they have learned language in the usual way. Special educators have developed a range of techniques for providing effective instruction to hard-of-hearing youngsters. It is also possible and desirable to mainstream many hard-of-hearing students into regular classrooms.

Deaf and hard-of-hearing children can be identified in the usual ways that other cases of exceptionality are identified: by physicians and parents, through preschool screening, and by the administration of annual hearing tests as part of the school program. In addition to these standard procedures, the classroom teacher should be alert to the following symptoms of hearing impairment:

1. Repeated failure to respond to one's name
2. Consistently cocking the head to one side
3. Difficulty in understanding, interpreting, and following directions
4. An inability to determine the source of a sound
5. Persistently watching others and following their movements
6. Frequently asking to have a word or a direction repeated
7. Persistently mispronouncing common words

Regular teachers need to develop sensitivity and skill in instructing hearing-impaired children who are mainstreamed into their classes. As is true of the mainstreaming of other exceptional children, it is necessary for special and regular teachers to cooperate in developing plans and strategies for the education of hearing-impaired students. Jack Birch, an authority on mainstreaming, has identified the following factors that have an impact on the education of hearing-impaired students:

1. What is the nature of the hearing defect? Is it in the speech range? While loss of hearing for high- and low-pitched sounds creates some problems in instructing hearing-impaired children, the most serious difficulties occur when the child cannot hear ordinary conversation.
2. What is the degree of the hearing impairment? Where does the hearing defect fall on a scale from a total to a relatively limited loss? A total hearing loss creates serious instructional problems as it closes off oral communication and renders a hearing aid useless. If the hearing impairment is limited, a hearing aid can be of immense use in the education of a hearing-impaired child.

13. Jack W. Birch, *Hearing Impaired Pupils in the Mainstream* (Minneapolis: Leadership Training Institute/Special Education, University of Minnesota, 1975), p. 8.

3. When did the hearing loss begin? At what age was hearing lost or impaired? The later the time of the hearing impairment, the greater the opportunity to acquire a language foundation. The earlier in childhood that the hearing impairment occurred, the more serious — depending on the degree of hearing loss — the instructional problem.

4. What is the hearing-impaired child's level of intelligence? As is generally true with all the children, the more intellectually able child — including the hearing-impaired child — will have a greater probability of academic success. So that the hearing-impaired child's academic potential can be assessed accurately and realistically, the interdisciplinary support team should have the professional evaluation of a school psychologist. It is important that teachers do not underestimate the intelligence of hearing-impaired children.

5. What kind and amount of stimulation should be given to hearing-impaired children? Unless efforts are made to encourage the hearing-impaired child's comprehension, use, and communication of language, the child's language development and speech quality is likely to deteriorate. Sustained, concerted, and regular stimulation of language comprehension and communication can minimize the effects of hearing impairment and maximize the constructive impact of special instruction.[14]

As in other areas of special education, a technology has developed to aid in the education of hearing-impaired persons. The *audiometer*, an instrument that emits tones of different frequencies at controlled loudness levels, is used to help identify students with impaired hearing and to measure the degrees of hearing. The *hearing aid*, an electronic device, is used to pick up and amplify sound for hearing-impaired persons who have residual hearing. The *radio ear* is an instrument that is used to magnify the human voice so that students can hear.

Ameslan, or American Sign Language, is a separate and distinct language used to communicate with the deaf. In Ameslan, actions represent concepts. The manual alphabet, in which the letters are spelled by different finger positions of the hand, can also be used. In the manual alphabet, each position of the fingers represents one of the 26 letters.

Visual Impairment   Millions of Americans have visual impairment. Visual impairment, restricted vision, includes both the blind and the low-visioned person. Fortunately, milder impairments such as myopia (nearsightedness), hyperopia (farsightedness), and astigmatism (imperfection in the thickness and curvature of the cornea) can be alleviated by corrective lenses.

Visually impaired children are often identified by parents, physicians, and preschool screenings. Because there may be changes in vision as the child matures, periodic examinations are useful both in the school setting or as part of a regular physical checkup. The following brief terminology is useful to teachers who will encounter students with vision problems in their classrooms:

Visually impaired child: blind and low-visioned children with restricted vision.
Low-visioned child: visually impaired children who use print as a primary learning medium.
Blind child: visually impaired children who use braille as a primary learning medium.

14. Ibid., pp. 11–17.

A special education teacher provides guided instruction to a child with handicaps.

Functional vision: information about a child's vision that has educational relevance. It refers to the child's effective use of the vision that she or he possesses.

Vision teacher: a special educator who provides service to visually impaired children.[15]

The regular classroom teacher can be alert to recognizing children who have vision problems and can refer to them for further examination. The incidence of children who need some eye care is estimated at approximately 25 percent of the school-age population. Teachers should be aware of those with vision problems, such as children who

1. Make frequent and repeated mistakes with words or numbers
2. Are unable to study without eye discomfort or who complain about headaches
3. Hold their heads in peculiar and awkward positions and who frequently squint or frown
4. Hold their books very close or very far from their eyes
5. Are able to see objects at a distance more clearly than those at close range
6. Are unable to see objects at a distance
7. Exhibit redness or swelling of eye lids or inflamed or watery eyes

As in teaching other handicapped children, teachers who have visually impaired youngsters in their classes should use the general principles and procedures that govern sound instruction. For example, each child should be regarded as a

15. This terminology is based on Glenda J. Martin and Mollie Hoben, *Supporting Visually Impaired Students in the Mainstream* (Reston, Va.: Council for Exceptional Children, 1977), p. 28.

unique individual who has basic human needs. All children should be treated fairly and consistently. Teachers need to be flexible enough to adapt their methods to the needs of the children for whom they have educational responsibility. While these pedagogical guidelines apply to teaching generally, it will be necessary for teachers to make some adaptation for visually impaired children.

The following suggestions may be helpful to teachers who have visually impaired students in their classrooms:

1. Develop an attitude in which you give reasonable assistance to visually handicapped children but avoid pity or too much help. Do not underestimate the ability of the visually handicapped child to learn and to cope with school.
2. In planning seating arrangements, locate visually impaired children in areas that have adequate light. They may need to be seated near the front of the room so that they can see the teacher and the chalkboard.
3. Read assignments, instructions, and explanations that are written on the chalkboard.
4. Provide occasions for visually impaired children to use and to exercise their existing and unused vision.
5. Be familiar with the technology used to assist in instructing visually impaired children, such as books and typewriters with large type, voice tapes, and audio equipment.

Gifted and Talented Learners

Although there has been much research on identifying and educating gifted and intellectually talented children, the development of gifted-education programs in many American public school systems has been slow and uneven.[16] Critics of American public schools often have asserted that the massiveness of the system and the emphasis on equality of educational opportunity have contributed to an attitude that stresses sameness and the average rather than the unique.

In an effort to respond to the national unevenness in educating gifted children, Congress enacted the Gifted and Talented Children's Act of 1978 (PL 95–561). According to PL 95–561, gifted and talented children and youth are those "who are identified at the preschool, elementary, or secondary level as possessing demonstrated or potential abilities that give evidence of high performance capabilities in areas such as intellectual, creative, specific academic, or leadership ability, or in the performing and visual arts, and who by reason thereof, require services or activities not ordinarily provided by the school." Unlike its efforts in mandating education for children with handicaps, Congress has not been as successful in efforts to legislate the improvement of the education of gifted individuals. Federally sponsored programs have been inadequately funded and implemented. The effort to define giftedness through legislation has also been questioned. Most students of American education still argue that the education of the nation's gifted children is a sorely neglected problem that needs attention, financial assistance, and curricular development.

Because of their very creativity and uniqueness, it is difficult to catalogue and categorize the characteristics of gifted children. Although listing of the characteris-

16. For definitions of giftedness, see Robert J. Sternberg and Janet E. Davidson, *Conceptions of Giftedness* (New York: Cambridge University Press, 1986).

tics of gifted children is difficult, a statement of some of the obvious qualities of gifted children is useful to teachers. Gifted children generally

1. Have keen powers of observation, abstraction, and conceptualization; they are interested in understanding cause-and-effect relationships and enjoy inductive learning and problem-solving situations.
2. Are adept at and enjoy divergent thinking; they resist the tendency to a premature closure of a problem that sees only a single solution; they prefer to hypothesize and structure alternative solutions to a problem.
3. Enjoy reading and exhibit verbal proficiency, facility in expression, and an extensive vocabulary.
4. Tend to be intellectually curious and enjoy individualized study and independent work.
5. Are critical thinkers who challenge commonly accepted styles of thought.

This list of characteristics can be extended. It should also be stated that giftedness is found throughout the various races, nationalities, and ethnic groups of humankind. Nor is giftedness a matter of color, creed, or sex.

The Academically or Intellectually Gifted

While no universal definition of the mentally gifted is generally accepted by educators, IQ as measured by the Stanford-Binet or Wechsler Intelligence Scale is often used to identify mentally gifted persons. An IQ that exceeds 125 is often used to identify the gifted person. In addition, teacher's judgments and academic records may be used to identify gifted children. It has been estimated that approximately 5 percent of the school population is within the gifted range.

Giftedness may exhibit itself in a particular academic area but not in all areas. For example, a child may be gifted in mathematics but not in art or music or history. While the greatest attention has been devoted to the intellectually gifted, consideration also needs to be given to the creatively gifted and the psychosocially gifted. These last two categories are not well defined, but teachers will recognize students who exhibit creative and leadership potential. The creatively gifted demonstrate consistent superior ability in originative, flexible, and productive thinking. Those who are socially gifted exhibit a strong tendency to political and social leadership. They have skill in interpersonal relationships and in determining and facilitating the attainment of group goals.

Instructing Gifted Learners

Various approaches exist to organizing instruction for gifted learners. Among them are grouping, acceleration, enrichment, and independent study.

Grouping of students is not new in education. One of the oldest patterns, historically, has been to group students according to age. Homogeneous grouping is used to cluster students in terms of intellectual readiness and ability and skill. Some high schools may schedule students into ability tracks. Other schools may use more flexible scheduling in which an individual student may be placed in a lower- or higher-level group in a particular subject.

Homogeneous grouping has long been the subject of considerable controversy among teachers. Those who favor homogeneous grouping argue that it makes it possible to organize materials and instruction according to the ability of a particular group of students. Opponents contend that it fosters intellectual elitism in that students in the higher-ability group may develop attitudes of superiority to those in lower groups. They also claim that ability grouping does not encourage realistic socialization.

Acceleration is an arrangement in which gifted students are promoted through school more rapidly than others. Gifted students may enter certain grades at an earlier age than the average student and may skip grades. In ungraded situations, it is also possible to accelerate or advance students into more complex subjects in which they demonstrate proficiency. The major argument used against acceleration is that it may place students in social situations for which they lack adequate social and emotional readiness and maturity.

Enrichment is designed to provide gifted students with a broad and varied experience within a given subject. If a student has mastered the essentials of a given subject matter, then he or she can broaden his or her knowledge by readings or assignments that add to the core knowledge. For example, if a student in a high school course in American history has mastered the material relating to the Civil War and Reconstruction, then he or she can pursue other topics that relate to the central theme, such as biographies of military and political leaders, military campaigns, or civil rights legislation.

Independent study can be used to individualize instruction for all students, including the academically gifted. It can provide for in-depth learning in a particular skill or subject that is part of the regular curriculum. Independent study projects or problems can also be interdisciplinary and related to several subject matter areas.

Conclusion

Public schools in the United States exist to educate the children of all the American people. Historically, this has meant that public education has served the needs of an increasingly diverse student population. To maximize the educational opportunities of the students, educators have designed instructional programs and patterns of school organization that meet the needs of individual students. Today, public schools, their administrators, and teachers are working to meet the needs of special learners in settings that not only maximize their educational opportunities in schools but also integrate them as productive citizens in the larger society.

DISCUSSION QUESTIONS

1. Identify the major provisions of the Education of All Handicapped Children Act of 1975 (PL 94–142) and comment on their implications for education.

2. Discuss the various components of an individualized education plan (IEP) and devise a model to be used in developing such plans.

3. Define the concept of "exceptionality." Is this term adequate or inadequate for use in school situations and in parent–teacher conferences and meetings?

4. Read a recent book on one of the categories of exceptionality. Report to the class on the author's contentions and the possible effects on classroom instruction.

5. What is mainstreaming? Consider the implications of mainstreaming for the grade level or subject matter area that you are preparing to teach. How should you prepare yourself to be an effective teacher in the mainstreamed classroom?

6. Define the following kinds of exceptionality: (a) learning disabled, (b) mentally retarded, (c) educable mentally retarded, (d) behaviorally disabled, (e) speech and language impaired, (f) hearing impaired, (g) visually impaired, (h) gifted.

7. Describe the characteristics of the intellectually gifted child.

8. Describe the various ways in which the regular classroom and special education teachers need to cooperate in instructional planning and delivery.

FIELD EXERCISES

1. Examine the physical plant—classrooms, libraries, elevators, lavatories—of the college or university in which you are enrolled. Discuss how physical facilities can aid or hinder the education of the handicapped person.

2. Arrange an in-class interview with a handicapped person that focuses on that individual's education.

3. Arrange an in-class interview with a special education and a regular classroom teacher that focuses on their cooperative activities.

4. Contact a school district and arrange to visit a mainstreamed class and a special education class. Report on your observations and share them with other students.

5. Contact a school district and arrange to visit a class for gifted students. Report on your observations and share them with other students.

6. Do preliminary research on how an interdisciplinary staffing is conducted. Simulate a staffing and prepare an IEP for a hypothetical student.

SUGGESTED READINGS

ASH, PAUL. *Educator's Guide to Exemplary Special Education Curricula: Results of a National Field Based Survey.* Indianapolis, Ind.: Council for Exceptional Children, 1985.

ASHMAN, ADRIAN F., AND CONWAY, ROBERT N. F. *Cognitive Strategies for Special Education: Process-Based Instruction.* New York: Routledge, 1989.

BAUER, ANNE M., AND SHEA, THOMAS M. *Teaching Exceptional Students in Your Classroom.* Boston: Allyn & Bacon, 1989.

BIRCH, J. W. *Mainstreaming: Educable Mentally Regarded Children in Regular Classes.* Reston, Va.: Council for Exceptional Children, 1974.

———. *Hearing Impaired Pupils in the Mainstream.* Minneapolis: Leadership Training Institute/Special Education, University of Minnesota, 1975.

———, AND JOHNSTONE, B. K. *Designing Schools and Schooling for the Handicapped.* Springfield, Ill.: Charles C. Thomas, 1975.

BLANKENSHIP, COLLEEN, AND STEPHEN, LILLY M. *Mainstreaming Students with Learning and Behavior Problems: Techniques for the Classroom Teacher.* New York: Holt, Rinehart and Winston, 1981.

BLITON, GILBERT, AND SCHROEDER, HENRY J. *The New Future for Children with Substantial Handicaps: The Second Wave of Least Restrictive Environment.* Bloomington, Ind.: Division of Special Education, Indiana Department of Education and Developmental Training Center, Indiana University, 1986.

CARTWRIGHT, G. PHILLIP, CARTWRIGHT, CAROL A., AND WARD, MARJORIE E. *Educating Special Learners*. Belmont, Calif.: Wadsworth, 1989.

CHAMBERS, JAY G., AND HARTMAN, WILLIAM T., EDS. *Special Education Policies: Their History, Implementation, and Finance*. Philadelphia: Temple University Press, 1982.

A Common Body of Practice for Teachers: The Challenge of Public Law 94-142 to Teacher Education. Washington, D.C.: American Association of Colleges of Teacher Education, 1980.

COUNCIL FOR EXCEPTIONAL CHILDREN. *The Education for All Handicapped Act—P.L. 94-142*. Reston, Va.: Council for Exceptional Children, 1977.

HALLAHAN, DANIEL P., AND KAUFFMAN, JAMES M. *Exceptional Children: Introduction to Special Education*. Englewood Cliffs, N.J.: Prentice-Hall, 1988.

HENDERSON, JOHN. *Making Regular Schools Special*. New York: Schocken Books, 1986.

HERLIHY, JOHN G., AND HERLIHY, MYRA T., EDS. *Mainstreaming in the Social Studies*. Washington, D.C.: National Council for the Social Studies, 1980.

HUME, MAGGIE. *A Mandate to Educate: The Law and Handicapped Children*. Alexandria, Va.: Capitol, 1987.

MCNAMARA, BARRY F. *The Resource Room: A Guide for Special Educators*. Albany: State University of New York Press, 1989.

MAROZAS, DONALD S., AND MAY, DEBORAH C. *Issues and Practices in Special Education*. White Plains, N.Y.: Longman, 1988.

MINDEL, EUGENE E., AND MCCAY, VERNON, EDS. *They Grow in Silence: Understanding Deaf Children and Adults*. San Diego: College-Hill Press, 1987.

MORRIS, RICHARD J., AND BLATT, BURTON, EDS. *Special Education: Research and Trends*. New York: Pergamon Press, 1986.

REYNOLDS, MAYNARD C., AND BIRCH, JACK W. *Adaptive Mainstreaming: A Primer for Teachers and Principals*. New York: Longman, 1988.

SHORE, KENNETH. *The Special Education Handbook: A Comprehensive Guide for Parents and Educators*. New York: Teachers College Press, 1986.

SMITH, DEBORAH DEUTSCH. *Teaching Students with Learning and Behavior Problems*. Englewood Cliffs, N.J.: Prentice Hall, 1989.

STERNBERG, ROBERT J., AND DAVIDSON, JANET E. *Conceptions of Giftedness*. New York: Cambridge University Press, 1986.

STERNLICHT, MANNY. *Special Education: A Source Book*. New York: Garland, 1987.

TAYLOR, STEVEN J., BIKLEN, DOUGLAS, AND SEARL, STANFORD J. *Preparing for Life: A Manual for Parents on Least Restrictive Environment*. Boston, Mass.: The Federation for Children with Special Needs, 1986.

INDEX